HANDBOOK
of
NEW MEDIA

D0709212

HANDBOOK
of
NEW MEDIA

Social Shaping and
Social Consequences of ICTs

Updated Student Edition

Edited by
LEAH A. LIEVROUW
and SONIA LIVINGSTONE

Los Angeles | London | New Delhi
Singapore | Washington DC

Contents

Acknowledgements   vii

The Editors   ix

The Contributors   x

Introduction to the Updated Student Edition   1
Leah A. Lievrouw and Sonia Livingstone

Introduction to the First Edition (2002)   15
The Social Shaping and Consequences of ICTs
Leah A. Lievrouw and Sonia Livingstone

Part One: New Media, Culture and Society   33

1   Interpersonal Life Online   35
   Nancy K. Baym

2   Creating Community with Media: History, Theories
   and Scientific Investigations   55
   Nicholas W. Jankowski

3   Children and New Media   75
   David Buckingham

4   Perspectives on Internet Use: Access, Involvement and Interaction   92
   Ronald E. Rice and Caroline Haythornthwaite

5   New Media and Small Group Organizing   114
   Andrea B. Hollingshead and Noshir S. Contractor

6   Culture and New Media: A Historical View   134
   Mark Poster

7   Cultural Studies and Communication Technology   141
   Jennifer Daryl Slack and J. Macgregor Wise

8   Power and Political Culture   163
   Timothy W. Luke

Part Two: Technology Systems, Design and Industries   185

9   New Media History   187
    Patrice Flichy

10 Exploring Models of Interactivity from Multiple Research
    Traditions: Users, Documents and Systems   205
    Sally J. McMillan

11 How to Infrastructure   230
    Susan Leigh Star and Geoffrey C. Bowker

12 New Media Design and Development: Diffusion of
    Innovations v Social Shaping of Technology   246
    Leah A. Lievrouw

13 New Media and New Economy Cluster Dynamics   266
    Philip Cooke

14 Globalization and the Structure of New Media Industries   287
    Terry Flew and Stephen McElhinney

15 Universal Access to the New Information Infrastructure   307
    Heather E. Hudson

Part Three: New Media, Institutions and Governance   327

16 The Regulation of Digital Content   329
    Stefaan G. Verhulst

17 From Hierarchies to Network Firms   350
    François Bar with Caroline Simard

18 New Media and the Economics of Information   364
    Don Lamberton

19 New Media and Trade Policy   386
    Anders Henten and Knud Erik Skouby

20 The Governance of Media Markets   405
    Bella Mody, Harry M. Trebing and Laura Stein

21 New Global Media and the Role of the State   415
    Laura Stein and Nikhil Sinha

22 The Information Society Revisited   443
    Frank Webster

Index   458

Acknowledgements for the Updated Student Edition

For this Updated Student Edition of the Handbook, we would like to acknowledge the ideas, efforts and enthusiasm of everyone involved. The contributors responded readily when we asked them to review, update and expand their original chapters, with only a couple of months to complete the work. Our International Advisory Board provided months of reviewing and careful commentary on the draft chapters for the first edition, and the strength of the chapters we have selected to include here still reflects their good advice. We have been saddened by the deaths of Board members Everett Rogers and Rob Kling since the first edition was published. Although they worked in somewhat different domains (communication/ sociology, and computer science/science and technology studies, respectively), each helped to shape and lay the groundwork for new media studies as a coherent field of research and scholarship.

We could not have completed the *Handbook* without significant institutional support, in terms of time and resources. We would therefore like to thank our colleagues at UCLA and LSE, who provided administrative and intellectual support (as well as the occasional airfare). Many thanks also to Shenja Vandergraaf at LSE, who has helped us with the updated student edition, working with intelligence, accuracy and good humour throughout.

Our commissioning editor at Sage, Julia Hall, was crucial to the success of the first edition, and was largely responsible for devising the student edition format, which is a new venture for Sage. We said it in the first edition, and it's still true: Julia is patient, strict, cheerful, resolute, reasonable, funny and much else as needed – the sort of commissioning editor any academic author would want.

And again, of course, we thank our partners, Dan Danzig and Peter Lunt, for their enthusiasm and steady support. In the years since we began working on the *Handbook* a simple professional collaboration has grown into a delightful four-way friendship. We look forward to many more productive and enjoyable years together.

We hope that you, the reader, find this *Handbook* as useful and inspiring as we have tried to make it.

Leah Lievrouw
University of California, Los Angeles

Sonia Livingstone
London School of Economics and Political Science

The Editors

Leah A. Lievrouw is a Professor in the Department of Information Studies, part of the Graduate School of Education and Information Studies, at the University of California, Los Angeles. She is also affiliated with UCLA's undergraduate program in Communication Studies. Her research and writing focus on the social and cultural changes associated with information and communication technologies and the relationship between new media technologies and knowledge, particularly problems of social equity, differentiation, and intellectual freedom. Her other books include *Mediation, Information and Communication: Information and Behavior*, vol. 3 (co-edited with Brent Ruben; Transaction, 1990) and *Competing Visions, Complex Realities: Social Aspects of the Information Society* (co-edited with Jorge Reina Schement; Ablex, 1987). From 2000 to 2005 she was co-editor of the journal *New Media & Society*, and the author of numerous journal articles, proceedings papers and book chapters on ICTs and society. Dr. Lievrouw received a Ph.D. in communication theory and research in 1986 from the Annenberg School for Communication at the University of Southern California, and holds an M.A. in biomedical communications from the University of Texas Southwestern Medical Center in Dallas and a Bachelor of Journalism from the University of Texas at Austin. She was formerly a member of the faculties of the Department of Telecommunication and Film at the University of Alabama in Tuscaloosa, and of the Department of Communication at Rutgers University in New Brunswick, NJ.

Sonia Livingstone is Professor of Social Psychology and a member of the Department of Media and Communications at the London School of Economics and Political Science. She has published widely on the subject of media audiences. Her recent work concerns children, young people and the Internet, as part of a broader interest in the domestic, familial and educational contexts of new media access and use (www.children-go-online.net). Books include *Making Sense of Television* (2nd edition, Routledge, 1998), *Mass Consumption and Personal Identity* (with Peter Lunt, Open University Press, 1992), *Talk on Television* (with Peter Lunt, Routledge, 1994), *Children and Their Changing Media Environment* (edited with Moira Bovill, Erlbaum, 2001), *Young People and New Media* (Sage, 2002), *Audiences and Publics* (edited, Intellect, 2005) and, her current project, *Children and the Internet* (Polity, for 2006). Sonia Livingstone has been visiting Professor at the Universities of Copenhagen, Stockholm, Milan, Bergen and Illinois at Urbana-Champaign, and is on the editorial board of several leading journals in the field, including *New Media & Society, The Communication Review, Journal of Communication, Journal of Broadcasting and Electronic Media* and the *European Journal of Communication*. She is Non-Industry Vice Chair of the Internet Watch Foundation.

The Contributors

François Bar is Associate Professor at the Annenberg School for Communication, University of Southern California. He previously served on the Communication faculty at Stanford University and at UC San Diego, and as a member of the Berkeley Roundtable on the International Economy (BRIE), at UC Berkeley. He has held visiting faculty appointments at the University of Toronto, the University of Paris-XIII, Théséus, and Eurécom. He received his Ph.D. from the UC Berkeley and holds a Diplôme d'Ingénieur from the Ecole Nationale des Ponts et Chaussées in Paris. Professor Bar's current research interests include comparative telecommunication policy, as well as economic, strategic and social dimensions of computer networking, new media and the Internet. His research has been published in books of collected studies, policy reports, and journals such as *Telecommunications Policy*, *The Information Society*, *Infrastructure Economics and Policy*, *Communications & Strategies*, *Réseaux*, *Organization Science*, and the *International Journal of Technology Management*.

Nancy K. Baym is an Associate Professor of Communication Studies at the University of Kansas, where she teaches communication on the Internet, interpersonal communication, nonverbal communication, and qualitative methods. Her ethnographic research into online community and television fandom appears in the book *Tune In, Log On: Soaps, Fandom, and Online Community* (Sage) and in several articles in journals and edited collections. In addition to online community, she has studied how the social life that takes place on the Internet is woven into the full fabric of mediated and unmediated interpersonal communication, work published in *New Media & Society* among other places. She served as President of the Association of Internet Researchers (2002–2005) and coordinated that association's first annual conference, 'Internet Research 1.0: The State of the Interdiscipline' in 2000. She is an editor of *The Internet Research Annual*, Volume I (2004, Peter Lang), a volume bringing together the best papers from the first three years of Association of Internet Researcher conferences. With Annette Markham, she is an editor of a forthcoming book examining key questions for the conduct of high-quality Internet research, which will likely be published in 2006. She serves on the editorial boards of *New Media & Society*, *The Information Society*, *The Journal of Communication*, and *Research on Language and Social Interaction*.

Geoffrey C. Bowker is Executive Director, Regis and Dianne McKenna Professor Center for Science, Technology and Society, Santa Clara University. He was previously Professor in and Chair of the Department of Communication, University of California, San Diego. His Ph.D is in History and Philosophy of Science at Melbourne University. He studies social and organizational aspects of the development of very large-scale information infrastructures. His first book (*Science on the Run*, MIT Press) discussed the development of information practices in the oil industry. He has written with Leigh Star a book on the history and sociology of medical classifications (*Sorting Things Out: Classification and Practice* – published by MIT Press in September 1999). This book looks at the classification of nursing work, diseases, viruses and race. He has co-edited a volume on computer support cooperative work (*Social Science, Technical Systems and Cooperative Work: Beyond the Great Divide*, LEA Press, 1997). He has, since his invitation to join the biodiversity sub-committee of the President's Committee of Advisors on Science and Technology, been working in the field of biodiversity and environmental informatics. He has recently completed a digital government-funded project on long-term databases in environmental science (http://pal.lternet.edu/dm/projects/02bdei/). His next book, entitled *Memory Practices in the Sciences*, about formal and informal record-keeping in science over the past 200 years, which includes extensive discussion of biodiversity informatics, will be published by MIT Press in 2005. He was 2002–2003 member of an OECD working group on international data sharing in science (http://dataaccess.sdsc.edu/ – the report can be found at this address). He is currently working on an NSF-funded project at the San Diego Computer Center on organizational and social dimensions of developing scientific cyberinfrastructures. More information, including a number of publications, can be found at his website: http://epl.scu.edu/~gbowker.

David Buckingham is Professor of Education at the Institute of Education, London University, where he directs the Centre for the Study of Children, Youth and Media (www.childrenyouthandmediacentre.co.uk). He has directed several major funded projects on media education, and on children's and young people's interactions with electronic media. He is the author, co-author or editor of 18 books, including *Children Talking Television* (Falmer, 1993), *Moving Images* (Manchester University Press, 1996), *The Making of Citizens* (Routledge, 2000), *After the Death of Childhood* (Polity, 2000) and *Media Education* (Polity, 2003). His work has been translated into 15 languages, and he has taught and addressed conferences in more than 25 countries around the world. He is currently directing research projects on young people's engagement with video games; informal learning and creativity in media education; the uses of digital media by migrant/refugee children across Europe; and young people's responses to sexual content in the media.

Noshir S. Contractor is a Professor in the Departments of Speech Communication and Psychology at the University of Illinois at Urbana-Champaign. He is a Research Affiliate of the Beckman Institute for Advanced Science and Technology, Director of the *Science of Networks in Communities* (SONIC) Research Group at the National Center for Supercomputing Applications, and Co-Director of the *Age of Networks* Initiative at the Center for Advanced Study at the University of Illinois at Urbana-Champaign. His current research program is investigating factors that lead to the formation, maintenance, and dissolution of dynamically linked knowledge networks among profit, non-profit, government as well as non-government agencies involved in issues of public interest including emergency response, food safety, public health, environmental engineering. His research has been funded continuously for the past decade by major grants from the U.S. National Science Foundation, as well as additional support from NASA, the National Cancer Institute, and the Rockefeller Foundation. His research has been published in journals including *Academy of Management Review, Communication Research, Computational and Mathematical Organizational Theory, Decision Science, Human Communication Research, Journal of Broadcasting & Electronic Media, Journal of Cultural Economics, Organization Science, Small Group Research, and Social Psychology Quarterly*. His papers have received top-paper awards from both the International Communication Association and the National Communication Association. His book titled *Theories of Communication Networks* (co-authored with Professor Peter Monge, Oxford University Press) received the 2003 Book of the Year award from the Organizational Communication Division of the National Communication Association. He is the lead developer of *IKNOW* (Inquiring Knowledge Networks On the Web), a web-based social networking software (http://iknow.spcomm.uiuc.edu) and *Blanche*, a software program to simulate the dynamics of social networks (http://csu1.spcomm.uiuc.edu/Projects/Teclab/Blanche/).

Philip Cooke is University Research Professor and founding Director (1993) of the Centre for Advanced Studies, University of Wales, Cardiff. His research interests lie in studies of economics of biotechnology (partner in CESAGen Research Centre), regional innovation systems, knowledge economies, and policy actions for business clusters and networks. As a field leader in knowledge and innovation sciences he has coordinated and participated in six FP projects since 1995. He co-edited a book entitled *Regional Innovation Systems* in 1998, a fully revised 2nd edition of which is published in 2004. He co-authored a book on network governance called *The Associational Economy*, also published in 1998, and is co-author of *The Governance of Innovation in Europe* published in 2000. His recent book *Knowledge Economies: Clusters, Learning and Cooperative Advantage* was published by Routledge in 2002. In 2004 he published *Regional Economies as Knowledge Laboratories* (Edward Elgar). Professor Cooke was adviser to Lord Sainsbury's Biotechnology Clusters mission in 1999 and subsequently UK Government Cluster Policy, and Innovation Review Adviser. He has been EU Adviser on Regional Foresight, Universities & Regional Development, and in 2004–2005 Chairs the EU Committee on Constructing Regional Advantage. He is OECD Adviser on Knowledge Economies, and UNIDO Adviser on Innovation Systems. In addition to the books, he is author of more than 100 research and scholarly articles in leading journals. He is also Editor of *European Planning Studies*, a bi-monthly journal devoted to European urban and regional governance, innovation and development issues. In 2003 he was elected Academician of the UK Academy of Social Sciences (AcSS). In 2004 he was made Distinguished Research Fellow (PRIME) of the University of Ottawa Management School.

Dr Terry Flew is Associate Professor and Head of Media and Communication in the Creative Industries Faculty, Queensland University of Technology, Brisbane, Australia. He is the author of *New Media Technologies: An Introduction* (Oxford, 2005, second edition), and *Understanding Global Media* (Palgrave, 2006). He has authored six research monographs, 21 book chapters and 31 refereed journal articles, including a chapter on 'Creative Economy' to J. Hartley (ed.), *Creative Industries* (Blackwell, 2005). His research interests include new media technologies; media policy and regulation; creative industries theory and policy; the culture of services; media globalization; international trade agreements; censorship and classification; virtual communities and Internet theory; popular music and music policy; and broadcasting and cultural diversity. He is also Reviews Editor of *Continuum: Journal of Media and Cultural Studies*, and Treasurer of the Australia and New Zealand Communications Association.

Patrice Flichy is Professor in the Department of Sociology at the University of Marne la Vallée in France, and editor of *Réseaux*, a French journal on communication studies. His research and writing focus on innovation and uses in ICT, in the past and today. His books include *L'imaginaire d'Internet* (La Découverte, 2001, English translation forthcoming at MIT Press); *Dynamics of Modern Communication: The Shaping and Impact of New Communication Technologies* (Sage, 1995). *L'innovation technique* (La Découverte, 1995); *European Telematics: The Emerging Economy of Words* (co-edited with Paul Beaud and Josiane Jouët, Elsevier, 1991).

Professor Flichy received a PhD in sociology in 1971 from the University of Paris-I. He also holds a degree in business management from the Ecole des Hautes Etudes Commerciales. He was formerly head of the Laboratory of Sociology of France Telecom Research Development.

Caroline Haythornthwaite is Associate Professor at the Graduate School of Library and Information Science, University of Illinois at Urbana-Champaign. Her research focuses on the way computer-mediated interaction supports and affects interaction for work, learning, the exchange of information, and the construction of knowledge. Ongoing work includes social network studies of the way computer media affect members of distance learning environments and research collaboratives, with emphasis on social, communal, and conversational aspects. Her work appears in *The Information Society, Journal of Computer-Mediated Communication, New Media & Society*, Jones' *Doing Internet Research*, Gackenbach's *Psychology and the Internet*, and Renninger and Shumar's *Building Virtual Community*. She recently co-edited with Barry Wellman *The Internet in Everyday Life* (2002), and with Michelle M. Kazmer, *Learning, Culture and Community in Online Education: Research and Practice*.

Anders Henten is Associate Professor at the Center for Information and Communication Technologies (CICT)at the Technical University of Denmark. He is a graduate in communications and international development studies from Roskilde University in Denmark and holds a PhD from the Technical University of Denmark. His main areas of research are socioeconomic implications of information and communication technologies including e-commerce and business models, internationalization of services, and regulations of communications. He teaches courses in 'e-commerce – markets and business models', 'standardization in telecommunications', and 'regulation of telecommunications'. Anders Henten has worked professionally in the areas of communications economy and policy for more than a decade. He has published, nationally and internationally, more than 150 academic publications in international journals, books, anthologies, and conference proceedings.

Andrea B. Hollingshead is Associate Professor of Communication in the Annenberg School for Communication. Her research concerns how people in groups learn, store, retrieve, communicate, and use knowledge – in particular knowledge from and about others in the group. She seeks to identify the factors and processes that lead to effective knowledge sharing in groups including those that are technologically based. Professor Hollingshead has been an investigator on three large collaborative projects on information technology and knowledge sharing in organizations supported by the National Science Foundation. Her publications include two books, *Theories of Small Groups: Interdisciplinary Perspectives* (2005, co-edited with Marshall Scott Poole) and *Groups Interacting with Technology* (1994, with Joseph E. McGrath). Her many articles have appeared in top-tier journals in the fields of communication, psychology and management. Professor Hollingshead is currently Senior Editor of *Organization Science*, and has served on many journal editorial boards.

Heather E. Hudson is Director of the Telecommunications Management and Policy Program in the School of Business and Management at the University of San Francisco. Dr Hudson has planned and evaluated communication projects in northern Canada, Alaska, and more than 50 developing countries in Africa, Asia and the Pacific, the Middle East, and Latin America. She has also consulted for government agencies, consumer and native organizations, foreign governments, telecommunications companies, and international organizations including the World Bank, the ITU, UNDP, UNESCO, USAID, CIDA, International Development Research Centre (IDRC), and the Commonwealth of Learning.

Dr Hudson received an Honours BA in English from the University of British Columbia, MA and Ph.D in Communication Research from Stanford University and JD from the University of Texas at Austin. She is the author of several books including *Global Connections: International Telecommunications Infrastructure and Policy; Communication Satellites: Their Development and Impact; When Telephones Reach the Village,* and co-author of *Rural America in the Information Age* and *Electronic Byways: State Policies for Rural Development through Telecommunications.* Dr Hudson has also published more than 100 articles and book chapters, and presented numerous conference papers, as well as providing expert testimony on telecommunications applications and domestic and international policy issues such as universal service, information infrastructure, and telecommunications planning for socioeconomic development.

Nicholas W. Jankowski (Ph.D., University of Amsterdam) is Associate Professor in the Department of Communication, Radboud University Nijmegen and Adjunct Professor, Department of Communication, University of Leuven. He has been involved in the investigation of community media and other small-scale communication facilities since the mid-1970s. His publications include: *The People's Voice: Local Radio and Television in Europe*; *The Contours of Multimedia*; *Community Media in the Information Age*; and *A Handbook of Qualitative Methodologies for Mass Communication Research*. He is preparing a methodology textbook on new media research. His research interests include study of initiatives designed to contribute to public discourse through online environments and the role played by the Internet during electoral campaigns. Jankowski is co-editor of the journal *New Media & Society* and board member of the European Institute for Communication and Culture.

Don Lamberton is Adjunct Professor, Creative Industries Faculty, Queensland University of Technology and Adjunct Professor in Communication, University of Canberra. He edits *Information Economics and Policy* and *Prometheus*, and is a member of other editorial boards. His recent books are: *The Economics of Communication and Information* (1996), *The New Frontiers of Communications Policy* (1997), *Communication and Trade* (1998), *Managing the Global: Globalization, Employment and Quality of Life* (2002), and *The Economics of Language* (2002). He received his BEc degree from the University of Sydney and his D.Phil. from Oxford University. He has held appointments at many universities and research centres in the US and UK. He served as a member of Australian Government committees of inquiry (public libraries, industrial property, and marine industries science and technology) and as a consultant to OECD, UNESCO, ITU, UNCTC, Australian Bureau of Statistics, Australia Post, and Prices Surveillance Authority.

Timothy W. Luke is University Distinguished Professor of Political Science and co-director of the Center for Digital Discourse and Culture at Virginia Polytechnic Institute and State University in Blacksburg, Virginia. His research interests are tied to the politics of information societies, international affairs, and ecological criticism. He has just completed a new critical study of ideological politics at a number of major museums in the United States, which is entitled *Museum Pieces: Probing the Powerplays at Culture, History, Nature, and Technology Museums* (University of Minnesota Press, forthcoming). His most recent books are *Capitalism, Democracy, and Ecology: Departing from Marx* (University of Illinois Press, 1999), and *Ecocritique: Contesting the Politics of Nature, Economy, and Culture* (University of Minnesota Press, 1997). He is also the author of *Shows of Force: Politics, Power and Ideology in Art Exhibitions* (Duke University Press, 1992).

Stephen McElhinney is Director of the Bachelor in International Communication at the Macquarie University Centre for International Communication (MUCIC) in Sydney, Australia. Prior to completing his PhD and joining MUCIC, he worked for the Special Broadcasting Service, the Australian government in areas of communications, intellectual property and arts policy and as a policy researcher with the Communications Law Centre. His research interests include the factors inhibiting the establishment of the knowledge society and the representation of international events on Australian television news. He has published on universal service in telecommunications and on the film and television preferences of Australian and Thai adolescents.

Sally J. McMillan is an Associate Professor in the Advertising Department School of Advertising and Public Relations at the University of Tennessee-Knoxville. Her research focuses on definitions and history of new media and the impacts of communication technology on organizations and society. She has a particular interest in the nature and role of interactivity in computer-mediated environments. She has also published several articles related to methodologies for online research. Her research has been published in journals such as *Journalism and Mass Communication Quarterly*, the *Journal of Computer Mediated Communication, New Media & Society, Journal of Advertising*, and the *Journal of Advertising Research*. Prior to earning her PhD in Communication and Society at the University of Oregon, McMillan worked for 15 years in communication- related roles in book publishing, newspaper reporting, public relations consulting, non-profit management, and executive-level marketing and management for computer technology firms. She teaches graduate and undergraduate courses in interactive advertising, advertising research, and advertising management.

Bella Mody holds the de Castro Chair in Global Media Studies at the School of Journalism and Mass Communication at the University of Colorado in Boulder. She specializes in the political economy of media in developing countries and in design research on public service applications of communication media. Dr Mody's books include *International and Development Communication: A 21st Century Perspective* (ed., Sage, 2003), *The Handbook of International and Intercultural Communication* (co-ed., Sage, 2001), *Telecommunication Politics* (co-ed., Lawrence Erlbaum, 1995), and *Designing Messages for Development Communication* (Sage, 1991). Her research articles have been published in *Communication Theory, The Journal of International Communication, The Information Society, The Journal of Communication, Telecommunication Policy, Media Development, Telematics and Informatics, Gazette, International Development Review, Educational Broadcasting International, Communication Research, Journal of Research in Personality*, and the *Journal of Social Psychology*. She was formerly a social scientist with the Satellite Instructional TV Experiment in the Government of India's space agency and a faculty member at Stanford University and San Francisco State University.

Mark Poster is a member of the Department of Film and Media Studies and a member of the History Department at the University of California, Irvine. He has courtesy appointments in the Department of Information and Computer Science and the Department of Comparative Literature. He is a member of the Critical Theory Institute. His recent and forthcoming books are: *Information Please: Culture and Politics in a Digital Age; What's the Matter with the Internet?: A Critical Theory of Cyberspace* (University of Minnesota Press, 2001); *The Information Subject* in Critical Voices Series (Gordon and Breach Arts International, 2001); *Cultural History and Postmodernity* (Columbia University Press, 1997); *The Second Media Age* (London: Polity and New York: Blackwell, 1995); and *The Mode of Information* (London: Blackwell and Chicago: University of Chicago Press, 1990).

Ronald E. Rice (PhD, MA, Stanford University, 1982) is the Arthur N. Rupe Professor of the Social Effects of Mass Communication in the Department of

Communication; Co-director of the Center for Film, Television and New Media, at University of California, Santa Barbara; and incoming President of the International Communication Association (2006–2007). He has co-authored or co-edited *Public Communication Campaigns* (3rd edn, 2000), *The Internet and Health Communication* (2000), *The New Media: Communication, Research and Technology* (1984), *Managing Organizational Innovation* (1987) and *Research Methods and the New Media* (1989). He has conducted research and published widely in communication science, public communication campaigns, computer-mediated communication systems, methodology, organizational and management theory, information systems, information science and bibliometrics, and social networks. His publications have won awards as best dissertation from the American Society for Information Science, and as best paper from the International Communication Association and the Academy of Management.

Caroline Simard (MA, Rutgers University, PhD, Stanford University) is a researcher at the Stanford Graduate School of Business. Her dissertation investigated the role of knowledge networks in the creation of regional clusters in the wireless industry. At the Graduate School of Business, she is part of a research project on the diffusion of managerial practices in the nonprofit sector. Her research interests include organizational behavior, new media, knowledge networks, the diffusion of innovations and regional clusters.

Nikhil Sinha is Associate Dean for Academic Affairs in the College of Communication at the University of Texas at Austin. He has also worked in the Information and Broadcasting Ministry of the Government of India and as a consultant to the Informatics and Telecommunications Division for the World Bank, and as an adviser to the Indian Telecommunications Commission and the Indian Planning Commission. He has published numerous articles and book chapters on international regulatory and policy issues on telecommunications and information technology.

Knud Erik Skouby is Professor and founding Director of the Center for Information and Communication Technologies (CICT) – a multidisciplinary teaching and research center at the Danish Technical University. His main area of research interest includes the techno-economics of the telecom sector and of new telecom applications and services. He has participated as a project manager and partner in a number of international, European and Danish research projects. He has served as a member of organizing boards and evaluation committees and as invited speaker to international conferences, published a number of Danish and international articles, books and conference proceedings in the areas of telecommunications regulation, technology assessment (information technology and telecommunications), demand forecasting and political economy.

Jennifer Daryl Slack is Professor of Communication and Cultural Studies at Michigan Technological University Department of Humanities. Her work on culture and technology is based on over 25 years of teaching and study. Notably, she has taught courses on culture and technology since 1981 and tracked the changes in her students' sense of the role and importance of technology. She is author of *Communication Technologies and Society* (Ablex, 1984), co-editor of *The Ideology of the Information Age* (Ablex, 1987), and author of numerous articles on culture and technology. *Culture and Technology: A Primer,* co-authored with J. Macgregor Wise, is in press from Peter Lang.

Susan Leigh Star is Senior Scholar at the Center for Science, Technology and Society at the University of Santa Clara. She is a Visiting Faculty at the Stanford Center for BioEthics, and president-elect of the Society for the Social Study of Science (4S). She writes about the social and historical aspects of science, information and technology, particularly on the values embedded in information technologies. With Geoffrey Bowker, she is the author of *Sorting Things Out: Classification and Its Consequences* (MIT Press, 1999), and has edited a number of other volumes, including *Ecologies of Knowledge* (SUNY, 1995), and with Martha Lampland, of *Formalizing Practices: Interpretive Approaches to Standardizing, Quantifying and Formalizing* (under review at Duke University Press). Her training was in the symbolic interactionist/pragmatist tradition in American sociology, which has grounded her research in the study of work, identity and meaning. She has also written on feminist theory, and is a poet.

Laura Stein is an Assistant Professor in the Radio-Television-Film Department at the University of Texas at Austin. She writes about communication law and policy, political communication, and alternative and public media. Her work appears in numerous journals and books, including *Communication Law and Policy, Media, Culture & Society, Javnost/The Public, Community Media in the Information Age,* and *Radical Media.* Her forthcoming book, entitled *Sustaining Speech Rights: The First Amendment, Democracy and the Media* (University of Illinois Press), explores the failure of speech rights to protect democratic communication in US media. She heads the Community Communication Division of the International Association for Media and Communication Research. Dr Stein began her career in the management, production, and distribution of public and educational media. She has an MA in Education from Columbia University, a Ph.D. in Communication from UT Austin, and a BA from the University of California at Berkeley.

Harry M. Trebing is Professor of Economics Emeritus and Senior Fellow at the Institute of Public Utilities, Michigan State University. Founder of the Institute, he served as its director from 1966 until his retirement in 1992. He has also served as Chief Economist, US Postal Rate Commission and US Federal Communications Commission, and as a member of advisory panels for government agencies and the Congressional Office of Technology Assessment. He currently serves as Chairman, Michigan Utility Consumer Participation Board (by appointment of the Governor). The author of numerous publications dealing with public utility regulation, he is the recipient of distinguished service awards from the National Association of State Utility Consumer Advocates, the National Association of Regulatory Utility Commissioners, five universities, and the Government of Guam, among others. He holds the BA and MA degrees from the University of Maryland and the Ph.D. degree from the University of Wisconsin.

Stefaan G. Verhulst is currently Chief of Research at the Markle Foundation. Prior to his arrival at Markle, where he held the previous positions of Director of Internet Governance and Director Policy for a Networked Society, Verhulst was the founder and director of the Programme in Comparative Media Law and Policy (PCMLP) at Oxford University, as well as Senior Research Fellow at the Centre for Socio-Legal Studies. In that capacity he was appointed the socio-legal Research Fellow at Wolfson College (Oxford). In addition, he was the UNESCO Chairholder in Communications Law and Policy for the UK. Before his move to Oxford in 1996, he had been a Lecturer on communications law and policy issues in Belgium and founder and co-director of the International Media and information-communications Policy and Law studies (IMPS) at the School of Law, University of Glasgow. Verhulst has served as consultant to various international and national organizations including the Council of Europe, the European Commission and Parliament, UNESCO, UNDP, USAID and DFID. He has published several books and numerous articles on communications law and policy issues and is invited regularly to speak at conferences globally. He is also the founder of the *International Journal of Communications Law and Policy* and the *Communications Law, in Transition* Newsletter.

Frank Webster is Professor of Sociology at City University London. He has published many books, including: *The New Photography: Responsibility in Visual Communication* (1980), *Information Technology: A Luddite Analysis* (with Kevin Robins, 1986), *The Technical Fix: Computers, Industry and Education* (with Kevin Robins, 1989), *The Postmodern University? Contested Visions of Higher Education* (with Anthony Smith, 1997), *Times of the Technoculture: From the Information Society to the Virtual Life* (with Kevin Robins) (1999); *Understanding Contemporary Society: Theories of the Present* (with Gary Browning and Abigail Halcli, 2000), and *Politics and Culture in the Information Age: A New Politics?* (2001), *The Virtual University* (with Kevin Robins, 2002), *Theories of the Information Society* (1995, 2nd edition 2002); *The Intensification of Surveillance* (with Kirstie Ball, 2003), *The Information Society Reader* (2004), and *Manuel Castells*, 3 vols (2004). He is currently preparing, with Howard Tumber, Front Line Correspondents and Information War and a 3rd edition of *Theories of the Information Society*.

J. Macgregor Wise (PhD, University of Illinois at Urbana-Champaign) is Associate Professor and Chair of Communication Studies at Arizona State University, West Campus. His work is situated at the intersection of cultural studies, media studies, and the sociology and philosophy of technology. He is author of *Exploring Technology and Social Space* (Sage, 1997), co-author (with Jennifer Daryl Slack) of *Culture and Technology: A Primer* (Peter Lang, 2005), and co-author (with Lawrence Grossberg, Ellen Wartella, and D. Charles Whitney) of *Media Making: Mass Media in a Popular Culture*, 2nd edition (Sage, in press).

Introduction to the Updated Student Edition

LEAH A. LIEVROUW AND SONIA LIVINGSTONE

The manuscript for the first edition of the *Handbook of New Media* went to the London publisher in mid-2001. In that volume, we and our contributing authors made numerous observations about the history, role, functions, meanings and implications of new media technologies and uses across a diverse range of social, cultural and institutional settings. Perhaps the most accurate was our sense of how rapidly the study of networked information and communication technologies was spreading across disciplines, specialities and perspectives. If anything, the proliferation and fragmentation of work we identified has accelerated since the first edition appeared in print. In the introduction (which is included in the present volume), we argued that the intellectual eclecticism and openness of new media studies was one of its great strengths, difficult as it might be to survey or synthesize the field from any single point of view. We offered the *Handbook* then, as we do now, as our effort to counter the 'Balkanization' of new media studies that was dividing the field into dozens of specialized, non-communicating academic niches.

Some of the changes anticipated in the first edition were fairly predictable. New media (with 'the Internet' at the top of the list as a kind of archetype) have become everyday technologies, thoroughly embedded and routinized in the societies where they are most widely used. New media have not replaced older media, any more than broadcasting replaced print in the mid-twentieth century. Rather, people's information and communication environments have become ever more individualized and commodified, integrating print, audio, still and moving images, broadcasting, telecommunications, computing, and other modes and channels of communication and information sharing.

As this last point suggests, the convergence of new media with other media and information sources and services has also continued apace, although the rush of technological innovation and novelty in the 1990s has given way to more incremental refinements and adaptations in the 2000s. ICTs have gone from radical to routine, in part because of two major events that neither we nor our contributors foresaw. In 2001, the dot.com bubble was about to evaporate, and the events of September 11 of that year would soon bring the dangers of global technology networks employed in the interests of radical ideologies – and of those who would suppress those ideologies – into stark relief.

Reduced economic expectations and the hovering threat of terrorist violence, both vividly portrayed in the mass media, quickly dampened what many analysts considered to be an 'overheated' and speculative information technology sector, and created new demands for ICT systems that were safe, stable, and ubiquitous. Popular interest in new media shifted from invention, novelty and risk to regulation, reliability and safety. Among researchers, perspectives on social change likewise turned from revolutionary to evolutionary processes. As several contributors to the fifth anniversary issue of the journal *New Media & Society* noted in 2004, the previous five years had been notable for the 'banalization' of ICTs, and their assimilation and reconfiguration to suit the demands, norms and expectations of everyday life, including expectations about communication itself and its constitutive role in society (Lievrouw, 2004).

None of these changes, however, has caused new media studies to lose momentum – far from it. It is precisely the astonishing success of new media that now confronts researchers with new questions of scale and capacity, of network architecture and infrastructural robustness, of international legal and regulatory frameworks, and of public trust, security and e-crime (Livingstone, in press). The routinization of new media has also required richer and more sophisticated theorizing, and in this volume the chapter authors identify multiple paths ahead and maintain a healthy scepticism as they examine the claims for change, weigh evidence, seek to clarify concepts and, always, acknowledge the limits as well as the insights of research.

As research has continued to pursue what we called the 'moving target' of social and technological innovation, certain milestones have been noted. For example, in his contribution to the special issue of *New Media & Society* mentioned earlier, Wellman (2004: 124) describes three 'ages of Internet studies'. The first age, beginning in the mid-1990s, was what he called 'punditry rides rampant': the optimistic celebration of the transformative potential of the Internet, peppered with dystopian prognostications from the sceptics. Then, with the dot.com bust at the turn of the twenty-first century, the second age turned to a more serious engagement with evidence, seeking to document users and uses of the Internet; or as Wellman and Haythornthwaite (2002: 4) put it, researchers sought to study the Internet 'as it descends from the firmament and becomes embedded in everyday life'. Our hope is that this updated edition of the *Handbook* will contribute to the present, third age and the move 'from documentation to analysis' (Wellman, 2004: 27).

DEFINITIONS, REVISITED

In the first edition, we also rejected definitions of new media based solely on particular technical features, channels or content. Instead, deliberately incorporating both technological and social, political and economic factors, we defined them as 'information and communication technologies and their associated social contexts' (p. 23, this volume), and specifically (following the lead of our contributors Susan Leigh Star and Geof Bowker) as infrastructures with three components: the *artefacts or devices* used to communicate or convey information; the *activities and practices* in which people engage to communicate or share information; and the *social arrangements or organizational forms* that develop around those devices and practices. For this updated edition, we have reorganized the chapters along these lines. The first part examines practices in cultural and social context. The second part focuses on the technologies themselves and their design and development. The third part takes a more macro-level, institutional view of the ways that new media technologies and practices are organized and governed. Within this three-part structure, we have asked all our chapter authors to provide the 'back story' to their topic – how did research get to where it is today, by making what assumptions, encountering which problems, and cross-fertilizing with which other fields?

Of course, all technologies – not just ICTs – can be framed and analyzed in terms of artefacts, practices and social arrangements. For communication research and related fields, the central question concerning technology today is whether the particular configurations of artefacts, practices, and social arrangements associated with new media differ, and in what ways, from those that characterized older information and communication technologies.

Our main conclusion is that new media require us to reconsider the longstanding dependence within media research on theories and phenomena of mass society. In the days of *mass* media, a related but different three-part framework, encompassing *production, text,* and *audience,* dominated media research and scholarship. As in our three-part scheme, each aspect is essential, and the dialogue among the various disciplines that has evolved to address each part has contributed to making media studies so engaging. The differences between the two frameworks are also important, however. Not only are *artefacts, practices,* and *social arrangements* broader terms than *production, text,* and *audience*; they are also more thoroughly 'socialized' and inherently culturally and historically conditioned.[1]

Most important, we do not specify *a priori* any set relationship among the three component processes of infrastructure. Where the mass communication tradition has spent decades struggling with and, more recently, unpicking the linear relationship among production, text, and audience (i.e., production makes texts which have effects or impacts on audiences, consistent with the sender–message–receiver model of communication), in new media research no such linear assumption is necessary. This is why we emphasize social shaping and social consequences together, in Michel Callon's term, as an *ensemble*: it is precisely the dynamic links and interdependencies among artefacts, practices and social arrangements that should guide our analytic focus. These dynamic interrelations are not infinitely flexible, however, and our use of the term *infrastructure* is intended to suggest that artefacts, practices, and social arrangements – and the relations among them – can and do become routine, established, institutionalized, and fixed to various extents, and so become taken for granted in everyday life.

As many of the following chapters demonstrate, new media studies have been strongly influenced by theories of post-industrial, late modern, or postmodern society, which posit 'the emergence of a new economic order characterised by the central importance of information and theoretical knowledge, and by a shift from a goods-producing to a service society' (Golding, 2000: 169; see Webster, Chapter 21 this volume). Signs of this shift, including the commodification of information, widespread diffusion of ICTs, diversity of message and content forms, interconnected social and technical networks, the rise of 'information work', and the privileging of abstract knowledge are all pivotal elements in accounts of new media technologies within the framework of post-industrial or information

society (Schement and Lievrouw, 1987), and are taken for granted in new media studies. But they play little if any role in theories of mass society and mass media.

The impressive array of literature that has now accumulated in new media studies demonstrates that in many ways, the relatively orderly terrain of mass society has been transformed into a new and emergent environment of network forms, roles, relations and dynamics. Mass production, distribution and economies of scale now contend with network externalities, cumulative advantage processes and power laws.[2] Research that formerly examined audiences, reception and effects must now account for users and uses, interactivity, reconfiguration, and reciprocity. Linear narratives and genres that were associated with particular media technologies and forms in the past – the novel, the Hollywood film, the LP record album, the crime drama – are absorbed into hyperlinked, hybrid content that is generated and shared via diverse channels. The inextricably linked phenomena of information, communication and mediation are no longer the sole province of communication research and a few related specialties; today they are the focus of intense interest and study across the social sciences, arts and humanities. Multidisciplinary approaches are thus essential in new media studies, even as they pose both theoretical and methodological challenges and bring hitherto distinct fields into conjunction (and sometimes, confrontation) with each other.

Communication and media research, then, is at a conceptual and disciplinary crossroads. As we argue below, it is time to rethink the role of 'the mass' in technology and society. First, however, we revisit the proposal that what make new media 'new,' and what distinguishes mediation today from the mass media of the past, are the distinctive ways in which the technologies develop – their *social shaping* – and their social *consequences*.

SOCIAL SHAPING OF ICTs

The term social shaping, borrowed from science and technology studies, is usually associated with the critique of strong technological determinism and a shift toward strong social determinism in the 1970s and 1980s in that field (MacKenzie and Wajcman, 1999). As Raymond Williams noted of mass communication research several decades ago, 'in *technological determinism*, research and development have been assumed as self-generating. The new technologies are invented as it were in an independent sphere, and then create new societies or new human conditions' (1974: 13, italics in original). Although recent writing about new media in cultural studies and media arts and design often takes a technologically deterministic tone (e.g. Manovich, 2001; Poster, 1990; Stone, 1995), new media researchers in the social sciences are virtually united in rejecting accounts in which technological innovation is the cause and society is the effect (see e.g. Woolgar, 2002). Instead, they have adopted the counter-view that 'the technological, instead of being a sphere separate from social life, is part of what makes society possible – in other words, it is constitutive of society' (MacKenzie and Wajcman, 1999: 23). This social-determinist view 'migrated' to communication research, cultural studies, information studies and other fields in the 1980s, and by the early 1990s it had displaced the technologically deterministic, 'new society' discourse common in communication research previously. It has subsequently become the dominant perspective in new media studies (Boczkowski and Lievrouw, forthcoming; Livingstone, in press).

The inclusion of 'social shaping' in the subtitle may thus seem to associate the *Handbook* with this strong social-determinist view. However, by social shaping we mean to suggest more of a mutual shaping process in which technological development and social practices are co-determining (for a fuller discussion, see Boczkowski, 2004). As we put it in the introduction to the first edition, 'On the one hand, there is a concern with agency and action; on the other, a concern with social effects, structure and impacts' (2002: 11). Or, to quote Bruno Latour's memorable phrase, 'technology is society made durable' (1991: 103). People always have choices about how technologies are created, understood and used. However,

when certain technologies become very extensive, embedded and taken for granted (e.g. voice telephony, broadcast television, newspaper publishing, and increasingly, the Internet), they can also constrain or limit the range of available choices. This too is a social process, as Agre points out when he observes that, 'every system affords a certain range of interpretations, and that range is determined by the discourses that have been inscribed into it' (2004: 27). Thus, technology, action and social context are inseparable phenomena, each influencing the other.[3]

Technology, action and social context are usefully located within the wider analytic framework of late modernity, a framework that identifies multiple vectors of change. Appadurai (1996: 33–6) identifies five key dimensions of change along which we can analyze the 'social' that prefaces the 'shaping' and 'consequences' of the *Handbook* title: the ethnoscape (the shifting landscape of persons, identities, diaspora), the technoscape (the fluid, networked configuration of technologies), the financescapes (the disposition of global capital), the mediascapes (the distribution of information, images and audiences) and the ideoscapes (the ideologies and counter-ideologies which link images and ideas to the power of states). Whether or not one agrees with these, especially the separation of technoscape and mediascape, his purpose, like that of many of our chapter authors, is, importantly, to examine the disjunctures between economy, culture and politics that arise from the interaction among diverse flows, thus opening up dynamic rather than a static conception of 'the social'.

Recombination

In the first edition, we focused our analysis of this dynamic in relation to two modes of social shaping which we believe distinguish new media from more conventional, linear, one-to-many, mass media processes and effects. The first is *recombination*, the 'continuous hybridization of both existing technologies and innovations in interconnected technical and institutional networks' (p. 23, this volume). Recombination has two main forms – convergence and divergence – both of which are readily observable in the development of new media technologies, message forms, social practices and cultural/economic institutions. As the product of an ongoing cycle of human action and available technical and cultural resources, new media technologies are continuously 'renewed'. Although they are usually created with particular purposes or uses in mind, they are commonly adopted and used in unanticipated ways – reinvented, reconfigured, sabotaged, adapted, hacked, ignored. This process, with its often unintended consequences, reinforces the persistent sense of 'newness' and pivotal change associated with ICTs.

Certainly, recombination and a sense of novelty are still associated with new media design and use. New features and options continue to be introduced, even if they currently tend to merge, elaborate or extend existing functions rather than constitute radically new and unfamiliar ones. As Star and Bowker point out in Chapter 11, like other established infrastructures, new media are 'built on an installed base'. However, unlike mass media, which by the late twentieth century had stabilized into a few major channels or forms (due to spectrum scarcity and the establishment of technical and formal standards), the forms and genres of new media continue to branch, recombine and proliferate. Marshall McLuhan (1964) observed that older media often become the content of newer media. Today, this has become an ongoing process of 'remediation' in which older media are appropriated, refashioned or absorbed by the new, therefore simultaneously shaping the new and reshaping the familiar (Bolter and Grusin, 1999).

To cite just a few examples, web logs (blogs), which have grown from an arcane curiosity to a common and popular mode of online communication in just a few years, are created with easy-to-use software that merges the graphic and hyperlinking features of web pages with those of older, collaborative, computer-mediated communication forms such as bulletin boards, teleconferencing, and e-mail (Coleman, 2004). Similarly, text messaging combines the tight, telegraphic style and 'emoticons' of ARPANET-era

e-mail messaging with the mobility and person-to-person access of cellular telephony (Ling, 2004). Multi-user games use web sites, hyperlinks and chat rooms as gateways to richly animated, cinematic 'worlds' in which hundreds of players participate and interact simultaneously, as both 'audiences' and 'players' (Gee, 2003). Each of these not only expands the range of information and communication possibilities, affording new or different forms of social relationships and experiences, but it also 'remediates' (rather than replacing or displacing) older forms such as diary writing, voice telephony, or video games.

The Network Metaphor

The second mode of social shaping of new media, the *network metaphor*, suggests that

> ... the point-to-point network has become ... the archetypal form of contemporary social and technical organization ... [it] denotes a broad, multiplex interconnection in which many points or nodes (persons, groups, machines, collections of information, organizations) are embedded. Links among nodes may be created or abandoned on an as-needed basis at any location in the system, and any node can be either a sender or a receiver of messages – or both. (p. 24, this volume)

Networks in this sense depart from the hierarchical, one-way distribution configurations typically associated with mass society, mass production and consumption, and mass media. To the extent that society is a 'network of networks' (Castells, 2002), researchers are rethinking the once dominant 'one-to-many' frame of mass communication and its role relative to one-to-one and many-to-many (or n-way) modes of communication. These multiple, shifting configurations have important implications for the management of authority, trust and participation in social relations, and the control and diffusion of information. Perhaps even this distinction – between n-way and mass or broadcast communication – is being surpassed by new and hybrid modes of communication and information seeking and sharing that incorporate whatever forms of transmission that best suit the purposes at hand. Certainly, the network metaphor

increasingly dominates cultural, social and
technological discourse in technologically
advanced societies. It is the basic assumption
underlying both the advocacy and the critique
of globalization, for example, and a central
trope in the discourses surrounding security,
community, migration, transportation, trade,
political mobilization and information flows,
among many others, that have evolved since
the events of 9/11.

CONSEQUENCES OF ICTs

The *consequences* of new media technologies –
the sociotechnical outcomes of the mutual
shaping process – also distinguish them from
mass media systems, mass communication
processes and mass audiences. In the first edition, we discussed two consequences in particular: ubiquity and interactivity.

Ubiquity

Ubiquity is the sense that new media technologies 'affect everyone in the societies where they
are employed' (p. 25, this volume), even if not
everyone in those societies actually use them.
One example of the sense of ubiquity – or,
more accurately, the sense that ubiquity is both
desirable and inevitable – was seen over a decade
ago when the existence of a 'digital divide' was
identified in the US (National Telecommunications and Information Administration, 1995;
1998).

Subsequently, this single issue stimulated an
enormous outpouring of empirical research
and commentary, both supporting and critical,
around the world. Some observers argued that
the uneven or inequitable distribution of ICTs
and the abilities to use them constituted a clear
and pressing social problem. Others questioned the extent and/or the significance of the
differences among social groups, or suggested
that the problem would solve itself as the technologies diffused (see Bucy and Newhagen,
2004; Compaine, 2001; Gandy, 2002; Lievrouw
and Farb, 2003; Light, 2001; Loader, 1998;
Murdock, 2002; Selwyn, 2004; Warschauer,

2003). The debates themselves generated a
variety of policy and regulatory schemes intended
to rectify various divides or gaps among ethnic
and economic groups, states, neighbourhoods,
nations, regions and so on, such as the e-rate subsidy for Internet access in US public schools and
libraries, and the European Union's Information
Society initiative.

Perhaps what is most notable about the
sheer volume of interest and work in this area
is that it has been built on the assumption that
the ubiquity of ICTs is a public good, with surprisingly little analysis of whether ICTs are,
indeed, to be uncritically promoted, or whether
gaining access to the Internet or other new
media technologies is so obviously a 'good
thing'. The model of access most often invoked
with regard to ICTs is that of voice telephony,
where telephone service is seen as a basic
necessity and therefore governed or regulated
on the basis of 'universal service' or 'universal
access' principles or obligations (Lievrouw,
2000). In contrast, the ubiquity of mass media
(or lack thereof) was not generally framed this
way. No literature sprang up to document and
criticize television or radio 'divides', for example, when those technologies were introduced.
On the contrary, considerable research effort
was devoted to controlling or minimizing
exposure to television – to reduce children's
viewing, or to regulate adult tastes for films,
video and electronic games.[4]

Another example of how expectations of
ubiquity have influenced the development and
use of ICTs is the growing use and versatility of
mobile technologies. As transistors, microchips,
and more recently, nanotechnologies have made
it possible to build smaller and more portable
electronic devices, expectations have also shifted
about where those devices can be used, by
whom, and for what purposes. 'Mobility' today
is an expectation predicated not only on minia-
turization, but also on ubiquitous, interoperable
transmission networks with common or 'con-
vertible' standards (e.g. tri- or quad-band GSM
for mobile phones, or 802.11b/Bluetooth/wi-fi
for wireless Internet access; Ling, 2004). In
traditional workplace, classroom and household
settings dominated by mass media, technologies
are physically fixed and typically shared; mobile

technologies today, in contrast, are designed as personal tools or accessories that provide access to a variety of individualized content and communications services, no matter where the users, services or resources happen to be (Livingstone, 2002).

Interactivity

The second consequence that, in our view, distinguishes new media from earlier mass media channels and content is the pervasive sense of *interactivity* associated with newer channels, that is, the selectivity and reach that media technologies afford users in their 'choices of information sources and interactions with other people' (p. 25, this volume). The immediacy, responsiveness and social presence of interaction via new media channels constitute a qualitatively and substantively different experience than what was possible via mass media channels (even those to which the term 'interactive' was sometimes too generously applied, such as remote control television). Although debates continue about the nature and quality of mediated interaction, especially in contrast with face-to-face conversation as the presumed 'ideal' mode of interpersonal communication (Lievrouw and Finn, 1990), mediated interactivity nonetheless has long been cited as a definitive difference between new media and mass media (see McMillan, Chapter 10 in this volume; also Ball-Rokeach and Reardon, 1988; Bryant and Street, 1988; Rafaeli, 1988; Reeves and Nass, 1996; Rice and Associates, 1984; Rogers, 1986).

FROM MASS MEDIA TO MEDIATION

Mediated communication today, then, differs from mass media 'processes and effects' in that it is recombinant, networked, ubiquitous and interactive. New media research and scholarship have moved away from a dependence on theories of mass society and toward post-industrial or postmodern theories of society. What are the implications of these developments for media and communication studies more generally?

As we noted in the first edition, the difficulties for the field are illustrated by the persistent problem of how to characterize people *collectively* with regard to their sociality and cultural practices via media and information technologies. As the dominance of mass communications began to unravel at the end of the twentieth century, audience researchers were already seeking different terms for understanding the power of the media – moving away from the language of effects or impacts, towards a conception of the active audience (Livingstone, 2004b), the diffused, embedded audience (Abercrombie and Longhurst, 1998), or more broadly, towards 'new audience studies' (Gray, 1999; see also Ang, 1990; Hartley, 1988). However, among audience researchers this rethinking, prompted by the interpretative and ethnographic turn that swept the social sciences more generally, remained focused primarily on television which, despite becoming more globalized, diversified, and even 'interactive', was (and still is) mainly used within the domestic domain of leisure and entertainment.

The convergence of ICTs that has been facilitated and shaped by the parallel convergence of entertainment, education, work and civic activities, and interpersonal communication, requires a more radical rethinking of people's relations with and understanding of ICTs. Today, mediated content and interaction are socially diversified (rather than directed primarily at the masses), channels are technologically convergent (rather than distinct systems), and mediated communication processes are interactive (rather than one-to-many, with separate producer and receiver roles). As we said in the first edition, 'new media and information technologies open up new, more active modes of engagement with media – *playing* computer games, *surfing* the Web, *searching* databases, *writing* and *responding* to email, *visiting* a chat room, *shopping* online, and so on' (2002: 10). These activities have since been joined by *blogging, mobbing, texting, IMing, spoofing*, and a dozen more. The list of new media uses, applications, activities and contents is in continual flux. Some of the terms are individual, some collective, some are mixed modes; some describe the content of the communication, some the act of communicating, some both.

Obviously, the single term *audience* does not capture this diversity of activity. We cannot say, *the internet audience*, though some try. 'Users' does not work either, though more try this. The word is too broad (having no particular relation to information or communication), too instrumental (if people are 'users' of computers or telephones, they are also users of pens, batteries, washing powder, automobiles and a host of other things that don't involve human contact), too individualistic (lacking both the collective status and power suggested by 'audience' and the relational sense of interaction and shared understanding), and too material (referring to the tools and techniques of communication rather than to content, meaning, interaction or shared understanding). *Internet users* works only because it is entirely vague: it doesn't exclude anything; neither does it suggest that there is anything specific about the ways people engage with or understand the technology. It's an empty term that homogenizes uses and 'users' as a category, contrasting them only with an equally empty category of 'nonusers'. So the language problem remains in conveying a sense of what might be new, and specifically related to communication and information, in contemporary engagement with ICTs.

What shall we say instead? *People* is as good a term as any, and better than some. This is not a trite suggestion: try putting *people* in place of *users* in social science and engineering accounts of ICTs. Immediately, human interests, concerns, knowledge and rights leap into focus (while it seems peculiar to talk about the civic potential of audiences, the rights of users, or the creativity of consumers). *People* captures their individuality and their collectivity; the word is neutral about their abilities and interests, but resolutely advances their needs and rights and takes their plurality and diversity for granted. *People* can be used by any academic discipline, introduces no new jargon, and includes us, the observers, in the frame of analysis. And it works in other languages besides English (unlike *audience, users,* and *consumers*; Livingstone, 2005).

The word also puts people's agency and action at the centre of new media studies, rather than the labels or categories we apply to them or to the devices they use. Again, this contrasts with most concepts of 'mass society', where individual and group agency tends to be underplayed or discounted, and of 'mass communication', where communicative behaviour is seen primarily as a response to stimulus, in terms of reception and effects, rather than in terms of action. Interestingly, the attempt by some media researchers to rescue and rehabilitate the term 'audience' by emphasizing audience members' agency and aligning them with creative, self-organizing publics (Livingstone, 2005), itself demonstrates a shift in focus from simple relation to the medium to a more contextualized account of agency in everyday life.

If we take agency and action seriously, we must reframe media and information technologies not just as powerful message-generating entities that influence behaviour and society, but also as resources that provide people with opportunities to cultivate their agency and as tools that allow them to act. By thinking of new media as resources for agency and action, we move away from the predominant view of 'mass media' as relatively fixed, stable and depersonalized institutional entities that have effects *on* people, to a view that considers what people do *with* media and each other – that is, we reorient communication research and scholarship toward the process of mediation.

Previously we defined new media as infrastructures for communication and information that comprise particular types of artefacts, practices and social arrangements; they are socially shaped in distinctive ways and have characteristic social consequences. We can further define *communication* as coordinated action that achieves understanding or shares meaning (Rogers and Kincaid, 1981), and *information* as the organized, expressed and intelligible representation or product of the communication process; the two phenomena are inextricably linked and interdependent (Lievrouw, 2001). *Mediation* therefore enables, supports or facilitates communicative action and representation. It is not simply the intervention or insertion of technology into the communication process or information production; it entails all three elements of infrastructure: artefacts (e.g. alphabets, electrical grids, keyboards and mice, operating systems, telephone switches, film stock, satellite dishes, money, etc.), practices (e.g. gestures, vocalization, telephone or email etiquette, language, manuscript formatting, typing, online file sharing, fashion, contract law, television program schedules, blogging, etc.), and social arrangements (e.g. single-parent families, recorded music labels, think tanks, national film boards, political campaigns, community advice networks, movie studios, etc.). The ubiquity of information and communicative action, recombinant modes of access, use and content, dynamic point-to-point network structures, and the sense of personal engagement and interactivity afforded by new ICTs can be thought of as contemporary modes or patterns of mediation that differ from those that were possible via mass media.

Several observers have already proposed that mediation itself should be a central framing idea in new media studies, for 'our communication society is based on mediations between texts and people, in that people pass and meet each other through texts, just as texts pass and encounter each other through people' (Fornas, 2002: 104). New information and communication technologies raise particular and challenging questions regarding these processes. For example, Stefaan Verhulst, in arguing for a 'new mediation ecology', points out that

> The arrival of new information and communication technologies led to a belief that we witnessed a decrease of the importance of mediation and the arrival of abundance. Yet, instead of the widely predicted process of disintermediation that was supposed to accompany emerging technologies, we are currently forced to confront a process of reintermediation, marked by new actors and methods of disseminating information and framing reality … we are only on the verge of understanding what the social implications of the new mediating forces might be … (2005)

Likewise, Roger Silverstone critiques the traditional, modernist view among some communication researchers that mass media technologies, and by extension mediation itself, distort or corrupt an otherwise idealized, symmetrical experience of interpersonal interaction. He suggests that mediation today must be understood as both 'literal and metaphorical', as technologies, institutions, messages and meanings all interact and influence each other recursively (2005: 30).

Moves from mass society, singular, towards networked societies and relations, plural, have entailed corresponding shifts in people's engagement with media technologies and each other, from mass audiences (powerful in their collective response, yet contained in the realms of the domestic and the local) to a diverse repertoire of mediated and unmediated communication and information sharing (in which collective power and individual action are mutually shaped and often extend beyond domestic and local boundaries). These shifts are clear in all the domains included in this volume, though the ways in which people are positioned, or position themselves, in particular domains varies considerably. A new focus on mediation, rather than on media themselves, invites a new phase of critical and empirical examination for new media researchers.

HOW TO USE THE UPDATED STUDENT EDITION

With this Updated Student Edition of the *Handbook*, we depart from the usual model in academic publishing of simply reproducing the first edition in soft cover. Nor have we put together an entirely new second edition. The book still provides a current and comprehensive introduction for non-specialist colleagues and advanced students who are new to the field, as well as a reference for new media scholars. However, this edition of the *Handbook* is aimed primarily at students and instructors teaching at the upper-division undergraduate or introductory graduate level, either as a primary text or as required background reading that provides more depth and range than is possible with more superficial textbook treatments. For this edition we have selected contributions from the first edition that provide the most clearly structured overviews of major concepts and issues in new media studies. The authors have revised and updated their chapters in light of the most recent scholarship and developments in their respective specialties.

As noted earlier, we have reorganized and streamlined the original six sections into three broad areas that address culture and society, system design and industries, and institutions and governance, respectively. Each chapter focuses on a single key issue, concept or set of related questions, and each combines an overview of foundational literature with a conceptual organization or framework to help put the literature in larger perspective. Introductory courses might cover all three areas, for example; more advanced syllabi might focus just on one or two. Alternatively, instructors might choose their own selection of chapters according to the requirements of their particular programmes or specializations.

One reason we have taken this approach is that most students enrolling in new media studies courses today have grown up with the technologies and are already sophisticated users of mobile phones, personal computers, PDAs, wireless networks, and so on. Many author and host their own web pages and blogs, download music, video, and mobile phone ring-tones, play online games, chat online with or send text messages to family and friends, make long distance phone calls via the Internet, shop for everything online from clothing to textbooks, organize and participate in political and cultural groups via technology. Their technical sophistication is far greater than that of students ten or even five years ago.

What students are often missing, however, is a familiarity with the historical, economic, social or behavioural context of the technologies they use every day and take for granted. They lack the knowledge and background that would enable them to think critically about new media – where they come from, how they're used, who benefits and who is disadvantaged by the ways that systems are configured and run. The overviews provided here can help students understand more about their own communication and the devices they use to do it, as well as give them a base of

knowledge to help frame their future choices and uses of media.

We have asked chapter authors to identify and draw out the key debates and problems in their fields, in the context of their various intellectual and disciplinary traditions. Therefore, the student of new media should also pay keen attention to relations among the chapters and the sections. Do the different authors agree with each other, and are their views mutually compatible, therefore 'filling in' the picture of new media studies for a particular domain? Or do they present the reader with competing visions of new media studies that require the reader to choose which author to follow, which route to take through the tangle of alternate accounts?

For example, Nancy Baym's chapter on interpersonal relations online shares some themes with Nicholas Jankowski's chapter about how new media facilitate community-building. The student of new media might ask whether Baym's micro-level analysis, focused on interpersonal communication and relationships, fits well with Jankowski's meso-level approach, focused on groups and collectives (Alexander et al., 1987). Do they draw similar or different conclusions about mediated relationships, about the future research agenda, even about the most productive research methods? Are similar methods used and results found when mediated relationships are studied within organizations, as in the chapter by Andrea Hollingshead and Noshir Contractor? Does their focus on 'networks' offer a more useful framework for research than, say, 'communities' or 'relationships'?

Similar questions apply when sections of the volume are compared. For example, in Part One, David Buckingham sees children as uniquely individual new media users, even pioneers, in the digital age. Stefaan Verhulst's chapter in Part Three traces the regulatory frameworks that are intended to empower and protect the public as they encounter new media, especially the Internet. Children, or legal minors, are frequently thought of as more vulnerable to the dangers of indecent or violent media than other groups and thus in need of such protective laws. But is the picture of children as vulnerable targets consistent with the depiction of them as heterogeneous, pleasure-seeking, and participatory, presented in Buckingham's chapter? Do either of these authors, from their different perspectives, take into account the three forms of interactivity that Sally McMillan proposes in Part Two? Or, perhaps, do they add to or elaborate her classification by focusing on even newer forms of interactive media? We encourage students to undertake a critical and comparative reading across the chapters and sections of the *Handbook*: the outcome is likely to be both unpredictable and stimulating.

Students and instructors alike should also consider the ideas that we (Lievrouw and Livingstone) have presented in this introduction and in the 'Introduction to the First Edition'. We have proposed that new media differ from mass media in terms of the recombinant and networked ways they develop, and their ubiquitous and interactive consequences. How, and to what extent, are these four themes reflected in the other chapters? Where and how should we look for evidence of recombination, the network metaphor, ubiquity or interactivity? Have we left out other characteristics that might be just as (or more) important? What are the comparable characteristics of mass media? Based on the record of new media research, we also take the position that communication studies should shift its primary focus from mass media to the mediation process itself. Do you agree? Should mass and new media be studied differently, that is, using different theories and research methods? If so, which theories and methods are best in each case?

We close this edition of the *Handbook* with a chapter by Frank Webster, a prominent 'new media sceptic'. Like several of the other chapter authors, Webster is rightly wary of hyperbolic claims made for new media and the breathless language of 'cyber', 'hyper', 'wired', and 'virtual' that are so often invoked by governments, technologists, industries and in popular culture. As we said previously, new media research has been strongly influenced by theories of post-industrial, postmodern, and information society; Webster sets some tough standards for deciding whether the 'information society' has actually arrived. He suggests that if we look at

large-scale economic processes, rather than the customized, personal, interactive experience of 'going online', contemporary society remains crucially hierarchical. Like some of the other authors here, and in line with a longstanding 'continuity' perspective in critical communication research regarding the information society (Schement and Lievrouw, 1987; Schiller, 1981; Turow, 1990), he insists that questions of power, resources and inequality still matter. Readers should test their ideas against this argument as well.

We wish to make one final point about the role research and scholarship can or should play in social change. A persistent theme running through new media studies, and in popular culture generally, is the pace and even urgency of social and technological change associated with ICTs. The hype surrounding new media is usually enough to generate a sceptical response from the academy: there are genuine difficulties in knowing social change when we see it, and in measuring and evaluating it when we do. But this caution also presents a challenge for new media researchers who seek to critique, intervene, or otherwise influence the political and economic management of new media. Just as we must not bypass conventional standards of intellectual and empirical rigour in our assessments of new media, neither should the academy itself risk being bypassed by neglecting questions about new media when they rise to the top of public and policy agendas. This is not simply a matter of the trade-off between academic standards and timely policy intervention; it also reflects the long-standing debate within media and communication studies between so-called administrative and critical traditions of research (Lazarfield, 1941; Levy and Gurevitch, 1994; see also Ferment in the Field, 1983). Ultimately, new media researchers must ask: is it the responsibility of research actively to shape social and technological change? Or is it more appropriate to evaluate the social shaping process independently, from a distance? Should new media research produce knowledge in order to inform or to critique the strategic activities of powerful or established interests? How will the public interest be served?

NOTES

1. As, of course, were *production, text*, and *audience* –
yet the effect of the administrative research tradition in
communication studies was to detach these phenomena
from the contexts that constituted them.

2. For more on network externalities, see Lievrouw, in
this volume. For a concise explanation of cumulative
advantage processes and power laws, especially in relation
to the Internet, see Huberman (2000).

3. Here MacKenzie and Wajcman's (1999) distinction
between technological determinism as a theory of technology
and as a theory of society proves useful. As the former,
technological determinism clearly fails: technological
innovation is a thoroughly social process, from conception, design, production, marketing, diffusion, appropriation, use and consequences. But as a theory of society
and social change, one may agree with MacKenzie and
Wajcman (1999: 3) that technological determinism contains 'a partial truth'. In other words, provided it is firmly
understood that technologies are social products which
embed human relations in their very constitution, we may –
for convenience in our arguments and discussion – cast
them in the role of actors, along with other kinds of actor,
when explaining social processes, whether education,
political life, childhood, labour and so forth. But this is
only a shorthand, for 'precisely because technological
determinism is partly right as a theory of society (technology
matters not just physically and biologically, but also to our
human relations to each other), its deficiency as a theory of
technology impoverishes the political life of our societies'
(1999: 5).

4. It can be argued that historically, the single exception
related to mass media has been print literacy and reading,
long considered a prerequisite to economic, social and
political participation, self-efficacy, and self-determination
in developed Western societies. The basic necessity and
'right' of literacy thus underpins publicly funded education, libraries and postal services. In recent years the language of literacy and reading has been appropriated to
discuss other types of media use and consumption, and
thus to draw parallels between literacy and other types of
communication and information skills, and thus the 'right'
to those other skills (see e.g. Kellner, 2002; Kress, 2003;
Livingstone, 2004a; Luke, 1989; Manguel, 1996; Snyder,
1998). Analogously, access to the telephone system has
been framed in terms of universal service in the US since
the 1934 Communications Act, but telephony has not been
considered a mass medium, or indeed a 'medium' at all, in
communication studies until relatively recently (Sawhney
and Barnett, 1999).

REFERENCES

Abercrombie, N. and Longhurst, B. (1998) *Audiences:
A Sociological Theory of Performance and
Imagination.* London: Sage.

Agre, P. (2004) 'Internet research: For and against',
in M. Consalvo et al. (eds), *Internet Research
Annual*, Volume 1. New York: Peter Lang,
pp. 25–36.

Alexander, J.C., Giesen, B., Munch, R. and Smelser, N.J.
(eds) (1987) *The Micro-macro Link.* Berkeley, CA:
University of California Press.

Ang, I. (1990) *Desperately Seeking the Audience.*
London: Routledge.

Appadurai, A. (1996) *Modernity at Large: Cultural
Dimensions of Globalization.* Minneapolis:
University of Minnesota Press.

Ball-Rokeach, S.J. and Reardon, K. (1988) 'Monologue, dialogue, and telelog: Comparing an emergent form of communication with traditional
forms', in R.P. Hawkins, J.M. Wiemann, and
S. Pingree (eds), *Advancing Communication
Science: Merging Mass and Interpersonal Processes.*
Beverly Hills, CA: Sage, pp. 135–61.

Boczkowski, P.J. (2004) *Digitizing the News:
Innovation in Online Newspapers.* Cambridge,
MA: MIT Press.

Boczkowski, P. and Lievrouw, L.A. (forthcoming)
'Bridging S&TS and communication studies:
Research on media and information technologies',
in E.J. Hackett, O. Amsterdamska, M. Lynch, and
J. Wajcman (eds), *New Handbook of Science and
Technology Studies.* Cambridge, MA: MIT Press.

Bolter, J.D. and Grusin, R. (1999) *Remediation:
Understanding New Media.* Cambridge, MA: MIT
Press.

Bryant, J. and Street, R.L. Jr. (1988) 'From reactivity to
activity and action: An evolving concept and
Weltanschauung in mass and interpersonal communication', in R.P. Hawkins, J.M. Wiemann
and S. Pingree (eds), *Advancing Communication
Science: Merging Mass and Interpersonal Processes.*
Beverly Hills, CA: Sage, pp. 162–90.

Bucy, E.P. and Newhagen, J.E. (eds) (2004) *Media
Access: Social and Psychological Dimensions of New
Technology Use.* Mahwah, NJ: Lawrence Erlbaum.

Castells, M. (2002) *The Internet Galaxy: Reflections
on the Internet, Business, and Society.* Oxford:
OUP.

Coleman, S. (2004) 'Blogs as listening posts rather
than soapboxes', in R. Ferguson and M. Howell
(eds), *Political Blogs: Craze or Convention.*
London: Hansard Society.

Compaine, B.M. (ed.) (2001) *The Digital Divide:
Facing a Crisis or Creating a Myth?* Cambridge
MA and London: MIT Press.

Ferment in the Field (1983) Special issue of the
Journal of Communication, 33 (3), summer.

Fornas, J. (2002) 'Passages across thresholds: Into the
borderlands of mediation', *Convergence*, 8 (4): 89–106.

Gandy, O.H. (2002) 'The real digital divide: Citizens versus consumers', in L. Lievrouw and S. Livingstone (eds) *Handbook of New Media*. London: Sage, pp. 448–600.

Gee, J.P. (2003) *What Video Games Have to Teach Us About Learning and Literacy*. New York: Palgrave Macmillan.

Golding, P. (2000) 'Forthcoming features: Information and communications technologies and the sociology of the future', *Sociology*, 34 (1): 165–84.

Gray, A. (1999) 'Audience and reception research in retrospect: The trouble with audiences', in P. Alasuutari (ed.), *Rethinking the Media Audience*. London: Sage, pp. 22–37.

Hartley, J. (1988) 'The real world of audiences', *Critical Response*, 5 (3): 234–43.

Huberman, B.A. (2000) *The Laws of the Web: Patterns in the Ecology of Information*. Cambridge, MA: MIT Press.

Kellner, D. (2002) 'New media and new literacies: Reconstructing education for the new millenium', in L.A. Lievrouw and S. Livingstone (eds), *The Handbook of New Media: Social Shaping and Consequences of ICTs*. London: Sage, pp. 90–104.

Kress, G. (2003) *Literacy in the New Media Age*. London: Routledge.

Latour, B. (1991) 'Technology is society made durable', in J. Law (ed.), *A Sociology of Monsters: Essays on Power, Technology and Domination*. London: Routledge, pp. 103–31.

Lazarfeld, P.F. (1941) 'Remarks on administrative and critical communication research', *Studies in Philosophy and Social Science*, 9: 2–16.

Levy, M.R. and Gurevitch, M. (eds) (1994) *Defining Media Studies: Reflections on the Future of the Field*. New York: Oxford University Press.

Lievrouw, L.A. (2000) 'The information environment and universal service', *The Information Society*, 16 (2): 155–9.

Lievrouw, L.A. (2001) 'New media and the "pluralization of life-worlds": A role for information in social differentiation', *New Media and Society*, 3 (1): 7–28.

Lievrouw, L.A. (2004) 'What's changed about new media? Introduction to the fifth anniversary issue', *New Media & Society*, 6 (1): 9–15.

Lievrouw, L.A. and Farb, S.E. (2003) 'Information and social equity', *Annual Review of Information Science and Technology*, 37: 499–540.

Lievrouw, L.A. and Finn, T.A. (1990) 'Identifying the common dimensions of communication: the Communication Systems Model', in Brent D. Ruben and Leah A. Lievrouw (eds), *Mediation, Information and Communication: Information and Behavior*, volume 3. New Brunswick, NJ: Transaction Publishers, pp. 37–65.

Lievrouw, L.A. and Livingstone, S. (2002) 'Introduction: The social shaping and consequences of new media', in L.A. Lievrouw and S. Livingstone (eds), *Handbook of New Media: Social Shaping and Consequences of ICTs*. London: Sage, pp. 1–15.

Light, J. (2001) 'Rethinking the digital divide', *Harvard Educational Review*, 71 (4): 710–34.

Ling, R. (2004) *The Mobile Connection: The Cell Phone's Impact on Society*. San Francisco: Elsevier.

Livingstone, S. (2002) *Young People and New Media: Childhood and the Changing Media Environment*. London: Sage.

Livingstone, S. (2004a) 'Media literacy and the challenge of new information and communication technologies', *Communication Review*, 7: 3–14.

Livingstone, S. (2004b) 'The challenge of changing audiences: Or, what is the audience researcher to do in the internet age?', *European Journal of Communication*, 19 (1): 75–86.

Livingstone, S. (ed.) (2005) *Audiences and Publics: When Cultural Engagement Matters for the Public Sphere*. Bristol: Intellect Press.

Livingstone, S. (in press) 'Critical debates in internet studies: Reflections on an emerging field', in J. Curran and M. Gurevich (eds), *Mass Media and Society*, 4th edn. London: HodderArnold.

Loader, B. (ed.) (1998) *Cyberspace Divide: Equality, Agency and Policy in the Information Society*. London: Routledge.

Luke, C. (1989) *Pedagogy, Printing and Protestantism: The Discourse of Childhood*. Albany, NY: State University of New York Press.

MacKenzie, D. and Wajcman, J. (eds) (1999) *The Social Shaping of Technology*, 2nd edn. Buckingham: Open University Press.

Manguel, A. (1996) *A History of Reading*. New York: Penguin.

Manovich, L. (2001) *The Language of New Media*. Cambridge, MA: MIT Press.

McLuhan, M. (1964) *Understanding Media: The Extensions of Man*. New York: McGraw-Hill.

Murdock, G. (2002) 'Review Article: Debating digital divides', *European Journal of Communication*, 17 (3): 385–90.

National Telecommunications and Information Administration (1995, July) *Falling Through the Net: A Survey of 'Have Nots' in Rural and Urban America*. Washington, DC: United States Department of Commerce. URL (consulted April 13, 2005): http://www.ntia.doc.gov/ntiahome/fallingthru.html.

National Telecommunications and Information Administration (1998, July) *Falling Through the*

Net II: New Data on the Digital Divide.
Washington, DC: United States Department of
Commerce. URL (consulted April 13, 2005):
http://www.ntia.doc.gov/ntiahome/net2/falling.
html.

Norris, P. (2001) *Digital Divide: Civic Engagement,
Information Poverty, and the Internet Worldwide.*
Cambridge: Cambridge University Press.

Poster, M. (1990) *The Mode of Information:
Poststructuralism and Social Control.* Chicago:
University of Chicago Press.

Rafaeli, S. (1988) 'Interactivity: From new media to
communication', in R.P. Hawkins, J.M. Wiemann
and S. Pingree (eds), *Advancing Communication
Science: Merging Mass and Interpersonal Processes.*
Beverly Hills, CA: Sage, pp. 110–34.

Reeves, B. and Nass, C. (1996) *The Media Equation:
How People Treat Computers, Television and New
Media Like Real People and Places.* Stanford, CA:
CSLI, and Cambridge: Cambridge University Press.

Rice, R.E. and Associates (eds) (1984) *The New Media:
Communication, Research and Technology.* Beverly
Hills, CA: Sage.

Rogers, E.M. (1986) *Communication Technology: The
New Media in Society.* New York: Free Press.

Rogers, E.M. and Kincaid, D.L. (1981) *Communication Networks: Toward a New Paradigm for
Research.* New York: Free Press.

Sawhney, H. and Barnett, G.A. (eds) (1999) *Progress
in Communication Sciences, Vol. XV: Advances in
Telecommunications.* Stamford, CT: Ablex.

Schement, J.R. and Lievrouw, L.A. (1987) 'The fundamental assumptions of information society
research', in J.R. Schement and L.A. Lievrouw
(eds), *Competing Visions, Complex Realities:
Social Aspects of the Information Society.*
Norwood, NJ: Ablex, pp. 1–10.

Schiller, H.I. (1981) *Who Knows: Information in the
Age of the Fortune 500.* Norwood, NJ: Ablex.

Selwyn, N. (2004) 'Reconsidering political and
popular understandings of the digital divide',
New Media and Society, 6 (3): 341–62.

Silverstone, R. (2005) 'Mediation and communication',
in Craig Calhoun, Chris Rojek and Bryan S. Turner
(eds), *International Handbook of Sociology.* London:
Sage.

Smythe, D. (1981) 'On the audience commodity and
its work', in *Dependency Road: Communications,
Capitalism, Consciousness, and Canada.* Norwood,
NJ: Ablex, pp. 22–51.

Stone, A.R. (1995) *The War of Desire and Technology
at the Close of the Mechanical Age.* Cambridge, MA:
MIT Press.

Turow, J. (1990) 'The critical importance of mass
communication as a concept', in B. Rubin and
L.A. Lievrouw (eds), *Mediation, Information, and
Communication: Information and Behavior,* volume 2.
New Brunswick, NJ: Transaction, pp. 9–19.

Verhulst, S. (2005) Analysis into the Social
Implication of Mediation by Emerging Tech-
nologies. Draft position paper for the MIT-OII
Joint Workshop, *New Approaches to Research on
the Social Implications of Emerging Technologies.*
Oxford Internet Institute, University of Oxford,
April 15–16, 2005. http://www.oii.ox.ac.uk

Warschauer, M. (2003) *Technology and Social
Inclusion: Rethinking the Digital Divide.* Cambridge,
MA: MIT Press.

Wellman, B. (2004) 'The three ages of Internet studies: Ten, five and zero years ago', *New Media and
Society,* 6 (1): 123–9.

Wellman, B., and Haythornwaite, C. (2002) *The
Internet in Everyday Life.* London: Blackwell.

Williams, R. (1974) *Television: Technology and
Cultural Form.* London: Fontana.

Woolgar, S. (2002) 'Five rules of virtuality', in
S. Woolgar (ed.), *Virtual Society? Technology,
Cyberbole, Reality.* Oxford: OUP, pp. 1–22.

Introduction to the First Edition (2002) The Social Shaping and Consequences of ICTs

LEAH A. LIEVROUW AND SONIA LIVINGSTONE

As this is being written, 'new media' is a buzzword, shorthand for a volatile cultural and technology industry that includes multimedia, entertainment and e-commerce. However, in social research the term has a long history, having been used since the 1960s and 1970s by investigators studying the forms, uses and implications of information and communication technologies (ICTs) (e.g. Parker, 1970a; 1973b; Parker and Dunn, 1972). As our contributor and International Advisory Board member Ron Rice pointed out in his foundational collection, *The New Media* (1984), behind the usual meaning of gadgets and trends lie multilayered relationships among economic, political, behavioural, cultural and institutional as well as technological phenomena. Social researchers, critics, historians and designers have all sought to understand them.

A quick visit to a bookstore (online or 'live') immediately reveals the scatter of new-media-related research and scholarship across what are often Balkanized literatures. Any new research front, especially one that is 'transdisciplinary', undergoes an initial period of exploration and expansion. Scholars ask new questions, gather data that is often hard to characterize or manage, and borrow or invent all sorts of frameworks and models in attempts to speak meaningfully about what they find. The sheer diversity and proliferation can be exhilarating and liberating – and difficult to comprehend. Eventually, the pendulum swings back toward synthesis and efforts are made to find common threads or themes.

The present volume was conceived as a move in this direction for new media studies. However, our goal is not to create fixed boundaries for the area, to dictate a canonical literature, or even to argue for a single coherent speciality. Rather, we believe that the continuing openness of new media research, after decades of growth and diversity, continues to be one of its most compelling and productive strengths. Its transdisciplinary goals and structure are entirely appropriate at this moment in Western intellectual history, though they may pose challenges to institutional and disciplinary conventions that are closer to the nineteenth century than the twenty-first.

In this volume, we have attempted to identify major research areas where substantial or influential work has already been done, and to suggest parallel themes or concerns that have surfaced within and among them. Our aim is to deal with the scatter by encouraging, for example, economists of information or technology to consider identity and gender as they are understood in cultural studies; by asking cultural historians to look at the psychology of media use; by persuading sociologists of social change to think about regulatory regimes; and by leading system designers to think about human geography.

Of course, to some extent this strategy only highlights a familiar fact of life for new media scholars: regardless of their disciplinary training or affiliations (ours happen to be in communication and information studies and in social psychology, respectively), we must read and engage across multiple disciplines, whether scientific or humanist, interpretive or empirical. It is difficult, but essential, to be able to look across terminologies, descriptive and explanatory tools, illustrative cases, even assumptions about everyday life. (Happily, an outstanding synthesis like Castells' *Information Age* trilogy or Luhmann's *Social Systems* does occasionally arrive.) The task can be particularly fearsome for students or colleagues who are new to the area, and we have tried to keep these readers in mind as we organized the *Handbook*.

Given the pervasiveness and significance of media and communication technologies in contemporary society it may be surprising that no single volume has yet attempted to draw together the principal strands of research and scholarship that comprise the best current understanding of the relationship between new media and society. Certainly, the chapters and reference lists in this book testify that a huge body of relevant work has been published, particularly over the last 20 years. In the last five years alone perhaps a dozen new scholarly journals on the topic have been launched as venues for publishing research from many disciplines. And by the late 1990s, new media programmes and faculty could be found throughout the world.

Though the speciality dates back several decades, only in the 1990s was there a major impetus for dramatic expansion in the field. In many ways the recent growth of new media studies has coincided with that of the Internet, though of course it is by no means the only significant new media technology. Since the 1970s, when the first 'personal computers' were introduced and the ARPANET was built as an elite channel for technical communication, the Internet has become a platform for commerce, sociality and popular culture. At the same time, new media research has expanded from a handful of specialists in telecommunications regulation and policy, small-group processes, social network analysis, the social psychology of computing and media, organizational communication and 'man–machine studies' to become a major focus of research and scholarship in its own right. Only lately have large numbers of scholars been drawn to the field, creating the

need for a collection like this one which draws together so many diverse developments and identifies key themes and challenges for future research.

Therefore, in this introductory chapter we do several things to help frame contemporary social research and scholarship on new media as it is represented in the following chapters. First, we trace the research projects, problems and intellectual traditions that informed and set the stage for the beginnings of new media research. Second, we propose a definition for new media that acknowledges these early influences as well as the evolution of the field over the last couple of decades. Third, we identify and discuss several important characteristics that distinguish the 'social shaping and consequences' of new media. And fourth, we review some continuing issues and new developments in the methodology of new media research. Obviously, our approach cannot be exhaustive or definitive; instead, we offer observations that suggest the range of possible ways ahead. We end with some observations on the contents and organization of this volume.

EARLY INFLUENCES ON NEW MEDIA RESEARCH

There is, inevitably, some arbitrariness in setting a starting point for any historical review. For new media studies, the problem is compounded because the area has always been multidisciplinary and international, so different fields and specialities have entered the scene at different times in different places.[1] Its early influences include research projects and initiatives that developed outside the mainstream of, or at the intersection among, the major disciplines. Each had its distinct concerns or problematics, or examined particular social phenomena or contexts, so collectively this early body of work tended to be a somewhat scattered response to the innovative information and communication technologies of that era. Nonetheless, many of these projects and studies have had a guiding influence on more recent research, and several of their authors are contributors to, or members of the International Advisory Board for, the present volume. They continue to be cited and would be included in any 'core' bibliography of new media studies (for a more extensive overview, see Lievrouw et al., 2001).

For example, in economics, *Handbook* contributor and Board member Don Lamberton (1971), Kenneth Arrow (1979, 1984), Charles Jonscher (1983) and others worked out important conceptualizations of the economics of information. Their insights about information as an economic good or commodity laid the foundation for new understandings of intellectual property and of the value and significance of 'information work'. Fritz Machlup (1962) and Marc Porat (Porat and Rubin, 1977) conducted some of the first studies that identified and described the extent and significance of information work in the US. In 1978, Simon Nora and Alain Minc, *inspecteurs de finances* for the French government, issued their internationally cited report on the economic significance and challenge of *télématique* for French society (Nora and Minc, 1981 [1978]). Joseph Schumpeter's (1939) theories of 'long waves' of economic development were an important influence on information society theories (Shields and Samarajiva, 1993). *Handbook* Board member Youichi Ito and his collaborators at Keio University based their analysis of *johoka shakai*, or informationalized society, on measurements of the stocks and flows of information in Japan during the 1960s. Their *johoka* index incorporated the amount of information produced per year, the distribution of communication media, the quality of information activities, and a ratio of information expenditures as a proportion of total expenditures (Ito, 1981). This approach has continued to dominate information society analyses in Japan (Kurisaki and Yanagimachi, 1992).

In sociology, Daniel Bell's (1973) theory of 'post-industrial society' quickly became a point of departure for studies of information technologies and social change, though it was also widely criticized (for example, see Webster in this volume). Anthony Giddens (another of our Board members) analysed the changing perceptions of space and time associated with information technology, and later, media as instruments of social surveillance and control in modern societies (Giddens, 1979; 1984). In an extensive historical study, James Beniger (1986) described the 'control revolution' facilitated by communication technologies from the nineteenth-century industrial era onward.

Social psychology provided many early insights into the uses of ICTs. In the UK, Short et al. (1976) proposed that teleconferencing systems could be evaluated in terms of their 'social presence'. Similarly, Robert Johansen and his colleagues (1979) at the Institute for the Future (near Stanford University) formulated the concept of 'telepresence' based on their studies of meetings conducted via video conferencing technology. At the New Jersey Institute of Technology, Roxanne Hiltz and Murray Turoff (1993 [1978]) conducted one of the earliest studies of interaction among geographically dispersed work groups of scientists and engineers via computer-mediated communication. Lee Sproull, Sara Kiesler and their students and colleagues at Carnegie-Mellon University were among the first to note the effects of the anonymity and 'reduced social context cues' of computer-based messaging, which, they argued, contribute to disinhibited communication and 'flaming' (Kiesler et al., 1984; Sproull and Kiesler, 1991). At the Massachusetts Institute of Technology, Sherry Turkle observed both children and computer science students and faculty learning to program. Her seminal essay, 'Computer as Rorschach' (1980), and her subsequent book, *The Second Self* (1984), introduced the idea that computers are 'projective devices' that allow users to control many aspects of their self-presentation and interaction.

Important work was done by scholars in many other fields, including the political scientist Ithiel de Sola Pool (1977; 1983), telecommunications engineer Colin Cherry (1978 [1957]; 1985) and management expert Thomas J. Allen (1977). However, at the same time, while these other fields and disciplines responded to changes in modes of communication and information technology that they had previously taken for granted, communication research was also developing, constituting a central plank of new media studies. Indeed, the moment when the mass communication research literature developed an identifiable interest in 'new media' coincided with the break up of mass media in the 1970s, as broadcasting converged with digital telecommunications, information systems and computing (e.g. Parker, 1973a). Therefore, interest in new media, especially within the communication discipline, was inextricably tied up with the transformation of 'old' mass media from the outset. These transformations were thought to be associated with the evolution of mass society into a service-based 'information society', or alternatively a more differentiated, perhaps fragmented, perhaps more heterarchical, network society.

In this context, some mass media researchers began to redirect their attention to newer technologies and channels that did not fit the conventional 'mass' framework. Such channels, including the telephone, videotex, audio and video teleconferencing, photocopying, facsimile, and computer-mediated communication (CMC) via the fledgling ARPANET and other systems, had been neglected because they did not fit easily into either the mass media or interpersonal/speech communication specialities within communication research (Rogers, 1999). They also lay outside the main theoretical and methodological concerns of other social science and humanities disciplines. Of these technologies, only the telephone had a major presence in the home; researchers often had to study the others within the settings of the universities, government agencies or other large organizations where they were used.

Therefore, and doubtless for reasons to do with the availability of research funding and the 'applied' or 'administrative' nature of the questions being asked (Lazarsfeld, 1941; Melody and Mansell, 1983), many early studies of new media technologies within communication research took a somewhat traditional approach, considering the 'impacts' of new technologies on attitudes, behaviour, organizations, policy and so on. They focused on workers' perceptions of new technologies, the features and functions of different systems, the

types of communication or information services that the systems supported, and their 'effects' on work performance and productivity. Policy studies considered the implications of new media for different industry structures and regulatory options, or described changes in employment and occupational structures attributable to the rise of new technologies and 'information industries'. They examined the prospects for extending established frameworks for universal service obligations, cross-subsidies, rate regulation, and decency and privacy laws to new media systems. In short, a broadly administrative response to technological innovation, modelled primarily after the mass communication 'effects' tradition, came to dominate the field of new media research at an early stage, particularly in the US.

At Stanford University, for example, Edwin Parker and his associates explored the uses of computing for information retrieval and 'information utilities' (Parker, 1970b; 1973b). They also studied the effects of new technologies (such as slow-scan television, direct broadcast satellites and telephone systems) on what was then termed 'development communication' (Parker, 1978). Parker, *Handbook* Board member Everett Rogers, and others examined the role of new media technologies in social and economic development, applying diffusion of innovations theory to the provision of social and information services to rural or underserved areas and nations (Parker and Hudson, 1975; Parker and Mohammadi, 1977; Rogers, 1995; see also Heather Hudson's chapter in this volume). In Canada, government initiatives on computer-mediated communication and videotex in the 1970s produced clusters of new media researchers in Québec and elsewhere. By the early 1980s, the Annenberg School for Communication at the University of Southern California in Los Angeles had become a centre for new media research grounded in the social psychology of telecommunications, organizational communication, and communication law and policy.

The European tradition of new media research took a rather different direction in the beginning, emphasizing a cultural/critical studies approach to media content and industries, on the one hand, and a broadly Marxist political economy of media, on the other.[2] Just as the different theoretical, philosophical, methodological and political commitments of administrative and critical (or, variously, 'positivist' and 'relativist', or 'quantitative' and 'qualitative') research were being explicitly debated in media and communication research more generally (see e.g. Ferment in the Field, 1983), new media research underwent a similar divergence of its own. Eschewing the preference for middle-range theory that characterized administrative research (Boudon, 1991), European scholars on the whole became more critical of new media than their US counterparts (with some exceptions, noted below). They drew upon a variety of social theories, ranging from Bourdieu's analysis of the relation between economy and culture (Bourdieu, 1977 [1972]; 1980) to Foucault's linking of technology to the administrative imperatives, standardization processes and procedures of bureaucratic organization (Foucault, 1970 [1966]; 1980). Social theories of modernity and social change, including Bell's post-industrial society, Habermas' theory of the public sphere and Giddens' theory of structuration, also inspired new theoretical approaches that connected new media technologies to the co-determination of social structure and action.

British media studies, for example, took an explicitly cultural/critical approach to new media, as they had to mass media previously. Raymond Williams (1974) was a key figure in this tradition, not only in establishing a critical approach to the mass media, contextualizing them in relation to both political economy and cultural analysis, but also in developing the relation between studies of mass communication and the study of technology and technological innovation. This perspective carried over into early studies of new media content and industry structure in the UK and Europe and has, more recently, also stimulated the study of the social and cultural contexts of ICT consumption and use (Jouet, 1994; Miller and Slater, 2000; Silverstone and Hirsch, 1992).

The political economy of media was another significant influence in European (and later, in North American) new media studies, especially during the 1980s as critics mounted a response to post-industrialism and the popular vision of the 'information society' promulgated by industry and government. As argued by Handbook contributor Frank Webster and Kevin Robins (Robins and Webster, 1985; Webster, 1995; Webster and Robins, 1986; 1989) and Nicholas Garnham (1986; 1990; 1994), among others, new media systems and services tend to reinforce the economic and political power of existing systems and institutions. In effect, they argued, the information society is the latest stage of industrial capitalism, not a radical departure from the past.

This critique of the cultural, economic and political power of mass media was advanced forcefully by a number of European scholars, including Handbook Board members Armand Mattelart in France, and Cees Hamelink, Tapio Varis and Osmo Wiio in Finland. It was also well represented in North America by the late Herb Schiller and his colleagues at the University of California, San Diego (Schiller, 1981), George Gerbner at the University of Pennsylvania's Annenberg School for Communication, and Dallas Smythe and his research group at Simon Fraser University in Canada. Their colleagues and students carried the critical perspective forward to studies of new media content, ownership structures and technology development (see e.g. Gandy, 1993; Mosco, 1982, 1996; Schiller, 1982; Slack and Fejes, 1987).

These and related perspectives provided the key framework for the development of new media research in the UK. Central to this development was the decision, in 1985, of the Economic and Social Research Council to provide ten years of funding for the first coordinated research Programme on Information and Communication Technologies (PICT) (which was succeeded by the Virtual Society? Programme headed by Handbook Board member Steve Woolgar, followed in turn by the E-Society Programme). This multimillion-pound research programme not only served to make visible the various strands of research on new media already developed in the UK, but also drew on a wide array of academic disciplines to establish what has become a burgeoning tradition of new media research in the UK.

Combining critical and empirical approaches, the PICT legacy in particular is that of an active, policy-oriented research community committed to a broadly 'social shaping' position, concerned to understand and critique how governments, regions, organizations and households are shaping as well as being shaped by technological developments in the field of new media (for an overview of PICT-related research, see the edited volume by our Board member Bill Dutton, 1996).

While some observers have asked how far mass communication theory can be extended to the new media (e.g. McQuail, 1986; Morris and Ogan, 1996), the effects-type approach is still found in new media research in many countries (e.g. Lea, 1992; Reeves and Nass, 1996). Today, however, it is balanced by more complex levels of analysis and a more critical perspective that locate the changing perceptions and practices surrounding new media within a broader institutional, economic and cultural context.

Nonetheless, there are some 'blind spots'. For example, international and comparative studies are still relatively scarce. The new media research traditions of non-Western countries remain less familiar to, and so less influential for, the largely English-language scholars and literature we have traced here. It is fair to say that, until very recently, rather more comparative literature has been produced concerning traditional mass media (e.g. Blumler et al., 1992; Chaffee and Chu, 1992; Lull, 1988) than new media, though there are notable exceptions (such as George Barnett's world-systems theory approach to international telephone uses and networks: Barnett and Choi, 1995; Barnett and Salisbury, 1996). Several major international bodies, such as UNESCO, OECD and the European Commission, collate national- and regional-level data that are used in comparative studies (UNESCO, 2000).

In part, this limited 'internationalization' of the field reflects the flows and connections among research communities cross-nationally. It demonstrates that new media themselves have developed and diffused according to different time-scales in different places, which is largely though not exclusively a matter of

economics. Only recently, for instance, since 'Europe' expanded its borders after 1989, has there been research on new media within the context of ex-Soviet countries (Lengel, 2000). Within Europe in particular, however, pan-European work has burgeoned, stimulated by the increasingly unified European economic and policy community (e.g. Becker and Schoenbach, 1989; Livingstone and Bovill, 2001; McQuail et al., 1986; Robins and Morley, 1989; Schultz, 1992; Tydeman and Kelm, 1986). This policy-oriented research, which is informed by Habermas' theory of the public sphere in particular, reflects a formative trend in new media research at both the national and pan-European level, and contrasts with a great deal of US policy research. It has arisen in response to a growing sense that the strong public service tradition in European media is being undermined by changes within the European media environment (Burgelman, 1997; Calabrese and Burgelman, 1999; Ferguson, 1986;).

As new media research has progressed from its early efforts to its recent proliferation in the 1990s, it has become more specialized; some of that variety is illustrated by the diverse chapters that follow. However, today this drift toward specialization is being challenged by broader developments in social theory. For example, as sociologists, political scientists, economists and others debate phenomena like globalization (e.g. Beck, Giddens, Luhmann), they often assume but rarely focus on or theorize the central role of ICTs in these hotly contested, incompletely global transformations in politics, economics and culture. Today, new media researchers face the new and important challenge of making their concepts, arguments and findings count, and having their theories and methods taken seriously, in this wider playing field.

WHAT IS/ARE NEW MEDIA?

The thumbnail history outlined above provides a sense of just how many points of entry there have been to new media research, and the many ways in which new media might be defined. The field needs a definition that is abstract enough to accommodate the range of systems, contents, issues and settings that researchers consider essential, yet not so broad that new media cannot be distinguished from other established areas within communication research and other disciplines.

At the risk of oversimplification, we can say that researchers concerned with technological, economic, or behavioural issues have tended to define new media in terms of system features and services, industry structures and ownership, or the psychology of media users, respectively. Critical/cultural scholars, following the media studies tradition, have drawn more on definitions based on new media content and its forms.

Undoubtedly, most definitions of new media and ICTs to date have focused on their technological features. Wilbur Schramm (1977) classified communication media on the basis of channel characteristics that parallel human sensory perception, such as motion versus still visuals, sound versus silent, text versus picture, or one-way (simplex) versus two-way (duplex) transmission. He distinguished between inexpensive, small-scale 'little media' and 'big media' with large, complex, expensive infrastructures and organizational arrangements. Ithiel de Sola Pool, a political scientist and pioneer of new media research, defined *new communications technologies* as 'shorthand for about 25 main devices', which he duly listed (Pool, 1990: 19). Other definitions of new media technology have taken a similar classificatory approach (Durlak, 1987; Steuer, 1995).

Ron Rice stressed the two-way capabilities of computing and telecommunications, and defined new media as 'those communication technologies, typically involving computer capabilities (microprocessor or mainframe), that allow or facilitate interactivity among users or between users and information' (Rice and Associates, 1984: 35). The demassified, time-shifting features of new media have been contrasted with the one-to-many, one-way message flows of traditional mass media (Rogers, 1986). More recently, writers have emphasized the convergence of computing and telecommunications technologies (Baldwin et al., 1996).

Studies of human–computer interaction and interface design focus on system features that affect the perceptions and cognitive 'human factors' of technology users (Reeves and Nass, 1996).

Consistent with this orientation toward system features, user perceptions and the mass media effects tradition in US communication research (especially the Shannon–Weaver linear model of communication that includes channel as a variable in the communication process), early studies of new media tended toward technological determinism. They emphasized the effects or 'impacts' of ICTs *on* users, organizations and societies. Technological determinism – the belief that technologies have an overwhelming and inevitable power to drive human actions and social change – is often taken for granted in technologically advanced societies. The opposing 'social shaping of technology' approach (see Lievrouw in this volume) contends that technologies are continuously remade by the things users do with them. Some technologies certainly constrain action, but people can always make choices about using them.

While many new media scholars today have developed a view of technology that is closer to the social shaping perspective, and despite the somewhat relentless critique of technological determinism over the last two decades, the language of 'impacts' persists in both academic research and popular culture (Kling, 1999; MacKenzie and Wajcman, 1999; Smith and Marx, 1994). Yet, as Raymond Williams (1974) forcefully pointed out, the link between technological determinism and narratives of progress (or, less commonly, narratives of decline) – narratives which cast science (typically allied to commercial imperatives) as the driver of not only technological innovation but also social change, with 'improvements' in technology becoming readily aligned with 'progress' in society – can be misleading or even dangerous.

For example, as several of our contributors point out, the Internet is popularly portrayed as a single medium which sprung fully formed into our lives less than a decade ago. However, this is misleading in two senses. First, 'the Internet' is shorthand for a bundle of different media and modalities – e-mail, websites, news-groups, e-commerce and so forth – that make it perhaps the most complex and plural of the electronic media yet invented. Second, these different modes have their own communication characteristics, are subject to differing economic and social conditions of use and, significantly, have different histories stretching back over several decades. Clearly, these differences must be accounted for; they undermine any possibility of identifying singular impacts or effects because the (plural) meanings and consequences of the Internet are contingent on a wide range of specific historical and cultural conditions.

The dangers of defining communication media in terms of system features or 'impacts' are also illustrated by recent debates in American media law and regulation. Traditionally, media systems have been regulated in the US according to their technological configurations or infrastructures. Speech and publishing are largely unregulated (that is, their content cannot be censored) because historically those forms of communication are protected under the First Amendment of the US Constitution (though exceptions include pornography, libel and defamation, and speech that incites violence). First Amendment protection has been extended to other recording media as well, such as photography, film, audio and video, on the grounds that they too constitute 'speech'.

The American telephone system (essentially AT&T and a few smaller operators), in contrast, was regulated under the Communications Act of 1934 as a 'common carrier', a concept borrowed from transportation law. The common carrier metaphor suggested that because the telephone system was a natural monopoly, AT&T should be required to serve any customers who were willing to pay, without regard for the content of their messages. Broadcasting was also regulated under the 1936 Act because the 'airwaves' (like water, perhaps) were a scarce resource that should be rationed because there were fewer radio (and later, television) frequencies available than broadcasters who wanted to use them. Broadcast licences were awarded to owners of radio and television stations whose programmes would serve the 'public interest, convenience and necessity' – and could be revoked if licensees aired material that did not meet this deliberately vague requirement.

Today technological convergence has blurred these channel-based metaphors – speech, transportation, airwaves – with serious consequences for the regulatory schemes that invoke them (First Amendment, common carriage, licensing). For example, though American Internet users often assume that they have First Amendment speech rights online, or expect the same level of privacy that they have for telephone calls, Internet service providers insist that they are entitled to intercept, read and censor any messages that pass through their systems because they may be held financially and legally liable for those communications. Employees who might reasonably assume that their books, papers and other print materials are safe from 'unreasonable search and seizure' find that similar privacy protections do not always extend to computer disks or hard drives. 'Content providers' like newspaper and book publishers, movie studios, and record companies, on the other hand, maintain that they should have the same rights of expression (and property rights) online as they do in print or on film. In response to recent technological developments and pressures from the media industries, the US Telecommunications Act of 1996 rolled back or weakened many of the rules of the 1934 Act. These include restrictions on cross-ownership of broadcast and publishing media, and the number of outlets that a single owner may have in a given market. While the 1996 Act does not solve all of the regulatory or equity problems of new media, the current regulatory climate shows that it is obviously becoming more difficult to distinguish among media, or to regulate them, on the basis of system features or technology alone.

Beyond Features

No wonder, then, that contemporary discussions of new media have begun to incorporate more than technological characteristics. For the inaugural issue of the journal *New Media & Society*

(What's New about New Media?, 1999, a theme since revisited in a special issue of *New Media & Society* on the topic, 'What's Changed About New Media?' in 2004), editors asked several scholars (including one of the present authors) to respond to the question: what is 'new' about new media? What distinguishes them from other media, either technologically or socially? Some contributors mentioned channel characteristics or features like those reviewed above, or commented on the historical problem of labelling any technology as 'new' by definition. But others pointed out that new technologies give users an unprecedented ability to modify and redistribute content – contributing to what *Handbook* contributor Mark Poster called the 'underdetermination' of new media in comparison with traditional media. Rakow suggested that media research has not yet come to terms with the fact that new media allow any user to 'speak', an issue echoed by Sonia Livingstone's call for a reconceptualization of the notion of audience.

Kevin Robins, reviewing the recent work of Pierre Lévy, agreed that new media have produced a new kind of 'knowledge space' or 'communication space' that is 'de-referentialized', that is, disconnected from local, situated knowledge and experience. But unlike Lévy, who sees this development as an emancipatory break from older forms of knowledge that were linear, hierarchical and rigid, Robins argued that the new 'relation to knowledge' serves to further global corporate capitalism and the interests of a relatively small elite. In this environment, information and communication are valued not for their substance or meaning, but for their capacity to be processed, circulated, or connected for their own sake: 'contemporary knowledge culture is regarded as essentially about the acquisition of generic information skills and competencies' (1999: 20). In the same issue, Bill Melody proposed that new media are 'more influenced by economic factors' and more central to the new information economy than traditional media have been. The high degree of interconnectedness, and the volume of communication and information moving through networks, has created greater economic instability.

Insights like these bring us closer to a framework that more fully captures the rich interweaving of media technology, human action and social structure. While a single definition can hardly capture the variety of ways that the term is used today – or even in this book – we can still propose a framework for thinking about new media that goes beyond simple classification of systems and features. Therefore, by *new media* we mean information and communication technologies and their associated social contexts, incorporating:

- the artifacts or devices that enable and extend our abilities to communicate;
- the communication activities or practices we engage in to develop and use these devices; and
- the social arrangements or organizations that form around the devices and practices.

Together, we can think of the three aspects of media technology as an 'ensemble', in Michel Callon's phrase, or as infrastructure in the sense that Susan Leigh Star and Geof Bowker define it in this volume. The three elements are inextricable and mutually determining.

Clearly, from the viewpoint of this definition, many technologies are infrastructural, in that they combine elements of technology, practice and social organization. So what can we say distinguishes new media as a particular focus of study? Many apparently novel traits of new media have been described, including hyperreality, virtuality, anonymity, interactivity and so on. However, we believe that new media can be characterized more usefully in terms of, first, the particular ways that they are both the instrument and the product of social shaping and, second, their particular social consequences.

A number of the chapters here make the point that new media technologies both shape, and are shaped by, their social, economic and cultural contexts. More specifically for new media, however, such shaping is *recombinant*. That is, new media systems are products of a continuous hybridization of both existing technologies and innovations in interconnected technical and institutional networks. The recombinant/hybrid metaphor suggests that while ICTs are influenced by the existing technological context, and may have unintended consequences, to a great extent they are the result of human actions and decisions. They are not determined by an independent, inevitable causality or evolutionary process unique to technology itself; rather, designers, users, regulators and others can take advantage of the current state of technical knowledge, and recombine technologies and new knowledge to achieve their particular goals or purposes.

The metaphor also suggests the essentially continuous nature of new media development. Even technologies that are perceived as being unprecedented are found upon closer analysis to have been designed, built and implemented around existing technologies and practices. Change, then, comes in waves or cycles; occasionally, a wave may be of such magnitude that it appears to be a 'revolution' or a complete break with the past, but from a longer perspective it is still part of an ongoing process.

Certainly, some media technologies may work so well, or be adopted so broadly, that they become very stable and resistant to change (for example, the NTSC television broadcast standard in the US). But in the last few decades, the social, political and economic premium placed on innovation, as well as the digitization of different media systems, have tended to push new media technologies toward instability. In this context, hybridization has created an unstable sociotechnical landscape and has compelled researchers to treat systems and their uses as moving targets (for example, the rapid coevolution of technologies and social groups that share audio and video over the Internet). This characteristic was first seen in the technological convergence of traditional media with computing and telecommunications that prompted the early studies within communication research and other fields in the 1960s and 1970s. It also accounts for the persistent sense of 'newness' that has been associated with media systems ever since.

Another specific aspect of social shaping associated with new media is that the point-to-point 'network' has become accepted as the archetypal form of contemporary social and technical organization. Today, the *network metaphor* applies not just to new media technologies, but also to the patterns of social relations and organizing and the institutional formations associated with them. It can be argued that more traditional mass media technologies, as well as the organizations that employed them and the institutions that governed them, embodied industrial-era notions of social and work organization. For example, though broadcasting was often organized into systems called 'networks', such systems were usually hierarchical. This type of configuration supported the large-scale production and distribution of messages directed from a few media centres (ordinarily, major cities or cultural capitals) to 'mass' audiences. It ensured the smooth and rapid diffusion of information from the 'top' or 'centre' of the hierarchy to the bottom or periphery and provided little or no capacity for messages going the other way, so-called feedback. As it is understood today, however, the term 'network' denotes a broad, multiplex interconnection in which many points or 'nodes' (persons, groups, machines, collections of information, organizations) are embedded. Links among nodes may be created or abandoned on an as-needed basis at any location in the system, and any node can be either a sender or a receiver of messages – or both.

Certainly, high-tech firms, including new media services, tend to congregate in particular geographic places (the 'clusters' discussed by Cooke in this volume), and the network topographies of telecommunications, computing and media are far from evenly distributed around the world, or even across regions. But these hubs and regions do not necessarily dominate new media content as a few major cities and cultural centres did for mass media. New kinds of 'spaces and places' for sociality and culture have been created, as systems like the Internet have been designed specifically to allow any node to connect to any other with network access (Curry, 1998). This architecture was introduced with the telephone system (and to a lesser extent, by the telegraph system before that), and it is both physically and qualitatively different from the 'networks' of broadcasting and print. Indeed, economists and others first recognized that the positive 'network externalities' associated with the telephone system were different in kind from the economies of scale of broadcasting or print. The larger the network, the more valuable it becomes to every additional new user, as each user gains the advantage of links to more potential respondents and sources of information.

Not only are new media shaped in characteristic ways; they also have distinctive social consequences. Perhaps the most obvious, one that has been commented on since the days of McLuhan, is the *ubiquity* of new media. Though not every individual in a society may use (or indeed have access to) new media technologies, we can say they are ubiquitous because they affect everyone in the societies where they are employed. The reach of ICTs extends far beyond the obvious arenas of entertainment and the workplace. Banking systems, utilities, education, law enforcement, military defence, health care and politics, for example, are all dependent on extensive ICT systems for record-keeping, monitoring and transmitting information – activities that affect anyone who deals with these services or activities.

The sense of ubiquity underlies several major issues that are discussed in the chapters that follow. For example, though ubiquity might be assumed, new technologies and the resources to use them are not distributed evenly or fairly, as evidenced by the flurry of research and news coverage about the 'digital divide' in the late 1990s (see Rice and Haythornthwaite, in this volume). By the same token, any system with pervasive reach and influence prompts questions about the control of the system and the power and cultural influence it affords those who are in control; new media systems are no exception. And while the relationship among media messages, public opinion and political participation has been studied extensively, the Internet and other new media technologies have presented new arenas for discourse that challenge the definition and understanding of the public sphere and what constitutes political action (see Luke, in this volume).

Another consequence of new media is the sense of *interactivity* that they convey to users. Interactivity is the main topic of the chapter by Sally McMillan in this volume. Briefly, however, we can say that because switching is a pivotal part of new media systems, they afford users more selectivity in their choices of information sources and interactions with other people. Communication researchers have known for decades that mass media audiences attend to, perceive and retain information selectively. Yet new media also give users the means to generate, seek and share content selectively, and to interact with other individuals and groups, on a scale that was impractical with traditional mass media. This selectivity accounts for much of the sense of interactivity or social presence associated with new media, as well as their 'demassified', or individualized, targeted quality. In turn, the sheer proliferation and diversity of content and sources now available have raised concerns about the quality of the content (for example, its authenticity or reliability), as well as questions about the nature of online experience and interaction (for example, about anonymity or identity of participants in online interaction).

NEW MEDIA, NEW METHODS?

Because the *Handbook* is organized around major substantive areas of research and scholarship, we have not dedicated a chapter specifically to the methodology of new media research. However, new media studies pose a number of empirical and analytical challenges that merit a brief discussion here.

The chapters in this volume represent a significant collation of past and current empirical research, as well as conceptual frameworks for analysing new media in relation to their social shaping and social consequences. While the field abounds with new and pressing research questions, only recently has attention been paid to the methods by which these are being addressed. Beyond the challenges posed by the multidisciplinary nature of the field, which results in often conflicting conventions underpinning the conduct and evaluation of empirical research, *Handbook* readers may discern two broad methodological issues. First, do new media require new methods to observe and study them? Second, how does empirical research contribute to the shaping and consequences of the new media being studied?

In response to the first issue, and as is evident from the recent bounty of books and articles addressing the conduct of empirical media research, and new media research in particular, two positions have emerged. The first presumes, at least implicitly, that media research rests on the same, well-established methods as any other area of social science (or humanities). In relation to the new media, therefore, the use of surveys, interviews, case studies, observation, textual analysis and so forth is considered to be 'business as usual'. Those adopting this position would argue that in new media research as elsewhere (perhaps even more so here, given the rush to produce findings before they go out of date), traditional standards of reliability, validity, generalizability and so forth are crucial to the evaluation of good research (e.g. Webster in this volume). This is perhaps the most common perspective, and is clearly laid out in the well-used textbook by Williams et al. (1988). Similarly, Deacon et al. (1999) deal with the Internet solely as a new source of information for media and communication researchers. They offer guidelines to its effective use as a knowledge resource, but say little about it as a subject of empirical research in its own right.

The contrasting position tends to draw primarily on a qualitative or ethnographic tradition (e.g. Hine, 2000), arguing that traditional methods must be changed both conceptually and procedurally. To the extent that new media generally, and virtual environments in particular, challenge key concepts of media research – authority and power, production and consumption, community and identity, and so forth – then research must frame and operationalize its questions (and answers) in different ways (Lyman and Wakeford, 1999). So too, again particularly for virtual environments, many guidelines, practices and evaluative criteria regarding, for example, research ethics, the nature of naturalistic/unobtrusive versus participant observation, or criteria for survey sampling and evaluating response rates, must be reformulated (Mann and Stewart, 2000).

The second broad methodological consideration concerns the social uses of new media research. It will be apparent in many of the chapters that follow that a major research strategy is to track what are, in effect, real-world experiments, in which new communication infrastructures and changing social phenomena are observed. From these experiments, we can infer early indications of the likely future 'impacts' of these new media and see the social shaping of technology itself, occurring through a path-dependent process of technological change in which contingent histories of adoption matter (see Lievrouw in this volume).

However, because the media being observed are often new or provisional, the research itself may affect the course of its design, implementation or use more than it might for older media, which are more stable and where a critical or neutral distance is more readily sustainable. MacKenzie and Wajcman observe that 'the very process of adoption tends to improve the performance of those technologies that are adopted' (1999: 19); by the same token, researchers must also acknowledge that studies of this adoption feed back into the design process itself. In other words, in so far as new media technologies are shaped not only in the rarefied world of design and innovation but also through their early history of adoption and everyday use, such experiments, and the research that accompanies and assesses them, play a role in the social shaping and social consequences of new media.

Researchers vary in their response to this situation. For many, 'it would be an unforgivable dereliction of the responsibilities of intellectuals if the potentials offered by current developments were not fully explored, and a concerted effort made to shape their direction to bring about at least some of the much talked about utopian visions of communication in the electronic age' (Kress, 1998: 79; see also Biocca, 1993). For others, a critical distance between the researcher and the new media phenomena being researched is crucial to the independence of the research findings.

The very pace of change – both technological and social – poses a challenge to new media research. In other words, the field is in flux, not so much because it is new (indeed, it is at least

20 years old) but because the object of study itself and its social contexts have never been – nor are they likely to become – stable. Researchers working in the area must tolerate ambiguity and be comfortable with the study of moving targets. At the same time, anticipating the future significance of the new media is hazardous in the extreme. Boddy (1985) notes some of the widespread misconceptions, within both public and industry circles, that existed at the time of television's arrival as a mass medium. Many observers failed to anticipate the success of television in dominating culture, information, lifestyles and, more arguably perhaps, public and political life in the second half of the twentieth century. Interestingly, in his highly influential book *Television: Technology and Cultural Form*, Raymond Williams (1974) had similar difficulties with prediction. He conceptualized new technologies primarily in terms of the transformation of television; despite his considerable percipience, he did not anticipate the convergence between broadcasting, telecommunication and, especially, information technology.

We might end this section with a note on terminology. In researching new media, some of the terms from mass media research still apply – production, media institution, design – though they are undoubtedly more complex and less fixed than hitherto. Other terms, however, apply less well. *Text* is one, as new media exploit the intertextual or transtextual (Drotner, 1992), as the meanings conveyed by new media result from an interactive engagement between producers and consumers, and as the texts are mutable, transformed through processes of relocation, transmission, and recombination.

Even more problematically perhaps, there is an uncertainty over how to label people in terms of their relationship with new media. The term *audience*, which was and to some extent still is satisfactory for mass media research, fits poorly within the domain of new media. In a number of important ways, audiences are becoming 'users'. Analytically, audiences are being relocated away from the screen, their activities contextualized into the everyday lifeworld. They are also becoming users because they are grappling with the meaning of new and unfamiliar media objects (i.e. as technologies, or consumer goods), and this not only in their homes but also in schools and workplaces. Further, they are becoming users because new media and information technologies open up new, more active modes of engagement with media – *playing* computer games, *surfing* the Web, *searching* databases, *responding* to e-mail, *visiting* a chat room, *shopping* online and so on. Etymologically, the term 'audience' only satisfactorily covers the activities of listening and watching (though even this has been expanded to include the activities which contextualize listening and viewing). But the term 'user', despite its problematic histories (e.g. in uses and gratifications research, or its instrumental connotations in technology-driven studies of information retrieval, interface design and 'human factors', which suggest that users of media technologies differ little from users of washing machines or cars), better covers this variety of modes of engagement.

What is significant about people's uses of new media remains, in many ways, what was also significant about audiences for traditional media: that is, the extent to which media engagement is necessary for a common culture, for shared community values or, conversely, the extent to which media engagement undermines, fragments, manipulates or exploits people collectively (as publics, markets, nations and so on). In this sense, the term 'audience' is still appropriate. But grammatically it is awkward, as are 'communicators', 'consumers' or 'users'. One can only conclude, as do the authors of the chapters included here, that no one term can be expected to cover the variety of significant relationships which now exist between people and the media. Perhaps most important is that we use the array of available terms with care, and not lose sight of the observation that has become a consensus among audience researchers (Livingstone, 1999), that the nature of the relationship, rather than the artificial creation of a reified entity (audience, user, consumer), is most central to the analysis of new media and their social consequences. To focus on the relationship also serves to locate this relationship in a social context, for people are, first and foremost, workers, business people, parents, teachers, friends – thoroughly embedded social roles which precede their status as 'users' or 'audiences'.

OVERVIEW OF THIS VOLUME

In putting together this book, we have stressed research on socially situated technologies, and on studies that document circumstances where strong cultural concerns or social norms have developed around ICTs. As its subtitle suggests, the social contexts and uses of new media are as important as the technologies themselves. 'Social shaping' and 'consequences' suggest the evolving, dynamic nature of the systems and their related issues, as well as major approaches to research in the area. On the one hand, there is a concern with agency and action; on the other, a concern with social effects, structure and impacts. While the *Handbook* attempts to cover the field as comprehensively as is practical, no single approach can be said to characterize the whole work, though certain sections may illustrate widely held perspectives.

Overall, one principal purpose of this volume is to lay out the present boundaries of new media research so as to allow a clear view of the current state of the art. We agree that 'as new fields evolve, there are periodic attempts to take stock of what's happened so far, how things are going, and what still needs to be done' (Johansen, 1984). Consequently, the emphasis throughout the chapters that follow is on documenting the most significant social research findings and insights in areas where a substantial amount of work has already been accomplished, rather than on speculations about future technological directions or scenarios. Thus, one ambition of the *Handbook*, prosaically but perhaps most usefully, is that it sets out to draw together in a single place the key resources and trends among the rapidly diversifying variety of new media research. The goal is to make visible and readily accessible work which has already been conducted but which may not be familiar to specialists in particular disciplines. In some domains, the stress is on consolidating and building on significant contributions already made within the field, while in others it seems more important to incorporate key ideas and approaches from outside, given the interdisciplinary nature of new media research.

A more ambitious aim than that of collating new media research is that of facilitating the identification of key themes and debates which have thus far framed the major contours of new media research, in order to support both critical perspectives on research and the development of future research projects. Hence we have invited chapter authors to identify not only major trends but also problematic claims or assumptions, remaining gaps in the research record, and new domains to be explored. In such future developments it is our hope that researchers from different disciplines and perspectives will not only converge productively on the problematics of new media shaping and consequences, but also take back these perspectives into their home disciplines. For it seems that, at least until very recently, little new-media- or ICT-related research has found its way into the most prestigious, core or mainstream journals in communication research, sociology, social psychology, education, law, economics or political science.

New media research spans not only multiple disciplines but also many countries. Yet, as already noted, it has proved more challenging than anticipated, and perhaps we have been less successful than we had hoped in achieving a multinational coverage of new media research. Research communities tend to be national in orientation, addressing national policy developments, responsive to national funding sources in particular economic and cultural contexts, and networked within distinct linguistic and intellectual traditions. While we are aware of the advantages of learning from comparative research, to some extent, the challenges of developing a comparative overview in the field of new media remain for the future.

Therefore, we offer the *Handbook of New Media* as one in what we hope will be a series of useful surveys and syntheses of new media studies, as more questions are asked, as more comprehensive and creative answers are found, and as the field and its influence continue to grow.

NOTES

1 For a longer historical perspective, bearing in mind that all media were once 'new' and gave rise to various hopes and anxieties, readers are encouraged to review the opening chapter of Rice and Associates (1984) as well as several histories of media technologies that have informed the field, including books by Jim Beniger (1986), James Carey (1989), Claude Fischer (1992), Patrice Flichy, (1995 [1991]), Carolyn Marvin (1988) and, more recently, Brian Winston (1996), as well as the edited collection by Chandler and Cortada (2000).

2 This dichotomy is well summarized in the introduction to a collection of key articles from the journal *Media, Culture & Society* (Collins et al., 1986).

REFERENCES

Allen, T.J. (1977) *Managing the Flow of Technology: Technology Transfer and the Dissemination of Technological Innovation within the R&D Organization.* Cambridge, MA: MIT Press.

Arrow, K. (1979) 'The economics of information', in M.L. Dertouzos and J. Moses (eds), *The Computer Age: a Twenty-Year View.* Cambridge, MA: MIT Press. pp. 306–17.

Arrow, K. (1984) *Collected Papers.* Vol. 4: *The Economics of Information.* Oxford: Blackwell.

Baldwin, T.F., McVoy, D.S. and Steinfield, C. (eds) (1996) *Convergence: Integrating Media, Information and Communication.* Thousand Oaks, CA: Sage.

Barnett, G.A. and Choi, Y. (1995) 'Physical distance and language as determinants of the international telecommunications network', *International Political Science Review*, 16: 249–65.

Barnett, G.A. and Salisbury, J.G.T. (1996) 'Communication and globalization: a longitudinal analysis of the international telecommunication network', *Journal of World System Research*, 2 (16): 1–17.

Becker, L.B. and Schoenbach, K. (eds) (1989) *Audience Responses to Media Diversification: Coping with Plenty.* Hillsdale, NJ: Erlbaum.

Bell, D. (1973) *The Coming of Post-Industrial Society: A Venture in Social Forecasting.* New York: Basic.

Beniger, J.R. (1986) *The Control Revolution: Technological and Economic Origins of the Information Society.* Cambridge, MA: Harvard University Press.

Biocca, F. (1993) 'Communication research in the design of communication interfaces and systems', *Journal of Communication*, 43 (4): 59–68.

Blumler, J., McLeod, J.M. and Rosengren, K.E. (eds) (1992) *Communication and Culture across Space and Time: Prospects of Comparative Analysis.* Newbury Park, CA: Sage.

Boddy, W. (1985) '"The shining centre of the home": Ontologies of television in the "Golden Age"', in P. Drummond and R. Paterson (eds), *Television in Transition.* London: British Film Institute.

Boudon, R. (1991) 'What middle-range theories are', *Contemporary Social Psychology*, 20 (4): 519–24.

Bourdieu, P. (1977 [1972]) *Outline of a Theory of Practice*, trans. R. Nice. Cambridge: Cambridge University Press.

Bourdieu, P. (1980) 'The production of belief: contribution to a theory of symbolic goods', *Media, Culture & Society*, 2 (3): 261–93.

Burgelman, J.-C. (1997) 'Issues and assumptions in communications policy and research in Western Europe: A critical analysis', in J. Corner, P. Schlesinger and R. Silverstone (eds), *International Media Research: a Critical Survey.* London: Routledge.

Calabrese, A. and Burgelman, J.-C. (eds) (1999) *Communication, Citizenship, and Social Policy: Rethinking the Limits of the Welfare State.* Lanham, MD and Oxford: Rowman & Littlefield.

Carey, J.W. (1989) *Communication as Culture: Essays on Media and Society.* Boston and London: Unwin Hyman.

Chaffee, S.H. and Chu, G. (1992) 'Communication and cultural change in China', in J. Blumler, J.M. McLeod and K.E. Rosengren (eds), *Communication and Culture across Space and Time: Prospects of Comparative Analysis.* Newbury Park, CA: Sage. pp. 209–37.

Chandler, A.D. Jr and Cortada, J.W. (eds) (2000) *A Nation Transformed by Information: How Information Has Shaped the United States from Colonial Times to the Present.* Oxford and New York: Oxford University Press.

Cherry, E.C. (1978 [1957]) *On Human Communication*, 3rd edn. Cambridge, MA: MIT Press.

Cherry, E.C. (1985) *The Age of Access: Information Technology and Social Revolution. The Posthumous Papers of Colin Cherry*, compiled and edited by W. Edmondson. London: Croom Helm.

Collins, R., Curran, J., Garnham, N., Scannell, P., Schlesinger, P. and Sparks, C. (eds) (1986) *Media, Culture & Society: A Critical Reader.* London: Sage.

Curry, M.R. (1998) *Digital Places: Living with Geographic Informaiton Systems*. London and New York: Routledge.

Deacon, D., Pickering, M., Golding, P. and Murdock, G. (1999) *Researching Communications: a Practical Guide to Methods in Media and Cultural Analysis*. London: Arnold.

Drotner, K. (1992) 'Modernity and media panics', in M. Skovmand and K.C. Schroder (eds), *Media Cultures: Reappraising Transnational Media*. London: Routledge.

Durlak, J.T. (1987) 'A typology for interactive media', in M.L. McLaughlin (ed.), *Communication Yearbook 10*. Newbury Park, CA: Sage. pp. 743–56.

Dutton, W.H. (ed.) (1996) *Information and Communication Technologies: Visions and Realities*. Oxford: Oxford University Press.

Ferguson, M. (ed.) (1986) *New Communication Technologies and the Public Interest*. London: Sage.

Ferment in the Field (1983) Special issue of *Journal of Communication*, 33 (3), summer.

Fischer, C.S. (1992) *America Calling: A Social History of the Telephone to 1940*. Berkeley and Los Angeles: University of California Press.

Flichy, P. (1995 [1991]) *Dynamics of Modern Communication: The Shaping and Impact of New Communication Technologies*, trans. L. Libbrecht. London: Sage.

Foucault, M. (1970 [1966]) *The Order of Things: An Archaeology of the Human Sciences*, trans. A. Sheridan. New York: Pantheon.

Foucault, M. (1980) *Power/Knowledge: Selected Interviews and Other Writings 1972–1977*, trans. C. Gordon et al. New York: Pantheon.

Gandy, O.H., Jr (1993) *The Panoptic Sort: A Political Economy of Personal Information*. Boulder, CO: Westview.

Garnham, N. (1986) 'Contribution to a political economy of mass-communication', in R. Collins, J. Curran, N. Garnham, P. Scannell, P. Schlesinger and C. Sparks (eds), *Media, Culture and Society: A Critical Reader*. London: Sage. pp. 9–32.

Garnham, N. (1990) *Capitalism and Communication: Global Culture and the Economics of Information*. London: Sage.

Garnham, N. (1994) 'Whatever happened to the information society?', in R.E. Mansell (ed.), *The Management of Information and Communication Technologies: Emerging Patterns of Control*. London: Aslib, The Association for Information Management. pp. 42–51.

Giddens, A. (1979) *Central Problems in Social Theory*. Berkeley and Los Angeles: University of California Press.

Giddens, A. (1984) *The Constitution of Society: Outline of the Theory of Structuration*. Cambridge: Polity.

Hiltz, S.R. and Turoff, M. (1993 [1978]) *The Network Nation: Human Communication via Computer*, rev. edn. Cambridge: MIT Press.

Hine, C. (2000) *Virtual Ethnography*. London: Sage.

Ito, Y. (1981) 'The *johoka shakai* approach to the study of communication in Japan', in C. Wilhoit and H. deBock (eds), *Mass Communication Review Yearbook*, vol. 2. Beverly Hills, CA: Sage. pp. 671–98.

Johansen, R. (1984) 'Foreword', in R.E. Rice and Associates (eds), *The New Media: Communication, Research and Technology*. Beverly Hills, CA: Sage. pp. 7–8.

Johansen, R., Vallee, J. and Spangler, K. (1979) *Electronic Meetings: Technical Alternatives and Social Choice*. Reading, MA: Addison-Wesley.

Jonscher, C. (1983) 'Information resources and economic productivity', *Information Economics and Policy*, 1: 13–35.

Jouet, J. (1994) 'Communication and mediation', *Réseaux*, 2 (1): 73–90.

Kiesler, S.B., Siegel, J. and McGuire, T.W. (1984) 'Social psychological aspects of computer-mediated communication', *American Psychologist*, 39: 1123–34.

Kling, R. (1999) 'What is social informatics and why does it matter?', *D-Lib Magazine*, 5 (1). Available online: http://www.dlib.org/dlib/january99/kling/01kling.html

Kress, G. (1998) 'Visual and verbal models of representation in electronically mediated communication: the potentials of new forms of text', in I. Snyder (ed.), *Page to Screen: Taking Literacy into the Electronic Era*. London and New York: Routledge. pp. 53–79.

Kurisaki, Y. and Yanagimachi, H. (1992) 'The impact of information on the economic development of sub-regional centres: a trial application of an "information activity" index to the 43 cities in Japan', in C. Antonelli (ed.), *The Economics of Information Networks*. Amsterdam and London: North-Holland. pp. 71–89.

Lamberton, D.M. (ed.) (1971) *The Economics of Information and Knowledge*. Harmondsworth: Penguin.

Lazarsfeld, P.F. (1941) 'Remarks on administrative and critical communication research', *Studies in Philosophy and Social Science*, 9: 3–16.

Lea, M. (ed.) (1992) *Contexts of Computer-Mediated Communication*. New York: Harvester Wheatsheaf.

Lengel, L. (ed.) (2000) *Culture and Technology in the New Europe: Civic Discourse in Transformation in Post-Communist Nations*. Stamford, CT: Ablex.

Lievrouw, L.A., Bucy, E.P., Finn, T.A., Frindte, W., Gershon, R.A., Haythornthwaite, C., Köhler, T., Metz, J.M. and Sundar, S.S. (2001) 'Bridging the subdisciplines: an overview of communication and technology research', in W.B. Gudykunst (ed.), *Communication Yearbook 24*. Thousand Oaks, CA: Sage, for the International Communication Association. pp. 271–95.

Livingstone, S. (1999) 'New media, new audiences', *New Media & Society*, 1 (1): 59–66.

Livingstone, S. and M. Bovill, M. (eds) (2001) *Children and Their Changing Media Environment: A European Comparative Study*. Mahwah, NJ: Erlbaum.

Lull, J. (ed.) (1988) *World Families Watch Television*. Newbury Park, CA: Sage.

Lyman, P. and Wakeford, N. (1999) 'Going into the (virtual) field', *American Behavioral Scientist*, 43 (3): 359–76.

Machlup, F. (1962) *The Production and Distribution of Knowledge in the United States*. Princeton, NJ: Princeton University Press.

MacKenzie, D. and Wajcman, J. (eds) (1999) *The Social Shaping of Technology*, 2nd edn. Buckingham: Open University Press.

Mann, C. and Stewart, F. (2000) *Internet Communication and Qualitative Research: A Handbook for Researching Online*. London: Sage.

Marvin, C. (1988) *When Old Technologies Were New: Thinking about Electric Communication in the Late Nineteenth Century*. New York and Oxford: Oxford University Press.

McQuail, D. (1986) 'Is media theory adequate to the challenge of new communications technologies?', in M. Ferguson (ed.), *New Communication Technologies and the Public Interest: Comparative Perspectives on Policy and Research*. London: Sage.

McQuail, D., Siune, K. and Euromedia Research Group (eds) (1986) *New Media Politics: Comparative Perspectives in Western Europe*. London: Sage.

Melody, W.H. and Mansell, R.E. (1983) 'The debate over critical vs. administrative research: circularity or challenge', *Journal of Communication*, 33 (3): 103–16.

Miller, D. and Slater, D. (2000) *The Internet: An Ethnographic Approach*. London: Berg.

Morris, M. and Ogan, C. (1996) 'The Internet as mass medium', *Journal of Communication*, 46 (1): 39–51.

Mosco, V. (1982) *Pushbutton Fantasies: Critical Perspectives on Videotex and Information Technology*. Norwood, NJ: Ablex.

Mosco, V. (1996) *The Political Economy of Communication: Rethinking and Renewal*. London: Sage.

Nora, S. and Minc, A. (1981 [1978]) *The Computerization of Society: A Report to the President of France*. Cambridge, MA: MIT Press.

Parker, E. (1970a) 'The new communication media', in C.S. Wallia (ed.), *Toward Century 21: Technology, Society and Human Values*. New York: Basic. pp. 97–106.

Parker, E. (1970b) 'Information utilities and mass communication', in H. Sackman and N. Nie (eds), *The Information Utility and Social Choice*. Montvale, NJ: AFIPS. pp. 51–70.

Parker, E. (1973a) 'Technological change and the mass media', in I. Pool, W. Schramm, F. Frey, N. Maccoby and E. Parker (eds), *Handbook of Communication*. Chicago: Rand McNally. pp. 619–45.

Parker, E. (1973b) 'Implications of new information technology', *Public Opinion Quarterly*, 37 (4): 590–600.

Parker, E. (1978) 'Communication satellites for rural development', *Telecommunications Policy*, 2 (4): 309–15.

Parker, E. and Dunn, D. (1972) 'Information technology: its social potential', *Science*, 176: 1392–9.

Parker, E. and Hudson, H. (1975) 'Telecommunication planning for rural development', *IEEE Transactions on Communications*, 23 (10): 1177–85.

Parker, E. and Mohammadi, A. (1977) 'National development support communication', in M. Teheranian, F. Hakiszadeh and M. Vidale (eds), *Communications Policy for National Development: A Comparative Perspective*. London: Routledge & Kegan Paul. pp. 167–201.

Pool, I. de S. (ed.) (1977) *The Social Impact of the Telephone*. Cambridge, MA: MIT Press.

Pool, I. de S. (1983) *Technologies of Freedom*. Cambridge, MA: Harvard University Press.

Pool, I. de S. (1990) *Technologies of Boundaries: On Telecommunications in a Global Age*, edited by Eli M. Noam. Cambridge, MA: Harvard University Press.

Porat, M.U. and Rubin, M.R. (1977) *The Information Economy*. OT Special Publication 77–12, 9 vols. Washington, DC: US Department of Commerce, Office of Telecommunications.

Reeves, B. and Nass, C. (1996) *The Media Equation: How People Treat Computers, Television and New Media Like Real People and Places*. Stanford, CA: CSLI and Cambridge: Cambridge University Press.

Rice, R.E. and Associates (eds) (1984) *The New Media: Communication, Research and Technology*. Beverly Hills, CA: Sage.

Robins, K. and Morley, D. (1989) 'Spaces of identity: communications technologies and the reconfiguration of Europe', *Screen*, 30 (4): 11–34.

Robins, K. and Webster, F. (1985) '"The revolution of the fixed wheel": information, technology and social Taylorism', in P. Drummond and R. Paterson (eds), *Television in Transition*. London: British Film Institute. pp. 36–63.

Rogers, E.M. (1986) *Communication Technology: The New Media in Society*. New York: Free Press.

Rogers, E.M. (1995) *Diffusion of Innovations*, 4th edn. New York: Free Press.

Rogers, E.M. (1999) 'Anatomy of the two sub-disciplines of communication study', *Human Communication Research*, 25: 618–31.

Schiller, D. (1982) *Telematics and Government*. Norwood, NJ: Ablex.

Schiller, H.I. (1981) *Who Knows: Information in the Age of the Fortune 500*. Norwood, NJ: Ablex.

Schramm, W. (1977) *Big Media, Little Media: Tools and Technologies for Instruction*. Beverly Hills, CA: Sage.

Schultz, W. (1992) 'European media systems in transition: general trends and modifying conditions. The case of the Federal Republic of Germany', *Gazette*, 49: 23–40.

Schumpeter, J. (1939) *Business Cycles: A Theoretical, Historical and Statistical Analysis of the Capitalist Process*. New York: McGraw-Hill.

Shields, P. and Samarajiva, R. (1993) 'Competing frameworks for research on information-communication technologies and society: toward a synthesis', in S.A. Deetz (ed.), *Communication Yearbook 16*. Newbury Park, CA: Sage. pp. 349–80.

Short, J., Williams, E. and Christie, B. (1976) *The Social Psychology of Telecommunications*. New York: Wiley.

Silverstone, R. and Hirsch, E. (eds) (1992) *Consuming Technologies: Media and Information in Domestic Spaces*. London and New York: Routledge.

Slack, J.D. and Fejes, F. (eds) (1987) *The Ideology of the Information Age*. Norwood, NJ: Ablex.

Smith, M.R. and Marx, L. (eds) (1994) *Does Technology Drive History? The Dilemma of Technological Determinism*. Cambridge, MA: MIT Press.

Sproull, L. and Kiesler, S. (1991) *Connections: New Ways of Working in the Networked Organization*. Cambridge, MA: MIT Press.

Steuer, J. (1995) 'Defining virtual reality: dimensions determining telepresence', in F. Biocca and M.R. Levy (eds), *Communication in the Age of Virtual Reality*. Mahwah, NJ: Erlbaum. pp. 33–56.

Turkle, S. (1980) 'Computer as Rorschach', *Society/ Transaction*, January/February: 15–24.

Turkle, S. (1984) *The Second Self: Computers and the Human Spirit*. New York: Simon & Schuster.

Tydeman, J. and Kelm, E.J. (1986) *New Media in Europe: Satellites, Cable, VCRs and Videotex*. London: McGraw-Hill.

UNESCO (2000) *World Communication and Information Report, 1999–2000*. Paris: UNESCO.

Webster, F. (1995) *Theories of the Information Society*. London: Routledge.

Webster, F. and Robins, K. (1986) *Information Technology: A Luddite Analysis*. Norwood, NJ: Ablex.

Webster, F. and Robins, K. (1989) 'Plan and control: towards a cultural history of the information society', *Theory and Society*, 18: 323–51.

What's New about New Media? (1999) Special themed section of *New Media & Society*, 1 (1): 10–82.

Williams, F., Rice, R.E. and Rogers, E.M. (1988) *Research Methods and the New Media*. New York: Free Press.

Williams, R. (1974) *Television: Technology and Cultural Form*. London: Fontana.

Winston, B. (1996) *Media Technology and Society: a History. From the Telegraph to the Internet*. London and New York: Routledge.

Part One

New Media, Culture and Society

1

Interpersonal Life Online

NANCY K. BAYM

In concluding her 1984 analysis of experimental research on computer-mediated communication, linguist Naomi Baron wrote that 'computer mediated communication – at least as currently used – is ill suited for such "social" uses of language' (1984: 136). Fourteen years later, in a move indicative of the shift in this line of research, she argued that 'e-mail is, in many respects, an ideal tool for building or maintaining social relationships' (1998: 157). Although computer-mediated communication was not invented with interpersonal interaction in mind, the rise of the Internet has clarified that this technology is fundamentally social (Parks and Roberts, 1998; Sproull and Faraj, 1997). E-mail, used primarily for person-to-person contact, is the Internet's 'killer app' and the best predictor of whether new users will stay online (Kraut et al., 2000; Madden and Ranie, 2003). Even aspects of the Internet that do not seem particularly social, such as business sites, online magazines and information services, have integrated social opportunities such as chat spaces and bulletin boards into their sites (Parks and Roberts, 1998). The early failure of its inventors and scholars to grasp the social implications of this medium is typical of the history of many new media. As Kraut et al. (2000) have pointed out, the interpersonal implications of the telephone were also not apparent to its innovators or

early analysts. This chapter examines the Internet, and computer-mediated communication (hereafter CMC) more broadly, arguing that CMC's interpersonal opportunities are among its most important.

Research into CMC began in the 1970s, as networked computer systems were being installed in large organizational contexts and as maverick computer enthusiasts were creating interactive dial-in bulletin board systems. At the time, organizational computing systems which allowed multiple users to interact consisted primarily of local area networks that offered e-mail, group decision-making software and computer conferencing. Despite the early presence of recreational CMC, its use in organizational contexts set the research agenda through the 1980s. Today's forms of CMC include asynchronous media such as mailing lists (discussion forums organized by topic and distributed to subscribers through e-mail), newsgroups (publicly accessible discussion forums organized by topic which are similar in form to e-mail but do not require e-mail subscriptions), message boards, and blogs on the World Wide Web. Synchronous computer-mediated forms of communication include chat (multi-user 'channels' or 'rooms' in which people gather in small numbers to discuss topics both general and specific), MUDs and MOOs (multi-user 'places' elaborately constructed through text for purposes of role-playing games, social interaction and education), instant messages (a more targeted form of chat, in which users keep 'buddy' lists and can keep tabs on whether or not their friends are online and available to receive messages), and graphic user worlds (akin to MUDs and MOOs but graphical). A sense of the popularity of these media (at least in the United States) can be gained from a Pew Internet and American Life Project poll in late 2004. They found that on an average day 48 per cent of American net users (an estimated 30.7 million people) send e-mail, 12 per cent (primarily young people) send instant messages, and 4 per cent participate in chat rooms or online discussions.

Although organizations are far from the only context for CMC use, early organizational research codified core assumptions and comparisons to which much interpersonal CMC scholarship still reacts. I begin by elaborating this backdrop. I then explore contemporary thought about the characteristics of CMC. Having laid out these two frameworks for CMC research, the remainder of the chapter focuses on four areas of interpersonal meaning that have received the most attention: online language use, identity, personal relationships and social groups.

MEDIA CHARACTERISTICS

The Cues-filtered-out Perspective

Most early efforts at analysing CMC were based on the premise that media characteristics have consistent effects on communication. Drawing largely on small-group research from social psychology, in particular the work of Bales (1950), this research had practical goals. Early applications and studies (e.g. Martino, 1972; Price, 1975) were generally concerned with efficiency and effectiveness (Kiesler et al., 1984). This research agenda essentially asked what happened when face-to-face work groups meet via computer instead. Questions included how CMC affected the quality of group decisions, leadership, participation and time to decision (Rice and Love, 1987). Given

this concern, the basis of comparison was (and often remains) face-to-face communication, the key features of which were taken to be the ongoing provision of feedback and the clarity of participants' relative social status. Social presence theory (Short et al., 1976) and later media richness theory (Daft and Lengel, 1984), both of which argued that media differ in the information they can provide and therefore in the extent to which they are appropriate for different communication tasks, were combined into what Culnan and Marcus (1987) called the 'cues-filtered-out' approach. This work is summarized and critiqued at length elsewhere (e.g. Lea and Spears, 1995; Walther et al., 1994) so I hit only the highlights here.

Cues-filtered-out took the defining features of CMC to be the absence of regulating feedback and reduced status and position cues. This was taken to result in anonymity and deindividuation, with a variety of communicative consequences (e.g. Hiltz and Turoff, 1978; Kiesler et al., 1984). In experiments where small face-to-face groups were compared with small computer-mediated groups, researchers found that the latter took longer to complete tasks, single leaders were less likely to emerge, participation became more equal, and there was more uninhibited behaviour (e.g. Hiltz and Turoff, 1978; Siegel et al., 1986). Most famous of the 'uninhibited' behaviours is flaming, which Walther et al. (1994) in a meta-analysis defined operationally as name calling, swearing, insults, impolite statements, threats and put-downs, crude flirtations of a demeaning or sexually explicit nature, and attacks on groups or individuals.

The task-oriented claims made from this approach have held up reasonably well, but the interpersonal implications of the cues-filtered-out approach have been roundly criticized, and this deterministic perspective has for the most part been dropped (although, as I will discuss below, the issue of limited non-verbal cues remains central). The criticisms were methodological, empirical and conceptual. Methodologically, most of the lab studies brought together unrealistically small, zero-history groups for a median time period of 30 minutes (Rafaeli and Sudweeks, 1997; Walther et al., 1994; Weisband and Atwater, 1999). Among differences in research designs were group characteristics and members, communication system infrastructures, functions or tasks around which the groups were organized, and groups' temporal structures (Hollingshead and McGrath, 1995; Walther, 1992; Walther and Burgoon, 1992). However, these variations were rarely addressed within the work, confounding experimental designs with findings (Hollingshead and McGrath, 1995).

Empirically, the laboratory evidence for differences between face-to-face and computer-mediated communication was statistically significant, but the magnitude of difference was small (Walther et al., 1994). More importantly, research using a different methodological approach – the field study – turned up evidence that socioemotional communication not only existed in computer-mediated groups, but was more likely to be prosocial than antisocial. Hiltz and Turoff (1978) reported that users compensated for the coldness of the medium with extra efforts to be friendly, warm and personal. Social cues reported in early CMC field studies included ASCII art, salutations, degree of formality of language, paralanguage, communication styles and message headers (Hiltz and Turoff, 1978; Lea et al., 1992). In a content analysis of transcripts from a professionally oriented CompuServe forum, Rice and Love (1987) found that socioemotional content (defined as showing solidarity, tension relief, agreement, antagonism, tension and disagreement) constituted around 30 per cent of messages. Only 0.4 per cent of the content was negative, and 18 per cent showed solidarity. In their critique of the notion that flaming is rampant in computer-mediated systems, Lea et al. (1992) concluded that there was no comparative evidence that flaming is more common in CMC than in other media or face-to-face. The richer portrait of CMC revealed by field research has since led to more sophisticated conceptualizations of variables in experimental research.

Most conceptual criticisms of the cues-filtered-out perspective revolved around definitions of socioemotional communication and disinhibition. As Lea (1991) pointed out, Bale's category system, which was often used to code messages, has very restrictive definitions of socioemotional. It also requires that messages be identified as either socioemotional or task-oriented, whereas messages are usually multifunctional and can be both. Thus, even studies such as Rice and Love's, which found considerable socioemotional communication, may have underestimated its prevalence. Regarding disinhibition, many studies included positive as well as negative comments as uninhibited behaviour (Lea et al., 1992), so that most socioemotional or off-task communication was seen as disinhibited. Empirical evidence also showed that even flaming, which seemed to be the most clearly disinhibited behaviour, sometimes took inhibited forms (for instance, punctuation marks substituted for letters in swear words). Furthermore, flaming was shown to be context-dependent, occurring at different levels across computer-mediated groups (Lea et al., 1992). If the cues-filtered-out perspective was right that media characteristics have consistent effects, there was no way to account for the development of norms regarding the appropriateness of flaming, or the fact that over time groups came to sanction inappropriate behaviours (Hiltz and Turoff, 1978; Lea et al., 1992). I return to the issues of context and norm development throughout what follows.

Communication-relevant Qualities of Computer Media

Despite the criticisms, the experimental findings of cues-filtered-out research cannot simply be dismissed (Walther, 1992; Walther et al., 1994). Most CMC researchers have continued to rely on media characteristics to think through key questions. However, rather than positing limited cues as the primary independent variable, or assuming that limited cues invariably produce particular results, the challenge now is to explain the roles that media characteristics can play in shaping communication and to clarify the variables that produce differing results in varying contexts. This has led to more sophisticated methodological and conceptual analyses. The media qualities with the greatest interpersonal implications fall into roughly three categories: those having to do with spatiotemporal issues, with the participants, and with the electronic and (usually) written nature of the medium. I focus on the Internet in what follows, though most of the discussion can be generalized to other forms of CMC such as local area networks.

In terms of time and space, as long as one is in a country or region that has access, the Internet makes physical location largely irrelevant (e.g. Baron, 1998; Lea and Spears, 1995; McKenna and Bargh, 2000; Sproull and Faraj, 1997). Interaction between two people in the same building is indistinguishable from interaction between people half a world apart. This creates a kind of spaceless proximity that did not exist to this extent before, a sense enhanced by the speed of transmission and immateriality of time, especially in synchronous CMC (Baron, 1998; Carnevale and Probst, 1997; McKenna and Bargh, 2000). In asynchronous CMC, the fact that one can read and respond to messages in one's own time has been taken to expand the potential for interpersonal engagement and thus to be a critical feature of the medium. In a real break from earlier technologies such as the telephone, CMC dramatically reduces the costs associated with communication across distance (Baron, 1998; Pew, 2000; Sproull and Faraj, 1997). This explains in part why many people report that e-mail is good for keeping in touch with friends and family far away and also that they make fewer long-distance phone calls after going online (Dimmick et al., 2000; Pew, 2000).

A second characteristic of CMC is the limited information available regarding participants. The notion of reduced social cues remains central. However, the effort has shifted from asking simply what effect this has, to more nuanced efforts to understand the variety of possible consequences, the contexts which give rise to different options, and the creative ways in which communicators make use of, or compensate for, this media characteristic. The reduction of physical appearance cues, along with the evidence of status and attractiveness they bear, creates a kind of invisibility or anonymity (Carnevale and Probst, 1997;

McKenna and Bargh, 2000; Sproull and Faraj, 1997; Turkle, 1996), which opens the potential for multiplicity of identities (Stone, 1995; Turkle, 1996), a high degree of privacy (Baron, 1998), and a lower sense of social risk (Curtis, 1997) or accountability (Stone, 1995), among other possibilities (topics I return to in the discussion of identity).

In addition to obscuring information about participants as individuals, CMC can also hide information regarding the participant structure of interactions. The net blurs the boundary between interpersonal and mass media (Baym, 1996; Lea and Spears, 1995; Morris and Ogan, 1996; Rafaeli and Sudweeks, 1997). E-mail and instant messaging are usually clearly interpersonal given their specific addressees, but other forms of CMC are harder to categorize. As Culnan and Marcus (1987) argued, addressivity in CMC is fundamentally different from face-to-face communication, as there is usually no need to specify identity and location of recipient in the latter. Furthermore, in many forms of CMC, such as newsgroups and mailing lists, it can be difficult if not impossible to judge the size of one's audience (Carnevale and Probst, 1997). Finally, just as a producer loses control over who watches a television show once it is aired, there is usually little, if any, control over access to and participation in computer-mediated groups (Galegher et al., 1998). Interactions between two individuals can thus have consequences for social formations larger than pairs. Just as the mail, telegraph and telephone bridged time and space before the Net, anonymity and unclear participant structures occurred in pre-Internet days, but not on anything like their current scale.

Finally, computer-mediated messages can be stored in memory, replicated, retrieved at later dates, and edited prior to sending, which has also been taken to have interpersonal consequences (Carnevale and Probst, 1997; Cherny, 1999; Culnan and Marcus, 1987; Walther, 1996). Some (e.g. Hiltz and Turoff, 1978; Walther, 1996) suggest that the additional visual channel of written discourse combined with the ability to edit leads to better organized and better thought out statements than occur face-to-face. Again, all of the consequences of these media characteristics were possible before computers, but the Internet combines them in such a way and on such a scale as to represent a qualitative shift in mediated communication. These characteristics together form a backdrop for the discussion that follows.

Media Comparisons

In casting the characteristics of CMC in terms of space, time, visual and auditory cues, participant structure and storage capabilities, the basis of comparison is usually face-to-face communication, a fact that follows both from the early agenda of CMC research and from the tendency of CMC users to think of the medium as conversational. However, as suggested by those who view CMC as a cross between interpersonal and mass media, and those who have compared it to the telephone, face-to-face conversation is by no means the only basis for comparison. Discourse analysts, in particular, have paid a good deal of detailed attention to language forms in CMC, often comparing CMC to writing. Rather than drawing on social psychology, these scholars were more likely to be guided by linguistic anthropologists (e.g. Bauman and Sherzer, 1974; Gumperz and Hymes, 1972). While the former tradition often focuses on identifying variables through the decontextualized space of the laboratory, the latter seeks to describe language forms in naturally occurring contexts, and to explain these forms in terms of those contexts. Discourse analysts have rarely looked at organizations, focusing instead on classroom and recreational groups.

Early on, Baron (1984) noted the need to distinguish between the use of CMC to replace writing and its use to replace speech. In the time since, many (e.g. Baron, 1998, 2000; Ferrara et al., 1991; Wilkins, 1991) have explored the extent to which CMC compares to writing, usually concluding that CMC represents 'a hybrid language variety displaying characteristics of both oral and written language' (Ferrara et al., 1991: 10). Like writing, CMC involves participants who are often temporally separated and do not share physical co-presence. Communicators in CMC must make explicit much of the information that would be carried by the voice, gestures or other non-verbal cues in face-to-face conversation. Like speech, much CMC is direct, contextualized and interactive (e.g. Baym, 1996; Galegher et al., 1998). Writers can assume that their readers will share many referents, will be reading within a few days and will be able to respond. Messages are often open to reformulation.

These analyses of online interaction recognized that media characteristics influence linguistic forms. For instance, in synchronous CMC one sees many language features that can be attributed to the desire to increase speed by typing less (and, for heavy users, to minimize carpal tunnel syndrome). In Internet relay chat and MOOs, people use abbreviations, acronyms, shortened words, the deletion of subject pronouns, and contractions in response to the medium (Cherny, 1999; Werry, 1996), much as they did with the telegraph. However, participants in many CMC media also actively strive to make their language seem conversational (Werry, 1996), indicating that the medium is only one influence on language. Wilkins points to lexical repetition, which 'made it possible for the participants to follow the conversational sequence, to integrate entries with the appropriate preceding ones, and thus to experience the discourse as conversation' (1991: 63). Werry (1996) and Galegher et al. (1998) point to the informal style of much CMC. 'The discourse,' concluded Galegher et al. 'does not depart discernibly from oral and written patterns of conversation' (1998: 524). That CMC appears more similar to speech and writing than different also points to the limits of conceptualizing the medium as a core causal variable. Most of this research has been conducted in English-speaking groups, owing largely to the (now changing) historical predominance of the English language on the Internet and of the location of so many CMC researchers in the United States, Australia and England. Werry's work, however, examined both English and French-speaking groups and found these phenomena in both languages. Non-English CMC is an area ripe for research, and one which has begun to receive increased attention, as exemplified in a special issue of the *Journal of Computer-Mediated Communication* titled 'The Multilingual Internet' (Danet and Herring, 2003).

As is the case with flaming, language forms online are highly normative and vary across and within CMC contexts. These norms, argued Ferrara et al. (1991), are acquired through interactions with other users. As the technology evolves, the usership grows and the varieties of CMC evolve, it becomes increasingly difficult to differentiate claims about the medium from claims about participants or stage of normative development (Baron, 1998). Baron (1998) argued that e-mail should be considered a 'creole' language, in that it is a still emerging hybrid of other language varieties. I would argue this is true of all CMC. That the nature of Internet discourse is still emerging further suggests the limited causal power of the medium and the futility of making simple generalizations about online interaction.

Users' perceptions of CMC and their desires regarding these media are central to the forms computer-mediated discourse takes. As Lea (1991) showed, even perceptions of a single computer medium like e-mail are complex and varied. In his effort to explore users' perceptions of the similarities and differences between e-mail and other media, Lea used the repertory grid method in which subjects construct categories of meaning as bases for comparison. He found that e-mail was seen as written, asynchronous, spontaneous, informal, and slightly impoverished and impersonal. Perceptions varied as to whether e-mail was seen as consequential or inconsequential, or direct or indirect. Lea concluded that e-mail was in some ways more like note and letter writing, and in other ways more like face-to-face communication and telephoning. In a blow to what he termed 'rationalist' models that assume reduced cues will make CMC more efficient and businesslike, Lea's subjects didn't construe CMC as particularly information efficient or inefficient relative to other media.

Ultimately, computer media should not be understood as deficient versions of face-to-face communication (Culnan and Marcus, 1987), or as peculiar versions of the telephone,

the television or the written word. Instead, theoretical approaches need to consider CMC's unique and varied qualities, and understand how users draw on their existing communicative competencies in multiple media to actively construct social meaning within the challenges and opportunities posed by this medium. The next section examines four primary areas of interpersonal social meanings: language use, identity, relationships and social groups.

INTERPERSONAL ISSUES IN CMC

Computer-mediated Language Use

Rationalist conceptions of CMC assumed that cue deprivation would create discourse that was more serious and information-oriented than face-to-face communication (Lea, 1991; Rice and Love, 1987). Aside from the fact that sometimes people turned more nasty than reasonable, this idea has also been undermined by a wide variety of field studies that explored recreational CMC from qualitative linguistic, sociological, communication and anthropological perspectives and consistently found that language use online is often remarkably playful. In what may have been the first pair of studies along these lines, Myers (1987a, 1987b) studied role-playing game systems using participant observation and interviewing. Looking at the discourse, he concluded that there was a tremendous amount of play with punctuation and spelling (Myers, 1987b). He argued this resulted from a desire for spontaneity. Danet and her associates (1995, 1997, 2001), Werry (1996) and Cherny (1999) are among those who have shown similar play with phonetic and visual qualities of language use in synchronous computer media. Danet et al. (1997) argued that the computer medium is inherently playful because of its 'ephemerality, speed, interactivity, and freedom from the tyranny of materials'.

The most common variety of playful language activity online is probably humour, which seems to be more common online than off. In a large project (see Sudweeks et al., 1998) in which dozens of researchers from several countries and universities conducted a quantitative content analysis of thousands of messages from international Usenet newsgroups, BITNET lists and CompuServe, Rafaeli and Sudweeks (1997) found that more than 20 per cent of the messages contained humour. In my analysis of a Usenet newsgroup that discussed American soap operas (Baym, 1995), I found that 27 per cent of messages addressing a dark and troubling storyline were humorous. The forms of humour included clever nicknames for characters (e.g. Natalie, also called Nat, was dubbed 'Not' when a new actress took over the role, and became 'Splat' when the character was killed in a car accident), plot parodies, and many others. Surveys revealed that humour made both messages and participants stand out as especially likeable.

Language play is a form of performance. Bauman (1975) and Hymes (1975) described performance as communication that is marked as open for evaluation by an audience. As Danet et al. (1997) argued, online performance draws attention to the language and the medium, turning the lack of other cues into a communicative asset. Communicative performances serve a variety of social functions, among them displaying competence (often in the service of self-enhancement), entertaining an audience and facilitating group cohesion (Bauman, 1975). By making the language form and content performative and playful, participants in CMC enhance the appeal of the discourse, build online identities and foster fun relationships.

Computer-mediated Identities

Since language is so often the only form of communication in CMC, it becomes the primary means of managing and forming impressions of our own and others' selves. Perhaps no aspect of online social life has received as much attention as identity, in both (often conflated) senses of personal individuality and category membership. O'Brien (1999: 95) points to two 'conceptual clusters' that characterize online identity formation as well as the interests of scholars studying the phenomenon.

Most analytic attention (scholarly and popular) has focused on the cluster of 'disembodied/ multiplicity/fantasy', while most online identities are along the lines of 'embodied/authenticity/ reality'. In a prescient essay titled 'Anonymity is part of the magic' (a quote drawn from an interview), Myers (1987a) drew attention to how reduced cues opened up the potential for identity play. The users he interviewed took this to be one of the medium's primary appeals. Reid (1991) explored the postmodern nature of this phenomenon in Internet relay chat in an essay that was among the first to describe online gender swapping. As evidenced by Turkle (1996) and Stone (1995), the postmodern implications of anonymity and identity play can be theoretically intoxicating. By divorcing our selves from our bodies, from time and from space, the computer opens a realm in which the multiplicity of identity that is taken to characterize contemporary life (e.g. Gergen, 1991) reaches an apex. We can be multiple people simultaneously, with no one of these selves necessarily more valid than any other. These varied identities can have varied degrees of relation to the embodied 'self'. Organizational research, guided by its practical agenda, conceptualized anonymity as problematic. The research outlined here, guided by a postmodern theoretical agenda, conceptualizes anonymity as indicative of a broad cultural shift. Though popular media often view online anonymity as dangerous, Turkle (1997: 151) examined how some of the MUD users she interviewed used the Internet as a way to grapple with psychological issues such as parental relationships, and argued that MUDs are 'privileged spaces for thinking through and working through issues of personal identity'.

One possible outcome of these experiments in identity is the resolution of identity issues offline. Turkle (1996, 1997) wrote of the potential to work on identity issues involving control and mastery. Myers (1987a) argued that his subjects gained a sense of efficacy or power through the self-creation process. McKenna and Bargh (2000) proposed that constructing a new identity which is successful within a new peer group can allow for role changes that create real changes in self-concept. Some (e.g. Haraway, 1991) have suggested that this may ultimately go beyond individual effects to redefine identity categories such as gender in offline life. This argument is disputed by others (e.g. Donath, 1999) who point out that people tend not to erase or redefine gender online but to exaggerate it, so that men who pretend to be women usually portray themselves as exceptionally sexually attractive in highly stereotypical ways. This has also been found among adolescent women who misrepresent their appearance online (Clark, 1998). At this point, we are still a long way from knowing the offline consequences of online identity (McKenna and Bargh, 2000).

Most attention given to computer-mediated identity play has centered on MUDs. In this regard, it is instructive to remember the Pew finding that only a small percentage of American Internet users participate in any kind of online discussion groups on a given day, and a minuscule percentage of such groups are MUDs. In comparison with the numbers of people who use e-mail and instant messaging (which do not lend themselves to the same kind of anonymity), MUDs hardly represent typical online interaction. According to Curtis (1997), creator of the LambdaMOO, the most popular social MUD and site of much MUD research, even in MUDs, role-playing and gender-swapping are uncommon. Parks and Roberts (1998) argued that there are no data to indicate identity deception is either widespread or more common online. To the contrary, some research suggests that anonymity, and its associated lessening of social risk, may allow people to be more honest and take greater risks in their self-disclosures than they would offline (McKenna and Bargh, 2000). The Pew 2000 poll, for instance, found that Americans feel they can be more honest in e-mail with loved ones and friends than they can be in conversation. Bargh et al. (2002) found that people randomly assigned to interact over the Internet rather than face-to-face were better able to express their true selves. Rather than making us less like our embodied selves, CMC's reduced cues sometimes allow us to be more true to our embodied selves than we can be in the flesh.

Online identities are also made to correspond to embodied identities through contextualization. In an analysis of (woefully understudied) personal Web home pages, Wynn and Katz found that people 'pull together a cohesive presentation of self across eclectic social contexts in which individuals participate' (1998: 324). Rather than being multiple or anonymous, the online identities constructed through home pages were richly contextualized in offline social contexts and groups through self-descriptions, implied audiences, and links to websites of other people and groups. Wellman made a similar point in a review essay when he wrote that too many scholars and pundits 'treat life online as an isolated social phenomenon … They usually ignore the fact that people bring to their online interactions such baggage as their gender, stage in the life cycle, cultural milieu, socioeconomic status, and offline connections with others' (1997b: 446). Furthermore, it is clear that most online interactions are between people who have also talked on the telephone or met face-to-face (Miller and Slater, 2000; Pew, 2000; UCLA Center for Communication Policy, 2000, 2001, 2002). In short, the focus on disembodied identity reflects theoretical interests and the lure of the exotic rather than an effort to understand the typical.

A different approach to identity has been taken by Lea and Spears (1995), who seek a theoretical explanation for the variation in online identity. Their SIDE (social individuation and deindividuation) model is based on self-categorization theory (Tajfel and Turner, 1986; Turner et al., 1987) which conceptualizes self as a range of self-categories including both personal and social identities. SIDE theory tries to identify situational conditions that will invoke particular self-categories and make the behaviour normative to that self-category possible and appropriate (Lea and Spears, 1995). From this perspective, some online contexts will do little to make the self-categories associated with offline selves relevant, and these will be most likely to result in identity play, deception and other behaviours divorced from social contexts. Other contexts will make those categories more relevant, and will invoke self-representations and behaviour consistent with embodied versions of the self. Consistent with this theory, Myers (1987a) and Baym (2000) have argued that the selves constructed in online groups are dependent on the norms of the groups within which they are constructed, so that what is an appropriate identity in one context may not be in another. 'The process of self-creation,' wrote Myers, 'depends very heavily on continuous group negotiation within previously negotiated interaction contexts' (1987a: 259).

To summarize: to the extent that it exists in CMC, anonymity is used in varying ways in different contexts. In some cases, it offers the chance to explore untried identities or to falsify the self. In other cases, it offers the freedom to be more open and honest than one would otherwise be. In still other cases, anonymity is an obstacle to be overcome through various forms of self-disclosure. It is too often forgotten that in much – perhaps even most – CMC, however, anonymity is not an issue, as people are corresponding with people they also know offline and building online selves that are richly contextualized in their offline social networks.

Computer-mediated Relationships

The same forces that can affect identity online also offer new possibilities for developing and sustaining interpersonal relationships in this medium. Just as studies of online identity have gravitated toward novel identities, most of the attention regarding interpersonal relationships in CMC has explored the formation of new relationships, with particular attention to friendship and, to a lesser extent, romance. In their excellent review of relational theory and its implications for CMC, Lea and Spears (1995) argued that theories of personal relationships are biased toward face-to-face communication, and often define relationships in terms of face-to-face qualities, leaving them unable to explain relational development in CMC. They fault traditional theories such as Altman and Taylor's (1973) canonical social penetration model for their 'emphasis on physical proximity, face-to-face interaction, and nonverbal communication

and talk as the essential processes of relating, and a general tendency to use physical and spatial metaphors in describing and accounting for relationships' (Lea and Spears, 1995: 212). Lea and Spears also fault these theories for their tendency to ignore relationships that cross boundaries, don't lead to marriage or are negative. On the other side of the coin, they point out that perspectives on CMC that focus on disembodiment, such as those discussed in the previous section, also raise doubts about the possibility of forming genuine personal relationships through mediated means.

One of the wonderful things about CMC is that it gives us an opportunity to rethink theories of communication. In this case, despite the implications of many interpersonal and postmodern theories that people can't or won't form personal relationships through CMC, people do, and do so often and fairly successfully. CMC, and the Internet, offer new opportunities for creating relationships. The Internet's discussion groups broaden the field of potential relational partners beyond those physically proximate (Lea and Spears, 1995). Kraut et al.'s (2000) interviews suggest that online groups are the main way in which people start online relationships. Parks and Floyd (1996) conducted a survey of Usenet participants in which they found that almost a third had formed friendships through Usenet. In a follow-up study of MOOs, Parks and Roberts (1998) found that such a high percentage of their respondents had formed personal relationships through MOOs that they were statistically unable to compare them with those who had not. Utz (2001) likewise documents the formation of friendships in MUDS, with particular attention to the role of emoticons and user motivations in shaping those relationships. I documented many interpersonal friendships and occasional romances that had emerged through a Usenet group (Baym, 2000). Indeed, the people I studied often described the group as 'a bunch of close friends'. Relational opportunities online are also increased by the aforementioned reduction of social risk, which makes some people more willing to strike up conversations with strangers (Curtis, 1997). Furthermore, liking and attraction face-to-face are often based in the early stages on physical appearance (e.g. Duck, 1977). In CMC, people are more likely to be brought together by shared interests, giving them the chance to discover similarity in values and interests, and to focus on one another's conversational style without attending to appearance (McKenna and Bargh, 2000; Whitty, 2004). This is a devastating reversal for stage models of relational development such as social penetration which so often rely on physical attraction to explain the early stages of relational development (Lea and Spears, 1995). Computer-mediated relationships often follow a predictable developmental trajectory (Baker, 1998; Parks and Floyd, 1996), moving from public discussion, to e-mail, to the telephone and then to face-to-face meetings. Of the friendship pairs in Parks and Floyd's (1996) study, 98 per cent had spoken on the telephone and a third had met face-to-face. Eventually, CMC becomes just one way that relational partners interact (Wellman and Gulia, 1999).

Walther has conducted a line of research which seeks to explain relational development in the face of reduced cues. His social information processing theory proposes that, regardless of medium, people experience the need to reduce uncertainty and increase affinity. As a result, CMC users 'adapt their linguistic and textual behaviors to the solicitation and presentation of socially revealing, relational behavior' such as personal self-disclosures (Walther et al., 1994: 465). Walther and Burgoon (1992) showed that, over time, CMC becomes more similar to face-to-face communication in terms of socioemotional conversation and impression formation. In zero-history groups, Walther (1994) found that the expectation of future interaction increased the likelihood of the expression of immediacy and affection, similarity and depth, trust and composure. The differences between interpersonal information revelation and processing in CMC and face-to-face are issues not of quality, he argued, but of rate.

Some dismiss relationships formed via CMC as inferior to those formed face-to-face, raising the issue of relational quality. Wellman and Gulia (1999) argued that most relationships formed through the Net are specialized weak ties, encouraged by the lack of status and situational cues. However, Wellman and Gulia also argue that strong ties emerge online and, as is the case offline, these ties encourage frequent, companionable contact; they are voluntary, mutually reciprocal and supportive of partners' needs; and they create long-term contact. Lea and Spears (1995) argued for understanding CMC relationships through the eyes of those who have them, claiming that a lack of face-to-face meeting does not render relationships less real or significant to those involved. Parks and Floyd (1996) used scales that measure commitment in face-to-face relationships, and found that Usenet relationships were moderately committed, generally exceeding the scales' midpoints. Parks and Roberts (1998) did this too, and also asked people to make specific comparisons with an offline relationship. They found that MOO relationships were stronger than those formed through Usenet (a finding they attributed to the sense of co-presence created by synchronous communication) and as a whole showed moderate to high levels of development. Parks and Roberts (1998) did find some differences between MOO relationships and face-to-face ones. Offline relationships were slightly more developed, but there were no differences in depth and breadth of interaction; cross-sex friendships were more common in MOOs than in newsgroups or offline; and respondents spent significantly more hours per week with their offline relational partners than their online counterparts. The differences between Usenet and MOOs point again to the importance of context in understanding interpersonal dynamics in online environments. Whitty and Gavin (2000) found that Australian Internet users emphasized relational ideals in online relationships that are the same as those emphasized in offline relationships, including trust, honesty, and commitment.

At times, relationships formed online may be more appealing than those formed face-to-face, a phenomenon Walther (1996) labelled 'hyperpersonal interaction'. In hyperpersonal communication, users overestimate the attractiveness of their online relational partners, relative to people they know offline, making

CMC more socially desirable than face-to-face communication. Walther (1996) offers several explanations for this, including the freedom to idealize that the lack of visual cues provides, the ability for communicators to choose which aspects of the self to disclose and when to disclose them, the increased ability to devote attention to message formation, and the likelihood that these factors will combine such that computer-mediated messages show more self-awareness and introspection. To this list might be added Lea and Spears' (1995) point that when one meets in a group linked by common interest, it is easy to assume that the other is similar to the self in other ways as well. In an experiment, McKenna and Bargh (2000) found that people who met online once, then met face-to-face, liked each other more than people who met face-to-face both times. Like online language and identity, relationships formed online do not seem to differ radically from those formed face-to-face. Indeed, they often evolve into face-to-face relationships. They can be weak or strong, specialized or broad, committed or casual, idealized or well grounded.

A related area that has received attention concerns whether or not those most likely to use the Internet to form personal relationships find it more difficult to do so face-to-face. The findings on this are mixed. Wolak et al. (2003) found that among adolescents, the girls and boys who formed close online relationships were more highly troubled and had higher levels of conflict or lower levels of communication with their parents. Research with adults, however, suggests that those who are most likely to use the Internet for personal communication are those who are most likely to use the telephone and face-to-face communication. Matei and Ball-Rokeach (2002) found that people with stronger local ties in their communities were more likely to meet new people online.

The Internet also serves as a means for people with existing ties to maintain their relationships. In a study comparing Internet and telephone use, Stafford et al. (1999) found that e-mail was used to support and maintain meaningful relationships. International surveys (Chen et al., 2002; Quan-Haase et al., 2002) have compared communication using the Internet in relationships to communication using other media. These scholars have found that e-mail is the most-used medium for communication in long-distance relationships, especially friendship. Even in local friendships, 29 per cent of all contact was achieved through e-mail and 17 per cent of communication in local family relationships occurred online (Quan-Haase et al., 2002). A Pew (2000) poll found that e-mail increases contact with family and friends for significant majorities of online Americans, and that siblings who have e-mail use it more than they use the telephone to contact one another. Though the maintenance of existing relationships is less exotic a topic than the creation of entirely new ones, a more balanced understanding of the interpersonal implications of CMC will have to devote considerably more attention to this more common dimension of online life.

Computer-mediated Social Groups

From the earliest research into CMC, there has been a strong interest in groups. The organizational research, as we have seen, begins with the assumption that CMC groups are different from others, and examines the effect of computer mediation on small-group processes. A second strain of research explores voluntary social groups, often focusing on issues of community. The term 'community' has become almost synonymous with 'online group', especially when the term is advantageous for site developers. This implies that any group involved in social discussion is necessarily a community. However, as is the case in offline groups, online groups vary widely. Though 'community' may apply to some, it is forced with others. Rafaeli and Sudweeks (1997) argued that groups differ in terms of their interactivity, or the extent on a continuum to which sequences of messages relate to each other. Interactivity functions as a mechanism that makes people want to become involved in and stay with Internet groups.

A complete review of the literature on online social groups is beyond the scope of this chapter.

In keeping with my focus on interpersonal issues, I focus on three common and consistent findings in analyses of online groups: they are normatively regulated, hierarchical and often very supportive. As with language, identities and relationships, work on online social groups reveals that 'everything old is new again'. In many ways computer-mediated groups are not very different from other kinds of groups. I close this section with a glance at the ongoing debate concerning the label 'community'.

Many studies of online communities have described how groups develop norms for their interaction. The term 'ways of speaking' is used in the ethnography of communication to describe how group values, beliefs and social structures are embodied in language form and use. Emergent ways of speaking online range from the use of particular words, phrases or other routines to standards of appropriate and inappropriate conduct and means for handling behavioural violations. Lea et al. (1992) argued that norms in CMC are locally defined, created by the group rather than the medium. There are norms that run across groups; however, it is questionable that any behavioural standards apply to all computer-mediated groups. McLaughlin et al. (1995), for example, conducted a study of messages from several Usenet groups which chastised others' behaviour, and were able to derive 'a taxonomy of reproachable conduct' that applies across Usenet. Werry (1996) points to a general code of conduct for Internet relay chat. I have discussed Baron's (1998) claim that norms for e-mail use are still emerging, a claim true of other modes of CMC as well. I have argued that community in CMC is an emergent process (Baym, 1998), in which the pre-existing factors of system infrastructure, temporal structure, participant characteristics and external contexts are appropriated in unpredictable ways by users. The outcome is a set of social meanings that allow participants to experience the group as community. These social meanings include identities and relationships, as well as group-specific forms of expression and behavioural standards. Tepper (1997) has written about a Usenet group which uses the practice of asking stupid questions as a way to distinguish insiders (who know better

than to answer them) from outsiders (who plunge in with earnest responses). Cherny (1999) offers a rich description of many ways MOO participants developed unique ways of interacting and making jokes. All of these can be considered normative, in that they become normal within the group, while remaining unfamiliar (and often incomprehensible) to outsiders. Knowing the inner discourse of a group, with its codes, in-jokes, vocabulary and routines, can offer a sense of belonging that many find appealing. Other norms for appropriate behaviour within groups include those that regulate the appropriateness of flaming (Baym, 1993; Lea et al., 1992) and the use and misuse of anonymity (Baym, 2000). Galegher et al. (1998) showed differences in how one establishes legitimacy and authority depending on whether a group is recreational or explicitly supportive.

Online groups also take social form through the emergence of social hierarchies, a finding which runs counter to the experimental finding that computer mediation creates equality, but which is completely consistent with offline groups. In one-shot situations, it may be rare for single leaders to emerge and participation may be fairly evenly distributed in CMC. Over time, however, groups develop patterns of participation which are radically unequal. At the simplest level, one can distinguish heavy users, light users and lurkers. Baym (1993), Galegher et al. (1998) and others have shown patterns of participation in which the majority of participants write only once or never, while a tiny minority write the majority of the messages. Participants may gain status through a variety of means other than loquacity, including skilled use of the software (Myers, 1987a), shared expertise (Kollock, 1999) and clever performance (Baym, 1993), forms of social capital at play offline as well. Some computer-mediated groups have hierarchies built into their design, pointing again to the importance of context. MUDs, for instance, partition users into levels with differing degrees of control over the system. At one extreme are those who can delete other users; at the other are guests with no abilities to create lasting change (Reid, 1999). MUDs also develop emergent hierarchical structures; in adventure-based MUDs these are based on competition and strength, while in social MUDs they are based on contributions to the group (Reid, 1999).

Another finding from field research into voluntary groups which runs counter to the findings from short-term experimental groups is that online groups tend to be interpersonally supportive, even when they are not designed to be (Wellman and Gulia, 1999). Some groups are explicitly supportive, providing camaraderie and advice on fields such as medical conditions, addiction and abuse recovery. Other groups, while ostensibly organized to discuss hobbies or other lighter-weight topics, may nonetheless provide social support. In a content analysis comparing levels of empathy in online patient and emotional support groups with other sorts of online groups, Preece and Ghozati (1988) found that empathy is more prevalent in patient and emotional support groups, but that most groups use empathic communication. Kollock (1999) pointed out that online groups are notable for the provision of expert and informational support. Adapting social exchange theory (e.g. Ekeh, 1974; Roloff, 1981) to the Internet, he argued that the features of online interaction (specifically that gifts of information and advice are given to unknown recipients one might never encounter again and that one can't expect immediate reciprocation) change the costs and benefits of social action such that even a response to a single person becomes a public good. In addition to the potential of such offerings to increase one's own status within a group, Kollock (1999) located the motivations for contributing in this environment to anticipated future reciprocity and the sense of efficacy that can come from being able to help.

Wellman and Gulia (1999) have argued that there is something distinctive about the provision of support, information, affiliation and sense of belonging to a group of people one hardly knows. These qualities (among others) have led many to label these groups 'communities', a label much debated in both popular and scholarly discourse. Some are highly enthusiastic about such communities because they overcome barriers of time and space and offer access to others with a shared interest, that may

not be available locally (e.g. Rheingold, 1993). Others express concern that in an increasingly fragmented offline world, online groups substitute for 'real' (i.e. geographically local) community, falling short in several ways. Lockard, for instance, argued that 'to accept only communication in place of a community's manifold functions is to sell our common faith in community vastly short' (1997: 225). The most serious charges against calling online groups communities are their homogeneity and lack of moral commitment. Because participants can leave with a mere click, online communities 'do not oblige their participants to deal with diversity' (Healy, 1997: 63).

There have been several reviews of the concept of community and its applicability to CMC (e.g. Fernback, 1999; Komito, 1998), most of which point out that debates over the definition of 'community' far predate the Internet. Komito (1998), in an interesting analysis of different kinds of community, argued that many online groups are best likened to foraging communities. Foraging communities are aggregations of individuals, membership is temporary and voluntary, people move and groups are redefined based on ecological or personal factors, and they are typically egalitarian. Ultimately, however, Komito concludes that 'the most useful means of looking at Net communities may be to treat "community" as background, and focus instead on how individuals and groups cope with continuously changing sets of resources and constraints and how individuals make regular adjustments in their rules for social interaction' (1998: 104–5).

INTERPERSONAL CONSEQUENCES OF THE INTERNET

This review of interpersonal issues in online life just scratches the surface of a broad range of research that comes from many disciplines and makes use of multiple methods. I have focused on what happens in the online context, arguing that much of what happens there is highly sociable, and that this interpersonal interaction is among the greatest appeals of CMC. The simple picture of CMC and its effects painted by early experimental research has given way to a far more varied and complex portrait – or set of portraits – as the use of CMC has grown and people have found new ways to make use of it. Far from being impersonal, CMC is often playful and creative. People use it as a means to assert their own identities and to explore new means of self-presentation. New relationships ranging from weak acquaintanceships to deep romantic bonds are formed, and relationships with people formed offline are perpetuated through CMC. Social groups form that offer a sense of belonging, information, empathy and social status, among other rewards. All of these phenomena offer powerful incentives for people to become involved with CMC and to stay online once there.

However, as the controversy surrounding the use of the term 'community' indicates, there is concern from many quarters that our increased use of the Internet will have deleterious consequences for the rest of our lives. This concern has been bolstered by Kraut et al.'s (1998) unexpected finding that first-year users of the Internet became more socially isolated and depressed the more they went online, and by Nie and Erbring (2000) whose subjects reported becoming more socially isolated the more they used the Internet. These studies have both been attacked on methodological grounds. Kraut et al. (1998) have been criticized for their atypical sample, and for describing the Internet as causing depression when the users who showed increased symptoms of depression did not seem to meet clinical definitions of depression (Rierdan, 1999). Nie and Erbring's study has been challenged for its leading questions, for offering no assessment of the magnitude of reported reductions in social contact, and for assuming all online activities are 'non-social'. Kraut et al.'s (2000) follow-up analysis of their sample a year later found these negative associations were gone, suggesting the importance of user experience (see also La Rose et al., 2001). A questionnaire study of students at the University of Texas (Scherer, 1997) puts the issue into sharper perspective. Scherer found that 13 per cent of Internet users reported some signs of

dependency on the Internet, specifically that it interfered with academic work, professional performance or social life. Those reporting such 'Internet addiction' were significantly more likely to be male. This suggests that it may be a relatively small percentage of Net users for whom the Internet has negative consequences. A serious problem with all of these studies is their retreat to determinism; the Internet is conceptualized as a single entity, as though it makes no difference with whom one communicates online and as though all online contexts are identical.

Critics of the notion that online life lessens the quality of offline life argue that community and sociability are not 'zero-sum games' (Orleans and Laney, 2000; Wellman and Gulia, 1999). Wellman (1997a, 1997b; Wellman and Gulia, 1999) has been among the most vociferous proponents of the notion that use of the Internet is integrated into the rest of life (see Wellman and Haythornthwaite (2002) for a collection emphasizing this point). Wellman and Gulia (1999) argued that the problems with conceptualizing the Net as something that will divorce people from face-to-face life include the facts that online ties are strong and important, that the comparison between electronic communities and face-to-face ones is false given the overlap in online and offline contacts, and that people manage relationships in multiple media. Wellman wrote: 'community ties are already geographically dispersed, sparsely knit, specialized in content, and connected heavily by telecommunications (phone and fax). Although virtual communities may carry these trends a bit further, they also sustain in person encounters between community members' (1997a: 198). People who communicate heavily in one modality tend to communicate heavily in others; heavier users of CMC are also more likely to use the telephone and to have face-to-face conversations (Baym et al., 2004; Copher et al., 2002; Kraut and Attewell, 1997).

There is also evidence that people who use the Internet are as socially and culturally involved as those who do not. Robinson and Kestnbaum found that 'computer users are at least as active as, if not more active than, nonusers in most arts-related activities' (1999: 215). Robinson et al. (2002) found that Internet users spent three times more time attending social events and reported significantly more conversation than nonusers. In terms of interpersonal relationships, an observational study of children's home use of the computer determined that 'online communication was usually not a substitute for interpersonal communication; rather, both often occurred simultaneously' (Orleans and Laney, 2000: 65). The online world was a topic for children's conversation, children surfed the Net together to find commonly valued items, they used the Internet for shared social experimentation, and the Internet gave them the chance to show off esteemed knowledge and skills for one another. The Pew (2000) study found that Internet users were more active socially than non-users: 61 per cent of non-users reported visiting family or friends the day before, whereas 72 per cent of Internet users had done so. This included heavy and long-time Internet users. Even the Internet-dependent students in Scherer's (1997) study had more relationships face-to-face than they had online, although they were more likely to have a larger proportion of their relationships online. It may very well be that for some people the Internet has damaging personal and interpersonal consequences. For others, an online social life extends and complements the sociability they maintain offline. As a whole, however, we must conclude that, as McKenna and Bargh put it, 'there is no simple main effect of the Internet on the average person' (2000: 59). The questions that have yet to be asked will explore which individual variables combine with the many variables of Internet use and contexts and with what range of impacts.

SUMMARY AND FUTURE DIRECTIONS

Research into the interpersonal dynamics of CMC began with the naïve assumption that media characteristics would have determining effects on interaction. There are numerous ways in which media characteristics contribute to interpersonal social processes. Language takes on enhanced roles and hybrid forms as a result of the limited non-verbal cues and the written yet speedy nature of the medium. Identity play, self-revelation and the creation of new relationships are enabled by the cue and participant structures. Social group formation is encouraged by the spatiotemporal and inexpensive nature of the Net, qualities which also enable offline groups to move online and which let relationships that developed offline be perpetuated online. However, there are many other contributors to online interpersonal dynamics, including contexts, users and the choices those users make. The computer medium is far more complex and diverse than first imagined.

The shift from simplistic thinking to a recognition of the range of computer-mediated communication is in part a shift in methods and approach. Early research was characterized by a narrow and practical agenda which generally relied on laboratory experiments. These experiments often failed to recognize confounding variables, leading to the sense that any effects found must result from 'the computer'. Field research explored a broader range of CMC contexts, examining organizations, but also looking at role-playing and social groups in bulletin boards, IRC, Usenet and other recreational forms of CMC. This work in natural contexts revealed both the variables that had been confounded in experimental work, and the wealth of alternative scenarios for CMC. The diversity revealed by fieldwork has played back into laboratory work, so that more recent experimental work has been oriented toward discerning the range of variables that can cause a range of outcomes in a range of CMC contexts. The lesson is not that one method is better than another, but that regardless of method, researchers need to recognize the breadth of CMC contexts and the significant (and often unpredictable) inputs of users.

If we look at context, it is clear that what happens in a decision-making organizational group with zero history (e.g. levelling of status, anonymity, rudeness) is quite different from what happens in a recreational MOO with a built-in power structure and a long history, where one will find a status hierarchy, well-known participants (who are likely to have met offline), well-developed friendships, and standards for appropriate interaction. What happens in a social MOO differs from what happens in a social Usenet group; indeed MOOs differ from each other. E-mail between friends or family may not resemble any of these. The infrastructure of different kinds of computer-mediated interaction (e.g. one-to-one, one-to-many, many-to-many, real-time versus asynchronous, built-in power structure or not) also provides context that shapes what occurs within. There are also a variety of reasons for interacting via computers – among them work, play, relational maintenance, the seeking of social support – each of which gives rise to differing sets of expectations, brings different realms of background knowledge to bear, and otherwise shapes the basic context in which interaction takes place. Many contexts from offline life are imported into online inter-action, an area about which we still know far too little. Any assessment of the interpersonal import of CMC requires a complex under-standing of how the use of CMC fits into the overall distribution and conduct of people's interpersonal interactions.

Users must be considered for at least two reasons: they have critical individual differ-ences and they are creative. Far from being monolithic, people differ in their perceptions of the Internet, in what they want online, and in what they find online. Some find support and friendships that enhance their lives, others find their lives diminished by their time online. Nearly all of the research into CMC has been conducted at the level of the group, or averaged across individuals; we know too little about the individual differences that make a difference in computer-mediated experience.

Users are also creative, and they shape online contexts in ways that may not be predictable even from rich understandings of contexts and media. People who want their interaction to resemble conversation may create groups with a good deal of abbreviation and language play, while those who want their interaction to resemble writing may create spaces that look like formal letters. Rather than resigning themselves to 'cuelessness', people rose to the occasion and found alternative ways to express themselves. Though they will always have their place, predictive theories of CMC will always fall short.

There are no simple questions to ask about CMC, as there is no single thing that is CMC, any more than there is a single thing called 'telephone-mediated communication', or 'television-mediated communication'. Discussions about the quality of CMC, which are surely worth having, must be predicated on this more complicated and messy reality. The studies to be done should look at the varieties and dimensions of contexts, and the varieties, per-ceptions and creativity of users, and should explore both the predictable and the unpre-dictable social meanings that emerge from the many combinations of these variables. CMC's uses and implications must be contextualized in the offline worlds in which they are embed-ded. In short, we must remember that the computer may be new, but like the many new media that came before, it is only a medium.

REFERENCES

Altman, I. and Taylor, D.A. (1973) *Social Pene-tration: The Development of Interpersonal Relationships*. New York: Holt, Rinehart & Winston.

Baker, A. (1998) 'Cyberspace couples finding romance online then meeting for the first time in real life', *Computer Mediated Communication Magazine*. Available online: http://www.december.com/cmc/mag/1998/jul/baker.html

Bales, R.F. (1950) *Interaction Process Analysis: A Method for the Study of Small Groups*. Reading, MA: Addison-Wesley.

Bargh, J.A., McKenna, K. and Grainne, M. (2002) 'Can you see the real me? Activation and expres-sion of the "true self" on the Internet', *Journal of Social Issues*, 58 (1): 33–48.

Baron, N.S. (1984) 'Computer mediated communi-cation as a force in language change', *Visible Language*, 18 (2): 118–41.

Baron, N.S. (1998) 'Letters by phone or speech by other means: the linguistics of e-mail', *Language and Communication*, 18: 133–70.

Baron, N.S. (2000) *Alphabet to Email: How Written English Evolved and Where It's Heading.* New York: Routledge.

Bauman, R. (1975) 'Verbal art as performance', *American Anthropologist,* 77 (2): 290–311.

Bauman, R. and Sherzer, J. (1974) *Explorations in the Ethnography of Speaking.* London: Cambridge University Press.

Baym, N. (1993) 'Interpreting soap operas and creating community: inside a computer-mediated fan culture', *Journal of Folklore Research,* 30 (2/3): 143–76.

Baym, N. (1995) 'The performance of humor in computer-mediated communication', *Journal of Computer-Mediated Communication,* 1 (2). Available online: http://www.ascusc.org/jcmc/vol1/issue2/baym.html

Baym, N. (1996) 'Agreement and disagreement in a computer-mediated group', *Research on Language and Social Interaction,* 29: 315–46.

Baym, N. (1998) 'The emergence of online community', in S. Jones (ed.), *Cybersociety 2.0: Revisiting Computer-mediated Communication and Community.* Thousand Oaks, CA: Sage. pp. 35–68.

Baym, N. (2000) *Tune In, Log On: Soaps, Fandom, and Online Community.* Thousand Oaks, CA: Sage.

Baym, N., Zhang, Y.B. and Lin, M. (2004) 'Social interactions across media: interpersonal communication on the Internet, telephone, and face-to-face', *New Media & Society,* 6 (3): 299–318.

Carnevale, P. and Probst, T.M. (1997) 'Conflict on the Internet', in S. Kiesler (ed.), *Culture of the Internet.* Mahwah, NJ: Erlbaum. pp. 233–55.

Chen, W., Boase, J. and Wellman, B. (2002) 'The global villagers: Comparing Internet users and uses around the world', in B. Wellman and C. Haythornthwaite (eds), *The Internet in Everyday Life.* Malden, MA: Blackwell. pp. 74–113.

Cherny, L. (1999) *Conversation and Community: Chat in a Virtual World.* Stanford, CA: CSLI.

Clark, L.S. (1998) 'Dating on the Net: teens and the rise of "pure" relationships', in S. Jones (ed.), *Cybersociety 2.0: Revisiting Computer-mediated Communication and Community.* Thousand Oaks, CA: Sage. pp. 159–83.

Copher, J.I., Kanfer, A.G. and Walker, M.B. (2002) 'Everyday communication patterns of heavy and light e-mail users', in B. Wellman and C. Haythornthwaite (eds), *The Internet in Everyday Life.* Malden, MA: Blackwell. pp. 263–90.

Culnan, M.J. and Markus, M.L. (1987) 'Information technologies', in F.M. Jablin, L.L. Putnam, K.H. Roberts and L.W. Porter (eds), *Handbook of Organizational Computing: An Interdisciplinary Perspective.* Newbury Park, CA: Sage. pp. 420–43.

Curtis, P. (1997) 'Mudding: social phenomena in text-based virtual realities', in S. Kiesler (ed.), *Culture of the Internet.* Mahwah, NJ: Erlbaum. pp. 121–42.

Daft, R.L. and Lengel, R.H. (1984) 'Information richness: a new approach to managerial behaviour and organizational design', *Research in Organizational Behaviour,* 6: 191–233.

Danet, B. (2001) *Cyberpl@y: Communicating Online.* Oxford: Berg.

Danet, B. and Herring, S. (eds) (2003), 'The Multilingual Internet', special issue of the *Journal of Computer-Mediated Communication.* Available online: http://jcmc.indiana.edu/vol9/ issue1

Danet, B., Ruedenberg-Wright, L. and Rosenbaum-Tamari, Y. (1997) '"HMMM … WHERE'S THAT SMOKE COMING FROM?': writing, play and performance on Internet relay chat', *Journal of Computer-Mediated Communication,* 2 (4). Available online: http://jcmc.indiana.edu/vol2/issue4/danet.html

Danet, B., Wachenhauser, T., Cividalli, A., Bechar-Israeli, H. and Rosenbaum-Tamari, Y. (1995) 'Curtain time 20:00 GMT: experiments in virtual theater on Internet relay chat', *Journal of Computer-Mediated Communication,* 1 (2). Available online: http://jcmc.indiana.edu/vol1/issue2/contents.html

Dimmick, J., Kline, S.L. and Stafford, L. (2000) 'The gratification niches of personal e-mail and the telephone: competition, displacement, and complementarity', *Communication Research,* 27 (2): 227–48.

Donath, J. (1999) 'Identity and deception in the virtual community', in M. Smith and P. Kollock (eds), *Communities in Cyberspace.* New York: Routledge. pp. 29–59.

Duck, S.W. (1977) *The Study of Acquaintance.* Farnborough: Teakfield–Saxon House.

Ekeh, P.P. (1974) *Social Exchange Theory: The Two Traditions.* Cambridge, MA: Harvard University Press.

Fernback, J. (1999) 'There is a there there: notes toward a definition of cybercommunity', in S.G. Jones (ed.), *Doing Internet Research: Critical Issues and Methods for Examining the Net.* Thousand Oaks, CA: Sage. pp. 203–20.

Ferrara, K., Brunner, H. and Whittemore, G. (1991) 'Interactive written discourse as an emergent register', *Written Communication,* 8 (1): 8–34.

Galegher, J., Sproull, L. and Kiesler, S. (1998) 'Legitimacy, authority, and community in electronic support groups', *Written Communication,* 15 (4): 493–530.

Gergen, K. (1991) *The Saturated Self: Dilemmas of Identity in Contemporary Life.* New York: Basic.

Gumperz, J.J. and Hymes, D. (1972) *Directions in Sociolinguistics: The Ethnography of Communication.* New York: Holt, Rinehart & Winston.

Haraway, D.J. (1991) *Simians, Cyborgs, and Women: The Reinvention of Nature.* London: Free Association.

Healy, D. (1997) 'Cyberspace and place: the Internet as middle landscape on the electronic frontier', in D. Porter (ed.), *Internet Culture.* New York: Routledge. pp. 55–71.

Hiltz, S.R. and Turoff, M. (1978) *The Network Nation: Human Communication via Computer.* Reading, MA: Addison-Wesley.

Hollingshead, A.B. and McGrath, J.E. (1995) 'The whole is less than the sum of its parts: a critical review of research on computer-assisted groups', in R. Guzzo and E. Salas (eds), *Team Effectiveness and Decision Making in Organizations.* San Francisco, CA: Jossey-Bass. pp. 46–78.

Hymes, D. (1975) 'Folklore's nature and the sun's myth', *Journal of American Folklore,* 88: 345–69.

Kiesler, S., Siegel, J. and McGuire, T.W. (1984) 'Social psychological aspect of computer-mediated communication', *American Psychologist,* 39 (10): 1123–34.

Kollock, P. (1999) 'The economies of online cooperation: gifts and public goods in cyberspace', in M. Smith and P. Kollock (eds), *Communities in Cyberspace.* New York: Routledge. pp. 220–42.

Komito, L. (1998) 'The Net as a foraging society', *The Information Society,* 14 (2): 97–106.

Kraut, R.E. and Attewell, P. (1997) 'Media use in a global corporation: electronic mail and organizational knowledge', in S. Kiesler (ed.), *Culture of the Internet,* Mahwah, NJ: Erlbaum. pp. 323–42.

Kraut, R., Mukhopadhyay, T., Szczypula, J., Kiesler, S. and Scherlis, B. (2000) 'Information and communication: alternative uses of the Internet in households', *Information Systems Research,* 10: 287–303.

Kraut, R., Patterson, M., Lundmark, V., Kiesler, S., Mukhopadhyay, T. and Scherlis, W. (1998) 'Internet paradox: a social technology that reduces social involvement and psychological well-being?', *American Psychologist,* 53 (9): 1017–31.

La Rose, R., Eastin, M.S. and Gregg, J. (2001), 'Reformulating the Internet paradox: social cognitive explanations of Internet use and depression', *Journal of Online Behavior,* 1 (2). Available online: http://www.behavior.net/JOB/v1n1/paradox. html

Lea, M. (1991) 'Rationalist assumptions in cross-media comparisons of computer-mediated communication', *Behaviour & Information Technology,* 10 (2): 153–72.

Lea, M. and Spears, R. (1995) 'Love at first byte?', in J. Wood and S. Duck (eds), *Understudied Relationships: Off the Beaten Track.* Thousand Oaks, CA: Sage. pp. 197–240.

Lea, M., O'Shea, T. and Spears, R. (1992) '"Flaming" in computer-mediated communication: observations, explanations, implications', in M. Lea (ed.), *Contexts of Computer-mediated Communication.* London: Harvester Wheatsheaf. pp. 89–112.

Lockard, J. (1997) 'Progressive politics, electronic individualism and the myth of virtual community', in D. Porter (ed.), *Internet Culture.* New York: Routledge. pp. 219–32.

Madden, M. and Ranie, L. (2003) 'America's online pursuits: the changing picture of who's online and what they do', Pew Project on the Internet and American Life. Available online: http://www.pewinternet.org/PPF/r/106/report_display.asp

Martino, J.P. (1972) *Technological Forecasting for Decisionmaking.* New York: American Elsevier.

Matei, S. and Ball-Rokeach, S. (2002), 'Belonging in geographic, ethnic, and Internet spaces', in B. Wellman and C. Haythornthwaite (eds), *The Internet in Everyday Life.* Malden, MA: Blackwell. pp. 404–30.

McKenna, K.Y.A. and Bargh, J.A. (2000) 'Plan 9 from cyberspace: the implications of the Internet for personality and social psychology', *Personality and Social Psychology Review,* 4 (1): 57–75.

McLaughlin, M.L., Osborne, K.K. and Smith, C.B. (1995) 'Standards of conduct on Usenet', in Steve Jones (ed.), *Cybersociety: Computer-mediated Communication and Community.* Thousand Oaks, CA: Sage. pp. 90–111.

Miller, D. and Slater, D. (2000), *The Internet: An Ethnographic Approach.* Oxford: Berg.

Morris, M. and Ogan, C. (1996) 'The Internet as mass medium', *Journal of Communication,* 46 (1): 39–50.

Myers, D. (1987a) '"Anonymity is part of the magic": individual manipulation of computer-mediated communication contexts', *Qualitative Sociology,* 19 (3): 251–66.

Myers, D. (1987b) 'A new environment for communication play: online play', in G.A. Fine (ed.), *Meaningful Play, Playful Meaning.* Champaign, IL: Human Kinetics. pp. 231–45.

Nie, N.H. and Erbring, L. (2000) *Internet and Society: A Preliminary Report.* Palo Alto, CA: Stanford Institute for the Quantitative Study of Society. Available online: http://www.stanford.edu/group/siqss

O'Brien, J. (1999) 'Writing in the body: gender (re)production in online interaction', in M. Smith and P. Kollock (eds), *Communities in Cyberspace*. New York: Routledge. pp. 76–106.

Orleans, M. and Laney, M.C. (2000) 'Children's computer use in the home: isolation or sociation?', *Social Science Computer Review*, 18 (1): 56–72.

Parks, M.R. and Floyd, K. (1996) 'Making friends in cyberspace', *Journal of Communication*, 46 (1): 80–97.

Parks, M.R. and Roberts, L.D. (1998) '"Making MOOsic": the development of personal relationships online and a comparison to their offline counterparts', *Journal of Social and Personal Relationships*, 15 (4): 517–37.

Pew (2000) *Tracking Online Life: How Women Use the Internet to Cultivate Relationships with Family and Friends*. Washington, DC: Pew Internet and American Life Project. Available online: www.pewinternet.org

Pew (2004) Available online 'Daily Internet activities', Pew Internet and American Life Project, Washington, DC. Available online http://www.pewinternet.org/trends/Daily_Activities_12.20.04.htm

Preece, J. and Ghozati, K. (1988) 'In search of empathy online: a review of 100 online communities', in *Proceedings of the 1998 Association for Information Systems Americas Conference*. pp. 92–4.

Price, C.R. (1975) 'Conferencing via computer: cost effective communication for the era of forced choice', in H.A. Linstone and M. Turoff (eds), *The Delphi Method: Techniques and Applications*. Reading, MA: Addison-Wesley. pp. 497–516.

Quan-Haase, A., Wellman, B., Witte, J. and Hampton, K.N. (2002), 'Capitalizing on the Net: social contact, civic engagement, and sense of community', in B. Wellman and C. Haythornthwaite (eds), *The Internet in Everyday Life*. Malden, MA: Blackwell. pp. 291–324.

Rafaeli, S., and Sudweeks, F. (1997) 'Networked interactivity', *Journal of Computer-Mediated Communication*, 2 (4). Available online: http://www.ascusc.org/jcmc/vol2/issue4/rafaeli.sudweeks.html

Reid, E.M. (1991) 'Electropolis: communication and community on Internet relay chat'. Masters Thesis, University of Melbourne, Australia.

Reid, E. (1999) 'Hierarchy and power: social control in cyberspace', in M. Smith and P. Kollock (eds), *Communities in Cyberspace*. New York: Routledge. pp. 107–33.

Rheingold, H. (1993) *The Virtual Community*. Reading, MA: Addison-Wesley.

Rice, R.E. and Love, G. (1987) 'Electronic emotion: socioemotional content in a computer-mediated communication network', *Communication Research*, 14 (1): 85–108.

Rierdan, J. (1999) 'Internet–depression link?', *American Psychologist*, 54 (9): 781–2.

Robinson, J.P. and Kestnbaum, M. (1999) 'The personal computer, culture, and other uses of free time', *Social Science Computer Review*, 17 (2): 209–16.

Robinson, J.P., Kestnbaum, M., Neustadtl, A. and Alvarez, A.S. (2002) 'The Internet and other uses of time', in B. Wellman and C. Haythornthwaite (eds), *The Internet in Everyday Life*. Malden, MA: Blackwell. pp. 244–262.

Roloff, M.E. (1981) '*Interpersonal Communication: the Social Exchange Approach*. Beverly Hills, CA: Sage.

Scherer, K. (1997) 'College life online: healthy and unhealthy Internet use', *Journal of College Student Development*, 38 (6): 655–65.

Short, J., Williams, E. and Christie, B. (1976) *The Social Psychology of Telecommunications*. Chichester: Wiley.

Siegel, J., Dubrovsky, V., Kiesler, S. and McGuire, T.W. (1986) 'Group processes in computer-mediated communication', *Organizational Behavior and Human Decision Processes*, 37: 157–87.

Sproull, L. and Faraj, S. (1997) 'Atheism, sex, and databases: the Net as a social technology', in S. Kiesler (ed.), *Culture of the Internet*. Mahwah, NJ: Lawrence Erlbaum. pp. 35–52.

Stafford, L., Kline, S.L. and Dimmick, J. (1999) 'Homee-mail: relational maintenance and gratification opportunities', *Journal of Broadcasting & Electronic Media*, 43 (4): 659–69.

Stone, A.R. (1995) *The War of Desire and Technology at the Close of the Mechanical Age*. Cambridge, MA: MIT Press.

Sudweeks, F., McLaughlin, M. and Rafaeli, S. (1998) *Networks and Netplay: Virtual Groups on the Internet*. Cambridge, MA: MIT Press.

Tajfel, H. and Turner, J.C. (1986) 'The social identity theory of intergroup behavior', in S. Worchel and W.G. Austin (eds), *Psychology of Intergroup Relations*. Chicago: Nelson-Hall.

Tepper, M. (1997) 'Usenet communities and the cultural politics of information', in D. Porter (ed.), *Internet Culture*. New York: Routledge. pp. 39–54.

Turkle, S. (1996) *Life on the Screen: Identity in the Age of the Internet*. New York: Simon & Schuster.

Turkle, S. (1997) 'Constructions and reconstructions of self in virtual reality: playing in the MUDs', in S. Kiesler (ed.), *Culture of the Internet*. Mahwah, NJ: Lawrence Erlbaum. pp. 143–55.

Turner, J.C., Hogg, M.A., Oakes, P.J., Reicher, S.D. and Wetherell, M.S. (1987) *Rediscovering the*

Social Group: a Self Categorization Theory.
Oxford: Blackwell.

UCLA Center for Communication Policy (2000) *'Surveying the digital future'.* Available online: http://ccp.ucla.edu/pages/internet-report.asp

UCLA Center for Communication Policy (2001) *'Surveying the digital future'.* Available online: http://ccp.ucla.edu/pages/internet-report.asp

UCLA Center for Communication Policy (2002) *'Surveying the digital future'.* Available online: http://ccp.ucla.edu/pages/internet-report.asp

Utz, S. (2001) 'Der Aufbau von interpersonalen Beziehungen in MUDS: Die Rolle von Motiven and Kommunikationsstrategien', *Gruppendynamik,* 32 (2): 145–60.

Walther, J.B. (1992) 'Interpersonal effects in computer-mediated interaction', *Communication Research,* 19 (1): 52–90.

Walther, J.B. (1994) 'Anticipated ongoing interaction versus channel effects on relational communication in computer-mediated interaction', *Human Communication Research,* 20 (4): 473–501.

Walther, J.B. (1996) 'Computer-mediated communication: impersonal, interpersonal and hyperpersonal interaction', *Communication Research,* 23 (1): 3–43.

Walther, J.B. and Burgoon, J.K. (1992) 'Relational communication in computer-mediated interaction', *Human Communication Research,* 18 (1): 50–88.

Walther, J.B., Anderson, J.F. and Park, D. (1994) 'Interpersonal effects in computer-mediated interaction: a meta-analysis of social and anti-social communication', *Communication Research,* 21 (4): 460–87.

Weisband, S. and Atwater, L. (1999) 'Evaluating self and others in electronic and face-to-face groups', *Journal of Applied Psychology,* 84 (4): 632–9.

Wellman, B. (1997a) 'An electronic group is virtually a social network', in S. Kiesler (ed.), *Culture of the Internet.* Mahwah, NJ: Lawrence Erlbaum. pp. 179–208.

Wellman, B. (1997b) 'The road to utopia and dystopia on the information highway', *Contemporary Sociology,* 26 (4): 445–9.

Wellman, B. and Gulia, M. (1999) 'Virtual communities as communities: Net surfers don't ride alone', in M. Smith and P. Kollock (eds), *Communities in Cyberspace.* New York: Routledge. pp. 167–94.

Wellman, B. and Haythornthwaite, C. (eds) (2002), *The Internet in Everyday Life.* Malden, MA: Blackwell.

Werry, C.C. (1996) 'Linguistic and interactional features of Internet relay chat', in S. Herring (ed.), *Computer-mediated Communication: Linguistic, Social, and Cross-cultural Perspectives.* Amsterdam: Benjamins. pp. 47–63.

Whitty, M. (2004) 'Cyber-flirting: an examination of men's and women's flirting behavior both offline and on the Internet', *Behavior Change,* 21 (2): 115–26.

Whitty, M. and Gavin, J. (2000) 'Age/sex/location: uncovering the social cues in the development of online relationships', *Cyberpsychology and Behavior,* 4 (5): 623–30.

Wilkins, H. (1991) 'Computer talk: long-distance conversations by computer', *Written Communication,* 8 (1): 56–78.

Wolak, J., Mitchell, K.J. and Finkelhor, D. (2003) 'Escaping or connecting? Characteristics of youth who form close online relationships', *Journal of Adolescence,* 26 (1): 105–19.

Wynn, E. and Katz, J.E. (1998) 'Hyperbole over cyberspace: self-presentation and social boundaries in Internet home pages and discourse', *The Information Society,* 13 (4): 297–328.

2

Creating Community with Media: History, Theories and Scientific Investigations

NICHOLAS W. JANKOWSKI

Of all the promises and prognoses made about old and new media, perhaps the most compelling has been the possibility of regenerating community through mediated forms of communication. This theme found expression during the development of radio in the 1920s and 1930s and later with television in the 1950s. It was particularly prominent during the introduction of community radio and television in the 1970s; it has reached extraordinary proportions with the more recent emergence of 'virtual communities' on Internet-based services.

This chapter traces the relationship between (new) media and community. The first section sketches three historical periods when the relation between community and media has been central. A brief description of new media is also provided here. The second section explores the transformation of the concept of community from early locality-oriented sociological studies to those conducted from a multi-disciplinary examination of Internet-based communication facilities where a geographical 'place' is absent. The third section provides illustrations of three types of studies relating community and media: small-scale electronic media, community information networks, and

public discussions and debates via electronic networks. The fourth and last section examines the main methodological approaches and suggests the contours of a research agenda oriented towards further exploration of the interface between community and new media.

COMMUNITY AND MEDIA: AN ONGOING AFFAIR

An abundance of claims, optimistic and pessimistic, have been made regarding what impact the media – and most recently the Internet – may have on society in general and community in particular. It seems as if each generation has been represented by its pundits on the contribution media may have on the human condition. During the Golden Age of radio, for example, that medium was promised to bring culture into every living room; later, television was destined to transform education (see e.g. Czitrom, 1982; Douglas, 1997; Head, 1972). Both of these media were equally feared as potential tools for political propaganda; television and movies, moreover, were suspected of being able to undermine the very fabric of society, deforming young minds and debasing cultural heritage. Most of such claims, initially, had little grounding in evidence, and when systematic and extensive studies were eventually conducted the results were, at best, mixed.[1]

Similar claims also accompanied the introduction of the Internet. This new communication technology, it is said, will eradicate the inequalities and evils in society. Education will improve exponentially; citizens will become concerned and active; commerce, under the stewardship of the 'new economy', will thrive. Some, such as the co-founder of the Electronic Frontier Foundation, envision the Internet as nothing less than 'the most transforming technological event since the capture of fire' (Barlow et al., 1995: 40). Rheingold (1993a, 1993b, 2000) is well known for his position that the Internet can help rediscover or reinvigorate community. In his widely cited book *The Virtual Community* (cited, once again, later in this chapter), he voices the general belief that the loss of traditional community values can be regained through communication via the Internet.

Such claims, as Fernback (1999) and others have observed, are more polemical expressions than considered assessments based on empirical evidence. Similarly, Wellman and Gulia (1999: 169) criticize such accounts as 'presentist and unscholarly' and historically uninformed. Most of these claims, they point out, fail to acknowledge the long-standing concern of sociologists regarding the impact of various facets of modernization – industrialization, urbanization, transportation – on society.

This section considers the special and ongoing relationship between communication and media across time. Primary attention is given to 'new media', and for that reason it is important to dwell, at least briefly, on what is meant by that term. First of all, it must be acknowledged that 'newness' is a relative notion with regard to both time and place. What is new today is old tomorrow, and what is new in one cultural context may be unknown or outmoded in another. This relativistic feature of the term has prompted some scholars (e.g. Fauconnier, 1973; Hamelink, 1980) to suggest

other identifiers: telematics, and information and communication technologies, are two such rivals. Other unique features of new media have also been addressed, coming to something of a climax in the series of essays published in the maiden issue of *New Media & Society* in 1999. There, 'what's new about new media' was considered by ten leading communications scholars. Although – understandably – no consensus was achieved, it is interesting to note that much of the newness addressed had to do with transformations in the ways individuals are able to relate to media and to determine the place and functions of these media in their everyday lives. New media are, to a large degree, socially constructed phenomena and often deviate substantially from the designer's original intent.

For the purposes of this chapter, the characteristics of new media outlined by McQuail (1994: 20–6) serve as a useful delineation of the term. New media, he suggests, generally involve decentralization of channels for the distribution of messages; an increase in the capacity available for transferral of messages thanks to satellites, cable and computer networks; an increase in the options available for audience members to become involved in the communication process, often entailing an interactive form of communication; and an increase in the degree of flexibility for determining the form and content through digitization of messages. Negroponte (1995) considers this last aspect the most fundamental feature, and digitization for him essentially means that the content of one medium can be interchanged with another.

The developments usually associated with new media are many and include such technologies as DVD and CD-ROM; cable television and computer networks; various computer-mediated communication (CMC) developments such as e-mail, newsgroups and discussion lists, and real-time chat services; telephony services such as SMS (short message service) and MMS (multimedia messaging service); and Internet-based news services provided by traditional newspapers and broadcasters. Many of these examples are technological in substance and have, by themselves, little to do with the communication process as embedded within specific historical, societal or personal contexts. New media, as considered in this chapter, are seen as developments in communication grounded within such contexts. For this reason, there is value in examining the relation of media, new for their time and place, with concern for community. Although the argument could be made that such examination might legitimately begin as far back as Gutenberg's invention of movable type or, even further, the Egyptian development of parchment, preference is given to sketching the special relationship between community and media evident since the early 1900s when community studies developed as a serious academic enterprise. The second 'wave' of studies concerned with community and media can be traced to the late 1960s and 1970s when small-scale electronic community media emerged on the scene. The third and last period to be sketched is the era of the Internet. Only a few of the striking highlights are mentioned here; more detailed illustrations of studies concerned with community and new media are reserved for the following section.

First Wave of Community and Media Studies

A concerted effort to investigate possible relations between media and community occurred under the auspices of the Chicago School in the 1920s and 1930s. In particular, Park (1922) was interested in the role of the community press regarding identity formation among immigrant groups. In a subsequent study he observed that newspaper reading was more a characteristic among residents in cities than in rural areas (Park, 1929). Also, Park found that different kinds of news were read in the city than in the country: in the city readers had more interest in news from outside the region and in the country readers preferred local news.

Merton (1949) followed up on this distinction in his study of 'Rovere' and identified two groups of residents: localites and cosmopolitans. Localites were oriented toward the local community, engaged in locally based social activities

and primarily attended to the local newspaper as a source for local news. Cosmopolitans, in contrast, had a broader orientation and range of social activities, and consumed media from outside the locality. Merton was suggesting, in other words, that media use and community participation were reflections of individual traits.

Janowitz (1952) took a different approach to the topic of community and media, and stressed the role of community structure with regard to local newspaper use. Like Park, Janowitz was concerned about the role of newspapers in integrating individuals into a community. He felt local newspapers could contribute to consensus within a local community, and he investigated the role of family, social cohesion and community participation on community newspaper readership. Janowitz found that community integration and community involvement are related to greater attention to local newspapers.

These and other contributions to the relation between media and community are reviewed by Stamm (1985) in his study of newspaper use and community ties. On the basis of this review, Stamm develops a model whereby community ties can be seen as either antecedents to or consequences of community media use. He suggests that an individual's tie to place (e.g. length of residence), to structure (e.g. membership of local organizations) and to process (e.g. participation in local activities) are associated with an individual's newspaper readership. Stamm's (1985: 8) model describes newspaper use across time and he postulates that at different points in time community newspaper readership contributes to establishing community ties, and at other times the opposite occurs: community ties contribute to newspaper use. This line of research has recently been extended by Westerik (2001) through construction and testing of a causal model involving these and other variables.

Second Wave: Electronic Community Media

With development of portable video recording technology and cable television distribution systems in the late 1960s and early 1970s, a new thrust of interest developed for geographically defined as well as spatially dispersed groups to employ these communication technologies for community initiatives and actions. Use of these electronic tools of communication was in many ways an extension of print technologies – the stencil machine and offset press technology – introduced a decade earlier during the 1960s when counter-culture and political groups established their own newspapers, known as the underground or alternative press (Denis and Rivers, 1974).

The media in these contexts were also coined 'community media', and this term referred to a diverse range of mediated forms of communication: electronic media such as radio and television, print media such as newspapers and magazines, and later electronic network initiatives embracing characteristics of both traditional print and electronic media. The manner in which community television is defined is typical of these small-scale initiatives: 'made by local people as distinct from professional broadcasters (Lewis, 1976: 61). Members of the community, often in alliance with professional station staff, are meant to be responsible for the ideas and production of the resulting programming. Community members are generally involved in all facets of station activities and exercise control over day-to-day and long-range policy matters.

New media such as community radio and television were the focus of studies across Western Europe (e.g. Halloran, 1977; Jankowski, 1988) and North America (e.g. Fuller, 1994; Widlok, 1992). Several reviews sketch how groups utilized such small-scale electronic media for political and cultural purposes (e.g. Downing, 1984, 2000; Girard, 1992; Jallov, 1997). European studies of this 'people's voice', undertaken during the 1970s and 1980s, were collected in an anthology documenting its development and impact (Jankowski et al., 1992). In the introduction to this volume the editors express their affinity with the goals of the *then* new media:

> We were … taken by the dreams of developing or rebuilding a sense of community within new housing estates and aging neighborhoods, and applying these new media to that task. Sometimes these new community-oriented media were meant to simply inform their audiences of events. Sometimes they went a step further and attempted to mobilize citizens in efforts to bring about change and improvement. Sometimes emancipatory objectives were embedded in station programming. (1992: 1)

In an assessment of those goals, Prehn (1992) points out that the initiators of community media frequently overestimated the need of people to express themselves via the media. This miscalculation often increased the difficulty of maintaining the necessary level of programming production for an established broadcasting schedule. And this problem led to the formation of a professional organizational structure antithetical to the original community-oriented objectives.

The legacy of this wave of activity relating community and media is mixed. Certainly the aspirations have remained intact, as will be demonstrated in the next section, but the results of the multitude of initiatives to achieve alternative voices reaching intended audiences are unclear. In an overall assessment of a national experiment with community electronic media in the Netherlands, the researchers suggest that the contribution of community media to community-building processes worked best in those situations where a sense of community was already well established (Hollander, 1982; Stappers et al., 1992). In residential areas short on social capital, it seems as if community media can do little to 'make things better' (see also Jankowski et al., 2001).

Concern with community media in localities gained revived interest with initiation of OURMedia, a group composed of both practioners and activist scholars. Since the first meeting in 2000, the group has mushroomed in size and scope, having met annually in both North and South America. The OurMedia website constitutes an extended and valuable resource for recent scholarship (see http://www.ourmedianet.org). Much of the work by members of this group has been inspired by discussion of 'citizens' media', initiated by Rodríguez (2001) and 'alternative media', elaborated by Atton (1999).

Third Wave: Era of the Internet

It is often difficult to pinpoint precisely when a new epoch has begun, but serious academic concern for the Internet can be traced to publication of a joint theme issue prepared by the *Journal of Communication* and the electronic upstart *Journal of Computer-Mediated Communication* (JCMC) in 1996. Another indication of the significance and importance of this third wave was the formation of the Association of Internet Researchers and the holding of its first international conference in September 2000 (see Jones, 2004). And, almost simultaneously across North America, Europe and Asia, new academic departments and research centres have been and are being established, all claiming niches in this new academic frontier. Some of these initiatives have taken virtual or online communities as objects of study.[2]

In terms of publishing, this new frontier has been no less than a gold rush and, for some, a lucrative gold mine. Major academic journals have recently been launched and others are on the drawing board.[3] The book publications regarding the Internet and aspects of community have quite literally exploded since publication of Benedikt's (1991) *Cyberspace: First Steps*. The series of volumes edited by Jones (1995a, 1997, 1998a, 1999) on cybersociety, virtual culture and Internet research rank as core contributions, as does a recent volume entitled *Communities in Cyberspace* (Smith and Kollock, 1999). The claim to key literature is also merited by a range of other studies on identity formation and the Internet (e.g. Stone, 1991; Turkle, 1995).

Yet another niche of literature in this area is concerned with the employment of electronic or computer networks in geographically based communities. Sometimes called public education networks (PENs), community information networks or community informatics, the literature around these developments is accumulating rapidly (e.g. Day and Schuler, 2004; Gurstein, 2000; Loader and Keeble, 2001; Schuler and Day, 2004). Several PhD dissertations have been or are nearing completion (e.g. Foth, 2005; Hampton, 2001; Malina, 2001;

Prell, 2001; Silver, 2000). Conferences on this facet of community and new media are becoming regular events, such as the Communities and Technologies conferences (http://www.cct2005.disco.unimib.it). An active discussion list and resource website is maintained by the Vancouver Community Network (http://www2.vcn.bc.ca); see also the Community Informatics Research Network (CIRN) site: http://www.ciresearch.net

In conclusion, much is in flux, and such movement impairs vision and reflection. Still, it seems fair to say that academic concern for community, particularly within Internet environments, is alive and well. Whether such robustness will continue may depend largely on the degree to which conceptual refinement is achieved during the coming years. How far that refinement has yet to go is sketched in the next section.

CHANGING FORMULATIONS OF COMMUNITY

Community has been called many things. Nisbet (1966: 47) considers it one of the 'most fundamental and far-reaching' concepts of sociology. Fundamental though it may be, sociologists have not succeeded in achieving consensus on what is exactly meant by the term. In an inventory taken during the heyday of sociological concern, Hillery (1955) collected 94 distinct definitions of the concept. This plethora of meanings has led some to doubt its scientific utility. In the entry in an authoritative dictionary of sociology, for example, the authors introduce the concept as 'one of the more elusive and vague in sociology and is by now largely without specific meaning' (Abercrombie et al., 1994: 75).

Community as a popular concept has proven strikingly resilient to such attacks, however, and has gained a new life in academic discourse since discussion of the various forms of virtual communities allegedly emerging in cyberspace. It has caught, once again, the collective imagination, so much so that some Internet scholars lament the 'use and overuse of "community" in the popular and scholarly press' (Dyson, cited in Cherny, 1999: 247). It is safe to say that the concept of community is as central to present-day studies of the Internet as it was during the earlier years of sociology. The main difference seems to be redirection of emphasis from geographic place to a feeling or sense of collectivity.

This section of the chapter traces the development and change of the main formulations of community from the early period of sociology through the decades of the Chicago School and subsequent follow-up studies. More recent theoretical and methodological reorientation, with emphasis on social ties, is considered thereafter. Finally, the discussions and efforts to define community within the context of the Internet are dealt with at some length, and new formulations of community within this environment are highlighted.

Early Sociological Conceptualizations of Community

Discussions of community within the discipline of sociology frequently begin with the contributions of Tönnies (1887/1957), particularly his formulations of *Gemeinschaft* and *Gesellschaft*. *Gemeinschaft*, usually translated as 'community', refers to relationships that are 'intimate, enduring and based upon a clear understanding of where each person stands in society' (Bell and Newby, 1972: 24). Found in pre-industrial societies, these relations were felt to be culturally homogeneous and strongly influenced by institutions such as the church and the family. The core of *Gemeinschaft* involves 'sentimental attachment to the conventions and mores of a beloved place enshrined in a tradition which was handed down over the generations from family to family' (Newby, 1980: 15).

Tönnies' term *Gesellschaft* is generally translated as 'society' or 'association', and refers to 'large-scale, impersonal, calculative and contractual relationships' (Newby, 1980: 15) believed to be increasing during the period of industrialization at the turn of the nineteenth century.

Actions are taken in light of their potential benefit for the individual. Relations are contractual and functionally specific. Because of the individual orientation, *Gesellschaft* is characterized by a continual state of tension.

These constructions should be seen as ideal types, as Tönnies intended. Further, it is important to realize that, for Tönnies, locality was but one of the factors of community. His term also involved consideration of a relationship meant to characterize the whole of society, of 'communion' as well as 'community' (Newby, 1980: 16). Nevertheless, emphasis in subsequent sociological studies stressed the locality dimension, as did Wirth's (1938) exposition on urban life and Redfield's (1947) elaboration of Tönnies' duality into a so-called rural–urban continuum. Wirth, for example, is noted for emphasizing that *where* we live has a profound influence upon *how* we live (Newby, 1980: 18). This idea – the centrality of locality – came under increasing challenge thanks to more recent research findings. Gans (1962), for example, took issue much later with the fundamental premise in the work of Wirth and Redfield, and argued that lifestyles are determined not by locality but by other variables, particularly social class and stage in the life cycle (Newby, 1980: 28).

Social Ties as Indicators of Community

The debate around community has, for some, the characteristics of a dead end. Stacey (1974), for example, feels sociologists should discard the concept of community altogether because of its normative lading and because of the substantial definitional disagreements. Her proposal is to concentrate on the role of institutions within specific localities.

Other proposals have also been made, and one of the most enticing is the argument made regarding social ties in understanding many of the issues previously assembled under the concept of community. The central approach being taken here is network analysis – examination of the relationships (ties) established between individuals, groups or institutions (nodes). This approach allows researchers to avoid the value-laden term 'community'. Equally important, the approach opens up investigation across localities: the rural with the urban, the suburban with the metropolitan.

Social network analysis has become the *cause célèbre* in much of the work of Wellman and colleagues (Garton et al., 1999; Wellman, 1997, 1999; Wellman and Berkowitz, 1988, 1997), and most recently in their investigation of the utilization of electronic networks within residential areas (e.g. Hampton and Wellman, 2000; Wellman and Hampton, 1999). In a discussion of what he calls the 'community question', Wellman (1999) explains the features and value of social network analysis. The network approach, he asserts, avoids individual-level research perspectives, focusing instead on the relations between the nodes or units of a network. This approach provides an opportunity to consider such features as the density and 'tightness' of relations, the degree of heterogeneity among units within a network, and the impact that connections and positions within a network may have on individual or collective action.

Virtual Community

As already mentioned, Rheingold is perhaps more responsible than anyone else for generating interest in and enthusiasm for virtual communities. His book *The Virtual Community: Homesteading on the Electronic Frontier* (2000) gives a personal glimpse of what life is like in the nether world of cyberspace. Drawing on many years of personal experience in one of the first virtual communities, the WELL (Whole Earth 'Lectronic Link), Rheingold elaborates on the range of activities participants engage in while in that virtual environment, a range about as broad as is conceivable:

> People in virtual communities use words on screens to exchange pleasantries and argue, engage in intellectual discourse, conduct commerce, exchange knowledge, share emotional support, make plans, brainstorm, gossip, feud, fall in love, find friends and lose them, play games, flirt, create a little high art and a lot of idle talk.

> People in virtual communities do just about everything people do in real life, but we leave our bodies behind. You can't kiss anybody and nobody can punch you in the nose, but a lot can happen within those boundaries. (1993b: 3)

Rheingold has been frequently criticized for taking an excessively euphoric and uncritical stance regarding virtual communities (e.g. Fernback and Thompson, 1995b) and for lacking theoretical sophistication in his approach. Both criticisms have a degree of truth, but both are at the same time misleading and misplaced. Although Rheingold is certainly hopeful about the contribution that virtual communities may make to enriching collective life, he is at the same time uncertain about whether the efforts will succeed and poses questions in this direction. For example, he speculates, 'fragmentation, hierarchization, rigidifying social boundaries, and single-niche colonies of people who share intolerances could become prevalent in the future' (1993b: 207).

Such foreboding has not impeded interest, however, and Jones has perhaps done more to place the study of online community on the academic agenda than any other individual. Largely through the two edited volumes on what he calls 'cybersociety' (Jones, 1995a; 1998a), but also through his collections on virtual culture (Jones, 1997) and Internet research (Jones, 1999), he has brought together a critical mass of scholars concerned with community in cyberspace.

Jones sets the stage in his introductory essays in the two volumes on cybersociety (Jones, 1995b, 1998b) for the remainder of the contributions. He discusses and problematizes the possibility of community that is based on forms of computer-mediated communication, and critiques the often unquestioned position taken by community sociologists who automatically associate community with locality, with geographic place. Jones, like Bender (1978) and others before him, contends such identification robs the concept of community of its essence and mistakenly gives priority to organizational ease. Jones also draws from the conceptualization of communication as a form of ritual, citing his mentor James Carey:

'Communication under a transmission view is the extension of messages across geography for the purposes of control, the ... case under a ritual view is the sacred ceremony that draws persons together in fellowship and commonality' (Carey, 1989: 18, cited in Jones, 1995b: 12).

There is an overwhelming feeling that new communities are being created, along with new forms of communities. The 'new form' these virtual communities may be taking is aptly expressed for Jones in a definition suggested by Stone (1991: 85): 'incontrovertibly social spaces in which people still meet face-to-face, but under new definitions of both "meet" and "face"... [V]irtual communities [are] passage points for collections of common beliefs and practices that united people who were physically separated' (cited in Jones, 1995b: 19).

A series of theoretical contributions about community in the Jones volumes has been prepared by Fernback (1997, 1999; see also Fernback and Thompson, 1995a, 1995b). Fernback addresses contributions from the early sociologists Tönnies and Simmel, but she also reviews contributions from Dewey and more recent literature from the 'new communitarians' Etzioni (1993) and Bellah et al. (1985). Unlike some earlier descriptions of community, she stresses the dynamic nature of the concept: 'as society evolves the notion of community evolves concomitantly' (Fernback, 1997). A current strain of the concept is known as virtual community which she defines as 'social relationship forged in cyberspace through repeated contact within a specified boundary or place (e.g. a conference or chat line) that is symbolically delineated by topic of interest' (Fernback and Thompson, 1995b).

One of the striking and problematic features of virtual communities, according to Fernback and Thompson (1995b), is the fluidity of association individuals may have with such communities. Individuals can become active and prominent quickly, and just as quickly disappear altogether: 'Leaving a virtual community might be as easy as changing the channel on a television set.' Such fluidity may have consequences, they point out, for the stability of virtual communities to a greater degree than is the case for 'real-life' or offline communities.

For this reason they are pessimistic about the potential of online communities to contribute to 'the already fragmented landscape of the public sphere'.

In a subsequent work Fernback compares characteristics of virtual communities and American culture. The principles of free speech, individualism, equality and open access are associated with virtual communities, she claims, and are 'the same symbolic interests that define the character of American democracy' (Fernback, 1997: 39). It remains to be demonstrated that the above characteristics attributed to virtual communities are universal, but even should that be the case it remains particularly ethnocentric to identify them with American cultural icons. Such parochialism seems out of place in a discussion of a form of community that, by definition, is not constrained by the geographical boundaries or the cultural manifestations of a particular nation-state.

Van Dijk (1998) takes a different approach to the topic of virtual communities from both Jones and Fernback. He sets, first of all, the task of determining whether such social constructions can compensate for the general sense of loss of community prevailing in society. He then provides a working definition of virtual communities similar to other formulations, noting that they 'are communities which are not tied to a particular place or time, but which still serve common interests in social, cultural and mental reality ranging from general to special interests or activities' (1998: 40). On the basis of a review of some of the available literature on communities, van Dijk distils four characteristics he says are common to all communities: having members, a social organization, language and patterns of interaction, and a culture and common identity. These characteristics are then used to compare virtual communities with real-life or what he prefers to call 'organic' communities. This exercise leads to a typology of ideal types wherein virtual communities are described as those with relatively loose relations, which are unconcerned with considerations of time and place, which contain a well-developed paralanguage, and which are pluralistic and heterogeneous in composition (see Table 2.1). As is the case with

Table 2.1 *Ideal types of organic and virtual communities*

Characteristic	Organic	Virtual
Composition and activity	Tight group (age)	Loose affiliation
	Several activities	Special activities
Social organization	Tied to place and time	Not tied to place and time
Language and interaction	Verbal and nonverbal	Verbal and paralanguage
Culture and identity	Total singular	Partial plural
	Homogeneous	Heterogeneous

Source: Van Dijk, 1998: 45

most efforts to construct ideal types, this profile of virtual communities falls short of adequately describing actual cases. Many virtual communities can be characterized by the strong ties among their members, are grounded in time and place, and reflect a homogeneous membership.

With this typology in hand, Van Dijk formulates the central question of his study: 'To what extent can virtual communities replace organic communities and provide forces to countervail the present social processes of fragmentation and individualization?' (1998: 48). Reviewing conclusions based on early CMC research, he asserts that electronic groups will come to resemble their organic counterparts regarding their structure and rules. His overall conclusion is that virtual communities cannot reclaim 'lost' community in society, largely because the cultures and identities created are 'too partial, heterogeneous and fluid to create a strong sense of membership and belonging' (1998: 59). He contends that the quality of discourse is 'poor' and genuine dialogue is missing. At best, virtual communities may supplement organic communities, but are unable to replace them, according to van Dijk.

The above assertions might serve as hypotheses, but it is too early to draw conclusions. The empirical studies necessary to substantiate such claims have not been conducted. In a review by one of the few persons to have undertaken an extended ethnographic fieldwork of an online community, Baym supports this criticism: 'we do not have the empirical grounds on which to assess how (or if) online community affects offline community' (1998: 38).

Baym (1995, 1998, 1999), in addition to providing rich insight into a Usenet newsgroup devoted to discussion of television soap operas, also elaborates on a theoretical model of online community. She is concerned with understanding how such communities develop and manifest themselves, and what occurs during the process of being online that leads participants to experience these virtual phenomena as communities. Baym develops what she calls an 'emergent model of online community' (1998: 38). She argues that five already existing features influence the character of an online community: external context, temporal structure, system infrastructure, group purposes and the characteristics of participants. These features impinge on the development of an online community regarding 'group-specific forms of expression, identities, relationships and normative conventions' (1998: 38).

The model Baym develops for online community can be represented schematically as illustrated in Table 2.2. Here, some of her original terms have been renamed, and the categories of temporal and system infrastructure have been combined. The cells within the table could contain summary data of a particular online community, such as the television soap opera newsgroup r.a.t.s. in the case of Baym's study. The model, once applied to a number of online communities, provides opportunity for comparative analysis. Baym notes that the overall purpose of her model is not to be predictive in nature, but to provide a framework for understanding how online communities develop. Although each community may be unique, as she argues, the model nevertheless provides guidelines for comparing online communities.

Another elaboration of the meaning of virtual community comes from the field of linguistics. In a case study of a multi-user dungeon (MUD), Cherny (1999) reviews definitions for

Table 2.2   *A model for online communities: characteristics and influences*

Characteristics	Influences			
	Communication	Identity	Relationships	Norms
Content				
Structure				
Objectives				
Participants				

Source: adapted from Baym, 1995, 1998

speech communities, discourse communities and communities of practice. Following Hymes (1972), Cherny (1999: 13) suggests that a speech community involves sharing rules for speaking and interpreting communicative performance. Members of a speech community use language to delineate the boundaries of the community, to unify its members and to exclude others.

'Discourse community', as elaborated by Gurak (1997: 11), is concerned with the 'use of discourse for purposeful social action in a public arena'. This form of community resembles the 'interpretive community' to which language composition scholars allude. Finally, 'community of practice' refers to relations maintained by persons across time who are involved in a collective set of activities. The 'academic community' could be considered an illustration of such a community of practice. One of the important features of this form of community is that it provides the overall conditions and basis for interpreting and making sense of events and activities. Participants share a general understanding of their activities and of the meaning ascribed to them. Although the distinctions between these terms are not always clear, they collectively suggest new avenues for understanding community from a perspective where use of language is central. The linguistics perspective seems particularly appropriate for computer-mediated communication because of its focus on forms of language and discourse.

Another current development is infusion of the concept 'social capital' into discussions and investigations of virtual communities (e.g. Blanchard and Horan, 1998). Popularized by Putnam (1993, 1995, 2000), social capital can be seen as a recent variant of the older tradition of community development, community work

and community action initiatives prominent in the United States in the 1960s. Riedel et al. (1998) examined the presence of social capital in a community network in a rural town in Minnesota, focusing on three components: interpersonal trust, social norms and association membership. Components of social capital were also used in a study of a digital community network in The Hague (Jankowski et al., 2001) as well as in the 'Netville' study in a Toronto suburb, described in more detail later (Hampton and Wellman, 2003).

ILLUSTRATIVE STUDIES OF NEW MEDIA AND COMMUNITY

The various formulations of community presented in the previous section have found reflection in many empirical studies of the media. Here, illustrations are provided for three areas of research: small-scale electronic media, physically based online communities, and public discussion and debate on the Internet. Although research from other areas could have been chosen (e.g. community development and design culture and language, identity formation and commercially oriented virtual communities),[4] the studies presented here illustrate some of the current work being conducted around community and (new) media.

Small-scale Electronic Media

A recent compilation of community media research (Jankowski, 2001) contains a section of four chapters devoted to issues and illustrations of the public sphere as related to community radio and television. There, Mitchell (2001) explores how women's community radio may serve as a tool for women's empowerment. With empirical data from women's radio stations and projects across Europe, Mitchell examines how radio can be used to develop a feminist public sphere. Coleman (2001) provides an analysis of phone-in radio programmes in the Irish Republic and considers how these programmes may contribute towards better exchange between disparate groups in that society. He argues that this form of discourse provides opportunity for communication that would otherwise be unlikely or difficult. A contribution by Stein (2001) assesses the role of public-access television in political communication in the United States. She examines the political uses of access television within radical media projects and argues that such media host a range of democratic speech absent from the traditional media industries. Finally, Barlow (2001) examines the policies and practices of three community radio stations in Australia regarding key features of that sector of broadcasting. While all of the stations seem to pay homage to the principles of access and participation, he finds that these three stations differ substantially in their practices. Moreover, all of the stations are subject to the strain caused by the concerns of professionalization, popularization and commercialization of community radio.

Physically Based Virtual Communities

There are basically two categories of virtual communities: those with a distinct relation to a geographical locality and those having no such binding with a particular space. Freenets, PENs, community information networks and digital cities are some of the types of physically based virtual communities. Preference is given to the term 'digital community network' to describe virtual communities in this category. Two recent studies of these virtual communities serve as illustrations of the research being conducted in this area.

The first investigation, conducted by Silver (2000), provides a comparative analysis of Blacksburg Electronic Village (BEV) in Virginia (see also Kavanaugh and Patterson, 2002) with the Seattle Community Network in the state of Washington. Silver is concerned with differences in the development, design and use of these two digital community networks. Regarding development, Silver notes that the Blacksburg Electronic Village is essentially a prototype of a 'top-down' approach whereby large amounts of capital were invested to construct a state-of-the-art facility. Silver suggests that a small group of actors – persons from local industry, government and the university situated in the town – conceived the initiative, financed it and brought it to operational level. Involvement of community organizations, groups and individual citizens during this process was minimal. Involvement by Blacksburg residents after site construction came to resemble the behaviour of consumers rather than of community members. According to Silver, the 'most common use of the BEV was for commercial purposes: to download coupons, check movie times, or purchase goods online' (2000: 282).

The Seattle Community Network, in contrast, was conceived by a broad assemblage of community organizations and groups from an early phase in its development. These community units engaged in what Silver and others (e.g. Harrison and Zappen, 2003; Schuler and Namioka, 1993) call participatory design, and they determined overall policy and structure for the community network. In this respect, the network reflected a 'bottom-up' initiative and was intended to serve as a tool for community development. The Seattle Community Network was promoted through workshops and outreach programmes, was made accessible through public facilities such as libraries and was provided free of charge to Seattle area residents. This community network, according to Silver, came to offer 'a culturally rich, civic-based online platform of resources, materials, and discussion forums with and within which residents of Seattle can share ideas, interact with one another, and build communities' (2000: 294).

The second investigation of digital community networks to be presented here involves 'Netville', a wired suburb located on the outskirts of Toronto. Netville is a complex of approximately 120 homes designed and built in the mid 1990s. A special feature of this suburb, distinguishing it from most others in

North America, is that it was equipped from the beginning with a local electronic network capable of providing high-speed Internet access; a computer videophone facility; a variety of music, health and entertainment services; and neighbourhood discussion forums. These features were widely promoted during the early sale of homes in the estate and a special research consortium was established to monitor technical and social developments.

The social science fieldwork was conducted by Hampton (2001) whose concern was to determine the influence such a state-of-the-art communication infrastructuture might have on the social relations that residents maintain with neighbours, friends, relatives and colleagues – within and outside Netville, online and offline.[5] The study was based on a long-standing premise developed and frequently argued by the 'Toronto School' of community studies (e.g. Wellman, 1979, 1999), suggesting that community is not of necessity locality-bound. This position argues that social ties constitute the central feature of community and not locality, and that these ties – be they weak or strong – should be the focus of empirical study of community. It is, in the words of Hampton and Wellman, 'the sociable, supportive, and identity-giving interactions that define community, and not the local space in which they might take place' (2000: 195).

Netville provided the opportunity for an extended field study of this premise, linked to the new 'variable' of an electronic network infrastructure with accompanying communication services. As part of this study, Hampton resided in Netville for a period of two years and integrated into the social life of the neighbourhood. He participated in both online and offline activities, the discussion lists and the barbecues, and conducted what Hampton and Wellman (1999) describe as a classical community ethnography. In addition, Hampton and Wellman conducted a survey of the residents regarding their network of social ties.

Findings from this survey suggest that the electronic network supported both weak and strong social ties ranging from those purely functional in nature to those grounded in social and personal issues. In probing for the breadth of social ties among residents, Hampton and Wellman (2000) report that those residents connected to the electronic network significantly differed from residents not connected: they knew more of their neighbours' names, they talked to and visited with them more often. The wired residents, in other words, maintained a broader ranger of social contacts than their non-wired counterparts. Hampton and Wellman suggest this may have had to do with the presence of the electronic network and particularly because of the neighbourhood e-mail list maintained on the network for residents. The network seemed to have been particularly valuable during periods of social action, i.e. during conflicts with the housing developer and especially during a conflict about an unexpected discontinuance of the network.

Internet and Public Discussion

The place of public discussion and debate has been a central feature of community media initiatives for decades, and this feature is equally central to many Internet-based facilities. Newsgroups, discussion lists, and specially constructed sites for debating social, political and cultural issues abound on the Internet. Empirical research is beginning to emerge around these phenomena, particularly from the perspective of the concept of public sphere (e.g. Dahlberg, 2001; Hagemann, 2002; Schirato, 2005). One of the most extensive studies to date has been carried out by Schneider (1996, 1997) around a Usenet discussion group concerned with abortion. During the period of a year, Schneider collected 46,000 messages posted on the site and examined them along four dimensions considered central to Habermas' (1989) notion of public sphere: *equality* of access to the arena of debate, *diversity* of opinions and topics relevant to a particular debate, *reciprocity* or degree of interaction between persons involved in a debate, and the *quality* or degree to which participants contribute information relevant to the topic.

Schneider operationalized each of these dimensions so that a quantitative analysis could be conducted on the entire number of postings during the period of study.[6] He found, overall, that contributions to the newsgroup were diverse in substance and that participants exhibited an acceptable degree of reciprocity. Although access to the discussion was theoretically open, actual involvement in the debate – a feature also relevant for the equality dimension of public sphere in this study – was strikingly low. Of the nearly 3000 contributors to the discussion during the year period, fewer than 0.5 per cent were responsible for more than 40 per cent of all postings. Put differently, some 5 per cent of the participants posted almost 80 per cent of the contributions. Finally, regarding the dimension quality, Schneider found that the most frequent contributors to the discussion were the least likely to post messages 'on topic', i.e. related to the issue of abortion. This feature, he suggests, exacerbated the inequality reflected in the discussion.

The findings from this study pose serious concerns regarding the contribution of Internet-based discussions to public debate. Although the potential of such discussions may be great, as Schneider and others (e.g. Jankowski and van Selm, 2000) continue to repeat, the actual degree of involvement is minuscule, and much of what is contributed is not relevant to the topic.

RESEARCHING NEW MEDIA AND COMMUNITY: METHODS AND QUESTIONS

No one research methodology or agenda of questions dominates work currently being undertaken around new media and community. As illustrated in the previous section, investigations are emerging from a variety of disciplines employing diverse tools of study and directed at different areas of concern. As pluralist as the field is, some overriding preferences for methods and questions can be discerned and are elaborated in this section.

Research Methods

Regarding research methods, about a decade ago an overview of the place of qualitative methods in studying community media was prepared (Jankowski, 1991). Then it appeared as if this approach was increasing in importance within the field of mass communication studies in general and within the more specialized concern of small-scale media in particular. The 'qualitative turn', it seemed, had arrived.

Now, looking at studies concerned with new media and community, it appears, once again, that qualitative or interpretive studies are prominent. Several of the empirical studies mentioned or presented earlier in this chapter feature characteristics of classical community study fieldwork (e.g. Baym, 1999; Malina, 2001; Silver, 2000). Others (e.g. Cherny, 1999; Jankowski and van Selm, 2000) develop a form of textual or discourse analysis. Yet others (Harrison and Stephen, 1999; Harrison et al., 2001; Hearn and Foth, 2005) integrate the conventional concerns of academic research with those regarding design and development of community information networks.

Quantitative approaches are also represented in current work. Schneider's (1997) study of public debate on a Usenet newsgroup represents a sophisticated quantitative analysis of a very large body of messages. Hampton (2001) employs survey research and network analysis within the context of a sociological field study. More generally, interest in online survey research is substantial. The first major text on this method has appeared (Dillman, 2000) and there has been a range of journal articles (e.g. Coomber, 1997; Mehta and Sivadas, 1995; Swoboda et al., 1997). It is only a matter of time before these data collection tools are applied to studies of new media and community.

Innovations in methods and methodologies are also being developed. For example, Stromer-Galley and Foot (2002) report on a study based on focus group interviews designed to explore the nature of public discussion and debate on the Internet. In another set of studies, innovative software and new strategies for website analysis are being developed (Foot and Schneider, 2002; Schneider and Foot, in press).

Many of the current and proposed investigations are constructed as case studies (e.g. Jankowski et al., 2001). This type of study has been subjected to severe criticism. In discussing community study as a method of research (similar to the case study method) Bell and Newby (1972: 17) summarize some of the commonly voiced reservations: excessive reliance on a single observer, lack of systematic data collection, insufficient distinction between researcher and object of study. Baym (1999: 18–21) eschews much of what presently passes for ethnography, but for different reasons. Following criticisms of ethnography developed by Nightingale (1996) and Press (1996), Baym notes that all too often studies of online audiences are limited to brief forays in the field coupled with individual and group interviews. She suggests, as a minimum standard, multiple forms of data collection undertaken during periods of extensive fieldwork.

In addition to Baym's suggestions, it should be mentioned that much refinement has been achieved in both qualitative data collection and analysis since Bell and Newby itemized the above reservations. For example, the systematic analysis procedures elaborated by Miles and Huberman (1994) and the utilization of computer programs to aid qualitative analysis and development of grounded theory (e.g. Hijmans and Peeters, 2000) are illustrative of these advances. These could be fruitfully applied to community media studies. Even with such technical perfections, it remains important to do more than simply increase the number of case studies. Core questions formulated within a theoretical framework are also essential, as argued below.

Research Agenda

In addition to developments in methods, advances are also being made in determining the key questions for community and media. For example, an overview is provided of the proposed research concerns shared by contributors to a recent volume on community media (Jankowski, 2001). For one specific area a model has been constructed within which research questions can be addressed. Hollander (2000) draws on the earlier work of Stamm (1985) and proposes a causal relation between community

structure, characteristics of individual community residents, the media landscape and community media use. He suggests that different causal relations may be dominant for different configurations of the variables related to each of the above factors. The model by Hollander has been further modified for application to investigations of digital community networks and thereby proposes a framework for formulation of a range of research interests (see Figure 2.1). The overriding research question for this model is: *to what degree and in what manner do aspects of community structure, individual characteristics and media landscape relate to the use of and involvement in digital community networks by local residents?*

Although not embedded within a model, the research questions formulated by Wellman and Gulia (1999) represent an extensive research agenda for virtual communities. They pose seven clusters of questions regarding the nature of online relationships and their relation to offline relationships and to community involvement.

Baym (1999: 210–16) in the conclusion of her study of an online community of television soap fans, formulates a more compact list of four questions:

- What forces shape online identities?
- How do online communities evolve over time?
- How does online participation connect to offline life?
- How do online communities influence offline communities?

She does not, however, extend these questions to the level of a model that could integrate findings, through which direction for further empirical study might be provided. In a sense, the observation made some years ago by Wellman and Gulia (1999: 185) is still relevant: 'It is time to replace anecdote with evidence … The answers have not yet been found. Indeed, the questions are just starting to be formulated'. I would only add that the time has also come to generate theoretically based models for emerging online communities and digital community networks, like the model presented above (see also Jankowski et al., 2001), that are relevant to other realms of new media and community.

Figure 2.1   *Components of community communication and digital community networks*
Source: Jankowski et al., 2001

Research questions embedded within such models will provide the needed direction and grounding missing from much of the current wave of disparate case studies concerned with community and new media.

NOTES

I wish to thank colleagues at home and abroad who contributed comments and suggestions during the preparation of this chapter, in alphabetical order: Nancy Baym, Hans Beentjes, Marcus Foth, Margot van der Goot, Ed Hollander, Steve Jones, Sonia Livingstone, Martine van Selm, David Silver, Barry Wellman and Henk Westerik. Responsibility for limitations inherent in this review rest, of course, with me.

1 See e.g. Gunter and Harrison (1998) for an overview of media violence studies.

2 Examples include the Center for the Study of Online Community at the University of California at Los Angeles,

the Centre for Urban and Community Studies at the University of Toronto, and the Electronic Learning Communities research programme at Georgia Institute of Technology. See also the Resource Center for Cyberculture Studies, presently located at the University of Washington (http://www.com.washington.edu/rccs/default.asp).

3 An incomplete list of academic journals concerned with new media includes: *The Information Society; Information, Communication & Society; New Media & Society; Television and New Media; Journal of Computer-Mediated Communication;* and *Journal of Online Behavior.* A more dynamic and thorough list may be found at: http://www.theorycommons.org

4 A primer for issues related to the construction of *community information networks* is Schuler's (1996) practically oriented volume. Harrison et al. (2001) explore design and research interventionist strategies for development of digital community networks. Regarding *collective and individual identity*, there is insufficient space to consider studies about multi-user dungeons (MUDs). The following authors provide a good introduction to this genre: Bromberg (1996), Cherny (1999), Dibbell (1993), Donath (1999), Reid (1994, 1999), Stone (1991), and – especially – Turkle (1995). As for *commercially oriented virtual communities,*

many e-commerce operations (e.g. Amazon.com, Participate.com) and Internet service providers (e.g. AOL) have incorporated this notion of community building. This development is also not addressed in this chapter, but Cherny (1999: 253–4) considers it briefly as do Hagel and Armstrong (1997).

5 A number of unpublished manuscripts, journal articles and book chapters have appeared on the Netville project (e.g. Hampton, 2003; Hampton and Wellman, 1999, 2000, 2003; Wellman and Hampton, 1999). The most complete publication is Hampton's (2001) PhD dissertation.

6 The theoretical perspective and method of analysis are described in detail by Schneider (1997) in his dissertation, available online: http://www.sunyit.edu/~steve A brief review of the four dimensions of public sphere and Schneider's findings may be found in Jankowski and van Selm (2000).

REFERENCES

Abercrombie, N., Hill, S. and Turner, B.S. (1994) *The Penguin Dictionary of Sociology*, 3rd edn (1st edn 1984). London: Penguin.

Ahern, R.K., Stromer-Galley, J. and Neuman, W.R. (2000) 'When voters can interact and compare candidates online: experimentally investigating political web effects'. Paper presented at the International Communication Association Conference, Acapulco, Mexico.

Atton, C. (1999) 'A re-assessment of the alternative press', *Media, Culture & Society,* 21: 51–76.

Barlow, D. (2001) 'Conceptions of access and participation in Australian community radio stations', in N.W. Jankowski (with O. Prehn) (ed.), *Community Media in the Information Age: Perspectives and Prospects.* Cresskill, NJ: Hampton.

Barlow, J.P., Birkets, S., Kelly, K. and Slouka, M. (1995) 'What are we doing on-line?', *Harper's,* August: 35–46.

Baym, N.K. (1995) 'The emergence of community in computer-mediated communication', in S.G. Jones (ed.), *Cybersociety: Computer-mediated Communication and Community.* Thousand Oaks, CA: Sage. pp. 138–63.

Baym, N.K. (1998) 'The emergence of on-line community', in S. Jones (ed.), *Cybersociety 2.0: Revisiting Computer-mediated Communication and Community.* Thousand Oaks, CA: Sage. pp. 35–67.

Baym, N.K. (1999) *Tune in, Log on: Soaps, Fandom, and Online Community.* Thousand Oaks, CA: Sage.

Bell, C. and Newby, H. (1972) *Community Studies: An Introduction to the Sociology of the Local Community.* New York: Praeger.

Bellah, R., Madsen, R., Sullivan, W., Swidler, A. and Tipton, S. (1985) *Habits of the Heart: Individualism and Commitment in American Life.* Berkeley, CA: University of California Press.

Bender, T. (1978) *Community and Social Change in America.* New Brunswick, NJ: Rutgers University Press.

Benedikt, M. (1991) *Cyberspace: First Steps.* Cambridge, MA: MIT Press.

Blanchard, A. and Horan, T. (1998) 'Virtual communities and social capital', *Social Science Computer Review,* 16 (3): 293–307.

Bromberg, H. (1996) 'Are MUDs communities? Identity, belongings and consciousness in virtual worlds', in R. Shields (ed.), *Cultures of Internet: Virtual Spaces, Real Histories, Living Bodies.* London: Sage. pp. 143–52.

Carey, J. (1989) *Communication as Culture.* Boston, MA: Unwin-Hyman.

Cherny, L. (1999) *Conversation and Community: Chat in a Virtual World.* Chicago: University of Chicago Press.

Coleman, S. (2001) 'BBC Radio Ulster's talkback phone-in: public feedback in a divided public space', in N.W. Jankowski (with O. Prehn) (ed.), *Community Media in the Information Age: Perspectives and Prospects.* Cresskill, NJ: Hampton.

Coomber, R. (1997) 'Using the Internet for survey research', *Sociological Research Online,* 2 (2). Available online: http://www.socresonline.org.uk/socresonline/2/2/2.html

Czitrom, D.J. (1982) *Media and the American Mind: From Morse to McLuhan.* Chapel Hill, NC: University of North Carolina Press.

Dahlberg, L. (2001) 'Computer-mediated communication and the public sphere: a critical analysis', *Journal of Computer-Mediated Communication,* 7 (1). Available online: http://www.ascusc.org/jcmc/vol7/issue1/dahlberg.html.

Day, P. and Schuler, D. (eds) (2004) *Community Practice in the Network Society: Local Action/Global Interaction.* London: Routledge.

Denis, E.E. and Rivers, W.L. (1974) *The Other Voices: New Journalism in America.* San Francisco: Canfield.

Dibbell, J. (1993) 'Rape in cyberspace', *The Village Voice,* 21 December: 38.

Dillman, D.A. (2000) *Mail and Internet Surveys: The Tailored Design Method.* New York: Wiley.

Donath, J.S. (1999) 'Identity and deception in the virtual community', in M.A. Smith and P. Kollock (eds), *Communities in Cyberspace.* London: Routledge. pp. 29–59.

Douglas, S.J. (1997) *Inventing American Broadcasting 1899–1922*. Baltimore, MD: Johns Hopkins University Press.

Downing, J. (1984) *Radical Media: The Political Experience of Alternative Communication*. Boston, MA: South End.

Downing, J. (2000) *Radical Media: Rebellious Communication and Social Movements*. Thousand Oaks, CA: Sage.

Etzioni, A. (1993) *The Spirit of Community: Rights, Responsibilities, and the Communitarian Agenda*. New York: Crown.

Fauconnier, G. (1973) *Massamedia en samenleving: inleiding tot de wetenschappelijke studie van de massa communicatie* (Mass Media and Society: Introduction to the Scientific Study of Mass Communication). Antwerp: De Nederlandsche Boekhandel.

Fernback, J. (1997) 'The individual within the collective: virtual ideology and the realization of collective principles', in S.G. Jones (ed.), *Virtual Culture: Identity and Communication in Cybersociety*. London: Sage. pp. 36–54.

Fernback, J. (1999) 'There is there there: notes toward a definition of cybercommunity', in S. Jones (ed.), *Doing Internet Research*. Thousand Oaks, CA: Sage. pp. 203–20.

Fernback, J. and Thompson, B. (1995a) 'Computer-mediated communication and the American collectivity: the dimensions of community within cyberspace'. Paper presented at the International Communication Association, Albuquerque, NM.

Fernback, J. and Thompson, B. (1995b) 'Virtual communities: abort, retry, failure?' Unpublished paper. Available online: http://www.well.com/user/hlr/texts/ VCcivil

Foot, K.A. and Schneider, S.M. (2002) 'Online action in Campaign 2000: An exploratory analysis of the U.S. political Web sphere', *Journal of Broadcasting & Electronic Media*, 46 (2): 222–44.

Foth, M. (2005) 'Towards a design methodology for online community networks to grow sustainable urban neighbourhoods'. PhD dissertation, Creative Industries Research and Applications Centre (CIRAC), Queensland University of Technology, Brisbane.

Fuller, L.K. (1994) *Community Television in the United States: A Sourcebook on Public, Educational, and Governmental Access*. Westport, CT: Greenwood.

Gans, H. (1962) *The Urban Villagers: Group and Class in the Life of Italian-Americans*. New York: Free Press.

Garton, L., Haythornthwaite, C. and Wellman, B. (1999) 'Studying on-line social networks', in S. Jones (ed.), *Doing Internet Research: Critical Issues and Methods for Examining the Net*. Thousand Oaks, CA: Sage. pp. 75–105.

Girard, B. (1992) *A Passion for Radio: Radio Waves and Community*. Montreal: Black Rose.

Gunter, B. and Harrison, J. (1998) *Violence on Television: An Analysis of Amount, Nature, Location and Origin of Violence in British Programmes*. London: Routledge.

Gurak, L. (1997) *Persuasion and Privacy in Cyberspace: The Online Protests over Lotis Marketplace and the Clipper Chip*. New Haven, CT: Yale University Press.

Gurstein, M. (2000) *Community Informatics: Enabling Communities with Information and Communication Technologies*. Hershey, PA: Idea Group.

Habermas, J. (1989) *The Structural Transformation of the Public Sphere: An Inquiry into a Category of Bourgeois Society*. Oxford: Polity.

Hagel, J. and Armstrong, A. (1997) *Net Gain: Expanding Markets through Virtual Communities*. Boston: Harvard Business School Press.

Hagemann, C. (2002) 'Participation in and contents of two Dutch political party discussion lists on the Internet', *Javnost–The Public*, 9 (2): 61–76.

Halloran, J. (1977) 'Communication and community: the evaluation of an experiment'. Report. Strasburg: Council of Europe.

Hamelink, C. (1980) *De Computer Samenleving* (*The Computer Society*). Baarn: In den Toren.

Hampton, K. (2001) 'Living the wired life in the wired suburb: Netville, globalization and civic society'. PhD dissertation, University of Toronto.

Hampton, K. (2003) 'Grieving for a lost network: collective action in a wired suburb', *The Information Society*, 19 (5): 1–13. Available online: www.mysocialnetwork.net

Hampton, K. and Wellman, B. (1999) 'Netville online and off-line: observing and surveying a wired suburb', *American Behavioral Scientist*, 43 (3): 475–92.

Hampton, K. and Wellman, B. (2000) 'Examining community in the digital neighborhood: early results from Canada's wired suburb', in T. Ishida and K. Isbister (eds), *Digital Cities: Technologies, Experiences, and Future Perspectives*. Berlin: Springer. pp. 475–92.

Hampton, K.N. and Wellman, B. (2003) 'Neighboring in Netville: how the Internet supports community and social capital in a wired suburb', *City and Community*, 2 (4): 277–311.

Harrison, T. and Stephen, T. (1999) 'Researching and creating community networks', in S. Jones (ed.), *Doing Internet Research: Critical Issues and Methods for Examining the Net*. London: Sage. pp. 221–41.

Harrison, T.M. and Zappen, J.P. (2003) 'Methodological and theoretical frameworks for the design of community information systems', *Journal of Computer-Mediated Communication*, 8 (3). Available online: http://www.ascusc.org/jcmc/vol8/issue3/harrison.html

Harrison, T., Zappen, J.P. and Prell, C. (2001) 'Transforming new communication technologies into community media', in N.W. Jankowski (with O. Prehn) (ed.), *Community Media in the Information Age: Perspectives and Prospects*. Cresskill, NJ: Hampton.

Head, S.W. (1972) *Broadcasting in America: A Survey of Television and Radio*, 2nd edn (1st edn 1956). Boston: Houghton Mifflin.

Hearn, G. and Foth, M. (2005) 'Action research in the design of new media and ICT systems', in K. Kwansah-Aidoo (ed.), *Topical Issues in Communications and Media Research*. New York: Nova Science. pp. 81–97.

Hijmans, E. and Peters, V. (2000) 'Grounded theory in media research and the use of the computer', *Communications: The European Journal of Communication Research*, 25 (4): 407–32.

Hillery, G. (1955) 'Definitions of community: areas of agreement', *Rural Sociology*, 20: 111–23.

Hollander, E. (1982) *Kleinschalige massacommunictie: lokale omroepvormen in West Europa* (Small-scale Mass Communication: Forms of Local Broadcasting in West Europe). The Hague: State.

Hollander, E. (2000) 'Online communities as community media: a theoretical and analytical framework for the study of digital community networks', *Communications: The European Journal of Communication Research*, 25 (4): 371–86.

Hymes, D. (1972) 'Models of the interaction of language and social life', in J. Gumperz and D. Hymes (eds), *Directions in Sociolinguistics*. New York: Holt, Rinehart, & Winston. pp. 35–71.

Jallov, B. (1997) 'Women's voices crossing frontiers: 1996 European directory of women's community radio stations and women's radio production collectives'. Report. Sheffield: AMARC–Europe Women's Network.

Janowitz, M. (1952) *The Community Press in an Urban Setting*. Glencoe, IL: Free Press.

Jankowski, N.W. (1988) 'Community television in Amsterdam: access to, participation in and use of the "Lokale Omroep Bijlmermeer"'. PhD dissertation, University of Amsterdam.

Jankowski, N.W. (1991) 'Qualitative research and community media', in K.B. Jensen and N.W. Jankowski (eds), *A Handbook of Qualitative Methodologies for Mass Communication Research*. London: Routledge. pp. 163–74.

Jankowski, N.W. (with Prehn, O.) (ed.) (2001) *Community Media in the Information Age: Perspectives and Prospects*. Cresskill, NJ: Hampton.

Jankowski, N. and van Selm, M. (2000) 'The promise and practice of public debate in cyberspace', in K.L. Hacker and J. van Dijk (eds), *Digital Democracy: Issues of Theory and Practice*. London: Sage. pp. 149–65.

Jankowski, N., Prehn, O. and Stappers, J. (eds) (1992) *The People's Voice: Local Radio and Television in Europe*. London: Libbey.

Jankowski, N., van Selm, M. and Hollander, E. (2001) 'On crafting a study of digital community networks: theoretical and methodological considerations', in B. Loader and L. Keeble (eds), *Community Informatics: Shaping Computer-Mediated Social Networks*. London: Taylor.

Jones, S.G. (ed.) (1995a) *Cybersociety: Computer-mediated Communication and Community*. Thousand Oaks, CA: Sage.

Jones, S.G. (1995b) 'Understanding community in the information age', in S.G. Jones (ed.), *Cybersociety: Computer-mediated Communication and Community*. Thousand Oaks, CA: Sage. pp. 10–34.

Jones, S.G. (ed.) (1997) *Virtual Culture: Identity and Communication in Cybersociety*. London: Sage.

Jones, S.G. (ed.) (1998a) *Cybersociety 2.0: Revisiting Computer-mediated Communication and Community*. Thousand Oaks, CA: Sage.

Jones, S.G. (1998b) 'Information, Internet, and community: notes toward an understanding of community in the information age', in S.G. Jones (ed.), *Cybersociety 2.0: Revisiting Computer-mediated Communication and Community*. Thousand Oaks, CA: Sage. pp. 1–33.

Jones, S.G. (ed.) (1999) *Doing Internet Research: Critical Issues and Methods for Examining the Net*. Thousand Oaks, CA: Sage.

Jones, S.G. (2004) 'Imagining an association', in M. Consalvo, N. Baym, J. Hunsinger et al. (eds), *Internet Research Annual: Selected Papers from the Association of Internet Research Conferences*. New York: Peter Lang. pp. 5–8.

Kavanaugh, A.L. and Patterson, S.J. (2002) 'The impact of community computer networks on social and community involvement in Blacksburg', in B. Wellman and C. Haythornthwaite (eds), *The Internet in Everyday Life*. Oxford: Blackwell, pp. 325–71.

Lewis, P. (1976) *Bristol Channel and Community Television*. London: IBA.

Loader, B. and Keeble, L. (eds) (2001) *Community Informatics: Shaping Computer-mediated Social Networks*. London: Taylor.

McQuail, D. (1994) *Mass Communication Theory: An Introduction*, 3rd edn (1st edn 1983). London: Sage.

Malina, A. (2001) 'Community building in cyberspace: a case study of a community network'. PhD dissertation, Queen Margaret College, Edinburgh, Scotland.

Mehta, R. and Sivadas, E. (1995) 'Comparing response rates and response content in mail versus electronic mail surveys', *Journal of the Market Research Society*, 37 (4): 429–39.

Merton, R.K. (1949) 'Patterns of influence: a study of interpersonal influence and communications behavior in a local community', in P.F. Lazarsfeld and F.N. Stanton (eds), *Communication Research 1948–49*. New York: Arno. pp. 180–219.

Miles, M.B. and Huberman, M. (1994) *Qualitative Data Analysis: An Expanded Sourcebook*. Thousand Oaks, CA: Sage.

Mitchell, C. (2001) 'On air/off air: defining women's radio space in European women's community radio', in N.W. Jankowski (with O. Prehn) (ed.), *Community Media in the Information Age: Perspectives and Prospects*. Cresskill, NJ: Hampton.

Negroponte, N. (1995) *Being Digital*. New York: Knopf.

Newby, H. (1980) *An Introduction to Sociology. Block 3: Comparison and Change: Community*. Milton Keynes: Open University Press.

Nightingale, V. (1996) *Studying Audiences: The Shock of the Real*. London: Routledge.

Nisbet, R. (1966) *The Sociological Tradition*. London: Heinemann.

Park, R.E. (1922) *The Immigrant Press and Its Control*. New York: Harper & Row.

Park, R.E. (1929) 'Urbanization as measured by newspaper circulation', *American Journal of Sociology*, 34: 60–79.

Prehn, O. (1992) 'From small scale utopianism to large scale pragmatism', in N. Jankowski, O. Prehn and J. Stappers (eds), *The People's Voice: Local Radio and Television in Europe*. London: Libbey. pp. 247–68.

Prell, C.L. (2001) 'The design and diffusion of a community network and its effect on social

capital'. PhD dissertation, Rensselaer Polytechnic Institute, Troy, NY.

Press, A.L. (1996) 'Towards a qualitative methodology of audience study: using ethnography to study the popular culture audience', in J.H.L. Grossberg and E. Wartella (eds), *The Audience and Its Landscape*. Boulder, CO: Westview. pp. 113–30.

Putnam, R.D. (with Leonardi, R. and Nanetti, R.Y.) (1993) *Making Democracy Work: Civic Traditions in Modern Italy*. Princeton, NJ: Princeton University Press.

Putnam, R.D. (1995) 'Bowling alone: America's declining social capital', *Journal of Democracy*, 6 (1): 65–78.

Putnam, R.D. (2000) *Bowling Alone: The Collapse and Revival of American Community*. New York: Simon & Schuster.

Redfield, R. (1947) 'The folk society', *American Journal of Sociology*, 52: 293.

Reid, E.M. (1994) 'Cultural formations in text-based virtual reality'. Master's thesis, University of Melbourne. Available online: ftp://ftp.lambda.moo.mud.org/pub/ MOO/papers/CulturalFormations.txt

Reid, E.M. (1999) 'Hierarchy and power: social control in cyberspace', in M.A. Smith and P. Kollock (eds), *Communities in Cyberspace*. London: Routledge. pp. 107–33.

Rheingold, H. (1993a) 'A slice of life in my virtual community', in L.M. Harasim (ed.), *Global Networks*. Cambridge: MIT Press. pp. 57–80. Draft version available online: http://home.ntt.com/eegtti/eeg_260html

Rheingold, H. (1993b) *The Virtual Community: Homesteading on the Electronic Frontier*. Reading, MA: Addison-Wesley. Available online: http://www.rheingold.com/vc/book

Rheingold, H. (2000) *The Virtual Community: Homesteading on the Electronic Frontier*, rev. edn. Cambridge, MA: MIT Press.

Riedel, E., Dresel, L., Wagoner, M.J., Sullivan, J.L. and Borgida, E. (1998) 'Electric communities: assessing equality of accesss in a rural Minnesota community', *Social Science Computer Review*, 15 (4): 370–90.

Rodríguez, C. (2001) *Fissures Mediascape: An International Study of Citizens' Media*. Creskill, NJ: Hampton Press.

Schneider, S. (1996) 'A case study of abortion conversation on the Internet', *Social Science Computer Review*, 14 (4): 373–93.

Schneider, S. (1997) 'Expanding the public sphere through computer-mediated communication: political discussion about abortion in a Usenet newsgroup'. PhD dissertation, Massachusetts Institute of Technology, Cambridge, MA. Available online: http://www.sunyit.edu/~steve

Schneider, S.M. and Foot, K.A. (in press) 'Web sphere analysis: an approach to studying online action', in C. Hine (ed.), *Virtual Methods: Issues in Social Research on the Internet*. Oxford: Berg.

Schirato, T. (2005) 'Cultural literacy, the media and the public sphere: implications for communication research', in K. Kwansah-Aidoo (ed.), *Topical Issues in Communications and Media Research*. New York: Nova Science. pp. 25–35.

Schuler, D. (1996) *New Community Networks: Wired for Change*. New York: ACM Press.

Schuler, D. and Day, P. (eds) (2004) *Shaping the Network Society: The New Role of Civil Society in Cyberspace*. Cambridge, MA: MIT Press.

Schuler, D. and Namioka, A. (eds) (1993) *Participatory Design: Principles and Practices*. Hillsdale, NJ: Lawrence Erlbaum Associates.

Silver, D. (2000) 'Cyberspace under construction: design, discourse, and diversity in the Blacksburg Electronic Village and the Seattle Community Network'. PhD dissertation, University of Maryland.

Smith, M. and Kollock, P. (eds) (1999) *Communities in Cyberspace*. London: Routledge.

Stacey, M. (1974) 'The myth of community studies', in C. Bell and H. Newby (eds), *The Sociology of Community*. London: Cass. pp. 13–26.

Stamm, K.R. (1985) *Newspaper Use and Community Ties: Toward a Dynamic Theory*. Norwood, NJ: Ablex.

Stappers, J., Olderaan, F. and del Wit, P. (1992) 'The Netherlands: emergence of a new medium', in N. Jankowski, O. Prehn and J. Stappers (eds), *The People's Voice: Local Radio and Television in Europe*. London: Libbey. pp. 90–103.

Stein, L. (2001) 'Democratic "talk", access television and participatory political communication', in N.W. Jankowski (with O. Prehn) (ed.), *Community Media in the Information Age: Perspectives and Prospects*. Cresskill, NJ: Hampton.

Stone, A.R. (1991) 'Will the real body please stand up: boundary stories about virtual cultures', in M. Benedikt (ed.), *Cyberspace: First Steps*. Cambridge, MA: MIT Press. pp. 81–118.

Stromer-Galley, J. and Foot, K.A. (2002) 'Citizens perceptions of online interactivity and implications for political campaign communication', *Journal of Computer-Mediated Communication*, 8 (1). Available online: http://www.ascusc.org/jcmc/vol8/issue1/stromerandfoot.html.

Swoboda, W.J., Mühlberger, N., Weikunat, R. and Schneeweiss, S. (1997) 'Internet surveys by direct mailing: an innovative way of collecting data', *Social Science Computer Review*, 15 (3): 242–55.

Tönnies, F. (1887/1957) *Community and Society*. New York: Harper Torchback.

Turkle, S. (1995) *Life on the Screen: Identity in the Age of the Internet*. New York: Simon & Schuster.

Van Dijk, J. (1998) 'The reality of virtual communities', *Trends in Communication*, 1 (1): 39–63.

Wellman, B. (1979) 'The community question: the intimate networks of East Yorkers', *American Journal of Sociology*, 84: 1201–31.

Wellman, B. (1997) 'An electronic group is virtually a social network', in S. Kiesler (ed.), *Culture of the Internet*. Mahwah, NJ: Lawrence Erlbaum. pp. 179–205.

Wellman, B. (ed.) (1999) *Networks in the Global Village*. Boulder, CO: Westview.

Wellman, B. and Berkowitz, S.D. (eds) (1988) *Social Structures: A Network Approach*. Cambridge: Cambridge University Press.

Wellman, B. and Berkowitz, S.D. (eds) (1997) *Social Structures: A Network Approach*, updated edn. Greenwich, CT: JAI Press.

Wellman, B. and Gulia, M. (1999) 'Net surfers don't ride alone: virtual communities as communities', in P. Kollock and M. Smith (eds), *Communities in Cyberspace*. Berkeley, CA: University of California Press. pp. 167–94.

Wellman, B. and Hampton, K. (1999) 'Living networked in a wired world', *Contemporary Sociology*, 28 (6): 648–54.

Westerik, H. (2001) 'De verklaring van het gebruik van lokale media' (Explanation of the use of local media). PhD dissertation, University of Nijmegen, the Netherlands.

Widlok, P. (1992) 'Der andere Hörfunk: community Radios in den USA' (The other form of broadcasting: community radio in the USA). PhD dissertation, University of Münster.

Wirth, L. (1938) 'Urbanism as a way of life', *American Journal of Sociology*, 44: 1–24.

3

Children and New Media

DAVID BUCKINGHAM

Some grand claims have been made about the impact of new media on children's lives. Like the idea of childhood itself, new technology is often invested with our most intense fantasies and fears. It holds out the promise of a better future, while simultaneously provoking anxieties about a fundamental break with the past. In this scenario, children are perceived both as the avant-garde of media users and as the ones who are most at risk from new developments. Childhood therefore provides a revealing lens through which many broader aspects of new media can be more clearly seen.

This chapter focuses on children's uses of new media (particularly computers) in the context of leisure time, in the home and in the peer group. The chapter begins by considering recent popular debates on these issues, drawing on material aimed at a general readership. Challenging generalized notions of 'childhood', it then moves on to consider the diverse social uses of new media among different groups of children. This is followed by a discussion of children's experiences of new media, focusing primarily upon computer games and 'online culture'; and a consideration of the 'educational' uses of new media by parents and children in the home. The chapter concludes with a brief discussion of implications for cultural and educational policy.

NIGHTMARES AND UTOPIAS

The advent of new cultural forms is often greeted by sharply divergent responses. This has been particularly true of digital media. On the one hand, these new media are seen to have enormous positive potential, particularly for learning; while on the other, they are frequently seen to be harmful to those perceived to be most at risk. In both cases, it is children – or more accurately, the *idea* of childhood – which is the vehicle for many of these aspirations and concerns.

Similar tensions were apparent in the early years of television. Amid current fears about the impact of television violence, it is interesting to recall that television was initially promoted to parents as an *educational* medium (Melody, 1973). Likewise, in the 1950s and 1960s, television and other new electronic technologies were widely seen to embody the future of education (Cuban, 1986). Yet even here, hopes of a utopian future were often balanced against fears of loss and cultural decline. Television was seen both as a new way of bringing the family together, and as something which would undermine natural family interaction. The medium was extolled as a way of nurturing children's educational development, and simultaneously condemned for taking them away from more wholesome activities (Spigel, 1992).

Contemporary responses to new media are similarly polarized. On the one hand, there is a form of visionary utopianism, particularly among educationists. Seymour Papert (1993), for example, argues that computers bring about new forms of learning, which transcend the limitations of older linear methods such as print and television. It is children who are seen to be most responsive to these new approaches: the computer somehow releases their natural creativity and desire to learn, which are blocked and frustrated by old-fashioned methods. Others have argued that computers empower children to communicate with each other, to express themselves and to participate in public life in ways that were previously impossible. Jon Katz (1996), for instance, regards the Internet as a means of children's liberation: it provides children with opportunities to escape from adult control, and to create their own cultures and communities. 'For the first time,' he argues, 'children can reach past the suffocating boundaries of social convention, past their elders' rigid notions of what is good for them' (1996: 122). Likewise, Don Tapscott (1997) argues that the Internet is creating an 'electronic generation' that is more democratic, more imaginative, more socially responsible and better informed than preceding generations. Digital technology, he argues, will eventually bring about a 'generational explosion', a 'social awakening' that will overthrow traditional hierarchies of knowledge and power. This kind of generational rhetoric is also powerfully reflected in advertising for computers. Children are typically seen to possess a natural wisdom in their relationships with technology that the majority of adults are seen to lack. Ads for Apple Macs or Microsoft focus not on the scientific specifications but on the magical promise of the technology: the computer is represented here as a window onto new worlds, a way of developing children's intuitive sense of wonder and thirst for knowledge (Nixon, 1998).

On the other hand, there is a much more negative account of the impact of these new media on children's lives. This account focuses not so much on their *educational* potential, but on their role as a means of *entertainment* – and it depends upon making an absolute distinction between the two. Some of the anxieties that are regularly rehearsed in relation to television have now been carried over to these new media. Thus, digital media are frequently seen to be a bad influence on children's behaviour – and particularly to cause imitative violence. Events like the shootings at Columbine High School in Colorado, USA in 1999 are frequently blamed on violent computer games or on children's access to 'hate sites' on the World Wide Web. The more 'realistic' graphic effects become, it is argued, the more likely they are to encourage 'copycat' behaviour (Provenzo, 1991). These new media are also seen to be bad for the brain – and indeed for the body. Thus, there have been numerous clinical studies of phenomena such as 'Nintendo elbow' and epileptic fits allegedly caused by computer games, through to research on computer 'addiction' and its negative effects on children's imagination and academic achievement (Griffiths, 1996). Meanwhile, new media are accused of making children antisocial, and of destroying normal human interaction and family life. The phenomenon of the 'Otaku-Zoku' or 'stay-at-home tribe' in Japan is seen as emblematic of the ways in which young people are coming to prefer the distance and anonymity of virtual communication to the reality of face-to-face interaction (Tobin, 1998). These media are also seen to have negative moral and ideological effects on children. Thus, games playing is seen to be a highly gendered activity, which reinforces traditional stereotypes and negative role models, and encourages male violence towards women. Meanwhile, there is increasing anxiety about the accessibility of pornography on the Internet, and about the dangers of children being seduced by online paedophiles. And finally, there is growing concern about the practice of online marketing to children, both through direct selling and through the gathering of market research data (Schor, 2004).

These arguments, like those about the effects of television, often involve a form of scapegoating. Like television, the computer becomes a convenient bad object, onto which we can displace a whole range of worries and frustrations. This often leads to calls for children's access to the medium to be restricted – whether through tighter regulation (such as ratings systems for computer games) or by means of a 'technological fix' (such as blocking software for the Internet). The effectiveness of such moves is debatable, but they undoubtedly enable legislators to show that they are 'doing something' about seemingly intractable social problems (Shuker, 1996). Meanwhile, there are renewed calls for educational intervention by parents and teachers – although such intervention often appears to be seen as a surrogate form of censorship, and hence may be something that children are inclined to resist (Buckingham and Sefton-Green, 1997).

As with debates around television, both the positive and the negative arguments here draw upon more general beliefs about childhood. On the one hand, children are seen to possess a natural, spontaneous creativity, which is somehow (perhaps paradoxically) released by the machine; while on the other, children are seen as vulnerable, innocent and in need of protection. These mythological constructions of childhood are in turn aligned with parallel mythologies about technology. Both positions are characterized by a powerful technological determinism – that is, a belief that technology will bring about social changes in and of itself (see Williams, 1974). Whether we see these changes as good or bad, they are seen to follow inexorably from the implementation or availability of the technology. Thus, computers are believed to produce 'fundamental shifts in the way we create and experience human identity' (Turkle, 1995). Through their encounters with new media, it is argued, contemporary children have become 'aliens': they represent a 'postmodern generation' whose subjectivity has been formed through the all-encompassing electronic habitat in which they live (Green and Bigum, 1993).

However overstated they may appear, these contrasting perspectives pose complex dilemmas for parents and others concerned with children's welfare. On the one hand, many parents feel that they should be exercising greater control in order to protect their children from harm; although, on the other hand, they are keen to exploit the educational potential of the technology. So to what extent can children be seen as technologically literate 'cyberkids' – or merely as victims seduced by the deceptions of the electronic screen? Can the broadly 'educational' benefits of these media be distinguished from their role as 'entertainment', and on what basis? And what should be the role of parents or teachers – or indeed the state – in regulating children's access to these new media?

FROM ACCESS TO USE

Children are undoubtedly one of the most significant target markets for new media. Even taking account of other social differences, households with children are much more likely to possess a multimedia computer or computer games console than those without children, and levels of access among children are increasing rapidly. Likewise, many of the new cultural forms made possible by these technologies are primarily identified with the young; and while this is most obviously the case with computer games, it is increasingly true of the Internet as well. Recent research in the UK (Livingstone and Bober, 2004) found that 74 per cent of children and young people (aged 9–19) have access to the Internet at home; while official statistics show that 99 per cent of UK schools now have Internet connections (DfES, 2003). The figures are broadly similar in other English-speaking countries (see, for example, Center for Media Research, 2004, and Rideout, 2003, on the US; Statistics Lamda, 2004, on Canada; and Colman, 2003, on Australia).

Nevertheless, we need to be aware of differences *within* the apparently homogeneous category of 'children'. There are significant inequalities in access between different social groups; and as other contributors to this volume indicate, these are particularly apparent in terms of social class and gender. In the UK, for example, Livingstone and Bober's (2004) study found that 88 per cent of middle-class children had home Internet access, compared with 61 per cent of working-class children. Socioeconomic status is also significant in relation to the *quality* of access at home (defined in terms of factors including the number, age and specification of computers and connection to dial-up or broadband). As with many other new technologies (not least television in the 1950s), those with greater disposable income are almost always the 'early adopters': they have newer and more powerful equipment, and more opportunities to develop the skills that are needed to use it.

Historically, researchers have also found that girls have less access to computers, are less interested in them and spend less time using them than boys (Cupitt and Stockbridge, 1996; Funk and Buchman, 1996; Kubey and Larson, 1990; Livingstone and Bovill, 1999). Both boys and girls are inclined to agree that computers are primarily 'for boys' (Bannert and Arbinger, 1996; Durndell et al., 1995). Even within comparatively 'media-rich' homes, girls are less likely than boys to own PCs or games consoles or have access to them in their bedrooms (Livingstone and Bovill, 1999). Nevertheless, more recent research (e.g. Livingstone and Bober, 2004) suggests that this gender gap may be narrowing as access increases, even if boys continue to express greater confidence in their dealings with technology. Perhaps the more significant differences now are to do with *purpose* and *content*: thus, it has been suggested that girls are more inclined than boys to use new media for the purpose of communication (Livingstone and Bovill, 1999), and their tastes in software are also quite different from those of boys (see below).

However, as Livingstone and Bovill (1999) point out, physical *access* to technology should not necessarily be equated with levels of *use*. Children who live in 'media-rich' homes do not necessarily have greater individualized access to media in their own bedrooms. These authors prefer to distinguish between different 'media use styles' – such as 'traditionalists', 'screen entertainment fans' and 'PC fans' – defined by clusters of age, class and gender variables. These different use styles reflect and in turn reproduce

particular sets of tastes and values, and particular philosophies of child-rearing. Children from different social groups possess not only different levels of access to technology, but also different attitudes and orientations towards it – or, in effect, different forms of 'cultural capital' (cf. Bourdieu, 1984). Research in the US suggests that this may also be related to ethnicity, as minority children may perceive computing to be a 'white' activity and hence avoid it (Straubhaar, 2000). Some commentators argue that these gaps between the 'technology rich' and the 'technology poor' will eventually disappear as an inevitable consequence of the diffusion of new media; while others fear a growing polarization, and the emergence of a 'media underclass' in which children will be disproportionately represented (Buckingham, 2000).

While this kind of research draws attention to social differences in the uses of technology, it tends to essentialize the differences between media. 'Computer games' or 'the Internet' are implicitly assumed to represent the same thing to all who use them. In this respect, broad demographic analyses need to be complemented by an understanding of how media and technologies are mediated through existing social relationships (Silverstone and Hirsch, 1992). Thus, we need to know more about how technology enters into the peer group and the family, how children gain access to it, how they learn about it, and how its use is regulated and controlled (for instance by parents). It is through such processes that technology comes to be defined as (for example) 'masculine' or 'feminine', 'educational' or 'entertaining', in ways that systematically favour access among particular social groups.

For example, research strongly refutes the popular idea that computer games playing is an antisocial activity (Buckingham, 1993; Carr et al., in press; Jenkins, 1993; Jessen, 1999; Livingstone and Bovill, 1999; Schott and Horrell, 2000). While the actual playing of games is sometimes an individual, isolated pursuit, it is also often collaborative, and the focus of a great deal of talk and interaction. Furthermore, the culture surrounding games is an important means of establishing and sustaining interpersonal relationships – from the swapping of games, advice and 'cheats', through to participation in the more public culture of games shops, arcades, magazines and TV shows. The culture of games playing involves an ongoing construction of an 'interpretive community' (cf. Radway, 1984) – and in this respect, as Jessen (1999) argues, it may be better suited to the pattern of children's play than older media such as books, which one is alone in consuming.

However, this social process is mediated by the operations of the market. Much of the discussion is about what you can buy, what you have bought, or what you are going to buy – and this is a discussion in which children are not equal. Furthermore, this surrounding culture is an arena for the 'border-work' that characterizes children's gender relationships (Thorne, 1993): it frequently serves to mark the boundaries between boys and girls, and thereby to prevent girls gaining access to technology or to the knowledge that is required to use it (Holloway and Valentine, 2003; Orr Vered, 1998). Through such processes, children are actively constructing and defining themselves, both as consumers and as gendered subjects. This kind of analysis potentially moves beyond the either/or dichotomy sketched above – the view of children either as passive recipients of adults' attempts at socialization, or alternatively as a sophisticated, 'media-literate' audience.

As this implies, we need to look beyond simple questions about children's access to media, and to look more closely at their diverse uses and experiences of these media. In moving on to address this issue, the following sections focus on two contrasting aspects of children's relationships with new media: computer games and 'online culture'.

ALL IN THE GAME?

Computer games now represent the fastest-growing sector of the global media and entertainment industries (see Herz, 1997; Kline et al., 2003). Games based in public arcades date back to the early 1970s, but it was the advent of home computer games in the late 1970s that resulted in a period of rapid expansion, led by manufacturers such as Atari. Following a collapse in the market around 1984, a 'second wave' of computer gaming, dominated by the Japanese companies Nintendo, Sega and Sony, followed in the second half of the 1980s. Growth in the market has been fairly inexorable since that time. The revenues from computer games now outstrip those of the Hollywood film industry; and major media companies such as Sony rely on the profitable 'synergies' between games and other media.

Children are by no means the only market for computer games – indeed, industry sources suggest that the average age of computer gamers is now 29 (Entertainment Software Association, 2003). The market penetration of games consoles is approaching saturation, at least among boys; although the regular succession of more powerful 'new generation' machines – combined with the rapid turnover of the younger market – means that hardware rapidly becomes obsolescent. Game software is comparatively highly priced, and since software platforms are incompatible (both between different systems and between successive 'generations' of machines), the profitability of the more popular games is extremely high.

Games have increasingly been integrated within what Marsha Kinder (1991) calls the 'transmedia intertextuality' of contemporary children's culture. Many of the most popular games use characters and scenarios from movies, while others have subsequently generated feature films and television shows in their own right. The global success of Nintendo's 'Pokémon' illustrates how such integrated marketing has become a key strategy for the 'digital empires' that increasingly dominate children's culture: simultaneously a computer game, a television series, a sequence of feature films and a trading card game, 'Pokémon' also generated an extensive range of books, comics, toys and other merchandise (Tobin, 2004). As Kinder suggests, media-based commodities of this kind have become a crucial factor in the social construction of children's peer group cultures. Meanwhile, educationalists such as Papert (1993) point out that games are now children's primary means of access to the world of computers; and that, rather than reinforcing distinctions between 'education' and 'entertainment', software designers need to capitalize on the educational potential of game play (Gee, 2003).

Although computer games have been a mass-market phenomenon for more than a quarter of a century, academic research in this field is a comparatively recent development. This is partly a result of the difficulty of keeping pace with change. Yet it may also reflect the fact that, unlike television, games do not immediately reveal themselves to the outside observer. The experience of game playing requires a great investment of time, and no small amount of expertise. As a result, many academics who have written about computer games have done so from a considerable distance. They have been inclined to generalize, without making fundamental distinctions between different genres or discussing particular games in any detail; they have concentrated on relatively superficial visual characteristics of games, without discussing the experience of game play; and they have imported conceptual and methodological approaches from studies of older media such as film and television without paying sufficient attention to the unique characteristics of the new medium.

THE LIMITS OF EFFECTS

Interestingly, much of the early research in this field – roughly coinciding with the 'first wave' of domestic computer games – focused on their positive effects. (A useful 'state-of-the-art' survey of this early work can be found in *Video Games and Human Behavior: A Research Agenda for the 80s*, 1983.) Patricia Greenfield (1984), for example, argues that game playing involves a whole range of cognitive skills – not merely hand–eye coordination, but also problem-solving, memory, inductive thinking, parallel processing, spatial awareness and so on. The notion that game playing is simply a 'mindless' activity is effectively refuted here; although the evidence on whether it actually *develops* these skills, or whether they transfer

to other domains of learning, is rather more questionable.

However, research in this field has been increasingly dominated by anxieties about the negative psychological, moral and behavioural effects of computer games. Thus, research studies have attempted to assess the impact of playing computer games on aggressive behaviour; on psychological variables such as self-esteem; on educational achievement; and on the development of stereotyped attitudes. Researchers have typically used survey methods, although there have been some more experimental studies of short-term effects. As some reviews have suggested (Durkin, 1995; Egenfeldt-Nielsen and Smith, 2004; Gunter, 1998), the findings of these studies have been uneven and inconsistent; and even less critical reviews (Funk et al., 1997; Griffiths, 1996; Sherry, 2001) have been fairly equivocal in their conclusions.

In many respects, the limitations of the research reflect those of parallel research on the effects of television (Barker and Petley, 2001). These would include the following.

1 *A crude approach to categorizing games 'texts':* Research studies rarely go further than superficial distinctions based on content. For example, distinctions are frequently made between 'violent' and 'non-violent' games, between 'educational' and 'non-educational' games, or between games that are judged to be more or less 'realistic'; but these distinctions are not based on subjects' own judgements, and are often inadequately defined.

2 *Inconsistent and/or unexplained findings:* Experimental studies of the effects of 'violent' games conducted in the late 1980s, for example, failed to generate consistent findings (e.g. Graybill et al., 1985, 1987); some only found effects among girls (Cooper and Mackie, 1986); while others simply failed to establish causal relationships at all (Winkel et al., 1987). Survey-based studies frequently establish correlations between game playing and 'negative' qualities such as poor self-esteem, although reliable evidence about the direction and significance of any *causal* relationship is

rarely provided (e.g. Funk and Buchman, 1996).

3 *Untested and inadequately theorized notions of the mechanisms by which effects are assumed to be caused*: As in television research, key terms such as 'addiction' (Griffiths, 1994), 'arousal' (Kubey and Larson, 1990), 'identification' (Funk et al., 1997) and 'modelling' (Funk and Buchman, 1996) are often loosely defined and measured. They are frequently offered as *post hoc* explanations, rather than hypotheses that are empirically tested by the research.

4 *A neglect of the social context of games playing, and of research itself*: Few effects studies pay attention to the social interaction that characterizes most game playing: they are solely concerned with the interaction between mind and screen. As in much media effects research, college students are frequently used as research subjects; yet the ability of students to recognize and respond to the 'demand characteristics' of research significantly limits the capacity for generalization.

Close attention to particular studies reveals more specific weaknesses. A paper by Funk and Buchman (1996) illustrates some of these. The study is concerned with the relationships between 'violent' games and adolescents' 'self-concept'. Apart from the many questions that one might raise about the methods used to measure these two variables, the authors themselves are bound to admit several crucial limitations to their analysis. Some of these, such as the unreliability of self-reports of media use and the fact that correlation does not establish proof of causality, are widely recognized in the field. In this instance, the analysis also throws up some apparently incongruous findings that the authors struggle to explain; and in fact only a small amount of the variance is accounted for by the key independent variables, and then only among girls. In effect, the authors fail to find what they are looking for – which is confirmation of the negative effects of violence in games, a finding which they regard as having been incontrovertibly established by research on television. And so, in their conclusion, they fall back on an entirely hypothetical construct, that

of the 'high-risk player' (who is, interestingly, male), even while admitting that their methods have been insufficiently sensitive to prove that he exists.

A rather different – though equally familiar – problem is raised by Eugene Provenzo's (1991) study. Provenzo's chosen method is content analysis; although in fact he analyses only the covers of the games rather than the actual games themselves – an approach which, as Jenkins (1993) points out, can be highly misleading. Here again, the categories used in the content analysis (such as 'violence') are inadequately defined and inconsistently applied; and the descriptions of particular games are very superficial. In comparing games with 'great literature', Provenzo persistently invokes received judgements of taste that he fails to justify. However, the most telling limitation of this study is its use of data about *texts* to support very powerful assertions about their *effects*. Provenzo asserts that games are 'powerful teaching machines and instruments of cultural transmission'; they 'socialize women to be dependent [and] men to assume dominant gender roles'; they are 'instruments of a larger social, political and cultural hegemony'; and they are ultimately 'dehumanizing'. These are all explicit claims about the *effectiveness* of texts; yet no evidence whatsoever is provided to support them.

GAME BOYS, GAME GIRLS

Much of the emphasis here has been on the role of games in gender socialization. Computer games are frequently defined, both by researchers and by children themselves, as 'boys' toys' (Jessen, 1999). Surveys consistently suggest that girls have less access to computer games, and play less often. Critics argue that this situation may be disadvantaging girls in their educational encounters with computers, and in their subsequent employment prospects, as high-status jobs increasingly require computing skills (Cassell and Jenkins, 1998a).

The causes and consequences of this situation have been interpreted in various ways, however. While the games industry is seeking to broaden its market, the majority of games still appear to be designed primarily with boys (or men) in mind. Provenzo's (1991) findings here largely remain true: there are few 'positive images' of women, and females often feature only as 'damsels in distress', awaiting rescue by the male adventurer. Some research (Subrahmanyam and Greenfield, 1998) suggests that girls generally do not favour the qualities that are characteristic of many computer games, such as an emphasis on 'action', contests between good and evil, fantasy settings and teams of characters (see also Cupitt and Stockbridge, 1996; Funk and Buchman, 1996; Kafai, 1998). Some studies find that boys are more 'aroused' than girls by the experience of new media, particularly when in the company of other boys (Kubey and Larson, 1990); although others have found the opposite (Cooper and Mackie, 1986).

However, such arguments can reinforce the essentialist notions of gender that they are outwardly concerned to challenge. Such research is often based on a fairly crude form of socialization theory, accompanied by a tendency to pathologize masculinity. Turkle (1984), for example, implicitly stigmatizes the rule-bound, 'hard' approach to computing which she defines as characteristic of boys, particularly during puberty. Alloway and Gilbert (1998) condemn computer game culture as a whole as 'masculinist, aggressive and violent', arguing that it simply reproduces oppressive forms of male subjectivity. Such arguments are reinforced by several of the researchers mentioned earlier (e.g. Funk and Buchman, 1996; Kubey and Larson, 1990; Provenzo, 1991). Here again, however, it is implicitly assumed that the 'messages' contained within the games are swallowed whole by their users. As Gailey (1993) suggests, this approach regards children as empty receptacles, and neglects the diverse ways in which the games are interpreted and used.

Both theoretically and empirically, some of these concerns are also beginning to appear rather outdated. The market in games is certainly skewed towards boys, but it is by no means exclusively confined to them: industry estimates from the US suggest that 39 per cent

of game players are female (Entertainment Software Association, 2003). Indeed, the move of games culture from the male-dominated public space of the arcades (Braun and Giroux, 1989; Panelas, 1983) to the domestic space of the living room or the child's bedroom has increased the potential access for girls, and there are extensive communities of 'girl gamers' (Cunningham, 1995; Schott and Horrell, 2000). As the games industry has increasingly reached out to girls, female characters have featured more strongly; although whether a character like Lara Croft (in 'Tomb Raider') would qualify as a 'positive image' is certainly open to debate. Games are also becoming more diverse, and some of the newer role-playing games are less obviously targeted at boys, at least in terms of the characteristics identified above. Meanwhile, computers themselves have become easier to operate, which may mean that they are less likely to be perceived as intimidatingly 'technological' and hence as 'masculine'.

Cassell and Jenkins (1998b) offer an intriguing analysis of one attempt to change this situation, in the form of the 'girl games movement' of the late 1990s. This movement resulted from a particular combination of feminist academics, young women players and those within the industry who were attempting to reach out to a female audience. This new form of 'entrepreneurial feminism' had to walk a difficult line between the attempt to satisfy the existing girls' market and the attempt to change gender relations. On the one hand, there was an effort to create and sustain a positive space for girls, albeit in a way which may appear to sustain gender stereotypes; while on the other, there was an attempt to make that space more 'empowering' for girls, thereby running the risk of alienating them. As Cassell and Jenkins explain, these dilemmas were manifested in many areas of games design, from the construction of narratives to the colour coding of the packaging.

The obvious 'absent presence' in Cassell and Jenkins' book, however, is that of boys (Sefton-Green, 1999). Jenkins' (1998) own contribution is alone in attempting to address the pleasures of masculinity, and to consider how these might be addressed by games. He argues that games could be seen as virtual 'play spaces' that compensate for the growing lack of such spaces in the real world, as children (and especially boys) have been increasingly confined to the home. According to Jenkins, the games (and the peer group culture that surrounds them) offer the same pleasures that used to be afforded to earlier generations of boys in outdoor play: the exploration and mastery of space, goal-driven activity, self-control rather than parental control, and male bonding. Rather than seeing these qualities as a kind of early training in 'masculinist violence', Jenkins attempts to understand them in their own terms.

Despite its fairly narrow focus, Cassell and Jenkins' book points towards the kind of multifaceted analysis of the games phenomenon that needs to be developed in future research. What remains lacking from their account, however, is an indication of how *effective* the 'girl games movement' actually was in reaching and engaging girl players. As this implies, investigations of industry strategies need to be combined with accounts of the experiences of games playing, and with much more detailed analyses of games 'texts' themselves.

GAMES AS TEXTS

As I have noted, analyses of children's relationships with computer games tend to rely on generalized assertions about games, or reductive categorizations of content. Detailed analyses of games themselves have been a relatively recent development. Early studies in this field used forms of literary and cultural theory to account for the nature of games, although in many cases at a high level of generality. Klein (1984), for example, argued that games like 'Pac-Man' reflected oral sadomasochistic fantasies of engulfment; Kestenbaum and Weinstein (1984) saw them as 'transitional objects'; while Skirrow (1986) regarded them as a form of fantasy resolution for male performance anxiety. In more overtly political terms, Stallybrass (1992) uses the work of Adorno and Benjamin to develop a theory of game

playing as a form of infantile regression promoted by capitalist consumer culture; while Fiske (1989) attempts to explain the appeal of games using an equally generalized account of popular culture as a form of 'ideological resistance'. Such arguments rarely make basic distinctions between different types of games, let alone refer to particular games in any detail.

However, the development of 'game studies' in recent years has seen a proliferation of new research looking at the nature of computer games as cultural texts. The key aim of many such studies has been to identify the qualities that are specific to games as a medium – their 'ludic' dimensions – and to develop new theories that might account for this (see, for example, the studies collected in Copier and Raessens, 2003; Goldstein and Raessens, in press; King, 2002; and Wolf and Perron, 2003; as well as the texts by Aarseth, 1997; Atkins, 2003; and Poole, 2000). Such analyses draw to some extent on play theory, for example in analyzing the nature of rules, the relationship between chance and strategy, the experience of time and the recursive nature of play. Rather than focusing on immediately observable content (such as the presence or absence of 'violence'), the emphasis here is on the different styles of interactivity (or what players call 'game play') offered by different games.

As Aarseth (2001) and others have argued, simply importing concepts and methodologies from studies of 'older' media to the analysis of new media such as computer games can be positively misleading. For example, notions of 'identification' taken from film studies may be inappropriate when it comes to characters who are simply devices to insert the player into the game. An emphasis on goal-driven narratives, and on the significance of narrative closure, may lead to a neglect of the pleasures of play for its own sake; and focusing on the experience of time in games may lead one to neglect the significance of space, and the metaphors of exploration and conquest around which they are organized (Fuller and Jenkins, 1995). Nevertheless, games clearly do possess a representational dimension as well as a ludic one; and while this may take a different form, and assume a different significance, in different game genres, it should not be ignored. To this extent, approaches derived from literary theory (such as narratology), from the study of visual iconography, or from fields such as semiotics, will continue to be relevant to analysing game texts (Carr et al., in press).

This kind of textual analysis is all the more significant as the games (and the cultures that surround them) continue to develop. As Provenzo (1991) and other critics have feared, computer games are indeed becoming more 'realistic' and 'graphic'; but they are also becoming significantly more complex and multilayered. To compare early games like 'Pong' or 'Space Invaders' with more recent games like the 'Final Fantasy' series or *The Sims* is to recognize the extraordinarily rapid evolution of the form. Technological developments will also offer new challenges here: the growing importance of multi-player games and online gaming reinforces the need for studies that pay much closer attention to the social context of games playing, and the culture that surrounds it.

CHILDREN'S ONLINE CULTURE

By contrast with the moral panics that have characterized discussion of computer games, debates about the potential of the Internet for young people have been significantly more positive. Rather than considering the Internet merely as a distribution medium, researchers have focused on the potential uses of chat groups, blogging, electronic mail and web pages as forms of autonomous creative expression. While these more 'creative' aspects of children's use of the medium are still confined to a minority, they are nevertheless growing at a remarkable rate. These are arenas in which, it is argued, children and young people are no longer constrained by the limitations of their parents' cultures (Tapscott, 1997).

Research on children's online communication has been hampered by the logistical and ethical difficulties of accessing private online activities. However, there have been some useful small-scale studies focusing on the linguistic structures of children's chat (e.g. Merchant, 2001) and the forms of 'identity work' that characterize online communication (e.g. Abbott, 1999; Tingstad, 2003; Willett and Sefton-Green, 2002). Thus, analyses of WWW home pages produced by children have seen them as instances of identity construction analogous to the decoration of bedroom walls (Chandler and Roberts-Young, 1998; Stern, 2004). Home pages and blogs are typically seen here as hybrid forms that combine aspects of public communication, (such as broadcasting or publishing) with those of private communication, such as the personal diary or the letter (Scheidt, in press). This hybridity is also reflected in the combination of written and spoken forms that characterizes these new media (Merchant, 2001). For some, the constant changes that characterize children's home pages are symptomatic of a 'postmodern' fluidity of identity (cf. Turkle, 1995); although others argue that the Net is a place where young people feel they can be 'truly themselves' (Tobin, 1998). Susannah Stern (1999) provides an account of three different types of home pages produced by teenage girls that begins to indicate the diverse styles and purposes of children's online culture. In Stern's categorization, 'spirited' sites convey buoyancy and cheerfulness, and are used as a form of 'self-glorification'; 'sombre' sites are disillusioned, angry and introspective, serving as 'an asylum from a difficult and hostile world'; while 'self-conscious' sites oscillate between the two, reflecting the authors' lack of confidence about sharing too much online. Like other researchers in this field, however, Stern appears uncertain about whether to view the sites as vehicles for 'self-construction' or (more straightforwardly) as 'self-expression' – and hence as a safe space in which girls can 'speak their experience'.

Similar issues arise in the analysis of Internet relay chat (IRC), although the possibility that children may 'pass' as adults, or adults as children, makes it very difficult to assess the reliability of data. Just as some have claimed that the anonymity of chat rooms can provide opportunities for play with gender identities, so the same may be true in relation to age (Smith and Curtin, 1998; Turkle, 1995).

Serious ethical dilemmas inevitably arise in this kind of research, particularly given the ease with which one can eavesdrop on apparently 'private' communications (Tingstad, 2003), and these may be particularly acute in relation to children. Nevertheless, some researchers have argued that children and young people may be particularly empowered by these online communities. Tobin (1998), for example, argues that online communication may provide a means for boys to share 'personal' concerns and problems that is denied to them in other social encounters; Abbott (1998) suggests that the use of oral linguistic forms in this context displays 'a striving for immediacy, response and dialogue, a sense of communion' which is only partially satisfied elsewhere; while Tingstad (2003) points to the potential for children to develop childhood identities that are not constrained by adult imperatives.

A related theme here is that of *pedagogy*. Tobin (1998) argues that online communication produces 'learning communities' that cross boundaries of age and geography, and that are more democratic and collaborative than traditional educational institutions. As in more general assertions about online communities (e.g. Rheingold, 1993), such arguments tend to neglect the occasionally *un*democratic and exclusionary nature of online communication; although the opportunities these media present for group interaction, when compared with equivalent older technologies such as the telephone, cannot be denied. Combined with assertions about the more self-managed, participatory learning *styles* developed by computers – by games as much as by 'educational' software (Gee, 2003) – these arguments lead towards a notion of a 'deschooled' society that comes close to that proposed by Ivan Illich more than 30 years ago (Illich, 1971; Snyder, 1998).

If research about computer games has been somewhat constrained by the 'carryover' of ideas from older media, work on children's online culture has only just begun to develop appropriate hypotheses and methods. As with games, researchers are dealing with forms of children's culture to which it is very difficult to gain access – and which, in many respects, seem almost deliberately designed to exclude them. Most of the studies mentioned here are highly descriptive, and some carry an almost colonialist air, as though they were reports from strange and distant lands. Future research will need to be much more detailed and sustained. Researchers will need to triangulate between the analysis of texts (such as home pages and IRC sessions) and interviews with their producers and users; analyse the evolution of particular pages and sites over time; consider the place of such activities in the context of 'real-life' relationships in the family and the peer group; and consider how far participants in online culture may be representative of broader social categories.

EDUCATION AND ENTERTAINMENT

As I have noted, much of the positive potential of new media for children has been seen to rest in their *educational* role. Longer-term fantasies of a deschooled, 'wired' society are perhaps the most utopian aspect of this; although claims about the educational value of home computing have long been a central aspect of the industry's marketing strategies (Buckingham et al., 2001; Nixon, 1998). Advertising for these media often represents them as a way of investing in children's future; and indeed as a means of compensating for what are seen to be the inadequacies of contemporary schooling. Thus, it is claimed that computer software will 'make learning fun' by using imagery and modes of address drawn from children's popular culture, and by employing what purport to be 'interactive' approaches. These new forms of 'edutainment' are offered both as an acceptable leisure-time pursuit, and as a glamorous alternative to the apparent tedium of much school work.

There have been some contrasting assessments of the educational value of these new media, however. Seymour Papert (1996), for example, waxes lyrical about children's 'love affair' with computers, arguing that they provide a more creative and spontaneous form of learning that can dramatically improve family relationships. By contrast, sceptics such as Jane

Healy (1998) argue that much of the learning that computers provide is superficial and trivial, and that claims about their educational potential are highly overstated. Despite these differences between them, however, such authors agree on the importance of high-quality software, support from parents and strong connections between home and school if this potential is to be realized.

In a substantial empirical study, Giacquinta et al. (1993) conclude that the educational 'promise' of this technology has been largely unfulfilled. While parents are likely to invest in computers and software with educational benefits in mind, and while they often have access to good-quality educational programs, they are rarely used. In general, children prefer to use home computers for playing games, and resist overtly 'educational' activities; and this is reinforced by the dominant view of the computer as a toy or plaything. Parents also lack the time and expertise to support their children's use of computers; while the uses of computers in schools are frequently limited, and there is little dialogue between parents and teachers on the issue. Finally, males are generally the major users and decision-makers in relation to home computing, while females (particularly mothers) are often defined as incompetent; and since mothers are generally the primary care-givers, this further reduces the potential for parental support. According to these authors, the benefits of technology will only be realized if we pay attention to the 'social envelope' – that is, to the sets of expectations, contexts and social practices – that surrounds it. Thus, for example, they suggest that schools can play a significant role as 'linking agents' to encourage educational computing in the home; but this will in turn require broader changes in the relationships between parents and teachers.

The Giacquinta et al. (1993) study was undertaken in the mid 1980s, before the advent of multimedia home computers and the Internet – although their findings are largely confirmed by several more recent studies (e.g. Buckingham and Scanlon, 2003, 2004; Facer et al., 2003; Holloway and Valentine, 2003). Similar arguments apply to the 'creative' potential

of home computing. Another relatively early study, by Sefton-Green and Buckingham (1996), found that while children were certainly aware of the potential of the technology, they were rarely in a position to exploit it. They understood in principle what their *computers* could do – for example in digital animation, design, sound and video editing, and 'multimedia authoring' – but they rarely engaged in such activities themselves. Some of the reasons for this were essentially 'technical'; and in this respect, the machines (or the advertisements for them) seemed to promise more than they were capable of delivering. However, there were also some important social reasons why the technology was not living up to its creative potential. Very few parents knew how to support their children in using the computer in this way; although children in middle-class families, whose parents or relatives were often more familiar with technology, were in a better position. For most children, however, using computers seemed to be a way of filling in time when they were bored. This sense of disconnectedness was also reflected in the lack of an *audience* for this material. Children described how they would show their work to their mum or stick it on their bedroom wall, but otherwise nobody ever saw or knew about it – a striking contrast with the intensely sociable culture of computer gaming.

There remains a need for further research on the *pedagogy* of computer use in the home – for example, how (and by whom) children are introduced to computers, and how parents encourage or regulate their use. We need to know more about how both groups perceive and balance out the 'educational' and 'entertainment' aspects of these new media, and understand their creative potential. While parents are encouraged to invest in computers for broadly 'educational' purposes, children are much more inclined to use them for 'entertainment' (Cupitt and Stockbridge, 1996; Downes, 1999; Facer et al., 2003). Over the past decade, these competing views have often been manifested in parents' decisions about whether to buy a PC or a games console; yet with the advent of games consoles that allow Internet access, these distinctions may prove more difficult to sustain. Meanwhile, the growing availability of the Internet may provide many more outlets for young people's creative work (Sefton-Green, 2004); but it remains to be seen how far these 'virtual audiences' can substitute for real audiences of family and peers.

TOWARDS NEW POLICIES

Many of the issues discussed in this chapter have significant implications for cultural and educational policy. The dangers of a polarization between the information rich and the information poor, and the various forms of 'social exclusion' that it might encourage, have been recognized since the early days of new media research (e.g. Chen and Paisley, 1985) and are now widely acknowledged by policy-makers. Governments have increasingly recognized that the diffusion of technology cannot be left to market forces, and that regulation and intervention are required in order to ensure that all homes and schools are 'wired' to electronic networks.

At the time of writing, much of the impetus here continues to focus on questions of physical *access*. However, access is not simply a matter of technology. It is also a question of the skills and competencies – the cultural and educational capital – that are required to use technology creatively and effectively. These forms of capital are also unevenly distributed: different social groups are positioned in very different ways in relation to public discourses about education, and in relation to the institution of the school. New technology is becoming a crucial part of many people's working lives, but it is doing so in very different ways for different groups of workers; and, in the process, new gaps of knowledge and skill may be opening up. Meanwhile, cutting across these moves are more familiar concerns about children's relationships with media. Growing anxieties about pornography on the Internet or online marketing to children have led to debates about the need for content regulation and parental control (Oswell, 1999; Waltermann and Machill, 2000). Yet it is far from clear how we can prevent children gaining access to 'harmful' content, while simultaneously encouraging them to make the most of the educational and cultural potential of these new media.

As this chapter suggests, policy-makers need to take much fuller account of the social contexts in which children encounter new media, and the kinds of support which are necessary in order to use them most effectively. This may require a fairly radical rethinking of the institutional contexts (such as schools) in which technologies are made available to children; and of the relationships between schools, homes and other sites of educational and cultural activity (Schon et al., 1999). Simply providing children with technology is not enough: we have to enable them to develop the intellectual and cultural competencies that are required to select, interpret and utilize it. Despite the optimism of some advocates, children do not automatically know how to use new media technology, let alone evaluate what it provides. Technology alone will not transform them into the autonomous 'cyberkids' of the popular imagination. We need to pay much closer attention to what is taking place in their interactions with these new media, and to the forms of support and education they need in order to make those interactions as productive as they promise to be.

REFERENCES

Aarseth, E. (1997) *Cybertext.* Baltimore, MD: Johns Hopkins University Press.

Aarseth, E. (2001) 'Computer game studies, year one', *Game Studies*, 1. Available online: www.gamestudies.org

Abbott, C. (1998) 'Making connections: young people and the Internet', in J. Sefton-Green (ed.), *Digital Diversions: Youth Culture in the Age of Multimedia.* London: UCL Press. pp. 84–105.

Abbott, C. (1999) 'Web publishing by young people', in J. Sefton-Green (ed.), *Young People, Creativity and New Technologies: The Challenge of Digital Arts.* London: Routledge. pp. 111–21.

Alloway, N. and Gilbert, P. (1998) 'Video game culture: playing with masculinity, violence and pleasure', in S. Howard (ed.), *Wired-up: Young*

People and Electronic Media. London: UCL Press. pp. 95–114.

Atkins, B. (2003) *More than a Game: The Computer Game as Fictional Form.* Manchester: Manchester University Press.

Bannert, M. and Arbinger, P.R. (1996) 'Gender-related differences in exposure to and use of computers: results of a survey of secondary school students', *European Journal of Psychology of Education,* 11 (3): 269–82.

Barker, M. and Petley, J. (eds) (2001) *Ill Effects: The Media Effects Debate,* 2nd edn. London: Routledge.

Bourdieu, P. (1984) *Distinction: A Social Critique of the Judgement of Taste.* London: Routledge & Kegan Paul.

Braun, C. and Giroux, J. (1989) 'Arcade video games: proxemic, cognitive and content analyses', *Journal of Leisure Research,* 21 (2): 92–105.

Buckingham, D. (1993) 'Just playing games', *English and Media Magazine,* 28: 21–5.

Buckingham, D. (2000) *After the Death of Childhood: Growing Up in the Age of Electronic Media.* Cambridge: Polity.

Buckingham, D. and Scanlon, M. (2003) *Education, Entertainment and Learning in the Home.* Buckingham: Open University Press.

Buckingham, D. and Scanlon, M. (2004) 'Connecting the family? "Edutainment" websites and learning in the home', *Education, Communication and Information* 4 (2/3): 271–91.

Buckingham, D. and Sefton-Green, J. (1997) 'From regulation to education', *English and Media Magazine,* 36: 28–32.

Buckingham, D., Scanlon, M. and Sefton-Green, J. (2001) 'Selling the digital dream: marketing educational technology to teachers and parents', in A. Loveless and V. Ellis (eds), *ICT, Pedagogy and the Curriculum: Subject to Change.* London: Routledge. pp. 20–40.

Carr, D., Buckingham, D., Burn, A. and Schott, G. (in press) *Computer Games: Text, Narrative and Play.* Cambridge: Polity.

Cassell, J. and Jenkins, H. (eds) (1998a) 'Chess for girls? Feminism and computer games', in J. Cassell and H. Jenkins (eds), *From Barbie to Mortal Kombat: Gender and Computer Games.* Cambridge, MA: MIT Press. pp. 2–45.

Cassell, J. and Jenkins, H. (eds) (1998b) *From Barbie to Mortal Kombat: Gender and Computer Games.* Cambridge, MA: MIT Press.

Center for Media Research (2004) Available online: http://www.centerformediaresearch.com/cfmr_brief.cfm?fnl=041027

Chandler, D. and Roberts-Young, D. (1998) 'The construction of identity in the personal home-pages of adolescents'. Available online: http://www.aber.ac.uk/~dgc/strasbourg.html

Chen, M. and Paisley, W. (eds) (1985) *Children and Microcomputers: Research on the Newest Medium.* Beverly Hills, CA: Sage.

Colman, A. (2003) 'Digital Divide', *Youth Studies Australia.* Available online: http://www.highbeam.com/library/doc0.asp?docid=1G1:99817463

Cooper, J. and Mackie, D. (1986) 'Video games and aggression in children', *Journal of Applied Social Psychology,* 16 (8): 726–44.

Copier. M. and Raessens, J. (eds) (2003) *Level Up: Digital Games Research Conference.* Utrecht: University of Utrecht/DIGRA.

Cuban, L. (1986) *Teachers and Machines: The Classroom Use of Technology since 1920.* New York: Teachers' College Press.

Cunningham, H. (1995) 'Moral kombat and computer game-girls', in C. Bazalgette and D. Buckingham (eds), *In Front of the Children: Screen Entertainment and Young Audiences.* London: British Film Institute. pp. 188–200.

Cupitt, M. and Stockbridge, S. (1996) *Families and Electronic Entertainment.* Sydney: Australian Broadcasting Corporation/Office of Film and Literature Classification.

Department for Education and Skills (DfES) (2003) *ICT in Schools Survey.* London: DfES.

Downes, T. (1999) 'Children's and parents' discourses about computers in the home and school', *Convergence,* 5 (2): 104–11.

Durkin, K. (1995) *Computer Games: Their Effects on Young People: A Review.* Sydney: Office of Film and Literature Classification.

Durndell, A., Glissov, P. and Siann, G. (1995) 'Gender and computing: persisting differences', *Educational Research,* 37 (3): 219–27.

Egenfeldt-Nielsen, S. and Smith, J.H. (2004) *Playing with Fire: How Do Computer Games Influence the Player?* Goteborg: Nordicom.

Entertainment Software Association (2003) Available online: www.theesa.com

Facer, K., Furlong, J., Furlong, R. and Sutherland, R. (2003) *Screen Play: Children and Computing in the Home.* London: Routledge Falmer.

Fiske, J. (1989) *Reading the Popular.* London: Unwin Hyman.

Fuller, M. and Jenkins, H. (1995) 'Nintendo and new world travel writing: a dialogue', in S. Jones (ed.), *Cybersociety: Computer-mediated Communication and Community.* London: Sage. pp. 57–72.

Funk, J. and Buchman, D. (1996) 'Playing violent video and computer games and adolescent self-concept', *Journal of Communication*, 46 (1): 19–32.

Funk, J., Germann, J. and Buchman, D. (1997) 'Children and electronic games in the United States', *Trends in Communication*, 2: 111–26.

Gailey, C.W. (1993) 'Mediated messages: gender, class and cosmos in home video games', *Journal of Popular Culture*, 27 (1): 81–97.

Gee, J. (2003) *What Video Games Have To Teach Us About Learning and Literacy*. London: Palgrave Macmillan.

Giacquinta, J.B., Bauer, J. and Levin, J.E. (1993) *Beyond Technology's Promise: An Examination of Children's Educational Computing at Home*. Cambridge: Cambridge University Press.

Goldstein, J. and Raessens, J. (eds.) (in press) *Handbook of Computer Game Studies*. Cambridge, MA: MIT Press.

Graybill, D., Strawniak, M., Hunter, T. and O'Leary, M. (1985) 'Effects of playing violent versus nonviolent video games on the aggressive ideation of aggressive and nonaggressive children', *Child Study Journal*, 15 (3): 199–205.

Graybill, D. Strawniak, M., Hunter, T. and O'Leary, M. (1987) 'Effects of playing versus observing violent versus nonviolent video games on children's aggression', *Psychology*, 24 (3): 1–8.

Green, B. and Bigum, C. (1993) 'Aliens in the classroom', *Australian Journal of Education*, 37 (2): 119–41.

Greenfield, P.M. (1984) *Mind and Media: The Effects of Television, Computers and Video Games*. London: Fontana.

Griffiths, M. (1994) 'Computer games: harmless or addictive?', *Education and Health*, 12 (2): 28–30.

Griffiths, M. (1996) 'Computer game playing in children and adolescents: a review of the literature', in T. Gill (ed.), *Electronic Children: How Children Are Responding to the Information Revolution*. London: National Children's Bureau.

Gunter, B. (1998) *The Effects of Video Games on Children: The Myth Unmasked*. Sheffield: Sheffield Academic Press.

Healy, J. (1998) *Failure to Connect: How Computers Affect Our Children's Minds – for Better and Worse*. New York: Simon & Schuster.

Herz, J.C. (1997) *Joystick Nation: How Videogames Gobbled Our Money, Won Our Hearts and Rewired Our Minds*. London: Abacus.

Holloway, S. and Valentine, G. (2003) *Cyberkids: Children in the Information Age*. London: Routledge Falmer.

Illich, I. (1971) *Deschooling Society*. New York: Harper & Row.

Jenkins, H. (1993) '"x logic": repositioning Nintendo in children's lives', *Quarterly Review of Film and Video*, 14 (4): 55–70.

Jenkins, H. (1998) '"Complete freedom of movement": video games as gendered play spaces', in J. Cassell and H. Jenkins (eds), *From Barbie to Mortal Kombat: Gender and Computer Games*. Cambridge, MA: MIT Press. pp. 262–97.

Jessen, C. (1999) *Children's Computer Culture: Three Essays on Children and Computers*. Odense: Odense University.

Kafai, Y.B. (1998) 'Video game designs by girls and boys: variability and consistency of gender differences', in J. Cassell and H. Jenkins (eds), *From Barbie to Mortal Kombat: Gender and Computer Games*. Cambridge, MA: MIT Press. pp. 90–114.

Katz, J. (1996) 'The rights of kids in the digital age', *Wired*, 4.07: 120–3, 166–70.

Kestenbaum, G. and Weinstein, L. (1984) 'Personality, psychopathology and developmental issues in male adolescent game use', *Journal of the American Academy of Child Psychiatry*, 24 (3): 329–37.

Kinder, M. (1991) *Playing with Power in Movies, Television and Video Games*. Berkeley, CA: University of California Press.

King, L. (ed.) (2002) *Game On: The History and Culture of Video Games*. London: Laurence King.

Klein, M. (1984) 'The bite of Pac-Man', *Journal of Psychohistory*, 2 (3): 395–401.

Kline, S., Dyer-Witheford, N. and de Peuter, G. (2003) *Digital Play: The Interaction of Technology, Culture and Marketing*. Montreal: McGill-Queens University Press.

Kubey, R. and Larson, R. (1990) 'The use and experience of the new video media among children and young adolescents', *Communication Research*, 17 (1): 107–30.

Livingstone, S. and Bober, M. (2004) *UK Children Go Online: Surveying the Experiences of Young People and Their Parents*. London: London School of Economics and Political Science.

Livingstone, S. and Bovill, M. (1999) *Young People, New Media*. Report of the Research Project 'Children, Young People and the Changing Media Environment'. London: London School of Economics and Political Science. Available online: http://psych.lse.ac.uk/young _people

Melody, W. (1973) *Children's Television: The Economics of Exploitation*. New Haven, CT: Yale University Press.

Merchant, G. (2001) 'Teenagers in cyberspace: language use and language change in Internet chatrooms', *Journal of Research in Reading*, 24 (3): 293–306.

Nixon, H. (1998) 'Fun and games are serious business', in J. Sefton-Green (ed.), *Digital Diversions: Youth Culture in the Age of Multimedia*. London: UCL Press. pp. 21–42.

Orr Vered, K. (1998) 'Blue group boys play *Incredible Machine*, girls play hopscotch: social discourse and gendered play at the computer', in J. Sefton-Green (ed.), *Digital Diversions: Youth Culture in the Age of Multimedia*. London: UCL Press. pp. 43–61.

Oswell, D. (1999) 'The dark side of cyberspace: Internet content regulation and child protection', *Convergence*, 5 (2): 42–62.

Panelas, T. (1983) 'Adolescents and video games: consumption of leisure and the social construction of the peer group', *Youth and Society*, 15 (1): 51–65.

Papert, S. (1993) *The Children's Machine: Rethinking School in the Age of the Computer*. New York: Basic.

Papert, S. (1996) *The Connected Family*. Atlanta, GA: Longstreet.

Poole, S. (2000) *Trigger Happy: The Inner Life of Video Games*. London: Fourth Estate.

Provenzo, E.F. (1991) *Video Kids: Making Sense of Nintendo*. Cambridge, MA: Harvard University Press.

Radway, J. (1984) *Reading the Romance*. Chapel Hill, NC: University of North Carolina Press.

Rheingold, H. (1993) *The Virtual Community: Homesteading on the Electronic Frontier*. Reading, MA: Addison-Wesley.

Rideout, D. and Foehr, U. (2003) *Kids and Media in America*. New York: Cambridge University Press.

Scheidt, L. (in press) 'Adolescent diary weblogs and the unseen audience', *Education, Communication, Information*, 5 (1).

Schon, D., Sanyal, B. and Mitchell, W. (eds) (1999) *High Technology and Low-income Communities*. Cambridge, MA: MIT Press.

Schor, J. (2004) *Born to Buy: The Commercialized Child and the New Consumer Culture*. New York: Scribner.

Schott, G. and Horrell, K. (2000) 'Girl gamers and their relationship with the gaming culture', *Convergence*, 6 (4): 36–53.

Sefton-Green, J. (1999) 'Playing the game: the critical study of computer games', *Convergence*, 5 (2): 114–20.

Sefton-Green, J. (2004) *Literature Review in Informal Learning with Technology Outside School*. Bristol: NESTA Futurelab.

Sefton-Green, J. and Buckingham, D. (1996) 'Digital visions: children's "creative" uses of multimedia technologies', *Convergence*, 2 (2): 47–79.

Sherry, J.L. (2001) 'The effects of violent video games on aggression: a meta-analysis', *Human Communication Research*, 27 (3): 409–31.

Shuker, R. (1996) 'Video games: serious fun', *Continuum*, 9 (2): 125–45.

Silverstone, R. and Hirsch, E. (eds) (1992) *Consuming Technologies: Media and Information in Domestic Spaces*. London: Routledge.

Skirrow, G. (1986) 'Hellivision: an analysis of video games', in C. MacCabe (ed.), *High Theory/Low Culture*. Manchester: Manchester University Press. pp. 115–42.

Smith, R. and Curtin, P. (1998) 'Children, computers and life online: education in a cyber-world', in I. Snyder (ed.), *Page to Screen: Taking Literacy into the Electronic Era*. London: Routledge. pp. 211–33.

Snyder, I. (ed.) (1998) *Page to Screen: Taking Literacy into the Electronic Era*. London: Routledge.

Spigel, L. (1992) *Make Room for TV*. Chicago: Chicago University Press.

Stallybrass, J. (1992) 'Just gaming: allegory and economy in computer games', *New Left Review*, 198: 83–106.

Statistics Lamda (2004) Available online: www. statscan.com Accessed November 2004.

Stern, S. (1999) 'Adolescent girls' expression on WWW home pages: spirited, sombre and self-conscious sites', *Convergence*, 5 (2): 22–41.

Stern, S. (2004) 'Expression of identity online: prominent features and gender differences in adolescents' WWW home pages', *Journal of Broadcasting and Electronic Media* 48 (2).

Straubhaar, T. (2000) 'Digital divide in East Austin'. Available online: ftp://uts.cc.utexas.edu/coc/rtf/digitaldivide/UT DigitalDivide.html

Subrahmanyam, K. and Greenfield, P.M. (1998) 'Computer games for girls: what makes them play?', in J. Cassell and H. Jenkins (eds), *From Barbie to Mortal Kombat: Gender and Computer Games*. Cambridge, MA: MIT Press. pp. 46–71.

Tapscott, D. (1997) *Growing up Digital: The Rise of the Net Generation*. New York: McGraw-Hill.

Thorne, B. (1993) *Gender Play: Girls and Boys at School*. New Brunswick, NJ: Rutgers University Press.

Tingstad, V. (2003) '*Children's Chat on the Net: A Study of Social Encounters in Two Norwegian Chat Rooms*'. PhD thesis, NTNU, Trondheim.

Tobin, J. (1998) 'An American Otaku (or, a boy's virtual life on the Net)', in J. Sefton-Green (ed.),

Digital Diversions: Youth Culture in the Age of Multimedia. London: UCL Press. pp. 106–27.

Tobin, J. (2004) *Pikachu's Global Adventure: The Rise and Fall of Pokémon.* Durham, NC: Duke University Press.

Turkle, S. (1984) *The Second Self: Computers and the Human Spirit.* New York: Simon & Schuster.

Turkle, S. (1995) *Life on Screen: Identity in the Age of the Internet.* New York: Simon & Schuster.

Video Games and Human Behavior: A Research Agenda for the 80s (1983) Papers and proceedings of a symposium at the Harvard Graduate School of Education. Cambridge, MA: Monroe C. Gutman Library and Harvard Graduate School of Education.

Waltermann, J. and Machill, M. (eds) (2000) *Protecting Our Children on the Internet: Towards A New Culture of Responsibility.* Gutersloh: Bertelsmann Foundation.

Willett, R. and Sefton-Green, J. (2002) 'Living and learning in chatrooms', *Éducation et Sociétés,* 10 (2): 57–77.

Williams, R. (1974) *Television: Technology and Cultural Form.* Glasgow: Fontana.

Winkel, M., Novak, D.M. and Hopson, H. (1987) 'Personality factors, subject gender and the effects of aggressive video games on aggression in adolescence', *Journal of Research in Personality,* 21: 211–23.

Wolf, M.J.P. and Perron, B. (eds) (2003) *The Video Game Theory Reader.* London: Routledge.

4

Perspectives on Internet Use: Access, Involvement and Interaction

RONALD E. RICE AND CAROLINE HAYTHORNTHWAITE

After a brief interlude when it looked like Internet growth, at least in the US, was showing signs of leveling off, more recent numbers show access has again risen sharply. Between December 2000 and April 2002, the proportion of the US population with access to the Internet remained at approximately 59 per cent (Nua.com, 2001). Yet, recent figures show a rapid rise, from 66 per cent in 2003 to 75 per cent in 2004, representing over 200 million people in the US (Nielsen//NetRatings, 2004). Worldwide, the top ten countries (Sweden, Hong Kong, US, Iceland, Netherlands, Australia, Canada, Switzerland, Denmark and South Korea) show similar Internet access statistics, with 62 to 74 per cent of each country's population having access (Internet World Stats, 2004). Numbers are dramatically different when examined by region, with only 1.4 per cent of Africa and 7 per cent of Asia and the Middle East with access (Internet World Stats, 2005), but so are growth rates – 187 per cent for Africa, 126 per cent for Asia, and 228 per cent for the Middle East (for other figures around the world, see ClickZ Stats, 2005). In all it is hard to dispute the increasing presence and penetration of the Internet around the globe.

Along with this increased access come many social changes. This rapid adoption brings with it new ways to seek and distribute information, communicate with others, foster communities, and produce, share and sell goods, culture products and services, which naturally raises a vast range of enduring as well as new social and policy issues. This chapter reviews relevant research on three primary issues – access, civic, political and community involvement, and social interaction and forms of expression – by grouping arguments and results into pessimistic and optimistic perspectives. Although the phenomena are occurring worldwide, the following addresses largely US outcomes.

ACCESS

The first fundamental concern is about access, including: who has or does not have access to the Internet; what motivates people to use the Internet; what barriers there are to usage; and what characterizes those who stop using the Internet (Katz and Aspden, 1997a, 1997b, 1997c). New technologies in general may bridge gaps between rich and poor, powerful and powerless, haves and have nots (for example, Downing, 1989; ECRL, 1999; NTIA, 2002; Schon et al., 1999). New technologies may enhance or hinder access to information in a democracy (Deetz, 1989a, 1989b; Dervin, 1980; Lievrouw, 1994; Murdock and Golding, 1989), in the workplace (Deetz, 1990; Garson, 1988; Kraut, 1989; US Congress, 1987; Zuboff, 1988) or in broader social or cultural contexts (Bourque and Warren, 1987; Krendl et al., 1989; Mulgan, 1991; Pool, 1983; US Congress, 1990; Weinberg, 1987). While new communication technologies can provide new ways of participating and interacting, they may also widen existing gaps, further blocking access to those already without access (Gillespie and Robins, 1989; Jansen, 1989; Schiller, 1996; Wresch, 1996).

Access is the major public policy area for those who see the Internet as a universal service and a significant influence on political and economic equity (Rice et al., 2001). The usual term for this differential access to and use of the Internet according to gender, income, race and location is 'the digital divide' (Cooper and Kimmelman, 1999; Hoffman and Novak, 1998; Hoffman et al., 1996; McConnaughey and Lader, 1998; Strover, 2003; see also the *Falling Through the Net* series by the US National Telecommunications and Information Administration (e.g. NTIA, 2002)).

While on the one hand the Internet and other communication and information technologies can increase human capital by providing better access to education and training, on the other hand those who do not have sufficient resources or experience will be further excluded from human and social capital (McNutt, 1998). Labour markets will prefer individuals with current or prior access to, experience with, and skills necessary for using communication networks. Learning new applications, software and technologies will be easier for those who already have a good understanding of the Internet and communication protocols (Carrier, 1998). Non-users are likely to face economic disadvantage: e.g. Bikson and Panis (1999: 156) discovered that employees who use computers in their jobs are paid 10 to 15 per cent more than non-computer users who hold similar positions. Besides economic benefits, communication technologies have greatly increased participation in and awareness of communication activities such as decision-making and discussions at the workplace (Carrier, 1998). So there are major social and economic rationales for investing in increased access to all citizens, such as through community networks (McNutt, 1998). For example, Neu et al. (1999) provide examples of how e-mail can provide access and general citizen information to the elderly and governmental information to social security beneficiaries. Others report on how access can help individuals weather emotional crises, as well as gain the information needed to deal with local events, as UK farmers did during the 2003 foot and mouth disease outbreak (Hagar, 2003; Haythornthwaite and Hagar, 2004; Wall, 2002).

Pessimistic Perspective

Access to Computers and the Internet

Pessimism about access stems from a concern about unequal access, and thus of unequal advantage being derived from its benefits. Many studies show that minorities such as African-Americans and non-white Hispanics are much less likely to possess home computers and have less access to networks than whites and Asians and therefore miss the opportunity to participate in Internet activities (Neu et al., 1999). Even as access in numbers becomes more similar, studies then show that other measures such as amount of time spent online are lower for minority groups. Howard et al. (2002) show that of those who have access, more of the men, whites, higher income earners, higher educated and more experienced users are likely to be online; while 57 per cent of men will be online on any particular day, only 52 per cent of women will be; while 56 per cent of whites will be online, 36 per cent of African-Americans, and 49 per cent of Hispanics will be.

A number of studies have also shown how access by those in traditionally disadvantaged sectors – lower education, female, higher age, lower income, non-US regions – are slow to come online and thus slow to overcome the lack of experience online. An ambitious study by the UCLA Center for Community Policy (UCLA,

2000) analysed a panel of 2096 representative households across time, comparing Internet users with non-users and with non-users who became users later on. It is part of a group of similar projects in other countries. The study found that while only 31.2 per cent of those who had not graduated from high school used the Internet in the fall of 2000, 86.3 per cent of those with at least a college degree did; 53.1 per cent of high school graduates and 70.2 per cent of those with some college education used the Internet. While access among American males and females is about even, with recent statistics even indicating more women than men online (81.7 per cent women aged 35–54, 77 per cent aged 25–34 compared to 80.2 per cent of men aged 35–54, and 75.6 per cent aged 25–34), the 2000 UCLA study showed a wide gender gap for those over 66 years old (18.4 per cent for females and 40.4 per cent for males). While the close of the gender gap in the US is a good sign, previously in North America – and currently in the rest of the world – more men than women were likely to have access to the Internet, thus still putting women in a catch-up position regarding use (Chen et al. 2002; Katz and Rice, 2002b; National Statistics Omnibus, 2000).

A study published by the non-profit Consumer Federation of America (Cooper, 2000), collected responses from a single statistically balanced panel ($n = 1902$) measured at two time periods (February 1999 and June 2000). They compared the *fully* connected (36 per cent of the population, with Internet service providers or high-speed Internet access at home), the *partially* connected (17 per cent, with basic Internet or e-mail service at home), the *potentially* connected (21 per cent, no home Internet service, but do have home computer or cell phone), and the *disconnected* (26 per cent, without Internet service, computer or cell phone) on measures associated with a large-scale 'life styles study'. The overall conclusion of the study was that 'the disconnected are, in fact, disadvantaged and disenfranchised' (2000: 1). The disconnected earn less than half the income of the fully connected ($25,500 versus $45,200), are much less likely to have a college degree (13 versus 46 per cent), and are

more likely to be black (12 versus 7 per cent), older (53 versus 44 years) and have smaller households (2.1 versus 2.8). Each of these significantly predicts differences across the four levels of connectedness, with income being the most powerful predictor. Overall, the study concludes that there is about a three- to five-year lag in penetration between those with above-median and below-median incomes. Cooper (2000: 1) agrees with the argument held by Castells and others that such differential timing in access to power and information – even if the later adopters catch up after several years – is itself a significant source of social inequality and unequal participation.

Often forgotten in considerations of connectivity are issues of dropouts. The UCLA (2000) study also notes that in mid 2000, 10.3 per cent of non-users are actually Internet dropouts (formerly used the Internet at least once a month, but no longer); Katz et al. (2001) and Katz and Rice (2002a) report that this 10 per cent figure is fairly consistent in surveys they conducted in 1995, 1996, 1997 and 2000. So, full connection rates should not be treated as a line that, once crossed, no longer needs to be addressed, but instead as a mark to constantly work towards.

Barriers, Influences and Consequences

Clearly, there are many physical and socio-economic barriers to equal access. Barriers to using the Internet reported by the UCLA (2000) study respondents include: no computer or terminal available (37.7 per cent), no interest (33.3 per cent), do not know how to use (18.9 per cent), too expensive (9.1 per cent) (and then various other factors). Not being able to find content online that has local or personal meaning, or represents one's culture, can also affect use of the Internet (Katz and Rice, 2002a; Warschauer, 2003).

Van Dijk (1999) identifies four general obstacles that affect the use of new media: (1) people, especially the elderly and unskilled, are intimidated by new technology or had a bad first experience with it; (2) no or difficult access to computers or networks; (3) lack of user

friendliness and unattractive usage style; and
(4) lack of significant usage opportunities.
A more invisible factor in this digital divide may
be embedded distinctions: 'the design of new
media techniques carries the imprint of the
social-cultural characteristics of its producers;
predominantly male, well-educated, English-
speaking, and members of the ethnic majority
in a particular country' (1999: 152). This is a
style that is said to not appeal to most women,
less educated people and ethnic minorities.
There is also a 'usage gap in which well-educated people use computers for work, private
business, education and other reasons whereas
those with less education and the young use
computers for entertainment and/or computer
games followed by education' (1999: 153).
These differences subdivide the potential user
populations, and rather than creating a range
from elite to excluded, the different uses may
contribute to the reinforcement of differences
across societal sectors.

Indeed, cultural, rather than strict economic, educational and racial differences are
receiving increased attention, from both government and commercial studies. Rojas et al.
(2004) identify other factors contributing to
the digital divide, such as the interrelations
among economic capital, cultural capital,
ethnicity, gender and age. Often, individuals
reside in a crossfire of competing and contrasting influences (such as family and peers,
cultural and social capital, educational and
consumer motivations, and early gender roles)
on computer and online technology. Similarly,
Haddon (2001) argues that 'social exclusion' is
context-dependent (neither necessarily economically based nor equivalent across all
domains of a person's life), involves not only
political and civic involvement but also
people's ability to occupy social roles, and may
also involve rejection of or lack of interest in
new technologies.

There are other aspects of access in the US
than just equal distribution across demographic
and national boundaries. People who have hearing, sight, movement and other disabilities may
also be disadvantaged by limitations on their
ability to access information, contacts and
opportunities for expression on the Internet.

Optimistic Perspective

Recent studies (ECRL, 1999; Howard et al.,
2002; Katz and Rice, 2002a) have been finding
that at least racial and gender differences in
Internet access disappear after other variables
are taken into account statistically.

There are efforts to overcome some of the
limitations on access that are due to disabilities.
In 1990, the government searched for a way
to provide universal service and include
persons with disabilities. In 1990, Title IV of the
Americans with Disabilities Act addressed disability issues by requiring all service carriers to
provide communication access for hearing-
impaired American citizens (Borchert, 1998: 56).
And 'Section 255 of the Telecommunications Act
requires that telecommunication services and
equipment providers make their goods and services accessible to individuals with disabilities'
(1998: 60). A good example of this is the recent
Windows operating systems, which offer program and application shortcuts for people with
disabilities. Through communication networks
which offer full duplex voice, data transmission,
graphics and video communication, there is the
potential for people with disabilities to overcome
these limitations.

CIVIC, POLITICAL AND COMMUNITY INVOLVEMENT

The second fundamental issue is whether the
Internet will decrease or increase political
participation and community involvement, fostering more diverse and better informed citizens, and mediated communities with greater
social capital.

Civic and Political Involvement

Pessimistic Perspective

The very differences associated with the
Internet digital divide, relative to traditional
outlets such as newspapers, radio and TV,
could narrow the basis of political participation and government legitimacy (White,
1997). Hill and Hughes report that 'Internet

users and activists (those who use it for political reasons) are considerably younger than the general public, with Internet activists averaging a very young 32.8 years' (1998: 29). This age may be even lower, as the survey only counted those over age 18. Males were the majority of Internet users and activists (72 per cent). There actually seems to be a higher percentage of non-white Internet activists, so 'there is no great "ethnic gap" in Internet activism'. However, Internet users and activists do have much more education than the general public, with 53 per cent and 56 per cent, respectively, having college degrees. These users are more involved in information gathering and more knowledgeable about current political events than is the general public (1998: 35). On Usenet's political newsgroups 'most threads are neutral but with clear right-wing anti-government overtones', possibly because right-wing people may not feel represented by the media – but they also might just be more active in posting to newsgroups (1998: 73). Chat rooms are heavily right-wing owing to greater activity by those members, and not because of a greater number of right-wing participants *per se* (1998: 128). Hill and Hughes find about an equal amount of left-wing and right-wing websites, but conservative sites are more in-depth and have 'higher production values'.

Others argue that the Internet could weaken the legitimacy of the governing process, by encouraging the spread of small, 'Net-savvy' special interest communities who could pursue their own narrow agenda at the cost of the public commonweal (Starobin, 1996). The quality and validity of material reported on the Internet are also increasingly problematic, leading to concerns about the corruption or debasement of elections, and a consequent reduction in political participation.

Some theorists have argued that the Internet is destroying community groups and voluntary associations that are necessary for the democratic process to succeed (Putnam, 2000; Turkle, 1996). Other critics fear that the Internet will absorb and dissipate the energy of the citizenry away from traditional political processes (Carpini, 1996; Rash, 1997). Van Dijk locates a central tension: 'Some would argue that

freedom, for example the freedom of choice for consumers, will increase because of the interactivity offered by this technology. Others paint a more pessimistic picture, and predict that freedom will be endangered by a decrease in privacy for the individual as a registered citizen, a "transparent" employee and a consumer screened for every personal characteristic, and by the growing opportunities for central control' (1999: 2). The Internet also often removes one layer of filtering of political information – that done by gatekeepers of the mainstream media. Further, self-selection plays a large role: those who were previously politically interested are those who make up the population of Internet users who utilize the web for political reasons (1999: 183).

Free speech can be both promoted and inhibited by the Internet. Theoretically, anyone can design a website and post any opinion on it. However, Shapiro and Leone (1999) suggest that free speech may actually suffer with the development of the Internet, because of both exposure and access issues. First, people may have a hard time finding an audience to reach because others may not be willing to listen. (Van Dijk (1999) believes that there will be so much information on the Internet that it would be hard to figure out what was valid, and thus will lead to faulty decision making.) People will not feel like responding to solicitations describing the opinions of others or they may filter their information so they only receive what directly interests them. Filtering and personalization of news via software agents can lead to narrow-mindedness and social fragmentation. Therefore, views that contradict or question any particular person's opinions may never reach that person, allowing that individual to remain ignorant of opposing perspectives. Second, not everyone will have the resources to pay for advertising one's opinions – in addition to the by now familiar access constraints such as technology and technological knowledge – thus limiting some people's right to free speech.

Indeed, the UCLA (2000) study shows that while 45.6 per cent of Internet users (versus 28.1 per cent of non-users) feel that the Internet helps people to better understand politics, only

29.3 per cent of users and 16.8 per cent of non-users feel that Internet use leads to people having greater political power. 'Likewise, debate and information-based discussion in the Usenet newsgroups and political chat rooms serves to reinforce pre-existing ideological positions, not to change them.' They also conclude that the Internet won't necessarily bring worldwide tolerance. Rash (1997) and others note that the Internet easily supports hate groups and conspiracy theorists in the political process.

Fallows (2000) argues that most of the predicted impacts of the Internet on politics have not (yet) appeared. However, two changes are already significant. The first is a reduced time for shifts in prevailing opinion and media narratives. The second is that the network economy has stimulated more and more concentrated media conglomerates using convergent bandwidth, as multinationals attempt to gain control over delivery channels of multimedia content. Fallows (2000), Hundt (2000) and McChesney (2000) all argue that this concentration of media reduces diversity in perspectives and opinions, and reinforces particular kinds of coverage and programming, leading to a much more powerful effect on political knowledge, participation and voting than any supposed consequence of extended Internet use by individuals and groups. And the inherent structural and power constraints of the political system are likely to limit the possibilities of the Internet for extensive political change (Margolis and Resnick, 2000).

Optimistic Perspective

Others strongly argue that the Internet may very well foster political involvement. In mid 2000, the online users in the AOL survey were particularly politically involved, as 84 per cent were registered to vote and 45 per cent intended to go online to get presidential candidate information (and 39 per cent for state candidate, 32 per cent for local candidate). Of the young people (between 9 and 17 years of age) in the companion AOL youth study (based on 505 young people in homes with online access), 41 per cent reported a greater interest in current events owing to being online (55 per cent reporting no difference). And they clearly feel that being online has had a much more positive influence on them than has television (57 versus 39 per cent).

Hill and Hughes (1998) summarize the perspectives of some optimists concerning the role of the Internet in citizen activism. Rheingold (1993) believes people will become more involved in the democratic process, such as through increased online debate, and Rash (1997) states that the Internet will open up the opportunity for new parties and ideas to develop. Shapiro and Leone (1999) associate the Internet with 'the control revolution', whereby control is being transferred from large institutions to individuals. This is due to six core features of the Internet that can enhance individual control. The first four already exist: (1) many-to-many interactivity; (2) digital content, making communication flexible 'in terms of how it can be stored, used, and manipulated' (1999: 16); (3) the design of the Internet as a distributed, packet-based network; and (4) the interoperability of the Internet, so that information can flow freely throughout a network without bottlenecks or barriers. The next two must be achieved in order to foster individual control: (5) broadband capacity and (6) universal access.

Certainly the Internet has already become a powerful tool for political parties, non-governmental organizations, congressional campaigns and local activist groups (Browning and Weitzner, 1996; Corrado, 2000; Davis, 1999; Rash, 1997). It allows political actors to monitor voting records, assess campaign contributions and financing, conduct online focus groups, increase voter access, keep up with recent and distant news, obtain campaign donations more quickly and efficiently (such as through online credit card payment), file contribution disclosure reports online, create and support mailing lists, get voters to the polling place, and more. Rash (1997), in particular, suggests that the impact of the Internet in the 1996 US presidential election was comparable to the role of television in the 1960 election.

Internet users in the UCLA (2000) study, compared with non-users, were slightly more likely to exercise and to participate in clubs/organizations, were slightly less likely to socialize with household members or to know neighbours by name, and had the same levels of socializing with friends, time spent sleeping, and number of friends outside their households. Further, users held fairly similar attitudes about various personal values, having slightly higher preference for visiting with friends, but slightly lower preference for attending religious services and for contributing to efforts to protect the environment. Nonusers reported slightly higher levels of life dissatisfaction, interaction anxiety, powerlessness and loneliness. Users in the Katz and Rice (2002a) study were more likely to participate in community and leisure organizations, but not religious organizations.

To some extent, the question of whether the Internet can foster political activism and knowledge of governance is somewhat simplistic, considering that the Internet itself involves considerable political, governmental, regulatory and economic institutions, and requires complex governance and even debates over what kinds of governance are appropriate and possible (Loader, 1997; Margolis and Resnick, 2000).

Community Involvement

Pessimistic Perspective

Simply put, some argue that cyberspace cannot be a source of real community and/or detracts from meaningful real-world communities (Beniger, 1988; Gergen, 1991; Kiesler et al., 1984; Stoll, 1995; Turkle, 1996; see also Jankowski, and Baym, this volume). Schement distinguishes two key elements of communities: primary and secondary relationships. Internet communities 'are really made up of secondary relationships' in which people only know each other in 'a single, or only a few, dimensions' in contrast to primary relationships in which people know each other in multiple dimensions (reported in Bollier, 1995: 10). John Seely Brown believes that 'it is not always clear where accountability and responsibility reside in virtual communities' because the lack of primary relationships may induce

'careless, irresponsible, and even anti-social' behaviour (1995: 12). The use of online systems to communicate with more distant others may reduce the vitality and integration of physical communities (Calhoun, 1986).

Shapiro and Leone warn that careless use of the Internet may lead to three fundamental problems: (1) overpersonalization, that is the use of information about users to target messages, products and control, and the use of filters and focused discussion groups to keep us from being exposed to diverse perspectives; (2) disintermediation, which may get out of hand as we forget the value of liaisons and gatekeepers in not only selecting but also verifying news, commerce and politics; and (3) the danger that 'we may rely too much on market-based solutions to problems such as protecting privacy' (1999: 104). Both Shapiro and Leone (1999) and Rice (1987a) point out that online ties are likely to be more ephemeral, less sustainable and more easily exitable compared with physical community relations. Along with the increased choice that online media provide comes an increased ability to 'disengage with little or no consequence' (Jones, 1999: 220).

Computer-mediated communication (CMC) 'may yet be the clearest evidence of Beniger's (1988) "pseudo-community", part of the "reversal" of a centuries-old trend from organic community based on interpersonal relationships to impersonal association integrated by mass means' (Jones, 1999: 369). 'The new mass media have an especially characteristic ability to create an illusion of apparently intimate face-to-face communication between a presenter and an individual viewer', thus creating what other researchers have called 'parasocial interaction' (Jensen, 1999). Further, differential access to and knowledge of these technologies create powerful boundaries between potential community members, and reinforce certain kinds of roles, statuses and social networks.

There's a subtle paradox involved in this issue of shared interests in online communities. What van Dijk (1999) calls an 'organic community' (comprising face-to-face interactions) is made up of a relatively homogeneous group of people because they have several interests in common, whereas a virtual community is relatively heterogeneous since only one interest links them. Therefore, an organic community has a better chance of building and maintaining its own culture and identity than a virtual community. Virtual communities can't replace organic communities since they are limited, but perhaps they can supplement and strengthen organic communities.

However, Wellman (2001) emphasizes that traditional communities were controlled by social class, management of labour power, access to resources, fixed capital, limited mobility and a few powerful gatekeepers, all embedded in a primary network. Revolutionary challenges to these community networks were associated with changes in media and transportation: horses, railroads, automobiles and airplanes, books, telegraph, telephone, radio and television. Thus, paradoxically, because media have allowed community to move inside the home or the office by means of the telephone or other media, most North Americans have little interpersonal connection with their neighbourhood or the social control of a neighbourhood group (Johnson, 1997: 69). Putnam (2000) argues that active involvement and participation in community have been significantly declining in the United States, and Skocpol (2000) shows that interest groups with local constituencies and interaction have declined in general in the US, creating a vacuum filled by disconnected people committed to little more than commercialism. People entertain less frequently in their homes, donations in terms of constant dollars have declined, voting and trust in government are low, and church attendance continues its drop. It can be argued that because of new communication possibilities, people are no longer forced to interact with specific, physically proximate others in order to participate in community. People now tend to choose physical neighbourhoods for reasons of safety, schooling and medical services (Dear et al., 1996). A related consequence is that actual network ties leap over physically linked areas, so that the overall social geography corresponds much less to physical geography.

Optimistic Perspective

Cerulo (1997), somewhat rejecting Beniger's (1988) critique of the pseudo-community created by digital mass media, argues that we need to reconceptualize community owing to the rise of new communication technologies, based on evidence about social interaction and social bonding (see also Katz et al., 2004; Rice, 1987a). First, pervasive examples of parasocial interaction with mediated personalities, call-in radio shows, and emotional support in online discussion groups argue for a wider concept of social interaction that does not presume that mediated relations are necessarily fleeting, impersonal or deceptive. Second, while there are many concerns about the superficiality or isolation associated with online relations, new media are perhaps better characterized as 'changing the nature and character of social bonds' (Cerulo, 1997: 53).

A more forceful optimistic argument is that cyberspace involvement can create alternative communities that are as valuable and useful as our familiar, physically located communities (Pool, 1983; Rheingold, 1993). Network ties may exist in cyberspace but they still represent places where people connect concerning shared interests, support, sociability and identity (Wellman, 2000). This potential is largely due to a combination of several factors: increased bandwidth, continuous access, wireless portability, globalized connectivity and personalization (such as collaborative filtering and content associated by shared users, individual e-mail profiles and web portals, and online communities of interests). People may use online communities to bypass constraints and inequity in unmediated interactions (Stone, 1991). Rather than being seen as disconnected from a group or a locale, these communities transcend these constraints, shifting from door-to-door relations to person-to-person and role-to-role interactions.

CMC 'brings us a form of efficient social contact'; it is a 'technology, medium, and engine of social relations', allowing us to move in terms of 'status, class, social role[s], and character' (Jones, 1999: 224–5). The vastly increased ability to share information is a crucial factor in community formation. Johnson echoes this argument: 'Instead of being a medium for shut-ins and introverts, the digital computer turns out to be the first major technology of the twentieth century that brings strangers closer together, rather than pushing them farther apart' (1997: 69). For example, the soc.culture hierarchy on Usenet includes over 150 newsgroups whose memberships include nearly all of the ethnic and national cultural communities in the world. The Cultural Access Group's (2001) study of ethnic differences among online users reported that 59 per cent of their African-American and 73 per cent of their Hispanic respondents said that the Internet keeps them connected to their ethnic community, and that the content on African-American (79 per cent) or Hispanic (69 per cent) websites is meaningful to them.

Turkle disputes the argument that Internet communities promote only secondary relationships, as suggested by Schement and Bollier (reported in Bollier, 1995: 10–12). She gives the example of one SeniorNet member who received dozens of calls and cards from her cyberfriends as she lay dying in the hospital. Virtual communities may become 'a counter-hegemonic movement in which socially or politically marginalized groups find expressive space on the Internet in which to locate like-minded others, speak freely, and forge solidarity' (Lindlof and Shatzer, 1998: 174).

Stacey Horn's (1998) account of ECHO, the New-York-based virtual salon whose members also physically meet at monthly gatherings, reinforces the idea that online behaviours, relations and concerns are essentially the same as those of physical communities. Online communities can reinforce and complement, even create and foster, physical communities and interest in local culture. Cherny's (1999) study of a MUD also reinforces the notion that online communities can develop cohesion, unity, shared history and close relationships using only appropriately varied forms of online, text-based language.

Other research shows that people interact happily and fruitfully online (for the most part) and in ways similar to face-to-face contact (Wellman and Gulia, 1999b). For example, Hampton and Wellman (2000) found, in their study of a leading-edge, broadband wired suburb near Toronto called 'Netville', that online users are more active neighbours (knowing about 25 neighbours) than are non-users (about eight), and they range more widely throughout the neighbourhood. They also found that once the learning curve was overcome, family members helped each other with the computers and shared their online discoveries, rather than watching television.

Shapiro and Leone (1999) describe the effectiveness of a supplemental community network in Blacksburg, Virginia, where over 60 per cent of the citizens participate. Parents and teachers communicate online and citizens participate in surveys regarding municipal government. They also describe the development of a community network in a London neighbourhood in which neighbours were given computers and Internet access. Those neighbours participated in debates over local parking rules and came to know each other better. Other studies of community networks point out a variety of advantages, challenges and developments (Gurstein, 2000; Kahin and Keller, 1995; Schon et al., 1999; Schuler, 1996; Tsagarousianou et al., 1998). While much attention is paid to the exotic and social aspects of online communities, they also represent consequential social policy issues, such as supporting neighbourhood and community relations, local school systems, and public access to government services and information (Doheny-Farina, 1998), especially health information and services (Rice and Katz, 2001).

Rheingold (1993) concludes that the Internet, Usenet and e-mail allow for people to access and transmit information that may not be allowed to surface in other communities. For example, Slack and Williams (2000) studied the Craigmillar Community Information Service (CCIS), developed for a town outside Edinburgh where many citizens are poor and underemployed. Countering positions that argue that online networks will foster isolated, inequitable and ahistorical societies, they argue that 'The growth and uptake of ICTs provides a point of contact at which the local and global intersect, wherein there is a potential for each to influence the other' (2000: 321). Before the CCIS, Craigmillar exhibited no sense of community feeling, showed no motivation to socialize, and offered no social or cultural activities. By means of the CCIS, however, 'Craigmillar has … developed a strategy of self-presentation that counters external representations and which works by being grounded in the highly spatialized notion of a tightly knit community' (2000: 322).

SOCIAL INTERACTION AND FORMS OF EXPRESSION

Although the actual architecture, and initial intention, of the Internet was to connect computers, one of its major social uses and consequences is as a complex medium of communication, neither completely interpersonal nor a mass medium. Thus the third issue is whether the Internet will hinder or foster social interaction, expression and new forms of identity (Gergen, 1991; Hiltz and Turoff, 1995; Parks and Floyd, 1996; Turkle, 1996; Wynn and Katz, 1997; see also Baym, this volume).

Pessimistic Perspective

This perspective holds that CMC technology is too inherently antithetical to the nature of human life, and too limited technologically for meaningful relationships to form (Stoll, 1995). Thus, cyberspace cannot be a source of meaningful friendships (Beniger, 1988). Many have argued for the socially isolating and psychologically depressing effect of (at least extreme) Internet use (Kraut et al., 1998; Kroker and Weinstein, 1994; Nie and Erbring, 2000; Stoll, 1995; Turkle, reported in Bollier, 1995). Online relationships may involve lower interdependence, commitment and permanence (Parks and Roberts, 1998; Rice, 1987a).

Computer-mediated communication can foster 'experimentation' (such as lying to others who cannot immediately know what the truth is) about one's identity and qualities. Such an atmosphere can be dominated by trickery, lechery, manipulation and emotional swindles. So much posturing, 'gender switching' and faking of identities can take place that it is extremely difficult for any real relationships to be created and maintained (Turkle, 1996). For example, online chat room discussions often remind Johnson of graffiti of the worst kind: 'isolated declarations of selfhood, failed conversations, slogans, and tag lines. You don't see a community in these exchanges; you see a group of individuals all talking past one another, and talking in an abbreviated, almost unintelligible code' (1997: 70).

Shapiro and Leone feel that 'the more time we spend online, the less time we will have to interact directly with our families, our neighbours, and other community members' (1999: 118). For example, Nie and Erbring (2000) found that web TV users spent less unmediated time with others. They argue that Internet use focuses on the individual, whereas watching TV may at least provide 'some sort of shared experience' (2000: 118). We may develop relationships online but may let our relationships with those around us suffer. The same tremendous ease with which users can 'personalize' the presentation, results and use of the Internet also facilitates a narrowing of focus and exposure to diverse perspectives. Further, it helps advertisers and other information providers in targeting their services, products and opinions to users identified by their online preferences and usage patterns (Schroeder and Ledger, 1998; Shapiro and Leone, 1999).

One's freedom of expression on the Internet is another's predation and indecency, especially when the users are children (Schroeder and Ledger, 1998). Tapscott (1997) identifies some possible disadvantages of the increased individuality and interactivity provided to young users by the Internet, such as disconnection from formal institutions, misleading and dangerous representations of information and identities, flaming, overload, lack of evaluation by informed gatekeepers, and emphasis on the short term.

Optimistic Perspective

Increased Frequency and Diversity of Interactions

The optimistic perspective increasingly sees the Internet as a medium for social interaction. Numerous case studies of CMC have shown that 'the social' is an important glue that binds together the task-oriented aspects of CMC, and in some cases even supplants them (Rice, 1987b). This work has been complemented by research on the functioning of medical discussion lists and newsgroups, health and psychological support groups, Internet relay chats, multi-user dungeons, object-oriented MUDS, and even online dating services, all of which are essentially social- and affect-oriented as opposed to task-oriented (Rice, 2001). A good proportion of those searching and participating in health information sites and discussion groups do so as 'third-party' intermediaries, seeking information and support for their significant others, for themselves to help them deal with illnesses of significant others, or to bring information from the Internet to stimulate, challenge or engage their health care providers (Aspden and Katz, 2001). The growth and persistence of Web-based chat rooms and 'instant messaging' offering 'community' would seem to provide additional evidence refuting the 'non-social' nature of CMC.

Baym summarizes a decade of research as revealing that 'the ways in which people have appropriated the commercial and non-commercial networks demonstrate that CMC not only lends itself to social uses but is, in fact, a site for an unusual amount of social creativity' (1995: 160). Porter's (1997) edited book provides a variety of additional perspectives, including the problem of interacting with virtual bodies.

Van Dijk (1999: 201–12, 239–40) summarizes some of the benefits of CMC: people can compensate for missing cues in images, sounds, texts and data by using available textual cues; people can focus more on the content of the text by reading e-mails; people can engage in more informal conversations and settings; and electronic group conversations often encourage normally quiet people and women to participate more. Walther (1996) shows that mediated interaction is usually personal, especially when participants have time and interest, and mediated interaction may even be 'hyperpersonal', managing interaction and impressions more than is possible face-to-face. Straus (1997) similarly found that CMC is not necessarily less personalized than face-to-face communication. Further, unmediated communication is highly constrained by the need for geographic and temporal proximity, limited processing and storage potential.

Hamman's (1999) ethnographic study concluded that Internet communication complements real-world relations, and Wellman and Gulia's (1999a) review of research on Internet communities argued that offline relationships may be strengthened as well as weakened. Surveys by Parks and colleagues found evidence of intimate and well-developed online relationships, often leading to real-world interactions, even though the frequency and duration of online relationships tend to be shorter (Parks and Roberts, 1998), and involve issues extending beyond the Internet communities (Parks and Floyd, 1996). Scherer's (1997) survey of college students showed no difference in sociability between those who exhibited Internet dependencies and regular users, even though they use Internet communication more and had fewer face-to-face social interactions. A Pew Research Center (2000) poll reported that Internet users indicated that e-mail had improved their social and kinship connections, and more so for those who had used the Internet longer and more frequently. Indeed, there were fewer social isolates among users than non-users, and users had a greater number of recent social contacts and greater access to social support. Riphagen and Kanfer (1997) showed that e-mail users and non-users had similar numbers of relationships, but users had more distant relationships, suggesting that e-mail reduced local interactions. Katz and Rice (2002a) found similar results, except that users had more offline relationships in general.

Survey results show diverse, extensive and growing use of the Internet for social interaction. In 2000, those online activities reported by the greatest percentage of the AOL (2000) respondents were doing research (91 per cent), communicating with friends and family (90 per cent), getting information about products to buy (80 per cent), getting news (76 per cent) and getting health information (70 per cent), and then there were many others (less than 60 per cent). The percentages reporting these activities, especially for doing research and getting health information, were higher for those online for more years. Of 12 new activities mentioned by the AOL (2000) respondents, the greatest interest was for sending/receiving pictures to and from family/friends (92 per cent). Of the AOL respondents, 44 per cent reported that they were more in touch with brothers/sisters, 40 per cent more in touch with aunts/uncles/cousins, 23 per cent more in touch with parents, 12 per cent more in touch with grandparents, and 38 per cent more in touch with other relatives, because of being online. Amazingly, 41 per cent reported that they had reconnected with people they had lost touch with – for an average of 12 years! And these percentages were somewhat greater for those who had been online for more years. People also spent time together online: 80 per cent with their children, and 68 per cent with their spouse. In the AOL survey, overall, people still preferred the telephone to online for communicating with friends (57 versus 35 per cent) and family (71 versus 24 per cent), but these differences decrease for those people who have been online more years.

Initial results from a study of survey responses to the National Geographic Society's website in the fall of 1998, from 35,000 Americans, 5000 Canadians and 15,000 others, showed that (1) high e-mail contact does not reduce other forms of interaction; (2) younger people used e-mail more for friends, near and far; (3) older people used e-mail more for kin, near and far; (4) women used e-mail more with kin at a distance; but (5) overall, communication frequencies for men and women were basically the same for all media.

The Internet at Home and in School

Tapscott (1997) discusses the generation that is growing up with the Internet, what he calls N-Gen (the Net generation, consisting of those aged 2 to 27 in 1997). This generation watches less TV, and is able to communicate through e-mail, develop web pages and start businesses. He emphasizes that these young users take advantage of the Internet to play, explore their world, try out different identities, express themselves through personal web pages, develop relationships with friends and family and become socialized. These activities are centred in interactive use of the medium and communication with others, as opposed to the more passive use of traditional mass media, and are (still) centered in a text-based medium, which promotes written literacy (see also Cherny, 1999). Tapscott suggests that early online communication will foster greater value for collaborative skills, based on 'peer-oriented relationships rather than hierarchies within families and companies' (1997: 212).

A third of the respondents in the AOL (2000) youth study felt that going online had made them a better student, 31 per cent said it had improved their language skills, and 56 per cent preferred going online for help with their homework, compared with 27 per cent for the library and other resources. Sixty-one per cent reported going online at least once with their parents, 44 per cent (52 per cent for those 15–17 years old) said they had some influence in getting their parents or family members to go online, and 66 per cent said that they had helped their parents get online or use the Internet (see also Buckingham, this volume).

Respondents to the UCLA (2000) study indicate that their use of the Internet helps to create and maintain friendships as well as communicate with the family. Indeed, the two most popular Internet activities reported by users were web surfing/browsing (81.7 per cent) and using e-mail (81.6 per cent) – that is, general information seeking and communicating with others. Concerning the attributes of the Internet, respondents were most satisfied with their 'ability to communicate with other people' – more so than with relevant information, goods and services, ease of finding information, and connection speed. Most (89.0 per cent) of the parents in the study reported that their children spent about the same time with their friends since they started using the Internet; 4.0 per cent indicated more time, and 7.0 per cent less time. While 27.5 per cent reported spending no time on the Internet together with other household members, 47.1 per cent reported doing so at least some time each week. Indeed, more people reported feeling ignored because of others' television use (36.5 per cent) than Internet use (24.7 per cent). Overall, 91.8 per cent indicate no change in the time members of the household spend together since becoming connected to the Internet. On average, Internet users feel that the Internet has slightly increased the number of people regularly contacted, and extent of communicating with family and friends; 26.2 per cent reported having online friends (on average, almost 13 friends) that they have never met, and 12.4 per cent have met in person someone they first met online (on average 5.6 such new friendships). A 2002 AOL survey of 6700 teenagers and parents of teens reported that 81 per cent of teens aged 12–17 use the Internet to e-mail friends or relatives, and 70 per cent use it for instant messaging; for teens aged 18–19, usage rises to 91 per cent and 83 per cent, respectively.

Associations with Other Media Use

Kayany and Yelsma (2000) argue that households comprise both social and technological dimensions; so the addition of new elements such as online media affects the organization of roles, relationships and functions. Their study of 185 people in 84 households showed that online use affects time spent mostly in TV viewing, some in telephone use, some in newspaper reading, and a small amount in family conversations, with greater declines reported by children. Both informational and entertainment functions of media were rated as more important by more frequent online users. The authors concluded that online media seem to be displacing informational functions for TV,

but not entertainment functions for either TV or newspaper.

James et al. (1995) studied home-based media via an online questionnaire, finding that computer bulletin board use reduced time spent using TV, books, telephone, and letters. Robinson et al. (1997), analysing data from a national probability telephone survey in 1994 and 1995, found that print media and CMC use seem to reinforce the use of each other, but there was no relationship to radio or TV use. Thus, displacement effects are most likely among functionally equivalent media, and among media that depend on the same limited resources, as well as provide similar resources, uses and gratifications. Other studies find that use of computer and Internet decreases some other media use. Reagan (1987) reported that young computer users are less likely to use radio, newspapers, local and network TV. The Pew Research Center (1997) found that online news consumers viewed TV news less, and the GVU (1997) online surveys reported that Web surfing replaces weekly TV viewing. Coffey and Stipp (1997) analysed home media diaries, finding only a very small percentage of respondents use their computers during prime time; few people have a computer in the same room as television (Media Metrix, 1997); heavy computer users are not heavy TV viewers (Crispell, 1997); and greater computer use is associated with greater use of print media (Perse and Dunn, 1998). Jessel (1995) and Miller and Clemente (1997) also show that nearly a third of online users reported spending less time watching television than before their online usage. AOL's (2000) representative national Internet users' survey also found declines in other media use. Users reported watching less television (24 per cent compared with 16 per cent in 1999), reading fewer print newspapers (19 versus 13 per cent) and reading fewer print magazines (18 versus 11 per cent), and those percentages generally increase the more users have been online.

Internet users report that they use more media overall than non-users (UCLA, 2000), especially books, video games, recorded music and radio. However, users report watching about 28 per cent less television per week than do non-users. More (67.3 per cent) also rate the Internet as an 'important' or 'extremely important' information source, compared with 53.1 per cent for television and 46.8 per cent for radio.

One study applying the uses and gratifications approach (Ferguson and Perse, 2000) analysed data from an online survey and a three-day media-use diary from over 200 college students at two universities that had extensive Internet access. Entertainment was the most salient motivation for Web use, after required school activities; after search engines, the most frequently visited sites were entertainment and sports. Thus, the play component of the Web may displace TV viewing, as entertainment is a primary gratification from TV. However, little Web surfing seems motivated by the need to pass time. The second most important motivation for watching TV is for relaxation, but Web use was not much motivated by this, probably because it requires active choice and cognition. Finally, companionship motivations were not salient for Web use: 'There was little evidence that the World Wide Web can substitute for personal interaction' (2000: 170), or even much parasocial interaction, but this may change with greater bandwidth, which would allow for streaming video and responsive Internet telephony.

Applying a uses and gratifications perspective to survey responses from 279 students, Papacharissi and Rubin (2000) found that the Internet was used as a 'functional alternative to face-to-face communication for those who are anxious about face-to-face communication and who did not find face-to-face communication to be rewarding' (2000: 188). Those who rated the Internet as providing more social presence were more likely to say they used the Internet to help pass time, for convenience and for entertainment. They note that interpersonal utilities and information seeking are distinct types of uses; for those with satisfying interpersonal relations, the Internet was used more for information seeking; for those with unrewarding or anxiety-inducing interpersonal relations, the Internet was used as an alternative medium for

social interaction, and such users had a greater affinity for the Internet.

Franzen (2000) analysed differences between responses to an online survey from 15,842 Internet users (20 per cent response) and a mailed survey to a control group of 1196 non-users (50 per cent response). Franzen's study found few differences in network size (in fact non-users reported 10 while users reported 12) or time spent with friends between users and non-users (though users had 23 per cent more friends), controlling for a variety of demographic, social and media factors. There was no effect of the number of months since first starting to use the Internet on network size. Consequentially, however, he shows that the number of people contacted online via e-mail increased the number of close friends, but longer or more intensive time spent on the Internet did not affect that number, or time spent socializing with others, though it did slightly reduce overall network size. So it is the ability to contact others via the Internet that leads to the associated increase in social networks. Respondents also reported many positive effects of e-mail usage on social networks. He concludes that 'Internet users are, on average, not socially isolated but quite to the contrary a relatively socially active group', and also suggests that larger social networks lead to greater e-mail contacts which in turn generates larger networks.

Increasing Diversity of Voices

The Internet can be a great communication tool for those who have a hard time meeting new friends owing to physical handicaps, diseases or even poor social skills (Wallace, 1999). These people can easily find others like them throughout the country and around the world, providing support and a chance to decrease loneliness or low self-esteem. Jones (1997) emphasizes that online communities can especially support otherwise marginalized cultures – both those discriminated against, and those acting as sources of discrimination against others. For example, the 7800 older SeniorNet members from the US and Canada say the network helps them ease their loneliness: 'It hosts welcoming events, celebrates anniversary parties, and mourns when one of its members dies' (Bollier, 1995: 3). The WELL is another example of an Internet community; WELL members live in the San Francisco Bay Area and often meet face-to-face (Rheingold, 1993). Other online communities include health support groups for people with illnesses that are not frequent enough to foster local physical communities (Rice, 2001).

Certainly the Internet has provided possibilities for viable communicative spaces for feminist networking and interaction (see Harcourt, 1999; Terry and Calvert, 1997). Harcourt in particular considers how the Internet might be used to support women's empowerment in developing countries, to bridge cultures, both local and global, and to coordinate women's issues at international conferences and working groups.

Internet users may increase their tolerance for a greater diversity of views, because the content of the message, not the physical appearance of the messenger/writer, is emphasized. However, as Hill and Hughes (1998: 184) point out, just because people have the opportunity to build friendships does not mean that they will be amiable. New forms of online expression also include virtual sex, alternate cyber identities and electronic stalking (Civin, 1999; Odzer, 1997). Odzer, in particular, argues that while the interaction occurs in virtual and fantasy environments, the psychological and emotional relations are real in both experience and consequence. Indeed, she puts forth online eroticism as a valid form of emotional relationship and self-growth. Others, however, analyse online sex as one manifestation of loneliness, isolation and depression.

At the other extreme of social relations, Cobb (1998) discusses how online technology and spirituality are reinforcing and convergent. Indeed, the transcendent transformations in technology can be seen as ongoing God-inspired creation. And what might it mean about human nature when artificial intelligence does satisfactorily mirror human actions, intentions and communication? Certainly there are many online religious communities and websites (from the most orthodox to the most fantastic), all supporting humans' needs for and expressions of spirituality. On the other hand, as with critiques of online communities in general, it may be difficult to avoid overemphasizing the individual's own experience, at the cost of real, personal religious relations with other humans, and with the inherent self-submerging nature of great religions.

Potential Transformations

More extravagantly, Levy (1997) suggests a transformation not only from a material economy to an information economy, but farther into a 'social economy', or a collective intelligence mediated through cyberspace, where interactions, relationships and communication become the central resource and social infrastructure, fostered by information and communication technology. This is precisely the argument of social capital, where the value-added and positive network externalities (or public goods) aspects of shared knowledge, collaboration and social networks cannot be captured, processed and mass produced. This rise of the role of social interactions, now unimpeded by physical, cultural, language and temporal boundaries, will bring great challenges to traditional notions of countries, nationalities and economies.

Others, such as Robertson (1998), argue that because scientific theory or our analytic ability, now augmented and even superseded in some cases by computing power, can generate cumulative as well as discontinuous change, the current transformation is clearly revolutionary. Indeed, he argues that the computer and information revolution will be more transcendent than language, writing and printing, in terms of consequences for knowledge, culture, education, entertainment and ordinary life. Johnson (1997) makes a somewhat similar claim, equating the rise of various computer interfaces (the hardware, software and usage patterns) with the development of literacy. One of the ways he constructs this argument is to reject the dichotomy between technology and art, so as to be able to consider artifacts such as Gothic cathedrals and hypertext both as instances of interfaces.

CONCLUSION

This chapter has reviewed research literature and results concerning three primary social issues surrounding the increased use of the Internet: access, civic and community involvement, and social interaction and new forms of expression.

While some evidence indicates that the digital divide is decreasing or even disappearing with respect to gender and race, differences in income and education are still great, and in some studies increasing. The general lag in access and use may create enduring and consequential negative social consequences, persisting even after later adopters achieve full access. There are many barriers, obstacles and challenges to more equitable access, and some of those may be deeply embedded in social and cultural contexts and differences.

Many critics are quite pessimistic about the impact of Internet use on civic, political and community involvement. People may use a less diverse range of media, individuals' actions may be less private, online activists may be more extreme, users may have difficulty assessing the vast amounts of information available, people may basically reinforce their prior beliefs by participating only in selected interest groups, and the greatest current threat may be the growing concentration across media industries. Some conceptualizations of the attributes of the Internet and communities reject the notion that organic communities can thrive in mediated, online form, as they constitute secondary and distant relationships. Further, individual privacy is threatened, especially by commercial interests, and online communities typically are bound only by a single shared interest. More fundamentally, the nature of current 'real' communities can be debated, as some evidence shows that various forms of social involvement have been declining for many years in the US, and that very few people actually interact densely with physically proximate neighbours; rather, they participate in thin local communities and dispersed family and work networks.

On the other hand, recent studies and surveys find that Internet users tend to be more interested in current events; campaigns and political activists have already started using the Internet for a variety of purposes; users are more involved in civic and political activities than non-users; and many government offices provide e-mail and Web access. Nonetheless, real online dialogue among different interest groups is rare, and government access is typically one-way. However, many communities are strengthened through online interaction, if only because of the lower obstacles, such as time, distance and need to initially know others personally before communicating. It's probably more appropriate to think of online interaction as complementing physical communities. Nonetheless, there are many vibrant and long-lived mediated communities, ranging from health support groups to dispersed cultural and ethnic groups. The very growth and intensity of online communities may well speak to the perceived decline in real communities, as humans seek out social support and interaction. Indeed, many aspects of relationships, emotions and identities are experienced as just as real through the Internet as they are over other media (such as the telephone) or face-to-face. There are several case studies showing that small communities have been reinvigorated through online systems.

Finally, concerning social interaction and expression, pessimistic perspectives claim that not only does mediated communication impoverish the nature of interactions, but online interactions can be deceiving, simplistic, hateful and transient. Some conclude that high or extended Internet use leads to isolation and depression, as weak mediated relations replace strong unmediated ones, and narrowly focused relations replace more diverse ones. However, both survey and ethnographic studies show that rich, fertile, diverse and expanded interactions are possible through the Internet. There are many online groups with impassioned members providing emotional and other resources to each other, and users regularly rate communicating with others – family, friends and new people they have met online – as their most favourite and important activity. Some studies show that interactive Internet usage replaces passive television watching, but that overall Internet users are greater media participants. The Net generation may well be more literate, creative and socially skilled because of their early familiarity with the Internet, including trying out various aspects of their developing identity online. Interacting with teachers and other students is easier when supported by the Internet, and both students and patients are more likely to talk about sensitive issues online, possibly because of the protection of anonymity. A noticeable percentage of users meet new people they come to call friends online, and go on to meet these people in person. Several studies have specifically countered some prior research linking Internet use with isolation or depression, showing indeed that experienced Internet users may find greater support online, become more satisfied with their interactions and communication, and generate new relationships through the ability to contact others more easily. Indeed, some speculate that the Internet can also foster greater tolerance through exposure to a wider diversity of voices, and even support transcendent and spiritual growth. All these possibilities may lead to major growth in our concepts of identity, groups and society.

While the uses and effects of many major communication technologies (such as the pen, telegraph, telephone, photocopier, memo), have been studied retrospectively, if at all, the recent rapid growth of the Internet affords communication researchers a unique opportunity to describe, assess, predict and evaluate short-term changes as well as long-term developments. If the current speculation and research seem to indicate diverse, contradictory and simultaneous consequences, at several levels of analysis, this may be because that is fundamentally the nature of social change. However, it is far better to ground this understanding of the complexity of this major phenomenon in research than in speculation and assertion.

NOTE

Ron Rice thanks Drs James Katz and Philip Aspden for inviting him to be part of their Syntopia project on studies of the Internet, and helping him to articulate the three primary themes of this chapter.

REFERENCES

AOL (2000) *American Online/Roper Starch Cyberstudy 2000*. Roper CNT375.

AOL (2002) *America Online Announces Top Teen Wired Cities in America*. Available online: http://media.aoltimewarner.com/media/press_view.cfm?release_num=55252413

Aspden, P. and Katz, J. (2001) 'Assessments of quality of health care information and referrals to physicians: a nationwide survey', in R.E. Rice and J. Katz (eds), *The Internet and Health Communication*. Thousand Oaks, CA: Sage. pp. 107–19.

Baym, N.K. (1995) 'The emergence of community in computer-mediated communication', in S.G. Jones (ed.), *Cybersociety: Computer-mediated Communication and Community*. Thousand Oaks, CA: Sage. pp. 138–63.

Beniger, J. (1988) 'The personalization of mass media and the growth of pseudo-community', *Communication Research*, 14 (3): 352–71.

Bikson, T. and Panis, C. (1999) *Citizens, Computers, and Connectivity*. Santa Monica, CA: RAND.

Bollier, D. (ed.) (1995) *The Future of Community and Personal Identity in the Coming Electronic Culture*. Washington, DC: Aspen Institute.

Borchert, M. (1998) 'The challenge of cyberspace: Internet access and persons with disabilities', in B. Ebo (ed.), *Cyberghetto or Cybertopia: Race, Class, and Gender on the Internet*. New York: Praeger. pp. 45–64.

Bourque, S.C. and Warren, K.B. (1987) 'Technology, gender, and development', *Daedalus*, 116 (4): 173–98.

Browning, G. and Weitzner, D. (1996) *Electronic Democracy: Using the Internet to Influence American Politics*. White Plains, NY: Information Today, Inc.

Calhoun, C. (1986) 'Computer technology, large-scale societal integration and the local community', *Urban Affairs Quarterly*, 22: 329–49.

Carpini, M.X.D. (1996) 'Voters, candidates, and campaigns in the new information age: an overview and assessment', *Harvard International Journal of Press/Politics*, 1: 36–56.

Carrier, R. (1998) 'Training the information-poor in an age of unequal access', in B. Ebo (ed.), *Cyberghetto or Cybertopia: Race, Class, and Gender on the Internet*. New York: Praeger. pp. 153–68.

Cerulo, K. (1997) 'Reframing sociological concepts for a brave new (virtual?) world', *Sociological Inquiry*, 67 (1): 48–58.

Chen, W., Boase, J. and Wellman, B. (2002) 'The global villagers: comparing Internet users and uses around the world', in B. Wellman and C. Haythornthwaite (eds), *The Internet in Everyday Life*. Oxford: Blackwell. pp. 74–113.

Cherny, L. (1999) *Conversation and Community: Discourse in a Social MUD*. Chicago: Chicago University Press.

Civin, M. (1999) *Male, Female, Email: The Struggle for Relatedness in a Paranoid Society*. New York: Other Press.

ClickZ Stats (2005) *Population Explosion!* Available online: http://www.clickz.com/stats/sectors/geographics/print.php/5911_151151

Cobb, J. (1998) *Cybergrace: The Search for God in Cyberspace*. New York: Crown.

Coffey, S. and Stipp, H. (1997) 'The interactions between computer and television usage', *Journal of Advertising Research*, 37 (2): 61–7.

Cooper, M. (2000) *Disconnected, Disadvantaged, and Disenfranchised: Explorations in the Digital Divide*. New York: Consumer Federation of America.

Cooper, M. and Kimmelman, G. (1999) *The Digital Divide Confronts the Telecommunications Act of 1996: Economic Reality versus Public Policy*. Washington, DC: Consumer Union. Available online: http://www.consunion.org/other/telecom2-0299.htm

Corrado, A. (2000) *Campaigns in Cyberspace: Toward a New Regulatory Approach*. Queenstown, MD: Aspen Institute.

Crispell, D. (1997) 'The Internet on TV', *American Demographics*, 19 (5): 32–3.

Cultural Access Group (2001) *Ethnicity in the Electronic Age: Looking at the Internet through Multicultural Lens*. Los Angeles: Access Worldwide Communications, Inc.

Davis, R. (1999) *The Web of Politics: The Internet's Impact on the American Political System*. New York: Oxford University Press.

Dear, M.J., Schockman, H. and Hise, G. (eds) (1996) *Rethinking Los Angeles*. Thousand Oaks, CA: Sage.

Deetz, S. (1989a) 'Communication technology policy and interest representation: Habermas' theory of communicative action'. Paper presented to the International Communication Association Meeting, San Francisco, 30 May.

Deetz, S. (1989b) 'Representation of interests and communication technologies: issues in democracy and policy', in S. Deetz (ed.), *Introduction to Communication*, 2nd edn. Needham Heights, MA: Ginn. pp. 128–45. Reprinted from S. Deetz, *Communication and the Culture of Technology*. Washington State University Press, 1980.

Deetz, S. (1990) 'Suppressed conflict, consent, and inequitable interest representation'. Paper presented at the annual meeting of the International Communication Association, Dublin, Ireland, June.

Dervin, B. (1980) 'Communication gaps and inequities: moving toward a reconceptualization', in B. Dervin and M.J. Voigt (eds), *Progress in Communication Sciences*, vol. 2. Norwood, NJ: Ablex. pp. 73–112.

Doheny-Farina, S. (1998) *The Wired Neighbourhood*. New Haven, CT: Yale University Press.

Downing, J.D.H. (1989) 'Computers for political change: PeaceNet and public data access', *Journal of Communication*, 39 (3): 154–62.

ECRL (1999) 'The evolution of the digital divide: examining the relationship of race to Internet access and usage over time', Electronic Commerce Research Laboratory. Tennessee: Vanderbilt University, Owen Graduate School of Management. Available online: http://www.ecommerce.vanderbilt.edu

Fallows, J. (2000) 'Internet illusions', *New York Times Book Review*, 16 November: 28–31.

Ferguson, D. and Perse, E. (2000) 'The World Wide Web as a functional alternative to television', *Journal of Broadcasting & Electronic Media*, 44 (2): 155–74.

Franzen, A. (2000) 'Does the Internet make us lonely?', *European Sociological Review*, 16 (4): 427–38.

Garson, B. (1988) *The Electronic Sweatshop: How Computers are Transforming the Office of the Future into the Factory of the Past*. New York: Simon & Schuster.

Gergen, K. (1991) *The Saturated Self: Dilemmas of Identity in Contemporary Life*. New York: HarperCollins.

Gillespie, A. and Robins, K. (1989) 'Geographical inequalities: the spatial bias of the new communications technologies', *Journal of Communication*, 39 (3): 7–19.

Gurstein, M. (ed.) (2000) *Community Informatics: Enabling Communities with Information and Communications Technologies*. Hershey, PA: Idea Group.

GVU (1997) *GVU's 7th WWW User Survey*. Graphics, Visualization and Usabilities Center.

Available online: http://www.guv.gatech.edu/
user_surveys/survey-1997-04

Haddon, L. (2001) 'Social exclusion and information and communication technologies', *New
Media & Society*, 2 (4): 387–406.

Hagar, C. (2003) 'Community in Crisis: The UK 2001
foot-and-mouth outbreak'. Presented at the
'Information & Communication Technology in
Rural Communities – Is the Net Working?'
International Conference on Communities and
Technologies, Amsterdam, 19–21 September 2003.

Hamman, R. (1999) 'Computer networks linking
communities: a study of the effects of computer
network use upon pre-existing communities', in
U. Thiedke (ed.), *Virtual Groups: Characteristics
and Problematic Dimensions* (in German).
Wiesbaden: Westdeutscher. Available online:
http://www.socio.demon.co.uk/mphil/short.
html

Hampton, K. and Wellman, B. (2000) 'Examining
community in the digital neighbourhood: early
results from Canada's wired suburb', in T. Ishida
and K. Isbister (eds), *Digital Cities*. Heidelberg:
Springer. pp. 475–92.

Harcourt, W. (1999) *Women@Internet: Creating
New Cultures in Cyberspace*. New York: Zed.

Haythornthwaite, C. and Hagar, C. (2004) 'The social
world(s) of the Web', *Annual Review of Information
Science and Technology*, 39: 311–46.

Hill, K.A. and Hughes, J. (1998) *Cyperpolitics:
Citizen Activism in the Age of the Internet*.
New York: Rowman & Littlefield.

Hiltz, S.R. and Turoff, M. (1995) *Network Nation*,
rev. edn. Cambridge, MA: MIT Press.

Hoffman, D. and Novak, T. (1998) 'Information
access: bridging the racial divide on the Internet',
Science, 280 (5362): 390–1.

Hoffman, D., Kalsbeek, W. and Novak, T. (1996)
'Internet and Web use in the U.S.', *Communications of the ACM*, 39 (12): 36–46.

Horn, S. (1998) *Cyberville: Clicks, Culture, and the
Creation of an Online Town*. New York: Warner.

Howard, P., Rainie, L. and Jones, S. (2002) 'Days and
nights on the Internet', in B. Wellman and
C. Haythornthwaite (eds), *The Internet in Everyday
Life*. Oxford: Blackwell. pp. 45–73.

Hundt, R. (2000) *You Say You Want a Revolution: A
Story of Information Age Politics*. New Haven, CT:
Yale University Press.

Internet World Stats (2004) 'Top ten countries on
Internet with the highest penetration rate'.
Available online: http://www.internetworldstats.
com/top10.htm

Internet World Stats (2005) 'Internet usage
statistics – the big picture: world Internet users

and populations stats'. Available online: http://
www.internetworldstats.com/stats.htm

James, M., Wotring, C. and Forrest, E. (1995) 'An
exploratory study of the perceived benefits of
electronic bulletin board use and their impact on
other communication activities', *Journal of
Broadcasting & Electronic Media*, 39: 30–50.

Jansen, S.C. (1989) 'Gender and the information
society: a socially structured silence', *Journal of
Communication*, 39 (3): 196–215.

Jensen, J. (1999) 'Interactivity', in P. Mayer (ed.),
Computer Media and Communication. New York:
Oxford University Press. pp. 160–87.

Jessel, M. (1995) 'Internet begins to cut into
TV viewing', *Broadcasting and Cable*, 40: 318–30.

Johnson, S. (1997) *Interface Culture: How New
Technology Transforms the Way We Create and
Communicate*. New York: Harper Edge.

Jones, S. (ed.) (1997) *Virtual Culture: Identity and
Communication in Cybersociety*. Thousand Oaks,
CA: Sage.

Jones, S. (1999) 'Understanding community in the
information age', in P. Mayer (ed.), *Computer
Media and Communication*. New York: Oxford
University Press. pp. 219–40.

Kahin, B. and Keller, J. (eds) (1995) *Public Access to
the Internet*. Cambridge, MA: MIT Press.

Katz, J. and Aspden, P. (1997a) 'Motives, hurdles, and
dropouts: who is on and off the Internet and why',
Communications of the ACM, 40 (4): 97–102.

Katz, J. and Aspden, P. (1997b) 'A nation of strangers',
Communications of the ACM, 40 (12): 81–6.

Katz, J. and Aspden, P. (1997c) 'Motivations for and
barriers to Internet usage: results of a national
public opinion survey', *Internet Research:
Electronic Networking Applications and Policy*,
7 (3): 170–88.

Katz, J. and Rice, R.E. (2002a) *Social Consequences of
Internet Use: Access, Involvement and Social
Interaction*. Cambridge, MA: MIT Press.

Katz, J. and Rice, R. (2002b) 'Syntopia: access, civic
involvement and social interaction on the Net', in
B. Wellman and C. Haythornthwaite (eds), *The
Internet in Everyday Life*. Oxford: Blackwell.
pp. 114–38.

Katz, J., Rice, R.E. and Aspden, P. (2001) 'The internet 1995–2000: access, civic involvement, and
social interaction', *American Behavioural Scientist*,
45 (3): 404–19.

Katz, J. Rice, R.E., Acord, S., Dasgupta, K. and David,
K. (2004) 'Personal mediated communication and
the concept of community in theory and practice',
in P. Kalbfleisch (ed.), *Communication and
Community: Communication Yearbook 28*. Mahwah,
NJ: Erlbaum. pp. 315–71.

Kayany, J. and Yelsma, P. (2000) 'Displacement effects of online media in the socio-technical contexts of households', *Journal of Broadcasting & Electronic Media*, 44 (2): 215–29.

Kiesler, S., Siegel, H. and McGuire, T.W. (1984) 'Social psychological aspects of computer-mediated communication', *American Psychologist*, 39 (10): 1123–34.

Kolko, B., Nakamura, L. and Rodman, G. (eds) (1999) *Race in Cyberspace*. New York: Routledge.

Kraut, R.E. (1989) 'Telecommuting: the trade-offs of home work', *Journal of Communication*, 39 (3): 19–47.

Kraut, R., Lundmark, V., Patterson, M., Kiesler, S., Mukopadhyay, T. and Scherlis, M. (1998) 'Internet paradox: a social technology that reduces social involvement and psychological well-being?', *American Psychologist*, 53 (9): 1017–31.

Krendl, K.A., Broihier, M.C. and Fleetwood, C. (1989) 'Children and computers: do sex-related differences persist?', *Journal of Communication*, 39 (3): 85–93.

Kroker, A. and Weinstein, M. (1994) *Data Trash: The Theory of the Virtual Class*. New York: St Martin's.

Levy, P. (1997) *Collective Intelligence: Mankind's Emerging World in Cyberspace*, trans. R. Bononno. New York: Plenum.

Lievrouw, L.A. (1994) 'Information resources and democracy: understanding the paradox', *Journal of the American Society for Information Science*, 45 (6): 350–7.

Lindlof, T. and Shatzer, M. (1998) 'Media ethnography in virtual space: strategies, limits and possibilities', *Journal of Broadcasting Electronic Media*, 42 (2): 170–89.

Loader, B. (ed.) (1997) *The Governance of Cyberspace: Politics, Technology and Global Restructuring*. New York: Routledge.

Margolis, M. and Resnick, D. (2000) *Politics as Usual: The Cyberspace 'Revolution'*. Thousand Oaks, CA: Sage.

McChesney, R. (2000) *Rich Media, Poor Democracy: Communication Politics in Dubious Times*, rev. edn. New York: New Press.

McConnaughey, J. and Lader, W. (1998) *Falling through the Net II: New Data on the Digital Divide*. Washington, DC: US Department of Commerce. Available online: http://www.ntia.doc.gov/ntia-home/net2/falling.html

McNutt, J. (1998) 'Ensuring social justice for the new underclass: community interventions to meet the needs of the new poor', in B. Ebo (ed.), *Cyberghetto or Cybertopia: Race, Class, and Gender on the Internet*. New York: Praeger. pp. 33–44.

Media Metrix (1997) Online press release: http://www. mediametric.com/pcmpr33.htm

Miller, T. and Clemente, P. (1997) *1997 American Internet User Survey*. New York: FIND/SVP Emerging Technologies Research Group. Available online: http://etrg.findsvp.com/internet/findf.html

Mulgan, G.J. (1991) *Communication and Control: Networks and the New Economies of Communication*. New York: Guilford.

Murdock, G. and Golding, P. (1989) 'Information poverty and political inequality: citizenship in the age of privatized communications', *Journal of Communication*, 39 (3): 180–95.

National Statistics Omnibus (2000) *Internet Access*. Available online: www.statistics.gov.uk

Neu, C.R., Anderson, R.H. and Bikson, T.K. (1999) *Sending Your Government a Message: E-mail Communication between Citizens and Government*. Santa Monica, CA: RAND.

Nie, N. and Erbring, L. (2000) 'Internet and society'. Available online: http://www.stanford.edu/group/siqss/Press_Release/Preliminary_Report.pdf

Nielsen//NetRatings (2004) 'Three out of four Americans have access to the Internet, according to Nielsen//NetRatings'. Available online: www. nielsennetratings.com/pr/pr_040318.pdf

NTIA (2002) *A Nation Online*. Washington, DC: National Telecommunications and Information Agency. Available online: http://www.ntia.doc.gov/ntiahome/ dn/index.html

Nua.com (2001) 'How many online? Canada & USA'. Available online: http://www.nua.ie/surveys/how_many_online/n_america.htm

Odzer, C. (1997) *Virtual Spaces: Sex and the Cyber Citizen*. New York: Berkley.

Papacharissi, Z. and Rubin, A. (2000) 'Predictors of Internet use', *Journal of Broadcasting & Electronic Media*, 44 (2): 175–96.

Parks, M.R. and Floyd, K. (1996) 'Making friends in cyberspace', *Journal of Communication*, 46 (1): 80–97.

Parks, M.R. and Roberts, L.D. (1998) '"Making MOOsic": the development of personal relationships online and a comparison to their offline counterparts', *Journal of Social and Personal Relationships*, 15 (4): 517–37.

Perse, E. and Dunn, D. (1998) 'The utility of home computers: implications of multimedia and connectivity', *Journal of Broadcasting & Electronic Media*, 42: 435–56.

Pew Research Center (1997) 'TV news viewership declines'. Available online: http://www.people press.org/mediaque.htm

Pew Research Center (2000) 'Tracking online life: how women use the Internet to cultivate relationships with family and friends'. Available online: http://www.pewinternet.org/reports/toc.asp?Report=11

Pool, I. de Sola (1983) *Technologies of Freedom.* Cambridge, MA: Belknap.

Porter, D. (ed.) (1997) *Internet Culture.* New York: Routledge.

Putnam, R. (2000) *Bowling Alone: The Collapse and Revival of American Community.* New York: Simon & Schuster.

Rash, W. (1997) *Politics on the Nets: Wiring the Political Process.* New York: Freeman.

Reagan, J. (1987) 'Classifying adopters and non-adopters of four technologies using political activity, media use and demographic variables', *Telematics and Informatics,* 4: 3–16.

Rheingold, H. (1993) *The Virtual Community: Homesteading on the Electronic Frontier.* Reading, MA: Addison-Wesley.

Rice, R.E. (1987a) 'New patterns of social structure in an information society', in J. Schement and L. Lievrouw (eds), *Competing Visions, Complex Realities: Social Aspects of the Information Society.* Norwood, NJ: Ablex. pp. 107–20.

Rice, R.E. (1987b) 'Computer-mediated communication and organizational innovation', *Journal of Communication,* 37: 65–94.

Rice, R.E. (2001) 'The Internet and health communication: a framework of experiences', in R.E. Rice and J.E. Katz (eds), *The Internet and Health Communication: Experiences and Expectations.* Thousand Oaks, CA: Sage. pp. 5–46.

Rice, R.E. and Katz, J.E. (eds) (2001) *The Internet and Health Communication: Experiences and Expectations.* Thousand Oaks, CA: Sage.

Rice, R.E. and Katz, J.E. (2003) 'Comparing Internet and mobile phone usage: digital divides of usage, adoption, and dropouts', *Telecommunications Policy,* 27 (8/9): 597–623.

Rice, R.E., McCreadie, M. and Chang, S.-J. (2001) *Accessing and Browsing Information and Communication: A Multidisciplinary Approach.* Cambridge, MA: MIT Press.

Riphagen, J. and Kanfer, A. (1997) 'How does e-mail affect our lives?' National Center for Supercomputing Applications. Available online: http://www.ncsa.uiuc.edu/edu/trg/e-mail/index.html

Robertson, D. (1998) *The New Renaissance: Computers and the Next Level of Civilization.* New York: Oxford University Press.

Robinson, J., Barth, K. and Kohut, A. (1997) 'Social impact research: personal computers, mass media and use of time', *Social Science Computer Review,* 15 (1): 65–82.

Rojas, V., Roychowdhury, D., Okur, O., Straubhaar, J. and Estrada-Ortiz, Y. (2004) 'Beyond access: cultural capital and the roots of the digital divide', in E. Bucy and J. Newhagen (eds), *Media Access: Social and Psychological Dimensions of New Technology Use.* Hillsdale, NJ: Erlbaum. pp. 107–30.

Scherer, K. (1997) 'College life on-line: healthy and unhealthy Internet use', *Journal of College Student Development,* 38: 655–65.

Schiller, H. (1996) *Information Inequality: The Deepening Social Crisis in America.* London: Routledge.

Schon, D., Sanyal, B. and Mitchell, W. (eds) (1999) *High Technology and Low-income Communities.* Cambridge, MA: MIT Press.

Schroeder, K. and Ledger, J. (1998) *Life and Death on the Internet.* Menasha, WI: Supple.

Schuler, D. (1996) *New Community Networks: Wired for Change.* New York: ACM.

Shapiro, A. and Leone, R. (1999) *The Control Revolution: How the Internet Is Putting Individuals in Charge and Changing the World We Know.* New York: Public Affairs Century Foundation.

Skocpol, T. (2000) *The Missing Middle: Working Families and the Future of American Social Policy.* New York: Norton.

Slack, R.S. and Williams, R.A. (2000) 'The dialectics of place and space: on community in the "information age"', *New Media & Society,* 2 (3): 313–34.

Starobin, P. (1996) 'On the square', *National Journal,* 25 June: 1145–9.

Stoll, C. (1995) *Silicon Snake Oil: Second Thoughts on the Information Highway.* New York: Doubleday.

Stone, A. (1991) 'Will the real body please stand up? Boundary stories about virtual cultures', in M. Benedikt (ed.), *Cyberspace: First Steps.* Cambridge, MA: MIT Press. pp. 81–119.

Straus, S. (1997) 'Technology, group processes, and group outcomes: testing the connections in performance in computer-mediated and face-to-face groups', *Human–Computer Interaction,* 12: 227–66.

Strover, S. (2003) 'Remapping the digital divide', *The Information Society,* 19 (4), whole issue.

Tapscott, D. (1997) *Growing up Digital: The Rise of the Net Generation.* New York: McGraw-Hill.

Terry, J. and Calvert, M. (eds) (1997) *Processed Lives: Gender and Technology in Everyday Life.* New York: Routledge.

Tsagarousianou, R., Tambini, D. and Bryan, C. (eds) (1998) *Cyberdemocracy: Technology, Cities and Civic Networks.* New York: Routledge.

Turkle, S. (1996) 'Virtuality and its discontents: searching for community in cyberspace', *The American Prospect,* 24: 50–7.

UCLA (2000) *The UCLA Internet Report: Surveying the Digital Future*. UCLA Center for Communication Policy. Available online: http://www.ccp.ucal.edu

US Congress (1987) *The Electronic Supervisor: New Technology, New Tensions*. Office of Technology Assessment OTA-CIT-333. Washington, DC: US Government Printing Office.

US Congress (1990) *Critical Connections: Communication for the Future*. Office of Technology Assessment. OTA-CIT-407. Washington, DC: US Government Printing Office.

Van Dijk, J. (1999) *The Network Society: Social Aspects of New Media*, trans. L. Spoorenberg. Thousand Oaks, CA: Sage.

Wall, M. (2002) 'Online lifeline for farmers', *The Sunday Times*, 10 November, pp. 51–2.

Wallace, P. (1999) *The Psychology of the Internet*. New York: Cambridge University Press.

Walther, J. (1996) 'Computer-mediated communication: impersonal, interpersonal, and hyperpersonal inter action', *Communication Research*, 23 (1): 3–43.

Warschauer, M. (2003). *Technology and Social Inclusion*. Cambridge, MA: MIT Press.

Weinberg, S. (1987) 'Expanding access to technology: computer equity for women', in B.D. Wright, M.M. Ferree, G.O. Mellow, L.H. Lewis, M.-L.D. Samper, R. Asher and K. Claspell (eds), *Women, Work, and Technology: Transformations*. Ann Arbor, MI: University of Michigan Press. pp. 281–90.

Wellman, B. (2001) 'Physical place and cyberspace: the rise of networked individualism', *International Journal of Urban and Regional Research*, 25, 227–52.

Wellman, B. and Gulia, M. (1999a) 'Virtual communities as communities: Net surfers don't ride alone', in M.A. Smith and P. Kollock (eds), *Communities in Cyberspace*. New York: Routledge. pp. 167–94.

Wellman, B. and Gulia, M. (1999b) 'Net surfers don't ride alone', in B. Wellman (ed.), *Networks in the Global Village*. Boulder, CO: Westview. pp. 331–66.

White, C.S. (1997) 'Citizen participation and the Internet: prospects for civic deliberation in the information age', *Social Studies*, 88: 23–8.

Wresch, W. (1996) *Disconnected: Haves and Have-Nots in the Information Age*. New Brunswick, NJ: Rutgers University Press.

Wynn, E. and Katz, J. (1997) 'Hyperbole over cyberspace: self-presentation and social boundaries in Internet home pages and discourse', *The Information Society*, 13 (4): 297–329.

Zuboff, S. (1988) *In the Age of the Smart Machine: The Future of Work and Power*. New York: Basic.

5

New Media and Small Group Organizing

ANDREA B. HOLLINGSHEAD AND
NOSHIR S. CONTRACTOR

Traditionally, small groups have been defined by researchers as collectives ranging from a minimum of two, and in most cases three, to a maximum of 15 or so members (cf. McGrath, 1984). Members of groups have interdependent goals, are acquainted with and interact with one another and have a sense of belonging. Recent developments in digital communication technologies have brought about a radical change in our collective notion of what constitutes a group. Members of groups no longer need to be formally constituted or to be co-present (in time or place) to collaborate, share information or socialize. Instead new technologies facilitate the creation, maintenance and dissolution of groups among individuals who use different devices (such as phones, mobiles, laptops, personal digital assistants) to interact over one or more of a variety of channels (audio, video, text and graphics) offered by several forums (such as Internet newsgroups, online chat sessions via Instant Messenger, and corporate intranets). Indeed, we are witnessing the emergence of new media not simply as a *conduit* but also as an *agent* within groups driving or regulating the group's decision process by dynamically structuring the group's interaction (Contractor, 2002; DeSanctis and Gallupe, 1987). They often

serve as important 'nodes' acting as 'non-human' agents or associates within the group. They can facilitate collaboration among human agents by offering the group information or 'gisted' summaries relevant to the current discussion or managing floor control by inviting contributions from group participants who have not contributed.

These developments have triggered a shift in conceptualizations of groups from the traditional notion of 'same time, same place' to 'any time, anywhere' and, some would argue apocryphally, 'all the time, everywhere'. In addition to the physical and temporal constraints, developments in new media have also eliminated constraints on the size of groups. In traditional face-to-face groups, the size of the group is likely to be relatively small and its membership is by definition a closed set. This is also true for some geographically distributed work teams that collaborate using communication technologies such as video and computer conferencing. However, that is not the case in many Internet-based newsgroups, where there are literally hundreds of participants (Alexander et al., 2002). These participants may coalesce as a group because of a common 'practice', such as the development of a new computer operating system, or because of a common 'interest', such as their concerns about the use of 'sweatshop' labour practices or their interest in downloading a particular genre of music. As a global community of consumers and producers we are grappling with the opportunities and challenges of these new, fluid 'group forms' of organizing (Contractor and Monge, 2002; Katz et al., 2004, 2005; Monge and Contractor, 2003).

As researchers, we are challenged to redefine the theoretical and methodological apparatus to study how new media shape, and are in turn shaped by, the ways in which we organize in groups. Before the development of the World Wide Web and the Internet, research on groups with technological support was driven by three basic goals: to examine how adequately new media could permit groups to overcome time and space constraints, to evaluate the impact of technologies on the range and speed of members' access to information, and to evaluate the impact of technologies on the groups' task performance (McGrath and Hollingshead, 1994). Much of the theory and research addressed when and how the structure, interaction and performance of technologically enabled groups were similar to and different from face-to-face groups. As such, the focus of this research was on examining the ways in which new media served to substitute and enlarge communication among group members (Contractor and Bishop, 2000; Monge and Contractor, 2003). With the surge in digital communication technologies, researchers started to reckon with the idea that most technologically enabled groups were inherently different from face-to-face groups, and that they were worthy of study as entities in their own right rather than simply to be benchmarked against equivalent face-to-face groups. Many of the premises of existing theories were being challenged by technological developments and risked becoming less relevant at best, and obsolete at worst. Researchers are currently rethinking their definitions of groups and are developing new theories to explain and predict their behaviour, and are designing new methods to study them.

This chapter examines the role of new media at the group level of analysis. In contrast to Baym's chapter in this volume, where she explores the social and interpersonal aspects of new media, this chapter focuses on new media and groups at work. Its emphasis is on how technology shapes and is shaped by the behaviour of groups, rather than on issues relating to the design of hardware and software systems for group collaboration. The organization of this chapter reflects the evolution in theory and research on groups and new media. As we shall see, the theory and research also reflect our evolving definitions of 'new media' – starting with early experiments in teleconferencing (audio and video conferencing) in the 1970s, and continuing with proprietary computer-mediated communication systems in the 1980s, the rise of the Internet and the Web as 'open' communication networks in the 1990s, and the ubiquitous, pervasive and mobile communication environment that ushers us into the twenty-first century. The chapter begins with a brief description of an early, but influential, classification of technologies that support group interaction. The second and third sections examine the theory and empirical findings of research that investigated how technologically enabled group collaborations are similar and different from face-to-face collaborations. As will become evident, most of this research was conducted, or at least premised, on conceptualizations of groups prior to recent developments in digital technologies and the Internet. The fourth section presents a reconceptualization of groups that takes into account the new forms of organizing enabled by new media. This reconceptualization allows for a more fluid, dynamic and activity-based definition of groups and technology, and is drawn from a network perspective. It presents a knowledge network approach to the study of groups and technology.

A CLASSIFICATION OF TECHNOLOGIES THAT SUPPORT GROUP INTERACTION

Collaboration among group members entails cognitive as well as emotional and motivational aspects of communication. Group members transmit, receive and store information of various kinds, from one another and from various other sources. These exchanges were viewed as distinct functions carried out by group members. Hence, not surprisingly, scholars conceptualized the technologies that support these functions to also be distinct. With an eye towards retrospective synthesis of research in this area, McGrath and Hollingshead (1993, 1994) presented a classification system for communication systems based on the functional role of technologies to support group collaboration. The four categories of the classification system are based on whether the technology: (1) provides within-group communication (i.e. group communication support systems or GCSS); (2) supplements information available to the group or its members by information drawn from databases (i.e. group information support systems or GISS); (3) supports communication with those outside the group (i.e. group external support systems or GXSS); and (4) structures group task performance processes and task products (i.e. group performance support systems or GPSS). The classification system was developed in the early 1990s when the World Wide Web was in its infancy. It was later updated to include communication technologies available on the Internet (Hollingshead, 2001). While the classification system was developed at a time when distinct technologies supported these different functions, it continues to be a viable framework to organize and examine contemporary technologies that typically support more than one of these four functions.

GCSS: Technologies That Mediate or Augment Within-group Communication

The signature feature of GCSS is its ability to permit group members to communicate using new media. In some cases GCSS may mediate communication among members spatially separated from one another while they are communicating. Examples would include video conferencing, or text messaging on mobile phones. In other cases, GCSS may augment face-to-face communication, for example, by the use of PowerPoint and LCD projectors

for showing graphics. Some GCSS support communication for group members interacting in different time periods such as e-mail; others require that group members interact synchronously such as instant messenging. As these examples illustrate, GCSS vary in the communication channels that are available to group members: visual, auditory, text and graphics and often support multiple channels.

Most research on GCSS has been based on the premise that the fewer modalities afforded by technologically mediated communication would 'filter' out some of the cues in face-to-face communication (Culnan and Markus, 1987). Based on this assumption, the research agenda sought to examine how the performance of groups using GCSS was moderated by the particular task(s) and activities in which the group was engaged, the experience of the group with the technology, and the degree to which group members have a shared conceptualization of relative expertise (Hollingshead, 1998a, 1998b; Hollingshead et al., 1993). In addition to examining the performance of groups using GCSS, some research has focused on the interaction process among group members. This research (McGrath and Hollingshead, 1994) has found evidence that the sequencing, synchrony and timing of messages among group members using GCSS is moderated by the size and nature of the groups, as well as the level of ambiguity among group members.

Table 5.1 provides examples of GCSS organized by the communication channels provided by the technology (video, audio, text/graphics) and the temporal distribution of members, i.e. whether they are communicating at the same time, synchronously, or at different times, asynchronously. As noted at the start of this section, GCSS can support communication between members who are co-present or are geographically distributed. However, as we shall see in the review of empirical research, the preponderance of research on GCSS has been among geographically distributed groups. Culnan and Markus (1987) argue that this bias reflects an early preoccupation with the role of GCSS to mediate rather than to augment face-to-face communication.

Table 5.1 *A typology of group communication support systems*

Modalities available	Synchronous	Asynchronous
Visual	Video conference	DVD exchange
Audio	Phone conference	Voice mail
Text, graphics	Computer conference, instant messaging, chat rooms	Fax, e-mail, text messaging, newsgroups, discussion groups, home pages, websites, blogs, wikis

GISS: Supplementing Information Available to the Group

Group members have access to many repositories of information or knowledge besides other group members. These repositories include databases, archives and intranets. Intranets are secure websites that support knowledge sharing among employees. Depending on configuration, intranets can support (a) *individual activities* such as updating personnel records or changing benefit choices; (b) *formal information dissemination*, such as company news or policy manuals; (c) *pointers to knowledge and knowledge holders*, such as experts directories, search engines and hyperlinks (Contractor, Zink and Chan, 1988); (d) individual and group *data, information and knowledge sharing*, such as document exchange, or jointly maintained knowledge repositories such as project websites; and (e) *group interaction*, such as group discussions, forums, Net meetings, or joint creation and editing of documents (Hollingshead et al., 2002). Other examples of GISS are information management programs that organize schedules, files, contacts and other information to facilitate information exchange with other members. Microsoft Outlook, which comes preloaded on many PC-compatible computers, is one such information management program. More recent examples include software agents such as 'webbots', or Web-based robots, that execute searches regularly and automatically on intranets and/or via the Internet, and update members with new information whenever webbots encounter it.

GXSS: Supporting External Communication

The GXSS function is a special case of both the GCSS function and the GISS function. Communication between group members and key external 'human' agents can be done with any of the GCSS systems described earlier. At the same time, one can consider interaction with non-human agents (such as webbots) external to the group as accessing yet another kind of information database, thus making it a special case of GISS.

Organizations are increasingly able to interconnect seamlessly the human agents and non-human agents on their intranets with those of their clients, partners, suppliers or subcontractors, via secure Web-based 'extranets' (Bar et al., 1998). As such, extranets serve as a unified infrastructure for GXSS that reaches beyond the traditional organizational boundary or its digital analogue, the corporate 'firewall'.

GPSS: Modifying the Group's Task Performance

For several decades, researchers have designed and evaluated strategies to structure the interaction among group members to enhance their effectiveness. These strategies, often under the guidance of a facilitator or supervisor, constrain and structure the communication, the task information available, and/or the form and sequence of task responses permitted and required of the group. Some examples of such strategies are brainstorming, the Delphi method and the nominal group technique (NGT) (for a summary, see McGrath, 1984).

More recently, technologically enabled group performance support systems (GPSS) have been deployed to assist with these strategies. An influential effort has focused specifically on technologically enabled strategies to enhance decision-making among groups. These GPSS are also called GDSS or group decision support systems (see Jessup and Valacich, 1993, for discussion). In the late 1980s and early 1990s, most GPSS were in the form of decision rooms – specially equipped rooms with networked computers supporting synchronous groups with co-located members. Most groups used these systems to augment their face-to-face decisions. These systems varied as to the type of task support provided to groups, the size of groups that could use the system, and whether a trained facilitator was necessary to augment the GPSS. Those that provided direct task support for groups usually incorporated an array of 'modules', each of which structures a different subset of a group's tasks or different portions of the group process on a given project. For example, a GPSS might include tools or modules for electronic brainstorming; for structuring various forms of evaluation and voting (rating, ranking, weighing, pick one, pick any, etc.); for identifying stakeholders and bringing their assumptions to the surface; or for exchanging anonymous or identified comments on any or all topics. Efforts are under way to develop these systems to support asynchronous and synchronous groups on the Internet. More recently, GPSS have been designed to encompass more than just decision-making. Current efforts in the area of workflow management, enterprise resource planning and computer-supported cooperative work (discussed by Star and Bowker and others elsewhere in this volume) underscore efforts to enhance group performance beyond simply decision-making.

THEORETICAL PERSPECTIVES

Most prior theory and research have focused primarily on how groups using technology accomplished their tasks differently from groups without access to technology. More specifically, much of the early theory relevant to the study of groups and technology addressed how the interaction and performance of groups that were separated in space and time differed from face-to-face groups. This research centred on those technologies classified as GCSS. One set of theories dealt with the topic of media choice or media selection: how people make choices about different media to use in their communication with others. Another set dealt with the topic of media effects: how technologies can impact group interaction processes and group outcomes. A third stream of theorizing explored the interrelations between technologies and group interaction by attempting to integrate the arguments offered by media choice and media effects theorists. Specifically, adaptive structuration theory (AST) examined how the structures that are imposed by technologies shape and in turn are shaped by group interaction. Most of the empirical investigations of this perspective were conducted with technologies classified as GPSS. Finally, the most current theory that relates to groups and technology deals with the complexity of group processes, and suggests that technology is only one of many factors that can influence group processes and outcomes.

The various streams of theorizing previewed above parallels the extant research on new media in a variety of social contexts. Contractor (2002) notes that there is an enduring and fundamental intellectual tension between what, at two extremes, constitute the 'organizational imperative' and the 'technological imperative' (Markus and Robey, 1988). Scholarship from an organizational imperative seeks to explain changes in the use of technology based on organizational constraints. This reflects the 'media choice' stream of theorizing discussed in the following section. Research from a technological imperative seeks to find changes resulting from changes in the technology. This stream of research coincides with the 'media effects' literature discussed in a subsequent section. Finally, there is a growing body of theorizing and research that embraces the 'emergent' perspective. The emergent perspective seeks to strike a balance by acknowledging the role of the technologies in triggering impacts but also explicitly incorporating the organizational imperatives that might moderate the influence of the technology. The emergent perspective is best exemplified here by the third stream of theorizing mentioned above. Theories based on an emergent perspective, such as adaptive structuration theory (DeSanctis and Poole, 1994), seek to understand the recursive and often unanticipated patterns that emerge by examining the interrelationships between the use of new media and the organizational structures and norms that influence, and are in turn influenced by, their use.

Media Choice

Some of the earliest theoretical work on media choice was conducted before computer use was widespread, and hence dealt with communication systems other than computers. Short et al. (1976) proposed the *social presence model* to predict which media individuals will use for certain types of interactions. Social presence refers to the degree of salience of the other person involved in the interaction, and was therefore assumed to be an 'objective' dimension that could be calibrated by a researcher independent of the users. They hypothesized that media differed in their social presence, and that individuals are aware of and agree on this difference and use it as a basis of their media choice. For instance, they argued that text-based communication has a lower social presence than video conferencing, which in turn has a lower social presence than face-to-face communication. Further they argued that individuals would select a communication medium that had a social presence commensurate with the task they were trying to accomplish. Specifically, they predicted that individuals avoid a given medium for a given type of interaction if they perceive that medium as not providing a high enough degree of social presence for that type of interaction. They also predicted that communication using media low in social presence would be more appropriate for task-related communication while media high in social presence, such as face-to-face communication, were more appropriate for transacting interpersonal (or socioemotional) content.

Daft and Lengel (1986) extended the ideas embodied in the social presence model in their theory of *media richness*. They proposed that different forms of communication differ in the 'richness' of the information that they provide. Richness was defined as the ability of a medium to provide multiple cues (verbal and nonverbal), and immediate (or quick) feedback, using multiple modalities (text, video, audio and graphics). Based on these criteria they arrayed the various media from very lean (company policy manuals for rules and regulations) to lean (formal information systems) to somewhat rich (direct contact) to very rich (group meetings). Further, they argued that the various information processing tasks conducted by group members could also be objectively arrayed in terms of their equivocality and uncertainty. Some communication tasks, such as finding the latest sales figures, entailed reducing uncertainty (that is, finding the right answer to a question). Other tasks, such as crafting a sales strategy, required reducing equivocality (that is, determining what is the right question to answer). Media richness theory proposed that 'rich' media were more appropriate to reduce equivocality and 'lean' media were more appropriate to reduce uncertainty. Daft and Lengel argued that managers use (and should use) different communication methods of appropriate degrees of richness to deal with situations that differ in equivocality and uncertainty. Hence, different communication media, or structural mechanisms in their terminology, need to be used for different types of organizational tasks. The more equivocality a situation involves, the richer the information required to deal with it. They presented seven structural mechanisms ordered along an information richness continuum based on capacity for resolving equivocality versus reducing uncertainty. The seven mechanisms included: group meetings, integrators, direct contact, planning, special reports, formal information systems, and rules and regulations.

At the time media richness theory was first proposed, e-mail was not widely available in organizations; however, this theory was featured quite prominently in early empirical research that addressed predictors of e-mail usage in organizations. It was argued that managers whose choice of media reflected the equivocality or uncertainty of the task were perceived to be more competent. Some researchers (Trevino et al., 1990) found support for this argument, but many others did not (e.g. El-Shinnawy and Markus, 1997). One of the early criticisms of the model was that, like social presence theory, it assumed that media richness was considered to be an objective dimension; that is, each medium provided the same amount of richness, predetermined by the inherent attributes of the technology, regardless of who was using it (Culnan and Markus, 1997). Other scholars proposed that media richness was a subjective dimension. For example, e-mail may be perceived as a richer medium by people experienced with that technology than by those who are not. Still others noted that most tasks involved varying degrees of uncertainty and equivocality and that it was often not feasible to parse the task into subtasks that were uniformly high or low in terms of their uncertainty or equivocality. As such, for these unbundled tasks it did not make much sense to dictate the use of lean or rich media.

Social presence theory and media richness theory were influential early attempts to understand media choice among group members. The lack of consistent empirical support for these theories was attributed to the theories' assumptions about ascribing objective attributes (social presence or media richness) to different communication technologies. As a result, alternative media selection theories were put forward that could account for these inconsistent findings.

One such theoretical formulation was the *social influence model*. Fulk et al. (1990) contended that the media richness model is more normative than descriptive of communication patterns in organizations. They argued that individual perceptions of the information richness of various media can vary, and that it was important to measure those perceptions rather than to rely solely on an objective assessment. They contended that objective features of media richness can and do influence individual perceptions of media richness, but there are other sources of such influence, such as social interaction. Drawing upon earlier research on social learning theory and social information processing theory, they argued that social interaction in the workplace shapes

the creation of shared meanings, and that those shared meanings provide an important basis for shared patterns of media selection (Fulk et al., 1990; Schmitz and Fulk, 1991).

The social influence model hypothesized that media perceptions and use: (1) are subject to social influence; (2) may be subjectively or retrospectively rationalized; (3) are not necessarily aimed at maximizing efficiency; and (4) may be designed to preserve or create ambiguity to achieve strategic goals. Schmitz and Fulk (1991) found that perceived (as distinct from objectively defined) e-mail richness predicted individuals' e-mail assessments and usage and that the opinions of colleagues influenced others' media assessments. These results supported the notion that other group members can influence how individuals perceive and use technology.

The social influence model of media selection explicitly recognized the role of group members' communication networks in shaping their perception of media richness. An important implication, not addressed by the social influence theory, was how media selection in turn influenced the subsequent structure of the communication network itself (Contractor and Eisenberg, 1990). For instance, group members may be socially influenced by other members in their primarily face-to-face communication network to begin using e-mail. However, once these members begin to use e-mail, the new contacts available through this new medium may enlarge and possibly modify their pre-existing communication network. That is, it is possible that the networks that socially influence individuals' media choices may in turn occasion a restructuring in their communication network. In essence, this observation points to a 'media effect' resulting from a 'media choice'. The following section describes an influential stream of research on the effects of media use on groups.

Media choice theories may be rendered less relevant today by developments in technologies. Increasingly, the convergence to a unified multimodal (audio, video, text and graphic) forum for communication makes interest in the distinctions between media, and hence the question of media choice, more complex. Not only can mobile phone users talk with others synchronously, but most can also leave a voice mail, text message, send photos, e-mail, and video conference. Unlike the context in which media selection theories were developed, today it is increasingly plausible for group members to simultaneously communicate via multiple modalities through a single device.

Media Effects

Hiltz and Turoff (1978) were among the first to describe differences between face-to-face and computer-mediated interaction in terms of social and psychological processes, and to discuss the importance of task–media contingencies. Hiltz and Turoff argued that groups communicating via computer had access to a narrower band of communication than groups communicating face-to-face. For example, non-verbal communication and paralanguage either were not available or were substantially reduced in computer-mediated communication. In some situations, such narrowband communication allowed information to be communicated with more precision and less noise, and afforded the opportunity for rational judgement processes to operate in the group with less intrusion of non-rational considerations. In other situations, computer conferencing needed to be supplemented by other media in which non-verbal communication and paralanguage were available. They were also among the first to present empirical findings that explored the effects of computer conferencing on the distribution of participation among members, on the amount of task and social communication, and on user responses to the availability and their satisfaction with the system (Hiltz et al., 1986).

Kiesler et al. (1984) provided a theoretical rationale as to why and how groups will differ when they use computer-mediated as compared with face-to-face communication. They proposed that computer-mediated communication depersonalizes the interaction process, with several concomitant effects. Individuals tend to lose mental sight of their interaction partners. At the same time, they lose access to a variety of cues that provide feedback to members regarding the impact of their behaviour on interaction

partners, their status and their individuality. Thus, computer-mediated communication removes substantial social information and eliminates much of the feedback that people ordinarily communicate to one another face-to-face. This can have both positive and negative influences on the interaction processes, task outcomes and responses of users (Sproull and Kiesler, 1991).

People feel less inhibited when interacting through a computer network as a result of the reduction in social cues that provide information regarding one's status in the group. Therefore, participants concentrate more on the messages and less on the persons involved in the communication. Individuals feel less committed to what they say, less concerned about it, and less worried about how it will be received by their communication partners. Because people communicating electronically are less aware of social differences, they feel a greater sense of anonymity and detect less individuality in others. As a consequence, individuals engaged in computer-mediated group interaction tend to:

- feel more anonymous and detect less individuality in their communication partners;
- participate more equally (because low-status members are less inhibited);
- focus more on task and instrumental aspects and less on personal and social aspects of interaction (because the context is depersonalized);
- communicate more negative and more uninhibited messages (because they are less concerned with politeness norms that tend to regulate communication in face-to-face groups); and
- experience more difficulty in attaining group consensus (both because of elimination of much interpersonal feedback, and because of reduced concern with social norms).

All of these effects have been demonstrated empirically (for a review, see Kiesler and Sproull, 1992), and will be revisited in greater detail later in this chapter.

McGrath and Hollingshead (1993, 1994), building on the work described above and applying it to work groups, maintained that group interaction and performance are greatly affected by the type and difficulty of the task that the group is performing, and that the effects of technology on group interaction and performance interact with task type. They hypothesized that the effectiveness of a group on a task will vary with the fit between the richness of the information that can be transmitted using that system's technology and the information richness requirements of the group's task. However, as groups developed more experience with a given communication technology, the richness of the information that could be transmitted effectively via that technology would increase.

McGrath and Hollingshead posited that group tasks differed in their information richness requirements. Information richness referred to how much the information contains surplus emotional, attitudinal, normative and other meanings, beyond the literal cognitive denotations of the symbols used to express it. They also posited that communication media differed in the richness of the information that they can and do convey. Face-to-face communication among interpersonally involved humans was the richest medium; communication in written form among strangers was the least rich. Computer communication among group members inexperienced with the technology is at the low-richness end of that continuum.

Drawing from McGrath's (1984) task typology, McGrath and Hollingshead hypothesized that groups working on generate tasks (e.g. simple brainstorming tasks) do not require the transmission of evaluative and emotional content. As a result, computer-supported groups may brainstorm more effectively than face-to-face groups. At the other end of the continuum, groups negotiating and resolving conflicts of views or interests may require the transmission of maximally rich information, including not only 'facts' but also values, attitudes, emotions, etc. As a result, groups interacting face-to-face should perform such tasks more effectively than groups interacting via computer. In between the two ends of the continuum are intellective tasks that have a correct answer or decision-making tasks that do not

have a correct answer, which may require some intermediary level of information richness. The predictions for generate tasks and negotiation tasks received empirical support (Gallupe et al., 1991; Hollingshead et al., 1993; Valacich et al., 1994), but not those for intellective and decision-making tasks (Hollingshead et al., 1993; Straus and McGrath, 1994).

McGrath and Hollingshead (1994) also predicted that communication technologies could provide information of increasing richness over time, as groups learned how to embed additional emotional, attitudinal, normative and other meaning through continued experience.

In summary, the theoretical arguments reviewed in this section offer three related perspectives on how technologies may influence the processes and outcomes of groups. While they vary in their levels of sophistication and theoretical complexity, all three theoretical approaches to media effects are based on the premise that technological attributes of different media influence key aspects of the interaction process. These key aspects include the availability of non-verbal cues, the potential for anonymous contributions, the ability to communicate status differentials, and the information richness of the medium. These key aspects in turn helped or hindered the group's interaction process (such as amount of participation, distribution of participation and negativity in communication on 'flaming'), as well as the group's outcomes (such as consensus, accuracy and speed of decision-making).

As such these theoretical perspectives on media effects acknowledge a modicum of technological determinism. Not unlike the media choice theories of social presence and media richness, discussed in the previous section, the theories of media effects described in this section do not privilege a socially constructed explanation for understanding media effects. The following section offers a theoretical framework that explicitly recognizes the social nature of technology and advocates an inextricable interrelatedness between media choice and media effects.

Adaptive Structuration Theory

Adaptive structuration theory (AST), proposed by Poole and DeSanctis (1990) and inspired by the influential theoretical contributions of Giddens' (1984) structuration theory, stresses the importance of group interaction processes, both in determining group outcomes and in mediating the effects of any given technology. Essentially, a social technology presents a structure of rules and operations to a group, but the group does not passively choose the technology in its pre-existing form. Rather, the group actively adapts the technology to its own ends, resulting in a restructuring of the technology as it is meshed with the group's own interaction system. Thus, a technology can be thought of as a set of social practices that emerge and evolve over time.

From this point of view, the structure of a group is not a permanent, concrete set of relations between members and their tasks. Rather, the structure is an evolving set of rules and resources available to them to produce and reproduce the apparently stable interaction systems that we observe. Thus, there is a recursive process between the structures (or the rules and resources in a group) and the systems (the interaction patterns in the groups). The rules or resources in the group shape the interaction patterns among group members. The interaction patterns among the group members, in turn, reify or subvert the rules and resources in the group. This recursive process is called adaptive structuration.

The rules and resources that groups use in the structuration process are sometimes created on the fly by the group, but more often they are *faithfully appropriated* by the group based on the social context in which it is embedded. *Appropriation* is the process by which a group selects features of a technology and socially constructs their meaning. It is through such appropriation that a group can choose to use a new technology. In some cases the group may not appropriate a technology in ways that were intended by the designers of the technology. This situation is referred to as an *ironic appropriation*. For instance, a group may have access to a group decision support system (GDSS) that provides them with an opportunity to vote on their ideas. The voting tool is intended by the designers of the technology to facilitate democratic deliberation among group members. However, in some instances members of a group may use the voting tool to prematurely close off discussion of an issue. This action would illustrate an ironic appropriation of the GDSS. By faithfully or ironically appropriating a technology, each group invests meaning in, and thereby adapts for its use, the rules and resources that it draws upon. Both technology and context affect group processes and outcomes because they affect this appropriation process.

Empirical research has shown that different, but seemingly similar, groups appropriate the same technology in different ways (DeSanctis and Poole, 1997; Poole and DeSanctis, 1992; for a review see DeSanctis and Poole, 1994). Zack and McKenney (1995) offer an example of work in this tradition. They examined the appropriation of the same group authoring and messaging computer system by the managing editorial groups of two morning newspapers owned by the same parent corporation. Drawing upon Poole and DeSanctis' (1990) theory of adaptive structuration, they discovered that the two groups' appropriation of the technology, as indexed by their communication networks, differed in accordance with the different contexts at the two locations. Further, they found evidence that the groups' performance outcomes for similar tasks were mediated by these interaction patterns.

Adaptive structuration theory continues to be an increasingly influential perspective to understand the socially constructed ways in which groups' choice of media and the effects of media on groups coevolve. It provides a powerful analytic framework to account for stability and change in a group's appropriation of new media. While the utility of a structurational perspective to the study of groups' use of new media is compelling, there continues to be a debate about the extent to which empirical studies offer a 'test' as opposed to an illustration of structuration theory's ability to explain the unfolding of complex processes (DeSanctis and Poole, 1994). Indeed, in a review of empirical studies from a structurational perspective, one would be hard pressed to identify a single work which failed to find support for adaptive structuration theory. Such overwhelming endorsement of a theory belies an underlying concern about the potential falsifiability of the theory. An appropriate challenge therefore would be to come up with specific predictions from the theory that, if they were not empirically validated, would plausibly represent a refutation of the premises of adaptive structuration theory.

Complexity theory, discussed in the next section, offers a novel and useful approach to translate the richly evocative, but highly abbreviated, verbal explications of adaptive structuration theory into precise, falsifiable hypotheses that can be empirically validated (Poole, 1997).

Groups as Complex Systems

In the past decade there has been a plethora of scholarship calling for the extension of complexity theory – arguably a mainstay of many disciplines in the physical and life sciences – to social sciences in general, and to the study of groups in particular (Arrow et al., 2000; Contractor and Seibold, 1993; Contractor and Whitbred, 1997; Gersick, 1991; McGrath, 1991; Monge and Contractor, 2003). The motivation for this call stems from a widely shared frustration with extant theories, which have proven to be inadequate at untangling with precision the complexity in group processes. The phenomena described in verbal expositions of, say, adaptive structuration theory invoke a multitude of factors that are highly interconnected, often via complex, non-linear, dynamic relationships. Lamenting the failed promise of earlier forays into systems theory, Poole notes, 'Most often, systems theory became a metaphor, rather than an instrument of analysis' (1997: 50). Two streams of research that attempt to go beyond the use of complexity theory as a metaphor (Contractor, 1999) have been developed to deal with the complexity

of groups' use of new media: groups as self-organizing systems (Contractor and Seibold, 1993; Contractor and Whitbred, 1997) and groups as complex, adaptive and dynamic systems (Arrow et al., 2000; Monge and Contractor, 2003).

Groups as Self-organizing Systems

In general terms, 'self-organizing systems theory (SOST) seeks to explain the emergence of patterned behaviour in systems that are initially in a state of disorganization. It offers a conceptual framework to explicitly articulate the underlying generative mechanisms and to systematically examine the processes by which these mechanisms generate, sustain and change existing structures or elaborate new structures' (Contractor and Seibold, 1993: 536).

Ilya Prigogine and his colleagues proposed the theory of self-organization. In an effort that contributed to a Nobel Prize, Prigogine and his colleagues (Glansdorff and Prigogine, 1971) mathematically proved that systems that exhibit emergence of spontaneous order must meet the following logical requirements.

1   At least one of the components in the system must exhibit autocatalysis, i.e. self-referencing.
2   At least two of the components in the system must be mutually causal.
3   The system must be open to the environment with respect to the exchange of energy and matter.
4   The system must operate in a far-from-equilibrium condition.

These four requirements offer, at a very abstract level, the conditions under which any system can self-organize. Our interests here are in applying these concepts to the study of groups using new media. Contractor and Seibold (1993) developed a self-organizing systems model for groups' use of group decision support systems (GDSS). They developed a model based on the theoretical mechanisms specified by adaptive structuration theory (Poole and DeSanctis, 1990; discussed in the previous section) about the recursive interrelationship between the structures (the rules and resources within the group) and the systems (the interaction patterns among the group members). Contractor and Seibold (1993: 537–8) specified four generative mechanisms that were consistent with the theoretical tenets of adaptive structuration theory and met the logical requirements of self-organizing systems theory.

1 Members' expertise (or resources) with the task will reinforce the content and pattern of their communication during GDSS-based discussions.
2 The content and pattern of members' communication will reinforce their perceptions of the group's norms for structuring the GDSS-based discussion.
3 Members' expertise (or resources) with GDSS will reinforce their perceptions of the group's norms for structuring the GDSS-based discussions.
4 Members' perceptions of the group's norms for structuring the GDSS-based discussion will reinforce the content and pattern of their communication.

Using simulations, they showed that based on these four theoretical mechanisms the group's use of GDSS would self-organize only under a very specific range of initial conditions. A group using GDSS was considered to have self-organized when the group's structures (that is, its members' perceptions of the rules) were stable and the group members' interaction patterns were reproducing and reinforcing (rather than subverting) these stable structures. The simulation also provided precise conditions under which the groups would *not* successfully appropriate the technology. That is, the group might initially attempt to use the technology but would then discontinue its use. These results, theoretically grounded in adaptive structuration theory and logically consistent with self-organizing systems theory, represent plausible occurrences in groups' use of new media. They also respond to one of the criticisms levelled against adaptive structuration theory by making its explanations more amenable to falsification. In general terms, the approach illustrates how self-organizing systems theory can

offer the logical conditions and the analytic framework to discover precise, empirically falsifiable hypotheses about the use (and lack thereof) of new media by groups.

Groups as Complex, Adaptive and Dynamic Systems

Arrow et al. (2000) have proposed a general theory of complex systems, which embeds technology as one aspect of the system. This theory builds on the time, interaction and performance (TIP) theory proposed by McGrath (1991). TIP theory assumes that groups pursue multiple functions for multiple projects by means of complex time/activity paths. Arrow et al. (2000) extend this theory by proposing that all groups act in the service of two generic functions: (1) *to complete group projects* and (2) to *fulfill member needs*. A group's success in pursuing these two functions affects and depends on the viability and integrity of the group as a system. Thus, *maintaining system integrity* becomes a third function, instrumental to the other two. A group's system integrity in turn affects its ability to complete group projects and fulfill member needs.

Groups include three types of elements: (1) people who become group *members*; (2) goals that are embodied in group *projects*; and (3) resources that get transformed into group *technologies*. Technologies differ in how much they facilitate or constrain interpersonal activity, task activity and procedural activity; and in how effectively they support different instrumental functions (i.e. processing of information, management of conflict and consensus, and motivation, regulation and coordination of member behaviours).

A group pursues its functions by creating and enacting a coordinated pattern of member–task–tool relations, its *coordination network*. The full coordination network includes six component networks: (1) the *member network*, or pattern of member–member relations (such as status relations); (2) the *task network*, or pattern of task–task relations (e.g. the required sequence for completion of a set of tasks); (3) the *tool network*, or pattern of tool–tool relations (e.g. the procedure by which a

technology can be used most efficiently);
(4) the *labour network*, or pattern of member–
task relations (i.e. who is supposed to do what);
(5) the *role network*, or pattern of member–
tool relations (i.e. how members do their tasks);
and (6) the *job network*, or pattern of task–tool
relations (e.g. what piece of equipment must
be used for a given task).

The life course of a group can be characterized by three logically ordered modes that are
conceptually distinct but have fuzzy temporal
boundaries: *formation, operation* and *metamorphosis*. As a group forms, people, intentions and resources become organized into
an initial coordination network of relations
among members, projects and technology
that demarcates that group as a bounded
social entity. As a group operates over time
in the service of group projects and member
needs, its members elaborate, enact, monitor
and modify the coordination network established during formation. Groups both learn
from their own experience and adapt to
events occurring in their environment. If and
when a group undergoes metamorphosis, it
dissolves or is transformed into a different
social entity.

OVERVIEW OF MAJOR
EMPIRICAL FINDINGS

A number of scholars have written literature
reviews that examine communication technologies and groups (e.g. Benbasat and
Lim, 1993; Hollingshead and McGrath,
1995; Kiesler and Sproull, 1992; Kraemer
and Pinsonneault, 1990; McGrath and
Hollingshead, 1994; McLeod, 1992, 1996;
Seibold et al., 1994; Williams, 1977). Most
of these reviews have compared the interaction processes and outcomes of computer-
mediated groups with those of face-to-face
groups. Several of those reviews have reached
the same conclusions about the state of knowledge in this area: namely, that more theory-
guided and programmatic research is needed (e.g.
Hollingshead and McGrath, 1995; McLeod,
1992).

Interaction Patterns

Many studies have revealed that groups
interacting via computers have more equal
participation among members than groups
interacting face-to-face (e.g. Clapper et al.,
1991; Daly, 1993; Dubrovsky et al., 1991;
George et al., 1990; Hiltz et al., 1986; McLeod,
1992; Rice, 1984; Siegel et al., 1986; Straus,
1996; Straus and McGrath, 1994; Zigurs et al.,
1988). As described earlier, the general explanation for the effect is that people feel less
inhibited when interacting through a computer network as a result of the reduction in
social cues that provide information regarding
one's status in the group. Because people communicating electronically are less aware of
social differences, they feel a greater sense of
anonymity and detect less individuality in
others (Sproull and Kiesler, 1991). It is important to note some common elements across
this set of studies. These studies were conducted during one experimental session with
ad hoc groups consisting of students in a laboratory setting. However, it is also important
to note that this finding was observed across a
variety of communication technologies.

Many studies have also showed no evidence
of the participation equalization effect in
computer-mediated groups (Berdahl and Craig,
1996; Hollingshead, 1996b; Lea and Spears,
1991; McLeod and Liker, 1992; McLeod et al.,
1997; Saunders et al., 1994; Spears and Lea,
1992; Watson et al., 1988; Weisband, 1992;
Weisband et al., 1995). In fact, most showed
that status differences among participants were
displayed in their interaction in the computer-
mediated setting. One explanation for the
inconsistency of findings across studies is that
status differences among members within the
groups may have been differentially salient
across studies. When members' identities were
known or were available visually, the status
differences in the number of contributions
and the perceived influence of those contributions were maintained in the computer-
mediated setting. When they were not or when
members' contributions were anonymous, the
participation equalization effect was more
likely to occur.

It is also possible that the participation equalization may be an indication of how the medium reduces the baseline of each member's participation rather than how the medium leads to increased participation of low-status members during the group discussion (McGrath and Hollingshead, 1994; Spears and Lea, 1994). It takes more time to type a message on a computer network than it does to say that same message verbally. In the experiments cited earlier, the computer sessions were at least as long as those face-to-face group meetings; however, the amount and the rate of communication in the computer-mediated setting were much less. Another possible technological explanation for greater egalitarian participation patterns in computer-mediated settings is that electronic group members have the ability to participate without interruption, since turn-taking is not a norm in a computer-mediated environment (Weisband et al., 1995).

A number of studies have found that computer-mediated groups exchange less information and are less likely to repeat information in their decisions than face-to-face groups (Hollingshead, 1996a, 1996b; McLeod et al., 1997; Straus and McGrath, 1994). In some cases, this reduction can lead to poorer outcomes for newly formed groups (cf. Hollingshead, 1996a, 1996b).

Performance

Very few studies have demonstrated that groups communicating via computer perform better than groups interacting face-to-face, although many have demonstrated that computer-mediated groups perform less well than or equally as well as face-to-face groups (for reviews see McGrath and Hollingshead, 1994; McLeod, 1992, 1996). Even though computer-mediated groups generate less communication and use less information in their decisions, they take longer to make them (Hollingshead, 1996a). They are also less likely to reach consensus (for reviews see Hollingshead and McGrath, 1995; Kiesler and Sproul, 1992).

As described earlier, there seems to be an interaction effect of task and technology on the quality of group performance. Computer groups produce more ideas of higher quality on idea generation tasks. Face-to-face groups tend to have higher-quality products on intellective and negotiation tasks. However, it may be the structure that is imposed by the technology rather than the technology itself that is responsible for this effect (Hollingshead and McGrath, 1995). The task structure may include: procedures that simplify the handling of complex information; procedures that explicate agenda, thus making group process more organized; and procedures that expose conflict and help the group to deal with it. Some research showed that a paper and pencil version of the task structure imposed by the technology (i.e. without electronic communication) gave higher-quality decisions than the same task structure provided by a GPSS, which in turn was higher than the no-structure face-to-face condition (Hollingshead and McGrath, 1995; Watson et al., 1988). In some cases, newly formed groups on computers may have problems with task structure that require more complex information processing (Hollingshead, 1996a).

Longitudinal research comparing the impact of computer-mediated and face-to-face communication over time has brought into question previous findings of significant differences in performance between face-to-face and computer-mediated groups. That research has shown that computer-mediated communication hinders the interaction process and performance of groups initially, but over time, groups can adjust successfully to their mode of communication (see McGrath et al., 1993 and Arrow et al., 1996 for overviews). In addition, work on the interpersonal and relationship aspects of computer-mediated communication over time complements this finding. Walther and Burgoon (1992) showed that members of computer-mediated groups felt less connected to one another initially, but over time, members of computer-mediated groups expressed more positive feelings about one another that approximated those expressed by members of face-to-face groups. The transient effects of technology were also illustrated in a longitudinal study comparing the developments of norms in groups using GDSS with groups not using GDSS. Contractor et al. (1996) found that while members of non-GDSS groups were initially more likely than members of GDSS groups to socially influence one another's perceptions of the group's norms, this difference dissipated over time. That is, in the long term, groups using GDSS were no more likely than groups not using GDSS to socially influence one another's perceptions of the groups' norms.

THE RECONCEPTUALIZATION OF GROUPS AND NEW MEDIA AS KNOWLEDGE NETWORKS

While it should be evident that the study of groups and new media is a vibrant area for research, we now return to the opening statements of this chapter about the theoretical and analytic challenges that confront scholars who consider the ways in which the 'new' new media of the twenty-first century will influence our ability to organize in groups. In conclusion, we offer a reconceptualization of groups' use of new media from a knowledge networks perspective.

From Knowledge Management to Knowledge Networks

Knowledge management is a critical concern for contemporary organizations, and it is expected to become increasingly important in the future (Nonaka and Takeuchi, 1995). It has long been recognized that computers could increase the range, depth and speed with which information could be acquired, processed, presented for use and shared for collaborative efforts. However, research in this area has given little attention to theoretical or conceptual issues about information acquisition, processing and integration, and even less attention to theoretical issues about the antecedents and consequences of different patterns of information distribution within work groups, and the conditions under which information can be and is easily shared among group members. Recent developments

in technologies have shown their potential as knowledge management systems, although little is known about the social challenges and motivations for group members to use these systems effectively (Hollingshead et al., 2002). These challenges call for a knowledge network approach (Contractor and Monge, 2002; Monge and Contractor, 2001, 2003) and knowledge-based theories to understand groups' use of new media.

Groups as Knowledge Networks

The proliferation of digital technologies has dramatically changed the nature of work in groups. These technologies, as described previously, have the potential to provide many benefits to groups by linking people who have common goals and interests but are separated in time and space. They may enable organizations to develop effective teams from workers who are geographically distributed. Today, in stark contrast to just a decade ago, organizations consider having employees located in time zones far removed from one another (such as California, Ireland and India) as a competitive advantage rather than a disadvantage. Members of distributed work teams can work round the clock in order to meet the competitive demands of a global marketplace. In some cases the members of these teams are 'e-lancers' (electronic freelancers) who coalesce on a short-term project and then disperse. In other cases, the technologies have the potential to enable the organization to hire and retain the best people, regardless of location (Townsend et al., 1996). These changes have led scholars to call for a reconceptualization of groups as much more fluid, dynamic, multiplex and activity based (Goodman and Wilson, 2000).

Clearly these new technologies have the potential to nurture a team by linking the members not only to one another but also to a large number of internal and external knowledge repositories. Conceptually, therefore, it is increasingly useful to consider the group and its members as a network of agents, where some of the agents are human agents while others are non-human agents (such as knowledge repositories, avatars and webbots). Human agents communicate with one another by retrieving and allocating information relevant to their collective tasks. An increasingly vexing question that group members face in this networked environment is not which medium to use (as was addressed by earlier theories of media choice), but rather which agent to use.

Groups and the media they use can be usefully reconceptualized as a *knowledge network* (Contractor and Monge, 2002; Katz et al., 2004, 2005; Monge and Contractor, 2003). A network is made up of a set of nodes and relations between these nodes. The nodes that contain the knowledge can be people, databases, data files or other forms of repositories. The relations are the communication relations (that is, publishing, retrieving, allocating) among the nodes. The location of knowledge within this network of agents can vary along a continuum from centralized, where knowledge resides with only one agent, to distributed, where knowledge exists among many agents (Farace et al., 1977). Distributed knowledge may refer to the parts of a larger knowledge base, each possessed by separate actors within the network. In this form of distributed knowledge, actors bring relatively unique, non-redundant knowledge that enables a collective to accomplish complex tasks. Distributed knowledge occurs at many levels in the empirical world, including work groups, large-scale project teams, and interorganizational strategic alliances. Alternatively, distributed knowledge may refer to the flow or diffusion of knowledge, which increases the level of knowledge among all actors.

Communication networks, actual knowledge networks, and cognitive knowledge networks are different ways of conceptualizing the network of agents. Communication networks represent the degree to which individual agents interact with other agents in the network. Actual knowledge networks represent the actual distribution of knowledge among the network of agents. Cognitive knowledge networks represent individuals' perceptions of the distribution of knowledge in the network of agents. Knowledge networks are dynamic, in terms of both agents and linkages. Agents join or leave a knowledge network on the basis of tasks to be accomplished, and their levels of interests, resources and commitments. The links within the knowledge network are also likely to change on the basis of evolving tasks, the distribution of knowledge within the network, or changes in the agents' cognitive knowledge networks. New media, such as intranets, serve both as the nodes and as the infrastructure that supports the development of relations in the network and as the nodes in the network. In our own research, we have applied a knowledge network perspective to theories that investigate new media use in groups and organizations (Contractor and Monge, 2002; Hollingshead et al., 2002; Monge and Contractor, 2001, 2003). We believe there is tremendous potential for the development and extension of theories which seek to explain the development of a group's use of media as a knowledge network of human and non-human agents. The knowledge network perspective is especially well suited to test multiple theories and their contradictory or complementary influences on the evolution of the groups. Knowledge networks and their defining characteristics can be represented and analysed exceptionally well using techniques developed within the field of social network analysis (Wasserman and Faust, 1994). Further, recent advances enable us to assess group processes and outcomes using multi-theoretical multilevel (MTML) models (Contractor and Monge, 2003; Contractor, et al., in press; Monge and Contractor, 2003). These models enable researchers to use multiple theories to explain the dynamics of groups across multiple levels of analyses (individual, dyads, triads, groups). It is difficult to predict the diverse and unanticipated ways in which new media will configure and reconfigure the ways in which we organize in groups. Regardless of their forms, a knowledge network perspective offers a compelling theoretical and methodological apparatus that we will need to advance our understanding of the interrelationships between new media and organizing as groups.

REFERENCES

Alexander, S.C., Peterson, J. and Hollingshead, A.B. (2002) 'Support at your keyboard: a study of on-line support groups', in L. Frey (ed.), *Group Communication in Context*, vol. 2. Hillsdale, NJ: Erlbaum. pp. 309–334.

Arrow, H., Berdahl, J.L., Bouas, K.S., Craig, K.M., Cummings, A., Lebie, L., McGrath, J.E., O'Connor, K.M., Rhoades, J.A. and Schlosser, A. (1996) 'Time, technology, and groups: an integration', *Computer Supported Cooperative Work*, 4: 253–61.

Arrow, H., McGrath, J.E. and Berdahl, J.L. (2000) *Small Groups as Complex Systems: Formation, Coordination, Development, and Adaptation.* Thousand Oaks, CA: Sage.

Bar, F., Borrus, M. and Hanson, W. (1998) 'Web portfolios: leveraging intranets, extranets, and the Internet for strategic gain'. Stanford University working paper.

Benbasat, I. and Lim, L. (1993) 'The effects of group, task, context, and technology variables on the usefulness of group support systems: a meta-analysis of experimental studies', *Small Group Research*, 24: 430–62.

Berdahl, J.L. and Craig, K.L. (1996) 'Equality of participation and influence in groups: the effects of communication medium and sex composition', *Computer Supported Cooperative Work*, 4: 179–202.

Clapper, D.L., McLean, E.R. and Watson, R.T. (1991) 'An experimental investigation of the effect of group decision support on normative influence in small groups', in J.I. de Gross, I. Benbasat, G. DeSanctis and C.M. Beath (eds), *Proceedings of the Twelfth International Conference on Information Systems.* New York. pp. 273–82.

Contractor, N.S. (1999) 'Self-organizing systems research in the social sciences: reconciling the metaphors and the models', *Management Communication Quarterly*, 13: 154–66.

Contractor, N.S. (2002) 'New media and organizing: introduction', in S. Livingstone and L. Lievrouw (eds), *Handbook of New Media*. London: Sage. pp. 201–5.

Contractor, N.S. and Bishop, A.P. (2000) 'Reconfiguring community networks: the case of Prairie KNOW', in T. Ishida (ed.), *Digital Cities: Technologies, Experiences, and Future Perspectives*. Berlin: Springer. pp. 151–64.

Contractor, N.S. and Eisenberg, E.M. (1990) 'Communication networks and new media in organizations', in J. Fulk and C.W. Steinfield (eds), *Organizations and Communication Technology.* Newbury Park, CA: Sage. pp. 145–74.

Contractor, N.S. and Monge, P.R. (2002) 'Managing knowledge networks', *Management Communication Quarterly*, 16: 249–58.

Contractor, N.S. and Monge, P.R. (2003) 'Using multitheoretical multilevel models to study adversarial network', *Dynamic Social Network Modeling and Analysis: Workshop Summary and Papers.* Washington, DC: National Research Council. pp. 324–44.

Contractor, N.S. and Seibold, D.R. (1993) 'Theoretical frameworks for the study of structuring processes in group decision support systems: adaptive structuration theory and self-organizing systems theory', *Human Communication Research*, 19: 528–63.

Contractor, N.S. and Whitbred, R. (1997) 'Decision development in work groups: a comparison of contingency and self-organizing systems perspectives', in G. Barnett and L. Thayer (eds), *Organizational Communication: Emerging Perspectives. V: The Renaissance in Systems Thinking.* Greenwich, CT: Ablex. pp. 83–104.

Contractor, N.S., Seibold, D.R. and Heller, M.A. (1996) 'Interactional influence in the structuring of media use in groups: influence of members' perceptions of group decision support system use', *Human Communication Research*, 22: 451–81.

Contractor, N.S., Wasserman, S. and Faust, K. (in press) 'Testing multitheoretical multilevel hypotheses about organizational networks: an analytic framework and empirical example', *Academy of Management Review.*

Contractor, N.S., Zink, D. and Chan, M. (1998) 'I KNOW: A tool to assist and study the creation, maintenance and dissolution of knowledge networks', in T. Ishida (ed.), *Community Computing and Support Systems. Lecture Notes in Computer Science 1319.* pp. 201–17.

Culnan, M.J. and Markus, M.L. (1987) 'Information technologies', in F.M. Jablin and L.L. Putnam (eds), *Handbook of Organizational Communication: An Interdisciplinary Perspective.* Newbury Park, CA: Sage. pp. 420–43.

Daft, R.L. and Lengel, R.H. (1986) 'Organizational information requirements, media richness and structural design', *Management Science*, 32: 554–71.

Daly, B. (1993) 'The influence of face-to-face versus computer-mediated communication channels on collective induction', *Accounting, Management & Information Technology*, 3 (1): 1–22.

DeSanctis, G. and Gallupe, R.B. (1987) 'A foundation for the study of group decision support systems', *Management Science*, 33: 589–609.

DeSanctis, G. and Poole, M.S. (1994) 'Capturing the complexity in advanced technology use: adaptive structuration theory', *Organization Science*, 5: 121–47.

DeSanctis, G. and Poole, M.S. (1997) 'Transitions in teamwork in new organizational forms', in *Advances in Group Processes*, vol. 14. Greenwich, CT: JAI. pp. 157–76.

Dubrovsky, V.J., Kiesler, S. and Sethna, B.N. (1991) 'The equalization phenomenon: status effects in computer-mediated and face-to-face decision making groups', *Human–Computer Interaction*, 6: 119–46.

El-Shinnawy, M. and Markus, M.L. (1997) 'The poverty of media richness theory: explaining people's preferences for electronic mail and voice mail', *International Journal of Human Computer Studies*, 46: 443–67.

Farace, R.V., Monge, P.R. and Russell, H.M. (1977) *Communicating and Organizing*. Reading, MA: Addison-Wesley.

Fulk, J., Schmitz, J. and Steinfield, C.W. (1990) 'A social influence model of technology use', in J. Fulk and C.W. Steinfield (eds), *Organizations and Communication Technology*. Newbury Park, CA: Sage. pp. 117–40.

Gallupe, R.B., Bastianutti, L.M. and Cooper, W.H. (1991) 'Unblocking brainstorms', *Journal of Applied Psychology*, 76 (1): 137–42.

George, J., Easton, G., Nunamaker, J. and Northcraft, G. (1990) 'A study of collaborative group work with and without computer-based support', *Information Systems Research*, 1 (4): 394–415.

Gersick, C.J.G. (1991) 'Revolutionary change theories: a multilevel exploration of the punctuated equilibrium paradigm', *Academy of Management Review*, 32: 274–309.

Giddens, A. (1984) *The Constitution of Society: Outline of the Theory of Structuration*. Berkeley, CA: University of California Press.

Glansdorff, P. and Prigogine, I. (1971) *Thermodynamic Study of Structure, Stability and Fluctuations*. New York: Wiley.

Goodman, P.S. and Wilson, J.M. (2000) 'Substitutes for socialization', in M.A. Neale, E.A. Mannix and T. Griffith (eds), *Research on Managing Groups and Teams*. Vol. 3: *Technology*. Stamford, CT: JAI. pp. 53–78.

Hiltz, S.R. and Turoff, M. (1978) *The Network Nation: Human Communication via Computer*. Reading, MA: Addison-Wesley.

Hiltz, S.R., Johnson, K. and Turoff, M. (1986) 'Experiments in group decision making. 1: Communications process and outcome in face-to-face vs. computerized conferences', *Human Communication Research*, 13: 225–52.

Hollingshead, A.B. (1996a) 'Information suppression and status persistence in group decision making: the effects of communication media', *Human Communication Research*, 23: 193–219.

Hollingshead, A.B. (1996b) 'The rank order effect: decision procedure, communication technology and group decisions', *Organizational Behavior and Human Decision Processes*, 68 (3): 1–13.

Hollingshead, A.B. (1998a) 'Retrieval processes in transactive memory systems', *Journal of Personality and Social Psychology*, 74: 659–71.

Hollingshead, A.B. (1998b) 'Distributed knowledge and transactive processes in groups', in M.A. Neale, E.A. Mannix and D.H. Gruenfeld (eds), *Research on Managing Groups and Teams*, Vol. 1. Greenwich, CT: JAI. pp. 103–23.

Hollingshead, A.B. (2001) 'Communication technologies, the Internet, and group research', in M.A. Hogg and Scott Tindale (eds), *Blackwell Handbook of Social Psychology: Group Processes*. Malden, MA: Blackwell. pp. 557–73.

Hollingshead, A.B. and McGrath, J.E. (1995) 'Computer-assisted groups: a critical review of the empirical research', in R.A. Guzzo and E. Salas (eds), *Team Effectiveness and Decision Making in Organizations*. San Francisco: Jossey-Bass. pp. 46–78.

Hollingshead, A.B., Fulk, J. and Monge, P. (2002) 'Fostering intranet knowledge-sharing: an integration of transactive memory and public goods approaches', in P. Hinds and S. Kiesler (eds), *Distributed Work: New Research on Working across Distance Using Technology*. Cambridge, MA: MIT Press.

Hollingshead, A.B., McGrath, J.E. and O'Connor, K.M. (1993) 'Group task performance and communication technology: a longitudinal study of computer-mediated versus face-to-face work groups', *Small Group Research*, 24: 307–33.

Jessup, L.M. and Valacich, J.E. (eds) (1993) *Group Support Systems: New Perspectives*. New York: Macmillan.

Katz, N., Lazer, D., Arrow, H. and Contractor, N. (2004) 'Network theory and small groups', *Small Group Research*, 35: 307–32.

Katz, N., Lazer, D., Arrow, H. and Contractor, N. (2005) 'The network perspective on small groups: theory and research', in M.S. Poole and A.B. Hollingshead (eds), *Theories of Small Groups:*

Interdisciplinary Perspectives. Newbury Park, CA: Sage.

Kiesler, S. and Sproull, L. (1992) 'Group decision making and technology', *Organizational Behavior and Human Decision Processes,* 52: 96–123.

Kiesler, S., Siegel, J. and McGuire, T.W. (1984) 'Social psychological aspects of computer-mediated communication', *American Psychologist,* 39: 1123–34.

Kraemer, K.L. and Pinsonneault, A. (1990) 'Technology and groups: assessments of the empirical research', in J. Galegher, R. Kraut and C. Egido (eds), *Intellectual Teamwork: Social and Technological Foundations of Cooperative Work.* Hillsdale, NJ: Erlbaum. pp. 373–404.

Lea, M. and Spears, R. (1991) 'Computer-mediated communication, de-individuation, and group decision making', *International Journal of Man–Machine Studies,* 34: 283–301.

Markus, M.L. and Robey, D. (1988) 'Information technology and organizational change: causal structure in theory and research', *Management Science,* 34: 583–98.

McGrath, J.E. (1984) *Groups, Interaction, and Performance.* Englewood Cliffs, NJ: Prentice-Hall.

McGrath, J.E. (1991) 'Time, interaction, and performance (TIP): a theory of groups', *Small Group Research,* 22: 147–74.

McGrath, J.E. and Hollingshead, A.B. (1993) 'Putting the "G" back in GSS: some theoretical issues about dynamic processes in groups with technological enhancements', in L.M. Jessup and J.E. Valacich (eds), *Group Support Systems: New Perspectives.* New York: Macmillan.

McGrath, J.E. and Hollingshead, A.B. (1994) *Groups Interacting with Technology.* Newbury Park, CA: Sage.

McGrath, J.E., Arrow, H., Gruenfeld, D.H., Hollingshead, A.B. and O'Connor, K.M. (1993) 'Groups, tasks, technology, and time: an integration', *Small Group Research,* 24: 406–20.

McLeod, P.L. (1992) 'An assessment of the experimental literature on the electronic support of group work: results of a meta-analysis', *Human–Computer Interaction,* 7 (3): 257–80.

McLeod, P.L. (1996) 'New communication technologies for group research: toward an integrative framework', in R. Hirokawa and M.S. Poole (eds), *Communication and Group Decision Making.* 2nd edn. Thousand Oaks, CA: Sage. pp. 426–62.

McLeod, P.L. and Liker, J.K. (1992) 'Electronic meeting systems: evidence from a low structure environment', *Information Systems Research,* 3: 195–223.

McLeod, P.L., Baron, R.S., Marti, M.W. and Kuh, Y. (1997) 'The eyes have it: minority influence in face-to-face and computer-mediated group discussion', *Journal of Applied Psychology,* 82: 706–18.

Monge, P.R. and Contractor, N.S. (2001) 'Emergence of communication networks', in F.M. Jablin and L.L. Putnam (eds), *New Handbook of Organizational Communication.* Newbury Park, CA: Sage. pp. 440–502.

Monge, P.R. and Contractor, N. (2003) *Theories of Communication Networks.* New York: Oxford University Press.

Nonaka, I. and Takeuchi, H. (1995) *The Knowledge-Creating Company: How Japanese Companies Create the Dynamics of Innovation.* New York: Oxford University Press.

Poole, M.S. (1997) 'A turn of the wheel: the case for renewal of systems inquiry in organizational communication research', in G. Barnett and L. Thayer (eds), *Organizational Communication: Emerging Perspectives. V: The Renaissance in Systems Thinking.* Greenwich, CT: Ablex. pp. 47–63.

Poole, M.S. and DeSanctis, G. (1990) 'Understanding the use of group decision support systems: the theory of adaptive structuration', in J. Fulk and C. Steinfield (eds), *Organizations and Communication Technology.* Newbury Park, CA: Sage. pp. 175–95.

Poole, M.S. and DeSanctis, G. (1992) 'Microlevel structuration in computer-supported group decision making', *Human Communication Research,* 19: 5–49.

Rice, R.E. (1984) 'Mediated group communication', in R.E. Rice and Associates (eds), *The New Media: Communication, Research, and Technology.* Beverly Hills, CA: Sage. pp. 129–54.

Saunders, C., Robey, D. and Vaverek, K. (1994) 'The persistence of status differentials in computer conferencing', *Human Communication Research,* 20: 443–72.

Schmitz, J. and Fulk, J. (1991) 'Organizational colleagues, media richness, and electronic mail: a test of the social influence model of technology use', *Communication Research,* 18: 487–523.

Seibold, D., Heller, M.A. and Contractor, N. (1994) 'Review and critique of empirical research on group decision support systems', in B. Kovacic (ed.), *Organizational Communication: New Perspectives.* Albany, NY: State University of New York Press. pp. 143–68.

Short, J.A., Williams, E. and Christie, B. (1976) *The Social Psychology of Telecommunications.* London: Wiley.

Siegel, J., Dubrovsky, V., Kiesler, S. and McGuire, T.W. (1986) 'Group processes in computer-mediated communication', *Organizational Behavior & Human Decision Processes*, 37: 157–87.

Spears, R. and Lea, M. (1992) 'Social influence and the influence of the "social" in computer-mediated communication', in M. Lea (ed.), *Contexts of Computer-mediated Communication*. London: Harvester-Wheatsheaf. pp. 30–65.

Spears, R. and Lea, M. (1994) 'Panacea or panopticon? The hidden power in computer-mediated communication', *Communication Research*, 21: 427–59.

Sproull, L.S. and Kiesler, S. (1991) *Connections: New Ways of Working in the Networked Organization*. Cambridge, MA: MIT Press.

Straus, S. (1996) 'Getting a clue: the effects of communication media and information distribution on participation and performance in computer-mediated and face-to-face groups', *Small Group Research*, 27: 115–42.

Straus, S. and McGrath, J.E. (1994) 'Does the medium matter? The interaction of task type and technology on group performance and member reactions', *Journal of Applied Psychology*, 79: 87–97.

Townsend, A.M., DeMarie, S.M. and Hendrickson, A.R. (1996) 'Are you ready for virtual teams?', *HR Magazine*, 41: 122–6.

Trevino, L.K., Daft, R.L. and Lengel, R.H. (1990) 'Understanding managers' media choices: a symbolic interactionist perspective', in J. Fulk and C.W. Steinfield (eds), *Organizations and Communication Technology*. Newbury Park, CA: Sage. pp. 71–94.

Valacich, J.S., Paranka, D., George, J.F. and Nunamaker, J.F. (1994) 'Communication concurrency and the new media: a new dimension for media richness', *Communication Research*, 20 (2): 249–76.

Walther, J.B. and Burgoon, J.K. (1992) 'Relational communication in computer-mediated interaction', *Human Communication Research*, 19: 50–88.

Wasserman, S. and Faust, K. (1994) *Social Network Analysis: Methods and Applications*. New York: Cambridge University Press.

Watson, R., DeSanctis, G. and Poole, M.S. (1988) 'Using a GDSS to facilitate group consensus: some intended and unintended consequences', *MIS Quarterly*, 12: 463–78.

Weisband, S.P. (1992) 'Group discussion and first advocacy effects in computer-mediated and face-to-face decision making groups', *Organizational Behavior and Human Decision Processes*, 53: 352–80.

Weisband, S.P., Schneider, S.K. and Connolly, T. (1995) 'Electronic communication and social information: status salience and status differences', *Academy of Management Journal*, 38: 1124–51.

Williams, E. (1977) 'Experimental comparisons of face-to-face and mediated communication: a review', *Psychological Bulletin*, 84 (5): 963–76.

Zack, M.H. and McKenney, J.L. (1995) 'Social context and interaction in ongoing computer-supported management groups', *Organization Science*, 6: 394–422.

Zigurs, I., Poole, M.S. and DeSanctis, G. (1988) 'A study of influence in computer-mediated group decisionmaking', *MIS Quarterly*, 12: 625–44.

6

Culture and New Media: A Historical View

MARK POSTER

Culture has become a problem for everyone. What was once a safe ground of enquiry has shifted as if by some earthquake whose effects long went unmeasured on academic Richter scales. Culture is now an unstable terrain marked by the scars of two decades of discursive rumbles. Where you stand on the culture question immediately places you, a bit too precisely for the comfort of many, on the map of scholarly and even political dispute. The humanities, the arts and the social sciences are now fractured into contentious subgroupings that run across disciplinary boundaries, all by dint of that little word 'culture'. Everyone wants to claim the term as their own, yet when they do so 'culture' receives new, unexpected meanings. Historians now practise empirical cultural history but find themselves slammed in the face by literary criticism and theory. Sociologists want to quantify culture, only to provoke the complaints of humanists who set in opposition number and subtlety, magnitude and meaning. Aestheticians decry the attribution of the term to popular culture. Anthropologists deconstruct culture and practise ethnography in the 'advanced' societies. Adepts of cultural studies wonder if their discourse can survive departmentalization.

Minorities and subcultures of great variety raise the banner of culture and insist on recognition. Conservatives defend what they see as culture as if it were under attack by communism, terrorism and Arab fundamentalism. National cultures collapse into multiplicity. Avant-garde cultures are considered modern and therefore paradoxically retrograde. Youth cultures are not simply rebellious but trickle up the social ladder, so to speak, to influence adult styles and habits. Genders are not biological but cultural, multiplying with the preferences and styles of their claimants. The most unstable groupings lay their claims to privileged cultural status: border cultures (Anzaldua, 1987) and even refugee camp cultures (Malkki, 1995) become models for the rest.

Culture has lost its boundary. The high and the low are mixed together. The finest creative sensibilities design packaging for commodities. The separation of culture from nature is in question. Scientists create animals in the laboratory. The air, the water and the skies are polluted by the social activities of high-tech nations. Nothing stands outside the cultivatable and so culture itself must be regarded as constructed rather than as given, historically contingent rather than timeless and certain. So sceptics ask if everything is constructed, then perhaps nothing is constructed. If everything emerges from a cultural process, the word has lost its specificity and coherence.

Despite this conflicted cacophony the term 'culture' remains useful, even essential, for studying new media. The paradox is this: without a concept of culture, the study of new media incorporates by default the culture of the dominant institutions in society. The state wishes to perfect its system of control over the population so as to secure its territorial boundaries. Corporations and entrepreneurs want nothing more than to glean greater profits. These are the cultures of the state and the economy, these are their characteristic gestures and motivations. Imposing these aims upon new media, the state and the economy regard them as tools for a more convenient implementation. In short, they colonize new media with the culture of instrumentality or performativity. In their approach to the Internet, the state and the economy frame it as something that is useful to them, something that may improve their pre-existing practices, make things go faster or more smoothly. Or not. These institutions are also concerned that the Internet might disrupt or hamper their ongoing activities: the state might be threatened by terrorists using the Net,[1] or banks and other financial institutions might be vulnerable to hackers. In either case, the question for them is instrumental: how will the Net benefit or harm their existing goals? Even when the state and the corporations look to the Internet for new ways of doing things, they do not put into question their foundations.

As long as we remain within an instrumental framework we cannot question it, define its limits, look to new media in relation to how they might generate new cultures. In this way, the culture of instrumentality obstructs research on the Internet, research that might open up the question of culture, of possible new cultural formations, of postmodern cultures.

The state and the economy are not the only institutions or groups which approach the Net in terms of their own culture: some of the democratizing political tendencies within the academy often exhibit similar impulses. The problem in this case is not exactly the culture of instrumentality, although at times it may be: it is rather the question of the subject,

the self. In a collaborative volume on 'race, class and gender on the Internet', the editor Bosah Ebo frames the work with the following question: 'Will the Internet create a cybertopia or will it exacerbate class divisions by creating a cyberghetto?' (1998: 9). If the state and the corporations look to the Internet to perpetuate their positions of domination, scholars like Ebo look to it for signs of change among groups in positions of subordination. He asks if groups determined by race, class and gender will, as a consequence of the Internet, improve their standing or recede further from positions of power. Here again the Internet serves as a tool for determining the fate of groups *as they are currently constituted*. Although this question is certainly legitimate, it is not critical of current cultural forms. Ebo and the authors in his book do not ask, in this regard, another question: how may the Internet mediate the transformation of existing cultural figures, or how may new cultural forms emerge which do not necessarily improve the position of existing groups as they are currently constituted but change them in unforeseeable ways? The question of culture in relation to the Internet involves a risk, a step into the unfamiliar precisely with respect to the figure of the self. If this question is foreclosed, one cannot examine critically the political culture of new media. One can merely put forward existing cultural figures of the self – race, class and gender, or citizen, manager and worker – to test the role of new media in furthering their positions as they see themselves and as they are. Such a framework is instrumental and overlooks systematically the constitutive character of media not in some form of technological determinism but as a space which encourages practices and which, in turn, serves to construct new types of subjects.

There is a perhaps more subtle way in which critical studies refuses the cultural question of the Internet. In this case scholars do not so much presuppose existing forms of race, class and gender. The uniqueness of the Internet is here fully recognized. But it is configured as a threat, not to specific groups but to general types of practice that are characterized as 'human'. Margaret Morse, for instance, argues 'there is a basic human need for reciprocity and the reversibility of "I" and "you" in discourse – seeing and being seen, recognizing others and being recognized, speaking, listening and being listened to'. And again: 'there is a human need for and pleasure in being recognized as a partner in discourse, even when the relation is based on a simulation that is mediated by or exchanged with machines' (1998: 10, 14). The virtual quality of the Internet, Morse continues, undermines these human needs by its machinic mediation. She continues the lament noted above that the Internet promotes patriarchy and capitalism but she especially is concerned that it erodes the 'sociality' of 'a well-functioning society' (1998: 35). For this cultural critic the Internet destabilizes community and undermines the felicity of face-to-face relations. As an aside one must ask why, if humans are so needful of bodily presence, they so regularly turn away from each other and bury their heads in books and newspapers, stare vacantly at television, move catatonically with portable music players blaring in their ears, or gaze with fascination at a networked computer screen. If one assumes, as a cultural critic, that whatever intercedes between relations of presence detracts from the human condition, then one cannot investigate potentials for rendering cyberspace inhabitable, one cannot ask the *political* question of what to do about the Internet. Cultural critics are better served by acknowledging the innovation of the Internet and examining how democratic groups might explore it and act politically so as to ensure its most beneficent configuration (McRobbie, 1994).

To approach the cultural question of the Internet is no easy task. Computer-mediated communication fundamentally shifts the registers of human experience as we have known them in modern society and even as they have been known through the ages. Time and space, body and mind, subject and object, human and machine are each drastically transformed by practices carried out on networked computers. Even if one is aware of this and consciously acts in cyberspace as one does in territorial space, reproducing the motivations of the world of bodily presence, the effects of machinic

mediation work just as surely to alter the human experience. What then can be the culture or cultures of cyberspace?

It is important not to pose this question in too stark terms. Cyberspace is surely no total departure from all previous history. Historians are right to remind us that the Internet does not mark the first reshuffling of the basic conditions of cultural formation as enumerated in the couplets above. From cave painting and smoke signals to writing and the alphabet, decisive shifts in the system of signification have accompanied humans throughout the past. In *Information Ages: Literacy, Numeracy, and the Computer Revolution* (1998), Michael Hobart and Zachary Schiffman point out the long heritage of computer-generated information. What occurs with networked computing, they argue, began at least as far back as writing: the commutation of signification into information. 'Information', they contend, 'is … wedded to writing insofar as writing gives stability to the mental objects abstracted from the flow of experience, such that one can access them readily and repeatedly' (1998: 30). Writing thus changes the time and space of signification, making it endure and shifting it from resonating air to papyrus or paper. It changes the relation of signification to the body and mind, abstracting it from living beings and securing it in bound volumes. It alters the relation of subject and object, confirming signification as a practice of the subject but also affirming that signification subsists in the world of objects. Finally, writing has shifted the relation of human to machine since the onset of printing: signification would now require elaborate crafts, masses of capital and collective labour.

If Hobart and Schiffman are wise to connect the Internet to earlier practices of signification, their insights need not deter us from formulating a problematic of the cultural novelty of cyberspace. We must turn to history for guidance in this project so as to acknowledge the constructedness of the Internet and to recognize its relations with earlier forms. Historical understanding alone enables the scholar to estimate the contours of the object under investigation as contingent and unfounded.

But we must also turn to those deviant and most controversial historians of culture, Friedrich Nietzsche and Michel Foucault, who corrected a surreptitious reintroduction of foundationalism when historians see only the continuity of the present object with the past. The problem Nietzsche and Foucault raise for historians is to connect the present with the past in a way that undercuts the unreflective legitimacy of the present, that acknowledges lineage while allowing for innovation, that traces the links of rationalities while holding open the emergence of the unexpected.

The study of the culture of the Internet then must seek in the analytics of man/machine, subject/object, body/mind, time/space a new configuration of the construction of the subject. Several authors have sought to accomplish at least some of these goals, especially Kate Hayles (1999), Mark Hansen (2003), Richard Doyle (2003) and Eugene Thacker (2004). Rather than presenting a review of this literature, however, I shall discuss in more detail the question of the subject. For it must not be assumed that this term is automatically useful in examining the Internet cultures.

We need to distinguish between the terms 'individual', 'self', 'identity' and 'subject'. The 'individual' may be taken as an empirical given, an empty term that requires elaboration to specify its parameters in a given time and place. Similarly the term 'self' refers in an undefined way to the mind, personality, soul, psyche of the individual. By contrast, the terms 'identity' and 'subject' are currently deployed in cultural analysis laden with much heavier meaning, much more theoretical and political weight than the former terms. 'Subject' is used as the modern configuration of the self, best expressed in Descartes as ontological separateness from material objects, as the profound centre of the individual, affording a distance from the world that enables the exercise of reason, reason that may grasp reality as certain truth. The figure of such an individual provides the legitimacy for most modern institutions – representative democracy, law, capitalist economics, science, education. Only if there is a prior and general sense that such a figure of the individual is viable does any argument make sense for citizenship,

the rational economic man, systematic and discursive investigations of nature, long years of education in reading and writing. Of course all of this is determined in discourse at the ideological level. The 'subject' then is the cultural basis for modern society.

'Identity' comes into discursive play when the coherence of the individual as a cultural figure begins to collapse. Identity was used seriously as an analytic term first in the 1950s by Erik Erikson (1968) precisely to step back from the Freudian subject and take an easier attitude toward the self, one that gave importance to questions of ego maintenance, continuity and stability, features of the psyche that Freud may be said to have assumed. Instead of an autonomous agent who might control his or her destiny, instead of the subject of the progressive, humanist vision, Erikson presents an individual who is deeply confused about who he/she is (Gleason, 1996: 470). Erikson's self, far from being a heroic bourgeois subject, experiences life as a series of crises, forming an ego that has a tentative stability, always under threat of difusion or even disintegration. This continually negotiated, fragile ego is what Erikson means by the term 'identity'. Identity then is a renegotiated figure of the subject that accounts for the failure of modernity to realize the metanarrative of progress. We need to keep in mind this massive cultural shift when we examine identity in relation to new media. The term 'identity' is the recognition of the failure of Western culture, a failure inscribed in the massive disasters of the twentieth century. It is an ideological compromise that saves and masks traditional individualism, adjusts it to changes in culture such as the disappearance of the proletariat, the emergence of consumer culture, the diffusion of electronic media, the demise of Europe from world hegemony, the end of the West as an alleged basis for universality. When the term is carried over into the new social movements of women, minorities, sexual preference and post-colonialism, it carries with it the burdens of its past. Individuals defined as their identity are hardly agents in the sense of the figure of the subject.

The difference between the individual as subject and the individual as identity becomes exigent in relation to new media. Individuals are constituted as subjects or identities (as cultural selves) in linguistic practices. In repeated enunciations, individuals become interpellated and recognized as coherent selves who function in a social world. Increasingly the process of interpellation occurs through mediations of information machines in addition to face-to-face interactions. First printed pages, then broadcast media and now networked computing shift the scene in which the individual becomes and continues to practise selfhood. I use the term 'postmodernity', however contested it has become, to designate the shift in incidence from a combination of face-to-face and print arenas of interpellation to one that includes to an important degree broadcast media and networked computing.

The term 'postmodern' designated for Lyotard (1984) the collapse of modern culture's metanarrative of progress and for Jameson (1991) a change in the culture of capitalism. In both instances postmodernity registered not an institutional transformation or an alteration of practices so much as a new figure of the self. Postmodernity for them certainly referred to social phenomena like the collapse of the distinction between high and low culture, or even to a more general blurring of boundaries in all areas of everyday life. But the weight of the category bore most heavily on the process of subjectivation or the constitution of the self. For Lyotard the self had become disengaged from historicity and for Jameson in addition it was now fragmented, dispersed, low in affect and one-dimensional. These theorists discerned a new figure of the self only through the backdrop of the older modern subject, the heroic bourgeois/proletarian agent. In both cases the trope for the change was tragedy, a fall from a higher place. In the analysis of the culture of new media, the reader needs to keep this theoretical heritage in mind but also to recognize the importance of framing the change to postmodernity in a way that opens the analysis to political possibilities, rather than closes the discussion with a large sigh of regret.

Those who would further the critical cultural study of the media have begun to recognize the need for a deployment of the term

'postmodern' in a manner that makes it suitable for analysis without either a celebratory fanfare or sarcastic smirks. In the study of broadcast media, for instance, Lynne Joyrich (1996: 63) argues persuasively that television brings consumer desires to the individual with an immediacy that undermines the separation of subject and object, the basic condition for the constitution of the self as subject. If this is the case, the cultural study of new media has no choice but to register this transformation with the use of some term. Like Joyrich, I suggest the term 'postmodernity' for this purpose.

The danger of the term, as she recognizes, is that it illicitly incorporates a certain universalism. Lyotard and Jameson certainly suffer from this tendency. Since the category of the subject was discursively inscribed as universal, even though it betrayed its conditions of birth in white, Western male culture, the suggestion that it has collapsed incorporated the same universalist gesture. The problem rests not with the aspiration for the universal as such but rather with the fact that the universal can only escape clandestine hierarchical resonances if it is enunciated universally, a condition that has never been possible in human history. Lacking such a condition, the universal must be approached with great caution. Until the enunciative conditions exist for the articulation of the universal we must always stress the contingent quality of discursive claims, the situatedness of knowledge, as Donna Haraway (1991) says. The issue is not really who speaks but how they speak, how they recognize themselves and inscribe themselves in their discourse in relation to the Western pattern of the all-knowing, unconditioned subject. As a corrective to the universalist inscription of the term 'postmodern' I suggest a focus on the specificity of the media in the process of self-construction.

Joyrich deploys the category of gender to very much the same end. Gender operates to render specific and contingent the epistemological position of enunciation. But gender – along with race, class, sexual preference and age – is not enough to deflect enunciation from the tendency to reinscribe foundational identity. We can escape better, if never completely, this danger if we include the machinic and the space/time configuration specific to the mediated scene of interpellation. If we are to study the culture of new media we need to take into account the information machines that increasingly mediate our symbolic practices. And these machines (be they print, broadcast or networked computing) extract us from territorial spaces and phenomenological time, repositioning us in strange new ways. These media of course are not themselves born innocent but arise from existing patterns of hierarchy in relation to class, race and gender. But they enable practices that fit badly with earlier complexes of domination, putting them into question and thereby opening the field – if we are not too defensive about and beholden to these older patterns – to new spaces of politics. Joyrich recognizes the destabilizing effects of the multiple, fragmented self of postmodernity. She proposes a most promising stance toward the phenomenon: 'I am trying neither to celebrate nor to lament postmodern fragmentation. Instead I hope to reveal the ways in which the sexed and cyborg body have been linked in both the televised and the critical imagination' (1996: 132). In her analysis she applauds television shows like 'Peewee's Playhouse', 'Max Headroom' and 'Moonlighting' for their transgressive potential, although she reminds readers of their commercial and discursive limitations, even of their recuperating closures. What she pays less attention to, however, is the machinic level, that is, television as an information machine of the broadcast model that sets into play practices of self-constitution whose specificity and difference from other such devices, in particular books and networked computing, require elaboration. If television, like consumption, is associated in critical writing with the feminine, as she argues, those discourses also deal poorly with the machinic quality of this visual medium, either ignoring it or instrumentalizing it. It is this crucial mediation, with particular reference to new media, that requires a great deal of attention from scholars.

Jennifer Daryl Slack and J. Macgregor Wise, in their chapter 'Cultural Studies and Communication Technology', introduce this aspect of the question of culture and new media with a broad examination of the relation of technology to culture, in particular with reference to the discourse of cultural studies. The question of the relation of technology to culture is a vexed one, with many pitfalls along the path to productive analysis. Slack and Wise review many of these problems, in particular the notorious issue of technological determinism, but also questions of causality and progress that are commonplace in discussions of media technology. In much of the humanities and social sciences, the mere mention of media as an important ingredient in social and cultural analysis is enough to raise the red flag of determinism. Slack and Wise explore this issue with subtlety, going on to open the other side of the issue, that of culture and cultural analysis. In some detail they discuss the traditions of cultural studies in relation to media, but expand beyond this to positions like those of Deleuze and Foucault. They review the literature on the relation of technology to culture in terms of four central issues: agency, genealogy, identity and inequality, and social space and the body. These more focused topics allow them to thread their way through the vast and dense thicket of the media technology question. Their conclusion is that while many important studies have been accomplished, much remains to be done in developing analytics of technology from a cultural studies point of view.

Many scholars have recently taken up the important cultural issue of the relation of space to technology. Michael Bull (2000) examines the use of portable music players in relation to urban space, arguing that such use complicates the relation of the individual to the specificity of place. When listening to music while say riding a bicycle or travelling in the underground one's sense of place doubles so to speak. One does not hear the sounds in the immediate environment but 'other' sounds that displace the individual or better multiply their spatiality. Another example of the cultural study of media in relation to space is Anna McCarthy's (2001) ethnography of televisions outside the home. In bars and airports, for example, television alters the spatial relation of individuals to architecture. Some years ago Lyn Spigel's (1992) important work raised the question of the placement of televisions inside the home in the 1950s. Now Mark Nunes (2005) extends a cultural studies approach to space and the Internet. Studying blogs, e-mail and distance learning, he argues that these sites of communication transform our experience of space into a virtual event. The new media of cyberspace, itself incorporating a spatial term, opens the question of territory, of nation, of specificity of place and abstraction of mapping in productive but puzzling ways.

In conclusion, the salient issue that emerges from posing the question of the culture of the Internet is that of the need for comparative media studies. It has become clear that numerous dangers confront the study of the culture of the Internet if it is not set in the context of earlier and contemporary media. Even if one regards media as integrated into social practice one must nonetheless be able to discriminate between the cultures that emerge in different mediated practices. This research agenda requires the collaboration of scholars from many disciplines, the humanities and social sciences but also the arts and computer science. Such a requirement for interdisciplinarity in the study of the Internet elicits a new culture among researchers, even if some of them might gainsay the cultural novelty of new media.

NOTE

1 *Wired News* reports that 20 nations attempt to keep the Internet out of their borders, that 45 nations seriously censor it, and that this is an improvement in Internet 'freedom' over the recent past (McCabe, 1999).

REFERENCES

Anzaldua, G. (1987) *Borderlands/La Frontera: The New Mestiza*. San Francisco: Aunt Lute.

Bull, M. (2000) *Sounding Out the City: Personal Stereos and the Management of Everyday Life*. New York: Berg.

Doyle, R. (2003) *Wetware: Experiments in Postvital Living*. Minneapolis: University of Minnesota Press.

Ebo, B. (ed.) (1998) *Cyberghetto or Cybertopia? Race, Class, and Gender on the Internet*. Westport, CT: Praeger.

Erikson, E. (1968) *Identity: Youth and Crisis*. New York: Norton.

Gleason, P. (1996) 'Identifying identity: a semantic history', in W. Sollors (ed.), *Theories of Ethnicity: A Classical Reader*. New York: New York University Press. pp. 460–87.

Hansen, M. (2003) *New Philosophy for New Media*. Boston: MIT Press.

Haraway, D. (1991) *Simians, Cyborgs and Women: The Re-invention of Nature*. New York: Routledge.

Hayles, N.K. (1999) *How We Became Posthuman: Virtual Bodies in Cybernetics, Literature, and Informatics*. Chicago: University of Chicago Press.

Hobart, M. and Schiffman, Z. (1998) *Information Ages: Literacy, Numeracy, and the Computer Revolution*. Baltimore, MD: Johns Hopkins University Press.

Jameson, F. (1991) *Postmodernism, or, the Cultural Logic of Late Capitalism*. Durham, NC: Duke University Press.

Joyrich, L. (1996) *Re-viewing Reception: Television, Gender, and Postmodern Culture*. Bloomington, IN: Indiana University Press.

Lyotard, J.-F. (1984) *The Postmodern Condition*. Minneapolis: University of Minnesota Press.

McCarthy, A. (2001) *Ambient Television: Visual Culture and Public Space*. Durham, NC: Duke University Press.

Malkki, L. (1995) *Purity and Exile: Violence, Memory, and National Cosmology among Hutu Refugees in Tanzania*. Chicago: University of Chicago Press.

McCabe, H. (1999) 'The Net: enemy of the state?', *Wired News*.

McRobbie, A. (1994) *Postmodernism and Popular Culture*. New York: Routledge.

Morse, M. (1998) *Virtualities: Television, Media Art, and Cyberculture*. Bloomington, IN: Indiana University Press.

Nunes, M. (2005) *Virtual Topographies: The Internet and the Spaces of Everyday Life*. Minneapolis, MN: University of Minnesota Press.

Spigel, L. (1992) *Make Room for TV: Television and the Family Ideal in Postwar America*. Chicago: University of Chicago Press.

Thacker, E. (2004) *Biomedia*. Minneapolis: University of Minnesota Press.

7

Cultural Studies and Communication Technology

JENNIFER DARYL SLACK AND J. MACGREGOR WISE

Relating technology to culture – an admirable, if elusive, pursuit – has a long and rich history. For decades, at least, scholars and policy-makers have argued against approaches to technology that posit it as a mere technical tool and for approaches that acknowledge technology in relation to culture – 'in context' as it is often put. The difficulty is of course that the relationship between culture and technology is every bit as much a theoretical problem as it is a task of description, and technological practitioners are often unaware of the work performed by their own theoretical assumptions.[1] A particularly pervasive tendency when discussing new technologies (including new communication and information technologies such as satellite, cable, digital broadcast and narrowcast, the Internet, the World Wide Web) is to treat them as if they were completely revolutionary, capable of (*sui generis* as it were) changing everything and likely to do so. Cultural studies is especially suited to revealing and critiquing the work of tendencies such as this and to positing an alternative way of understanding and shaping the relationship between technologies and culture.

Cultural studies' emphasis on the radical contextuality of phenomena under study and its use of articulation as both analytic tool and model of practice put it in a position to critique the assumptions embedded in technological practice and to contribute to the ongoing development of a more dynamic approach to new media technology. In this chapter, we sketch the most salient components of a developing cultural studies approach to technology and culture. In doing so we draw as much as possible on work on new media that, as we clarify below, 'counts' as cultural studies. But because explicit cultural studies treatments of technology are few, we focus as much on the implications for thinking about new media from a cultural studies perspective. Our treatment of the issue, then, folds in several purposes: first, to utilize a cultural studies perspective to show how contemporary issues involving new media are embedded within (and against) a long genealogy of issues and debates; second, to characterize an emerging cultural studies approach to technology; third, to draw attention to scholarship that contributes specifically to a cultural studies approach to new media; fourth, to consider problems that a cultural studies approach to new media faces; and finally, to speculate on directions for further research.

WHAT COUNTS AS CULTURAL STUDIES

Cultural studies is not and never has been one thing, but that does not mean that it is anything and everything (Hall, 1990: 11). It is, rather, like an ongoing conversation: a series of regroupings and revisionings, issues considered, questions asked, responses offered, topics explored, risks taken and directions tried. Because the conversation takes place within changing historical moments, the shape of the conversation is connected to historical events, political realities, institutional situations and theoretical and intellectual influences. The longer and/or more intensely a participant has engaged in the conversation, the more likely they have become part of it and the more likely they are to understand its nuances. Cultural studies is thus more like art than science. In the same way that an artistic movement is shaped loosely by the goals, concerns, challenges and interests of the participating artists and evolves along with the changes they instantiate, so too is cultural studies shaped loosely by the participants in the conversation, evolving as the conversation changes. In the same way that questions designed to clarify what constitutes belonging to a particular artistic movement are most difficult at the 'edges' of what seem to be (conjuncturally) central to definitions of the movement ('is this piece cubist or surrealist?'), so too is it difficult to discern at the edges exactly what is or is not cultural studies.

That having been said, there are a number of worthwhile positions explaining what cultural studies has been. As long as one understands that these positions are themselves only a part of the conversation, they are instructive. They can help us envision what 'counts' as a cultural studies approach to technology generally and to new media technology specifically. Nelson et al.'s (1992) Introduction to *Cultural Studies* is one of the more helpful as it offers an excellent bibliography to the definitional task (pre-1992), is widely read, and remains historically close to crucial dynamics of the ongoing conversation. Nelson et al. point to the following:

Cultural studies is an interdisciplinary, transdisciplinary, and sometimes counterdisciplinary field. (1992: 4)

Cultural studies is ... committed to the study of the entire range of a society's arts, beliefs, institutions, and communicative practices. (1992: 4)

Culture is understood *both* as a way of life – encompassing ideas, attitudes, languages, practices, institutions, and structure of power – and as a whole range of cultural practices: artistic forms, texts, canons, architecture, mass-produced commodities, and so forth. (1992: 5)

Its practitioners see cultural studies not simply as a chronicle of cultural change but as an intervention in it, and see themselves not simply as scholars providing an account but as politically engaged participants. (1992: 5)

[An] emphasis on contingencies is central to contemporary cultural studies, to a theory of articulation, and to models for carrying out conjunctural analysis – analysis, that is, which is embedded, descriptive, and historically and contextually specific. (1992: 8)

The last requires additional explanation. An emphasis on contingency suggests that cultural theorists understand what something 'is' as constituted in a particular historical conjuncture. Thus, as opposed to having an essential, independent identity, what something 'is' is contingent on a particular configuration of relationships. This 'radical contextuality' insists that a context is not something 'out there', independent, into which other independent things move, are inserted or removed. Context and phenomena are, rather, mutually constitutive. The analysis of any phenomenon is precisely the act of contextualizing it. This mode of analysis is termed 'articulation', which points to the double-pincered work of describing the connection (following Deleuze and Guattari, 1987, we refer to this as 'tracing') as well as the act of drawing or making the connection (again following Deleuze and Guattari, we refer to this as 'mapping').

The distinction between tracing and mapping is a crucial one, because radical contextuality and articulation theory recognize that theories, methods and practices are always embedded in, reflective of and limited by their historical circumstances. Theories, methods and practices are seen as particular ways of engaging and giving shape to these circumstances. The act of theorizing is not therefore a case of getting something right or wrong, and cultural studies does not purport to advance one correct theory (or even the idea that there can be one correct theory), or one correct methodology, or even one correct political practice. However, this is not a theoretical, methodological or political relativism; one theory, practice or method is not just as good as any other. Instead, cultural studies works to understand the embedded contexts of theories, methods and practices and their institutional and disciplinary specificity, at the same time that it undertakes analysis of the specific phenomenon under investigation. Cultural studies thus demands the ongoing work of theorizing in relation to the ongoing analysis of changing historical conjunctures. This makes cultural studies work tremendously difficult when done rigorously.

Drawing on these broad parameters, we can say that the analysis of culture necessitates at some point an analysis of technology, since technology in some form will always be part of the context of everyday life. Historically, understanding the role of technology in culture seems particularly pressing as: (1) new media technology plays a central role in changing global political economic configurations; (2) new media technology contributes to defining a new organization of knowledge, the information age; and (3) new media technology plays a conspicuous role in popular culture.

Theoretically, cultural studies works with and against a series of problematics that have shaped understanding of, and debate about, the relationship between technology and culture. The problematics that have most dominated work on culture and technology are as follows:

- *The question of causality*: Does technology drive cultural change (technological determinism)? Or is technology a neutral tool, its effects and politics determined solely by its uses ('guns don't kill people, people kill people')? At the heart of this issue is not only the direction of causality (culture versus technology), but the nature of that causality (absolute determinism, relative determinism, expressive causality, etc.).
- *The question of technological dependence*: Have we become so dependent on our tools that we have created a de facto technological determinism? Have we become slaves to our own machines?

- *The question of progress*: What is the relationship between technology and progress? Technology has become central to discourses on progress and development. The pervasive sense is that technology is instrumental in moving cultures inevitably and inexorably toward a state of perfection. By this logic, more technology equals progress equals a better life.

To say that these problematics are 'worked with and against' is to mitigate against simply dismissing them as 'wrong', worthy only of being discarded. Instead, in 'working with' these problematics, cultural studies recognizes and critiques their power in shaping a role for technology. In 'working against' these problematics, cultural studies recognizes that the role of technology can change – in part – by changing the terms of the debate. To put this very concretely, we (those of us who study culture and technology) have long since accepted that technology is not neutral, that technology does not cause cultural change (or vice versa) in any simple way, that the relationship between technology and culture is contingent not determined, that neither we nor technology are slave to the other, and that technological development is not necessarily progress. Okay, so what then? Where do we go after that? There is a pressing need in this techno-fetishistic culture to cultivate an understanding of technology that insists on theories that challenge current practices, that give us somewhere to go and provide us with direction. Work in the cultural studies of technology is finding its way there.

These problematics, then, as the following discussion illustrates, are being transformed by what we take to be four major problematics of cultural studies: agency; genealogy; identity, politics and power; and social space and corporeality. Each of these has important applications and implications for understanding the relationship between culture and new media technology.[2]

In the process of discussing the work that makes these advances, we acknowledge that we have chosen to see and represent that work as an emerging cultural studies approach to technology. In this way we add not only to the discussion of new media technology and culture but to the discussion of what – theoretically – constitutes cultural studies. Readers may note that from time to time we draw on figures (such as Bruno Latour and Langdon Winner) from the social studies of technology (SST) or science, technology and society (STS) approaches prevalent in many of the other contributions to this collection. The commonality of these works points to articulations between sociological and cultural approaches to the study of technology. However, in citing them here we often rearticulate their theories and case studies, drawing them into the context of cultural studies. Differentiating a cultural studies approach to technology from an SST or STS approach entails more than the observation that one focuses on culture and the other on society. Indeed, the distinctions between what constitutes 'culture' and what constitutes 'society' have always been a source of contention, if not significant overlap. Rather, what differentiates the cultural studies approach to technology from the SST or STS approaches is the radical nature of the contextuality that cultural studies foregrounds and the deep commitment to theory as an essential part of the analysis, as we outlined earlier.

FROM CAUSALITY TO AGENCY

Questions of causality – in many guises – have haunted the study of technology throughout history. Although the questions have been formulated in many different ways, the underlying problematic has been 'what causes what'. Perhaps the oldest formulation assuming that technology has effects – Plato's exploration of the effects of writing technology – dates this concern at least as far back as the fourth century BC. The delineation of effects (and side-effects) has occupied much contemporary work on new media technology, in studies by the Office of Technology Assessment for example. The delineation of kinds of side-effects has been taken almost to the level of absurdity by Edward Tenner in *Why Things Bite Back* (1996). Conversely, the position that technology is a

neutral tool that merely responds to (is an effect of) the needs and desires of the culture permeates treatments of technology. There have been many ways to characterize the causal possibilities, all of which tend to suggest the operation of a binary distinction: autonomous versus non-autonomous technology (Winner, 1977); mechanistic versus non-mechanistic causality (Slack, 1984); substantive versus instrumental theory (Borgmann, 1984; Feenberg, 1991); and technological versus social determinism (Wise, 1997).

The binary distinctions fail on two counts. First, the binary cannot adequately explain the complexity of either everyday discourse about, or mobilization of, technology. What is, perhaps, most interesting about the theoretically rigorous attempt at making binary distinctions is the fact that in everyday life we tend to rely on atheoretical, opportunistic combinations of claims about causality as the circumstances demand: technology is treated as both a neutral instrument *and* a powerful cause of cultural change. Second, the binary is inadequate to the task of explaining the theoretically acknowledged complex imbrication of technology and culture. The history of debates in technology studies, philosophy of technology, SST and STS points to the fact that the causal relationship between technology and culture is neither one way nor the other. The fundamental mistake seems to be the fact that the binary assumes that technology and culture are separate phenomena. The theoretical problem is, rather, to find a way to understand the role of technology, acknowledging that technology is always already a part of culture, not a cause or an effect of it. At the same time the challenge remains to distinguish the ways in which technology is effective, for it clearly does make a difference which technologies we use.

Both of these failings have been recognized by virtually all contemporary critical and cultural theorists studying technology. In place of the constricting binary, theorists have developed a variety of figures designed to comprehend technology as effective, but as irreducible to either cause or effect. Raymond Williams, in his pivotal book, *Television: Technology and Cultural Form* (1975), introduces the notion of a 'community of selected emphasis and intention' (1975: 18) in order to argue that new media technologies (television in this case) emerge within a configuration of emphasis, interests and intentions, as part of that configuration. The configuration, or complex, that contextualizes the emergence of television for Williams is 'mobile privatization', in which the technology serves 'an at once mobile and home-centered way of living' (1975: 26). Interestingly, Williams' model for understanding the emergence of new media technologies never really generated studies in its image. In part, this may be because it took far longer for cultural studies to accept widely the importance of studying media technology (as opposed to media content). Further, when cultural studies finally directed its attention to technology, it moved beyond Williams' expressive causal commitments (Slack, 1984: 73–8).

The new direction is paved, instead, by Winner's (1986) idea of technology as forms of life; Slack's notion of technology as articulation (1989); Latour's (1988, 1996; Callon and Latour, 1981) and Haraway's (1992) conceptions of technological agency; and Wise's (1997) technology as assemblage. Each of these figures resists the common-sense equation of technology with 'things', with the comforting sense that the boundaries of what any particular technology is can be clearly delimited. For example, cultural theorists resist studying the computer as if it was simply the hardware, the software and the networks that connect the computer to other computers and other media. Rather, they are drawn to understanding the technology to be a form of life, an articulation, an apparatus or an assemblage within which agency flows.

One way to characterize the shift is to see it as a change from focusing on 'what causes what' to attending to 'how things happen'. The shift blurs the vision of the 'whats': technology, culture, effects. Instead the mechanisms of stasis, resistance and change, not categories of identity, become the objects of study. Langdon Winner's 'forms of life', though never widely adopted, was an early formulation of this shift. He argued that as the devices, techniques and systems that we commonly understand to be technology 'become woven into the texture of

everyday existence', they 'shed their tool-like qualities to become part of our very humanity'. They become '[d]eeply insinuated into people's perceptions, thoughts, and behaviour'. They become, in short, 'an indelible part of modern culture' (Winner, 1986: 12). It becomes impossible to talk about the effect of one on the other, since earlier innovations are both reflections of culture and the conditions of further cultural development. Drawing on the Marxist conception that the forms within which we live our lives define who we are, Winner focuses on how technologies embody ways of engaging the world: of making it, reproducing it, changing it. Indeed, Winner points out the danger of separating technology from the culture and society: it allows one to be easily swayed by the rhetoric of revolution that accompanies new media technologies (a belief he terms 'mythinformation (1986: 105)) and allows for serious misconceptions about the possibilities for democracy with new technologies such as the computer. Rather, he argues, new technologies tend to reinforce the overall power structure, not overthrow it. Winner, however, does not offer a theoretical approach, model or method sufficiently developed to go much beyond acknowledging that technologies *are* forms of life and that they *do* tend to reinforce existing structures of power. Also, persistent in Winner's formulation is a tendency to characterize technologies as 'things'. Winner's work illustrates how difficult it is to move beyond our cultural habit of understanding technologies as things, even in the act of arguing against it.

A more recent work which raises the same promise—and issues—that Winner does is Andy Clark's *Natural-born Cyborgs: Minds, Technologies, and the Future of Human Intelligence* (2003). Clark borrows the term 'scaffolding' from psychologist Lev Vygotsky to rethink not only the mind–body problem but the human–technology one as well. He writes:

It is the problem of understanding how human thought and reason is born out of looping interactions between material brains, material bodies, and complex cultural and technological environments. We create these supportive environments, but they create us too. We exist, as the thinking things we are, only thanks to a baffling dance of brains, bodies, and cultural and technological scaffolding. (2003: 11)

However, the concept of scaffolding itself, though potentially generative, isn't much developed beyond this. So, although Clark's book seeks to establish how permeable and hybrid humans are, it tends to fall back into the language of the mind *and* the scaffolding rather than the mind *as* scaffolding. On the one hand he describes a 'biotechnological matrix' which problem-solves, consisting of the brain, papers, scribbled notes, computer programs, and so on. But on the other hand rather than focusing on this matrix he returns to the language of the brain and its team members (2003: 26).

Following Stuart Hall (1986), who formulated one of the earliest and most influential accounts of the concept of articulation, Jennifer Daryl Slack argues that technology can be understood as an articulation, as 'a non-necessary connection of different elements that, when connected in a particular way, form a specific unity' (1989: 331). If technology (she uses the example of the personal computer) is itself an articulation of elements (hardware, software, network, etc.) that can be connected in different ways with other elements (economics, ideology, politics, policy, gender, etc.), then technology as a generic term and any specific common-sense technology (such as the computer) are contingent rather than determined, dispersed rather than discrete. The question of the relationship between technology and culture is thus reframed to foreground the connections that constitute technology.

A still more dramatic shift away from the problematic of causality occurs when the idea of agency is taken up and radically transformed. Those most responsible for developing this concept in relation to technology are Bruno Latour, Donna Haraway and J. Macgregor Wise. Latour begins to transform the idea of agency by revisioning what it means to be an actor. An actor for Latour is not limited to humans as agents, but is 'any element which bends space around itself, makes other elements dependent upon itself and translates their will into a language of its own' (Callon and Latour, 1981: 286). The resulting aggregate of elements is an 'actor network'. Agency, it follows, is the ability to achieve effects either through physical contact or through non-corporeal means (Wise, 1997: xv). Agency structures movement; it distributes and organizes entities (human and other than human), spaces and places. Latour (1988, 1993, 1996) was particularly influential in introducing the notion that, in this sense, technology is an actor or agent that exercises agency. Technology can bend space around itself, render other elements dependent on it, and translate the will of others into a language of its own. Technology structures movement; it distributes and organizes entities, spaces and places. A dramatic example is the electric eye door opener, which allows people to move from one place to another. If a person is too short, the electric eye will not sense them, the door will not open, and the short person's movement in space will be restricted (a form of discrimination). If the electricity is shut off, the door will indiscriminately prohibit movement through that particular space (see Latour, 1988, for a parallel example of an automatic door closer, which we will return to below). Latour goes so far as to give technology a voice: in *Aramis, or the Love of Technology* (1996), Aramis, a failed new transportation technology, speaks of the reasons for its own death.

Donna Haraway, influenced by Latour's actor-network theory, links the notion of actors with the concept of articulation. She writes that actors 'take provisional, never-finished shape in articulatory practices' and observes that 'humans and unhumans' (technology, for example) 'articulate ... in a social relationship' (1992: 313). Rapidly receding here are the once comfortable notions that technology is an identity with identifiable boundaries, that there is a clear-cut distinction between technology and humans, and that only humans exercise agency. Consequently the binary problematic of determination (what causes what) begins to recede. Not entirely, however, for the 'thingness' of actors sneaks back in the guise of the construction that *actors exercise agency*. For example, Haraway works with constructions such as 'jaguars, among other actors' (1992: 313) and Latour works with statements such as 'Humans and nonhumans take on form by redistributing the competencies and performance of the multitude of actors that they hold on to and that hold on to them' (1996: 225). This return to 'actors exercising agency' seems always to reintroduce the seductive and familiar distinction between things (technologies) and culture, and hence the causal problematic.

The cultural studies conception of technology does finally move dramatically away from the ultimately binary conception of 'thingness' under the influence of the work of Gilles Deleuze and Félix Guattari. Lawrence Grossberg (1996), drawing on the work of Deleuze and Guattari, asserts that agency is not a property of an identity, an agent. Rather, agency is a flow that circulates through and produces a sense of agents. Grossberg puts it this way: 'Agency is the product of diagrams of mobility and placement which define or map the possibilities of where and how specific vectors of influence can stop and be placed' (1996: 102). It is the work of agency that lets abstract identities stand as identities: human; animal; technology in general; specific technologies, etc. Each abstraction is produced in relations of agency.

J. Macgregor Wise (1997) develops this Deleuzoguattarian sense of agency in *Exploring Technology and Social Space*. He argues that 'machinic assemblages' (in lieu of technology) are articulations of physiochemical, organic and enunciative strata. Likewise, 'assemblages of enunciation' (in lieu of language) are also articulations of physiochemical, organic and enunciative strata. These assemblages articulate (taking the form of a double articulation) to 'mark the territory', that is, they delineate 'how things happen' as well as 'what does not happen' (1997: 57–80). Agency in this conception 'is not a given, but is distributed, differentiated, and territorialized. The resultant actor-network can thus be understood and critiqued without falling back on the problematic notion of a rational network builder' (1997: 70). Agency, in this sense, works to avoid the conundrum of the binary that adheres to the problematic of identity. From this Deleuzoguattarian perspective, technologies – particular artifacts or services – are seen as 'habits ... contractions of action, substance, and thought, a condensation of technology and language' (1997: 71). While grasped as wholes (what Deleuze and Guattari term 'molarities'), they are in fact abstract, differentiated assemblages.

The language of Deleuze and Guattari used by Wise and others (for example, Elmer, 2004) is difficult to be sure – and therefore a decided disadvantage if the goal is to develop a broad-based cultural studies approach to new technology. But it is hardly surprising that a challenge to the tenacious articulation of technology as 'thing' existing in a binary relationship with culture would be a difficult link to sever and that it would take radical language and thought to challenge it. Jonathan Sterne (1999) has pointed directly to the difficulty of applying such an approach to specific new media technology such as the Internet. The difficulty, as illustrated for Sterne in Wise's work, is that one 'focuses more on discourses about and around the Internet than on attempting a description of the Internet itself' (1999: 275). However, the real challenge for culture theorists, as illustrated in Sterne's own complaint, is a deep-seated loyalty to 'the Internet [or any new media technology] *itself*' (emphasis added). As if there were such a thing.

FROM THE INEVITABILITY OF PROGRESS TO GENEALOGY

Cultural studies' conception of technology deeply undercuts the common-sense cultural commitment to the equation of progress with the development of new technology. Just as attention to articulation moves the understanding of technology from causal terms to a conception of agency, so too does it displace conceptions of inevitability and progress. Inevitability is supplanted by contingency; progress with genealogy; and idealist conceptions of freedom with an understanding of responsibility as defined and distributed within differentially structured terrains.

It has long been the case that Western (and now increasingly global) culture has equated the development of new technology with progress. The progress 'narrative', as described by Nisbet (1980), holds that the human species – by nature – is developing steadily toward increasing perfection here on earth. And technology has long been seen as a marker of that progress – as its (causal) agent (see Smith and Marx, 1994). For example, international development projects beginning in the 1940s have often used new media technologies as indicators of degrees of 'civilization' (Lerner, 1958). So deeply held is the assumption that new technology and progress are linked that David Noble (1982) once claimed that it was 'heretical' to even ask the question: is it so?

The concept of technological progress depends on a unidirectional, evolutionary model of change (Berland, 2000), a teleologically driven conception of history where origins are decidable and origins determine endings. But cultural studies is in some sense predicated on the idea that origins do not determine endings (Carey, 1975/1989), that there are no 'guarantees' (Hall, 1983), and that connections, outcomes, effects are always 'contingent' rather than determined. Hall, in his widely quoted interview on articulation, emphasizes the role of contingency:

> An articulation is thus the form of the connection that *can* make a unity of two different elements, under certain conditions. It is a linkage which is not necessary, determined, absolute and essential for all time. You have to ask, under what circumstances *can* a connection be forged or made? So the so-called 'unity' of a discourse [or any abstract identity, such as technology or progress] is really the articulation of different, distinct elements which can be rearticulated in different ways because they have no necessary 'belongingness'. (1986: 53)

Indeed, the interventionist commitments of cultural theorists of the new media technology lead them, on the one hand, to trace significant articulations and, on the other hand, to unhinge them, so to speak, to map or rearticulate them. For example, Charles Acland, in tracing the articulations of IMAX (large-format cinema technology) in Canada, insists that it must be seen 'as a multiple articulation of technological system, corporate entity and cinema practice invested in the notion of expanded cinema, or what Andre Bazin ... called the myth of total cinema' (1998: 431). For Acland, this particular configuration is a symptom of a general shift in patterns of leisure

toward the reintroduction of a technologically mediated form of the tourist gaze, about which he is obviously critical. Although Acland does not map explicit directions for change, one cannot read his argument without considering what might make it possible to rearticulate this configuration.

Often, cultural studies of new media technology are timid in exposing the intent of their work as mapping the need (if not the direction) for rearticulating the terrain. It is sometimes a frustrating weakness of these studies that superficially they profess only to describe (trace) a developing historical conjuncture when, theoretically, they really are mapping strategies. It is almost as though cultural theory has developed in powerful ways a bit beyond our ability to exploit it. Our work is often – perhaps merely (though not insignificantly) for local political reasons – tamed. Dare we be explicit about the fact that not all technological development is progress? The terrain of study of new media technology is rife with criticism of those who suggest too much that might be taken as negative. Jill J. McMillan and Michael J. Hyde's (2000) case study of the pressure to adopt a technological progress narrative at Wake Forest University illustrates the difficulties of challenging particular technological developments, and even of posing questions that might be considered critical of technology. This is the conjuncture, after all, where appropriate political rhetoric includes positions taken by President William Clinton in his 1996 State of the Union Address announcing 'America's Technological Literacy Campaign', where the goal is 'to make every young person technologically literate', the assumption being that this will 'provide all our children with a greater opportunity to learn the skills they need to thrive into the next century' (America's Technology Literacy Challenge, 1996). The 'politically correct' position to take with regard to technology in this conjuncture is, 'yes, it is inevitable; yes, it is the way forward; we just need to be smart enough to use it for good not ill'. As if the effects of technologies were only about the use of things – after the fact.

Methodologically, cultural studies has an affinity with the practice of genealogy, as it has come down to us from Nietzsche, via Foucault. Genealogy is explicitly opposed to the progress narrative. It does not assume a single, evolutionary direction; it does not assume that ideas or practices retain their logic. It looks instead to the way in which multitudes of elements career, crash, invade, struggle, plunder and play, such that complex and changing arrangements characterize an apparatus (for Deleuze and Guattari, an assemblage) within which we would understand technology to be disbursed. The task of genealogy is, as Foucault puts it, to record the singularity of events outside any monotonous finality; it must seek them in the

> most unpromising places, in what we tend to feel is without history – in sentiments, love, conscience, instincts; it must be sensitive to their recurrence, not in order to trace the gradual curve of their evolution, but to isolate the different scenes where they engaged in different roles. Finally, genealogy must define even those instances where they are absent, the moment when they remained unrealized. (1977b: 139–40)

A genealogical method thus displaces the 'object' of study away from an analysis of things (such as a particular new media technology) and toward a patient tracking of the apparatus within which things take on particular meanings and play particular roles. Thomas Tierney's *The Value of Convenience* (1993) provides an example of this method. This is not a book about particular technologies; it is about the context within which particular kinds of technologies are produced and consumed. It is about the emergence of a notion of a need for convenience (a need to overcome the bodily limits of time and space) and the way that particular kinds of technologies are sought after, used to fill that need, and contribute to it. Tierney does not depict a linear, evolutionary path to explain technologies in any reductionist or essentialist way. Instead, this is a book about conceptions of privacy, the economic work of consumption practices, the settlement of the American West, changing modes of transportation, the devolution of Protestantism, the development of the idea of labour as a calling, the 'death' of God, the fear of death, etc. But yes, it tells us an enormous amount about why, for example, we simply have to have cell phones or faster computers, and why we have to teach our

children certain kinds of literacy skills as though those were *the* skills that ensured their survival into the twenty-first century. There are *things* in Tierney's account, but interestingly they are not the point.

Genealogy is hard and frustrating work – never complete, and always open to revision and contestation. It is not about objects that stand still for scrutiny. It is, like cultural studies generally, a conversation, a mapping project, in which the exploration of possibilities for rearticulation is the point.

IDENTITY, POLITICS AND THE BIAS OF TECHNOLOGY

The issue of identity has always been central to cultural studies work, from its disputes with Marxism's class determination of identity to the importance of the idea of identity to culture (and culture to identity). Marxist positions suggest that the individual is determined by class position, but it has been cultural studies' argument that such relations are non-necessary, that is, they are articulated. The connections between class, culture and identity are the result of struggle; they are not natural but can be rearticulated with work. This, again, is not a relativism. Individuals and groups construct their identity within and against unequal structures of power. As Marx once wrote in the *Eighteenth Brumaire of Louis Bonaparte*: 'Men make history, but they do not make it just as they please' (quoted in Feuer, 1959: 321).

Cultural studies also argues against essentialist positions on identity. Rather identity is the product of social relations and experience. Following Williams (1958/1989) in 'Culture is ordinary', identity is formed in the relations among traditions and heritage and a whole way of life, that is, in the living of that heritage and the negotiation of the challenges that experience raises to that heritage. From this we can identify two problematics of cultural studies work. The first is the question of identity: how is identity created? The second is the question of reproduction: how are social relations – and especially social inequalities – reproduced? What is the role of cultural practices in the reproduction of social relations?

Technology interjects its role in these problematics in three ways: (1) How is technology a constituent of identity? (2) How is technology a cultural practice (part of the broader theme of this essay)? (3) How do technologies reproduce social inequalities; in other words, how are technologies political and how do they factor in issues of power? Though we can identify work on gender, race and class bias of technologies, little work has been done within a cultural studies approach to technology and identity apart from the more Foucauldian notion of technologies of the self (though this work is important) (Foucault, 1988; Probyn, 1993).

When talking about the *politics* of technology, at least two things can be meant. One is the more generally circulated argument around the political *uses* of technology. Often these debates rely on a neutral view of technology, that a technology's politics are determined by its uses. However, Winner (1986) has persuasively argued that we should consider that the technological arrangement itself, prior to its specific use, not only reflects but imposes a social order. His examples are by now well known: the bridges on Long Island were designed by Robert Moses to be too low for buses to be let through, thus cutting off access to the island to the poor and minorities who were more likely to use public transport; campuses were designed (and redesigned) to make it difficult for students to organize after the student protests of the 1960s; expensive industrial machines were installed in Cyrus McCormick's reaper manufacturing plant in order to replace workers and force out the unions (the machines were taken out after the unions were defeated); the mechanical tomato harvester developed by University of California researchers favoured large farms over smaller farms and had a significant impact on farm labour in California and also on the types of tomatoes grown; buildings are designed that discriminate against the disabled; and so on. Technologies, Winner argues, are ways of building order into the world, and design decisions can affect populations for generations. In addition, he argues that some technologies are by

their very nature political in that they tend to favour centralization or decentralization, egalitarian organization or non-egalitarian organization, or tend to be repressive or liberating. His example here is nuclear energy, which by the truly dangerous nature of its material demands security, elite control and centralization. Winner acknowledges that the level of determination varies on a case-by-case basis. Some technologies require certain social conditions and arrangements to work (for example, a ship at sea in a storm cannot be run via participatory democracy), and some technologies are more or less compatible with different social systems (for example, solar energy is potentially more democratic than nuclear energy). Iain Boal argues that all technologies have a 'value slope', that is, 'they conduce to certain forms of life and of consciousness, and against others' (1995: 12).

In writing about communication technology, Harold Innis (1951) introduced the idea of the *bias* of a technology: bias towards centralization or decentralization of power. For example, Eric Michaels (1989), in an essay on the Aboriginal Australian use of television, notes that broadcast television is by its nature highly centralized (one-to-many broadcasting) and prone to elite control. It is also prone to homogenization and the imposition of values from one location on a broader area: 'The bias of mass broadcasting is concentration and unification; the bias of Aboriginal culture is diversity and autonomy' (1989: 13). Aboriginal culture, which values time, locality and kinship, runs at odds with the standard broadcast model that threatens Aboriginal culture.

When we discuss bias we mean tendency; these are not absolute determinations. It is very possible to have democratic television (for example, public-access, low-power local stations, as the Aboriginal Warlpiri developed) or radio (for example, pirate radio stations which often cover only a few blocks), but such uses are discouraged (and are often illegal).

When we talk about the bias of electronic communication technologies we should, of course, immediately think of new media such as the Internet and World Wide Web. These technologies are biased towards decentralization, though as Andrew Shapiro (1999) points out, democracy on the Internet – despite its bias – is not a sure thing. We hear from proponents of these technologies many of the same promises for democracy, equality and world peace which were proposed for the telegraph, telephone, radio, television, etc. Indeed, cyberspace itself has its roots in the nineteenth century (see, e.g. Standage, 1998). Jon Stratton (1997) argues that its origins can be found in attempts to speed up the circulation of commodities. Drawing on Carey's (1983/1989) germinal work on the cultural and social impact of the telegraph (especially on markets), Stratton places the origins of cyberspace within capital's processes of deterritorialization and reterritorialization. Electronic communication technologies are fundamentally associated with industrial and finance capital's attempts at control (cf. Beniger, 1986). Public space, that of either the imagined community, the public sphere or the mass audience, is structured to ensure general passivity on the part of the public (the public is represented by others and therefore becomes a spectator to democracy as well as television). Stratton writes that the fragmentation of the mass media through new technologies of cable, satellite and video, plus the global flows of people, technologies, ideas and so on (described by Appadurai, 1996), plus the increase in interactivity, result in a 'qualitative shift' which works to undermine the old mass media (and political) model of centre and periphery. This shift is being countered, and the democratizing potentials constrained, by the rearticulation of the Internet into the information superhighway in which the Internet becomes another mass media delivery vehicle (with portals such as Yahoo! replacing networks). In addition, Stratton writes that frequent appeals to the trope of community in relation to the Internet hark back to a narrowly ideological and culturally specific view of what constitutes a community. The lesson to draw from Stratton is not that these technologies are inherently one way or the other, but that the Internet is the site of political struggle among (at least) information technology's value slope, capitalistic institutions, and the cultures through which it is developed and disseminated.

The political biases of technology have frequently been addressed through the lens of gender. The work on gender and technology is fairly extensive, including work on new media (for example, Balsamo, 1996; Cherny and Weise, 1996; Consalvo and Paasonen, 2002; Green and Adam, 2001; Haraway, 1985; Miller, 1995; Rakow, 1988; Shade, 2002; Stone, 1995). That technologies have a gender bias is evident from Ruth Schwartz Cowan's work, *More Work for Mother* (1983). This classic study found that so-called labour-saving household appliances actually increased the amount of time that women were required to do housework and reinforced the social roles of women in the household and men out at work. Laura Miller's (1995) influential essay, 'Women and children first: gender and the settling of the electronic frontier', illustrates that technological gender bias has political uses. She argues, for example, that the depiction of cyberspace as a realm biased against, if not overtly hostile to, women serves the political function of increasing broad regulation and control over the Internet.

Beyond questions of gender bias and its political uses, cultural theorists have raised questions of gender identity as well. MUDs, MOOs, IRCs and other text-only media do not display a user's gender, thus allowing for passing or gender-bending online, about which great numbers of both academic and popular essays have been written (for example, see Spender, 1996; and essays in Cherny and Weise, 1996; Consalvo and Paasonen, 2002; Green and Adam, 2001; and Jones, 1998). The ability to elide or bend gender has the potential to be politically empowering by evening the playing field. For example, the usual gendered tactics of dominating a conversation can be lessened, and ideas can be more readily evaluated on the basis of their merit rather than on the appearance of the speaker. Online gender-bending throws into question the nature of gendered identity and enters into debates over essentialist versus anti-essentialist frameworks for understanding gender. Basically the questions become: *can* a person mask their gender effectively online? Can a man successfully masquerade as a woman, and vice versa? Or will gender always out? Dale Spender (1996), for example, drawing on decades of research on language, believes that a user's gender will eventually make itself known. This argument tends to fall back into an essentialist position, but not necessarily. It could be seen as recognizing the point that one cannot so easily shrug off years of socialization. For Miller, these arguments lead her to question how 'adequate those [gender] roles are to the task of describing real human beings' anyway (1995: 57).

Similar issues arise in relation to race and online environments. Though works on the racial bias of new media are not as extensive as those on gender, these issues are being addressed under the phrase 'the digital divide', a phrase taken up by the Clinton administration in the spring of 2000 to discuss the wiring of inner-city schools, native American reservations, and other 'have nots'. Issues of racial identity online have been addressed only recently (Kolko et al., 2000; Nakamura, 1995, 2002; Nelson et al., 2001). The starting point of these discussions is the alleged erasure of race in cyberspace (accompanying erasures of gender, class, ability and so forth). An MCI advertisement entitled 'Anthem' (discussed in Kolko et al., 2000: 15, 134, 180) sets out the utopian scenario: 'There is no race. There is no gender. There is no age. There are no infirmities. There are only minds. Utopia? No, Internet'. Though we may wish for a utopian society where, to echo Martin Luther King Jr, we judge people at last by the content of their character and not the colour of their skin, a world where prejudice does not play any role in our reactions, interactions and exchanges, the reality is something different. When the trope of 'no race in cyberspace' is not only established in discourses about the Internet but also built into the architecture of the system itself (there often isn't even a command in virtual environments to indicate race), the elision of race only serves to support the culturally unspoken dominant: whiteness. When one's race is not mentioned, the default assumption is that one is white. Tara McPherson (2000) labels this a version of 'covert' racism where race is simply ignored, but segregation nonetheless ensues. This reinforces the point that cyberspace exists not in a vacuum but in a particular social and cultural conjuncture. As Kolko et al. write:

You may be able to go online and not have anyone know your race or gender – you may even be able to take cyberspace's potential for anonymity a step further and masquerade as a race or gender that doesn't reflect the real, offline you – but neither the invisibility nor the mutability of online identity makes it possible for you to escape your 'real world' identity completely. Consequently, race matters in cyberspace precisely because all of us who spend time online are already shaped by the ways in which race matters offline, and we can't help but bring our own knowledge, experiences, and values with us when we log on. (2000: 4–5)

One limitation to approaching technology in terms of the bias or value slope of a technology is that, careful as they are, these accounts are still haunted by the spectre of technological determinism, in that social problems tend to be seen as technology's 'fault'. What is needed is an approach which exorcizes this ghost. For this, cultural theorists of technology turn to Latour. Latour's work explains how effectivity occurs in the parallel processes of delegation and prescription. Delegation occurs when a task is assigned to someone or something. Latour offers the example of a door. For a door to work effectively, that is, to keep undesired things out and to permit desired passage through, it needs to be consistently shut after it has been opened (or else why have a door?) The task of shutting a door can be delegated to humans: either hire someone to stand there and open or close the door, or train people to shut the door behind them. Neither option is completely foolproof (one may hire a fool or have foolish people pass through one's door, leaving it standing open). One could delegate the task to a machine: an automatic door closer (or groom) which does the task quietly, efficiently and consistently. In this way we delegate tasks to non-humans (stoplights instead of traffic cops, etc.). Technologies are our lieutenants; they stand in place of (in lieu of) our own actions.

However, we cannot consider the process of delegation alone. To do so would be to fall into a naïve social constructionism, as though technologies merely embodied social desire. This is naïve because once technologies are in place, they prescribe behaviours back on us. The door closer will work in a certain way (too fast, too slow, too stiff) and we must adjust to the properties of this particular machine (just as we know which copying machine to use and which jams more frequently, or which elevator is faster). One must be able to push on a door with a certain amount of force and then hold it from slamming back. Further, technology prescribes behaviour back on *all* those who encounter it, not just those who initially delegate the task (for example, designers, city planners, engineers and so on). Those who delegate and those who are impinged upon can be (and often are) quite disparate groups of people (Star, 1991). In this way Latour argues that technologies are moral. They impose 'correct' behaviour and foster 'good' habits. 'In spite of the constant weeping of moralists, no human is as relentlessly moral as a machine, especially if it is (she is, he is, they are) as "user friendly" as my computer' (1988: 301). In addition, the technology may be discriminatory, making it difficult for small children, the elderly, or the physically challenged to move through the door.

No one feels the prescription of new information and communication technologies (ICTs) more than those who are forced to work with them every day and whose livelihoods depend on them. Data-intensive work can lead easily to physical effects, such as carpal tunnel syndrome, eye strain and so on. The impact of ICTs on the nature of the labour market as a whole is enormous (Aronowitz and DiFazio, 1994; Dyer-Witheford, 1999). New ICTs provide myriad opportunities for surveillance, such as the counting of key strokes. The emphasis on speed is a means of extending management control over the workforce. As Andrew Ross has put it, 'let's not forget that for every one of us who wants our PCs and software to go faster, there are fifty others who want them to go slower' (1998: 20).

But the process of prescription should not be taken on its own either. This leads straight to technological determinism, because it only considers how technology affects society. Rather, Latour emphasizes that we must grasp both processes. The politics of technology goes in both directions: what is delegated and what is prescribed. This is not to suggest that the equation of power balances out. Rather it is to

suggest that the same care that has been taken when examining the ideology, politics and power of cultural *texts* needs to be extended to cover technologies as well. But to do so we need to develop a subtle enough language which can adequately describe these processes.

SOCIAL SPACE AND CORPOREALITY

A more recent concern of cultural studies has been that of social space (Grossberg, 1993). When this problematic is applied to technology it means more than saying that technology is social or that the impact on society is socially determined. The social in this approach is inherently and predominantly spatial; the spatial dimensions of technology are social. Historically, arguments along these lines have fallen into a technological determinism. For example, Elizabeth Eisenstein (1979) argued that the printing press changed the shape of European society. But a spatial approach is not necessarily deterministic. Cultural studies approaches technology as a contingent social agent in everyday life.

One approach to this view of technology has been through the nexus of time, space, orality and literacy. Drawing on the work of Carey (for example, 1989), Eric Havelock (for example, 1982), Innis (for example, 1951), Marshall McLuhan (for example, 1964) and Walter Ong (for example, 1982), this general approach examines how the characteristics of communication technologies shape the experience of the users and even mould society itself. For example, Innis has argued that communication technologies have a 'bias' not only towards either centralization or decentralization, but more crucially towards space or time. Carving on stone is a more permanent medium and serves to maintain a society longitudinally through time. Papyrus, though less permanent, is lighter and much more portable, and therefore has a bias toward space. The choice of medium, then, has consequences for the political shape of that society. Time-bias media focus on maintenance of community in time: space-bias media focus on control over space, and therefore promote empire. Yet, space-bias media also hold forth the possibility of the democratization of society. More recent scholars, such as Berland (1992) and Carey (1989), have argued that modern electronic technologies are space-biased and therefore fundamentally concerned with control. From the promises of global connectivity of the telephone companies to the 'World' in the World Wide Web, new media discourses emphasize space over time. This control of space is perhaps both exacerbated and foiled by the electronic language of new media that, as Mark Poster (1990) points out, can no longer be located in space and time. With its 'time–space coordinates undermined', electronic language 'is everywhere and nowhere, always and never. It is truly material/immaterial' (1990: 85).

The characteristics of a medium may have psychodynamic effects as well as social effects. For example, Ong (1982) discusses the physical characteristics of sound and sound reception and how these characteristics shape an orally based culture. Likewise, with limited extra-somatic resources, an oral society is dependent on mnemonics, repetition and ritualized questioning to create and pass along knowledge. The invention of writing and the printing press allowed for deeper, more unique thoughts and ideas to be expressed, though these also emphasized linear thought (McLuhan and Fiore, 1967). Recent cultural studies work has followed through on this thread, noting that social space is not just a visual space, but an aural and oral space as well (Sterne, 2003).

Social space, in this cultural tradition following Innis, is both a sphere of politics (community versus control) and a phenomenological space (living in an oral, or print, or electronic world). Contemporary cultural studies has begun to address issues of technology and social space in terms of agency and corporeality in an attempt to avoid the latent determinism of the earlier tradition. For example, following Deleuze and Guattari, Wise (1997: 57–82) has identified two types of agency, corporeal and incorporeal; the first is termed *technology*, and the second *language*. Key to understanding these concepts is the relation between them. Technology and language are articulated and

presuppose each other. Human social space is the result of this articulation and is always made up of both language and technology and a particular, contingent relation between them. For example, discourse on new media, especially in the United States, tends to emphasize linguistic agency over the technological. This is the foundation of democracy, the ability of the free citizen to instigate change through non-corporeal means: the vote. Indeed, trends in new media emphasize the democratic possibilities of the new technologies. With the power of language, we control machines that might otherwise overpower us. It is often made to seem as if new technologies are themselves incorporeal: the mere bits of cyberspace (for example, Mitchell, 1995; Negroponte, 1995). However, to the extent that social space is increasingly permeated by technologies (especially those of communication), we need to realize that these technologies also operate in the realm of corporeal agency, despite the seeming ephemerality of the digital.

Approaching technology in terms of corporeality involves considering the materiality of the technology itself, the system itself, the linkages and connections of the physical infrastructure. For example, if we consider virtual communities, non-corporeal agency involves the exchange of ideas, and the notion that these communities involve only the meeting of minds. But virtual communities are more than this; they are organizations and networks which have materiality. A virtual community is a network of corporeal procedures. We need to consider the effects of that corporeality on the communication within, the actions of, and the shaping of the network itself. Harrison and Stephen (1999) write that technologies, especially virtual communities, are *embodiments* of ideas. It is not just the ideas themselves which shape virtual communities, but how they are embodied in technologies which impinge back on the user and system, making corporeal demands of their own.

One of the key sites of corporeal agency, and a focus of postmodern treatments of technology, is the body itself. Serious consideration needs to be paid to the body and technology (called biotechnology) by both cultural studies and communication theory (on the latter, see Slack, forthcoming) As Slack wrote over a decade ago, one question cultural studies of technology might/must ask is how technology articulates in/with postmodern culture:

> What is the pleasure of using a PC? Are the techniques pleasurable (for example, the techniques of writing or bookkeeping)? Is the pleasure tactile, aural, visual? How does the body challenge/engage/disengage/control/master/command the PC? What is the nature of that interaction? Does the body become superfluous? (1989: 343)

Affect, we are arguing, is a corporeal aspect of new technologies. Affect is often cited in discourses around new technologies (especially work on virtual communities, for example, Rheingold, 1993) as a certain intensity of purpose behind new technologies. As Rheingold has written, virtual communities need to be more than simply virtual if they are to be more than merely ersatz communities (1993: 23). This means not just adding in physical meetings (picnics, get-togethers) to the composition of a virtual community, but considering affective responses to online activity as an embodied response.

Anne Balsamo's *Technologies of the Gendered Body* (1996) is an exemplar of a contemporary cultural studies approach to issues of the body. Though the book does spend time analysing the representations of body and how bodies signify (aspects of incorporeal agency), it also examines non-signifying aspects of the technocorporeal articulation. Balsamo asks, 'how is the body, as a "thing of nature", transformed into a "sign of culture"?' (1996: 3). The body is both a product of social forces and a process of identity creation. Her book concerns a range of new technologies from bodybuilding to cosmetic surgery, pregnancy to the plugged-in cyberpunk.

Information technology is accelerating us, Mark Dery argues, to an escape velocity. In *Escape Velocity* (1996) he describes subcultures caught up in the techno-transcendentalist movement that pushes the body to its limits, ultimately attempting to abandon the body in the pure space of cyberspace. Examples are numerous in writings on cyberculture where material structures (especially the body) are abandoned and subjects are left to play in 'the city of bits' (Mitchell, 1995; Moravec, 1988; Negroponte, 1995).

Decorporealization has its dangers, however, and it definitely has its blind spots. It ignores many of the effects of power and politics outlined in the previous section. For example, Brook and Boal have written:

> The wish to leave body, time, and place behind in search of electronic emulation of community does not accidentally intensify at a time when the space and time of everyday life have become so uncertain, unpleasant, and dangerous for so many – even if it is the people best insulated from risk who show the greatest fear ... But the flight into cyberspace is motivated by some of the same fears and longings as the flight to the suburbs: it is another 'white flight'. (1995: ix)

The focus on corporeal agency has other implications. Much of the work on technology, and not only in cultural studies, focuses on representation and the processes of signification: what technology means; how it is represented; what it represents; and so on. These questions are meant to get at the cultural aspects of technology. But a version of culture that deals only with representation and signification is a limited version of culture indeed. Culture is much more than simply signifying practices. Lefebvre (1991) argues, using a model of social space, that there are non-signifying aspects to space and culture.

In *The Production of Space*, Lefebvre presents three ways of thinking about space: spatial practice, representations of space, and representational space (or, more briefly, space as it is perceived, conceived and lived). Spatial practice 'embraces production and reproduction, and the particular locations and spatial sets characteristic of each social formation. Spatial practice ensures continuity and some degree of cohesion. In terms of social space, this cohesion implies a guaranteed level of competence and a specific level of performance' (1991: 33). Representations of space are abstract, conceptualized space, a plane of concepts (for example, modern social space is constructed around concepts of efficiency, newness/revolution, technicism and so on). Representational space (or, better and more literally, spaces of representation) is 'space as directly lived through its associated images and symbols, and hence the space of inhabitants and "users"' (1991: 39).

In terms of technology, then, we need to consider technology as a spatial practice, and technology's effect on spatial practices. We could consider the rearrangement of the work environment, even the dissolution of the work environment, into a virtual office. We could also consider the way devices such as personal stereos, pagers and ankle trackers articulate space. Changes in representations of space are particularly evident with new media, with new data-mapping technologies on the one hand and new geographies of cyberspace on the other (Elmer, 2004). Finally, spaces of representation present new media technologies as a new frontier (cf. Rheingold, 1993), a neighbourhood mall, a salon or café, and so on (see also discussions in Jones, 1997, 1998).

One of the more recent and, we believe, important articulations or discourses around the idea of social space comes from recent work in urban geography which brings together the spatial disciplines of geography (for example Massey, 1994) and the more corporeal/material approach of urban studies that considers urban space. An exemplary work in this area is the book *Telecommunications and the City* (1996) by Stephen Graham and Simon Marvin, which looks at the idea of city space from a variety of perspectives, taking into account the telecommunications infrastructure (that is, in this case, the telephone system), the changing nature of the urban landscape, urban planning and economics, and Latourian notions of agency, plus how such things contribute to the construction of space, the construction of private and public through new media technologies (see also Droege, 1997).

Approaches to technology and social space overlap approaches to technology, politics and power in the issue of surveillance. Graham and Marvin write, 'telecommunications, combined with computers and media technologies, are at the most fundamental level control and surveillance technologies' (1996: 213). Such control technologies 'have allowed large and complex industrial societies to develop' (1996: 214). While acknowledging the dystopian spin that is often placed on issues of surveillance and

control, Graham and Marvin rightly point out that surveillance is not one singular thing but occurs in a variety of contexts, and the diverse means of surveillance are not yet centralized.

Deriving from the work of Foucault (especially 1977a), the principle of surveillance has been used to talk about a number of issues, for example how architecture (including streets, schools, prisons and so on) can be structured under the idea of the gaze. This is a visual model of surveillance. Demanding consideration is work that puts surveillance in a historical context, as Foucault did, but which is sometimes forgotten, with the effect that surveillance is used as a more universalist principle. Some of the last writing of Deleuze (1995) was on new forms of surveillance and control, outlining a regime of control that differs from the more institutionally based disciplinary society of the nineteenth century which Foucault delineated. It is also important to note non-visual aspects of surveillance, especially the management of personal data and new organizations of, and linkages between, previously disparate databases of information to create superprofiles. The idea of consumer surveillance, for example, has most prominently been discussed from a political economy standpoint (Gandy, 1993). But there have been other attempts to discuss both the social effects of surveillance (Lyon, 1994, 2001, 2003; Poster, 1990) and the cultural effects of surveillance (Bogard, 1996; Elmer, 2004; Staples, 1997).

In terms of Lefebvre's notion of social space, we can see surveillance as articulating a spatial practice (the construction of public/private space), the changing nature of representations of space (the wavering line between public and private) and representations of space. Surveillance is a practice that creates a physical setup (arena, panopticon, practice) that assesses representations of space (video monitors of a public square) according to ideologically loaded presumptions of criminality and identity. Surveillance has moved from watching and then catching after the fact to predicting, then watching, then catching *before* the fact. This applies to visually oriented notions of surveillance as well as to other forms of data surveillance, including marketing (Gandy,

1993). What is established is a crucial linkage between surveillance and simulation (Bogard, 1996; see also Graham's, 1998, response to Bogard).

The question to ask here, especially post-9/11, is, what would a more explicitly cultural studies approach to surveillance look like? Following from our analysis in this chapter, we suggest examining the articulations and stratifications of discourse and technology, what technologies are purported to represent or mean and how they fit in within broader discourses of society (especially discourses of terror, security, and fear). But we also need to think through how surveillance becomes part of culture, how notions of privacy and control articulate to *practices* of surveillance and the materiality of shaped social space. As such, Steve Mann's (2001) work on surveillance and everyday life, sousveillance (watching the watchers) as resistance, and the cyborg as contemporary condition is promising.

In addition to issues of corporeality and surveillance, contemporary cultural studies work on social space also addresses dimensions of everyday life and globalization. The work on everyday life derives jointly from cultural studies' ethnographic tradition (for example, Hall and Jefferson, 1976; Willis, 1977) and more recently from the works of Lefebvre (1991) and Michel de Certeau (1984). Yet except for studies of technology in the home (particularly television, see Silverstone and Hirsch, 1992; for IT in the home, see Noble, 1999), technology remains absent. Perhaps a cultural studies of everyday life inflected via Latour's notion of technology as social actors might prove generative in future studies. If nothing else, the Y2K computer issue (the so-called millennium bug) pointed out the ubiquity of technology in the daily lives of industrialized countries, as people worried about their toasters not working after New Year's Day 2000.

A contemporary cultural studies perspective on technology and everyday life is especially important given the proliferation of ICTs and their embedding in the environment. Older notions of ubiquitous computing and smart rooms have come much closer to reality. From networks of texting/voicing/imaging mobile telephones (see e.g. Katz, 2003; Katz and Aakhus, 2002), PDAs and other such devices to embedded location-aware/communication-enabled technologies in everyday objects and settings, new media have rapidly become part of the everyday habits and settings of contemporary urban culture. Such ambient technologies (Aarts and Marzano, 2003), with their abilities to create smart environments and smart mobs (Rheingold, 2003), require careful cultural analysis.

Most work on globalization focuses on political economy, though more studies are addressing the cultural aspects of the process (Bird et al., 1993; Tomlinson, 1999; Waters, 1995). Few, however, have addressed globalization in terms of both culture and technology. Stratton (1997) is an exception, though his essay ends up being more political economy than culturally oriented. Most discourses of globalization fail to engage issues of culture and technology despite the fact that most accounts of globalization do not fail to note that globalization is dependent upon new media, communication and information technologies connecting financial markets, factories and so on. The area demands further work (see Abbas and Erni, 2005).

CONCLUSION

To undertake cultural studies of new media technology is neither exact nor scientific. It is always provisional. This makes the question of responsibility decidedly tricky. If we do not conceive of easily identifiable agents who (or that) exercise agency in any easily identifiable way, how can we hold anyone or anything responsible in any way? The risk of disbursing agency (especially across both humans and non-humans) is that it becomes possible to so disburse responsibility as to create either paralysis or the total denial of any responsibility. However, even though the self and subjectivity are in a sense abstractions, different conceptions of self and subjectivity enable and constrain possibilities with potentially enormous consequences in relations of power. As Grossberg explains:

Obviously, within cultural studies, the question of agency involves more than a simple question of whether or how people control their own actions through some act of will. In classical modern terms, the issue of agency raises questions of the freedom of the will, or of how people can be responsible for their determined actions. But in broader cultural terms, questions of agency involve the possibilities of action as interventions into the processes by which reality is continually being transformed and power enacted. (1996: 99)

There is a pressing need in cultural studies to link these theoretical insights to practical decision-making, with, for example, decisions regarding the new media technology. There is a need to consider dimensions of agency, politics and space in the design, implementation and use of new media.

It is always easy to make these suggestions or critiques of other people in other places (designers, policy-makers, the public), but if we are to hold on to the conjunctural aspect of cultural studies we must also address our own practices which most often are within the context of higher education. As it has aptly been put by Calvin O. Schrag, 'A university that does not respond to the technological developments of the current age can be said to be both nonresponsive and irresponsible in the moral sense' (quoted in McMillan and Hyde, 2000). We are commanded to respond responsibly in ways that cultural studies has not yet determined how to do. Sterne, like other cultural theorists, is characteristic in claiming that 'Cultural studies' usefulness to Internet research should … be measured by the degree to which it can get its readers to think beyond the technophilic–technophobic dichotomy, beyond the rhetoric of millennial [now in 2006, we can substitute revolutionary] transformation' (1999: 282). Okay, but what then do we do? And what sense do we make of the construction 'we do'?

A cultural studies that 'lets us off the hook' is antithetical to the impulses that still articulate to the motivations of most of its practitioners. Yet, quite honestly, because cultural studies (in North America at least) is so firmly ensconced within technophilic and corporatizing universities, it is difficult to find a theoretical and practical path that does not result in the identification of the cultural theorist as technophilic, technophobic or opportunistic. There clearly is work yet to be undertaken.

NOTES

1 For example, see Carol Cohn (1989) for an analysis of the gendered ways that defence intellectuals characterize their technologies and practices; see Richard Coyne (1995) on the philosophical assumptions of information technology designers.

2 We are aware of, and uncomfortable with, the inadequacy of our occasional use of the construction 'the relationship between culture and technology', which gives the impression that culture is one thing and technology is another. While cultural studies works actively against such a construction, the phrase is so widely used in the discourse on technology that it is difficult to find a replacement that does not sound ridiculously theoreticist. Likewise we are aware of, and uncomfortable with, the almost inevitable slides in the meaning of technology as, on the one hand, an object of analysis in the abstract sense (as in technology and culture) and, on the other hand, an object of analysis in the more concrete sense of a particular technology or technological apparatus.

REFERENCES

Aarts, Emile and Marzano, Stefano (2003) *The New Everyday: Views on Ambient Intelligence*. Rotterdam: 010 Publishers.

Abbas, Ackbar and Erni, John Nguyet (eds) (2005) *Internationalizing Cultural Studies: An Anthology*. Malden, MA: Blackwell.

Acland, Charles (1998) 'IMAX technology and the tourist gaze', *Cultural Studies*, 12 (3): 429–45.

America's Technology Literacy Challenge (1996) 15 February. Available online: www.whitehouse.gov/WH/New/edtech/2pager.html

Appadurai, Arjun (1996) *Modernity at Large: Cultural Dimensions of Globalization*. Minneapolis: University of Minnesota Press.

Aronowitz, Stanley and DiFazio, William (1994) *The Jobless Future: Sci-Tech and the Dogmas of Work*. Minneapolis: University of Minnesota Press.

Balsamo, Anne (1996) *Technologies of the Gendered Body: Reading Cyborg Women*. Durham, NC: Duke University Press.

Beniger, James (1986) *The Control Revolution: Technological and Economic Origins of the Information Society*. Cambridge, MA: Harvard University Press.

Berland, Jody (1992) 'Angels dancing: cultural technologies and the production of space', in

Lawrence Grossberg, Cary Nelson and Paula A. Treichler (eds), *Cultural Studies*. New York: Routledge. pp. 38–51.

Berland, Jody (2000) 'Cultural technologies and the "evolution" of technological cultures', in Andrew Herman and Thomas Swiss (eds), *The World Wide Web and Contemporary Cultural Theory: Magic, Metaphor, Power*. New York: Routledge.

Bird, Jon, Curtis, Barry, Putnam, Tim, Robertson, George and Tickner, Lisa (eds) (1993) *Mapping the Futures: Local Cultures, Global Change*. New York: Routledge.

Boal, Iain (1995) 'A flow of monsters: Luddism and virtual technologies', in James Brook and Iain Boal (eds), *Resisting the Virtual Life: The Culture and Politics of Information*. San Francisco: City Lights. pp. 3–15.

Bogard, William (1996) *The Simulation of Surveillance: Hypercontrol in Telematic Societies*. Cambridge: Cambridge University Press.

Borgmann, Albert (1984) *Technology and the Character of Contemporary Life: A Philosophical Inquiry*. Chicago: University of Chicago Press.

Brook, James and Boal, Iain A. (eds) (1995) *Resisting the Virtual Life: The Culture and Politics of Information*. San Francisco: City Lights.

Callon, Michel and Latour, Bruno (1981) 'Unscrewing the big leviathan: how actors macro-structure reality and how sociologists help them do so', in K. Knorr-Cetina and A. Cicourel (eds), *Advances in Social Theory and Methodology: Toward an Integration of Micro- and Macro-Sociologies*. Boston: Routledge & Kegan Paul. pp. 277–303.

Carey, James W. (1975/1989) 'A cultural approach to communication', reprinted in *Communication as Culture: Essays on Media and Society*. Boston: Unwin Hyman. pp. 13–36.

Carey, James W. (1983/1989) 'Technology and ideology: the case of the telegraph', reprinted in *Communication as Culture: Essays on Media and Society*. Boston: Unwin Hyman. pp. 201–30.

Carey, James W. (1989) 'Space, time, and communications: a tribute to Harold Innis', in *Communication as Culture: Essays on Media and Society*. Boston: Unwin Hyman. pp. 142–72.

Cherny, Lynn and Weise, Elizabeth Reba (1996) *Wired_Women: Gender and New Realities in Cyberspace*. Seattle: Seal.

Clark, Andy (2003) *Natural-born Cyborgs: Minds, Technologies, and the Future of Human Intelligence*. New York: Oxford University Press.

Cohn, Carol (1989) 'Sex and death in the rational world of defense intellectuals', in Micheline R. Malson, Jean F. O'Barr, Sarah Westphal-Wihl and Mary Wyler (eds), *Feminist Theory in Practice and Process*. Chicago: University of Chicago Press. pp. 107–38.

Consalvo, Mia and Paasonen, Susan (eds) (2002) *Women & Everyday Uses of the Internet: Agency and Identity*. New York: Peter Lang.

Cowan, Ruth Schwartz (1983) *More Work for Mother: The Ironies of Household Technology from the Open Hearth to the Microwave*. New York: Basic.

Coyne, Richard (1995) *Designing Information Technology in the Postmodern Age: From Method to Metaphor*. Cambridge, MA: MIT Press.

de Certeau, Michel (1984) *The Practice of Everyday Life*, trans. Steven Rendall. Berkeley, CA: University of California Press.

Deleuze, Gilles (1995) *Negotiations: 1972–1990*, trans. Martin Joughin. New York: Columbia University Press.

Deleuze, Gilles and Guattari, Félix (1987) *A Thousand Plateaus: Capitalism and Schizophrenia*, trans. Brian Massumi. Minneapolis: University of Minnesota Press.

Dery, Mark (1996) *Escape Velocity: Cyberculture and the End of the Century*. New York: Grove.

Droege, Peter (ed.) (1997) *Intelligent Environments: Spatial Aspects of the Information Revolution*. New York: Elsevier.

Dyer-Witheford, Nick (1999) *Cyber-Marx: Cycles and Circuits of Struggle in High-technology Capitalism*. Urbana, IL: University of Illinois Press.

Eisenstein, Elizabeth (1979) *The Printing Press as an Agent of Change: Communications and Cultural Transformations in Early Modern Europe*. New York: Cambridge University Press.

Elmer, Greg (2004) *Profiling Machines: Mapping the Personal Information Economy*. Cambridge, MA: MIT Press.

Feenberg, Andrew (1991) *Critical Theory of Technology*. New York: Oxford University Press.

Feuer, Lewis S. (ed.) (1959) *Marx and Engels: Basic Writings on Politics and Philosophy*. Garden City, NY: Anchor.

Foucault, Michel (1977a) *Discipline and Punish: The Birth of the Prison*, trans. Alan Sheridan. Harmondsworth: Penguin.

Foucault, Michel (1977b) 'Nietzsche, genealogy, history', in *Language, Counter-memory, Practice: Selected Essays and Interviews*, trans. D.F. Bouchard and S. Simon. Ithaca, NY: Cornell University Press.

Foucault, Michel (1988) *Technologies of the Self: A Seminar with Michel Foucault*, edited by Luther H. Martin, Huck Gutman and Patrick H. Hutton. Amherst, MA: University of Massachusetts Press.

Gandy, Oscar H., Jr (1993) *The Panoptic Sort: a Political Economy of Personal Information.* Boulder, CO: Westview.

Graham, Stephen (1998) 'Spaces of surveillant simulation: new technologies, digital representations, and material geographies', *Environment and Planning D: Society and Space,* 16: 483–504.

Graham, Stephen and Marvin, Simon (1996) *Telecommunications and the City: Electronic Spaces, Urban Places.* New York: Routledge.

Green, Eileen and Adam, Alison (2001) *Virtual Gender: Technology, Consumption and Identity.* New York: Routledge.

Grossberg, Lawrence (1993) 'Cultural studies and/in new worlds', *Critical Studies in Mass Communication,* 10 (1): 1–22.

Grossberg, Lawrence (1996) 'Identity and cultural studies: is that all there is?', in Stuart Hall and Paul DuGay (eds), *Questions of Cultural Identity.* London: Sage. pp. 87–107.

Hall, Stuart (1983) 'The problem of ideology – Marxism without guarantees', in Betty Matthews (ed.), *Marx 100 Years on.* London: Lawrence & Wishart. pp. 57–84.

Hall, Stuart (1986) 'On postmodernism and articulation: an interview with Stuart Hall', by Lawrence Grossberg, *Journal of Communication Inquiry,* 10 (2): 45–60.

Hall, Stuart (1990) 'The emergence of cultural studies and the crisis of the humanities', *October,* 53: 11–23.

Hall, Stuart and Jefferson, Tony (eds) (1976) *Resistance through Rituals: Youth Subcultures in Post-War Britain.* London: Unwin Hyman.

Haraway, Donna (1985) 'A cyborg manifesto: science, technology and socialist-feminism in the 1980s', *Socialist Review,* 80: 65–108.

Haraway, Donna (1992) 'The promises of monsters: a regenerative politics for inappropriate/d others', in Lawrence Grossberg, Cary Nelson and Paula A. Treichler (eds), *Cultural Studies.* New York: Routledge. pp. 295–337.

Harrison, Teresa M. and Stephen, Timothy (1999) 'Researching and creating community networks', in Steve Jones (ed.), *Doing Internet Research: Critical Issues and Methods for Examining the Net.* Thousand Oaks, CA: Sage.

Havelock, Eric (1982) *The Literate Revolution in Greece and its Cultural Consequences.* Princeton, NJ: Princeton University Press.

Innis, Harold Adams (1951) *The Bias of Communication.* Toronto: University of Toronto Press.

Jones, Steve (1997) *Virtual Culture: Identity and Communication in Cybersociety.* Thousand Oaks, CA: Sage.

Jones, Steve (ed.) (1998) *Cybersociety 2.0: Revisiting Computer-mediated Communication and Community.* Thousand Oaks, CA: Sage.

Katz, James E. (ed.) (2003) *Machines That Become Us: The Social Context of Personal Communication Technology.* New Brunswick, NJ: Transaction Publishers.

Katz, James E. and Aakhus, Mark (2002) *Perpetual Contact: Mobile Communication, Private Talk, Public Performance.* New York: Cambridge University Press.

Kolko, Beth E., Nakamura, Lisa and Rodman, Gilbert B. (2000) *Race in Cyberspace.* New York: Routledge.

Latour, Bruno (alias Jim Johnson) (1988) 'Mixing humans and nonhumans together: the sociology of a door-closer', *Social Problems,* 35 (3): 298–310.

Latour, Bruno (1993) *We Have Never Been Modern,* trans. C. Porter. Cambridge, MA: Harvard University Press.

Latour, Bruno (1996) *Aramis, or the Love of Technology,* trans. C. Porter. Cambridge, MA: Harvard University Press.

Lefebvre, Henri (1991) *The Production of Space,* trans. D. Nicholson-Smith. Cambridge, MA: Blackwell.

Lerner, Daniel (1958) *The Passing of Traditional Society: Modernizing the Middle East.* Glencoe, IL: Free Press.

Lyon, David (1994) *The Electronic Eye: The Rise of Surveillance Society.* Minneapolis: University of Minnesota Press.

Lyon, David (2001) *Surveillance Society: Monitoring Everyday Life.* Buckingham and Philadelphia: Open University Press.

Lyon, David (2003) *Surveillance After September 11.* Cambridge: Polity Press.

Mann, Steve with Niedzviecki, Hal (2001) *Cyborg: Digital Destiny and Human Possibility in the Age of the Wearable Computer.* Toronto: Doubleday Canada.

Massey, Doreen (1994) *Space, Place, and Gender.* Minneapolis: University of Minnesota Press.

McLuhan, Marshall (1964) *Understanding Media: the Extensions of Man.* New York: Signet.

McLuhan, Marshall and Fiore, Quentin (1967) *The Medium Is the Massage: An Inventory of Effects.* New York: Bantam.

McMillan, Jill J. and Hyde, Michael J. (2000) 'Technological innovation and change: a case study in the formation of organizational conscience', *Quarterly Journal of Speech,* 86 (1): 19–47.

McPherson, Tara (2000) 'I'll take my stand in Dixie-net: white guys, the South, and cyberspace', in Beth E. Kolko, Lisa Nakamura and Gilbert B. Rodman (eds), *Race in Cyberspace.* New York: Routledge. pp. 117–31.

Michaels, Eric (1989) *For a Cultural Future: Francis Jupurrurla Makes TV at Yuendumu.* Sydney: Art and Text.

Miller, Laura (1995) 'Women and children first: gender and the settling of the electronic frontier', in James Brook and Iain A. Boal (eds), *Resisting the Virtual Life: The Culture and Politics of Information.* San Francisco: City Lights. pp. 49–57.

Mitchell, William J. (1995) *City of Bits: Space, Place and the Infobahn.* Cambridge, MA: MIT Press.

Moravec, Hans (1988) *Mind Children: The Future of Robot and Human Intelligence.* Cambridge, MA: Harvard University Press.

Nakamura, Lisa (1995) 'Race in/for cyberspace: identity tourism and racial passing on the Internet', *Works and Days,* 13 (1–2): 181–93.

Nakamura, Lisa (2002) *Cybertypes: Race, Ethnicity, and Identity on the Internet.* New York: Routledge.

Negroponte, Nicholas (1995) *Being Digital.* New York: Knopf.

Nelson, Alondra and Tu, Thuy Linh N. with Hines, Alicia Headlam (eds) (2001) *Technicolor: Race, Technology, and Everyday Life.* New York: NYU Press.

Nelson, Cary, Treichler, Paula A. and Grossberg, Lawrence (1992) 'Cultural studies: an introduction', in Lawrence Grossberg, Cary Nelson and Paula A. Treichler (eds), *Cultural Studies.* New York and London: Routledge. pp. 1–16.

Nisbet, Robert (1980) *History of the Idea of Progress.* New York: Basic.

Noble, David (1982) 'Introduction', in M. Cooley, *Architect or Bee? The Human/Technology Relationship.* Boston: South End.

Noble, Greg (1999) 'Domesticating technology: learning to live with your computer', *Australian Journal of Communication,* 26 (2): 59–76.

Ong, Walter (1982) *Orality and Literacy: the Technologizing of the Word.* London and New York: Routledge.

Plato (1952) *Phaedrus,* trans. R. Hackforth. Cambridge: Cambridge University Press.

Poster, Mark (1990) *The Mode of Information: Poststructuralism and Social Control.* Chicago: University of Chicago Press.

Probyn, Elspeth (1993) *Sexing the Self: Gendered Positions in Cultural Studies.* London and New York: Routledge.

Rakow, Lana F. (1988) 'Gendered technology, gendered practice', *Critical Studies in Mass Communication,* 5 (1): 57–70.

Rheingold, Howard (1993) *The Virtual Community: Homesteading on the Electronic Frontier.* New York: HarperCollins.

Rheingold, Howard (2003) *Smart Mobs: The Next Social Revolution.* Cambridge, MA: Perseus.

Ross, Andrew (1998) *Real Love: in Pursuit of Cultural Justice.* New York: New York University Press.

Shade, Leslie Regan (2002) *Gender and Community in the Social Construction of the Internet.* New York: Peter Lang.

Shapiro, Andrew L. (1999) 'The net that binds: using cyberspace to create real communities', *The Nation,* 21 June: 11–15.

Silverstone, Roger and Hirsch, Eric (eds) (1992) *Consuming Technologies: Media and Information in Domestic Spaces.* New York: Routledge.

Slack, Jennifer Daryl (1984) *Communication Technologies and Society: Conceptions of Causality and the Politics of Technological Intervention.* Norwood, NJ: Ablex.

Slack, Jennifer Daryl (1989) 'Contextualizing technology', in Brenda Dervin, Lawrence Grossberg, Barbara J. O'Keefe and Ellen Wartella (eds), *Rethinking Communication.* Vol. 2: *Paradigm Exemplars.* Newbury Park, CA: Sage.

Slack, Jennifer Daryl (ed.) (forthcoming) 'Communication, biotechnology, and the body', *Communication Theory* (special issue).

Smith, Merritt Roe and Marx, Leo (eds) (1994) *Does Technology Drive History? The Dilemma of Technological Determinism.* Cambridge, MA: MIT Press.

Spender, Dale (1996) *Nattering on the Net: Women, Power and Cyberspace.* Melbourne: Spinifex.

Standage, Tom (1998) *The Victorian Internet: The Remarkable Story of the Telegraph and the Nineteenth Century's On-line Pioneers.* New York: Walker & Company.

Staples, William G. (1997) *The Culture of Surveillance: Discipline and Social Control in the United States.* New York: St Martin's Press.

Star, Susan Leigh (1991) 'Power, technology and the phenomenology of conventions: on being allergic to onions', in J. Law (ed.), *A Sociology of Monsters? Power, Technology, and the Modern World.* Oxford: Blackwell. pp. 27–57.

Sterne, Jonathan (1999) 'Thinking the Internet: cultural studies versus the millennium', in Steve Jones (ed.), *Doing Internet Research: Critical Issues and Methods for Examining the Net.* Thousand Oaks, CA: Sage. pp. 257–87.

Sterne, Jonathan (2003) *The Audible Past: Cultural Origins of Sound Reproduction.* Durham, NC: Duke University Press.

Stone, Allucquère Rosanne (1995) *The War of Desire and Technology at the Close of the Mechanical Age.* Cambridge, MA: MIT Press.

Stratton, Jon (1997) 'Cyberspace and the globalization of culture', in D. Porter (ed.), *Internet Culture*. New York: Routledge. pp. 253–75.

Tenner, Edward (1996) *Why Things Bite Back: Technology and the Revenge of Unintended Consequences*. New York: Vintage.

Tierney, Thomas F. (1993) *The Value of Convenience: a Genealogy of Technical Culture*. Albany, NY: State University of New York Press.

Tomlinson, John (1999) *Globalization and Culture*. Chicago: University of Chicago Press.

Waters, Malcolm (1995) *Globalization*. New York: Routledge.

Williams, Raymond (1958/1989) 'Culture is ordinary', reprinted in Robin Gable (ed.), *Resources of Hope: Culture, Democracy, Socialism*. New York: Verso. pp. 3–18.

Williams, Raymond (1975) *Television: Technology and Cultural Form*. New York: Schocken.

Willis, Paul E. (1977) *Learning to Labor: How Working Class Kids Get Working Class Jobs*. Farnborough: Saxon House.

Winner, Langdon (1977) *Autonomous Technology: Technics-out-of-Control as a Theme in Political Thought*. Cambridge, MA: MIT Press.

Winner, Langdon (1986) 'Technologies as forms of life', in *The Whale and the Reactor: A Search for Limits in an Age of High Technology*. Chicago: University of Chicago Press. pp. 3–18.

Wise, J. Macgregor (1997) *Exploring Technology and Social Space*. Thousand Oaks, CA: Sage.

8

Power and Political Culture

TIMOTHY W. LUKE

Whether one examines the saavy use of the Web by Osama bin Laden and Al Qaeda or Donald Rumsfeld and the USA's Department of Defense, it is difficult to ignore how online technologies affect power and political culture. Consequently, this chapter rethinks the remediations of political culture and power, which are unfolding on what is called 'the Internet', or the ever-changing network of networks that are knit together out of information and communication technologies (ICTs). Rapid change in the digital domains of the Internet is widely acknowledged, so to write about the net effects of new media emerging on the Internet is a hazardous enterprise. In that respect, this analysis is not much different from many others, which either precede, or now parallel, its examination of Internet politics. In other ways, however, this chapter is different in as much as it explores the power effects of computer networks, digital discourses and online organizations on political culture and institutions by re-examining what is technologically new as well as what is socially new (Meikle, 2002; Nye, 2004).

For better or worse, many fields of human agency – both individual and collective – and of social structure – on all levels of aggregation – are being repolarized, because computer-mediated communication (CMC) 'rewraps', as Poster (1990) argues, who dominates whom, where, when and how. Few questions are either as interesting or as significant as this one at this historical juncture, because the *modi operandi* of most social practices are being reshaped out of bits for bits and with bits by the new media of ICTs. The rewrapping of terrorism around CMC, for example, was made perfectly clear when Al Qaeda hijackers struck the USA on 9.11.01. Subsequent investigations of that attack, and the global network that supported the attackers, discovered how dependent these terrorists were upon the Internet for their flexiblized, just-in-time, distributed modes of operation (Luke, 2001). At another turn in history, one could ask to see a foundational text, which had been accepted as the definitive articulation of order. As Walker (1993: 26–49) maintains, there were once princes, principalities and *The Prince* interoperating in triangular constellations of energy, form, intelligence, matter and will to decode the emergent (dis)order of sovereignty, nationality and economy in modernity. The royal 'we' of action imposed its conditions for thought and practice, even as it erased its own autonomous authority with jurisdictive myths, constitutional mechanisms and violent manhandlings. Similar changes are afoot today, but digitalization appears to be re(con)textualizing all those foundations into ones and zeros so thoroughly that one cannot find 'the programmer'. This analysis, then, seeks to understand how political culture today, in large part, ultimately can circulate online (Bukatman, 1993; Poster, 1995). In this environment, systemcraft can be soulcraft, and the crafted soul acquires digital forms of being from the system (Rushkoff, 1994). For the latest profile of these discourses, one must turn to the 'blogsphere', or the burgeoning networks of 'Web logs', devoted to innumerable topics in a new populist politics (Hewitt, 2005). The technology itself guarantees that much of what is said in this volume will be partly outmoded after the presses roll simply because of rapid changes at the interface.

Historically, the Internet was the creation of the United States of America – the 'hyperpower' allegedly at the heart of post Cold War world order (Abbate, 1999). Yet, the legal authority, managerial acumen and administrative effectiveness of various national and international bodies now nominally in charge of the Net, like the Internet Architecture Board (IAB), the Internet Engineering Task Force (IETF), the International Corporation for Assigned Names and Numbers (ICANN), or the Internet Society (ISOC) itself, are quite uncertain. As a 1997 FCC policy brief observed:

> Most of the underlying architecture of the Internet was developed under the auspices, directly or indirectly, of the United States Government. The government has not, however, defined whether it retains authority over Internet management functions, or whether these responsibilities have been delegated to the private sector. The degree to which any existing body can lay claim to representing 'the Internet community' is also unclear. (Cited in Abbate, 1999: 208)

In this power vacuum, which has been created and maintained by state and non-state interests, political groups – from Al Qaeda to the UN to the Sierra Club to the USA's Republican Party – are reimagining human community (Anderson, 1991; Bimber, 2003b), pushing their own ideologies and interests in pursuit of neoliberal utopias and non-liberal resistances (Luke, 1989). In an ironic twist to Engels' famous characterization of socialism, the ICTs associated with the Internet are moving societies from the government of people to the administration of things, which, in turn, remediates new modes of control into governance over people and things (Kroker and Weinstein, 1994; Mueller, 2002; van der Pjil, 1998).

Out on the networks, people who are not of the same race, gender, class, nationality or locality are interacting in cyberspace through operational interfaces that reduce their identities to strings of text, synthesized speech or stylized graphics (de Kerckhove, 1998). Once on the Net, they seek to leverage cyberspace to serve various offline agendas (Gibson, 1984). Their efforts to operate together and alone in the digital domain, however, are also creating cultural commonalities, or conventional understandings manifest in act and artifact that characterize their shared forms of life, which are pitched against their offline interests. Face-to-face interactions between persons become online events with digital beings; material systems with well-proven redundancies, proven safeguards and fixed practices are supplanted by unstable clusters of code in fragile telematic networks; locatable sites in real space under identifiable, albeit perhaps not effective, governmental control are displaced by cyberspatial addresses under very little or no governmental oversight (Grisham, 1999; Slouka, 1995). Yet, all of this expresses a new kind of productive power (Foucault, 1980; Lessig, 2000; Luke, 1997) articulated as ones and zeros.

The Net also provides social forces with alternative modes of action and types of artifacts to organize their cultural interactions, institutionalize political movements, and advance economic demands on a deterritorialized metanational basis in 24/7 time frames (Anderson, 1991; Chayko, 2002; Hauben, 1997). The networks are operational venues whose assignment, sale and use generate a new governance challenge: how to create, border, police and use virtual spaces (Castells, 2001; Slevin, 2000). Some Net-ready interests realize that these spaces, and hence the legal jurisdictions, strategic alliances, cultural norms and communal rituals which will prevail in them are up for grabs (Everard, 2000). Cyberspace, as both its emerging 'hacktivist' and 'Netizenship' practices indicate (Hauben, 1997), will be contested space in so far as the operational effects of informatics can be simultaneously experienced everywhere and nowhere. One recent study found the United States to be the most common domain source of Usenet messages, for example, in the 1990s, but 'anonymous', or no territorial region of origin, was the 15th most common source in Usenet messages (Smith and Kollock, 1999: 197) of the nearly 200 states and government entities with top-level domains. If the governmentality problematic is, as Foucault claims, the challenge of conveniently arranging things and people to organize the conduct of conduct, then the Web poses tremendous new transnational challenges for governance, especially who governs whom, where, when and how (Jordan, 1999; Luke 1995; Trippi, 2004).

Individuals and groups can become fully enmeshed within the tactics and strategies of complex forms of normalizing power, which can be political regimes or technical regimens, whose institutions, procedures, analyses and techniques loosely organize mass populations and their material environments in different highly politicized symbolic material economies (Ihde, 1990; Poster, 1990). It provides an inexact set of bearings, but Foucault asserts:

> it is the tactics of government which make possible the continual definition and redefinition of what is within the competence of the state and what is not, the public versus the private, and so on; thus the state can only be understood in its survival and its limits on the basis of the general tactics of governmentality. (1991: 103)

Because governmentalizing practices are always at the centre of political struggle, the online interactions of populations in highly organized economies now compel state regimes to redefine continually what is within their administrative competence throughout the informationalizing process (Beck, 1997; Luke, 1994).

The devotees of digitalization among the digerati, like Nicholas Negroponte, overrate the positive aspects of telematic life, while they underplay how most negative social and political tendencies will continue in cyberspace like they are offline. For Negroponte, 'the change from atoms to bits is irrevocable and unstoppable' (1995: 4), and digitalization ultimately means dematerialization. To mark this turning point in human history, he asserts 'computing is not about computers any more. It is about living' (1995: 6). His claim in all too many ways is true. Here is the political and ethical problematic of 'the polis' – living how, living where, living for whom, and by whose leave – only now while online.

Much of the literature on ICTs misses the Internet's governmentality to the degree it presumes the existence of positive affinities rooted in artifacts (Adas, 1989; Cooper, 1999; Franda, 2003). Stefnik, for example, asserts that the Net is redrawing the edges of groups and individuals, and this power is the source of its transformative power as well as the contra-transformative pushbacks against it:

> New technologies bring change. When they are fundamental to transportation and communication they affect more than just the mechanics of how we work and live. Because of them, we find ourselves interacting with people from different cultures who hold different values, people who used to be very far away. We learn to operate in a global space – experiencing cultural clashes and making cultural accommodations. Technological changes lead to cultural changes – especially changes in the social and legal institutions that are now coevolving with the technology of the Internet. (1999: 1)

Consequently, Stefnik maintains that new edges get fixed in this process of technological change:

> Groups can have edge just as individuals have edges. In a group, confusion at the edge usually shows up as lack of agreement about the right course of action. Members may express contradictory and shifting views. Over time the people in a group may align themselves to make a change, then back off, only to try again later ... This is why the edge for technologies of connection is open to conflict between global and local values. Such a conflict can evoke resistance, a pushback, as people seek stability and attempt to preserve the status quo. The pushback thus acts to preserve cultural diversity. (1999: 2, 3)

As one of the Xerox Corporation's leading in-house scientists, Stefnik can propound this sense of the network society, and get an audience. Yet his vision is tremendously self-serving. People and organizations like Stefnik and Xerox bring change, not 'technologies'. The 'we' whose work and life are being affected is not large, not cohesive, and not an agent as such, but Stefnik turns to technology to create an artifactual affinity. And this 'we' then becomes conscious and cohesive, and copes with a cultural give-and-take along the edges of an apparently open, free-flowing and consensual search for stability. Some – both inside and outside the group – resist and push back, but others go along with the new connections. At one level, this account is not entirely false, but on many other levels it is almost untrue (Feenberg, 1999).

Only Deibert's sophisticated analysis of the social epistemologies and political technics of media as environments begins to approach the complexity of networked economies and societies with real insight. Deibert's *Parchment, Printing, and Hypermedia: Communication in World Order Transformation* (1997) rearranges the connections of different historical periods, ranging from the medieval to the modern and the postmodern, into distinctive communicative technics, represented as parchment manuscripts, printed literature and electronic hypermedia. A change is identified in the relations between the informers and the informed. While this might not represent a new mode of information, as Poster claims, the workings of postmodern decentredness and electronic hypermedia are altered as a result of the fit 'between this social epistemology and the emerging hypermedia environment' (1997: 200).

The culture of network society owes a lot to new companies, institutions and organizations that create new digital media, and then exploit their capabilities to redefine and then satisfy new human needs (Trippi, 2004; Trumbull, 2004). Thus, the Internet becomes the focus of everyday life. 'The Net is not a separate environment that individuals can choose or not choose to utilize'. Instead, as Martin asserts:

> In an Internet-worked world, networks will be the backbone of social and economic life. Just as governments help organize society, and just as cities help organize the daily activities of individuals, networks will increasingly become the primary tool for organizing information. The choice not to participate automatically removes these groups or individuals from the mainstream. (1997: 211)

To not go online then is to choose antiquation, anachronism and anti-progressiveness (Tapscott, 1997).

Like all previous technological generations of new practices, whether the telephone, automobile, radio, aeroplane or television, the Net is producing the politics and culture of a 'new generation' (Tapscott, 1997). According to Martin, 'This is a generation united under the banner of interactivity, which thrives on

making connections. This group of online, interactive, digital individuals are the consumers in the Digital Estate' (1997: 211). Tapscott, Martin and Negroponte all regard these interactive generation populations, 'I-Generation' individuals, as the vanguard of universal virtuality. They have that special knowledge the members of any vanguard require: 'They know it will not be long before interactivity is taken for granted and that memories of pre-internetworking will be tantamount to realizing the days before machines could fly. After critical mass, everyone will already belong' (Martin, 1997: 211). The intrinsic value to adding more nodes to the Net turns its new media into a concrete normativity that assumes, or assures, everyone will belong (Hassan, 1977).

In most respects, informatics are only the latest wrinkle in 'modernity' (Harvey, 1989; Mumford, 1963). Once again, a fresh set of cultural transformations, resting in a destructively productive new technics with its own unformed social mores, appears as the source and goal of yet another universalizing moral order, uniform vision of nature, and univocalized economic model (Mumford, 1970). Bits, like most modern things defined by commodified commercial operations, are privileged objects, which can go from anywhere to anywhere at anytime for anybody (Slouka, 1995; Stauffer, 2002; Trumbull, 2004). Yet this potential omnipresence, first, mostly glosses over how much 'anywhere' actually remains (in world systems terms) as a set of very limited venues, or truly 'manywheres', albeit often widely distributed geographically; second, ignores how most movements go from somebody at one privileged site to somebody, or actually 'manybodies', at another special place; and third, discounts how speeds in anytime are arrayed in 'manytimes' as a function of willingness to pay, salience of authority, or quality of connectivity (Luke, 1997: 121–44).

POLITICS AND CULTURE IN CYBERSPACE

The fractalizing power of cyberspace as a political culture construct can be tracked out into several philosophical patches and theoretical thickets (Grusin and Bolter, 1999; Kelly, 1998; Levy, 1997; Miller, 1996; Shane, 2004). Perhaps we never have been modern (Latour, 1993), but one promising perspective leads into the critiques of postmodernity. These writings puzzle through the emergence of transnational space by reconsidering the relationships of territory to the earth, and their deterritorializing remediations in contemporary thought and practice.

On one level, following Lyotard, the concept of postmodernity might mark the decline of modernity's grand narratives, which have until quite recently embedded Western capitalist humanity's and society's economic, political and social-technological practices in some deeper metaphysical substance. These meta-narratives, or the fables of reason and freedom, see science and technology bring gradual, but inevitable, progress to individuals and societies through the unfolding of history. Lyotard, however, saw this historical period closing during the 1960s and 1970s with the transition to post-industrialism. His analysis is based

upon the perception of the existence of a modern era that dates from the time of the Enlightenment and that now has run its course: and this modern era was predicated on the notion of progress in knowledge, in the arts, in technology, and in human freedom as well, all of which was thought of as leading to a truly emancipated society: a society emancipated from poverty, despotism and ignorance. But all of us can see that the development continues to take place without leading to the realization of any of these dreams of emancipation. (1984: 39)

With this rising distrust in any metanarratives of truth, enlightenment or progress, Lyotard sees science and technology falling under the sway of 'another language game, in which the goal is no longer truth, but performativity – that is, the best possible input/output equation' (1984: 46).

On another level, following Jameson, the mediations of performativity are found in 'a new social system beyond classical capitalism', proliferating across 'the world space of multi-national capital' (1992: 59, 54). More specifically, as Harvey argues, this new regime for multinational capital began by disintegrating the Fordist regime of industrial production,

capital accumulation and state intervention patched together on a national basis during the 1930s through the 1970s by welfare states. In its place, new arrangements for flexible accumulation, productive specialization and public deregulation have surfaced within many loosely coupled transnational alliances since the 1970s. As Harvey observes, 'flexible accumulation typically exploits a wide range of seemingly contingent geographical circumstances, and reconstitutes them as structured internal elements of its own encompassing logic ... the result has been the production of fragmentation, insecurity, and ephemeral uneven development within a highly unified global space economy of capital flows' (1989: 294, 296). On the horizon drawn by flexible accumulation, Lyotard's cultural vision of performativity is what anchors 'the new world order' of the 1990s and 2000s, as most spatial barriers and all time zones collapse in the cultural compression caused by transnational businesses' acceleration of production and consumption. Today, 'the State and/or company must abandon the idealist and humanist narratives of legitimation in order to justify the new goal: in the discourse of today's financial backers of research, the only credible goal is power. Scientists, technicians, and instruments are purchased not to find truth, but to augment power' (Lyotard, 1984: 46).

Corporate enthusiasts, such as Cairncross (1997), see this development as 'the death of distance'. In this vein, Jameson argues, 'we are back in the spatial itself', and critical analysis

infers a certain supplement of spatiality in the contemporary period and suggests that there is a way in which, even though other modes of production ... are distinctively spatial, ours has been spatialized in a unique sense, such that space is for us an existential and cultural dominant, a thematized or foregrounded feature or structural principle standing in striking contrast to its relatively subordinate and secondary ... role in earlier modes of production. (1992: 365)

Even though this new world spatiality might be an existential and social dominant, its networked qualities remain fairly vague (Castells, 1996–8). Indeed, this phenomenon lacks much permanence, closure or primordialism. Jameson reaches for common household technological referents, like channel surfing on cable TV with a remote control, to substantiate his sense of this new consciousness. His discussion lacks theoretical heft, because he also ignores and underplays cyberspace, when it, in fact, seems to be a much richer instantiation of 'the new space that thereby emerges [and which] involves the suppression of distance (in the sense of Benjamin's aura) and the relentless saturation of any remaining voids and empty places, to the point where the postmodern body ... is now exposed to a perceptual barrage of immediacy from which all sheltering layers and intervening mediations have been removed' (Jameson, 1992: 412–13).

Out in the digital domain, one slips into spaces of suppressed distance shorn of sheltering mediations and brimming with buckets of immediacy. This is what saturates the final remaining hidden zones of world markets. While he does not state it in these terms, Jameson captures many of the qualities found in the telematic environments of the Net. Out online, the peculiar spatial quality of cyberspace as a cultural domain for dispersion, decentring and discontinuity comes into its own (Agger, 2003). Hence 'we', the networked subjects enveloped in the world spaces of transnational capital, and then remediated in connected clusters of code, 'turn out to be whatever we are in, confront, inhabit, or habitually move through, provided it is understood that under current conditions we are obliged to renegotiate all those spaces or channels back and forth in a single Joycean day' (Jameson, 1992: 373). Cyberspace contains layer upon layer of multiple interrelating, and diversely channelled, ephemeral constructs which everyone moves through, inhabits and confronts on every single day of their Joycean existences (Kelly, 1994; Poster, 1995; Shenk, 1997). The browser histories from such online odysseys will mark these renegotiations all too well as a 'multidimensional set of radically discontinuous realities' which replicates itself online throughout every last void and empty place of the world from the poorest rural household up to the richest global marketplace. Jameson misconstrues these changes as an 'unimaginable decentering of global capital itself' (1992: 413),

when, in fact, it is the radical recentering of the imagination behind valorizing exchange that now occurs 24/7 in the digital domain.

The analysis of concrete power arrangements for the Net ranges from the new idealism of the digital digerati, such as Kelly (1994) or Negroponte (1995), to the more sophisticated materialist perspectives of analysts such as Deibert (1997) or Mattelart (2000). Communications media are a perfect illustration of the normalizing mediations of proactive power put forward by Foucault. To paraphrase McLuhan, who saw all technologies as media providing 'extensions of man' psychically and physically (1964: 19–67), men and women online become psychic and physical peripheral plug-ins for other central processing units, leaving men and women to impersonate 'being digital' as variable extensions of digital technologies. Connectivity as a mechanism of power depends upon the cultivation of the body as well as the mind, and getting online anywhere all the time allows businesses to extract time, energy and labour from a new culture of production and consumption as ones and zeros. The material functionalities of connectivity can be liberating, but only in the very peculiar fashions permitted by the mode of information. Big businesses do not want to maintain today's digital divides between those online with access and those offline without access (Martin and Schumann, 1997). In fact, it is only by granting new commodified freedoms to more people in the digital domain that global businesses can constantly 'increase subjected forces' and 'improve force and efficacy of that which subjects them' (Foucault, 1980: 104) in the rapid circulation of commodified goods and services. The digital divides in world society between white, Hispanic, black or Asian computer use are destined to close. Until bits can command many more atoms of all classes, creeds and colours, digital being will remain incomplete.

ICTs do not operate autonomously or discretely (Hobart and Schiffman, 1998). Rather, contemporary informatics, as they intermesh with the circuits of commodity production and consumption, permit one to see how fully metanationalized cyberspace can amalgamate online with both: '(1) Technologies of production, which permit us to produce, transform, or manipulate things', and, '(2) technologies of the self, which permit individuals to effect by their own means or with the help of others a certain number of operations on their own bodies and souls, thought, conduct, and way of being, so as to transform themselves in order to attain a certain state of happiness, purity, wisdom, perfection, or immortality' (Foucault, 1988: 18). These coaligned technologies of production and the self fuse invirtual environments. And, it is the transnational spaces of the Net that are promoting 'the ultimate realization of the private individual as a productive force. The system of needs must wring liberty and pleasure from him as so many functional elements of the reproduction of the system of production and the relations of power that sanction it' (Baudrillard, 1981: 85).

NETWORKS: GOVERNING WITH OR THROUGH TECHNOLOGY

To rethink the cultural limits and political possibilities of exercising power over the Internet, one must gauge the social, political and economic changes being caused by this new technological system (Nye, 1990; Rutsky, 2000). Too many approaches to the technology and culture of the Net are plagued by a mindset of naïve instrumentalism. That is, the Net is simply a tool like any other, and it is being used consciously and rationally by autonomous human agents to serve effectively the instrumental ends of its users. According to these views, democracies online basically will be just like democracies offline except that their officials and constituents will use e-mail and/or have webchat (Rash, 1997; Rheingold, 1993). Even though we know democracies with newspapers, televisions and telephones are not entirely like those without them because a new mediated technoculture of mass communications (Deibert, 1997) reshapes their operations, the naïve instrumentalism of too many political analyses of the Net rehashes reality in this unproductive fashion. On one level, a political

reading of the Internet can focus upon 'governing with technology'. This approach sees the Net as a tool to rationalize and redirect many processes of government (Anderson and Cornfield, 2002; Norris, 2001; Poster, 2001). On a second level, one also can examine how the Net constitutes a regime of 'governance through technology'. By rethinking how technologies have 'anonymous histories' (Giedion, 1948) that shape space, temper time and package performance apart from the conscious intention of their users, this approach to politics – as it is conducted through computer-mediated communications over information networks – would re-examine the practices and values of how political subjectivity would change in digital environments in many fundamental ways (Bimber, 2003a; Heim, 1998). Digital networks can be used by existing governments to govern, but they also can create new operational domains with their own cultural discourses and practices beyond the scope of today's territorial sovereignty as it works now (Adams, 1998; Mattelart, 1994; Ohmae, 1990). In this manner, 'Netizenship' is potentially far more than 'citizenship', because the Net is much more expansive than any city, *polis* or state (Bimber, 2003b).

Most importantly, the current commercialization of cyberspace is transforming the political realities of online life (Virilio, 1995). The initial interface of disembodied subjectivity, distributed community and cybernetic play celebrated in the early days the Net is rapidly being eclipsed by newer interface values tied to reimagining cyberspaceas hyperreal estate, virtual markets and online e-commerce (Brin, 1998; Gates, 1999; Grossman, 1997). Negroponte is not entirely mistaken when he puffs up the potentialities of 'being digital' (1995: 11–20) as the latest grand transition of modernization. In his digital materialism, the economies and societies still organized around making and moving matter, or 'atoms', will be slipsliding away into a new domain focused upon inventing and integrating information, or 'bits'. Space will be occupied by reworked atoms, but this occupation will also be filled by the flow of continuously upgraded bits (Bukatman, 1993). Without saying so, Negroponte essentially recasts digital technics as a nascent form of nanotechnology with which bits reach out and reshape atoms at will as part and parcel of digital being.

This recognition acquires articulation in Bill Gates' views on personal computing. He outlines another style of being digital in elaborate tales about his, and allegedly 'everyone' else's, experiences of 'growing up' since the 1970s with computers:

> In the minds of a lot of people at school we became linked with the computer, and it with us ... In doing so, we caused a kind of revolution – peaceful, mainly – and now the computer has taken up residence in our offices and homes ... Inexpensive computer chips now show up in engines, watches, antilock brakes, facsimile machines, elevators, gasoline pumps, cameras, thermostats, treadmills, vending machines, burglar alarms, and even talking greeting cards ... Now that computing is astoundingly inexpensive and computers inhabit every part of our lives, we stand on the brink of another revolution. This one will involve unprecedentedly inexpensive communication; all the computers will join together to communicate with us and for us. (1996: 2–5)

For Gates and Microsoft, computers are just what will remake built environments for the betterment of all. Like it or not, digital being on this hyperreal estate is the place where human beings find computers are linked to us, computers tie us into networks, and computers colonize other artifacts to communicate with each other and, of course, us (Mitchell, 1995). Hence, governance through technology is inescapable.

Unlike the public projects underpinning the *polis*, this odd remembrance by Gates belies larger corporate agendas for private profit and power to sustain an informatic 'subpolis'. What is more, the financial, professional and technical development networks behind this subpolis leave its possibilities for collective action and imagination caught somewhere between the traditional vision of politics and non-politics. This idea snags something quite significant out of the bitstream. As Beck suspects, big technological systems, like cybernetic networks, telecommunications grids or computer applications, are becoming

> a third entity, acquiring the precarious hybrid status of a *sub-politics*, in which the scope of social changes precipitated varies inversely with their legitimation ... The direction of development and results of technological

transformation become fit for discourse and subject to legitimation. Thus business and techno-scientific action acquire a *new political and moral dimension* that had previously seemed alien to techno-economic activity ... now the potential for structuring society migrates from the political system into the sub-political system of scientific, technological, and economic modernization. *The political becomes non-political and the non-political political* ... A revolution under the cloak of normality occurs, which escapes from possibilities of intervention, but must all the same be justified and enforced against a public becoming critical ... The political institutions become the administrators of a development they neither have planned for nor are able to structure, but must nevertheless somehow justify ... Lacking a place to appear, the decisions that change society become tongue-tied and anonymous ... What we *do not* see and *do not want* is changing the world more and more obviously and threateningly. (1992: 186–7)

In the name of digital materialism, Gates and thousands of other far more anonymous and usually more tongue-tied computer geeks like him are mounting a revolution from their desktops by designing, building and owning new subpolitical spaces (Roszak, 1994). Digitalization generated out on the WWW, from within the Wintel operating system, or with ASCII code, all too often is neither seen nor wanted. Nevertheless, the collective decisions taken through these codes and systems by technicians and tradesmen to structure the economy and society around such 'sub-political systems of scientific, technological, and economic modernization' (Beck, 1992: 186) are changing the world without much, if any, state regulation, political planning structure or civic legitimation.

Thus, corporate campaigns for the expanded ownership and control of public goods, like cyberspace, are frequently dressed out in a new pluralism of open-ended popular decisions (Lessig, 2004). Because hackers, debuggers and other users are always running an ongoing open review of past design decisions, Microsoft and other vendors design feedback from their customers and their users. Either way, the network of networkers out on the Net builds and then maintains the multilayered complexities of this digital domain as a computer-mediated subpolis. Network connectivity, then, is 'your passport' into 'a new, mediated way of life' (Gates, 1996: 5). More than an object, not quite yet a subject, online connectivity can provide a pass, a port and a presence for entering into a new way of life.

George Gilder's celebration of 'the new age of intelligent machines' (1989: 381) sees this coming e-formation of our world of matter-centred manufacture attaining absolute immanence in societies under the sway of information-denominated 'Mind'. Conflating the Cold War with cyberwar in 1989, Gilder asserts:

> The overthrow of matter in business will reverberate through geopolitics and exalt the nations in command of creative minds over the nations in command of land and resources. Military power will accrue more and more to the masters of information technology. Finally, the overthrow of matter will stultify all materialist philosophy and open vistas of human imagination and moral revival. (1989: 18)

This effusion of humans and machines in a progressive pact of transcendent unity over ten years later, however, is leading more toward MP3 downloads, $8 online stock trades on Ameritrade, 24/7 swap meets on eBay, and cyberporn on demand, than it is to an opening of communal concord between all humans. Oddly enough, Gilder fails to show how the old materialist philosophy has been stultified. Instead it returns in the discursive discipline of an informatic materialism in which silicon, fibre and code will reknit humans and their machines into new subpolitical collectives of economic development. This utopian talk is no different from that made by other technological determinists who attributed these same powers over the past century to rayon, radio and railroads and it raises the question of how to govern with technology (Nye, 1996).

The wide open spaces of the Internet are administered loosely by the Internet Society (ISOC), which also is the home of the Internet Engineering Task Force (IETF) and the Internet Architecture Board (IAB). Drawing together people from transnational telecoms, big software houses, national scientific agencies, professional-technical groups and media companies, ISOC is a major force in the management of the informatic subpolis. Its programmes, however, are metanational in as much as its members seek to maintain the Net's uniquely metanational qualities by safeguarding 'the viability and global scaling of the Internet' in ways that 'assure the open development, evolution, and use of the Internet for the benefit of all people throughout the world' (http://www.isoc.org/mission).

Another interpretation of this dynamic partnership between people and intelligent machines finds its voice in singing the praises of 'friction-free capitalism' out on the Net (Gates, 1999). Its reflexive epistemology also sees the wired world's digital exchanges in global terms (Lewis, 1997). As Bill Gates observes:

> The global information market will be huge and will combine all the various ways human goods, services and ideas are exchanged. On a practical level, this will give you broader choices about most things, including how you earn and invest, what you buy and how much you pay for it, who your friends are and how you spend your time with them, and where and how securely you and your family live. Your workplace and your idea of what it means to be 'educated' will be transformed, perhaps almost beyond recognition. Your identity, of who you are and where you belong, may open up considerably. In short, just about everything will be done differently. (1996: 6–7)

Opening up the norms of identity – who you are and where you belong – here becomes a credo for reconfiguring the entire globe into a vast internal market for transnational exchange: this perhaps is the essence of digital being. In the network society, we are becoming bits, everything is becoming bits, and globalization is just being digital (Castells, 1996–8).

This development is not 'friction-free'. Instead, as Lyotard suggests, 'economic powers have reached the point of imperiling the stability of the State through new forms of the circulation of capital that go by the generic name of *multinational corporations*', and these new modes of revalorizing exchange 'imply that investment decisions have, at least in part, passed beyond the control of the nation-states' (1984: 5). Even though it probably was not what Hayles (1999) envisioned when she cast posthumanism as that condition in which no organism can be entirely differentiated from its environment, no self is separate from society, and no agency lacks structure, corporate powers are growing so pervasive online that bits are becoming almost monetized. Emergent knowledges framed as bits begin circulating along the same lines as money, instead of for its 'educational' value or political (administrative, diplomatic, military) importance; the pertinent distinction would no longer be between knowledge and ignorance, but rather, as is the case with money, between 'payment knowledge' and 'investment knowledge' – in other words, between units of knowledge exchange in a daily maintenance framework (the reconstitution of the work force, 'survival') versus funds of knowledge dedicated to optimizing the performance of a project. (Lyotard, 1984: 6)

Online, bits can meld payment and investment knowledge into a single performative flow that pays out by drawing new investments, and draws new investments as its payoff (Drahos with Braithwaite, 2003).

By fabricating digital domains, and then continually struggling to master their telemetrical terrain, posthumans also fulfil Lyotard's prophecies about 'the postmodern condition'. That is, 'knowledge in the form of an informational commodity indispensable to productive power is already, and will continue to be, a major – perhaps *the* major – stake in the worldwide competition for power'; in fact, the struggle over cyberspace intranationally and transnationally illustrates how fully the residents of nation-states must fight for 'control of information, just as they battled in the past for control over territory, and afterwards for control of access to and exploitation of raw materials and cheap labour' (1984: 5). Online mediations of digital being work through data/information/knowledge in accord with familiar liberal humanist goals. Online and offline, information 'is and will be produced in order to be sold, it is and will be consumed in order to be valorized in a new production: in both cases, the goal is exchange' (1984: 4). In these spaces, everything in society, the marketplace and culture:

> is made conditional on performativity. The redefinition of the norms of life consists in enhancing the system's competence for power. That this is the case is particularly evident in the introduction of telematic technology: the technocrats see in telematics a promise of liberalization and enrichment in the interactions between interlocutors; but what makes this process attractive for them is that it will result in new tensions in the system, and these will lead to an improvement in its performativity. (1984: 64)

Once again, the system is the solution, and solutions come from accepting the systems.

Still, as this transnational informatic subpolis and neoliberal marketplace grow, the role and stature of the traditional polis – whatever this might be – in many nation-states could well decline. Even though everyone currently remains captured as bodies within some type of face-to-face political system, their civic abilities to exercise certain practices of rule making, rule applying and rule adjudication offline do not map over to the subpolitical domains of online technics. Democracy offline may become the engine of collective inaction or, worse, the audience for endless spectacles of quasi-theatrical scandal. In turn, new decisive revolutions will be made metanationally, as Beck maintains, *'under the cloak of normality'* (1992: 186) thanks to telematic global powers such as Microsoft and Bill Gates or AOL and Steve Case. 'In contemporary discussions', as Beck suggests, 'the "alternative society" is no longer expected to come from parliamentary debates on new laws, but rather from the application of microelectronics, genetic technology, and information media' (1992: 223).

Other openly transnationalist organizations, like the Electronic Frontier Foundation (EFF), espouse the principles of offline human rights for the online settlement and improvement of cyberspace as an e-public domain. While EFF seeks to leverage offline state authorities to protect online freedoms, its image of the 'electronic frontier' is essentially metanational. Indeed, it wants 'to make [the electronic frontier] truly useful and beneficial not just to a technical elite, but to everyone' (http://www. eff.org/EFF docs). Similarly the Global Internet Liberty Campaign (GILC) also pushes metanational ideas, claiming 'there are no borders in cyberspace' and joining together its multinational membership 'to protect and promote fundamental human rights such as freedom of speech and the right of privacy on the Net for users everywhere' (http://www.gilc.org/about/ members.html). As Trippi argues, 'the Internet is tailor-made for a populist, insurgent movement. Its roots in the open source ARPAnet, its hacker culture, and its decentralized, scattered architecture make it difficult for big, establishment candidates, companies, and media to gain control of it' (2004: 102).

One of the most significant effects of the Net, then, is the tendency for connectivity to disintegrate, or at least disrupt, those long-standing forms of institutional action in markets, governments or cultures that have presumed fixed built environments and face-to-face human engagement (Cooper, 1999). Such operations relied upon physical sites of political power (agency offices, election booths, service bureaucracies), economic production (corporate headquarters, sales offices, managerial suites), personal consumption (brokerage offices, new bookstores, car dealerships) and cultural reproduction (public libraries, civic centres, graduate schools), but these venues can easily be morphed into online sites in a fashion that reduces costs, cuts employment, enhances service and raises consumer satisfaction. Physical collocation and geographic contiguity continue to be important on many levels, but online 'electronic proximity' (Dertouzos, 1997: 229) is cross-cutting many institutional practices that have evolved in the real time, real life, real space of what William Gibson (1984) calls 'the meat world'. In these cross-cuts, the shapeshifting outlines of 'e-proximate' interactions surface out of every e-commerce transaction, e-media page download, e-schooling lesson and e-governance contact made with ICTs.

Dertouzos envisions the networks as 'the information marketplace'. Open 24/7, these electronic sites, or I-marts, are an 'e-proximate' space in which 'people and computers buy, sell, and freely exchange information and information services' in round-the-clock transactions that 'involve the processing and communication of information under the same economic motives that drive today's traditional marketplace for goods and services' (1997: 9–10). As Marx warns us, the ever-growing socialization of production is coupled with the increasing privatization of ownership and control behind such digital domains (Shapiro, 1999). This tendency does not trouble Dertouzos. Instead, he opines that 'the profit motive' drives today's traditional markets, so there is no reason for it not to persist in cyberspace. The information marketplace exists in order to amplify and extend its existence by collecting consumers, satisfying their needs with need satisfactions, and reselling the information about all or any of these individual and collective choices (Lyon, 1994). Whose service, who serves, who is served, what kind of service, when service works, how service happens in such I-marts, however, would all depend upon economic, political and social decisions, not technical choices *per se*. Yet these realities are painted over in the colours of a constructive interaction that can occur only in/of/for/by the informatic tools of such infostructures. Technics completely occludes the essentially hyperpolitical nature of the I-Mart (Servon, 2002; Trippi, 2004).

Cultural scripts, sites and structures hammered out over decades or centuries by human beings, as physically collocated or institutionally mediated agents, cannot easily adapt to many online environments (Anderson, 1991). Consequently, new virtual forms of organization, or 'e-formations', are thrown together to match the surging flows of bits, both into and out of the e-proximities of online environments. The quasi-anarchic practices of the Net before 1994, which emphasized user autonomy, individuality, mutual aid, creativity and collective chaos, are still preferred by some, but state regulators, corporate salespersons, religious authorities and economic planners are all struggling to impose more familiar forms of bureaucratic regulation, self-interested profit seeking, and conventional morality upon cyberspace without much success. Hackivists and terrorists, before and after 9/11, show how difficult the governance task is (Hachten, 2002; Lessig, 2004; Verton, 2003).

Most of their new first-generation adaptations to the time and space compression of the Net also are uncomfortably, but perhaps all too predictably, privileging the corporate practices and freewheeling markets of transnational enterprise, which are already running roughshod over most of the world's territorial jurisdictions (Kelly, 1994). A Computer Economics analysis in 2002 suggested that 2004 transactions would only be $2.8 trillion and that 2006 figures would only rise to around $5.3 trillion (Waite, 2002). And many of the 'inefficiencies' B2B (business-to-business) commerce would be removing from 'the supply chain' or 'enterprise transactions' are people's jobs, national industries and regional ties.

The regimen of e-commerce, despite the pronouncements by dot.com utopians pushed every day on CNBC or CNNfn, is not yet fully defined or finally sealed with respect to its specific operations (Rochlin, 1997). It is instead ironically imagined now in the very collectivist terms of global business: personal connectivity determines social utility, intrusive smartness colonizes the objects of everyday life, data mining of everyone's Net work accelerates the surveillance of services, and general productivity depends upon individual e-lancing labour. Even though Bill Gates (1996, 1999) pretends 'the road ahead' is a friction-free path to greater economic liberty, most of the goods and services defining this freedom presume that those who experience e-proximity must endure tremendous levels of unrelenting psychodemographic monitoring – both online and offline. In retail e-commerce as well as B2B trade, the networks produce power that can rerationalize energy production, resource extraction, materials processing, service delivery and capital accumulation as system-supportive performativity.

NETIZENS AND NETIZENSHIP

To survive in the fast capitalist world of the twenty-first century, it is not enough for territorial states or political entities to maintain offline legal jurisdiction over their allegedly sovereign territories and/or constituent members. The Net is a governmentality engine, whose subpolitical assemblies of informatic artifacts create new collective subjectivities and collections of subjects beyond the territorial polis in the flows of transnational exchange (Saco, 2000). In online governmentality, the disciplinary articulations of software packages and hardware functionalities also centre upon enforcing 'the right disposition of things' between humans conducting their conduct in cybernetic environments as e-publics (Foucault, 1991).

Many agencies of subnational, national and transnational governmentality now must preoccupy themselves with the conduct of conduct by tracking digital e-haviours on informatic networks. Until the late 1990s, it was the offline involvements of people with family, community and nation – as public interests – that mostly guided civic conduct; at this juncture, however, growing Internet economies and societies seek to be accepted as another ethical e-public ground for normalizing any individual's behaviour. Cybernetic domains are spaces under a special kind of subnational self-policing supervision fulfilled in the free flight of packet switching. The prospects for an informatic prosperity, which are looming ahead on a global scale, will not be possible without some manner of governmentality to guide 'the controlled insertion of bodies into the machinery of production and the adjustment of the phenomena of population to economic processes' (Foucault, 1980: 141).

Despite Sunstein's (2002) worries, living in societies organized out of telematic networks will require a broad facility for coping with many different language games nested in new technocultures. Many decision-makers strive, however, to reduce such heterogeneous social, political and cultural elements to fit the logics of techno-economic performativity. That is, they struggle to manage

> these clouds of sociality according to input/output matrices, following a logic which implies that their elements are commensurable and that the whole is determinable. They allocate our lives for the growth of power. In matters of social justice and of scientific truth alike, the legitimation of that power is based on its optimizing the system's performance efficiency. The application of this criterion to all of our games necessarily entails a certain level of terror, whether soft or hard: be operational (that is, commensurable) or disappear. (Lyotard, 1984: xxiv)

Such decision rules acquire paramount importance for everyone in the telematic economies and societies of the current world system. The politics of networked places, connectivity spaces and digital domains, as Lyotard suggests, frequently revolve around one question: 'who decides what knowledge is and who knows what needs to be decided? In the computer age, the question of knowledge is now more than ever a question of government' (1984: 9). Whether the governed will be citizens or Netizens is an intriguing question. The pervasiveness of today's neoliberal market capitalist ideologies is rooted in a quest for focused efficiency; and, in turn, these basic cultural conditions of production are shaping the productive conditions of digitalization as much, or even more, than the boxes and wires themselves are remaking collective infrastructure.

Consequently, one finds that the online *bourgeois* of digital sites appears to have interests, capabilities and goals which appear as antithetical to those commonly shared by the offline *citoyen* of material cities. This flexible geometry of indefinite boundaries, open architectures and unfixed locations online in the 'Netropolis' of 'virtual life' constantly contradicts the fixed geometries of definite boundaries, closed communities and inflexible locations offline in the 'polis' still out there in 'the meat world' in 'real life'. Without a re-examination of new technology as lifeworld, we cannot assess the impact of new technologies on our existing lifeworlds (Ihde, 1990).

Netizenship as political culture can unfold within the containment vessels of the *polis* as digital democracy, electronic voting or online organizing, which would mark the Net reshaping the *polis* to support e-citizenship, e-governance and e-management inside existing territorial jurisdictions (Bryan et al., 1998; Cooper, 1999; Lessig, 2004; Sunstein, 2002). Graeme Browning's 'how-to' manual, for example, *Electronic Democracy: Using the Internet to Influence American Politics* (1996), is written to direct the Net toward this task. This 'cyberage book' has been urging readers since 1996 to use the Net 'to reach decision makers at all levels of government, research political issues, and effectively promote your causes' in the ever accelerating effort 'to become a successful online activist'. Yet, the Great Seal of the United States of America on a PC's VDT, and the unfurled Stars and Stripes under the keyboard, as they are photographed on the cover of Browning's manual for e-citizens, are only the first, and most obvious, application of this book's cybernetic remediation of citizens within the polis. Saco's *Cybering Democracy* (2000) addresses many of these concerns quite effectively. The Net can also generate innumerable

postnational, non-statal, territorial collectives of people in which any given *polis* is essentially accidental to the wiredness of some new Netropolis (Hauben, 1997). The interests of identity and community articulated at www.islamicity.com, for example, are not necessarily the same as those at www.whitehouse.gov, www.senate.gov or www.house.gov. Indeed, the 'actually transnational' qualities of the Net starkly contradict the 'nominally national' identities of their users (Reich, 1991).

Nevertheless, such a vision of Netizenship is essentially the naïve instrumentalist one that imagines ICT connectivity as such creates strong common interests, shared goals or communal values. Everyone on the Net allegedly wants unconstrained and free connectivity to something, but sharing access to, and the use of, a set of telematic tools may not automatically create a free and equal fraternity of meta-nationals. In fact, there are many different varieties of Netizens and Netizenship, and they are still entangled in the technical dictates of the online interface and the consumerist expectations of offline use. The Net is not one system with a single set of functionalities; it is instead a machinic collective of many things, diverse sites and varying capabilities resting upon multiple metanational links between both online and offline communities. And, as a result, many people in most nations end up 'falling through the Net' (National Telecommunications and Information Administration, 1995, 1998, 1999). A shared sense of common goals and interests still is in many ways incomplete, because the typical sources of its definition – a common economic life within shared markets or a common political life under a single sovereign authority that together might realize material security and physical safety – are not yet fully in place (Solomon, 1997). When, however, one's financial life is mostly nested with something like eTrade, one's commercial survival is tied to eBay, one's mass media consumption is dependent upon Yahoo!, one's family ties are maintained through AOL, and one's business affairs are conducted through Commerce One.com, then a transnational basis emerges for discrete, diverse and divided groups to develop a united opposition to offline political interests as well as to other online political forces (Lewis, 1997). The building waves of blogs devoted to government political issues, politics, and global affairs permits a 24/7 deliberative, discursive and delusive stream of organization networks to organize now around pressing opportunities or threatening crises. In electoral politics, Jerry Brown in California, Jesse Ventura in Minnesota, John McCain in Arizona or Howard Dean in Vermont all have mobilized the Internet to create movements, raise money, and organize major electoral campaigns. While powerful agencies and ruling parties now have websites and Net strategies, 'the most successful websites and blogs on the Net have about them the unruly whiff of rebellion' (Trippi, 2004: 103).

This tendency to normalize the Net and its political impact upon society is also found in Wayne Rash Jr's *Politics on the Nets: Wiring the Political Process* (1997). His celebration of the Internet highlights its ability to accelerate communication, open up multipoint communication to more audiences, and short-circuit the 'filtering processes' found in the mass media. While all of this is true, these positions tend to ignore other rapid forms of communication, downplay the problems of open multipoint communication, and suggest that the Net is not somehow filtered in its workings.

Similarly, Rash apparently believes that the Net will be accessible essentially all of the time to just about everyone. Waving off the negative impact of the Net on politics, he argues that the democratic base of politics is broadened with the Internet as 'a direct effect of opening electronic communications for the delivery of services and for the reception of interest and opinion' (1997: 152). Because of this alleged openness, 'outside of repressive societies politics and the nets will become one, and as a result it will look a lot like society because it will be a part of society' (1997: 167). This might open up the political process to more political parties and groups, but it is unlikely to open up all domains of the Net, or even most key decision-making centres on the Net, to everyone simply because technology can drop 'the price of entry onto the National

stage to a level that nearly anyone can afford' (1997: 169).

One increasingly may doubt, for example, the status and role of the territorialized national, or 'the citizen' born to subjectivity in a polis, or political structure, while revelling in the statuses and roles of a deterritorialized consumer/producer or 'buyer and seller' fulfilling the subjectivity of the agora or marketplace. As a consumer, it is an easy transition to adopt the status and role of a telematic node, or 'the Netizen' whose subjectivity opens in the Net. Caught up within many more complex language games, like other nodal points in a network, any individual can be a sender, a receiver and/or a referent in the relays routing informational flows. States with the techno-economic ability to mount national information infrastructure initiatives, like the United States or Singapore, may do so, and thereby recast the spaces filled by their territorialized nationality to suit telematic nodality. Many regimes, however, lack the industry, initiative and/or infrastructure to transmogrify their constituents' agency or state structures along such nationally informationalized lines. Consequently, other information infrastructure initiatives pursued by hardware makers, transnational telco alliances or dot.com entrepreneurs infiltrate most nations with performative protocols that suit the world's most dominant businesses and great powers.

Some (Ohmae, 1990) celebrate this 'borderless world', others see it as a creative chaos (Kelly, 1994), and still others fear its inhumane/unfair/anti-egalitarian qualities (Virilio, 1997). Most importantly, the older embedded identities of territorial nationality at physical sites are being tested by newer user identities tied to telematic nodes generated for, by and of digital cites (Luke, 1996: 320–39). Where the informational world system has occupied much of the psychosocial space left for the traditional lifeworld, multiculturalist politics remediate the push and pull of nodal social forces (Beck, 1997). A nodal identity permits one to be located practically anywhere, because the Net is almost everywhere. The 'Other' is just another 'self', and each self merely another other, always out there everywhere online and offline, so it pays to accept all other identities, communities, platforms and systems in the valorization of bits and commodities (Hillis, 1999). As long as basic connections can be maintained for sending and receiving the discursive core of any multiculturalized identity and community, the foundational referents of such metanational collectivities can easily flow anywhere in national spaces that their carriers' personal and professional lives take them (Everard, 2000; Luke, 1998; Lyotard, 1984).

Furthermore, the disconnection of networked telematic ties from grounded organic traditions could enable new discursive formations beyond those of any nation's kith and kin to reshape human identities in new cybernetic consumption communities formed around shared consumer goods, common mass media, mutual machine uses, coincident aesthetic preferences or parallel market niches (Jones, 1995). Spending one's limited supplies of time online screen-to-screen means not engaging one's attention and energy in the collective life of one's face-to-face coresidents and contemporaries offline. Instead, compatriots in the shared territorial space of a metropolis often can be ignored as more and more e-migrate into cyberspace (Gilster, 1997). In this e-migration, new quarters of the Netropolis begin to take shape:

> Thousands of users spend many hours each week 'living' in virtual communities, each with its own residents and laws and even politics. In these virtual communities, users interact with others whom they know only in their online personas, which may be quite different from who they are in their offline hours; thus the 'residents' of virtual communities are more welcoming – and even more real – than the world with which they spend the rest of their time. (Carter, 1998: 195–6)

Quasi-cultures with some real solidity, therefore, begin to reproduce themselves on a global basis around the e-haviour of e-lancing, e-commerce, e-voting, e-governance, and e-learning. Turkle's musings about 'life on the screen' easily support such visions of e-migration out on to the cyberscapes of online environments (Johnson, 1997). In cyberspace, society and community become composite materials concocted out of the various codes, discourses and games composing the bitstream (Horn, 1998).

New e-figurations for online collaboration 'blur the boundaries between self and game, self and rule, self and simulation' such that as one player observes, '"you are what you pretend to be … you are what you play." But people don't just become who they play, they play who they are or who they want to be or who they don't want to be' (Turkle, 1997: 192).

The WYSIWYG aesthetics of a graphic user interface in multitasked, window-driven, cross-platform connectivity out on the Net essentially become 'a powerful new metaphor for thinking about the self as a multiple, distributed system … The experience of this parallelism encourages treating on-screen and off-screen lives with a surprising degree of equality' (Turkle, 1997: 21). No one single screen necessarily has primacy, and all of them operate in parallel according to the contingent configurations most appropriate at that time for the individuals and groups choosing to collaborate in this or that fashion (Luke, 1989). These tendencies, as Turkle suggests, point to Netizens 'taking things at their interface value', or a political culture in which 'people are increasingly comfortable with substituting representations of reality for the real' (1997: 23). Jerry Everard takes on these issues of sovereignty in cyberspace in *Virtual States: The Internet and the Boundaries of The Nation-State* (2000). He quite correctly sees the state persisting into the era of networked economies and societies for quite solid material reasons: state domains, anchor economies and stage wars – all of these practices will continue in cyberspace. So Turkle might be right, but perhaps only within specific parameters.

In reviewing the contradictions of citizenship and Netizenship, any analysis must consider newly emergent tendencies and unfolding possibilities. Despite what many would-be Netizens claim, the Net is still a comparatively small realm of user domains with relatively few hard and fast rules. Virtual life along with e-commerce, e-schooling, and e-governance are quite promising, but from a global perspective only a very privileged few now enjoy such online services. As Markham (1998) notes, real experience in virtual space can be very different from real life offline. Most people remain in the corporeal, material, substantial tracks of a life offline, and nationality for them continues to be a major determinant of their life chances. Today's rhetorics of universal Netizenship, then, must be examined carefully. On one level, these literatures may only be the latest expression for very modern forms of technified utopianism, which embed an enthusiasm for universal access to a new technology at the base of new designs for social transformation. The PC touts in *Wired* only recapitulate the now long-past millenarian dreams spun over the years by railroaders, aviators, radiomen, motorists, rocketeers and TV people in *Popular Mechanics* or *Popular Science*, who have imagined their new technics would remake humanity anew and for the better. On another level, however, successful would-be Netizens also seem to be laying the foundations for cyber-secessionist movements from face-to-face markets, urban life, banks, public affairs, schools and social institutions, which only will accentuate and aggravate the already deep splits (Martin and Schumann, 1997; Reich, 1991) between the informationally competent classes (labelled by some as 'symbolic analysts' or 'the successful fifth') and the informationally obsolescent and superfluous classes (recognized by others as the deindustrialized underemployed or even underclass making up the unsuccessful remaining four-fifths of society).

CONCLUSIONS

On the Net, one finds points of coincidence, cooperation and cofiguration condensing into new modes of transnational cohabitation – separate and apart from existing maps of familiar behaviours. As online identity and community are turned into normative ideals by information rhetorics and cybertechnics, they will begin to normalize the behaviour of individuals and populations as the behaviour of online game players, Napster users and Usenet regulars all suggest. Consequently, the accumulation of all the Netoperational components now constitutes a

vast incorporeal engine of agency and structure in virtual realities (Kelly, 1998; Mattelart, 1994). Yet, these online cooperant possibilities are also finding other very concrete means for power to gain actualization, incarnation and effectuation offline in physical bodies and social groups. Being digital online is also digitalizing concrete modes of becoming offline in many remarkable ways. Therefore, the various ethical personae which are made in cyberspace as forms of digital being need to be tracked far more closely.

For three decades, the Internet, or the network of networks that this regrettably singular term still denotes, has evolved, first, in accord with military–bureaucratic plans and then, later, in concord with technical–corporate agendas. In both instances, the Net's techno–economic action remains shielded from the demands of democratic legitimation by its own constitution. At the same time, however, it loses its non-political character. It is *neither politics nor non-politics*, but a third entity: economically guided action in pursuit of interests. (Beck, 1992: 222)

On the Net, many varieties of economically guided action are pursuing national, corporate and personal monetary interests as performativity, just as Lyotard suggested. These dynamics, in which virtually everything in cyberspace becomes an I-mart, ironically and simultaneously also shield the networks from democratic legitimation, rob them of their non-political character, give them subpolitical powers, and lock their users into performativity games (Mattelart and Mattelart, 1992).

On one level, networks are simply rhetorical representations of various ideological projects, like Michael Dertouzos' 'information marketplace', Bill Gates' 'friction-free capitalism', and Nicholas Negroponte's 'being digital', that dress out cybernetic goods and services in the semantic costumes of more traditional activities. On a second level, networks are a new global infrastructure of material systems – chips and cables, routines and routers, modems and machines all stacked up upon themselves. Such physical assets cannot be discounted entirely from cyberspace, because without these components nothing would operate. And, on a third level, networks are institutionalized entities whose code-carried infostructure coevolves hand in hand with its machine-made infrastructure. Control over specific segments of capital, labour, knowledge and communication, however, turns such big informatic systems into public spheres with their own virtual and material assets to serve, protect and defend (Habermas, 1989). Here bits reach out, touch someone, organize something, and then reconstitute both human acts and non-human artifacts into subpolitical clusters of operational performativity. Politics, or who dominates whom, from both the inside and the outside of which systems, becomes the most significant question for any system's designers, owners and users as well as for the citizens of those nations that these networked systems criss-cross.

To explore these questions, this chapter has performed three tasks. First, it re-examined the politics and culture of an online economy and society in the lifeworld made by ICTs where national state structures, corporate market strategies and complex technoscience systems are all promoting highly individualized modes of life. Second, it reconsidered how governing with, and governance through, digital technics create new technically mediated identities and communities tied to online commerce, education and faith out of new media. Third, it reconsidered how existing literatures treat Netizenship in contrast to citizenship and it looked at current visions of digital democracy. In many ways, they are imagined only as more flexible, specialized articulations of the televisual consumerist modes of political participation that have developed in the US since the 1950s, or as a much more aterritorial/nonstatal Netropolitan life that might lead to forms of Netizenship based upon a government by Netizens, of the Netizenry, and for Netizenship in the workings of the Net itself (Hauben, 1997; Saco, 2000).

This chapter also approached the question of political culture online by moving past the current literatures, in which governing with cybernetic technologies, by such means as online voting, digital citizenship and cybernetic party building, typically are celebrated. Instead of seeing Netizenship as more of the same, only with computers, this discussion sought to problematize the performative sites and operational practices of citizenship by examining how intertwined they are with certain technics, built environments and machinic systems. Digital political behaviours are being imagined in today's cybernetic writings to be just like embodied civic behaviours, but they are not. This recognition must lead us to a more critical exploration of the imbricate coevolution of human subjects and non-human objects in which, first, citizens cannot be easily separated from cities and, second, netizens ought not to be thought about apart from networks. Likewise, such developments in political culture should not be examined apart from the ongoing processes of modernization in which new informational technologies are integrated as part and parcel of new forms of personal agency being valorized by e-commerce and e-government.

REFERENCES

Abbate, Janet (1999) *Inventing the Internet.* Cambridge, MA: MIT Press.

Adams, James (1998) *The Next World War: Computers Are the Weapons and the Frontline Is Everywhere.* New York: Simon & Schuster.

Adas, Michael (1989) *Machines as the Measure of Men: Science, Technology, and Ideologies of Western Dominance.* Ithaca, NY: Cornell University Press.

Agger, Ben (2003) *The Virtual Self: A Contemporary Sociology.* Oxford: Blackwell.

Anderson, Benedict (1991) *Imagined Communities,* rev. edn. London: Verso.

Anderson, David M. and Cornfield, Michael (2002) *The Civic Web: Online Politics and Democratic Values.* Lanham, MD: Rowman & Littlefield.

Baudrillard, Jean (1981) *For a Critique of the Political Economy of the Sign.* St Louis, MO: Telos.

Baudrillard, Jean (1993) *The Transparency of Evil: Essays on Extreme Phenomena.* London: Verso.

Beck, Ulrich (1992) *The Risk Society.* London: Sage.

Beck, Ulrich (1997) *The Reinvention of Politics.* Oxford: Polity.

Bimber, Bruce (2003a) *Information and American Democracy: Technology in the Evolution of Political Power.* Cambridge: Cambridge University Press.

Bimber, Bruce (2003b) *Campaigning Online: The Internet in US Elections.* Oxford: Oxford University Press.

Brin, David (1998) *The Transparent Society.* Reading, MA: Addison-Wesley.

Browning, Graeme (1996) *Electronic Democracy: Using the Internet to Influence American Politics.* Wilson, CT: Pemberton.

Bryan, Cathy, Tsagarousianou, Roza and Tambini, Damian (1998) 'Electronic democracy and the civic networking movement in context', in Roza Tsagarousianou, Damian Tambini and Cathy Bryan (eds), *Cyberdemocracy: Technology, Cities, and Civic Networks.* London: Routledge.

Bukatman, Scott (1993) *Terminal Identity.* Durham, NC: Duke University Press.

Businessweek (2000) 21 February: 41.

Cairncross, Frances (1997) *The Death of Distance: How the Communications Revolution Will Change Our Lives.* Boston: Harvard Business School Press.

Carter, Stephen (1998) *Civility: Manners, Morals, and the Etiquette of Democracy.* New York: Basic.

Castells, Manuel (1996–8) *The Information Age,* Vols I–III. Oxford: Blackwell.

Castells, Manuel (2001) *The Internet Galaxy: Reflections on the Internet, Business, and Society.* Oxford: Oxford University Press.

Chayko, Mary (2002) *Connecting: How We Form Social Bonds and Communities in the Internet Age.* Albany: SUNY Press.

Cooper, Jonathan (1999) *Liberating Cyberspace: Civil Liberties, Human Rights and the Internet.* London: Pluto.

Deibert, Ronald J. (1997) *Parchment, Printing, and Hypermedia: Communication in World Order Transformation.* New York: Columbia University Press.

De Kerckhove, Derrick (1998) *Connected Intelligence: The Arrival of the Web Society.* Toronto: Somerville.

Dertouzos, Michael (1997) *What Will Be: How the New World of Information Will Change Our Lives.* New York: HarperCollins.

Drahos, Peter with John Braithwaite (2003) *Information Feudalism: Who Owns the Knowledge Economy?* New York: New Press.

Everard, Jerry (2000) *Virtual States: The Internet and the Boundaries of the Nation-state.* London: Routledge.

Feenberg, Andrew (1999) *Questioning Technology.* New York: Routledge.

Foucault, Michel (1980) *History of Sexuality,* Vol. I. New York: Vintage.

Foucault, Michel (1988) *Technologies of the Self.* Amherst, MA: University of Massachusetts Press.

Foucault, Michel (1991) *The Foucault Effect: Studies in Governmentality,* edited by Graham Burchell, Colin Gordon and Peter Miller. Chicago: University of Chicago Press.

Franda, Marcus (2003) *Launching into Cyberspace: Internet Development and Politics in Five World Regions (Ipolitics: Global Challenges in the Information Age).* Boulder, CO: Lynne Rienner.

Gates, Bill (1999) *Business @ the Speed of Thought: Using a Digital Nervous System.* New York: Warner.

Gates, Bill with Myhrvold, Norman and Rinearson, Peter (1996) *The Road Ahead.* New York: Viking.

Gergen, Kenneth (1991) *The Saturated Self: Dilemmas of Identity in Contemporary Life.* New York: Basic.

Gibson, William (1984) *Neuromancer.* New York: Ace.

Giedion, Sigfried (1948) *Mechanization Takes Command: A Contribution to Anonymous History.* New York: Norton.

Gilder, George (1989) *Microcosm.* New York: Simon & Schuster.

Gilster, Paul (1997) *Digital Literacy.* New York: Wiley.

Grisham, Gordon (1999) *The Internet: A Philosophical Inquiry.* London: Routledge.

Grossman, Wendy (1997) *net.wars.* New York: New York University Press.

Grusin, R. and Bolter, J. (1999) *Remediation: Understanding New Media.* Cambridge, MA: MIT Press.

Habermas, Jürgen (1989) *The Structural Transformation of the Public Sphere.* Cambridge, MA: MIT Press.

Hachten, William A. (2002) *The World News Prism: Global Media in an Era of Terrorism,* 6th edn. Ames, IA: Iowa State Press.

Harvey, David (1989) *The Condition of Postmodernity.* Oxford: Blackwell.

Hassan, Ihab (1977) 'Prometheus as performer: towards a posthumanist culture', in Michael Benamou and Charles Caramella (eds), *Performance in Modern Change.* Madison, WI: Coda.

Hauben, Michael (1997) *Netizens: On the History and Impact of USENet and the Internet.* Los Alamitos, CA: IEEE Computer Society Press.

Hayles, N. Katherine (1999) *How We Became Posthuman: Virtual Bodies in Cybernetics, Literature, and Informatics.* Chicago: University of Chicago Press.

Heim, Michael (1998) *Virtual Realism*. Oxford: Oxford University Press.

Hewitt, Hugh (2005) *Blog: Understanding the Information Reformation That's Changing Your World*. New York: Nelson Books.

Hillis, Ken (1999) *Digital Sensations: Space, Identity and Embodiment in Virtual Reality*. Minneapolis: University of Minnesota Press.

Hobart, M. and Schiffman, Z. (1998) *Information Ages*. Baltimore, MD: Johns Hopkins University Press.

Horn, Stacey (1998) *Cyberville*. New York: Warner.

Ihde, Don (1990) *Technology and the Lifeworld: From Garden to Earth*. Bloomington, IN: Indiana University Press.

Jameson, Fredric (1992) *Postmodernism, or the Cultural Logic of Late Capitalism*. Durham, NC: Duke University Press.

Johnson, Steven (1997) *Interface Culture*. San Francisco: Harper Edge.

Jones, Stephen G. (ed.) (1995) *Cybersociety: Computer-mediated Communication and Community*, 2nd edn. London: Sage.

Jordan, Tim (1999) *Cyberpower: The Culture and Politics of Cyberspace and the Internet*. New York: Routledge.

Kelly, Kevin (1994) *Out of Control: The Rise of Neo-biological Civilization*. Reading, MA: Addison-Wesley.

Kelly, Kevin (1998) *New Rules for the New Economy*. New York: Viking.

Kroker, A. and Weinstein, M. (1994) *Data Trash: The Theory of the Virtual Class*. New York: St Martin's Press.

Latour, Bruno (1993) *We Have Never Been Modern*. London: Harvester Wheatsheaf.

Lessig, Lawrence (2000) *Code and Other Laws of Cyberspace*. New York: Basic Books.

Lessig, Lawrence (2001) *The Future of Ideas: The Fate of the Commons in a Connected World*. New York: Random Press.

Lessig, Lawrence (2004) *Free Culture: How Big Media Uses Technology and the Law to Lock Down Culture and Control Creativity*. New York: Penguin.

Levy, Pierre (1997) *Becoming Virtual*. New York: Plenum.

Lewis, T.G. (1997) *The Friction-free Economy: Marketing Strategies for a Wired World*. New York: Harper Business.

Luke, Timothy W. (1989) *Screens of Power: Ideology, Domination, and Resistance in Informational Society*. Urbana, IL: University of Illinois Press.

Luke, Timothy W. (1994) 'Placing powers/siting spaces: the politics of global and local in the new world order', *Environment and Planning D: Society and Space*, 12: 613–28.

Luke, Timothy W. (1995) 'New world order or neo-world orders: power, politics and ideology in informationalizing glocalities', in Mike Featherstone, Scott Lash and Roland Robertson (eds), *Global Modernities*. London: Sage. pp. 91–107.

Luke, Timothy W. (1996) 'Identity, meaning and globalization: space–time compression and the political economy of everyday life', in Scott Lash, Paul Heelas and Paul Morris (eds), *Detraditionalization: Critical Reflections on Authority and Identity*. Oxford: Blackwell. pp. 109–33.

Luke, Timothy W. (1997) 'The politics of digital inequality: access, capabilities, and distribution in cyberspace', *New Political Science*, 41–2 (Fall): 121–44.

Luke, Timothy W. (1998) 'Running flat out on the road ahead: nationality, sovereignty, and territoriality in the world of the information superhighway', in Gearóid Ó Tuathail and Simon Dalby (eds), *Rethinking Geopolitics*. London: Routledge. pp. 274–94.

Luke, Timothy W. (2001) 'On 9.11.01', *Telos*, 120 (Summer): 129–42.

Lyon, David (1994) *The Electronic Eye: The Rise of Surveillance Society*. Minneapolis: University of Minnesota Press.

Lyotard, Jean-François (1984) *The Postmodern Condition: A Report on Knowledge*. Minneapolis: University of Minnesota Press.

Markham, Annette (1998) *Life Online: Researching Real Experience in Virtual Space*. Walnut Creek, CA: Altamira.

Martin, Chuck (1997) *The Digital Estate: Strategies for Competing, Surviving and Thriving in an Internet Worked World*. New York: McGraw-Hill.

Martin, Hans-Peter and Schumann, Harald (1997) *The Global Trap: Globalization and the Assault on Democracy and Prosperity*. London: Zed.

Mattelart, Armand (1994) *Mapping World Communication: War, Progress, Culture*. Minneapolis: University of Minnesota Press.

Mattelart, Armand (2000) *Networking the World, 1794–2000*. Minneapolis: University of Minnesota Press.

Mattelart, Armand and Mattelart, Michele (1992) *Rethinking Media Theory*. Minneapolis: University of Minnesota Press.

McLuhan, Marshall (1964) *Understanding Media: The Extensions of Man*. New York: Signet.

Meikle, Graham (2002) *Future Active: Media Activism and the Internet*. New York: Routledge.

Miller, Steven E. (1996) *Civilizing Cyberspace*. New York: ACM Press.

Mitchell, William J. (1995) *City of Bits*. Cambridge, MA: MIT Press.

Mueller, Milton L. (2002) *Ruling the Root: Internet Governance and the Taming of Cyberspace*. Cambridge, MA: MIT Press.

Mumford, Lewis (1963) *Technics and Civilization*. New York: Harcourt Brace Jovanovich.

Mumford, Lewis (1970) *The Pentagon of Power*. New York: Harcourt Brace.

National Telecommunications and Information Administration (1995) *Falling through the Net: A Survey of 'Have Nots' in Rural and Urban America*. Washington, DC: US Department of Commerce. Available online: http://www.ntia.doc.gov/ntiahome/fallingthru.html

National Telecommunications and Information Administration (1998) *Falling through the Net II: New Data on the Digital Divide*. Washington, DC: US Department of Commerce. Available online: http://www. ntia.doc.gov/ntiahome/net2

National Telecommunications and Information Administration (1999) *Americans in the Information Age: Falling through the Net*. Washington, DC: US Department of Commerce. Available online: http://ntia.doc. gov./ntiahome/digital divide

Negroponte, Nicholas (1995) *Being Digital*. New York: Knopf.

Norris, Pippa (2001) *Digital Divide: Civic Engagement, Information Poverty, and the Internet Worldwide*. Cambridge: Cambridge University Press.

Nye, David E. (1990) *Electrifying America: Social Meanings of a New Technology*. Cambridge, MA: MIT Press.

Nye, David E. (1996) *The Technological Sublime*. Cambridge, MA: MIT Press.

Nye, Joseph, S., Jr (2004) *Soft Power: The Means to Success in World Politics*. New York: Public Affairs.

Ohmae, Kenichi (1990) *The Borderless World: Power and Strategy in the Interlinked Economy*. New York: Harper & Row.

Poster, Mark (1990) *The Mode of Information*. Chicago: University of Chicago Press.

Poster, Mark (1995) *The Second Media Age*. Chicago: University of Chicago Press.

Poster, Mark (2001) *What's the Matter with the Internet?* Minneapolis: University of Minnesota Press.

Rash, Wayne Jr (1997) *Politics on the Nets: Wiring the Political Process*. New York: Freeman.

Reich, Robert (1991) *The Work of Nations: Preparing Ourselves for 21st Century Capitalism*. New York: Knopf.

Rheingold, Howard (1993) *The Virtual Community*. Reading, MA: Addison-Wesley.

Rochlin, Gene (1997) *Trapped in the Net: The Unanticipated Consequences of Computerization*. Princeton, NJ: Princeton University Press.

Roszak, Theodore (1994) *The Cult of Information*, 2nd edn. Berkeley, CA: University of California Press.

Rushkoff, Douglas (1994) *Cyberia: Life in the Trenches of Hyperspace*. San Francisco: HarperCollins.

Rutsky, R.L. (2000) *High Techuê: Art and Technology from the Machine Assistance to the Postman*. Minneapolis: University of Minnesota Press.

Saco, Diana (2000) *Cybering Democracy*. Minneapolis: University of Minnesota Press.

Servon, Lisa J (2002) *Bridging the Digital Divide: Technology, Community, and Public Policy*. Oxford: Blackwell.

Shane, Peter M. (2004) *Democracy Online: The Prospects for Political Renewal Through the Internet*. New York: Routledge.

Shapiro, Andrew (1999) *The Control Revolution*. New York: Public Affairs Press.

Shenk, David (1997) *Data Smog*. San Francisco: Harper Edge.

Slevin, James (2000) *The Internet and Society*. Oxford: Polity.

Slouka, Mark (1995) *War of the Worlds: Cyberspace and the High-tech Assault on Reality*. New York: Basic.

Smith, Gary and Kollock, Peter (1999) *Communities in Cyberspace*. New York: Routledge.

Solomon, Elinore Harris (1997) *Virtual Money: Understanding the Power and Risks of Money's High-speed Journey into Electronic Space*. Oxford: Oxford University Press.

Stauffer, Todd (2002) *Blog On: Building Online Communities with Web Logs*. Berkeley, CA: McGraw-Hill/Osborne.

Stefnik, Mark (1999) *The Internet Edge: Social, Technical, and Legal Challenges for a Networked World*. Cambridge, MA: MIT Press.

Sunstein, Cass (2002) *Republic.com*. Princeton, NJ: Princeton University Press.

Tapscott, Don (1996) *The Digital Economy: Promise and Peril in an Age of Networked Intelligence*. New York: McGraw-Hill.

Tapscott, Don (1997) *Growing up Digital: The Rise of the Net Generation*. New York: McGraw-Hill.

Trippi, Joe (2004) *The Revolution Will Not Be Televised: Democracy, the Internet, and the Overthrow of Everything*. New York: HarperCollins.

Trumbull, Gunnar (2004) *Silicon and the State: French Innovation Policy in the Internet Age*. Washington, DC: Brookings Institution.

Turkle, Sherry (1997) *Life on the Screen: Identity in the Age of the Internet*. New York: Touchstone.

Van der Pjil, Kees (1998) *Transnational Classes and International Relations*. London: Routledge.

Verton, D. (2003) *Black Ice: The Invisible Threat of Cyber-terrorism*. New York: McGraw-Hill/Osborne.

Virilio, Paul (1995) *The Art of the Motor*. Minneapolis: University of Minnesota Press.

Virilio, Paul (1997) *Open Sky*. London: Verso.

Waite, Beverly (2002) 'Internet B2B transaction by continent 2002 to 2006', *Computer Economics*. Available online: www.computereconomics.com/article.cfm?id=598

Walker, R.B.J. (1993) *Inside/Outside: International Relations as Political Theory*. Cambridge: Cambridge University Press.

Part Two

Technology Systems, Design and Industries

9

New Media History

PATRICE FLICHY

Many histories of information and communication could be written: the history of institutions and firms, the history of programmes and creative works, the history of techniques, and the history of practices and uses which, in turn, can be related to that of work and leisure but also to that of the public sphere. All these histories are related to very different fields of social science, and the information and communication sector is far too vast to present all these perspectives here. I have chosen to take as the main theme of this chapter the question of relations between ICTs and society. With this point of view we are at the heart of a number of debates: debate on the effects of communication, which for a long time mobilized sociologists of the media; extensive debate on determinism among historians of techniques; and debate around the sociotechnical perspective which has now been adopted by most sociologists of science and technology.

We shall focus on three points in particular: the launching and development of ICTs, their uses in a professional context and, lastly, their uses in a leisure context.

INNOVATION IN ICTS

Does Technology Drive History?

In many histories of computing, the transistor, then the microprocessor, are considered to be the determining elements. Behind this very common theory lies the idea that technical progress is inevitable and globally linear. Electronic components and basic technologies such as digitization are seen as determining the form of the technical devices we use. Similarly, these new machines have been expected to determine the organization of work (Friedmann, 1978), our leisure activities and, more broadly, our ways of thinking (McLuhan, 1964) or even society at large (Ellul, 1964).

By contrast, other researchers such as the historian David Noble (1984) clearly show, through the case of automatically controlled machine tools, that there is no one best way, and that the effect of a technique cannot be understood without simultaneously studying its use and the choices made by its designers. After the Second World War two alternatives were explored to automate production: record–playback (automatic analogue) machines and numerical control machines. The former recorded the design of a part drawn by a human operator and then automatically produced copies. The numeric machine, by contrast, did not need to memorize human knowhow; it was capable of programming design and production. If the numeric option triumphed, it was not because it was more reliable or easier to implement, but because it corresponded to the representations that designers and corporate managers (future buyers) had of automated industrial production:

> Numerical control was always more than a technology for cutting metals, especially in the eyes of its MIT designers who knew little about metal cutting: it was a symbol of the computer age, of mathematical elegance, of power, order and predictability, of continuous flow, of remote control, of the automatic factory. Record–playback, on the other hand, however much it represented a significant advance on manual methods, retained a vestige of traditional human skills; as such, in the eyes of the future (and engineers always confuse the present and the future) it was obsolete. (Noble, 1979: 29–30)

Studying Successes and Failures

One conclusion can be drawn from Noble's study: there is never a single technical solution; as a rule, several solutions are studied in parallel. The historian has to study these different solutions and analyse both successes and failures (Bijker et al., 1987). The RCA videodisk is a good example of failure. Margaret Graham (1986) showed that the television corporation RCA had everything it needed to launch its new product successfully: one of the best US research laboratories, positive market research, support from the media and, lastly, access to a very large programme catalogue. Despite all these assets, RCA sold no more than 500,000 copies of its videodisk player in three years. Another technical system, the VCR, developed in Japan, was to dominate the market with a resulting loss for RCA of $600 million. The company that had launched television in the US was eventually bought out by General Electric and then by the French company Thomson. Thus, as many computer manufacturers were to discover, a company can pay very dearly for a failure. The main lesson that Graham draws from this case is that technical or commercial competencies are not enough if they are not properly coordinated. That was the underlying cause of the videodisk's failure. As sociologists of technology have shown, 'rather than rational decision-making, it is necessary to talk of an aggregation of interests that can or cannot be produced. Innovation is the art of involving a growing number of allies who are made stronger and stronger' (Akrich et al., 1988: 17; see also Latour, 1987). This strategy of

alliances was what enabled France Télécom to successfully launch its videotex (the minitel) in the early 1980s. A few months before the new medium was launched, this telematic project collided with a virulent combination of media and political opposition. In fact, France Télécom, which at the time was still the French Post Office (PTT), wanted to create and run the whole system on its own. It hoped not only to provide the network and terminals but also to install all the information to be offered to the public on its own servers. Other European post and telecommunications authorities had opted for the same schema. However, faced with intense opposition France Télécom backed down and decided to move from a closed to an open system in which any firm could become a service provider. France Télécom simply transported the information and took care of the billing (with a share of the revenue paid back to the supplier). Owing to partnerships with service providers and especially with the press, 20 per cent of French households adopted the new service (Flichy, 1991).[1]

Boundary Objects

Behind the questions of coordination of designers within a company or of partnerships with the outside, lies the question of the mobilization of the different parties concerned by innovation: R&D engineers, marketing specialists, salespeople, repairers, partner companies (manufacturers of components, content providers, etc.) but also users. In an interactionist approach, sociologists have used the notion of boundary objects. These are objects situated at the intersection of several social worlds, which meet the needs of all worlds simultaneously. 'They are objects which are both plastic enough to adapt to local needs and the constraints of the several parties employing them, yet robust enough to maintain a common identity' (Star and Griesemer, 1989: 393). A boundary object is the result of complex interaction between the different actors concerned. This is the exact opposite of the naïve idea of innovation spawned ready-made by the inventor's mind. The history of Macintosh clearly illustrates this point. Two computers using the principle of graphic windows were produced concurrently at Apple: Lisa, a failure, and Macintosh, the Californian company's leading machine. Lisa was designed in a rather cumbersome organizational frame, with a strict division of tasks between teams. Macintosh, by contrast, was developed by a small, tightly knit team in which choices made by individuals were always discussed collectively. The software developers gave their opinions on the hardware and vice versa. Moreover, the people in charge of building the factory and of marketing and finance were also included in these discussions. This continuous negotiation caused the project to be amended more than once. A computer that was originally designed for the general public was eventually substituted for Lisa as an office machine. The simplicity of its use, imagined from the outset, was one of this computer's most attractive features (Guterl, 1984). The Macintosh is a computer situated on the boundary between hardware and software, between the computer specialist and the layperson.[2]

Path Dependency

While the perspective of boundary objects is very useful for the study of specific cases, other perspectives are needed to analyse more long-term phenomena. The path-dependency concept devised by economist and historian Paul David is particularly illuminating. Through the paradigmatic example of the typewriter keyboard which has not evolved since its invention, David (1985) builds a model that compares dynamic growth to a tree. At each branch the actors face a choice. This choice may sometimes be linked to a minor element, but once a solution has been chosen by a large number of actors it becomes relatively stable. The outcome of initial choices is relatively unpredictable but a time comes when a technique or an industrial mode of organization is imposed, with a resulting phenomenon of lock-in.

IBM's entry into the PC market is an interesting example of path dependency. Big Blue was aware that this was an entirely new market and that it needed to find a specific mode of organization to produce a fundamentally different computer. A task force was set up to produce and market this microcomputer, independently of the rest of the company. Unlike Apple and in the true IBM tradition, it chose an open architecture not protected by patents. This meant that users could buy peripherals and software from other companies. The task force also decided to break away from IBM's traditional vertical integration. The central processing unit would thus be bought from Intel and the operating system from a startup, Microsoft. There were two main reasons for this policy: the desire to be reactive and to short-circuit the usual functioning; and the desire to show the Department of Justice that IBM had stopped its monopolistic behaviour. The strategy was a success. In 1982, the first full year of production, IBM's microcomputer revenues totalled £500 million and in 1985 £5.5 billion, 'a record of revenue growth unsurpassed in industrial history' (Chandler, 2000: 33). But it also had a whole series of unexpected effects. While the appearance of rivals (producers of clones and specialized software) was part of the game, the key position that this afforded Intel and, to an even greater extent, Microsoft (Cusumano, 1995) was far less predictable. These two companies rapidly became the two main players in the microcomputing industry, at IBM's expense. Finally, in 2004, IBM decided to abandon the PC market.

The Internet is another case of a path-dependent history. It has sometimes been said that ARPANET, the ancestor of the network of networks, was built so that the US Army could maintain communication links in case of a Soviet attack. In fact, this network had a far more modest aim: it was to link the computing departments of universities working for ARPA, the US Defense Department's advanced research agency (Edwards, 1996; Hafner and Lyon, 1996: 41, 77). Telecommunication companies and especially AT&T refused to build this new data network. It was therefore designed by computer specialists who had a new view of computing, suited to communication between machines with the same status. This computer-mediated communication was profoundly different from IBM's centralized and hierarchized computing system or from a telephone network. From the outset ARPANET was a highly decentralized network which stopped at the university entrance. This technical architecture left a large degree of leeway to each computing site which could organize itself as it wished as regards hardware and software and could create its own local area network. The only constraint was the need to be able to connect to an interface. These technical choices in favour of decentralization were also to be found in the organization of work needed to develop the network. Construction of the network was entrusted to a small company closely linked to MIT. This company dealt with no technical problems posed by data exchange beyond the interface, considering that they were the universities' responsibility. Unlike the time-sharing system developed by IBM, in particular, where the central computer is in a master–slave position to the terminals, in ARPANET host computers were on an equal footing with terminals.

Whereas ARPANET was launched and coordinated by ARPA, Usenet, which constituted another branch of what was to become the Internet, was developed cooperatively by research centres not linked to ARPANET. Usenet did not have its own financing. The administrators of the system were computer scientists who participated on a voluntary basis, making space on their hard disks to record news and transmitting it by telephone.

The Internet was designed in the second half of the 1970s as an 'internetwork architecture', that is, a metaprotocol for interaction between networks built on different principles. The idea of an open architecture leaves total autonomy to each network. Since the metaprotocol manages only interaction between networks, each individual network can maintain its own mode of functioning. Furthermore, the Internet has no central authority. The Internet society is only an associative coordination structure. Applications proposed on the ARPANET or Internet (e-mail, newsgroups, database sharing and, later, the World Wide Web) were proposed by different designers and can be used by anyone who wants to (Abbate, 1999; Norberg and O'Neill, 1996).

The two main principles of decentralization and free access in which the Internet is grounded stem essentially from the academic functioning of its founders. When the Internet subsequently became a system of communication for the general public, these two principles were perpetuated to a large extent. The network is still not managed by a single operator, and a large amount of software, especially browsers, circulates freely on the Web, at least in its most basic form.

Engineers' Representations

The initial choices that will profoundly influence the trajectory of a technology are related not only to contingent decisions but also to the representations of the designers (Flichy, 2001). Thus, the founding fathers of the Internet, such as Licklider or Engelbart, thought that computing was not only a calculation tool but also a means of communication. Hiltz and Turoff considered that once computer-mediated communication was widespread 'we will become the Network Nation, exchanging vast amounts of both information and social-emotional communications with colleagues, friends and strangers who share similar interests, who are spread out all over the nation' (1978: xxvii–xxiv). This theme of the creation of collective intelligence through networking was to mobilize many computer specialists in the 1970s and 1980s, and to appeal strongly to users. The Californian bulletin board the WELL, for example, functioned around that idea (Rheingold, 1993).

We similarly find a common project among hackers, those young computer enthusiasts who were to play an essential part in the design of the first microcomputers (Freiberger and Swaine, 1984). They shared the same principles:

- access to computers should be unlimited and total;
- all information should be free;
- mistrust authority, promote decentralization;
- hackers should be judged by their hacking, not bogus criteria such as degrees, age, race or position;

- you can create art and beauty on a computer;
- computers can change your life for the better. (Levy, 1985: 40–5)

They considered that computing was a device to be made available to all, which would help to build a new society.

Technological imagination is a key component of the development of technology. Without the myths produced by the American counter-culture in the early 1970s, the microcomputer would probably have remained a mere curiosity. The ideology of computing for all, in a decentralized form, suddenly lent a whole new dimension to hackers' tinkering in their garages. However, we can talk of the influence of the counter-culture on the microcomputing project only if we consider that there were hackers who chose to associate the values of the counter-culture with their passion for computing. They defined the problems that they chose to grapple with. The community ideology alone did not create the microcomputer; at best, it produced a mythical frame of use. The basis of hackers' activity was immersion both in the counter-culture and in the world of computer tinkering; these two components were not only juxtaposed but also very closely linked. The ties needed for the establishment of a permanent sociotechnological frame were built by the actors; the technological or social dreams thus had no power other than supplying resources for the action.

This type of study of the representations of designers of information tools has also been made by Simon Schaffer (1995) on Babbage's calculating engine, generally considered to be the computer's mechanical ancestor. Babbage, a Victorian mathematician, also conducted research on the division of labour observed in factories and at the Greenwich Royal Observatory where dozens of employees did calculations from morning till night to prepare mathematical tables. To make the production of goods and calculations more efficient, it was necessary to automate the factory system. Just as Jacquard had mechanized weaving with his famous loom, so too Babbage wanted to mechanize the production of numeric tables. He hoped to speed up the production of tables which were perfectly accurate and rid of all human error. But Schaffer does more than point out the analogy between Babbage's machine and the factory system. He draws a map of the places and networks in which the credibility of Babbage's machine was regularly evaluated. Although the machine was never totally operational, it was exhibited often enough to contribute towards the production of a need that it could not entirely fulfil.

Representations of the Media

Representations of techniques are interesting to observe, not only in inventors but also in the first users. Susan Douglas studied enthusiasts of the wireless, whose passion for this new technology was to popularize Marconi's invention and attract the attention of the press. A short story from 1912 is a good example of these representations of the new medium. In it Francis Collins describes the practices of new users of the wireless:

> imagine a gigantic spider's web with innumerable threads radiating from New York more than a thousand miles over land and sea in all directions. In his station, our operator may be compared to the spider, sleepless, vigilant, ever watching for the faintest tremor from the farthest corner of his invisible fabric ... These operators, thousands of miles apart, talk and joke with one another as though they were in the same room. (Douglas, 1987: 199)

This is clearly a new imaginary type of communication that Collins is proposing. But this utopian discourse, which not only described potential users but also indicated everything that the wireless could do for society and individuals, was becoming a reality. Everyone could communicate instantly and independently with persons very far away, whenever they wanted to. Communication was free in that it did not depend on telegraph or telephone operators and therefore did not have to be paid for. As Susan Douglas says: 'The ether was an exciting new frontier in which men and boys could congregate, compete, test their mettle, and be privy to a range of new information. Social order and social control were defied' (1987: 214).

After the First World War a new 'wireless mania' appeared. This time it concerned wireless telephony, soon to become radio broadcasting. This new device was also to create a new community feeling. Douglas, in 'The social destiny of radio' wrote: 'How fine is the texture of the web that radio is even now spinning! It is achieving the task of making us feel together, think together, live together' (Douglas, 1987: 306).

Internet utopias, which in a sense are related to those of radio, also changed when the new technology left the world of designers in universities and groups of hackers (Flichy, 2001). For example, the first manuals for the public at large gave a fairly coherent representation of the Net that combined characteristics of scientific communities and those of communities of electronics enthusiasts. One of these guides considered that internauts 'freed from physical limitations ... are developing new types of cohesive and effective communities – ones which are defined more by common interest and purpose than by an accident of geography, ones on which what really counts is what you say and think and feel, not how you look' (Gaffin and Kapor, 1991: 8–9). Rheingold (1993) considers that virtual communities bring together individuals from all corners of the globe who exchange information or expertise. More broadly, they build ties of cooperation and develop conversations that are as intellectually and emotionally rich as those of real life. It is a world of balanced interaction between equals. In short, the net can make it possible not only to work collectively but also to re-establish a social link that is slackening, and to breathe life into public debate and democratic life.

Later the press started to write extensively about the Internet. In 1995 an editorial in *Time* noted that:

> most conventional computer systems are hierarchical and proprietary; they run on copyrighted software in a pyramid structure that gives dictatorial powers to the system operators to sit on top. The Internet, by contrast, is open (non-proprietary) and rabidly democratic. No one owns it. No single organization controls it. It is run like a commune with 4.8 million fiercely independent members (called hosts). It crosses national boundaries and answers to no sovereign. It is literally lawless ... Stripped of the external trappings of wealth, power, beauty and social status, people tend to be judged in the cyberspace of Internet only by their ideas. (*Time*, special issue, March 1995: 9)

Newsweek made 1995 Internet Year. It opened its year-end issue with the following phrase stretched across four pages: 'this changes ... everything' (*Newsweek*, special double issue, 2 January 1996). The editorial noted that the Internet is 'the medium that will change the way we communicate, shop, publish and (so the cybersmut cops warned) be damned'.

Thus, with the Internet, like the wireless, we find two examples of the 'rhetoric of the sublime technology' that Leo Marx (1964) already referred to regarding the steam engine. This rhetoric nevertheless takes on a specific form with communication systems, for it concerns not only a particular domain of productive activity but also social links and, more generally, the way society is constituted. The communication utopias of wireless and Internet are therefore fairly similar. They successively refer to interpersonal communication, group communication and, later, mass communication. In so far as both technologies soon acquired an international dimension, so that they could cover the entire planet, the utopias also granted much importance to the feeling of ubiquity found less strongly in other electric or electronic media. Finally, these utopias emphasized the principles of liberty and free access that characterize the development of these two technologies. They were defined in contrast to the two main technical systems of the time: telegraph and telephone in the case of wireless technology; and the absence of compatibility between computing systems, along with the centralized and hierarchical view of data networks that IBM incarnated, in the case of the Internet.

ICTS IN THE PROFESSIONAL SPHERE

Historical comparisons between the nineteenth and twentieth centuries are equally enlightening as regards the role of ICTs in economic activity. James Beniger shows that the industrial revolution was accompanied by what he calls 'the control revolution'. Changes in the scale of productive activity necessitated new modes of organization, for example the bureaucratic organization developed by railways, the organization of material processing established in industries, telecommunications used by distribution, and mass media used by marketing. For him, information is at the centre of this control revolution which continued developing in the second half of the twentieth century. 'Microprocessing and computing technology, contrary to currently fashionable opinion, do not represent a new force only recently unleashed on an unprepared society but merely the most recent instalment in the continuing development of the Control Revolution' (1986: 435).

The First Generation of Office Machines

Let us consider in more detail these nineteenth-century information and communication tools that were to facilitate the organization of business and markets. The telegraph was a decisive element in the organization of markets, first of all the stock market. In Europe the transmission of stock market information was the first use to which the telegraph was put, in the 1850s, and it facilitated the unification of values (Flichy, 1995: 46–50). In the United States the telegraph, in conjunction with the railroad, made it possible to unify regional markets and to create a large national market from east coast to west (DuBoff, 1983). It also facilitated the creation of large-scale business enterprises which made huge economies of scale and scope possible. The telegraph and railway companies were the prototype of such enterprises. Circulating messages or goods from one end of the North American continent to the other demanded complex coordination and could not be organized by the market alone. It necessitated the creation of large multisite corporations that decentralized responsibilities and simultaneously created functional coordination in finance and technical research (Chandler, 1977). The railway companies that used the telegraph to control traffic processed these data and thus developed the first management methods subsequently applied in other industrial sectors. With the increase in the size of firms the coordination of work was profoundly modified. In small

pre-industrial firms the owner and a few skilled artisans organized the work verbally. Writing was reserved for communication with the outside. By contrast, in large industrial firms writing was to be used extensively in internal coordination. Managers were thus to standardize production processes through handbooks or circular letters. Sales manuals were given to sales agents in order to standardize prices and the sale process itself. The development of accounting, which made it possible to calculate costs precisely and to better determine prices, also used writing (Yates, 1989). In industrial work, this use of the written document was to be systematized, at the end of the century, in Taylorism. The existence of written instructions given by the methods department to each worker was one of the basic elements of the scientific organization of work (Taylor, 1911). Office work also increased substantially. In the US the number of clerical workers rose from 74,000 in 1870 to 2.8 million in 1920 (Yates, 2000: 112).

To produce and manage this paper, various tools appeared: the typewriter, the roneo machine, the calculator, but also furniture to file and store documents, etc. All these devices were, in a sense, the first generation of data processing machines. We thus witness several parallel evolutions: growth in the size of firms, increase in the number of written documents, and appearance of new machines. But Joanne Yates (1994) has clearly shown that these evolutions would not necessarily have been articulated to one another without a locus of mediation and incentives to change. The managerial literature that developed at the time, as well as the first business schools, were to propose management methods and recommend the use of new office machines. For this new managerial ideology, writing was the most appropriate procedure to set up efficient coordination between the different actors in the firm. This systematic management also proposed management tools.

Mainframe and Centralized Organization

Computing, designed to meet scientists' and the defence force's needs (Campbell-Kelly and

Aspray, 1996), did not immediately find its place in managerial activity. Ten years after the advent of computing, a pioneer such as Howard Aiken could still write: 'if it should ever turn out that the basic logics of a machine designed for the numerical solution of differential equations coincide with the logics of a machine intended to make bills for a department store, I would regard this as the most amazing coincidence that I have ever encountered' (quoted by Ceruzzi, 1987: 197). The shift from calculating machines to management machines was made by companies that already had extensive technical and commercial experience in punch card tabulating technology, such as NCR, Burroughs and of course IBM (Cortada, 1993).

So, when IBM built the first mainframe computers it knew business organization so well that it could conceive a structure well adapted to the dominant form of organization: the multidivisional functional hierarchy. A database system like IMS (Information Management System) clearly reflected this organizational hierarchy (Nolan, 2000: 220).

This parallel between technical and organizational structures was also observed by French sociologists of labour who noted that, despite the utopian discourse of computer specialists on the structuring effects of computers in the processing and circulation of information, computing introduced no change in the firm; on the contrary, it reproduced the existing order (Ballé and Peaucelle, 1972). To understand this, we need to examine in detail the work of computer specialists in firms. To rationalize the circulation and processing of information they started by drawing up computer guidelines. They first analysed the existing functioning but, since few of them had any particular skills regarding the best modes of organization, they simply formalized written rules. When there were no such rules they had them formulated by the hierarchy. The computer program was thus to incorporate all these rules into an automatic data processing and circulation system. The bending of rules that characterize any bureaucracy thus became more difficult. In this way computerization rigidified procedures rather than renewing

them. We can consider, like Colette Hoffsaes, that:

> faced with the inability to know the rules of functioning of organizations, the past was repeated ... Computer specialists had a project for change but they were not in a position to change the aims that were known by and embodied in the operatives. Rather, they were to help them to do better what they already did. They thus intervened at the process level, the stability of which they tended to increase. (1978: 307)

Computing did nevertheless bring some changes. The role of those that Peter Drucker (1974) calls 'knowledge workers' or 'professional managers' increased. Their new mission in the firm was no longer to control others; on the contrary, they defined themselves by their own work. Moreover, executive tasks became more routine and less qualified. The division of labour was accentuated and a Taylorization of tertiary work emerged. While data were codified by the departments that produced them (pay, accounting, etc.), they were then captured in large centralized workshops where card punchers and then controllers processed them. Punch cards were then processed by keyboard operators in large computer rooms. Lastly, the data were returned to the service that had produced them.

Data telecommunications and the use of 'dumb terminals' were to modify the process a little. They made it possible to integrate on a single machine the codification and keying in of data as well as their updating. Big computing workshops were consequently fragmented and data capture activities, which in the meantime had become more qualified, moved closer to the data production services or in some instances even became part of them. In parallel, the number of junior management posts were sharply reduced. The division of work and its control were henceforth done by the computing system rather than by the hierarchy. Yet corporate organization changed little. Those first computing networks were extremely hierarchized and the new device had been designed and organized centrally by the data processing division.

From the managers' point of view, the situation was somewhat different. Owing to the possibilities afforded by management computing, each manager, at corporate management level and in the divisions and even the departments, had a financial statement at regular intervals. With quasi-immediate access to this information, the US corporate model, in which each manager is responsible for the revenue generated by his/her unit, was able to function efficiently (Nolan, 2000: 229).

Microcomputing and the Temptation to Decentralize

While mainframe computing was initialized and developed by managers in order to automate routine data processing tasks, microcomputing was adopted at grassroots level. Another current of French sociology of labour, which studies not phenomena of reproduction but elements of transformation, facts which impact on the future, closely studied the diffusion of microcomputing. These sociologists have shown that it was often employees who had a fair amount of autonomy in the organization of their work (personal secretaries, archivists, etc.) who grasped this new tool and proposed small applications adapted to their immediate environment: management of leave, monitoring budgets, bibliographic database, etc. (Alter, 1991).

These innovative people later became experts in microcomputing and thus acquired a new legitimacy and a little more power. In a new technical world which was particularly uncertain because users received no support from the data processing divisions, which were opposed to PCs at the time, these first users soon became resource persons who not only mastered the new technology but were also capable of using it to improve their own productivity. This situation corresponds to an innovation model studied by von Hippel (1988). He considers that end users are often essential innovators. They do not need much technical expertise to find new uses. Their strength derives from close contact with daily problems that the new devices have to solve. This model of uncontrolled diffusion was to spread particularly fast because investments in microcomputers were sufficiently small to enable many departments to take decisions in

this respect on their own. Thus, contact was made directly between sellers and users, along the lines of a model resembling a market for the public at large rather than a business market.

Yet these innovators did encounter a good deal of opposition. Apart from the data processing divisions which saw the PC as a technological alternative which they did not control, middle management also saw it as a potential challenge to the organization, with greater autonomy for employees. By contrast, top management saw microcomputers as an opportunity to create a counter-power *vis-à-vis* the data processing division. It therefore left local initiatives to develop, as an experiment. Initially it accepted a diversity of models of computerization in the various services.

While this fragmented innovation model made it possible to mobilize multiple initiatives, it was potentially also a source of disorder and inefficiency. Thus, in a second stage top management took over the reins, in collaboration with the data processing divisions who were forced to include the PC in their plan. The project was to replace partial computerization in islands of the organization by a totally integrated information system (Cerruti and Reiser, 1993). The setting up of such a system posed not only technical but also organizational problems, for these new machines allowed for automation but also for a different way of thinking and managing. Zuboff (1988) has clearly shown that informating and automating are the two faces of computers in firms.

Digital Network and Interactive Deployment

While we can roughly say that mainframe computing developed in a centralized way, while microcomputing started off being decentralized, intranet and network data communications correspond to a more interactive mode in the development of computing. Bar et al. (2000) have thus constructed a cyclical model of the development of digital networks. Initially, intranet was used to automate existing work processes, for example to organize the circulation of documents in a firm. It was a way of enhancing efficiency and improving productivity. Once the network was available it could be used for other purposes, such as information searches on request or simple administrative procedures, for example ordering supplies, requests for leave and so on. Through this experimental phase, new communication technologies fitted into the organization better. The third phase could then begin, in which the firm was to be reorganized and to modify its digital network simultaneously.

Research on French firms has reached similar conclusions (Benghozi et al., 2000). These authors also note development in phases, although computerization was initiated either by local experimentation or by a decision by top management. Yet the network expanded fully only if there was articulation between the two phases. The idea was to construct a learning device in a context of controlled disorder. If we now review the setting up of digital networks, we note that effects on organization were diverse. Within a single business sector, such as the press, diametrically opposed organizational choices have been observed. At a newspaper in the west of France, local editorial staff devote as little time as possible to computing which is left to employees previously responsible for setting the newspaper. This is a case where computerized workflow has not undermined the division of work. By contrast, at a newspaper in the north, the introduction of an integrated computing system radically modified the organization of work. In local offices the same person does investigative work and typesetting (Ruellan and Thierry, 1998). These two contrasting models clearly show that in these cases the introduction of network computing does not, in itself, induce a new organization. Thus, even if there is no technical determinism, is there organizational determinism? It would appear so, given that in many cases the setting up of intranet or of cooperative devices in smaller businesses is related to substantial organizational change. In reality, such reorganization is actually an opportunity to introduce these new tools.

The various studies cited, both in the US and in France, are thus grounded in a conception where technology coevolves with the organization and its members (Leonard-Barton, 1988; Orlikowski, 1992). They therefore contrast with current discourse on the revolution in the organization of work generated by digital networks.

ICTs AND PRIVATE LIFE

The Gradual Slide from Public to Private Sphere

The history of information technology in the private sphere, as in the business world, originates in the nineteenth century. Public life changed profoundly during that period. Richard Sennett (1977) considers that it lost its character of conviviality and interaction, to become a space in which people mixed together in silence. With regard to this 'public private life' he talks of 'daydreaming', referring to the same phenomenon as did Edgar Allan Poe in 'The man of the crowd' (1971) or Baudelaire (1978) in his study of the stroller. In that work Baudelaire presented an individual who is both out of his home and at home everywhere. This articulation between public and private is also characteristic of the theatre. For a good part of the century, the theatre was above all a place for social interaction. The box was a sort of drawing room where people could converse, observe others and watch the show. Gradually, it became more usual to switch off the lights in the hall and to focus on the stage. Audiences had to listen in silence. New theatres were designed to enable audiences to see the stage, above all. Theatres thus received a solitary crowd; the public was an entity in which individuals experienced their emotions separately (see Flichy, 1995: 152–5).

We also find this dialectic between public and private spheres with the beginnings of photography. In the mid nineteenth century the photo portrait, a private image, became the main use of the new medium. But photographers who took these pictures set themselves up in the most frequented urban places. Their studios became veritable urban attractions.

Inside, they were decorated like parlours; outside, collections of portraits several metres high were displayed on the pavement. In their windows copies of diverse portraits were exhibited, for example, crowned heads, artists, individuals who by nature have to show themselves, but also portraits of ordinary people (Mary, 1993: 83–4). Thus, if the man in the street had his portrait taken to give to his family, his picture also became public.

This play between public and private images appeared in several respects. Ordinary people were photographed in stereotyped poses; they chose the décor from a catalogue and the photographer often touched up the picture to make it closer to current standards of beauty. Important people, on the other hand, displayed details of their private lives in addition to their official poses. Furthermore, with the multiplication of copies photography was no longer used only for private souvenirs; it became a medium. People usually had between 10 and 100 copies of their 'portrait card' or 'photo visiting card' printed, but in some cases tens of thousands of copies were made. These photo portraits were put into albums with not only photographs of family and friends but also portraits of celebrities bought from specialized publishers. The binding of the albums played on the secret/representation ambiguity; they were often beautifully decorated and sometimes had a lock to protect the owner's privacy.

The debate between private and collective media also appeared with the beginnings of the cinema. Edison thought his kinetoscope would be installed in public places, to be used by individuals (Clark, 1977). The success of the projector proposed by Lumière and other inventors was, by contrast, partly owing to the fact that it fitted into a tradition of collective shows. The content proposed, like that of the other visual media, turned around the dual attraction of daily life and fantasy. The idea was to show something that surprised by both its familiarity and its strangeness. Lumière focused more on the former, with scenes from daily life in both the private sphere ('Le déjeuner de bébé', 'La dispute de bébé', etc.) and in public ('La sortie des usines Lumière', 'L'arrivée du train en gare de la Ciotat', etc.). Lumière's first projectionists were

also cameramen. They filmed scenes in the towns in which they were and showed them the same evening to an audience that was likely to recognize itself in the film.

This fairground cinema made people familiar with the new medium but it eventually bored them. The real success of the cinema appeared when it started telling stories, that is, when it became a narrative medium. The success of narrative film-makers such as William Paul in England and Charles Pathé in France was based on their entry into an industrial economy. The French industrialist soon discovered that it was in his interests to make a large number of copies and to distribute them throughout the world. He developed a system of industrial production similar to that of the press, in which he produced one film per week and later several (Abel, 1995).

Going to the cinema soon became a regular habit. Audiences behaved as they did at café concerts. For example, in 1912 a Venetian journalist wrote:

> the most beautiful cinema is that of San Margeria, where working class women go ... Oh! How they applaud in certain scenes. Hordes of children sometimes go to see series of landscapes and discover vulgar scenes: 'one doesn't kiss on the mouth' and the public answers 'si' ('yes one does'); 'no one touches my lips' and the public again choruses 'si'. (Turnaturi, 1995)

In the United States the new entertainment medium attracted a large immigrant population in particular (Sklar, 1975). The narrative cinema was to become a big consumer of scenarios, sometimes found in legitimate literature. That was how the cultured classes were to become interested in this new medium that gradually became the seventh art. As the Italian historian Gabriella Turnaturi (1995) notes, on the eve of the First World War 'a slow and difficult process of unification of customs, culture and traditions took place through the learning of a common language in the obscurity of cinema halls'.

While the cinema was part of the emergence of collective urban entertainment, the late nineteenth century also saw the advent of entertainment at home. Withdrawal into the home, pointed out by historians of private life, was reflected mainly in the appearance of private musical life which adopted the piano as the main instrument. The piano became an emblematic element of the middle classes' furniture. It was to bring public music into the domestic sphere, a transformation achieved through a very specific activity in the writing of music: reduction. Composers arranged scores written for an orchestra into pieces for piano. This same phenomenon of adaptation can be found at the beginning of jazz in the United States, where publishers simplified the rhythmic complexity of ragtime. In the tradition of the Frankfurt School, this activity of adaptation and reduction was often denounced: the capitalist market was killing art. Can we not consider, on the contrary, that these score sheets were the instrument of mediation between public and private music?

But music for amateur pianists was not only scholarly music. A very large market developed for sheet music for songs. In some cases over a million copies of the so-called 'royalty songs' were printed. Singing these songs, accompanied by the piano, was an important feature in the domestic entertainment of the upper and middle classes. It is estimated that by 1914 one quarter of English homes had a piano (Ehrlich, 1976).

It was in this context that the phonograph appeared. This device soon found a place in the domestic sphere. In the United States 3 per cent of all homes had one by 1900, 15 per cent by 1910 and 50 per cent by 1920. At first the catalogue consisted of songs, popular ballads or a few well-known symphonies. A second catalogue was later created, consisting of major operatic arias (Gelatt, 1965). While some singers were starting to be very popular, phonographic recordings were to enable people to remember tunes and popular songs they had already heard. As Walter Benjamin said, 'the art of collecting is a practical form of re-remembering' (1989: 222). This taste for collection concerned not only records but also photographs and postcards. The latter were used to send pictures of historical buildings to those who did not travel. The same applied to records which found a public among those who could not go to the opera and could thus listen to 'the most enchanting selection of the world's greatest singers'[3] at home.

Thus the phonograph, like the piano, was not only the instrument that allowed a private musical activity to be substituted for a public one. It was also owing to this device that music for shows was arranged for music at home (see Flichy, 1995: 67–75).

Radio and Television, Family Media

Between the two wars, radio was to replace records to a large extent. The new medium was presented as a tool enabling people to listen to plays or to music at home. Advertisements often presented the radio set as a theatre in the living room. Sets were 'designed to fit into all contexts of family life and the privacy of the home'.[4] Of the receiver it was said that 'all the waves in the world come to nest in it'.[5] We thus witness a privatization of the public sphere of entertainment. As many documents of the time show, reception was a family activity (Isola, 1990), a sort of ritual. It was often the father who tuned the radio and silence was demanded to listen to it. C.A. Lewis (1942), the first programme manager at the BBC, considered that

> broadcasting means the rediscovery of the home. In these days when house and hearth have been largely given up in favour of a multitude of other interests and activities outside, with the consequent disintegration of family ties and affections, it appears that this new persuasion may to some extent reinstate the parental roof in its old accustomed place.

This family medium was considerably successful. In the US in 1927, five years after the first broadcasts were launched, 24 per cent of all households had a wireless. In 1932, despite the economic crisis, this number had risen to 60 per cent. In the UK, 73 per cent of all households had a set on the eve of the Second World War, and listened to the radio on average four hours a day (Briggs, 1965: 253).

From the end of the 1940s television entered the domestic sphere. Yet its introduction into the home took place differently to that of the phonograph and radio. Whereas in the Victorian world there was a profound break between the public and private spheres, and the home was designed to be a closed space, the domestic space of post-war North American suburbs was built on a complex interaction between public and private. According to Lynn Spigel, 'in paradoxical terms, privacy was something which could be enjoyed only in the company of others'. Middle-class suburbs described in magazines at the time 'suggested the new form of social cohesion which allowed people to be alone and together at the same time' (1992: 6).

A typical feature of the model home of that period was the large open living room and 'American kitchen'. Rooms opened onto the outside, giving the impression that public space was a continuation of domestic space. It was this new conception of space articulating public and private that prevailed at the birth of television. In 1946 Thomas Hutchinson published an introduction to this new medium, called *Here is Television: Your Window on the World* for the general public. Four years later, in another book for the general public, called *Radio, Television and Society*, Charles Siepmann wrote: 'television provides a maximum extension of the perceived environment with a minimum of effort ... It is bringing the world to people's door' (Spigel, 1992: 7).

This theme can also be found in advertisements from that period. While adverts for the phonograph focused on the decorative aspect of the machine as a part of the furnishings of a room,[6] those for radio emphasized the same point but added the idea that the set brought sounds of the world into the home ('all the world's roads lie before you, it's a beautiful, splendid adventure ... right in your armchair!').[7] Advertisements for television showed the world. Photographs of a TV set featured the Eiffel Tower, Big Ben or the Statue of Liberty, for example. One advertisement showed a baseball field with an armchair and a TV set on it, with a baseball player on the screen.

This association of the domestic sphere with historical buildings or famous cities is also found in the first television series. In 'Make Room for Daddy', the hero's apartment has a splendid view of the New York skyline. One of the key characters in 'I Love Lucy' sees the hills of Hollywood from his bedroom window. These characters thus act against a backdrop of prestigious sites (Spigel, 1992: 10). Another

theme runs through advertising during that period: the dramatization of the domestic sphere. Certain advertisements referred to television as a 'family', 'chairside' or 'living room' theatre (1992: 12). Some showed a woman in a black evening gown watching television at home. But it was also the great ritual events of our societies that television brought into the home: national celebrations, coronations and major sports events (Dayan and Katz, 1992).

The association between daily life and the entertainment world was furthermore found in new ways in which the American middle classes decorated their homes. What in Europe is called an American kitchen enabled the housewife to prepare meals while watching television. Very popular TV programmes in the 1950s also show the wish to include the entertainment world in daily life. In certain episodes of 'I Love Lucy' famous Hollywood actors are invited to dinner in ordinary homes (Mann, 1992: 44).

By contrast, television in the 1980s no longer tried to mix the two or to orchestrate major societal rituals. Instead, small family rituals were organized. In this new form that Italian sociologists have called 'neo-television' (Casetti and Odin, 1990; Eco, 1985), the content of interaction or the personality of the participants is of little consequence; the only thing that matters is their presence. Television displays daily life but also becomes a reference to serve as a standard for daily life. We thus witness a constant play in which television and society mirror each other.

Live Together Separately

As the family gathered together around television to watch it collectively (Meyrowitz, 1985), it abandoned radio which became an individual medium. Owing to the portability and low cost of transistor radios, everybody could listen alone in their bedroom while doing something else. This new family could 'live together separately' (Flichy, 1995: 158). It was probably with rock music, which appeared at that time, that use of the transistor and the related medium, the record player, appeared in full force. Whereas in the 1950s collective listening around the jukebox was decisive, listening was subsequently done at home, especially by teenage girls whose culture became a 'culture of the bedroom, the place where girls meet, listen to music and teach each other make-up skills, practise their dancing' (Frith, 1978: 64). Rock music listened to on a transistor radio or record player gave teenagers the opportunity to control their own space. This behaviour was part of the 'juxtaposed home'; it allowed teenagers to remove themselves from adult supervision while still living with their parents (Flichy, 1995: 160–5). This shift in listening from the living room to the bedroom was therefore far more than a new mode of listening, it was a way of asserting oneself, of creating a peer subculture. Was this individualization of listening to become generalized and affect television? In the mid 1980s that was far from being the case. David Morley's (1986) ethnographic study shows the family television to be a perpetual source of tension within the family between men, women, parents and children. As families acquired more and more sets, living room wars (Ang, 1996) were expected to disappear. Yet the TV set did not, as in the case of the transistor radio, disappear from the living room. It has remained the main set around which the family gathers, while sets in bedrooms are used less.[8]

What about the new media? Research in this area is beginning (Livingstone, 2002; Livingstone and Bovill, 2001) and it is still too early to draw final conclusions. The current literature nevertheless allows us to make some comments. In Europe the mobile phone is the communication device that has developed the fastest.[9] Like radio in the 1950s, it has spread rapidly among the youth. Once again, this device has enabled them to become more autonomous as regards the family cell, to live in it but to be elsewhere. This new media is complying with a symbolic demand following the individualist trend of modern society (Katz and Aakhus, 2002). Yet, the cell phone, which is above all an individual communication device, does not seem to be causing the disappearance of the fixed phone which is still used at home, as a collective tool of the family.

Despite discourse on the information society revolution, one has to agree that the microcomputer followed by its connection to the Internet have not spread as fast in homes as radio and television.[10] In the US, for example, it took about 20 years before households were equipped with at least one computer. It seems that in many cases one member of the family tends to appropriate the set. A French study shows that in wealthy families it is often the father and that in working-class families it is, by contrast, a child and often the oldest son. In this case the set is installed in his bedroom (Jouët and Pasquier, 1999: 41). Yet, contrary to widespread belief, the computer does not isolate its user from others. It is characterized by a high level of sociability within peer groups. Young people exchange software and various tips for more efficient use of hardware and software. Video games are often played collectively. Alongside these horizontal social networks, Kirsten Drotner sees the emergence of vertical networks that function between generations: skills are passed on no longer from oldest to youngest but from teenagers to adults (1999: 103–4). Teenagers act as the technological gurus for the household (Kiesler and al., 2000). The Internet has continued this trend of living in different networks (Wellman and Haythornthwaite, 2002).

Virtual Communication

Although computing and the Internet, unlike radio and television and like the mobile phone, are personal tools, they are nevertheless characterized by complex social relations in peer groups and between generations. Sociability among internauts also has another degree of complexity: the fact that the individual can communicate anonymously behind a pseudonym and simultaneously have several pseudonyms and therefore several personalities. French sociologists had already noticed the phenomenon with the minitel. Users of minitel forums wanted not only to give themselves a new identity but also to take advantage of their mask to have different social behaviour, to reveal other facets of themselves and thus to better display their true identity (Jouët, 1991; Toussaint, 1991). Sherry Turkle studied the question of multiple identities on the Internet and especially in MUDs. One of her interviewees declared: 'I'm not one thing, I'm many things. Each part gets to be more fully expressed in MUDs than in the real world. So even though I play more than one self on MUDs, I feel more like "myself" when I'm MUDding' (1997: 185). These different lives can be lived out simultaneously in different windows of the same computer screen. 'I split my mind, say another player, I can see myself as being two or three or more. And I just turn on one part of my mind and then another when I go from window to window' (Turkle, 1996: 194). Are we heading for an identity crisis? Or can we consider, like Turkle, that this coexistence of different identities is one of the characteristics of our postmodern age?

Velkovska (2002), who has studied identities and relations arising through real-time written interactions in web chats. has a different conclusion. Relations which are built via chats are characterized by a tension between intimacy and anonymity. This kind of distant and personal communication gives the opportunity to have different occupations simultaneously while remaining a single person.

CONCLUSION

Today the Internet constitutes the last phase in the history of information and communication technologies. But the network of networks is also a particularly interesting case since it enables us to recap most of the points considered in this chapter. This is simply one of the possible versions of digital networks. It is the result of a long history that started in the late 1960s. While IBM and AT&T had the competencies to launch a digital network, it was the collaboration of academics and hackers, with military funding, that spawned this network. The initial choices were profoundly marked by the representations of these actors who dreamed of a communicating, free, universal and non-hierarchized network. It was this

same utopia that was spread by the media in the early 1990s. By contrast, the diffusion of the new technology in the corporate world combines a centralized model from mainframe computing and an open model launched by microcomputing. At home, the Internet combines the characteristics of several means of information and communication. It is a tool for interpersonal interaction and collective communication in virtual groups, but also a new medium with multiple sources of information. But this multiform information and communication tool also tends to undermine the separation between the professional and private spheres. It makes it easy to work from home and sometimes to attend to personal things at work. Unlike radio and television on the one hand and the telephone on the other, which were quickly standardized around an economic model and a media format, the Internet is fundamentally heterogeneous. This diversity is a key asset. As a result, use of the Internet cannot be unified around an economic model or a communicational format. It is not a medium but a system which is tending to become as complex as the society of which it is claimed to be a virtual copy.

NOTES

1 By contrast, in the 1990s the minitel stagnated. The France Télécom monopoly impeded all development of the system. This device soon seemed obsolete compared with the Internet.

2 On the history of Macintosh see also Levy (1994), and more broadly on the history of Apple see Carlton (1997).

3 Advertising slogan for the red label launched by the Gramophone Company in 1902.

4 'Le 12ème salon de la TSF', *L'Illustration*, 12 October 1935, Supplement: xx.

5 *L'Illustration*, 7 September 1935, Annonces: viii.

6 See the catalogue *Archeofon* (1989), Milano, Electra.

7 'Le 12ème salon de la TSF', *L'Illustration*, 12 October 1935, Supplement: xxi.

8 Sonia Livingstone (1999: 81) contests this thesis and is surprised that I have not seen the similarity between the evolution of radio and that of television. Although habits changed a great deal in the 1990s, the fact remains that the individualization of TV viewing has been only partial, unlike that of radio listening.

9 Historical comparisons are difficult in this domain. In the audiovisual media the number of sets per household

are counted, and in telecommunications the number of sets per 100 inhabitants. This ratio does not distinguish business equipment from domestic equipment, and for mobile phones one has to take into account that the purchase is more often individual than collective.

10 Many authors defend the opposite point of view. See the table by the Morgan Stanley Research Group which classifies speed of penetration of the main communication technologies, cited in 'State of the Internet: USIC's report on use and threats in 1999' (available online: http://www.usic.org/usic99). This difference of evaluation stems from the fact that these authors take the invention of the technique, and not the beginning of its distribution in society at large, as the starting point of that diffusion.

REFERENCES

Abbate, Janet (1999) *Inventing the Internet.* Cambridge, MA: MIT Press.

Abel, Richard (1995) 'The perils of Pathé or the Americanization of the American cinema', in Leo Charney and Vanessa Schwartz (eds), *Cinema and the Invention of Modern Life.* Berkeley, CA: University of California Press.

Akrich, Madeleine, Callon, Michel and Latour, Bruno (1988) 'A quoi tient le succès des innovations?', *Annale des Mines. Gérer et comprendre* (11).

Alter, Norbert (1991) *La Gestion du désordre en entreprise.* Paris: L'Harmattan.

Ang, Ien (ed.) (1996) *Living Room Wars: Rethinking Media Audiences for a Postmodern World.* London: Routledge.

Ballé, Catherine and Peaucelle, Jean-Louis (1972) *Le pouvoir informatique dans l'entreprise.* Paris: Les Editions d'Organisation.

Bar, François, Kane, Neil and Simard, Caroline (2000) 'Digital networks and organizational change: the evolutionary deployment of corporate information infrastructure'. Paper presented at the International Sunbelt Social Network Conference, Vancouver, 13–16 April 2000.

Baudelaire, Charles (1978) *The Painter of Modern Life and Other Essays.* New York: Garland.

Benghozi, Pierre-Jean, Flichy, Patrice and d'Iribarne, Alain (2000) 'Le développement d'intranet dans les entreprises françaises. Premiers constats', *Réseaux,* (104).

Beniger, James (1986) *The Control Revolution: Technological and Economic Origins of the Information Society.* Cambridge, MA: Harvard University Press.

Benjamin, Walter (1989) *Paris, capitale du XIXème siècle.* Paris: Le Cerf.

Bijker, Wiebe, Hughes, Thomas and Pinch, Trevor (1987) *The Social Construction of Technological Systems: New Directions in the Sociology and History of Technology.* Cambridge, MA: MIT Press.

Briggs, Asa (1965) *The History of Broadcasting in the United Kingdom.* Vol. 2: *The Golden Age of Wireless.* London: Oxford University Press.

Campbell-Kelly, Martin and Aspray, William (1996) *Computer: A History of the Information Machine.* New York: Basic.

Carlton, Jim (1997) *Apple: The Inside Story of Intrigue, Egomania, and Business Blunders.* New York: Times Business/Random House.

Casetti, Francesco and Odin, Roger (1990) 'De la paléo à la néo-télévision. Approche sémio-pragmatique', *Communications,* 51.

Cerruti, G. and Reiser, V. (1993) 'Information systems, computer systems and new strategies of rationalization', in Martin Heidenreich (ed.), *Computers and Culture in Organizations: The Introduction and Use of Production Control Systems in French, Italian, and German.* Berlin: Edition Sigma.

Ceruzzi, Paul (1987) 'An unforeseen revolution: computers and expectations, 1935–1985', in Joseph Corn (ed.), *Imagining Tomorrow: History, Technology and the American Future.* Cambridge, MA: MIT Press.

Chandler, Alfred, Jr (1977) *The Visible Hand: The Managerial Revolution in American Business.* Cambridge, MA: Harvard University Press.

Chandler, Alfred, Jr (2000) 'The information age in historical perspective', in Alfred Chandler Jr and James Cortada (eds), *A Nation Transformed by Information.* New York: Oxford University Press. pp. 3–37.

Clark, Ronald (1977) *Edison: The Man Who Made the Future.* New York: Putnam.

Cortada, James (1993) *The Computer in the United States: From Laboratory to Market, 1930 to 1960.* Armonk, NY: Sharpe.

Cusumano, Michael (1995) *Microsoft Secrets: How the World's Most Powerful Software Company Creates Technology, Shapes Markets, and Manages People.* New York: Free Press.

David, Paul (1985) 'Clio and the Economics of QWERTY', *American Economic Review,* 75 (2): 332–7.

Dayan, Daniel and Katz, Elihu (1992) *Media Events: The Live Broadcasting of History.* Cambridge, MA: Harvard University Press.

Douglas, Susan (1987) *Inventing American Broadcasting (1899–1922).* Baltimore, MD: Johns Hopkins University Press.

Drotner, Kirsten (1999) 'Netsurfers and game navigators: new media and youthful leisure cultures in Denmark', *Réseaux*, 7 (1): 83–108.

Drucker, Peter (1974) *Management: Tasks, Responsibilities, Practices*. New York: Harper & Row.

DuBoff, Richard (1983) 'The telegraph and the structure of markets in the United States, 1845–1900', *Research in Economic History*, 8: 253–77.

Eco, Umberto (1985) 'TV la transparence perdue', in Umberto Eco, *La guerre du faux*. Paris: Grasset.

Edwards, Paul (1996) *The Closed World: Computers and the Politics of Discourse in Cold War America*, Cambridge, MA: MIT Press.

Ehrlich, Cyril (1976) *The Piano: A History*. London: Dent.

Ellul, Jacques (1964) *The Technological Society*. New York: Knopf.

Flichy, Patrice (1991) 'The losers win. A comparative history of two innovations: videotext and the videodisc', in Josiane Jouët, Patrice Flichy and Paul Beaud (eds), *European Telematics: The Emerging Economy of Words*. Amsterdam: North-Holland. pp. 73–86.

Flichy, Patrice (1995) *Dynamics of Modern Communication: The Shaping and Impact of New Communication Technologies*. London: Sage.

Flichy, Patrice (2001) *L'imaginaire d'internet*. Paris: La Découverte. English version forthcoming, MIT Press.

Freiberger, Paul and Swaine, Michael (1984) *Fire in the Valley: The Making of the Personal Computer*. Berkeley, CA: McGraw-Hill.

Friedmann, Georges (1978) *The Anatomy of Work: Labor, Leisure and the Implications of Automation*. Westport, CT: Greenwood.

Frith, Simon (1978) *The Sociology of Rock*. London: Constable.

Gaffin, Adam and Kapor, Mitchell (1991) *Big Dummy's Guide to the Internet*. Available online: http://www.thegulf.com/InternetGuide.html

Gelatt, Roland (1965) *The Fabulous Phonograph: From Edison to Stereo*. New York: Appleton-Century.

Graham, Margaret (1986) *RCA and the VideoDisc: The Business of Research*. New York: Cambridge University Press.

Guterl, Fred (1984) 'Design case history: Apple's Macintosh', *IEEE Spectrum*, December: 34–43.

Hafner, Katie and Lyon, Mathew (1996) *Where Wizards Stay Up Late: The Origins of the Internet*. New York: Simon & Schuster.

Hiltz, Starr and Turoff, Murray (1978) *The Network Nation: Human Communication via Computer*. Cambridge, MA: MIT Press.

Hoffsaes, Colette (1978) 'L'informatique dans l'organisation: changement ou stabilité?', *Sociologie du travail* (3).

Isola, Gianni (1990) *Abbassa la tua radio, per favore: storia dell'ascolto radiofonico nell'Italia fascista*. Firenze: La Nuova Italia.

Jouët, Josiane (1991) 'A telematic community: the Axiens', in Josiane Jouët, Patrice Flichy and Paul Beaud (eds), *European Telematics: The Emerging Economy of Words*. Amsterdam: North-Holland. pp. 181–202.

Jouët, Josiane and Pasquier, Dominique (1999) 'Youth and screen culture', *Réseaux*, 7 (1): 31–58.

Katz, James and Aakhus, Mark (eds) (2002) *Perpetual Contact: Mobile Communication, Private Talk, Public Performance*. Cambridge: Cambridge University Press.

Kiesler, S., Zdaniuk, B., Lundmark, V. and Kraut, R. (2000) 'Troubles with the Internet: The dynamics of help at home', *Human-computer Interaction*, Special Issue, 15 (4): 323–51.

Latour, Bruno (1987) *Science in Action: How to Follow Scientists and Engineers through Society*. Cambridge, MA: Harvard University Press.

Leonard-Barton, Dorothy (1988) 'Implementation as mutual adaptation of technology and organization', *Research Policy*, 17 (5): 251–67.

Levy, Steven (1985) *Hackers, Heroes of the Computer Revolution*. New York: Dell.

Levy, Steven (1994) *Insanely Great: The Life and Times of Macintosh, the Computer that Changed Everything*. New York: Viking.

Lewis, C.A. (1942) *Broadcasting from Within*. London: Newnes.

Livingstone, Sonia (1999) 'Young people and the new media: on learning lessons from TV to apply to the PC', *Réseaux*, 7 (1): 59–81.

Livingstone, Sonia (2002) *Young People and New Media: Childhood and the Changing Media Environment*. Thousand Oaks, CA: Sage.

Livingstone, Sonia and Bovill, Moira (eds) (2001) *Children and Their Changing Media Environment: A European Comparative Study*. Mahwah, NJ: Lawrence Erlbaum Associates.

Mann, Denise (1992) 'The spectacularization of everyday life: recycling Hollywood stars and fans in early variety shows', in Lynn Spigel and Denise Mann (eds), *Private Screenings: Television and the Female Consumer*. Minneapolis: University of Minnesota Press.

Marx, Leo (1964) *The Machine in the Garden: Technology and the Pastoral Ideal in America*. New York: Oxford University Press.

Mary, Bertrand (1993) *La photo sur la cheminée: naissance d'un culte moderne*. Paris: Métailié.

McLuhan, Marshall (1964) *Understanding Media: The Extensions of Man.* New York: McGraw-Hill.

Meyrowitz, Joshua (1985) *No Sense of Place: The Impact of Electronic Media on Social Behavior.* New York: Oxford University Press.

Morley, David (1986) *Family Television: Cultural Power and Domestic Leisure.* London: Comedia.

Noble, David (1979) 'Social choice in machine design: the case of automatically controlled machine tools', in Andrew Zimbalist (ed.), *Case Studies on the Labor Process.* New York: Monthly Review Press.

Noble, David (1984) *Forces of Production: A Social History of Industrial Automation.* New York: Knopf.

Nolan, Richard (2000) 'Information technology management', in Alfred Chandler and James Cortada Jr (eds), *A Nation Transformed by Information.* New York: Oxford University Press.

Norberg, Arthur and O'Neill, Judy (1996) *Transforming Computer Technology: Information Processing for the Pentagon (1962–1986).* Baltimore, MD: Johns Hopkins University Press.

Orlikowski, Wanda (1992) 'The duality of technology: rethinking the concept of technology in organizations', *Organization Science*, 3 (3): 398–427.

Poe, Edgar Allan (1971) 'The man of the crowd', in Edgar Allan Poe, *Tales of Mystery and Imagination.* New York: Everyman.

Rheingold, Howard (1993) *The Virtual Community: Homesteading on the Electronic Frontier.* New York: HarperCollins.

Ruellan, Denis and Thierry, Daniel (1998) *Journal local et réseaux informatiques: travail coopératif, décentralisation et identité des journalistes.* Paris: L'Harmattan.

Schaffer, Simon (1995) *Babbage's Intelligence: Calculating Engines and the Factory System.* Available online: http://www.wmin.ac.uk/media/schaffer/schaffer01.html

Sennett, Richard (1977) *The Fall of Public Man.* New York: Knopf.

Sklar, Robert (1975) *Movie-made America: A Cultural History of American Movies.* New York: Random House.

Spigel, Lynn (1992) 'Installing the television and domestic space 1948–1955', in Lynn Spigel and Denise Mann (eds), *Private Screenings: Television and the Female Consumer.* Minneapolis: University of Minnesota Press.

Star, Susan and Griesemer, James (1989) 'Institutional ecology, translations and boundary objects: amateurs and professionals in Berkeley's Museum of Vertebrate Zoology (1907–1939)', *Social Studies of Science*, 19: 387–420.

Taylor, Frederick (1911) *The Principles of Scientific Management.* New York: Harper.

Toussaint, Yves (1991) 'Concealment and dissimulation on the messageries', in Josiane Jouët, Patrice Flichy and Paul Beaud (eds), *European Telematics: The Emerging Economy of Words.* Amsterdam: North-Holland. pp. 229–49.

Turkle, Sherry (1996) 'Who am we?', *Wired*, January.

Turkle, Sherry (1997) *Life on the Screen.* New York: Touchstone.

Turnaturi, Gabriella (1995) 'Les métamorphoses du divertissement citadin', in Alain Corbin (ed.), *L'avènement des loisirs 1860–1960.* Paris: Aubier.

Velkovska Julia (2002) 'L'intimité anonyme dans les conversations électroniques sur les webchats' *Sociologie du travail*, 44 (2): 193–213.

Von Hippel, Eric (1988) *The Sources of Innovation.* New York: Oxford University Press.

Wellman, Barry and Haythornthwaite, Caroline (eds) (2002) *The Internet in Everyday Life*, Malden, MA: Blackwell.

Yates, JoAnne (1989) *Control through Communication: The Rise of System in American Management.* Baltimore, MD: Johns Hopkins University Press.

Yates, JoAnne (1994) 'Evolving information use in firms, 1850–1920: ideology and information techniques and technologies', in Lisa Bud-Frierman (ed.), *Information Acumen: The Understanding and Use of Knowledge in Modern Business.* London: Routledge.

Yates, JoAnne (2000) 'Business use of information and technology during the industrial age', in Alfred Chandler Jr and James Cortada (eds), *A Nation Transformed by Information.* New York: Oxford University Press. pp. 107–35.

Zuboff, Shoshana (1988) *In the Age of the Smart Machine: The Future of Work and Power.* New York: Basic Books.

10

Exploring Models of Interactivity from Multiple Research Traditions: Users, Documents and Systems

SALLY J. McMILLAN

Interactivity. We 'know it when we see it', but what is it? When asked to define the term, many individuals – even scholars of new media – may feel stumped. Rafaeli noted some of the common conceptions about interactivity in the mid 1980s:

> Interactivity is generally assumed to be a natural attribute of face-to-face conversation, but it has been proposed to occur in mediated communication settings as well. For example, interactivity is also one of the defining characteristics of two-way cable systems, electronic text systems, and some programming work as in interactive video games. Interactivity is present in the operation of traditional media, too. The phenomena of letters to the editor, talk shows on radio and television, listener participation in programs, and in programming are all characterized by interactivity. (1988: 110)

In the early 1990s, use of the term 'interactivity' exploded in the popular, trade and scholarly press (McMillan, 1999). Researchers are actively engaged in scholarship that explores how people interact through media, the nature of interactive content, and how individuals interface with the computers and telecommunications tools that host interactive communication.

Interactivity is generally considered to be a central characteristic of new media. But it is not enough to say that new media are interactive. It is important to understand what makes them interactive. It is also important to realize that interactivity means different things to different people in different contexts. Understanding interactivity can help practitioners create environments that facilitate interaction. Individuals who use new media can more effectively utilize interactivity if they understand it. And for scholars, understanding interactivity is central to developing theory and research about new media.

This chapter begins with a brief overview of new media and basic definitions of interactivity in new media environments. Three traditions of interactivity research are identified: human-to-human interaction, human-to-documents interaction and human-to-system interaction. Within each of these traditions, definitions of interactivity both before and after the evolution of new media are examined. Central characteristics of interactivity as identified in each of these three traditions are used to develop models that illustrate multiple types of interactivity. Finally, some suggestions are made for future study of interactivity.

NEW MEDIA AND INTERACTIVITY

Interactivity is not unique to new media. This chapter will illustrate ways in which the concept of interactivity has emerged from multiple long-standing research traditions. But new media do facilitate interactivity in new environments. And, it is in the context of new media that the concept of interactivity has become a widely recognized subject of exploration. Thus, it is important to have a basic understanding of new media and key concepts related to interactivity in the context of these new media before examining interactivity in more depth.

New Media

Many observers tend to write about 'new media' such as networked computing and telecommunications as if they had been recently discovered in their fully developed state. Huhtamo wrote that 'One of the most common features of many technocultural discourses is their lack of historical consciousness' (1999: 97). These new media are not completely new phenomena. They have been growing out of 'old media' for some time. Furthermore, the concept of new technology is not unique to the current digital revolution. Marvin wrote that: '*New technologies* is a historically relative term. We are not the first generation to wonder at the rapid and extraordinary shifts in the dimensions of the world and human relationships it contains as a result of new forms of communication' (1988: 3).

Some researchers have consciously attempted to make historical linkages between new media and old. For example, Leonhirth et al. (1997) explored metaphors for the concept of the online mailing list, comparing it to the telegraph, the round table and the bonfire. But other authors have suggested that terms used to define new media are too dependent on old media forms. For example, Murray (1997) argued that the term 'multimedia', which most authors use to mean the 'digital integration of media types within a single technological system' (Jankowski and Hanssen, 1996: 4), is a

word with little descriptive power. Murray compared the word 'multimedia' as a descriptor of new technology to the term 'photo-play' which was used to describe early films. She suggested that such additive, catchall phrases are evidence that a medium is 'in an early stage of development and is still depending on formats derived from earlier technologies instead of exploiting its own expressive power' (1997: 67).

Williams et al. (1994) defined new media as applications of microelectronics, computers and telecommunications that offer new services or enhancement of old ones. Marvin (1988) also focused on the interplay between new and old purposes in new media. She suggested the tension created by the coexistence of the old and new becomes a focus of interest because it is novel.

Other authors have identified specific characteristics of new media. For example, Negroponte (1995) suggested that one of the things that differentiates new media from old is that new media are based on the transmission of digital bits rather than physical atoms. Pavlik (1998) indicated that for the media consumer, the major differences between old media and new are greater user choice and control. Williams et al. (1988) identified three characteristics of new media: interactivity, demassification and asynchronicity. New media not only demassify, but they also 'create a continuum between formerly discrete categories of interpersonal and mass-mediated communication' (Rice and Williams, 1984: 57). Chaffee (1972) suggested that most new communication technologies, with the exception of the telephone, have advanced the art of mass communication. However, he indicated that the latest batch of new technologies seems to be shifting the balance toward interpersonal communication. Cathcart and Gumpert (1983) also identified ways in which new technologies facilitate 'mediated interpersonal communication'.

While much of the current analysis of new media focuses on technologies such as the World Wide Web and collaborative decision-making systems, relatively recent research has focused on other forms of new media technologies such as video telephones (Carey, 1989), electronic bulletin board systems

(Rafaeli, 1986; Rafaeli and LaRose, 1993), videotex, and teletext and other forms of interactive television (Bretz, 1983; Feenberg, 1992; Paisley, 1983; Pavlik, 1998). However, much of the literature on new media reflects Murray's optimism about the networked computer, in which: 'All the major representational formats of the previous five thousand years of history have now been translated into digital form' (1997: 27). Nevertheless, this new digital technology, despite its synthetic capabilities, does not yet seem to be eliminating other media. Rather, a recent study reported that many individuals actually use their computers concurrently with other older media such as television (Coffee and Stipp, 1997).

Many scholars have observed that the term 'interactivity', while frequently used in conjunction with the discussion of new media, is often either undefined or underdefined (Hanssen et al., 1996; Heeter, 1989, 2000; Huhtamo, 1999; Miller et al., 1997; Rafaeli, 1988; Schultz, 2000; Simms, 1997; Smethers, 1998). But there is a growing body of literature that attempts to remedy this situation. Researchers have begun to seek definitions of interactivity by examining various characteristics of the new media environment. Several researchers have pointed out that interactivity has several different characteristics (Liu and Shrum, 2002; McMillan and Hwang, 2002; Tremayne and Dunwoody, 2001). The most important characteristics seem to be interactive features, perceived interactivity, and interactive exchange.

Interactive Features

Some of the earliest research on interactivity in new media focused on the properties and/or features of the message and/or the medium. For example, consensus derived from an international symposium in 1980 resulted in a definition of interactivity as 'a style of control and interactive systems that exhibit that style' (Guedj et al., 1980: 69). Other definitions of interactivity in this tradition include Markus' (1990) suggestion that interactivity is a characteristic of technologies that enables multidirectional communication.

Other definitions that embed interactivity in the features of the message/medium include conceptions of interactivity as being based in functionality such as user control and participation (Jensen, 1998; Latchem et al., 1993b; Lieb, 1998; Morrison, 1998; Murray, 1997; Street and Rimal, 1997). Some studies have begun the process of operationalizing specific features that can be identified and categorized as interactive (Ahren et al., 2000; Ha and James, 1998; Massey and Levy, 1999; McMillan, 2000b; Schultz, 1999, 2000). Others have associated these interactive features with specific strategies such as mass customization, virtual stores and collaborative learning (Blattberg and Deighton, 1991; Day, 1998; Landow, 1992).

Perceived Interactivity

In contrast to scholars who seek to identify 'features' of interactivity, others have suggested that interactivity may be 'in the eye of the beholder' (Lee, 2000; McMillan, 2000a; McMillan and Downes, 2000; Morrison, 1998; Newhagen et al., 1996). Heeter (2000) proposed that orientation to interactivity is a personality characteristic and Kiousis (2002) also suggested that interactivity resides, at least in part, in individuals' perceptions.

A recent study (Burgoon et al., 2000) suggested that one way to conceptualize interactivity is based on the qualitative experiences that users equate with interactivity. Morrison (1998) noted that it is important to understand how individuals perceive interactivity in order to grasp the influence of newer media technologies in their lives. Newhagen and his colleagues have insisted that the individual and individual perceptions must take conceptual centre stage in studies of new media (Newhagen, 1998; Newhagen et al., 1996). Wu (1999) and McMillan (2000a, 2002) found that users' attitude toward websites is positively related to their perceived interactivity of the website. Reeves and Nass (1996) suggested that, in general, perceptions are far more influential than reality in terms of individuals' interactions with computers. Lee (2000) suggested that the most important thing to be examined in measuring the level of interactivity is not the provision of technological features, but rather how users perceive and/or experience those features. A promising recent trend in the literature is the development of scales for measuring perceived interactivity (Liu, 2003; McMillan and Hwang, 2002).

Interactive Exchange

Rafaeli, one of the most cited scholars on the subject of interactivity, identified interactivity as being located in the relatedness of information exchange among participants rather than in either features or perceptions. He defined interactivity as going beyond simple one-way 'action' or two-way 'reaction' that may not be truly responsive. He wrote: 'Interactivity is an expression of the extent that in a given series of communication exchanges, any third (or later) transmission (or message) is related to the degree to which previous exchanges referred to even earlier transmissions' (1988: 111).

Other authors have also focused on the exchanges among participants in interactive media (Haeckel, 1998; Rice and Williams, 1984). Ha and James defined interactivity as 'the extent to which the communicator and the audience respond to, or are willing to facilitate, each other's communication needs' (1998: 461). A subset to this literature addresses the idea that interactive exchanges make sender and receiver roles interchangeable (Bretz, 1983; Rice, 1984). Additionally, literature that focuses on interactivity as exchange often focuses on the importance of reducing the time lag between exchanges (Bretz, 1983).

Mahood et al. (2000) identified two kinds of interactive exchange: the dialogue view and the message-based view. They suggested that the dialogue view, based in literature on role exchange and mutual discourse, focuses primarily on conversational-style exchanges. In contrast, the message-based view deals more with the relationships between messages sent previously and how those messages relate to those that precede them. However, it seems that both the dialogue view and the message-based view of interactivity focus primarily on communication exchanges.

Also within this tradition is examination of 'actual' interactions or exchanges. Whereas interactive features are often studied by examining the manifest content and/or features of sites and perceived interactivity resides within the mind of the individual, interactive exchange can be observed. The Web offers an ideal forum for observing and tracking the actual interactions of individuals as they navigate and communicate (Coyle and Thorson, 2001; McMillan and Hwang, 2002, McMillan et al., 2003).

Multidimensional Perspectives

Several scholars have suggested that interactivity cannot be neatly defined based on features, perceptions or exchanges. Instead, they define interactivity as a multidimensional construct. Heeter (1989) provided an early attempt to conceptualize multiple dimensions of interactivity in new media. She suggested a six-dimensional choice based on: complexity of user choice, effort users must exert, responsiveness to the user, monitoring information use, ease of adding information, and facilitation of interpersonal communication. Attempts to operationalize her conceptual definition have met with limited success (Massey and Levy, 1999; McMillan, 1998b). Massey and Levy suggested that one reason that they had to adapt Heeter's conceptual definition was that they found two broad meanings for interactivity in online journalism. One dimension they identified as interpersonal interactivity, or the extent to which audiences can have computer-mediated conversations in the 'spaces' created for them by journalists. The other dimension they defined as content interactivity in which journalists technologically empower consumers over content. Schultz (2000) also indicated that two types of interactivity characterize journalistic websites: reader-to-reader and journalist-to-reader.

This dual approach to interactivity is reflected in other areas of new media research. For example, Lee (2000) indicated that two broad types of interactivity are interacting with people and interacting with technology. Hoffman and

Novak (1996) described person interactivity and machine interactivity. Stromer-Galley (2000) identified human-to-human and human-to-media interaction. Carey defined interactive media as: 'Technologies that provide person-to-person communications … and person-to-machine interactions' (1989: 328).

Other researchers have suggested more dimensions are needed to explore different ways of interacting with new media. For example, Szuprowicz (1995) identified three levels of interactivity: user-to-user, user-to-documents and user-to-computer (or user-to-system). Others have identified similar three-dimensional constructs (Barker and Tucker, 1990; Haeckel, 1998; Jensen, 1998). Kayany et al. (1996) suggested that within these three types of interactivity users exert three types of control: relational (or interpersonal), content (or document-based) and process/sequence (or interface-based) controls. Additional interactivity dimensions have been identified that are setting-specific. For example, Stromer-Galley and Foot (2000) identified 'citizen–campaign interaction' in political websites and Chesebro and Bonsall (1989) added dimensions for program-dominated interaction and artificial intelligence.

However, the three-dimensional construct of user-to-user, user-to-documents and user-to-system interactivity seems to encompass the primary literature on interactivity in new media. Furthermore, this three-part construct parallels historical developments in the concept of interactivity that predated new media. The following section will examine these three types of interactivity as they have evolved both before and after the advent of new media.

THREE TRADITIONS OF INTERACTIVITY

The user-to-user, user-to-documents and user-to-system traditions of interactivity have been evolving for decades. However, in many ways distinctions among these traditions are arbitrary. For example, the user-to-user tradition focuses on human communication, but subjects such as how readers respond to newspaper editors, while clearly part of the human communication tradition, also cross over into the user-to-documents literature that addresses how people interact with content and content creators. Yet, despite the relatively arbitrary nature of the distinctions, these three research traditions do provide a basic framework for investigation of the past, present and future of interactivity. While each tradition is treated separately, areas of overlap among the traditions will also be probed. In particular, the three models designed to illustrate the nature of interactivity in these three traditions clearly show some commonalities such as the importance of the concept of 'control'.

User-to-user Interaction

User-to-user interaction focuses on ways that individuals interact with each other. This tradition is based in human communication research. User-to-user interaction clearly predates new media and extends back to the earliest communication between sentient beings. Among many users of new media, the concept of interactivity is closely tied to the discovery of new tools for facilitating old techniques of human communication. Several research traditions related to user-to-user communication both before and after the advent of new media are briefly reviewed below.

Interpersonal Interaction

Goffman's (1967) analysis of the 'interaction ritual' placed human interaction at the forefront of communication research. Goffman wrote that 'the proper study of interaction is not the individual and his psychology, but rather the syntactic relations among the acts of different persons mutually present to one another' (1967: 2). Co-presence was central to Goffman's work that examined glances, gestures and other verbal and non-verbal elements that influence communication. Argyle's (1969) work also examined the visible, audible, intentional and unintentional signals that are central to co-present interpersonal communication.

Berger (1979) identified various stages for dealing with uncertainty in interpersonal relationships. These begin with passive strategies, then move to active strategies, and then go on to interactive strategies. Among the interactive strategies that he identified were verbal interrogation, self-disclosure, and detection of deception in the communication exchange. He also noted that anticipated future interaction might impact on the strategy that an individual selects for addressing uncertainty in interpersonal interactions. Other researchers also examined dimensions of interpersonal interaction (see, for example, Wish et al., 1976).

Symbolic Interaction

Goffman's (1967) work also led to the development of the field of symbolic interaction. Blumer (1969) identified three premises that underlie the concept of symbolic interaction. First, human beings act toward things on the basis of the meanings that those things have for them. Second, the meanings of such things are derived from, or arise out of, the social interaction that an individual has with others. And finally, those meanings are modified through an interpretive process used by individuals in dealing with the things they encounter.

Blumer suggested that in non-symbolic interaction, individuals respond directly to one another's gestures or actions; in symbolic interaction, they interpret each other's gestures and act on the basis of the meaning yielded by that interpretation. He further noted that mutual role taking is central to symbolic interaction. The symbolic interaction approach served as the foundation for a body of literature that examined webs of interaction in non-technology environments (see, for example, Miller et al., 1997; Ruben, 1975).

Social Interaction

Bales' (1950) work on categorizing small-group interaction underlies much of the subsequent literature on interaction in groups and organizations. Bales identified stages in group interaction. Later research built on Bales' work on social interaction by examining communication rules for cooperation or competition in groups (Shimanoff, 1988), relationships between task and interaction (Poole, 1985),

and the impact of time limits and task quality on group interaction and group performance (Kelly and McGrath, 1985; McGrath, 1990, 1991; Straus and McGrath, 1994).

By the late 1980s, scholars who studied social interaction in face-to-face group settings had begun to equate the terms 'interaction' and 'communication'. For example, Hirokawa (1988) wrote that 'interaction profiles' were a common technique used by researchers to examine who tends to interact with whom – in other words, who communicates directly with whom in a group setting.

But it is important to recognize that face-to-face communication does not necessarily lead to social interaction. Schudson (1978) pointed out that many communication scholars hold an 'ideal of conversation' which assumes that face-to-face interpersonal communication is characterized by continuous feedback and egalitarian norms which make mass media seem inferior to conversation. However, he argued that most conversations don't match this ideal and, in some cases, mass media have actually helped to improve standards of interpersonal communication. Thus, Schudson suggested that social interaction can be facilitated by mediated communication. Lievrouw and Finn (1990) also pointed out that all communication is mediated: even face-to-face communication is mediated through one or more of the five senses.

Interaction as Feedback

Another long-standing research tradition examines interaction between individuals who are often characterized by their roles as either source or receiver. This form of interaction is often explored within the limited framework of the 'feedback' that receivers give to the senders of professionally prepared communication vehicles such as newspapers. Clearly this tradition is related to both user-to-user interaction and user-to-documents interaction. It is briefly reviewed here because the primary focus is not on mass communication but rather on the ways that individuals have limited capability to interact with the individuals who create content.

Even before Wiener (1948) developed cybernetic theory which led to increased interest in media 'feedback' tools, some communication scholars had begun to explore the ways in which members of the audience can interact with content creators through letters to the editor. For example, Sayre (1939) examined the contents of fan mail sent to a radio station. Other researchers later conducted more in-depth analysis of radio fan mail (Bierig and Dimmick, 1979; Turow, 1974, 1977), letters to editors of print media such as newspapers (Davis and Rarick, 1964; Forsythe, 1950; Grey and Brown, 1970; Lander, 1972; Rafaeli, 1990), and letters to television news providers (Gans, 1977; McGuire and Leroy, 1977).

In general, the authors suggested that letters to media content providers can fulfil some needs for audience interaction and can also provide feedback to content creators. However, the studies tend to suggest that opinions expressed in the letters are not generally representative of the larger audience and such opinions rarely change editorial positions or actions. Thus, 'feedback' would seem to be similar to the 'reaction' stage which Rafaeli (1988) identified as the middle step in the action/reaction/interaction process.

User-to-user Interaction in New Media

Unquestionably, new media bring change to human communications. Fundamentally, media such as computer networks and telecommunication systems add a layer of technology between communicating partners (Chilcoat and DeWine, 1985). Walther (1996) noted that the impulse to interpersonal communication seems inherently human, yet may be more easily enacted via technology. Among the new media that enable social uses are: electronic mail, networked electronic bulletin boards, chat and electronic shopping (Chesebro and Bonsall, 1989). However, as Lievrouw and Finn (1990) pointed out, communication behaviours rather than communication technologies drive the evolution of meaning in communication systems.

Much of the literature on human interaction can serve as a foundation for examination of user-to-user interaction, which is also widely known as computer-mediated communication (CMC). Hesse et al. asserted that CMC 'provides us with a medium in which to test, modify, and expand our understanding of human social interaction' (1988: 162). Reeves and Nass suggested that as individuals interact through new media they expect those media to obey 'social and natural rules. All these rules come from the world of interpersonal interaction, and from studies about how people interact with the real world. But all of them apply equally well to media' (1996: 5).

As Danowski (1982) noted, many of the research techniques used for evaluating human communication in CMC are similar to those techniques used for evaluating other human communication. Among the effects that have been explored are the impacts of CMC on ability to form impressions of communicators in the absence of non-verbal cues (Lea and Spears, 1992; Rafaeli and Sudweeks, 1997; Walther, 1995), idea generation and group participation (Bikson et al., 1989; DeVries, 1996; Fredin, 1983; Romiszowski, 1993; Shaw et al., 1993; Siegel et al., 1986; Valacich et al., 1993; Walther, 1996), personal identity and decision-making (Bezjian-Avery et al., 1998; Cooley, 1999; Garramone et al., 1986; Sherblom, 1988; Yom, 1996), and sociability and engagement (Ha and James, 1998; Kiesler, 1986; Rafaeli and Sudweeks, 1997).

Direction of Communication

Within the CMC tradition, a fundamental assumption is that the medium serves primarily as a conduit for communication that flows back and forth among communication participants. Pavlik wrote that 'interactivity means two-way communication between source and receiver, or, more broadly multi-directional communication between any number of sources and receivers' (1998: 137). Many other authors have echoed this view (Beniger, 1987; Bretz, 1983; Chesebro, 1985; Duncan, 1989; Durlak, 1987; Garramone et al., 1986; Kirsh, 1997; Rafaeli and Sudweeks, 1997; Zack, 1993).

Within some of the literature, two-way communication is characterized by an egalitarian notion of mutual discourse and mutual role taking (Ball-Rokeach and Reardon, 1988; Burgoon et al., 2000; Hanssen et al., 1996; Williams et al., 1988). For example, Hanssen and his colleagues wrote: 'new communication technologies make possible creation of virtual environments in which the traditional roles of senders and receivers no longer apply' (1996: 61).

Among other scholars, the multidirectional capabilities of new media serve more for providing feedback than for truly mutual discourse. Ha and James asserted that 'despite its importance, discussions of interactivity have been filled with a restrictive assumption that requires reexamination. This assumption is that reciprocal, two-way communication is a common desire of both the communicator and the audience' (1998: 460). Other scholars who consider CMC from the marketer's perspective tend to focus on feedback from consumers to marketers (see, for example, Duncan and Moriarty, 1998), but even though this form of feedback may not be egalitarian it is still often viewed as empowering. Day wrote that 'the essence of interactive marketing is the use of information *from* the customer rather than *about* the customer' (1998: 47). Newhagen et al. (1996) provided evidence that the feedback function corresponds to self-efficacy among individuals who send e-mail to a news site. However, Nielsen (2000) warned that site designers should not build in feedback tools unless they are willing to respond to messages – an effort that can require substantial resources.

Within the CMC tradition, direction of communication has been shown to play a unique role in the diffusion of interactive technologies. Mahler and Rogers wrote: 'because the main purpose of an interactive telecommunications innovation is to connect the potential adopter with others who have adopted the innovation, the innovation has little perceived utility for an individual until others with whom the individual wishes to communicate have adopted' (1999: 724). Thus, the concept of critical mass becomes very important in diffusion of technologies that allow for multidirectional communication (Allen, 1988; Mahler and Rogers, 1999; Markus, 1990; Williams et al., 1988, 1994).

Control

New media also provide new tools that enable communicators to have more control over their communication experience. Beniger (1986) suggested that the industrial revolution spawned a 'control revolution' in which systems were put into place for managing increases in production and changes in distribution. New media also provide new kinds of controls. Many scholars have noted that a key benefit of computer-mediated communication is that it allows participants to communicate without being bound by constraints of time or geography (Ball-Rokeach and Reardon, 1988; Bikson et al., 1989; Burgoon et al., 2000; Cathcart and Gumpert, 1983; Danowski, 1982; Hesse et al., 1988; Hiltz and Turoff, 1993; Hoffman and Novak, 1996; McGrath, 1990; Shaw et al., 1993; Walther, 1994, 1996; Walther and Burgoon, 1992; Walther et al., 1994). For example, Cathcart and Gumpert wrote that 'interpersonal mediated communication refers to any person-to-person interaction where a medium has been interposed to transcend the limitations of time and space' (1983: 271).

CMC can also shift patterns of control among communication participants. Kiesler noted that 'to some degree all communication technologies weaken the controls over information distribution that people have in dealing with each other face to face' (1986: 48). She further observed that CMC tends to break down hierarchies and cut across organizational boundaries. McGrath (1990) also observed flattened hierarchies in CMC-based communication. Landow (1992) noted that CMC results in power shifts in the educational environment as well, and suggested that these shifts have the potential to transform roles of teacher and pupil.

A Proposed Model for User-to-user Interactivity

Directionality of communication and level of control over the communication environment are, as noted above, central to interactivity in CMC environments. Figure 10.1 proposes four

Direction of communication

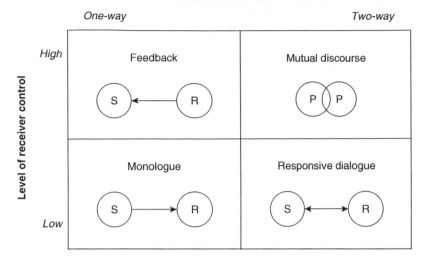

Figure 10.1   *Four models of user-to-user interactivity*
S = sender, R = receiver, P = participant (sender/receiver roles are interchangeable)

models of user-to-user interactivity based on the juxtaposition of those two dimensions.

The monologue model, which utilized primarily one-way, sender-controlled communication, can be witnessed in some marketing communications and political communications environments that focus primarily on 'getting the word out'. Feedback is often added to such sites when the communicator wants to add 'interactivity' to the environment. However, while feedback tools such as e-mail links might theoretically open two-way communication channels, such tools often provide the person who is giving the feedback with relatively little control over the communication exchange.

Responsive dialogue meets the criteria set forth in Rafaeli's (1988) popular definition in that each message reflects awareness of all earlier messages. However, in the responsive dialogue model, the message sender still retains primary control. This model might be found at websites that provide customer service or e-commerce. Mutual dialogue is responsive, but it also gives more egalitarian control to all participants so that sender and receiver roles become indistinguishable. Chat rooms and instant messaging tools often facilitate mutual discourse.

User-to-documents Interactivity

People interact with each other, but they also interact with documents and the creators of those documents. This user-to-documents interactivity can be seen in the ways that active audiences interpret and use mass media messages. New forms of interaction with documents are also emerging in new media as evidenced in areas such as active navigation of websites and active participation in creation of interactive fiction. As illustrated in the following sections, user-to-documents interactivity applies to both old media and new media and involves both perceived interaction with content creators and actual creation of content.

Parasocial Interaction

Parasocial interaction illustrates ways in which limited forms of interaction with content creators can be achieved even when actual mechanisms for interactivity are limited. Horton and Wohl suggested that radio, television and film can give the illusion of face-to-face relationships with the performer:

The conditions of response to the performer are analogous to those in a primary group. The most remote and illustrious men are met *as if* they were in the circle of one's peers; the same is true of a character in a story who comes to life in these media in an especially vivid and arresting way. We propose to call this seeming face-to-face relationship between spectator and performer a *para-social relationship*. (1956: 215)

Again, the distinctions between research traditions are blurred. Clearly, parasocial interaction is a form of user-to-user interaction (or at least it simulates that kind of interpersonal interaction). But it is reviewed here because it is in the context of mass media, which focus predominantly on user-to-documents interaction, that the concept of parasocial interaction has primarily been applied.

Levy (1979) suggested that the parasocial relationship requires time to develop and is based on the perceived 'shared' experiences with media personalities. Beniger (1987) suggested that feelings of 'intimacy' can be developed between individuals who are associated with the media and members of their audience. Houlberg (1984) found evidence of such parasocial relationships between viewing audiences and local television newscasters. Norlund (1978) suggested that parasocial interaction depends on the development of media personalities for the audience to 'interact' with. He suggested that media have varying levels of interaction potential based on: the extent to which the medium is able to approximate reality, whether the content is characterized by the presence of dominating characters, and whether the content is characterized by individuals who appear regularly.

Rafaeli (1990) identified some concerns that may arise in parasocial interaction. He suggested that the attempt to form a bond of emotional intimacy between television celebrities and members of the audience was a type of manipulation designed primarily to result in a larger, more loyal audience. Beniger (1987) also warned that the personalization of mass media might lead to the development of a sense of 'pseudo-community' in which parasocial interactions substitute for 'real' interactions.

Norlund also warned of potential negative side-effects of parasocial interaction: 'It seems that media interaction can lead to greater dependency on mass media as well as a tendency to use the mass media (rather than for instance interacting with people) in certain situations of stress and loneliness' (1978: 171–2). Williams et al. (1994) also noted the potential for individuals to depend on media for fulfilling social interaction needs. They suggested links between such media use and media dependency theory (Ball-Rokeach et al., 1984), which states that the power of the media is a function of dependencies of individuals, groups, organizations and systems on the scarce information resources that are controlled by the media.

Creating Content

In addition to parasocial interaction with content creators, other forms of user-to-documents interactivity have also emerged in traditional media. In particular, some forms of user-to-documents interactivity actually rely on the active audience members to supply the content of traditional media.

Telephone calls to radio stations allow for audience participation in the creation of content. The call-in show has a substantial history as a subset of radio programming (Crittenden, 1971). Some researchers (Bierig and Dimmick, 1979) suggest that such shows function as a substitute for face-to-face communication, and others (Turow, 1974) suggest that calls to 'talk stations' are rooted in the need for personal communication with the 'outside world'. However, there is also evidence that radio (Crittenden, 1971) and television (Newhagen, 1994) talk shows are related to self-efficacy, or the sense of being able to cope with the political system.

Some forms of mediated communication actually require participation. For example, citizen's band radio would be devoid of content were it not for the individuals who broadcast their messages. Citizen's Band (CB) communication is built on a unique form of interpersonal discourse (Powell and Ary, 1977) and CB radio has faced a unique history of regulation (Marvin and Schultze, 1977) that is based in part on its unique interactive nature. Dannefer and Poushinsky (1977) defined interactivity in CB radio as 'step reflexivity' because it permits two-way communication, but only one person can talk at a time.

Interacting with Old Media

Some media, such as newspapers, seem to have limited capacity for parasocial interaction or interaction through participation. However, other older media forms do have interactive potential. For example Standage (1998) suggested that the telegraph, with its two-way wired communication, was a precursor to the Internet. Researchers have also identified strong parallels between the development of the radio and development of the Internet in terms of cultural history (Douglas, 1987; Lappin, 1995) and market evolution (McMillan, 1998a; Smulyan, 1994). The interactive potential and early interactive uses of radio are noted in much of this work.

Before the radio, the invention of the telephone heralded a new age in mediated interactive communication. Bretz (1983) noted that despite its availability to a great mass of people, few individuals today think of the telephone as a mass medium. He suggests that the primary reason for this perception is that radio is distributed in only one direction, thus lending it to 'broadcast' and mass communication. By contrast the telephone requires two wires that facilitate a kind of back-and-forth communication that seems more appropriate to interpersonal interactions. However, this distinction between radio as broadcast and telephone as interpersonal was by no means self-evident in the early developmental stages of these media. Experiments existed in telephone broadcasts (Marvin, 1988), and when telephone was introduced many managers envisioned it as a device for transmitting orders and information to their employees (Kiesler, 1986). Nevertheless, the telephone has evolved primarily as an interpersonal communication tool upon which individuals rely for feelings of connectedness and control over their environments (Wurtzel and Turner, 1977). However, the continued evolution of telephony into the mobile era has signalled further changes as the telephone now becomes the receiver for everything from e-mail to news and even place-based advertising.

Interacting with New Media

Research on new media has further explored interactivity with both the content and the creators of content in those new media environments. Rafaeli and LaRose noted that 'Collaborative mass media systems, in which the audience is the primary source of media content as well as its receiver, represent a new and significant departure from mass media forms. They expand the very definition of mass media from "one-to-many" to "many-to- many" communication' (1993: 277).

A key theme that emerges in literature which examines interaction with content and content creators is that the 'audience' is not a passive receiver of information, but rather an active co-creator. A key characteristic of the active audience is that individuals have control over both presentation and content (Barak and Fisher, 1997; Bezjian-Avery et al., 1998; Chesebro and Bonsall, 1989; Fredin, 1989; Hanssen et al., 1996; Latchem et al., 1993a; Looms, 1993; Miles, 1992; Morrison, 1998; Steuer, 1992; Street and Rimal, 1997; Tucker, 1990; Williams et al., 1988).

In many cases, the literature suggests that the individual's control of content extends beyond simply navigating through a standard set of options. Researchers have suggested that interactive content should dynamically respond to individual actions. Straubhaar and LaRose wrote that interactivity should be used to 'refer to situations where real-time feedback is collected from the receivers of a communications channel and is used by the source to continually modify the message as it is being delivered to the receiver' (1996: 12). Similar concepts have been explored in applied fields such as education (Barker and Tucker, 1990; Hester, 1999) and marketing (Blattberg and Deighton, 1991; Xie, 2000).

Despite the role of the active audience, the role of professional content creators has not been eliminated. Communication professionals create content for online newspapers, educational CD-ROMs and interactive fiction.

Nature of audience

Figure 10.2   *Four models of user-to-documents interactivity*
S = sender, R = receiver, P = participant (sender/receiver roles are interchangeable)

Mass communication researchers who have begun to examine interactive journalism have found that journalists seem to be providing few opportunities for audiences to be either active or interactive (Newhagen et al., 1996; Schultz, 1999). Media such as 'interactive television' offer little more than a menu of choices for services such as movies on demand (Pavlik, 1998), and news-on-demand systems often offer little opportunity for interchange between the audience and the content creators (Mayburry, 2000). However, some research has looked at issues such as ways that e-mail is being used as a tool for communication between content creators and the audience (Newhagen et al., 1996). Journalists must recognize that new media tools such as the Internet can be a mass medium (Morris and Ogan, 1996), but they must also recognize that new media tools must offer some substantial improvements over existing media if they are to change relationships between audience and content creators (Fredin, 1989). Interactive journalism must address issues such as the 24-hour news cycle (Borden and Harvey, 1998), but such studies should more directly address interactivity at multiple levels. The emergence of web logs (or blogs) represent a possible major new direction in journalism as they seem to offer the opportunity for anyone to post news and opinion

that is both read and commented upon by growing numbers of new media users.

Interactive fiction has also attracted comment and observation as an emerging form of interactive content. Landow suggested that interactive fiction, which allows readers to have some level of control over the outcome of a story, 'blurs the boundaries between reader and writer' (1992: 5). Scholars have also examined other issues related to interactive fiction such as the role of playfulness in content (Bolter, 1991), linearity and structure (Fredin, 1997; Hunt, 2000; Iser, 1989; Murray, 1995, 1997, 1999).

A Proposed Model for User-to-documents Interactivity

The dimensions of communication direction and participant control that were identified in the earlier section on user-to-user interactivity can also be applied in conceptualizing user-to-documents interactivity. The active audience is central to the concept of communication direction and content creators tend to either retain or relinquish control of content. Figure 10.2 proposes four models of interactivity based on the juxtaposition of those two dimensions.

The packaged content model grows out of the mass media tradition in which content creators package content and deliver it to relatively passive audiences. This limited form of user-to-system interactivity can be found at many online newspapers and magazines. The content-on-demand model assumes a more active audience. But the audience is not a creator of content. Rather, individual members of the audience customize the content to meet their individual needs. This model is reflected in some of the information science literature and is also implemented in customized web pages that deliver news, weather, sports and other content as specified by individual preferences.

Content exchange assumes that all participants can be either senders or receivers of content. Bulletin boards are an example of this type of information exchange that often occurs asynchronously. Co-created content assumes that all participants share in the creation of content. Group decision support systems are designed to create this kind of environment. Blogs, interactive fiction, MUDs and MOOs might provide other examples of situations in which multiple active individuals create the content that provides the building blocks for an interactive environment.

User-to-system Interactivity

Individuals interact with each other through new media; they interact with documents and document creators, too. But a third form of interactivity is also central to new media – the interaction between people and the computer (or other type of new media system) itself. The study of human interaction with computers is not new and this section provides an overview of that history. Additionally, some key theories related to uses of new media systems are briefly explored and the balance of control in the human relationship is considered.

Early Explorations of Human–Technology Interfaces

In the mid 1900s computer scientists began using the term 'interactivity' to describe a new form of interface that was different from, and more user-friendly than, batch processing (Alter, 1977; Miles, 1992; Zeltzer, 1992). The ability to issue commands to the computer directly was viewed as more 'conversational' and 'interactive' and more supportive of management decision-making (Vasarhelyi, 1977).

However, even before interactive processing replaced batch processing of commands, scholars had begun to think about how humans might interact with machines. Turing's (1956) often cited test of computer intelligence proposed that a computer and a human being are equally intelligent if other human beings are unable to distinguish between the responses of a computer and those of a human being. Ten years after Turing proposed his test of computer–human interaction, MIT professor Joseph Weizenbaum developed a computer program that he named ELIZA. The program was able to carry on a 'conversation' by replaying sentences typed into it. While users of the system were not likely to confuse the machine with a person, its natural-language responses often resembled the 'conversation' that a patient might have with a Jungian psychologist (Murray, 1997).

The study of user-to-system interactivity grows out of the field of human factors research which studies the ways that humans respond to information presented to them by a computer (Guedj et al., 1980). Biocca wrote that 'the words *human factors* refer to important aspects of human performance, behaviour, and desire that must be considered in the design of any machine, hardware, program, or information system' (1993: 63).

Much of the human factors literature focuses on design of the experience that users will have when they interact with the computer system. Kay suggested that 'the dawn of user interface design first happened when computer designers finally noticed, not just that end users had functioning minds, but that a better understanding of how those minds worked would completely shift the paradigm of interaction' (1990: 192). Design of the user interface is often considered to be both an art and a science (Guedj et al., 1980; Kirsh, 1997; Salzman and Rosenthal, 1994; Simms, 1997) and is central to the future of interactive processes. In the 1970s, as computer scientists began to explore not only the design but also the consequences of interactive versus batch processing, they noted the importance of understanding human interaction as a way of improving human–computer interaction (Chapanis et al., 1972). And some researchers began to apply Bales' (1950) work on symbolic interaction to human–computer interactions (Alter, 1977).

Media Richness and Social Presence

Symbolic interaction also provided the basis for a body of literature that began to develop in the late 1980s that examined how a dynamic web of communications could impact on the content richness of media, symbolic cues provided by the medium, and situational determinants of media choice such as time and distance (Daft et al., 1987; Trevino and Webster, 1992; Trevino et al., 1987, 1990). For example, Trevino et al. (1987) found that managers tended to select face-to-face communication for content and symbolic reasons, whereas electronic mail and the telephone were more often chosen because of situational constraints such as time or geography.

The richness of the medium can sometimes reduce the sense of distance between communicators. Closely related to media richness is the study of social presence that explores the ways that the communication systems enable individuals to feel as if they are co-present even when they are not physically in the same place or time. Social presence research grows out of the telecommunications tradition and explores the use of long-standing technologies (such as the telephone) that enable mediated interpersonal communication. Short et al. (1976) used the principles of social psychology to develop the field of social presence research. They indicated that: 'the capacity to transmit information about facial expression, direction of looking, posture, dress and non-verbal vocal cues, all contribute to the Social Presence of a communication medium' (1976: 65).

Researchers used the concept of social presence to further examine mediated interpersonal communication (see, for example, Burke et al., 1999; Rice and Williams, 1984) and issues such as relationships between social presence, anticipated future interaction and

group performance (Berger, 1979). This work provided the basis for additional research on media richness and telepresence in the late 1980s and the 1990s (Daft et al., 1987; Fulk and Boyd, 1991; Fulk et al., 1991; Lea and Spears, 1992; Schmitz and Fulk, 1991; Steuer, 1992; Trevino et al., 1987, 1990; Walther, 1992, 1994; Walther and Burgoon, 1992; Walther et al., 1994; Zack, 1993).

Social presence theory has also been applied to computer-mediated communication in ways that illustrate shifting patterns of control in CMC (Chesebro, 1985; d'Ambra and Rice, 1994; Fulketal, 1992; Hiltz et al., 1989; Kiesler et al., 1984; Lea and Spears, 1992; Schmitz and Fulk, 1991; Sherblom, 1988; Sproull and Kiesler, 1986; Straus and McGrath, 1994; Trevino et al., 1990; Walther, 1992; Zack, 1993). For example, Schmitz and Fulk (1991) conducted a study that investigated the effects of perceived social influences from organizational colleagues on the uses and assessments of electronic mail. They found that 'an explicit consideration of social influences aids in understanding how individuals perceive and use information technology' (1991: 487). In other words, social influence provides controls that help individuals adapt to new technologies.

The Human–Computer Equation

Within the field of human factors or human–computer interaction (HCI) research, definitions of interactivity tend to focus on the ways that the human communicates directly with computers and other new media systems (Burgoon et al., 2000; Hanssen et al., 1996; Huhtamo, 1999; Milheim, 1996; Murray, 1997; Paisley, 1983; Preece, 1993; Reardon and Rogers, 1988; Tan and Nguyen, 1993; Trevino and Webster, 1992). Typically, research in this tradition defines the interaction between a single human and a single computer as the most elemental form of interactivity (Shaw et al., 1993). Crawford (1990) depicted the communication between human and computer as a kind of 'interactive circuit' through which the user and computer are in continuous communication. In briefly tracing the history of HCI studies, Laurel wrote:

When the concept of the interface first began to emerge, it was commonly understood as the hardware and software through which a human and computer could communicate. As it has evolved, the concept has come to include the cognitive and emotional aspects of the user's experience as well. (1990a: xi)

Reeves and Nass noted that, in the study of human–computer interaction, 'one of the two words surrounding the hyphen usually leads' (2000: 65). Some studies focus more on human perception, others more on computer design.

Among the studies that focus on the human side are those that examine how individuals interpret computer personality (Moon and Nass, 1996), the level of agency that individuals perceive they have in working with the computer (Huhtamo,1999; Murray, 1997), individual decision styles (Vasarhelyi, 1977), and goals that the individual brings to the system (Belkin et al., 1993; Xie, 2000).

A subset of the literature that focuses on the human side of the HCI equation addresses the concept of flow (Csikszentmihalyi, 1975), which 'represents the user's perception of the interaction with the medium as playful and exploratory' (Trevino and Webster, 1992: 540). Ghani and Deshpande wrote:

Flow, which is characterized by intense concentration and enjoyment, was found to be significantly linked with exploratory use behaviour, which in turn was linked to extent of computer use. Flow was itself determined by the individual's sense of being in control and the level of challenge perceived in using computers. (1994: 381)

Scholars have suggested that increased flow can lead to positive outcomes such as improved attitude (Trevino and Webster, 1992), more depth of interchange with computer systems (Hesse et al., 1988), heightened creativity and reduced anxiety (Webster and Martocchio, 1992), enhanced marketing opportunities (Hoffman and Novak, 1996), and insights into problem-solving skills (Ord, 1989).

Studies that focus more on the computer side of the human–computer equation tend to examine issues such as interfaces and input devices (Baecker, 1980; Biocca, 1993; Laurel, 1990b; Naimark, 1990; Nielsen, 2000; Schneiderman, 1998; Simms, 1997), navigation tools (Heeter, 2000; Nielsen, 2000), interactive features that allow for user choice and input (Belkin et al., 1993; Daft et al., 1987; Durlak, 1987; Hanssen et al., 1996; Looms, 1993; Mahood et al., 2000; Steuer, 1992; Zeltzer, 1992), and system activity (Milheim, 1996; Valacich et al., 1993).

A subset of this literature focuses specifically on hypertextuality and the ways in which linked text can be used to manage non-linear communication (Belkin et al., 1993; Klein, 2000; Landow, 1992; Mayhew, 1998; Schaffer and Hannafin, 1986; Sundar et al., 1998, 1999). Hypertext is generally defined as blocks of text and the electronic links that join them. The concept of hypertext was developed by Theodor H. Nelson in the 1960s and has earlier roots in Vannevar Bush's (1945) article on mechanically linked information retrieval systems (Landow, 1992). The primary advantage of hypertext is the control that it gives to the user who navigates through a computer-based system.

A Proposed Model for User-to-system Interactivity

The dimensions that were incorporated into Figures 10.1 and 10.2 can also be adapted and applied to user-to-system interaction. The control dimension, which was central to both Figures 10.1 and 10.2, remains central in this model as well. However, the issue changes slightly. The question becomes: who is in control, the computer or the human(s) interacting with it? The second dimension parallels the direction of communication dimension in Figure 10.1 and the nature of audience dimension in Figure 10.2. In HCI the second key issue is the interface. How much is the interface apparent enough to require user attention versus becoming a transparent part of the user's experience? Figure 10.3 proposes four models of interactivity based on the juxtaposition of those two dimensions.

Computer-controlled interaction assumes that the computer will 'present' information to persons who will respond to that information. Users are very aware that they are sitting in front of a computer. Much computer-based instruction uses this kind of interactivity. Filling in Web-based forms is an example. By contrast,

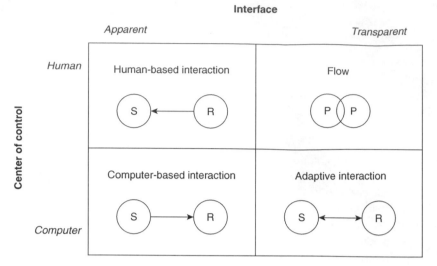

Figure 10.3   *Four models of user-to-system interactivity*
S = sender, R = receiver, P = participant (sender/receiver roles are interchangeable)

human-controlled interaction assumes a much more active individual who uses interface tools provided by programmers and designers to manipulate the computer and obtain information. For example, this form of interactivity would occur when individuals use tools such as databases, spreadsheets and word processors to manipulate and organize data so that the data are more useful to them and their colleagues.

Adaptive communication assumes that the computer is still in command of the interaction, but that it is more responsive to individual needs. For example, advanced gaming and educational systems are able to adapt to changes in the individual's skill level. The state of flow is generally assumed to be characterized by a state of high user activity in which the computer becomes virtually transparent as individuals 'lose themselves' in the computer environment. Virtual reality systems seek this level, but it may also be characteristic of gaming environments and other situations in which the user interfaces seamlessly with the computer.

FUTURE DIRECTIONS

Figure 10.4 suggests a way to bring together the interactive characteristics of new media identified at the start of this chapter with the three traditions of interactivity that have been reviewed at length. The items in each cell are meant to be representative rather than exhaustive. Clearly, when one speaks of interactivity it is important to know what is meant by that term. Different characteristics and features will lead to different forms of analysis.

For example, content or feature analysis may be the most appropriate way to examine interactive features. But coders must know whether they are looking for user-to-user, user-to-document, or user-to-system interactivity (or some combination of those types of interactivity). Measures of perceived interactivity will, undoubtedly be influenced by interactive characteristics, but carefully developed perceptual measures will be able to determine other factors (such as involvement) that might also influence perceptions of interactivity. Finally, new media offer exciting opportunities to analyse interactive exchange. Most forms of digital media leave 'trails' that researchers can follow as they examine interactivity. For example, they might analyse the actual content of exchanges in chat rooms, they might examine patterns of user-posted product/service reviews, and they might examine what organizations actually do with all the data they collect through Web-based forms.

	Interactive features	Perceived interactivity	Interactive exchange
User-to-user	Chat room	Perception that presence of chat space makes a site interactive	Participating in an online chat
User-to-document	Customer reviews	Perception that customer reviews enhance interactivity of site	Posting a product/ service review
User-to-system	Web-based forms	Belief that Web-based form will elicit a response	Filling in a Web-based form

Figure 10.4 *Bringing together characteristics and traditions of interactivity*

The proposed models presented in Figures 10.1, 10.2 and 10.3 offer a way of organizing and making sense of the many different perspectives and definitions of interactivity. If 'interactivity' is to move beyond its current status as a widely used but poorly conceptualized term, we must recognize that there are three fundamentally different types of interactivity that grow out of three research traditions. Scholars and others who use the term should indicate whether they are focusing on user-to-user, user-to-documents or user-to-system interactivity, or some combination of the three.

Within each of these traditions of interactivity, an important factor to consider is the locus of control. As control shifts among senders and receivers and between humans and computer systems, the nature of interactivity shifts. Studies that focus on user-to-user interactivity should also carefully consider the direction of communication between and among senders and receivers who interact in computer-based environments. Studies that focus on user-to-documents interactivity should carefully consider the audience: how active do members of the audience wish to be? And studies that focus on user-to-system interactivity should focus on the human–computer interface: how transparent can and should that interface be?

These models may provide direction for scholars who seek to explore specific aspects of interactive communication. For example, studies of role taking in interactive environments are probably most appropriately based in the user-to-user literature, while studies of interactive fiction are probably centred in user-to-documents literature, and studies involving

virtual reality centre on user-to-system issues. However, these classifications should not be viewed as either mutually exclusive or all-inclusive. For example, virtual reality studies need to incorporate human communication factors from the user-to-user model, and content creators who are considering how users interact with documents also need to address interface issues from the user-to-system model. And some forms of interactivity and new media may not fit into any of these categories at all.

In sum, when approaching interactivity at the surface level we may be able to 'know it when we see it'. But we can understand it better if we recognize that it is a multifaceted concept that resides in the users, the documents and the systems that facilitate interactive communication.

NOTE

The author thanks Kyoungtae Nam for his research assistance on this chapter.

REFERENCES

Ahren, R. Kirkland, Stromer-Galley, Jennifer and Neuman, W. Russell (2000) 'Interactivity and structured issue comparisons on the political Web: an experimental study of the 2000 New Hampshire presidential primary'. Paper presented at the International Communication Association Annual Conference, Acapulco, 1–5 June.

Allen, David (1988) 'New telecommunications services: network externalities and critical mass', *Telecommunication Policy*, 12 (3): 257–71.

Alter, Steven (1977) 'Why is man–computer interaction important for decision support systems?', *Interfaces*, 7 (2): 109–15.

Argyle, Michael (1969) *Social Interaction*. New York: Atherton.

Baecker, Ronald (1980) 'Towards an effective characterization of graphical interaction', in R.A. Guedj, P.J.W. ten Hagen, F.R. Hopgood, H.A. Tucker and D.A. Duce (eds), *Methodology of Interaction*. Amsterdam: North-Holland. pp. 127–47.

Bales, R.F. (1950) 'A set of categories for the analysis of small group interaction', *American Sociological Review*, 15: 257–63.

Ball-Rokeach, Sandra J. and Reardon, Kathleen (1988) 'Monologue, dialogue, and telelog: comparing an emergent form of communication with traditional forms', in R.P. Hawkins, J.M. Wiemann and S. Pingree (eds), *Advancing Communication Science: Merging Mass and Interpersonal Process*. Newbury Park, CA: Sage. pp. 135–61.

Ball-Rokeach, Sandra J., Rokeach, M. and Grube, J.W. (1984) *The Great American Values Test: Influencing Behavior and Belief through Television*. New York: Free Press.

Barak, Azy and Fisher, William A. (1997) 'Effects of interactive computer erotica on men's attitudes and behavior toward women: an experimental study', *Computers in Human Behavior*, 13 (3): 353–69.

Barker, John and Tucker, Richard N. (1990) *The Interactive Learning Revolution: Multimedia in Education and Training*. London: Kogan Page.

Belkin, N.J., Marchetti, P.G. and Cool, C. (1993) 'Braque: design of an interface to support users' interaction in information retrieval', *Information Processing & Management*, 29 (3): 325–44.

Beniger, James R. (1986) *The Control Revolution: Technological and Economic Origins of the Information Society*. Cambridge, MA: Harvard University Press.

Beniger, James R. (1987) 'Personalization of mass media and the growth of pseudo-community', *Communication Research*, 14 (3): 352–71.

Berger, Charles R. (1979) 'Beyond initial interaction: uncertainty, understanding, and the development of interpersonal relationships', in H. Giles and R.N. St Clair (eds), *Language and Social Psychology*. Oxford: Basil Blackwell. pp. 122–44.

Bezjian-Avery, Alexa, Calder, Bobby and Iacobucci, Dawn (1998) 'New media interactive advertising vs. traditional advertising', *Journal of Advertising Research*, 38 (4): 23–32.

Bierig, Jeffrey and Dimmick, John (1979) 'The late night radio talk show as interpersonal communication', *Journalism Quarterly*, 56 (1): 92–6.

Bikson, Tora K., Eveland, J.D. and Guetek, Barbara A. (1989) 'Flexible interactive technologies and multi-person tasks: current problems and future prospects', in M.H. Olson (ed.), *Technological Support for Work Group Collaboration*. Hillsdale, NJ: Erlbaum. pp. 89–112.

Biocca, Frank (1993) 'Communication research in the design of communication interfaces and systems', *Journal of Communication*, 43 (4): 59–68.

Blattberg, Robert C. and Deighton, John (1991) 'Interactive marketing: exploiting the age of addressability', *Sloan Management Review*, 32 (1): 5–14.

Blumer, Herbert (1969) *Symbolic Interactionism: Perspective and Method*. Englewood Cliffs, NJ: Prentice-Hall.

Bolter, Jay David (1991) *Writing Space: the Computer, Hypertext, and the History of Writing*. Hillsdale, NJ: Erlbaum.

Borden, Diane L. and Harvey, Kerrick (1998) *The Electronic Grapevine: Rumor, Reputation, and Reporting in the New Online Environment*. Mahwah, NJ: Erlbaum.

Bretz, R. (1983) *Media for Interactive Communication*. Beverly Hills, CA: Sage.

Burgoon, Judee K., Bonito, Joseph A., Bengtsson, Bjorn, Ramirez, Artemio Jr, Dunbar, Norah E. and Miczo, Nathan (2000) 'Testing the interactivity model: communication processes, partner assessments, and the quality of collaborative work', *Journal of Management Information Systems*, 16 (3): 33–56.

Burke, Kelly, Aytes, Kregg, Chidambaram, Laku and Johnson, Jeffrey J. (1999) 'A study of partially distributed work groups: the impact of media, location, and time on perceptions and performance', *Small Group Research*, 30 (4): 453–90.

Bush, V. (1945) 'As we may think', *Atlantic Monthly*, 176 (July): 101–8.

Carey, John (1989) 'Interactive media', in *International Encyclopedia of Communications*. New York: Oxford University Press. pp. 328–30.

Cathcart, Robert and Gumpert, Gary (1983) 'Mediated interpersonal communication: toward a new typology', *Quarterly Journal of Speech*, 69 (3): 267–77.

Chaffee, Steven H. (1972) 'The interpersonal context of mass communication', in F.G. Kline and P.J. Tichenor (eds), *Current Perspectives in Mass Communication Research*. Beverly Hills, CA: Sage. pp. 95–120.

Chapanis, Alphonse, Ochsman, Robert B., Parrish, Robert N. and Weeks, Gerald D. (1972) 'Studies in interactive communication. I: The effects of four communication modes on the behavior of teams during cooperative problem-solving', *Human Factors*, 14 (6): 487–509.

Chesebro, James W. (1985) 'Computer mediated interpersonal communication', in B.D. Ruben (ed.), *Information and Behavior*, vol. 1. New Brunswick, NJ: Transaction. pp. 202–22.

Chesebro, James W. and Bonsall, Donald G. (1989) *Computer Mediated Communication: Human Relationships in a Computerized World.* Tuscaloosa, AL: University of Alabama Press.

Chilcoat, Yvonne and DeWine, Sue (1985) 'Teleconferencing and interpersonal communication perception', *Journal of Applied Communication Research*, 13 (1): 14–32.

Coffee, Steve and Stipp, Horst (1997) 'The interactions between computer and television usage', *Journal of Advertising Research*, 37 (2): 61–6.

Cooley, Tracy (1999) 'Interactive communication–public relations on the web', *Public Relations Quarterly*, 144 (2): 41–2.

Coyle, James R. and Thorson, Esther (2001) 'The effects of progressive levels of interactivity and vividness in Web marketing sites', *Journal of Advertising*, 30 (3): 65–77.

Crawford, Chris (1990) 'Lessons from computer game design', in B. Laurel (ed.), *The Art of Human–Computer Interface Design.* Reading, MA: Addison-Wesley. pp. 103–11.

Crittenden, John (1971) 'Democratic functions of the open mike forum', *Public Opinion Quarterly*, 35: 200–10.

Csikszentmihalyi, M. (1975) *Beyond Boredom and Anxiety.* San Francisco: Jossey-Bass.

d'Ambra, John and Rice, Ronald E. (1994) 'Multimedia approaches for the study of computer-mediated communication, equivocality, and media selection', *IEEE Transactions on Professional Communication*, 37 (4): 231–9.

Daft, Richard L., Lengel, Robert H. and Trevino, Linda Klebe (1987) 'Message equivocality, media selection, and manager performance: implications for information systems', *MIS Quarterly*, 12 (3): 355–66.

Dannefer, W. Dale and Poushinsky, Nicholas (1977) 'CB in perspective: language and community', *Journal of Communication*, 27 (3): 122–6.

Danowski, James A. (1982) 'Computer mediated communication: a network-based analysis using a CBBS conference', in M. Burgoon (ed.), *Communication Yearbook 6.* Beverly Hills, CA: Sage. pp. 905–24.

Davis, Hal and Rarick, Galen (1964) 'Functions of editorials and letters to the editor', *Journalism Quarterly*, 41 (1): 108–9.

Day, George S. (1998) 'Organizing for interactivity', *Journal of Interactive Marketing*, 12 (1): 47–53.

DeVries, Yousri Eldin (1996) 'The interactive component of distance learning implemented in the art studio course', *Education*, 117 (2): 180–4.

Douglas, Susan J. (1987) *Inventing American Broadcasting: 1899–1922.* Baltimore, MD: Johns Hopkins University Press.

Duncan, Starkey Jr (1989) 'Interaction, face-to-face', in *International Encyclopedia of Communications.* New York: Oxford University Press. pp. 325–7.

Duncan, Tom and Moriarty, Sandra E. (1998) 'A communication-based marketing model for managing relationships', *Journal of Marketing*, 62: 1–13.

Durlak, Jerome T. (1987) 'A typology for interactive media', in M.L. McLaughlin (ed.), *Communication Yearbook 10.* Newbury Park, CA: Sage. pp. 743–57.

Feenberg, Andrew (1992) 'From information to communication: the French experience with videotex', in M. Lea (ed.), *Contexts of Computer-Mediated Communication.* New York: Harvester-Wheatsheaf. pp. 168–87.

Forsythe, Sidney A. (1950) 'An exploratory study of letters to the editor and their contributors', *Public Opinion Quarterly*, 14 (1): 143–4.

Fredin, Eric S. (1983) 'The context of communication: interactive telecommunication, interpersonal communication, and their effects on ideas', *Communication Research*, 10 (4): 553–81.

Fredin, Eric S. (1989) 'Interactive communication systems, values, and the requirement of self-reflection', in J.A. Anderson (ed.), *Communication Yearbook 12.* Newbury Park, CA: Sage. pp. 533–46.

Fredin, Eric S. (1997) *Rethinking the News Story for the Internet: Hyperstory Prototypes and a Model of the User.* Columbia, SC: AEJMC.

Fulk, Janet and Boyd, Brian (1991) 'Emerging theories of communication and organizations', *Journal of Management*, 17 (2): 407–46.

Fulk, Janet, Schmitz, Joseph A. and Schwarz, Deanna (1992) 'The dynamics of context–behavior interactions in computer-mediated communication', in M. Lea (ed.), *Contexts of Computer-mediated Communication.* New York: Harvester Wheatsheaf. pp. 7–29.

Fulk, Janet, Schmitz, Joseph A. and Steinfeld, Charles W. (1991) 'A social influence model of technology use', in J. Fulk and C.W. Steinfeld (eds), *Organization and Communication Technology.* Newbury Park, CA: Sage. pp. 117–40.

Gans, Herbert J. (1977) 'Audience mail: letters to an anchorman', *Journal of Communication*, 27 (3): 86–91.

Garramone, Gina M., Harris, Allen C. and Anderson, Ronald (1986) 'Uses of political computer bulletin boards', *Journal of Broadcasting and Electronic Media*, 30 (3): 325–39.

Ghani, Jawaid A. and Deshpande, Satish P. (1994) 'Task characteristics and the experience of optimal flow in human–computer interaction', *Journal of Psychology*, 128 (4): 381–91.

Goffman, Erving (1967) *Interaction Ritual: Essays on Face-to-Face Behavior*. Chicago: Aldine.

Grey, David L. and Brown, Trevor R. (1970) 'Letters to the editor: hazy reflections of public opinion', *Journalism Quarterly*, 47 (1): 450–471.

Guedj, Richard A., ten Hagen, Paul J.W., Hopgood, F. Robert, Tucker, Hugh A. and Duce, David A. (1980) *Methodology of Interaction*. Amsterdam: North-Holland.

Ha, Louisa and James, Lincoln (1998) 'Interactivity re-examined: a baseline analysis of early business web sites', *Journal of Broadcasting & Electronic Media*, 42 (4): 457–74.

Haeckel, Stephan H. (1998) 'About the nature and future of interactive marketing', *Journal of Interactive Marketing*, 12 (1): 63–71.

Hanssen, Lucien, Jankowski, Nicholas W. and Etienne, Reinier (1996) 'Interactivity from the perspective of communication studies', in N.W. Jankowski and L. Hanssen (eds), *Contours of Multimedia: Recent Technological, Theoretical, and Empirical Developments*. Luton: University of Luton Press. pp. 61–73.

Heeter, Carrie (1989) 'Implications of new interactive technologies for conceptualizing communication', in J.L. Salvaggio and J. Bryant (eds), *Media Use in the Information Age: Emerging Patterns of Adoption and Computer Use*. Hillsdale, NJ: Erlbaum. pp. 217–35.

Heeter, Carrie (2000) 'Interactivity in the context of designed experiences', *Journal of Interactive Advertising*, 1 (1). Available online: http://www.jiad.org

Hesse, Bradford W., Werner, Carol M. and Altman, Irwin (1988) 'Temporal aspects of computer-mediated communication', *Computers in Human Behavior*, 4: 147–65.

Hester, Joe Bob (1999) 'Using a Web-based interactive test as a learning tool', *Journalism and Mass Communication Educator*, 54 (1): 35–41.

Hiltz, Starr Roxanne and Turoff, Murray (1993) *The Network Nation: Human Communication via Computer*, rev. edn. Cambridge, MA: MIT Press.

Hiltz, Starr Roxanne, Turoff, Murray and Johnson, Kenneth (1989) 'Experiments in group decision making. 3: Disinhibition, deindividuation and group processes in pen name and real name computer conferences', *Decision Support Systems*, 5: 217–32.

Hirokawa, Randy Y. (1988) 'Group communication research: considerations for the use of interaction analysis', in C.H. Tardy (ed.), *A Handbook for the Study of Human Communication: Methods and Instruments for Observing, Measuring, and Assessing Communication Processes*. Norwood, NJ: Ablex. pp. 229–45.

Hoffman, Donna L. and Novak, Thomas P. (1996) 'Marketing in hypermedia computer-mediated environments: conceptual foundations', *Journal of Marketing*, 60: 50–68.

Horton, Donald and Wohl, R. Richard (1956) 'Mass communication and para-social interaction: observations on intimacy at a distance', *Psychiatry*, 19: 215–29.

Houlberg, Rick (1984) 'Local television news audience and the para-social interaction', *Journal of Broadcasting*, 28 (4): 423–9.

Huhtamo, Erkki (1999) 'From cybernation to interaction: a contribution to an archaeology of interactivity', in P. Lunenfeld (ed.), *The Digital Dialectic: New Essays on New Media*. Cambridge, MA: MIT Press. pp. 96–110.

Hunt, Peter (2000) 'Futures for children's literature: evolution or radical break', *Cambridge Journal of Education*, 30 (1): 111–19.

Iser, Wolfgang (1989) 'Interaction between text and reader', in J. Corner and J. Hawthorn (eds), *Communication Studies: An Introductory Reader*. London: Arnold. pp. 160–4.

Jankowski, Nicholas W. and Hanssen, Lucien (1996) 'Introduction: multimedia comes of age', in N.W. Jankowski and L. Hanssen (eds), *The Contours of Multimedia: Recent Technological, Theoretical, and Empirical Developments*. Luton: University of Luton Press. pp. 1–21.

Jensen, Jens F. (1998) 'Interactivity: tracing a new concept in media and communication studies', *Nordicom Review*, 19 (1): 185–204.

Kay, Alan (1990) 'User interface: a personal view', in B. Laurel (ed.), *The Art of Human–computer Interface Design*. Reading, MA: Addison-Wesley. pp. 191–207.

Kayany, Joseph M., Wotring, C. Edward and Forrest, Edward J. (1996) 'Relational control and interactive media choice in technology-mediated communication situations', *Human Communication Research*, 22 (3): 399–421.

Kelly, Janice R. and McGrath, Joseph E. (1985) 'Effects of time limits and task types on task performance and interaction of four-person groups', *Journal of Personality and Social Psychology*, 49 (2): 395–407.

Kiesler, Sara (1986) 'Thinking ahead: the hidden messages in computer networks', *Harvard Business Review*, 27 (3): 46–60.

Kiesler, Sara, Siegel, Jane and McGuire, Timothy W. (1984) 'Social-psychological aspects of computer-mediated communication', *American Psychologist*, 39 (10): 1123–34.

Kiousis, Spiro (2002) 'Interactivity: a concept explication', *New Media and Society*, 4 (3): 355–83.

Kirsh, David (1997) 'Interactivity and multimedia interfaces', *Instructional Science*, 25: 79–96.

Klein, Leo R. (2000) 'The joys of interactivity', *Library Journal*, 12 (5): 20–2.

Lander, Byron G. (1972) 'Functions of letters to the editor: a reexamination', *Journalism Quarterly*, 49 (1): 142–3.

Landow, George P. (1992) *Hypertext: The Convergence of Contemporary Critical Theory and Technology*. Baltimore, MD: Johns Hopkins University Press.

Lappin, Todd (1995) 'Déjà vu all over again', *Wired*, May: 174–7, 218–22.

Latchem, Colin, Williamson, John and Henderson-Lancett, Lexie (1993a) 'IMM: an overview', in C. Latchem, J. Williamson and L. Henderson-Lancett (eds), *Interactive Multimedia: Practice and Purpose*. London: Kogan Page. pp. 19–38.

Latchem, Colin, Williamson, John and Henderson-Lancett, Lexie (1993b) *Interactive Multimedia: Practice and Purpose*. London: Kogan Page.

Laurel, Brenda (1990a) 'Introduction', in B. Laurel (ed.), *The Art of Human–computer Interface Design*. Reading, MA: Addison-Wesley. pp. xi–xvi.

Laurel, Brenda (1990b) 'Users and contexts', in B. Laurel (ed.), *The Art of Human–computer Interface Design*. Reading, MA: Addison-Wesley. pp. 91–3.

Lea, Martin and Spears, Russell (1992) 'Paralanguage and social perception in computer-mediated communication', *Journal of Organizational Computing*, 2 (3, 4): 321–41.

Lee, Jae-Shin (2000) 'Interactivity: a new approach', Paper presented at the Association for Education in Journalism and Mass Communication, Phoenix, AZ.

Leonhirth, William J., Mindich, David T.Z. and Straumanis, Andris (1997) 'Wanted … a metaphor of history: using past information system to explain Internet mailing lists', *Electronic Journal of Communication*, 7 (4). Available online: http://sss.cios.org/getfile/LEONHIRT_ V7N497

Levy, Mark R. (1979) 'Watching TV news as para-social interaction', *Journal of Broadcasting*, 23 (1): 67–89.

Lieb, Thom (1998) 'Inactivity on interactivity', *Journal of Electronic Publishing*, 3 (3). Available online: http://www.press.umich.edu/jep/03-/lieb 0303.html

Lievrouw, Leah A. and Finn, T. Andrew (1990) 'Identifying the common dimensions of communication: the communication systems model', in B.D. Ruben and L.A. Lievrouw (eds), *Mediation, Information and Communication: Information and Behavior*, vol. 3. New Brunswick, NJ: Transaction. pp. 37–65.

Liu, Yuping (2003) 'Developing a scale to measure the interactivity of websites', *Journal of Advertising Research*, 43 (2): 207–16.

Liu, Yuping and Shrum, L.J. (2002) 'What is interactivity and is it always such a good thing: implications of definition, person, and situation for the influence of interactivity on advertising effectiveness', *Journal of Advertising*, 31 (4): 53–64.

Looms, Peter Olaf (1993) 'Interactive multimedia in education', in C. Latchem, J. Williamson and L. Henderson-Lancett (eds), *Interactive Multimedia: Practice and Purpose*. London: Kogan Page. pp. 115–34.

Mahler, Alwin and Rogers, Everett M. (1999) 'The diffusion of interactive communication innovations and the critical mass: the adoption of telecommunication services by German banks', *Telecommunications Policy*, 23 (10/11): 719–40.

Mahood, Chad, Kalyanaraman, Sriram and Sundar, S. Shyam (2000) 'The effects of erotica and dehumanizing pornography in an online interactive environment'. Paper presented at the Association for Education in Journalism and Mass Communication, Phoenix, AZ, 9–12 August.

Markus, M. Lynne (1990) 'Toward a "critical mass" theory of interactive media', in J. Fulk and C. Steinfeld (eds), *Organization and Communication Technology*. Newbury Park, CA: Sage. pp. 194–218.

Marvin, Carolyn (1988) *When Old Technologies Were New: Thinking about Electric Communication in the Late Nineteenth Century*. New York: Oxford University Press.

Marvin, Carolyn and Schultze, Quentin J. (1977) 'CB in perspective: the first thirty years', *Journal of Communication*, 27 (3): 104–17.

Massey, Brian L. and Levy, Mark R. (1999) 'Interactivity, online journalism, and English-language Web newspapers in Asia', *Journalism & Mass Communication Quarterly*, 76 (1): 138–51.

Mayburry, Mark (2000) 'News on demand', *Communications of the ACM*, 43 (2): 33–4.

Mayhew, Deborah J. (1998) 'Introduction', in C. Forsythe, E. Grose and J. Ratner (eds), *Human Factors and Web Development*. Mahwah, NJ: Erlbaum. pp. 1–13.

McGrath, Joseph E. (1990) 'Time matters in groups', in J. Galegher, R.E. Kraut and C. Egido (eds), *Intellectual Teamwork: Social and Technical Foundations of Cooperative Work*. Hillsdale, NJ: Erlbaum. pp. 23–61.

McGrath, Joseph E. (1991) 'Time, interaction, and performance (TIP): a theory of groups', *Small Group Research*, 22 (2): 147–74.

McGuire, Bernadette and Leroy, David J. (1977) 'Audience mail: letters to the broadcaster', *Journal of Communication*, 27: 79–85.

McMillan, Sally J. (1998a) 'The role of advertising in new media: a historical analysis of radio with comparisons to computer-mediated communication', in D.D. Muehling (ed.), *Proceedings of the 1998 Conference of the American Academy of Advertising*. Pullman, WA: Washington State University. pp. 157–66.

McMillan, Sally J. (1998b) 'Who pays for content? Funding in interactive media', *Journal of Computer Mediated Communication*, 4 (1). Available online: http://www.ascusc.org/jcmc/vol4/issue1/mcmillan. html

McMillan, Sally J. (1999) 'Advertising age and interactivity: tracing media evolution through the advertising trade press', in M. Roberts (ed.), *Proceedings of the 1999 Conference of the American Academy of Advertising*. Gainesville, FL: University of Florida. pp. 107–14.

McMillan, Sally J. (2000a) 'Interactivity is in the eye of the beholder: function, perception, involvement, and attitude toward the web site', in M.A. Shaver (ed.), *Proceedings of the 2000 Conference of the American Academy of Advertising*. East Lansing, MI: Michigan State University. pp. 71–8.

McMillan, Sally J. (2002) 'A four-part model of cyber-interactivity: some places are more interactive than others', *New Media and Society*, 4 (2): 271–91.

McMillan, Sally J. and Downes, Edward J. (2000) 'Defining interactivity: a qualitative identification of key dimensions', *New Media and Society*, 2 (2): 157–79.

McMillan, Sally J. and Hwang, Jang-Sun (2002) 'Measures of perceived interactivity: an exploration of communication, user control, and time in shaping perceptions of interactivity', *Journal of Advertising*, 31 (3): 41–54.

McMillan, Sally J., Kim, Juran, and Hwang, Jang-Sun (2003) 'Searching for the riddle in the web site: coding interactivity in online content analysis', in Pat B. Rose (ed.), *Proceedings of the 2003 Conference of the American Academy of Advertising*. Miami, FL: University of South Florida.

Miles, Ian (1992) 'When mediation is the message: how suppliers envisage new markets', in M. Lea (ed.), *Contexts of Computer-mediated Communication*. New York: Harvester-Wheatsheaf. pp. 145–67.

Milheim, William D. (1996) 'Interactivity and computer-based instruction', *Journal of Educational Technology Systems*, 24 (3): 225–33.

Miller, Dan E., Katovich, Michael A. and Saxton, Stanley L. (1997) *Constructing Complexity: Symbolic Interaction and Social Forms*, vol. 3. Greenwich, CT: JAI.

Moon, Youngme and Nass, Clifford (1996) 'How "real" are computer personalities? Psychological responses to personality types in human–computer interaction', *Communication Research*, 23 (6): 651–74.

Morris, Merrill and Ogan, Christine (1996) 'The Internet as mass medium', *Journal of Computer Mediated Communication*, 1 (4). Available online: http://www.ascusc.org/jcmc/vol1/issue4/morris. html

Morrison, Margaret (1998) 'A look at interactivity from a consumer perspective', in J.B. Ford and E.J.D. Honeycutt (eds), *Developments in Marketing Science*, vol. 21. Norfolk, VA: Academy of Marketing Science. pp. 149–54.

Murray, Janet H. (1995) 'The pedagogy of cyberfiction: teaching a course on reading and writing interactive narrative', in E. Barrett and M. Redmond (eds), *Contextual Media: Multimedia and Interpretation*. Cambridge, MA: MIT Press. pp. 129–62.

Murray, Janet H. (1997) *Hamlet on the Holodeck: The Future of Narrative in Cyberspace*. New York: Free Press.

Murray, Janet H. (1999) 'Interactive design: a profession in search of professional education', *The Chronicle of Higher Education*, 23 April: B4–5.

Naimark, Michael (1990) 'Realness and interactivity', in B. Laurel (ed.), *The Art of Human–Computer Interface Design*. Menlo Park, CA: Addison-Wesley. pp. 455–9.

Negroponte, Nicholas (1995) *Being Digital*. New York: Knopf.

Newhagen, John E. (1994) 'Self-efficacy and call-in political television show use', *Communication Research*, 21 (3): 366–79.

Newhagen, John E. (1998) 'Hitting the agenda reset button for the Internet: the problem of matching research with development'. Paper presented at the International Communication Association Annual Conference, Jerusalem, July.

Newhagen, John E., Cordes, John W. and Levy, Mark R. (1996) 'Nightly@NbC.Com: audience scope and the perception of interactivity in viewer mail on the Internet', *Journal of Communication*, 45 (3): 164–75.

Nielsen, Jakob (2000) *Designing Web Usability*. Indianapolis: New Riders.

Norlund, Jan-Erik (1978) 'Media interaction', *Communication Research*, 5 (2): 150–75.

Ord, Jacqueline G. (1989) 'Who's joking? The information system at play', *Interacting with Computers*, 1 (1): 118–28.

Paisley, William (1983) 'Computerizing information: lessons of a videotext trial', *Journal of Communication*, 33 (1): 153–61.

Pavlik, John V. (1998) *New Media Technology: Cultural and Commercial Perspectives*, 2nd edn. Boston: Allyn and Bacon.

Poole, Marshall Scott (1985) 'Task and interaction sequences: a theory of coherence in group decision-making interaction', in R.L. Street and J.N. Capella (eds), *Sequence and Pattern in Communicative Behaviour*. London: Arnold. pp. 206–24.

Powell, Jon T. and Ary, Donald (1977) 'CB in perspective: communication without commitment', *Journal of Communication*, 27 (3): 118–21.

Preece, Jenny (1993) 'Hypermedia, multimedia and human factors', in C. Latchem, J. Williamson and L. Henderson-Lancett (eds), *Interactive Multimedia: Practice and Purpose*. London: Kogan Page. pp. 135–50.

Rafaeli, Sheizaf (1986) 'The electronic bulletin board: a computer driven mass medium', *Computers and the Social Sciences*, 2 (3): 123–36.

Rafaeli, Sheizaf (1988) 'Interactivity: from new media to communication', in R.P. Hawkins, J.M. Wiemann and S. Pingree (eds), *Advancing Communication Science: Merging Mass and Interpersonal Process*. Newbury Park, CA: Sage. pp. 110–34.

Rafaeli, Sheizaf (1990) 'Interacting with media: para-social interaction and real interaction', in B.D. Ruben and L.A. Lievrouw (eds), *Mediation, Information and Communication: Information and Behavior*, vol. 3. New Brunswick, NJ: Transaction. pp. 125–81.

Rafaeli, Sheizaf and LaRose, Robert J. (1993) 'Electronic bulletin boards and "public goods" explanations of collaborative mass media', *Communication Research*, 20 (2): 277–97.

Rafaeli, Sheizaf and Sudweeks, Fay (1997) 'Networked interactivity', *Journal of Computer Mediated Communication*, 2 (4). Available online: http://www.usc.edu/dept/annenberg/vol2/issue4/rafaeli.sudweeks.html

Reardon, Kathleen K. and Rogers, Everett M. (1988) 'Interpersonal versus mass media communication: a false dichotomy', *Human Communication Research*, 15 (2): 284–303.

Reeves, Byron and Nass, Clifford (1996) *The Media Equation: How People Treat Computers, Television, and New Media Like Real People and Places*. New York: Cambridge University Press/CSLI.

Reeves, Byron and Nass, Clifford (2000) 'Perceptual bandwidth', *Communications of the ACM*, 43 (3): 65–70.

Rice, Ronald E. (1984) 'New media technology: growth and integration', in R.E. Rice (ed.), *The New Media: Communication, Research, and Technology*. Beverly Hills, CA: Sage. pp. 33–54.

Rice, Ronald E. and Williams, Frederick (1984) 'Theories old and new: the study of new media', in R.E. Rice (ed.), *The New Media: Communication, Research, and Technology*. Beverly Hills, CA: Sage. pp. 55–80.

Romiszowski, Alexander J. (1993) 'Developing interactive multimedia courseware and networks: some current issues', in C. Latchem, J. Williamson and L. Henderson-Lancett (eds), *Interactive Multimedia: Practice and Purpose*. London: Kogan Page. pp. 57–78.

Ruben, B.D. (1975) 'Intrapersonal, interpersonal, and mass communication processes in individual and multi-person systems', in B.D. Ruben and J.Y. Kim (eds), *General Systems Theory and Human Communication*. Rochelle Park, NY: Hayden. pp. 164–90.

Salzman, Harold and Rosenthal, Stephen R. (1994) *Software by Design: Shaping Technology and the Workplace*. New York: Oxford University Press.

Sayre, Jeanette (1939) 'Progress in radio fan-mail analysis', *Public Opinion Quarterly*, 3 (2): 272–8.

Schaffer, Lemuel C. and Hannafin, Michael J. (1986) 'The effects of progressive interactivity in learning from interactive video', *Educational Communication and Technology*, 34 (2): 89–96.

Schmitz, Joseph and Fulk, Janet (1991) 'Organizational colleagues, media richness, and electronic mail: a test of the social influence model of technology use', *Communication Research*, 18 (4): 487–523.

Schneiderman, Ben (1998) *Designing the User Interface: Strategies for Effective Human–Computer Interaction*, 3rd edn. Reading, MA: Addison-Wesley.

Schudson, Michael (1978) 'The ideal of conversation in the study of mass media', *Communication Research*, 5 (3): 320–9.

Schultz, Tanjev (1999) 'Interactive options in online journalism: a content analysis of 100 US newspapers', *Journal of Computer Mediated Communication*,

5 (1). Available online: http://www.ascusc.org/jcmc/vol5/issue1/schultz.html

Schultz, Tanjev (2000) 'Mass media and the concept of interactivity: an exploratory study of online forums and reader e-mail', *Media, Culture & Society*, 22 (2): 205–21.

Shaw, Thomas, Aranson, Karl and Belardo, Salvatore (1993) 'The effects of computer mediated interactivity on idea generation: an experimental investigation', *IEEE Transactions on Systems, Man and Cybernetics*, 23 (3): 737–45.

Sherblom, John (1988) 'Direction, function, and signature in electronic mail', *Journal of Business Communication*, 25 (4): 39–54.

Shimanoff, Susan B. (1988) 'Group interaction via communication rules', in R.S. Cathcart and L.A. Samover (eds), *Small Group Communication: A Reader*, 5th edn. Dubuque, IA: Brown. pp. 50–64.

Short, John, Williams, Ederyn and Christie, Bruce (1976) *The Social Psychology of Telecommunications*. London: Wiley.

Siegel, Jane, Dubrovsky, Vitaly, Kiesler, Sara and McGuire, Timothy W. (1986) 'Group processes in computer-mediated communication', *Organizational Behavior and Human Decision Processes*, 37: 157–87.

Simms, R. (1997) 'Interactivity: a forgotten art?', *Computers in Human Behavior*, 13: 157–80.

Smethers, Steven (1998) 'Cyberspace in the curricula: new legal and ethical issues', *Journalism & Mass Communication Educator*, 53 (4): 15–23.

Smulyan, Susan (1994) *Selling Radio: the Commercialization of American Broadcasting, 1920–1934*. Washington, DC: Smithsonian Institution Press.

Sproull, Lee and Kiesler, Sara (1986) 'Reducing social context cues: electronic mail in organizational communication', *Management Science*, 32 (11): 1492–512.

Standage, Tom (1998) *The Victorian Internet*. New York: Walker.

Steuer, Jonathan (1992) 'Defining virtual reality: dimensions determining telepresence', *Journal of Communication*, 42 (4): 73–93.

Straubhaar, Joseph and LaRose, Robert (1996) *Communications Media in the Information Society*. Belmont, CA: Wadsworth.

Straus, Susan G. and McGrath, Joseph E. (1994) 'Does the medium matter? The interaction of task type and technology on group performance and member reactions', *Journal of Applied Psychology*, 79 (1): 87–97.

Street, Richard L. Jr and Rimal, Rajiv N. (1997) 'Health promotion and interactive technology: a conceptual foundation', in R.L. Street, W.R. Gold and T. Manning (eds), *Health Promotion and Interactive Technology*. Mahwah, NJ: Erlbaum. pp. 1–18.

Stromer-Galley, Jennifer (2000) 'Online interaction and why candidates avoid it', *Journal of Communication*, 50 (4): 111–32.

Stromer-Galley, Jennifer and Foot, Kirsten A. (2000) 'Citizens, campaigns, and online interactivity', Paper presented at the International Communication Association Annual Conference, Acapulco, Mexico, 1–5 June.

Sundar, S. Shyam, Narayan, Sunetra, Obregon, Rafael and Uppal, Charu (1998) 'Does web advertising work? Memory for print vs. online media', *Journalism & Mass Communication Quarterly*, 75 (4): 822–35.

Sundar, S. Shyam, Brown, Justin and Kalyanaraman, Sriam (1999) 'Reactivity vs. interactivity: impression formation effects of message contingency in political websites'. Paper presented at the International Communication Association Annual Conference, San Francisco, CA, 27–31 May.

Szuprowicz, Bohdan O. (1995) *Multimedia Networking*. New York: McGraw-Hill.

Tan, William and Nguyen, Ann (1993) 'Lifecycle costing models for interactive multimedia systems', in C. Latchem, J. Williamson and L. Henderson-Lancett (eds), *Interactive Multimedia: Practice and Purpose*. London: Kogan Page. pp. 151–64.

Tremayne, Mark and Dunwoody, Sharon (2001) 'Interactivity, information processing, and learning on the World Wide Web', *Science Communication*, 23 (2): 111–34.

Trevino, Linda Klebe and Webster, Jane (1992) 'Flow in computer-mediated communication: electronic mail and voice mail evaluation and impacts', *Communication Research*, 19 (5): 539–73.

Trevino, Linda Klebe, Lengel, Robert H. and Daft, Richard L. (1987) 'Media symbolism, media richness, and media choice in organizations: a symbolic interactionist perspective', *Communication Research*, 14 (5): 553–74.

Trevino, Linda Klebe, Daft, Richard L. and Lengel, Robert H. (1990) 'Understanding managers' media choices: a symbolic interactionist perspective', in J. Fulk and C. Steinfeld (eds), *Organizations and Communication Technology*. Newbury Park, CA: Sage. pp. 71–94.

Tucker, Richard N. (1990) 'Transitions in European education', in R.N. Tucker (ed.), *The Interactive Learning Revolution: Multimedia in Education and Training*. London: Kogan Page. pp. 34–45.

Turing, A.M. (1956) 'Can a machine think?', in J.R. Newman (ed.), *Machines, Music, and Puzzles*. New York: Simon & Schuster. pp. 2099–123.

Turow, Joseph (1974) 'Talk show radio as interpersonal communication', *Journal of Broadcasting*, 18 (2): 171–9.

Turow, Joseph (1977) 'Another view of "citizen feedback" to the mass media', *Public Opinion Quarterly*, 41 (4): 534–43.

Valacich, Joseph S., Paranka, David, George, Joey F. and Nunamaker, J.F. Jr (1993) 'Communication concurrency and the new media: a new dimension for media richness', *Communication Research*, 20 (2): 249–76.

Vasarhelyi, Miklos Antal (1977) 'Man–machine planning systems: a cognitive style examination of interactive decision making', *Journal of Accounting Research*, 15 (1): 138–53.

Walther, Joseph B. (1992) 'Interpersonal effects in computer-mediated interaction: a relational perspective', *Communication Research*, 19 (1): 52–90.

Walther, Joseph B. (1994) 'Anticipated ongoing interaction versus channel effects on relational communication in computer-mediated interaction', *Human Communication Research*, 20 (4): 473–501.

Walther, Joseph B. (1995) 'Relational aspects of computer-mediated communication: experimental observations over time in computer-mediated interaction', *Organization Science*, 6 (2): 186–203.

Walther, Joseph B. (1996) 'Computer-mediated communication: impersonal, interpersonal, and hyperpersonal interaction', *Communication Research*, 23 (1): 3–43.

Walther, Joseph B. and Burgoon, Judee K. (1992) 'Relational communication in computer-mediated interaction', *Human Communication Research*, 19 (1): 50–88.

Walther, Joseph B., Anderson, Jeffrey F. and Park, David W. (1994) 'Interpersonal effects in computer-mediated interaction: a meta-analysis of social and antisocial communication', *Communication Research*, 21 (4): 460–87.

Webster, Jane and Martocchio, Joseph J. (1992) 'Microcomputer playfulness: development of a measure with workplace implications', *MIS Quarterly*, 16 (2): 201–26.

Wiener, Norbert (1948) *Cybernetics: Or Control and Communication in the Animal and the Machine*. Cambridge, MA: Technology Press.

Williams, Frederick, Rice, Ronald E. and Rogers, Everett M. (1988) *Research Methods and the New Media*. New York: Free Press.

Williams, Frederick, Strover, Sharon and Grant, August E. (1994) 'Social aspects of new media technologies', in J. Bryant and D. Zillman (eds), *Media Effects: Advances in Theory and Research*. Hillsdale, NJ: Erlbaum. pp. 463–82.

Wish, Myron, Deutsch, Morton and Kaplan, Susan J. (1976) 'Perceived dimensions of interpersonal relations', *Journal of Personality and Social Psychology*, 33 (4): 409–20.

Wu, Guohua (1999) 'Perceived interactivity and attitude toward website'. Paper presented at the American Academy of Advertising Annual Conference, Albuquerque, NM, March.

Wurtzel, Alan H. and Turner, Colin (1977) 'What missing the telephone means', *Journal of Communication*, 27 (2): 48–57.

Xie, Hong (2000) 'Shifts of interactive intentions and information-seeking strategies in interactive information retrieval', *Journal of the American Society for Information Science*, 51 (9): 841–57.

Yom, Sue Son (1996) 'The Internet and the future of minority health', *Journal of the American Medical Association*, 275 (9): 735.

Zack, Michael H. (1993) 'Interactivity and communication mode choice in ongoing management groups', *Information Systems Research*, 4 (3): 207–39.

Zeltzer, David (1992) 'Autonomy, interaction, and presence', *Teleoperators and Virtual Environments*, 1 (1): 127–32.

11

How to Infrastructure

SUSAN LEIGH STAR AND GEOFFREY C. BOWKER

Resources appear, too, as shared visions of the possible and acceptable dreams of the innovative, as techniques, knowledge, know-how, and the institutions for learning these things. Infrastructure in these terms is a dense interwoven fabric that is, at the same time, dynamic, thoroughly ecological, even fragile.

(Bucciarelli, 1994: 131)

The central topic of this chapter is the infrastructure that subtends new media: overwhelmingly for our purposes this means the Internet in all its guises. We seek to explore the development and design of infrastructure; our main argument will be that a social and theoretical understanding of infrastructure is key to the design of new media applications in our highly networked, information convergent society.

When we think of infrastructure in a common-sense way, infrastructure is that which runs 'underneath' actual structures – railroad tracks, city plumbing and sewage, electricity, roads and highways, cable wires that connect to the broadcast grid and bring pictures to our TVs. It is that upon which something else rides, or works, a platform of sorts. This common-sense definition begins to unravel when we populate the picture, and begin to look at multiple, overlapping and perhaps contradictory infrastructural arrangements. For the railroad engineer, the rails are only infrastructure when she or he is a passenger. Almost anyone can flip an electric switch, for a variety of purposes. When the

switch fails, we are forced to look more deeply into the cause: first check the light bulb, then the other appliances on the same circuit, then look at the circuit breaker box, then look down the block to see if it is a power outage in the neighbourhood or city, and lastly, depending on one's home repair skills, consider calling an electrician. Finally, increasingly many of us are faced with infrastructures, designed by one group, that may not work for us. For instance, someone in a wheelchair appreciates the tiny (and not so tiny) barriers that are considered 'wheelchair accessible' by the able-bodied. Four steps can be a mountain if the specific conditions of usability are overlooked. So we have three separate themes here:

1 the moving target of infrastructure, from easy-to-use black box to active topic of work and research;
2 the breakdown of infrastructure that opens the taken-for-granted;
3 the relative usefulness of infrastructure for different populations.

One thing that unites each of these strands is the notion that infrastructure is not absolute, but relative to working conditions. It never stands apart from the people who design, maintain and use it. Its designers try to make it as invisible as possible, while leaving pointers to make it visible when it needs to be repaired or remapped. It is tricky to study for this reason.

Perhaps for these reasons, infrastructure is an often neglected aspect of communication studies, except in areas such as the specific regulation of an infrastructure, or the history of one type (such as the telephone, the automobile or the Internet). Both such kinds of studies are invaluable, and certainly central to the discipline of communication. Communication infrastructures include printing, telegraph, radio, fax, television, the Internet and the Web, and movie production and distribution. Under some circumstances the human body becomes infrastructure, such as in the study of face-to-face conversations. Interestingly, for example in the study of body language, human emotions and situations are the infrastructure, and the targets of study are facial and body muscles, posture and proximity. This chapter outlines several facets of importance to theory and research on the design, development and use of infrastructure. We will also refer to some policy articles for purely policy-related infrastructure issues, such as the regulation of telecommunications or the standards setting process for the Internet.

Given the above qualifications, what then are we left with that is infrastructure? Can it be anything? Like many concepts in communication, the relational quality of infrastructure talks about that which is between – between people, mediated by tools, and emergent (Jewett and Kling, 1991). Like the term 'communication' itself, and others such as 'meaning', 'audience', 'free speech', or 'regulation', the exact sense of the term 'infrastructure' and its 'betweenness' are both theoretical and empirical questions.

We will work from Star and Ruhleder's (1996) definition of the salient features of infrastructure in order to bound and clarify the term.

- *Embeddedness* Infrastructure is sunk into, inside of, other structures, social arrangements and technologies.
- *Transparency* Infrastructure is transparent to use, in the sense that it does not have to be reinvented each time or assembled for each task, but invisibly supports those tasks.
- *Reach or scope* This may be either spatial or temporal: infrastructure has reach beyond a single event or one-site practice.

- *Learned as part of membership* The taken-for-grantedness of artifacts and organizational arrangements is a *sine qua non* of membership in a community of practice (Lave and Wenger, 1991; Star and Ruhleder, 1996). Strangers and outsiders encounter infrastructure as a target object to be learned about. New participants acquire a naturalized familiarity with its objects as they become members.
- *Links with conventions of practice* Infrastructure both shapes and is shaped by the conventions of a community of practice, e.g. the ways that cycles of day–night work are affected by and affect electrical power rates and needs. Generations of typists have learned the QWERTY keyboard; its limitations are inherited by the computer keyboard and thence by the design of today's computer furniture (Becker, 1982).
- *Embodiment of standards* Modified by scope and often by conflicting conventions, infrastructure takes on transparency by plugging into other infrastructures and tools in a standardized fashion.
- *Built on an installed base* Infrastructure does not grow *de novo*; it wrestles with the inertia of the installed base and inherits strengths and limitations from that base. Optical fibres run along old railroad lines; new systems are designed for backward compatibility; and failing to account for these constraints may be fatal or distorting to new development processes (Monteiro and Hanseth, 1996; Schmidt and Werle, 1998).
- *Becomes visible upon breakdown* The normally invisible quality of working infrastructure becomes visible when it breaks: the server is down, the bridge washes out, there is a power blackout. Even when there are back-up mechanisms or procedures, their existence further highlights the now visible infrastructure.

Something that was once an object of development and design becomes sunk into infrastructure over time. Therefore a historical, archaeological approach to the development of an infrastructure like the Internet needs complementary sociological, regulatory and technical studies.

SOCIOHISTORICAL ANALYSES OF INFRASTRUCTURE

Much current work in the sociohistorical analysis of infrastructure has derived from the field of science and technology studies (STS). This is unsurprising, since over the past 50 years, science has been at the forefront of the testing and implementation of new information infrastructures – from the early days of the Internet to the visions of e-science (Europe) and cyberinfrastructure (USA) today. Latour and Woolgar's *Laboratory Life* (1979) helped open a window to a more qualitative, intensively observational set of studies of scientific work and practice. These authors drew particular attention to the role of the scientists' information infrastructure (articles, graphs, pieces of paper) in their work. By the 1990s, STS researchers began to turn their attention to the design and use of computing and information technologies (see e.g. Star, 1995). Woolgar has called this the 'technical turn' in STS. Using many of the same techniques as had laboratory studies of science, these researchers studied (and in some cases, worked in partnership with) the design, use, manufacture and distribution of information technology (Collins and Kusch, 1998; Downey and Lucena, 1994; Henderson, 1999; to name just a few).[1] A particularly exciting field now is that of the 'value sensitive design' of infrastructure (Friedman et al., forthcoming; Proceedings of the Participatory Design Conferences (PDC), held in conjunction with the larger ACM Computer-supported Cooperative Work conferences each year).

The combination of the technical turn and studies of materials brought infrastructure to the fore in STS (see e.g. Bowker, 2005; Latour and Hernant, 1999; Star and Ruhleder, 1996). The ethnographic eye that helped reveal the inner workings of science or technology research and development was helpful in interpreting infrastructure. Arguments about standardization, selection and maintenance of tools, and the right materials for the job of knowledge production have slowly come into centre stage via this synthesis (Clarke and Fujimura, 1992; Lampland and Star,

forthcoming). Along with this has come a rediscovery of some of the tools germane to cognate disciplines which had previously analysed material culture and the built environment. These have included, *inter alia*, fields such as architecture (where scholars sometimes read the built environment as a kind of text – cf the blend of organization theory and architecture in Boland and Collopy, 2004), literary theory (especially those aspects of literary theory that help surface hidden assumptions and narrative structure), social geography (where the values and biases inherent in such tools as maps are a lively topic of inquiry) and information science (Bowker and Star, 1999; *Library Trends*, 1998).

Thomas Hughes (1983), in his historical discussion of the rise of electricity networks in Europe and the United States, developed a suite of tools for analysing the development and design of infrastructure. He drew attention to the importance of *reverse salients* – technological, social or political sticking points which can slow the development of an infrastructure. Crucially, he argued that the solution to a reverse salient does not have to be from the same register as the problem: there might be a political solution to a technical problem and so forth (cf. Latour, 1996). Thus, for example, the technical problem of low-bandwidth communications in e-mail was partially solved by the social solution of using a complex set of 'emoticons' to provide a layering of the flat ASCII text. The design implication here is that there is no possible *a priori* assignation of different tasks to different bodies of specialists in the design of communication infrastructures for new media: the emergent infrastructure itself represents one of a number of possible distributions of tasks and properties between hardware, software and people (see Tanenbaum, 1996 for a full discussion of the variety of possible representations of the Internet, with different distributions between them).

Hughes (1983) further pointed out that the early electricity networks drew off skills developed in the design of gas networks before them and canals before that: each generation of engineers imports solutions from one infrastructure to the next. This trend has continued with the current design of the Web. This has both positive and negative consequences. On the positive side, it points to the fact that skills can be usefully transferred from one medium to the next. However, the negative side is that this can lead to a lack of imagination. Paul David (1995; cf. Landauer, 1995) has written about the 'productivity paradox' that saw productivity decline with the introduction of the electric dynamo in factories in the nineteenth century and with the introduction of the computer in organizations in the twentieth. He makes the strong point that it was not until ways of thinking through the new technology emerged that improvements occurred: the dynamo made a bad steam engine, the computer a bad typewriter, and so on. This draws attention to the importance of the metaphors that we use to think through technology: Mark Stefik (1996) speaks of a set of 'archetypes' that have been used to drive design on the Internet. It is important to recognize that these archetypes might also be traps (Woolgar, 2002).

David's argument works because infrastructures don't just exist by themselves – they are embedded in organizations of many kinds. Bowker (1994b) has developed the concept of infrastructural inversion to describe the fact that historical changes frequently ascribed to some spectacular product of an age are frequently more a feature of an infrastructure permitting the development of that product. Thus the rise of computing machinery in the late nineteenth century was consequent on (not causative of) changes in office organization; the twin rise of life expectancy and the medical profession at the same time was consequent on (not causative of) the development of water and sanitation infrastructures. Operating this inversion is a struggle against the tendency of infrastructure to disappear (except when breaking down). It means learning to look closely at technologies and arrangements which, by design and by habit, tend to fade into the woodwork (sometimes literally!). Infrastructural inversion foregrounds these normally invisible Lilliputian threads, and furthermore gives them causal prominence in many areas normally attributed to heroic actors, social movements or cultural mores. This inversion is similar to the argument made by Becker in his book *Art Worlds* (1982). Most history and social analysis of art has neglected the details of infrastructure within which communities of artistic practice emerge, instead focusing on aesthetics as devoid from these issues. Becker's inversion examines the conventions and constraints of the material artistic infrastructure, and its ramifications. For example, the convention of musical concerts lasting about two hours ramifies throughout the producing organization. Parking attendants, unions, ticket takers and theatre rentals are arranged in cascading dependence on this interval of time. An eight-hour musical piece, which is occasionally written, means rearranging all of these expectations – which in turn is so expensive that such productions are rare. Or paintings are about the size, usually, that will hang comfortably on a wall. They are also the size that fits rolls of canvas, the skills of framers, and the very doorways of museums and galleries. These constraints are mutable only at great cost, and artists must always consider them before violating them. The infrastructure designer must always be aware of the multiple sets of contexts her work impinges on. Frequently a technical innovation must be accompanied by an organizational innovation in order to work: the design of sociotechnical systems engages both the technologist and the organization theorist.

What comes through from a set of key texts (Bud-Frierman, 1994; Clarke and Fujimura, 1992; Fischer, 1992; Friedlander, 1995; Rosenberg, 1982) is that analysing infrastructure means problematizing this relationship between background and foreground. A given infrastructure may have become transparent, but a number of significant political, ethical and social choices have without doubt been folded into its development – and this background needs to be understood if we are to produce thoughtful analyses of the nature of infrastructural work. For example, a road network may be designed politically to prevent access by the poor to a given facility (Davis, 1997 makes this point about SeaWorld in San Diego; Winner, 1986 about beach access in New York). Equally, a highly standardized instrument like the census form folds in strong claims about the nature and importance of a particular set of ethnic categories (Bowker and Star, 1999). Web designers frequently wrap choices about the kind of visitor they want into their website (few sites are designed with access for the blind, say, since HTML is written in such a way that it does not force designers to produce alternative text for every image they produce); and complex sites often require a high-speed connection, so the less wealthy user with a slow modem will be excluded by his or her own understandable impatience.

HOW INFRASTRUCTURE HAPPENS

Both standardization and classification are essential to the development of working infra-structures. Work done on standards commit-tees and in setting up classification schemes is frequently overlooked in social and political analyses of infrastructure, and yet it is of crucial importance. In this section, we will review work that explores these issues.

There is no question that in the develop-ment of large-scale information infrastruc-tures, we need standards. In a sense this is a trivial observation: strings of bits travelling along wires are meaningless unless there is a shared set of handshakes among the various media they pass through. An e-mail message is typically broken up into regular size chunks, and then wrapped in various 'envelopes', each of which represents a different layer of the infrastructure. A given message might be encoded using the MIME (multipurpose Internet mail extensions protocol): this will allow various other mail programs to read it. It might then be chunked into smaller parts, each of which is wrapped in an envelope designat-ing its ultimate address and its order in the message. This envelope will be further wrapped in an envelope telling it how to enter the Internet. It will then quite possibly be wrapped in further envelopes telling it how to change from a configuration of electrons on a wire to a radio message beamed to a satellite and back

down again (Hurley and Keller, 1999; Tanenbaum, 1996). Each envelope is progres-sively opened at the end, and the original message reassembled from its contingent parts then appears 'transparently' on your desktop. It is the standards that let this happen.

One observation that we can make at once is that it is standards all the way down: each layer of infrastructure requires its own set of stan-dards. We might also say that it is standard all the way up. There is no simple break point at which one can say that communication proto-cols stop and technical standards start. As a thought experiment, let us take the example of a scientific paper. I write a paper about palaeoecology for the journal *Science*. I know that my immediate audience will not be leading-edge palaeoecologists, but a wider community who know only a little about Devonian plant communities. So I wrap the kernel in an introduction and conclusion that discuss in general terms the nature and signif-icance of my findings. A journalist might well write a more popular piece for the 'Perspectives' section which will point to my paper. If this is my first paper for *Science* then I will probably go through quite a complex set of negotiations through the peer review process in order to ensure the correct 'handshake' between my message and its audience: is it written at the right level, have I used the right tone of authority, and so forth. Yates (1989) has writ-ten about similar sets of standards/protocols that arose with the development of office memoranda in the nineteenth century; she and Orlikowski have observed similar effects in the development of e-mail genres (Orlikowski et al., 1993). I then need to be sure that the right set of economic agreements has been put into place so that my paper can be found on the Web by anyone at any time (Kahin and Keller, 1997).

This common vision of disciplinary, eco-nomic and network protocols serves the pur-pose of highlighting a central fact about infrastructures. It is not just the bits and bytes that get hustled into standard form in order for the technical infrastructure to work. People's discursive and work practices get hustled into standard form as well. Working infrastructures standardize both people and machines. A further example will clarify this point. In order for the large-scale states of the nineteenth century to operate efficiently and effectively, the new science of statistics (of the same etymological root as the word 'state') was developed. People were sorted into categories, and a series of information technologies was put into place to provide an infrastructure to government work (regular ten-year censuses; special tables and printers; by the end of the nineteenth century, punch card machines for faster processing of results). These standardized categories (male, African-American, professional, etc.) thus spawned their own set of technical standards (80-column sheets – later transferred to 80-column punch cards and computer screens). They also spawned their own set of standardized people. As Alain Desrosières and Laurent Thévenot (1988) note, different categories for professional works in the French, German and British censuses led to the creation of very different social structures and government programmes around them. Early in the nineteenth century, the differences between professionals in one country or the other was minimal. By the end of the century these differences had become entrenched and reified: unions had formed around them, informal dress codes had been adopted and so forth.

At both the technical and the social level, there is no guarantee that the best set of standards will win.[2] The process of the creation of standards for infrastructures is a long, tortuous, contingent one. The best-known stories here are the adoption of the QWERTY keyboard (good for its time in preventing keys jamming in manual typewriters; counterproductive now for most in that it puts most of the work onto the left hand, a hardship for many, but one appreciated by the southpaws (left-handers) among us, but so entrenched that there is no end in sight for it; David, 1986); the victory of the VHS standard over the technically superior Betamax standard; the victory of DOS and its successors over superior operating systems.

So why does the best standard not always win? In an infrastructure you are never alone: no node is an island. Suppose there are 500

users of DOS to every one user of a Macintosh. A software developer has less motivation to write software for Macs, which have a much smaller potential user base. So the strong get stronger. Going down one level into the infrastructure, companies are more likely to write APIs (application program interfaces – to allow communication between one program and another) for interoperation between a new program and an industry standard one than a rarely used one. More generally put, a new kind of economic logic has developed around the network infrastructures that have been created over the past 200 years – the logic of 'network externalities' (David, 1986; David and Greenstein, 1990; David and Rothwell, 1994; Mirowski, 2004). The logic runs as follows. If a person buys a telephone for $50 and there are only five people on the network, then owning a telephone is not worth very much, even if the five are fast friends. If 5000 more people buy telephones then the first five have not had to lay out another cent, but their phones are suddenly much more valuable. This situation describes positive externalities. *De facto* standards (such as DOS, QWERTY, etc.) gain and hold on to their position largely through the development of positive externalities. The design lesson here is that integration with existing programs is key to the success of new infrastructural tools.

Arguably some of the most far-reaching decisions of the past 50 years have been taken by standards setting bodies – although one does not find a 'standards' section of the bookshop alongside 'history' and 'new age'. Consider, for example, the political and social implications of the 'open source' movement. This movement has a long history, running deep into the origin of the Internet, proclaiming the democratic and liberatory value of freely sharing software code. The Internet, indeed, was cobbled together out of a set of freely distributed software standards. The open source movement has been seen as running counter to the dominance of large centralized industries: the argument goes that it puts power over the media back into the hands of the people in a way that might truly transform capitalist society (Poster, 1995). This promise of cyberdemocracy is integrally social, political and technical: it is promoted in part through centrally funded programmes in digital government and mobile government. While there is much talk of an 'information revolution' (though be it noted there has been fairly regular talk of the same since the 1830s; Bowker, 1994a), there is not enough of the ways in which people and communities are in part constituted by the new infrastructure. One important example here is the development of patient support groups on the Internet – allowing sufferers of a rare illness to share moral support, information about new drugs and medical trials and folk treatments. Such patient communities would have been impossible in the past in the case of very rare diseases; certainly, even for more common diseases, they permit patients from rural areas access to the dense information networks of the city. Groups such as these frequently organize face-to-face meetings after they have 'met' on the Internet (Baym, 2000).

There are many models for information infrastructures. The Internet itself can be cut up conceptually a number of different ways. There is over time and between models a distribution of properties between hardware, software and people. Thus one can get two computers 'talking' to each other by running a dedicated line between them or by preempting a given physical circuit (hardware solutions) or by creating a 'virtual circuit' (software solution) which runs over multiple different physical circuits. Or finally you can still (and this is the fastest way of getting terabits of data from San Francisco to LA) put a hard disk in a truck and drive it down (Tanenbaum, 1996). Each kind of circuit is made up of a different stable configuration of wires, bits and people, but they are all (as far as the infrastructure itself is concerned) interchangeable. One can think of standards in the infrastructure as the tools for stabilizing these configurations. There is a continuum of strategies for standards setting. At the one end of the spectrum is the strategy of one standard fits all. This can be imposed by government fiat (for example the Navy's failed attempt to impose ADA as the sole programming language for

their applications) or can take the form of an emergent monopoly (for example, Microsoft Windows/NT). At the other end of the spectrum is the 'let a thousand standards bloom' model. In such a case, one concentrates on producing interfaces such as APIs between programs and on such standards as the ANSI/NISO Z39.50 information retrieval protocol. Z39.50 is a standard that has been developed for being able to make a single enquiry over multiple databases: it has been very widely adopted in the library world. You can use whatever database program you wish to make your bibliographic database with, provided that the program itself subscribes to the standard. This means in essence that certain key fields like 'author', 'title' and 'keyword' will be defined in the database. Now, instead of having to load up multiple different database programs in order to search over many databases (a challenge of significance well beyond the library community, as large-scale heterogeneous datasets are coming into centre stage in a number of scientific and cultural fields) one can frame a single query using the Z39.50 standard and have your results returned seamlessly from many different sources. One metaphor about these two extremes is that the former is the 'colonial' model of infrastructure development where the latter is the 'democratic' model. There is some truth to the implied claim that one's political philosophy will determine one's choice; and there is some solace for democrats in the observation that with the development of the Internet the latter has almost invariably won out: most Internet standards have been cobbled together in such a way that they permit maximal flexibility and heterogeneity. Thus, for example, if one tracks the emergence and deployment of collaborative computing, one finds that large-scale stand-alone programs have done much worse than less powerful programs that permit easy integration with one's other programs and with the Internet (Star and Ruhleder, 1996).

There are utopian visions that when we get all the standards in place, there will be seamless access to the world's store of information from any place on the planet. The World Brain project (http://www.imagination-engines.com/

world.htm), for example, claims that it is developing 'not a mere kitten brain, not an on-line library, but a true synthetic genius that will deliver us from war, poverty, and suffering'; compare also the utopian vision of the Principia Cybernetica (http://pespmc1.vub.ac.be). Gregory (2000) has called such efforts 'incomplete utopian projects'. It is the incompleteness that we must turn to here: they always remain incomplete; they are always outnumbered, always outgunned by the forces against them. The World Brain, for example, echoes H.G. Wells' long-forgotten project of the same name, announced just as optimistically some 60 years earlier: 'An immense, an ever-increasing wealth of knowledge is scattered about the world today, a wealth of knowledge and suggestion that – systematically ordered and generally disseminated – would probably give this giant vision and direction and suffice to solve all the mighty difficulties of our age' (1938: 66–7, cited in Rayward, 1999).

The reason for pointing to these persistent failures is that they reflect some key features of infrastructures. They show that infrastructural development and maintenance require work, a relatively stable technology and communication. The work side is frequently overlooked. Consider the claim in the 1920s that with the advent of microfiche, the end of the book was nigh: everyone would have their own personal libraries; we would no longer need to waste vast amounts of natural resources on producing paper; all the largest library would need would be a few rooms and a set of microfiche readers (Abbott, 1988). A possible vision, and one that we should not discount just because it did not happen; MacKenzie (1990) reminds us that technological roads not taken can appear futile – for example, anyone who has used a microfiche reader will attest that it's a most uncomfortable experience – whereas if the same resources had gone into the failure as into the successful technology, it probably could have been a winner. However, the microfiche dream, like the universal digital library, runs up against the problem that someone has to sit there and do the necessary photography/scanning; and this takes a huge amount of time and resources. It is easy enough to develop a

potentially revolutionary technology; it is extremely hard to implement it.

Further, one needs a relatively stable technology. If one thinks of some of the great infrastructural technologies of the past (gas, electric, sewage and so forth) one can see that once the infrastructure is put into place it tends to have a long life. Electrical wiring from before World War II is still in use in many households; in major cities there is frequently no good map of sewage pipes, since their origin goes too far back in time. The Internet is only virtually stable – through the mediation of a set of relatively stable protocols: for this reason, Edwards (1998) suggests that we call it an Internetwork technology rather than a Hughesian (Hughes, 1983) network technology such as the electricity network. However, there is nothing to guarantee the stability of vast datasets. At the turn of the twentieth century, Otlet developed a scheme for a universal library which would work by providing automatic electromechanical access to extremely well-catalogued microfiches, which could link between each other (Rayward, 1975). All the world's knowledge would be put onto these fiches; his vision was a precursor to today's hypertext. He made huge strides in developing this system (though he only had the person power to achieve a minuscule fraction of his goal). However, within 40 years, with the development of computer memory, his whole enterprise was effectively doomed to languish as it does today in boxes in a basement. Why retrieve information electromechanically using levers and gears when you can call it up at the speed of light from a computer? Much the same can be said of Bush's never realized but inspirational vision of the Memex – an electromechanical precursor to the workstation (Bush et al., 1991). Large databases from the early days of the computer revolution are now completely lost. Who now reads punch cards – a technology whose first major use in this country was to deal with the massive datasets of the 1890 census, and which dominated information storage and handling for some 70 years? Closer to the present day, the 'electronic medical record' has been announced every few years since the 1960s – and yet it has not been globally attained. Changes in database architecture, storage capabilities of computers and ingrained organizational practices have rendered it a chimera. The development of stable standards together with due attention being paid to backwards compatibility provide in principle a fix to these problems. It can all unravel very easily, though. The bottom line is that no storage medium is permanent (CDs will not last anywhere near as long as books printed on acid-free paper) – so that our emergent information infrastructure will require a continued maintenance effort to keep data accessible and usable as it passes from one storage medium to another and is analysed by one generation of database technology to the next.

Finally, in order to really build an information infrastructure, you need to pay close attention to issues of communication. We can parse this partly as the problem of reliable metadata. Metadata ('data about data': Michener et al., 1997) is the technical term for all the information that a single piece of data out there on the Internet can carry with it in order to provide sufficient context for another user to be able to first locate it and then use it. The most widespread metadata standards are the Dublin Core, developed for library applications; and the Federal Geographic Data Committee (FGDC: http://www.fgdc.gov) standard developed for geographical information systems. If everyone can agree to standard names for certain kinds of data, then one can easily search for, say, authors over multiple databases. We have already seen this. Philosophically, however, metadata open up into some far deeper problems. Take the example of biodiversity science. It is generally agreed that if we want to preserve a decent proportion of animal and floral life from the current great extinction event (one of six since the origin of life on this planet) then policy-makers need the best possible information about the current species size and distribution, as well as the ability to model the effect of potential and current environmental changes. In order to do this, you need to be able to bring together data from many different scientific disciplines using many different information technologies (from paper to supercomputer). Now imagine that I am measuring lake water acidity in the Midwest in order to see if there are any effects from recent acid rain. I might be lucky and come across a very large dataset going back 80 or 100 years and giving lake water acidity levels at one-year intervals. However, this might well not be enough for me to actually use the data. It makes quite a difference if the measurement was taken immediately at the lake or later, when the samples were brought back to the laboratory: there will be different amounts of dissolved carbon dioxide in the sample. And as it happens, it makes a difference which technology of measurement I use: a new technology can provide a consistent jump in values for the same sample (see Bowker, 2000 for a detailed discussion of this and related cases of metadata problems). Now to make matters worse, I as a scientist am no expert in measuring lake water; I am an expert modeller, and I just want some data to plug into my model. But the point is that there is no such thing as pure data. You always have to know some context. And as you develop metadata standards you always need to think about how much information you need to give in order to make your information maximally useful over time. And here we circle back to the first difficulty with developing an information infrastructure: the more information that you provide in order to make the data useful to the widest community and over the longest time, the more work you have to do. Yet empirical studies have shown time and again that people will not see it as a good use of their time to preserve information about their data beyond what is necessary to guarantee its immediate usefulness. Thus Fagot-Largeault (1989) describes the medical culture of producing quick and easy diagnoses on death certificates in order to meet the administrative need and free time to get onto the next (live) patient.

So standards are necessary – from social protocols down to wiring size. Indeed, when you foreground the infrastructure of your lives, you will see that you encounter thousands of standards in a single day. However, as we have already seen, the development and maintenance of standards are complex ethical and philosophical problems: ethical since decisions taken at the stage of development standards can have enormous implications for user communities; and philosophical since standards frequently deal with very basic ways of splitting up the world (the base categories of Z39.50 sketch out an interestingly restricted ontology of 'authorship', for example). Further, standards implementation requires a vast amount of resources. Standards undergird our potential for action in the world, both political and scientific; they make the infrastructure possible.

Representation in a database can be a key means for a group or profession to gain recognition – yet there are frequently costs involved. For instance, a group of nurses in Iowa developed a Nursing Interventions Classification in order to carve out a place in hospital information systems for nursing work. However, they recognized while doing this that the scheme put them in danger both of being stripped of some of their work ('it doesn't take a skilled professional to do this') and of losing some of the essence of their contribution in the scheme (it is hard to code for 'humour', for example) (Bowker and Star, 1999). Such cases have proliferated with the development of interlocking large-scale information infrastructures.[3]

The installed base of a particular infrastructure carries huge inertia. And yet infrastructures do change over time, sometimes transforming remarkably rapidly, sometimes apparently discontinuously (a country going from postal communication to cellular phones without passing through landlines, for example). This is made more complicated by the ways in which the built environment (libraries, schools, offices, homes, traffic lights, airports, hospitals) is increasingly imbricated with information technologies of every sort (Taylor and van Every, 1993, 2000). These include sensors, databases, digital cameras, networked PCs and all forms of display units. A deeper sense of this comes with the realization that these forms of information technology are increasingly *integrated* (they can share information via protocols and standards) and *convergent* (they are delivered through a single point, such as web pages embedded in a cellular telephone,

where one's plane schedule for a connecting flight may be checked while on board the current flight). In some cases, this may result in serious privacy and ethical boundaries. An example of this would be the sale of a hospital to a pharmaceutical company, along with its records; the pharmaceutical company might use the list of patients and their illnesses to direct mail niche markets based on, for example, a chronic condition.[4] A similar issue may occur around any sort of record, where little regard is paid to the privacy boundaries of the people represented therein. So one may take the social security number from school records, join it with health or criminal records, use it to uncover 'tendencies', and, voila! A very different view of the graduate emerges from that which their 3.8 average alone might show. Legal? Unclear. Ethical? Not for many privacy advocates.

ACCESS AND USABILITY ISSUES

One of the places where the relational aspects of infrastructure appear most strongly is in the barriers presented to the poor or those with no access to hardware or training; those with disabilities; and the institutional racism and sexism that form barriers to usability. As aspects of the latter are covered in other chapters, we shall confine these remarks to resources and issues touching on infrastructure.

The sense that new networked media will create a two-class society – the 'information rich' and the 'information poor' – seems to be coming true. Access to training, hardware and maintenance is in general much more difficult, if not impossible, for the poor. Attempts to remedy this on the part of community and non-profit organizations, NGOs and governments have used a variety of means to mitigate this phenomenon. As with development work, many of the early efforts neglected local infrastructural considerations, such as availability of telephones for dialup access, costs of maintenance and supplies, and security. A typical scenario would be that large companies would donate slightly outmoded computers to a 'needy' classroom, not recognizing that these classrooms lacked a telephone, and that the teachers, while dedicated, were so overloaded that they had no time to catch up on their own computer skills. More recent work has begun to take these considerations into account. An important part of this is working locally, cooperatively designing solutions that work in their natural places.[5]

A cognate community organizing effort has come through the freenet and community networks social movements. Freenets are local efforts, usually voluntary or via a public library, to provide at least basic Internet access on a democratic basis.[6] One way to view these efforts is as a direct organizing attempt to address gaps in current local infrastructure. People living in low-income communities have a keen sense of the failures of imposed solutions that do not take account of their circumstances or their lack of infrastructural resources (or their often rich-in-other-senses resources that are not formally taken into account if one just counts money. These other resources may include support from churches, existing reform movements, or the social networks through which information travels; Bishop, 2001).[7]

There has been much hope expressed that, in the developing world, the new information infrastructure will provide the potential for a narrowing of the knowledge gaps between countries. Thus an effective global digital library would allow Third World researchers access to the latest journals. Distributed computing environments (such as the Grid[8]) would permit supercomputer grade access to computing to scientists throughout the world. The example of the use of cell phone technology to provide a jump in technology in countries without landlines has opened the possibility of great leaps being made into the information future. As powerful as these visions are, they need to be tempered with some real concerns. The first is that an information infrastructure like the Internet functions like a Greek democracy of old: everyone who has access may be an equal citizen, but those without access are left further and further out of the picture. Further, as noted above with respect to the school environment, access is never really equal: the fastest

connections and computers (needed for running the latest software) tend to be concentrated in the First World. Third, governments in the developing world have indicated real doubts about the usefulness of opening their data resources out onto the Internet. Just as in the nineteenth century the *laissez-faire* economics of free trade was advocated by developed countries with most to gain (because they had organizations in place ready to take advantage of emerging possibilities), so in our age the greatest advocates of the free and open exchange of information are developed countries with robust computing infrastructures. Some in developing countries see this as a second wave of colonialism: the first pillaged material resources and the second will pillage information. All of these concerns can be met through the development of careful information policies. Works such as Mansell and Wehn's (1998) both point to the extent of work that needs to be done and open up the very real possibilities that are emerging.

Much has been written on the social barriers for all women, and men of colour, in feeling comfortable in computing environments, including the Web. Since before the Web, feminists have analysed the 'chilly climate' for girls and women learning computing, as well as the glass ceiling in the information technology industries. Holeton (1998) has several excellent chapters devoted to gender issues; the series *Women, Work and Computing*, hosted by IFIPS Special Interest Group 8.1 and issued every four years for more than a decade, provides critiques of identity, design, employment and epistemology in the world of gender and computing (see for example Eriksson et al., 1991). The infrastructural aspects of this stretch in many directions, beginning with the early mathematics and physics (traditionally male- and white-dominated fields) orientation of much of computer science, forming a complex *a priori* barrier to advancement for women and for men of colour. Other issues have included sexism and racism in the content of websites and online conversations.[9]

The Internet has proven a good resource for community organizing on the basis of ecological racism, and for organizing indigenous peoples[10] (who are often scattered and unable to meet face-to-face on a regular basis). Within this movement, there are attempts to put dying or very remote indigenous languages (such as that of the Suomi people in Lapland) online, so that they may be remembered and spread. These are good examples of social movements and ethnic groups taking over the infrastructure for their own purposes.[11] An overlapping but distinct set of issues can also be found in the infrastructural barriers faced by people with disabilities. Blind people now have available (if they can afford it, or if a social service agency can provide it) Braille terminals (that translate text to a Braille keyboard); fast text readers with optical character recognition that transform text into speech; and on some websites, alternative 'text-only' pages with short descriptions of the graphics involved. It is, however, an ongoing difficulty to convince web page designers consistently to make this option available. For those living with an inability to move or to work a keyboard or voice recognition systems, a number of augmenting devices have been developed over the years. These include mice that can be operated by tongues, eye movements, toes or minor head movements. The impact of rapidly improving voice recognition systems on these communities is yet to be fully realized, especially for those living on restricted incomes, as is often true of disabled people. In addition, the basic communication processes carried by e-mail and the Web make self-employment and new kinds of networks and social participation available for many of these people.[12]

CONCLUSION: DESIGN IMPLICATIONS

In 1994, Stewart Brand wrote a wonderful book entitled *How Buildings Learn: What Happens After They Are Built*. He pointed out that we tend to view the architect as the designer of a given building, and as a result we overlook the massive modifications that any building undergoes in the course of its life. Much the same point can be made about designing infrastructures. The work of design

is in many ways secondary to the work of modification. A good information infrastructure is one that is stable enough to allow information to be able to persist in time (word processor programs, for this reason, are generally 'backwards compatible' – meaning that the newer version of a program can open files created with an earlier version). However, it should also be modifiable – at the individual level in terms of 'tailorability' (allowing a user to modify it for their own purposes: see Nardi, 1993), and at the social level in terms of being able to respond to emergent social needs (Web standards have developed quickly to cater for image and video manipulation on the Web).

Designing for flexibility is not an easy task. In general, the required flexibility is emergent. It is clear that you do not need a single great architect for an infrastructure. Eric Raymond's classic, though flawed, article 'The cathedral and the bazaar' (1999) says that unlike in the old days when a set of master blueprints was needed to build a cathedral, now we can see very large-scale infrastructures (he is talking of the Linux operating system) being designed in more of an evolutionary, distributed process. The flaw we are referring to is that his history is wrong: cathedrals themselves often do not have master planners (Turnbull, 1993) but were built in just such an *ad hoc* fashion. Raymond does, however, make the very strong point that complex, interoperating systems (and, we would add, cathedrals) can be built in a distributed fashion, providing you have a good set of protocols in place for receiving and vetting changes. These social arrangements (the protocols) are best developed and maintained by standards bodies containing representatives of all major stakeholders.

We have argued throughout this chapter that there are significant ethical and political concerns in the design of infrastructures. The Scandinavian school of 'participatory design' has successfully responded to this challenge. It developed in part in response to union demands for an input into the design of information technologies that would be implanted in the workplace. A key feature in its design process has been the use of ethnographers of work practice to analyse the ways in which work is carried on in order to anticipate and design for social and cultural effects as well as to produce a technically efficient design (see Bowker et al., 1997: Introduction). This design process has been adopted by some major 'infrastructure' companies and NGOs such as Intel, Hewlett Packard, Apple, and the Scandinavian Trades Unions. This movement suggests a complementary way of reading the design implications of our analysis of infrastructure in this chapter. This is that the most important thing is for the user of the infrastructure to first become aware of the social and political work that the infrastructure is doing and then seek ways to modify it (locally or globally) as need be. Infrastructures subtend complex ecologies: their design process should always be tentative, flexible and open.

NOTES

1 In addition, several detailed studies of the material culture of scientific work began to appear, many of which began to pick upon aspects of infrastructure (see e.g. Clarke, 1998).

2 See Callon (1992) for a fine general discussion of the development of technoeconomic networks; compare Grindley (1995) and Abbate and Kahin (1995).

3 See Suchman and Lynch (1990) for a good overview.

4 Graham and Marvin (1996) provide a comprehensive set of richly theoretical readings on the relationship between the built urban environment and the information/telecommunications infrastructure, ranging from the home and surveillance to city maps, teleshopping, manufacturing and the city itself as a node in an informatic network. From the socio-informatic-regional perspective, Kling et al. (1991) do a detailed analysis of the information economy of Orange County, California. Neumann et al. (2001) suggest some methodological challenges and approaches for the 'ethnography of infrastructure', beginning with the built environment and its classifications and standards.

5 Much good work along these lines can be found at the Participatory Design Conferences (PDCS) held in tandem with the computer-supported cooperative work (CSCW) annual conferences. More information about this can be found at the site for Computer Professionals for Social Responsibility (CPSR): http://www.cpsr.org This is also a good site for reviewing privacy and free speech issues. See also the foundational textbook by Greenbaum and Kyng (1991), the book by Namioka and Schuler (1993), and the report by the European Commission (1998) on the issues of globalizing and localizing information and communication technology.

6 A good overview can be found in Schuler (1996). A listing of specific freenets can be found at http://www.lights.com/freenet This listing is fairly international for the North and for Australia. *Bytes for All* is an e-zine (electronic magazine) devoted to universal access to IT, and can be found at http://www.bytesforall.org A specific example of federated projects in the city of Chicago gives links of several neighbourhood organizations and their emerging community-driven infrastructures: http://www.uic.edu/~schorsch

7 Schön et al. (1999) present a variety of compelling chapters about community organizing efforts, public policy and social empowerment, including many detailed case studies and theoretical foundations.

8 The term refers to a 'grid' of high-performance research networks. The Web-based Grid portal helps computer scientists, scientists and engineers by simplifying and consolidating access to advanced computing systems. It is one of a number of initiatives allowing distributed scientific collaboration.

9 See for example Kali Tal on 'The unbearable whiteness of being: African American critical theory and cyberculture', http://www.kalital.com/Text/Writing/Whitenes.html; Lisa Nakamura on 'Race in/for cyberspace', http://www.iup.edu/en/workdays/Nakamura.html, which addresses racism in MUDs and MOOs; and the University of Iowa's Communication Department resource page on 'Race and gender in cyberspace', http://www.uiowa.edu/%7Ecommstud/resources/GenderMedia/cyber.html. Kolko et al. (2000) review some interesting and wide-ranging cases.

10 A good link to indigenous people's Internet resources (mostly US, Canada and Australia) is found at: http://www.uiowa.edu/%7Ecommstud/resources/GenderMedia/native.html

11 See Summerton (1994) for a good overview of case studies of social movements aimed at changing large-scale infrastructure.

12 A comprehensive home page sponsored by WGBH, US public television, gives advice and links for access for people with several types of disabilities (and some international links): http://www.wgbh.org/wgbh/pages/ncam

REFERENCES

Abbate, Janet (1999) *Inventing the Internet.* Cambridge, MA: MIT Press.

Abbate, J. and Kahin, B. (eds) (1995) *Standards Policy for Information Infrastructure.* Cambridge, MA: MIT Press.

Abbott, Andrew (1988) *The System of Professions: An Essay on the Division of Expert Labor.* Chicago: University of Chicago Press.

Baym, Nancy K. (2000) *Tune In, Log On: Soaps, Fandom, and Online Community.* Thousand Oaks, CA: Sage.

Becker, Howard S. (1982) *Art Worlds.* Berkeley, CA: University of California Press.

Bishop, A.P. (ed.) (2001) *Digital Library Use: Social Practice in Design and Evaluation.* Cambridge, MA: MIT Press.

Boland, R. and F. Collopy (2004) *Managing as Designing.* Stanford, CA: Stanford Business Books.

Bowker, Geoffrey C. (1994a) 'Information mythology: the world of/as information', in Lisa Bud-Frierman (ed.), *Information Acumen: The Understanding and Use of Knowledge in Modern Business.* London: Routledge. pp. 231–47.

Bowker, Geoffrey C. (1994b) *Science on the Run: Information Management and Industrial Geophysics at Schlumberger, 1920–1940.* Cambridge, MA: MIT Press.

Bowker, Geoffrey C. (2000) 'Mapping biodiversity', *International Journal of GIS*, 14 (8): 739–54.

Bowker, Geoffrey C. (2005) *Memory Practices in the Sciences.* Cambridge, MA: MIT Press.

Bowker, Geoffrey C. and Star, Susan Leigh (1999) *Sorting Things Out: Classification and Its Consequences.* Cambridge, MA: MIT Press.

Bowker, Geoffrey, Star, Susan Leigh, Turner, William and Gasser, Les (eds) (1997) *Social Science, Technical Systems, and Cooperative Work: Beyond the Great Divide.* Mahwah, NJ: Erlbaum.

Brand, Stewart (1994) *How Buildings Learn: What Happens After They Are Built.* New York: Viking.

Bucciarelli, L.L. (1994) *Designing Engineers.* Cambridge, MA: MIT Press.

Bud-Frierman, Lisa (ed.) (1994) *Information Acumen: The Understanding and Use of Knowledge in Modern Business.* London: Routledge.

Bush, Vannevar, Nyce, James M. and Kahn, Paul (1991) *From Memex to Hypertext: Vannevar Bush and the Mind's Machine.* Boston: Academic.

Callon, Michel (1992) 'The dynamics of techno-economic networks', in Rod Coombs, Paolo Saviotti and Vivien Walsh (eds), *Technological Change and Company Strategies: Economic and Sociological Perspectives.* London: Harcourt Brace Jovanovich. pp. 72–102.

Clarke, Adele (1998) *Disciplining Reproduction: Modernity, American Life Sciences, and 'The Problems of Sex'.* Berkeley, CA: University of California Press.

Clarke, Adele E. and Fujimura, Joan H. (eds) (1992) *The Right Tools for the Job: At Work in Twentieth-century Life Sciences.* Princeton, NJ: Princeton University Press.

Collins, Harry M. and Kusch, Martin (1998) *The Shape of Actions: What Humans and Machines Can Do.* Cambridge, MA: MIT Press.

David, Paul A. (1986) 'Understanding the economics of QWERTY: the necessity of history', in W.N. Parker (ed.), *Economic History and the Modern Economist.* Oxford: Basil Blackwell.

David, Paul A. (1995) 'The dynamo and the computer: a historical perspective on the modern productivity paradox', *American Economic Review*, 80 (May): 355.

David, Paul A. and Greenstein, Shane (1990) 'The economics of compatibility standards: an introduction to recent research', in *Economics of Innovation and New Technology*, vol. 1. London: Harwood Academic. pp. 3–41.

David, Paul and Rothwell, Geoffrey S. (1994) *Standardization, Diversity and Learning: Strategies for the Coevolution of Technology and Industrial Capacity.* Stanford, CA: Center for Economic Policy Research, Stanford University.

Davis, Susan G. (1997) *Spectacular Nature: Corporate Culture and the SeaWorld Experience.* Berkeley, CA: University of California Press.

Desrosières, Alain and Thévenot, Laurent (1988) *Les catégories socio-professionnelles.* Paris: Découverte.

Downey, Gary and Lucena, Juan (1994) 'Engineering studies', in S. Jasanoff, G. Markle, J. Petersen and T. Pinch (eds), *Handbook of Science, Technology, and Society.* Newbury Park, CA: Sage.

Edwards, Paul N. (1998) 'Y2K: millennial reflections on computers as infrastructure', *History and Technology*, 15: 7–29.

Eriksson, I., Kitchenham, B. and Tijdens, K. (eds) (1991) *Women, Work and Computerization: Understanding and Overcoming Bias in Work and Education.* Amsterdam: North-Holland.

European Commission (1998) *Domesticating the World Wide Webs of Information and Communication Technology*, Per Hetland and Hans-Peter Meyer-Dallach (eds), Report COSTA4. Vol. 7 of 'Making the Global Village Local?' series. Brussels: European Commission.

Fagot-Largeault, Anne (1989) *Causes de la Mort: Histoire Naturelle et Facteurs de Risque.* Paris: Librairie Philosophique J. Vrin.

Fischer, Claude S. (1992) *America Calling: A Social History of the Telephone to 1940.* Berkeley, CA: University of California Press.

Friedman, Batya, Kahn, Jr, Peter H. and Borning, Alan (forthcoming) 'Value sensitive design and information systems' in P. Zhang and D. Galletta (eds), *Human–computer Interaction in Management Information Systems: Foundations.* New York: M.E. Sharpe, Inc. Available online: http://www.ischool.washington.edu/vsd/vsd-and-information-systems.pdf

Friedlander, Amy (1995) *Emerging Infrastructure: The Growth of Railroads.* Reston, VA: Corporation for National Research Initiatives.

Graham, Stephen and Marvin, Simon (1996) *Telecommunications and the City*. London: Routledge.

Greenbaum, Joan and Kyng, Morten (1991) *Design at Work: Cooperative Design of Computer Systems*. Hillsdale, NJ: Erlbaum.

Gregory, Judith (2000) 'Sorcerer's apprentice: creating the electronic health record, re-inventing medical records and patient care'. PhD thesis, University of California at San Diego.

Grindley, Peter (1995) *Standards, Strategy, and Policy: Cases and Stories*. Oxford and New York: Oxford University Press.

Henderson, Kathryn (1999) *On Line and on Paper: Visual Representations, Visual Culture, and Computer Graphics in Design Engineering*. Cambridge, MA: MIT Press.

Holeton, Richard (ed.) (1998) *Composing Cyberspace: Identity, Community, and Knowledge in the Electronic Age*. Boston: McGraw-Hill.

Hughes, Thomas P. (1983) *Networks of Power: Electrification in Western Society, 1880–1930*. Baltimore, MD: Johns Hopkins University Press.

Hurley, Deborah and Keller, James (1999) *The First 100 Feet: Options for Internet and Broadband Access*. Cambridge, MA: MIT Press.

Jewett, Tom and Kling, Rob (1991) 'The dynamics of computerization in a social science research team: a case study of infrastructure, strategies, and skills', *Social Science Computer Review*, 9: 246–75.

Kahin, Brian and Keller, James (1997) *Coordinating the Internet*. Cambridge, MA: MIT Press.

Kling, Rob, Olin, Spencer and Poster, Mark (eds) (1991) *Postsuburban California: The Transformation of Orange County Since World War II*. Berkeley, CA: University of California Press.

Kolko, Beth, Nakamura, Lisa and Rodman, Gilbert (eds) (2000) *Race in Cyberspace*. New York: Routledge.

Lampland, Martha and Star, Susan Leigh (Forthcoming) *Formalizing Practices: Interpretive Approaches to Standardizing, Quantifying and Formalizing*. Under review at Duke University Press, Durham, NC.

Landauer, Thomas K. (1995) *The Trouble with Computers: Usefulness, Usability, and Productivity*. Cambridge, MA: MIT Press.

Latour, Bruno (1996) *Aramis or the Love of Technology*. Cambridge, MA: Harvard University Press.

Latour, Bruno and Hernant, Emilie (1999) *Paris: Ville Invisible*. Paris: Découverte.

Latour, Bruno and Woolgar, Steve (1979) *Laboratory Life: The Construction of Scientific Facts*. Thousand Oaks, CA: Sage.

Lave, Jean and Wenger, Etienne (1991) *Situated Learning: Legitimate Peripheral Participation*. Cambridge: Cambridge University Press.

Library Trends (1998) Special issue on 'How Classifications Work: Problems and Challenges in an Electronic Age', 47 (2): 185–340.

MacKenzie, Donald A. (1990) *Inventing Accuracy: A Historical Sociology of Nuclear Missile Guidance*. Cambridge, MA: MIT Press.

Mansell, Robin and Wehn, Uta (1998) *Knowledge Societies: Information Technology for Sustainable Development*. United Nations Commission on Science and Technology for Development. Oxford and New York: Oxford University Press for and on behalf of the United Nations.

Michener, William K., Brunt, James W., Helly, John J., Kirchner, Thomas B. and Stafford, Susan G. (1997) 'Nongeospatial metadata for the ecological sciences', *Ecological Applications*, 7: 330–42.

Mirowski, P. (2004) *The Effortless Economy of Science?* Durham, NC: Duke University Press.

Monteiro, Eric and Hanseth, Ole (1996) 'Social shaping of information infrastructure: on being specific about the technology', in Wanda J. Orlikowski, Geoff Walsham, Matthew R. Jones and Janice I. DeGross (eds), *Proceedings of the IFIP WG8.2 Working Conference on Information Technology and Changes in Organizational Work, December 1995*. London: Chapman & Hall. pp. 325–43.

Namioka, A. and Schuler, D. (1993) *Participatory Design: Principles and Practice*. Hillsdale, NJ: Erlbaum.

Nardi, Bonnie A. (1993) *A Small Matter of Programming: Perspectives on End User Computing*. Cambridge, MA: MIT Press.

Neumann, Laura, Bowker, Geoffrey C. and Star, Susan Leigh (2001) 'Transparency beyond the individual level of scale: convergence between information artifacts and communities of practice', in A.P. Bishop (ed.), *Digital Library Use: Social Practice in Design and Evaluation*. Cambridge, MA: MIT Press.

Orlikowski, Wanda, Yates, JoAnne, Okamura, Kazuo and Fujimoto, Masayo (1993) 'Shaping electronic communication: the structuring and metastructuring of technology in the context of use', *Organization Science*, 6 (4): 423–44.

Participatory Design Conference Proceedings (n.d.) http://www.cpsr.org/prevsite/conferences/index.html pdc

Poster, Mark (1995) 'Cyberdemocracy', Available online: http://www.hnet.uci.edu/mposter/writings/democ.html

Raymond, Eric S. (1999) *The Cathedral and the Bazaar: Musings on Linux and Open Source by an Accidental Revolutionary*, foreword by Bob Young. Beijing and Cambridge, MA: O'Reilly.

Rayward, W. Boyd (1975) *The Universe of Information: The Work of Paul Otlet for Documentation and International Organisation*. Moscow: All-Union Institute for Scientific and Technical Information (VINITI) for International Federation for Documentation (FID).

Rayward, W. Boyd (1999) 'H.G. Wells's idea of a world brain: a critical re-assessment', *Journal of the American Society for Information Science*, 50 (15 May): 557–73.

Rosenberg, Nathan (1982) *Inside the Black Box: Technology and Economics*. Cambridge: Cambridge University Press.

Schmidt, S.K. and Werle, R. (1998) *Coordinating Technology: Studies in the International Standardization of Telecommunications*. Cambridge, MA: MIT Press.

Schön, Donald A., Sanyal, Bish and Mitchell, William J. (1999) *High Technology and Low-income communities: Prospects for the Positive Use of Advanced Information Technology*. Cambridge, MA: MIT Press.

Schuler, Douglas (1996) *New Community Networks: Wired for Change*. New York: ACM.

Star, Susan Leigh (ed.) (1995) *The Cultures of Computing*. Oxford: Basil Blackwell.

Star, Susan Leigh and Ruhleder, Karen (1996) 'Steps toward an ecology of infrastructure: design and access for large information spaces', *Information Systems Research*, 7: 111–34.

Stefik, Mark (1996) *Internet Dreams: Archetypes, Myths, and Metaphors*. Cambridge, MA: MIT Press.

Suchman, Lucy and Lynch, Michael (eds) (1990) *Representation in Scientific Practice*. Cambridge, MA: MIT Press.

Summerton, Jane (ed.) (1994) *Changing Large Technical Systems*. Boulder, CO: Westview.

Tanenbaum, Andrew S. (1996) *Computer Networks*. Upper Saddle River, NJ: Prentice-Hall.

Taylor, James R. and van Every, Elizabeth J. (1993) *The Vulnerable Fortress: Bureaucratic Organization and Management in the Information Age*. Toronto: University of Toronto Press.

Taylor, James R. and van Every, Elizabeth J. (2000) *The Emergent Organization: Communication as Its Site and Surface*. Mahwah, NJ: Erlbaum.

Turnbull, David (1993) 'The *ad hoc* collective work of building Gothic cathedrals with templates, string, and geometry', *Science, Technology & Human Values*, 18: 315–43.

Wells, H.G. (1938) *World Brain*. London: Methuen.

Winner, Langdon (1986) 'Do artifacts have politics?', in Judy Wacjman and Donald MacKenzie (eds), *The Social Shaping of Technology: How the Refrigerator Got Its Hum*. Milton Keynes: Open University Press.

Woolgar, S. (2002) *Virtual Society?: Technology, Cyberbole, Reality*. Oxford and New York: Oxford University Press.

Yates, JoAnne (1989) *Control through Communication: The Rise of System in American Management*. Baltimore, MD: Johns Hopkins University Press.

12

New Media Design and Development: Diffusion of Innovations v Social Shaping of Technology

LEAH A. LIEVROUW

Across many literatures technologies are described as having trajectories, stages, cycles and growth curves; they diffuse, transfer, are 'pushed' and 'pulled', and evolve. Many current observers agree that 'technology' includes not only the built devices themselves, but also the practices and knowledge related to them and the social arrangements that form around those devices, practices and knowledge (Dierkes and Hoffmann, 1992; MacKenzie and Wacjman, 1999; see also the Introduction to the First Edition (2002)). Thought of this way, technology is dynamic, even fluid: 'The interaction between material and nonmaterial components and coupling of technical and social components can be captured in the concept of technology as a project' (Rammert, 1992: 63). New media technologies are no exception. They develop in dynamic environments where users, designers, manufacturers, investors, regulators, distributors and others work out their interrelated and competing interests, cultural assumptions, desires and visions.

This chapter has two main purposes. The first is to review and compare two major bodies of research on technology and society that have been particularly influential in new media

research. *Diffusion of innovations theory* (Rogers, 1995) and the *social shaping of technology* (SST) perspective (Mackay and Gillespie, 1992; MacKenzie and Wajcman, 1999; Williams and Edge, 1996) are sometimes characterized as competing or even antithetical approaches to technological change. They might also be classified as 'mediated impact' and 'shaping' explanations of technological development, respectively (Boczkowski, 1999, 2004). While the two perspectives differ in important respects, they also share common concerns and theoretical grounding.

The comparison of diffusion and SST is illustrated by two examples. Electronic mail and videotex originated at about the same time in the 1960s and 1970s; e-mail was eventually adopted in universities, workplaces and homes, while videotex never found a 'niche' in the US and encountered considerable consumer resistance elsewhere. Both cases have been studied extensively, and the present discussion draws on those studies to show how diffusion and SST would frame the cases differently.

Based on the comparison of SST and diffusion and the two case studies, the second purpose is to characterize the development and use of new media technologies as a process that involves a constant tension between *determination* and *contingency*, that is, between the imposition of order and uncertainty. It is argued that determination and contingency are interdependent and iterative, and that this relationship can be seen at several key junctures or 'moments' in new media development and use. The chapter closes with a discussion of determination and contingency as common threads in both theoretical traditions.

THE DEVELOPMENT OF NEW MEDIA TECHNOLOGIES

As with other technologies, new media development is not just a matter of engineering or optimal solutions to technical problems; it can be characterized as a *sociotechnical* phenomenon (Bijker, 1995; Bijker and Law, 1992; Suchman, 1996). It brings together engineering specifications (such as interoperability, ergonomics, human factors, interface design, navigation, system implementation) and media production values (such as visual or sound quality, post-production techniques or style) in the changing social, institutional, economic, cultural and policy context of everyday reception and use.

It is often tempting to focus on the origins of technology, on design, invention or innovation, and to give designers or inventors priority in the process. But this can be a misleading approach because 'Technologies are created not by lone inventors or geniuses working in a social vacuum, but by a combination of social forces and processes' (Mackay and Gillespie, 1992: 688; see also McMillan and Flichy, in this volume). Bucciarelli explains that technology design is a fundamentally communicative process that brings objects, actions and social relationships together: 'design is best seen as a social process of negotiation and consensus, a consensus somewhat awkwardly expressed in the final product' (1994: 20–1).

Moreover, some observers argue that technology design continues in use (Suchman, 1987;

Suchman and Jordan, 1997). 'Design and use mutually shape one another in iterative, social processes' (Brown and Duguid, 1994: 29). Technology design has been said to lie somewhere between a technology-driven, science-influenced 'one best solution' approach, and claims that design simply responds to human 'needs' or markets (Bucciarelli, 1994). For new media, the idea of design-in-use suggests that development encompasses both channels and content. As formerly distinct forms and genres of content based on particular media technologies (for example, feature films, personal letters, pop music albums, radio programmes, printed books) have converged into a single digital bit stream that can be retrieved via different types of terminal equipment (wireless phones, PDAs, satellite-based multichannel systems), artists, designers and consumers alike have devised new ways to create, manipulate and capture those content streams.[1]

New information and communication technologies may be designed and intended from the outset to fulfil particular needs or purposes. However, we need only consider the histories of the telephone (Fischer, 1992; Umble, 1992), radio (Aitken, 1985; Slotten, 1995), computing (Abbate, 1999; Ceruzzi, 1998; Edwards, 1996; MacKenzie, 1991) or the typewriter (David, 1985; Knie, 1992) to find that some are likely to have open and unanticipated uses or consequences, while others become firmly – perhaps prematurely – entrenched. Other apparently good inventions never succeed.

COMPARING DIFFUSION AND SST

Two seminal social science research perspectives have sought to capture the complexity of the relationship between society and technology, including media technology. *Diffusion of innovations* theory and the *social shaping of technology* perspective have enjoyed widespread influence in studies of technology and social change. Both SST and diffusion study the origins and uses of new technologies. Both address the evolution and rate of technological development. Though they differ in emphasis, both contextualize technology relative to human action, social relationships and culture. Both examine the choices people make about technologies and, to differing degrees, both are concerned with the consequences of technology adoption and use. They also focus on information flows and communication relationships that foster new ideas and ways of doing things.

SST and diffusion also share theoretical roots in nineteenth-century European social thought and the interactionist tradition associated with the Chicago School of sociology.[2] Along with its close relative, structural or social network analysis, diffusion traces its foundations to the work of Georg Simmel. He conceptualized society as a fundamentally interactive and intersubjective 'web of affiliations' rather than a static, separate superstructure overshadowing human action (Emirbayer and Goodwin, 1994; Rogers, 1995; Rogers and Kincaid, 1981). Simmel's theories were a major influence among Chicago School sociologists in the 1920s and 1930s, particularly for Robert Park and Charles Cooley (Hamilton, 1996), who taught succeeding generations of social network researchers (for example, Fischer, 1982). Mitchell notes that the social network approach, given its focus on communication among network members and the meanings they attribute to their relationships, 'converges with that of the symbolic interactionists' (1975: 20, note 2). And Wellman (1988: 25) notes the 'Simmelian sensibility' that characterizes network or structural analysis, the premise that the structure of social relations determines the content of those relations, including norms and values.

In the SST tradition, too, scholars have been influenced by concepts and methods from Chicago School sociology. The social construction of technology perspective, discussed later, reflects many of the assumptions and empirical orientations of social interactionism and ethnomethodology. Simmel's 'pioneering sociology of consumption' (Holton, 1996: 45), which examined the effects of the emotional and aesthetic aspects of life on a society's popular culture, resonates with the SST emphasis on the 'consumption' or shaping of technology by its users (Mackay and Gillespie, 1992).

Despite these common influences and concerns, however, SST and diffusion have divergent histories, disciplinary roots, theoretical assumptions and methodologies. Their differences have given them windows with distinct views of technology and society.

Social Shaping of Technology

Several areas of theory and research coexist under the umbrella of social shaping of technology, but they all share a basic theoretical commitment: that technological determinism is an inadequate description or explanation of technological innovation and development, or of social change more generally (MacKenzie and Wacjman, 1999; Williams and Edge, 1996). Technological determinism has been a prominent theme in accounts of modernity and social progress; the idea is neatly captured in the motto of the 1933 Chicago World's Fair: 'Science Finds – Industry Applies – Man Conforms' (Rydell, 1993: 98–9). In contrast, SST emphasizes the importance of human choices and action in technological change, rather than seeing technology as politically and ethically neutral, an independent force with its own inevitable logic and motives, or as a mysterious black box that cannot be analysed socially. From the SST point of view, to talk about the 'impacts' of technology on society, as though technology is the hammer and society the nail, is to accept implicitly the basic premise of technological determinism.

In the 1960s several prominent critics began to question the prevailing assumption that technology drives social change (McDermott, 1969; Mumford, 1964, 1970). More recent critiques have also helped to discredit the deterministic view (for example, Winner, 1977, 1986). Despite nearly 30 years of SST research, however, deterministic assumptions and language continue to dominate popular culture in technologically advanced societies, to the distress of some observers (MacKenzie and Wacjman, 1999). Still, the critique of technological determinism has been a powerful influence in social science research about technology, and indeed in engineering. Many prestigious American engineering schools (including MIT, Georgia Tech, Virginia Tech, Cornell and the Rochester Polytechnic Institute), as well as prominent departments at Amsterdam, Delft, Paris, Sussex and Edinburgh, have courses and degree programmes in science, technology and society that incorporate the SST perspective.

SST takes a particular philosophical view of the nature of knowledge and its manifestations in society, specifically that knowledge and its products (including science and technology) are essentially social phenomena. The *sociology of scientific knowledge* or SSK has identified critical points of contingency in the process of scientific research when events (such as data collection, explanations, discoveries) could have gone differently, that is, when the people involved showed 'interpretive flexibility'. By conducting historical studies and ethnographic fieldwork, many sociologists of knowledge have concluded that scientists' own beliefs, opportunities and relationships are as important in the establishment of scientific facts or truths as the natural phenomena that they study (Knorr, 1981; Latour and Woolgar, 1986).

Despite the intense anxiety of some scientists who object to science and technological innovation being treated as objects of study in themselves (Gross and Levitt, 1994), anti-determinist and constructivist researchers in SST do not seek to deny or undermine the benefits of science and technology. Rather, the stated aim of SST is to formulate policies to guide technology development so that its benefits are more 'human-centred', usable, equitable, appropriate and responsive to everyday culture and practice (Williams and Edge, 1996).

The *strong programme* of SSK has provoked some of the greatest worries among scientist critics of SST. The strong programme is often identified with historian and philosopher David Bloor (1991) and his colleagues at the University of Edinburgh. He proposes that the creation and acceptance of *all* knowledge claims (including those of SSK) must be explained 'in social terms, rather than by reference to the natural world' (Williams and Edge, 1996: 869). Furthermore, its proponents say, this method should be applied equally both to knowledge that is considered factual and that which is considered biased, mistaken or fraudulent. The *weak programme* of SSK, on the other hand, examines only the social conditions of knowledge growth or the sources of biased or distorted knowledge, and not the 'rational acts of apprehending inferences and evidence' as facts, truths or errors (Bloor, 1992: 494).

Both the strong and weak programmes of SSK have influenced social studies of technology. Notably, the *social construction of technology* (SCOT) approach (Bijker and Law, 1992; Bijker et al., 1987) has borrowed the idea of interpretive flexibility to examine the choices available to designers, developers and users in the course of technological development. Given their focus on the social context of innovation and change, SCOT analyses have much in common with the weak programme of SSK.

Several research fronts employ the SCOT framework. For example, studies of *large technical systems* (LTS) (Hughes, 1987; LaPorte, 1991; Mayntz and Hughes, 1988; Summerton, 1994) have applied SCOT principles to the analysis of extensive, complex technologies such as electrical power grids (Hughes, 1983), supercomputing (MacKenzie, 1991) and videotex and telephone systems (Galambos, 1988; Mayntz and Schneider, 1988; Schneider, 1991, 1994, 2000). Also, the growing field of *social informatics* (Kling, 1996, 1999) has combined a broad SCOT approach with methods from industrial and organizational sociology to study the evolution of information systems and computing (see Kling and Scacchi, 1982; Star, 1995; Star and Ruhleder, 1986; Suchman, 1996). Leigh Star has elaborated a particular aspect of interpretive flexibility to argue that a given technology, for example computers, may be understood and used very differently by different social groups. They become 'boundary objects' whose forms and uses are negotiated among groups (Star and Griesemer, 1989; see the chapter by Flichy in this volume).

By emphasizing the influence of society on technology, rather than the reverse, SST has attempted to understand the complex society–technology relationship. Researchers have tried to transcend 'one-way' or linear accounts of technology and society that imply that progress is irreversible. However, in recent years SST's adherents have recognized that while they might have reversed the direction of causality, the hypothesis that society shapes technology remains an essentially linear explanation (MacKenzie and Wacjman, 1999).

One of the most compelling bodies of SST research, *actor-network theory* or ANT (Callon, 1986; Latour, 1993; Law and Hassard, 1999), shares many of the assumptions of SCOT but attempts to overcome the problem of linear causality. ANT rejects both strong technological determinism, on the one hand, and the strong social constructivist argument, on the other. Its proponents (including Bruno Latour, Michel Callon and their colleagues at the Centre de Sociologie de l'Innovation of the École Supérieure des Mines in Paris) consider people, technologies and institutions alike as 'actants' that have equal potential to influence technological development (Callon et al., 1986; Hughes, 1986). Neither technology 'push' nor market 'pull' can fully account for the shaping of technology, they argue; technologies and people alike should be thought of as interrelated nodes in constantly changing sociotechnical networks, which constitute the forms and uses of technology differently in different times and places for different groups. Furthermore, according to ANT, technologies are not infinitely flexible or negotiable; they tend to become embedded and stabilize within institutional and social structures and influence or even determine subsequent technological choices.

Diffusion of Innovations

As its name suggests, diffusion of innovations theory describes how new ideas or practices are introduced and adopted in a social system, with a special focus on the communication relations and information flows that promote adoption (Rogers, 1995). Diffusion is a specialization of communication research that combines theories of personal influence and persuasion with the analytical techniques and theories of social structural or network analysis in sociology (Blau, 1982; Wellman and Berkowitz, 1988). Diffusion of innovations is also a key construct

in the economics of information and technology transfer (Antonelli, 1991a, 1991b; Dosi et al., 1988; Griliches, 1988). Though diffusion processes are studied in many social contexts and disciplines (Valente, 1995), the diffusion of new ICTs has been studied most extensively in sociology, communication research and economics. Sociological/communication studies tend to emphasize social relations and interaction in the diffusion process, while economic studies stress industry and market structures and economic motives for adoption, such as profitability.

Diffusion theory models the dynamics of technology adoption, including the rate of adoption and the eventual spread of the innovation in a social system. A new technology (or other innovation) is introduced in a social group (community, organization, nation, market, industry), often by a change agent with an interest in promoting it (private firm, public agency or influential individual). Typically, a few actors are the first or early adopters; the success of the innovation often depends on their social status or influence. Other members of the group, who are either directly acquainted with or share similar interests with the early adopters, may be persuaded to adopt the innovation, and they in turn influence others. Successive waves of adoption continue until the innovation reaches a saturation point or *ceiling* that varies depending on the characteristics of the innovation and the social system. Important concepts in diffusion include the adoption *threshold*, the number of adopters necessary to induce one more actor to adopt an innovation (Valente, 1995), and *critical mass*, the point at which enough actors have adopted an innovation for it to succeed, based on the rate or momentum of adoption (Allen, 1983; Mahler and Rogers, 1999; Markus, 1987; Rogers, 1995).

The sociological/communication and economic traditions of diffusion research frame technology somewhat differently. Sociology and communication have a long-standing interest in the development and use of technology in particular social contexts (Rogers, 1995). On the other hand, in neoclassical economics technology has usually been treated as an exogenous factor, like 'manna from heaven' in Christopher Freeman's phrase (1991: 303; see also Antonelli, 1991; Dosi et al., 1988). Economists have tended to view technology as a 'black box' that could be an economic input or output, but not a component of the economy itself (Rosenberg, 1982).

However, difficulties arose with neoclassical analysis as economies shifted toward services and information technology in the 1960s and 1970s. Information technologies were no longer ancillary to the 'real' productivity of the manufacturing and extractive sectors, but had become the very centrepiece of developed economies. Critics argued that mainstream economics could not meet the analytical challenge (see Lamberton in this volume). In the 1970s and 1980s, Freeman and his associates, influenced by the early work of Joseph Schumpeter, called for a new economic approach to understanding technological innovation and development (Dosi et al., 1988; Henten and Skouby in this volume). They argued that, analogously to the paradigm shifts in science described by Thomas Kuhn, societies may undergo shifts in *sociotechnical paradigms* that have profound economic consequences.

Economic and sociological/communication diffusion studies share a fundamental theoretical and analytic focus on network structures and dynamics. In sociological network analysis, this emphasis has been called the 'anti-categorical imperative' (Emirbayer and Goodwin, 1994). That is, network analysts, including diffusion researchers, assume that the relationships or links among social actors explain more about their actions than does the conventional procedure of classifying actors according to their individual traits or characteristics, and then predicting action based on that classification. Action, network scholars say, must be considered within the context of complex and changing social relations that are directly observable, and not as the result of individual values, motivations or other psychological states that are difficult or impossible to observe.

Network analysis and diffusion studies have a generally holistic, inclusive orientation. Wellman and Berkowitz (1988) argue that the network approach is consistent with a late-twentieth-century intellectual shift in the sciences and social sciences away from atomistic, reductionist and cumulative explanations, and toward explanations of complexity in which parts are defined by their interactions. Likewise, economists of information and technological change contend that by definition networks have a high degree of complementarity, compatibility and strong interdependence among network elements (people, innovations, firms, etc.).

Another key concept is *network externalities* (see also the chapter by Star and Bowker in this volume). Sometimes called a 'snowball effect' (Bodet et al., 1991: 310), the idea is that the value of a network to a given member increases with the size of the network. Katz and Shapiro (1986: 146) have pointed out that 'This effect has long been recognized in the context of communications networks such as the telephone and telex ... the more subscribers there are on a given communications network, the greater are the services provided by that network' (quoted in Antonelli, 1991: 18, note 15). Ironically, analysts say, early adopters of a technology receive less of a benefit than later adopters do; in fact to some extent they subsidize the benefits of later adopters.

A basic axiom of network analysis and diffusion is that 'Networks structure competitive and collaborative activities to secure scarce resources' (Wellman, 1988: 46). Large, stable networks (those with greater externalities, to use the economic term) tend to maintain the resource or value status quo, and can actually impede the introduction and diffusion of innovations and create barriers to entry of new ideas or techniques (similar to the 'embeddedness' of some technologies noted by actor-network theorists). Technological development, especially in telecommunications, tends to have 'high levels of lock-in effects' (Antonelli, 1991: 12). Antonelli argues that since network externalities can inhibit technological change, network economics must balance competition and cooperation, in contrast to the exclusive focus on markets and competition in neoclassical economics (see also Flichy in this volume).

Both sociological and economic diffusion research have been criticized, often for similar reasons. Critics charge that diffusion theory is technologically deterministic because it treats innovations as given and focuses more on the effects or impact of innovations in social systems. Rogers (1995) calls this the 'pro-innovation bias' of diffusion theory. The perceived pro-innovation bias has led critics to question the impartiality of diffusion research because it seems to ally the interests of researchers with those of change agents or technology proponents. In economic diffusion research, the determinist tendency emerges in its treatment of technology as exogenous, though this has been modified somewhat by the growing emphasis on sociotechnical paradigms. Economists have also called for greater attention to the creation and development of the innovations themselves, along the lines of some SST studies (Dierkes and Hoffmann, 1992). However, most accounts of diffusion continue to depict the process as linear, for example by using the classic S-shaped diffusion curve to illustrate the rate of adoption or by describing technology use in terms of industry 'push' versus market 'pull'.

Diffusion is also criticized on the grounds that it assumes that technologies and other innovations are unitary, stable phenomena throughout the diffusion process. However, most sociologists, communication researchers and economists acknowledge that technological innovations are rarely singular inventions. Rather, they are constellations or 'clusters' of interrelated or complementary innovations (Freeman, 1991; Perez and Soete, 1988). Rice and Rogers (1980) have demonstrated that technologies are *reinvented* as they diffuse, creating a kind of punctuated equilibrium alternating between rapid growth and plateaus in the rate of diffusion, rather than a single S-curve. Koontz (1976) has characterized innovations as either tightly or loosely bound bundles of subinnovations. Tight bundles may diffuse more slowly, while loose bundles diffuse quickly because they allow users to adapt their components more flexibly. Freeman (1991) has distinguished between radical and incremental innovations, which produce different diffusion patterns. As Perez and Soete put it: 'There are plenty of reasons for expecting both the

innovation and its surrounding economic environment to change as diffusion proceeds' (1988: 462). Freeman concurs: '"diffusion" is seldom if ever a simple process of replication by unimaginative imitators' (1991: 305).

To recap some of the main points about SST and diffusion, SST is based in constructivist epistemology and rejects technological determinism. Diffusion derives from theories of social influence and persuasion and asserts that networks of relationships and shared meaning shape social action, including the adoption of technology (Rogers and Kincaid, 1981). Both struggle to transcend linear models of causality, with varying success. Diffusion is frequently associated with institutions that sponsor innovations and promote technological development; SST emphasizes the consumption side and the everyday use of technology. Diffusion research analyses adoption patterns of successful and unsuccessful innovations to formulate models that allow the prediction of future trends. SST advocates intervention in the development of technologies before they are 'pushed' into society.

Two Cases: E-mail and Videotex

Two brief case studies are offered here to illustrate the similarities and differences between SST and diffusion. Electronic mail and videotex are 'telematic' technologies, that is, they merge data processing/computation with telecommunications systems. Originally, e-mail required an expensive and esoteric technical infrastructure and served a very small community of highly specialized scientists and engineers. Today, however, e-mail has been adopted widely throughout the world. Videotex, on the other hand, merged computerized information databases with widely available broadcast and telephone systems, and provided broad-based news and community information for general audiences. Nonetheless, it never really found a niche in American households or business, and was adopted very slowly elsewhere. Even in France, where it has been most successful, videotex use has declined sharply in the face of competition from similar services available through the Internet.

Electronic Mail

By most accounts electronic mail arose accidentally as a by-product of the US Defense Advanced Research Projects Agency's ARPANET. The ARPANET project began in the late 1960s as a means to share data processing facilities at universities, military bases and other DARPA-funded research sites, via satellite and telecommunications networks. The system allowed researchers to move data files among sites and gave them access to remote computing facilities when local systems were unavailable or insufficient to handle a given job. The centrepiece of the system was the sabotage-resistant technique of packet switching, which divided files or data processing jobs into small chunks called packets. Packets were sent separately through any available network links, and reassembled into their original form at the destination computer. Packets could be moved through any open route among networked computers, even if some links or nodes in the network were damaged or unavailable. The ARPANET grew rapidly, from 11 nodes in 1970 to almost 90 in 1985; each node connected many computers to the network (Abbate, 1999; Ceruzzi, 1998; Jennings et al., 1986; Newell and Sproull, 1982).

Once the ARPANET was running in the 1970s, researchers at member sites quickly realized that they could use the system to exchange messages with colleagues at other sites as well as to exchange files or data processing jobs. E-mail 'emerged soon after the first few nodes were working' (Ceruzzi, 1998: 298). Specialized software was developed that performed most of the e-mail functions still used today, such as saving or responding to messages, or sending a message to a list of recipients. Soon, messaging overtook other uses, and computer scientists took note of what was perhaps the first 'killer app':

> The value of electronic mail came as a surprise to the developers of the ARPANET, who expected the network to be used principally for computer-to-computer communication for resource sharing but found instead that the dominant use was mail. (Newell and Sproull, 1982: 848)

> ARPANET was used less as a tool for sharing remote computational resources than it was for sharing information. The major lesson from the ARPANET experience is that information sharing is a key benefit of computer networking. (Jennings et al., 1986: 945)

However, network access was distributed unevenly from the outset; technical and administrative barriers slowed the spread of electronic mail for nearly 20 years. Given the esoteric nature of the research and the security constraints of defence projects, the designers of the ARPANET had always intended the system to link a relatively small, elite group of scientists and engineers. Therefore,

> ARPANET also had the negative effect of creating a have–have not situation in experimental computer research. Scientists and engineers carrying out such research at institutions other than the twenty or so ARPANET sites were at a clear disadvantage in accessing pertinent technical information and in attracting faculty and students. (Jennings et al., 1986: 945–6)

Other observers 'sensed a growing split in the community between those with ARPANET access and those without it' (Comer, 1983: 747–8), which included access to resources, facilities and scholarly interaction with colleagues at other institutions. To help alleviate the widening gaps, the National Science Foundation established NSFnet, which linked researchers at many US campuses to NSF supercomputer centres through the ARPANET (Comer, 1983; Jennings et al., 1986). A confederation of non-ARPANET computer science departments created CSNET in the early 1980s to connect with their colleagues at ARPANET sites (Comer, 1983).

As networked computing grew other barriers arose, particularly between scientists and engineers and other university-based scholars and researchers who recognized the potential benefits of high-speed asynchronous messaging for their own specialities, but did not have access to the network. 'In general, the existing ARPANET connections are in departments of computer science and electrical engineering and are not readily accessible by other researchers' (Jennings et al., 1986: 946). With the help of IBM, a consortium of non-ARPANET colleges and universities using IBM mainframes established BITNET (Because It's There Net) in 1981, with the first link between the City University of New York and Yale University (Abbate, 1999: 202; Ceruzzi, 1998). By 1985 BITNET connected about 600 computers in 175 institutions: 'It is not limited to specific academic disciplines, and may be used for any academic or administrative purposes' (Jennings et al., 1986: 947).

Abbate (1999) gives a detailed account of the transformation of the ARPANET into an NSF-supported 'backbone' that became the core of the Internet, and how separate networks like BITNET eventually were connected to the Internet. However, for a time interconnection between Internet and BITNET sites was often awkward; some scholars and researchers maintained both Internet and BITNET e-mail addresses to reach colleagues in different disciplines or institutions. There was also a persistent sense of a two-class system associated with BITNET, with Internet addresses (major government and research institutions with plenty of extramural funding) having more cachet than their BITNET counterparts. (Network address status distinctions resurfaced in the 1990s with the .edu, .org, .gov, .mil and .com domains of US Internet addresses, and continues in ICANN debates about the allocation of domain names.) Nonetheless, BITNET opened e-mail access to an unprecedented number of researchers and students, and established electronic mail, bulletin boards and discussion lists as a routine mode of communication throughout American academia.

At about the same time in the 1970s and 1980s, public data networks were being developed in Europe, Canada and the US for clients prohibited from using the non-profit research networks. These networks, such as Telenet in the US, were expensive; they conveyed files and data via dedicated transmission lines, much like a long-distance telephone call. Instead of the TCP/IP networking protocol used in the ARPANET, which connected many diverse computer networks, public data networks employed the X.25 protocol developed by national postal, telegraph and telephone ministries (PTTs) and adopted by the Consultative Committee on International Telegraphy and Telephony (CCITT) (Abbate, 1994). The framers of the X.25 protocol assumed that a uniform standard for computer networks would eventually emerge, such as the reliable, high-speed Ethernet local area network developed at XeroxPARC (Abbate, 1994; Ceruzzi, 1998).

Therefore another barrier was created, this time between the (mainly American) non-profit research- and university-based Internet on the one hand and (US and international) public data networks and private-sector organizational 'intranets' on the other. This barrier endured until the late 1980s, when moves began to privatize the Internet and so open it to commercial and entertainment uses (Abbate, 1999). The distinction virtually disappeared in the mid 1990s, when the hypertext transfer protocol (HTTP) for the World Wide Web, combined with the client–server network configurations that had originally been designed for Xerox's Ethernet, effectively bridged the TCP/IP and X.25 standards (Abbate, 1994).

As networked computing and the use of electronic mail spread from high-level, DARPA-funded research sites to computer science and engineering more generally, then throughout academia, and finally to the private sector, e-mail and the Internet became increasingly taken for granted as communication media, with all the social expectations and difficulties of other media. For example, users found that the style of interaction among computer scientists and engineers was not always appropriate in other contexts. Early ARPANET users – often students, using UNIX-based research workstations – had created news or discussion groups in which members posted messages and expressed their opinions on a wide range of topics. Writing in 1982, two prominent computer scientists observed that 'electronic mail has come to be used in an informal way ... messages have the informality of speech, perhaps because the sender views the message as an alternative to a telephone call' (Newell and Sproull, 1982: 848). E-mail and bulletin board discussions often became heated and lengthy, in part because members would use aliases to avoid being identified as the source or target of an often brutal, *ad hominem* style of criticism called 'flaming'. Flaming and aliases were understood and accepted within the relatively small, closed world of computing research, but were foreign to newcomers from other disciplines.

As computer networks proliferated, the Internet shifted to the private sector, and e-mail attracted more diverse users, social scientists had more opportunities to study the uses of e-mail and other computer-mediated communication (CMC) technologies (Garton and Wellman, 1995; Rice, 1980; Steinfield, 1986; see Rice and Haythornthwaite in this volume). E-mail users began to develop and enforce consensual rules of 'netiquette'. They cultivated a more civil style of interaction to limit the rhetorical excesses of the engineers' 'flame wars'.

Today, it can be argued that e-mail development has entered a new phase of consolidation and control. E-mail users must often adapt their work and communication patterns to established systems, and are prohibited from modifying systems to suit their own needs. While the technology has been adopted widely in private-sector work settings, managers routinely control e-mail content as well as access. E-mail records are routinely subpoenaed in legal actions. The original 'acceptable use policy' imposed by DARPA and the NSF, which restricted uses of the ARPANET and Internet to non-profit research and teaching activities, has given way to a flurry of organizational use policies that can severely restrict what users may or may not say about their workplaces, corporate sponsors or other private firms, or even about the provider of the Internet service being used. Voluntary 'netiquette' has given way in many organizations to strictly enforced, top-down controls on expression and the surveillance of employee messages by management. In a recent study by the Pew Internet and American Life Project (2002) nearly 70 per cent of survey respondents said that their e-mail use at work was monitored by employers. According to survey data gathered by the American Management Association, the percentage of major US firms that monitor employee e-mail increased from about 15 per cent in 1997 to 60 per cent in 2004 (American Management Association, 2001, 2004). Today, e-mail is a routine, and perhaps the most routinely monitored and sanctioned, form of interpersonal communication in the US and elsewhere.

Videotex

Though unfamiliar to most Americans, videotex information systems are common in other parts of the world, including Canada, Japan, Europe and the UK. Videotex systems link users' television sets or a specially dedicated terminal (or in more current systems, their PCs) to computerized information databases via telephone or cable lines. (A similar system, teletext, provides the same type of information over the air as part of the television broadcast signal.) Subscribers use a keypad device, such as a specially modified remote control channel changer or keyboard, to call up 'pages' of information that are displayed on the television screen. Pages incorporate text and very simple graphics; content ranges from news, sports scores and weather reports to telephone directory information, want ads, rail and airline schedules, stock prices and gardening tips. Early systems connected subscribers to a single centralized database; later systems incorporated networked computers and distributed databases. In some ways videotex can be seen as a precursor to today's World Wide Web, where users call up web pages from any one of millions of databases on demand.[3]

The first videotex system, Prestel, was introduced in the UK in 1979 by a division of the British Post Office (now British Telecom). By the mid 1980s the Bundespost in the Federal Republic of Germany had started the Bild-schirmtext system, based on Prestel technology; the Canadian government had launched its Telidon project; and in the UK Prestel was joined by the BBC's teletext service, Ceefax. The French Télétel service, based on a hybrid videotex/teletext platform called Antiope, was developed by the Direction Générale des Télécommunications section (DGT) of the French PTT ministry (now France Télécom). Télétel was distinctive because it displayed pages of text on small, specially designed terminals called minitels instead of television sets. The developers of all these systems envisioned them as 'information utilities' and anticipated rapid, widespread adoption in households and workplaces (Greenberger, 1964).

However, videotex got off to a slow start. In Britain, Prestel never grew as quickly as planners predicted. At its most extensive, the system attracted fewer than 100,000 subscribers; these numbers were soon surpassed by the BBC's Ceefax. The German Bildschirmtext system experienced similarly slow growth until Deutsche Telekom (the successor to the telecommunications branch of the state Bundespost) modified the system in the 1990s to be PC accessible via the Internet. Facing early consumer resistance, the operators of both Prestel and Bildschirmtext shifted their focus from households to business and professional users. In Canada, Telidon offered a technically superior system with better graphics, but the system never attracted enough subscribers to get past the trial stage.

In France, Télétel was the only real videotex success, owing partly to the free distribution of millions of minitel terminals to households and business telephone customers between 1983 and 1990 (Schneider, 2000). The French public was slow to adopt PCs in the 1980s, and minitels gave them access to basic French-language information and messaging services similar to those available in English over the Internet. Originally, the system provided only telephone directory assistance, but it was soon expanded to include personal messaging and bulletin-board-type services, for example 'erotic "conversation" groups' (Schneider, 2000: 320) called *messageries roses*. Students even used minitel messaging to organize nationwide protests in the 1980s. Since the mid 1990s, however, minitel use has declined as PC adoption and Internet use have grown in France.

In the US, videotex encountered even bigger problems during the 1980s. Information services similar to those offered on videotex systems were available online to subscribers with PCs and modems, including H&R Block's CompuServe, the Dow Jones Information Service, The Source from Reader's Digest, and later, IBM and Sears' Prodigy system and America Online (AOL). Several major media firms conducted videotex trials in selected US markets in the 1980s using Canadian, British and French technologies (Case, 1994; Mosco, 1982; Rogers, 1986). Knight-Ridder introduced the Viewtron system in Miami/Coral Gables, FL; the Times-Mirror Company built the Gateway system in Orange County, CA; IBM, Sears and CBS joined forces in the Trintex project; CBS and AT&T ran an experimental

system in New Jersey; and Time/Life planned a trial as well. Besides these firms, a number of others were involved in the design and development of terminal equipment, information services and system infrastructures (Mosco, 1982).

Despite millions of dollars spent on the various American trials, however, sponsors soon abandoned videotex systems because they attracted so few subscribers. Though media companies were involved in many of the trials, critics charged that they were never really interested in developing services that would rival their existing operations in publishing, broadcasting or online services. The trials, it was alleged, were virtually designed to fail, offering general-interest content that was readily available elsewhere and charging high prices for terminal equipment and connection time. Because most trials were conducted in affluent suburban neighbourhoods, there were doubts about the general appeal of the services. By the late 1980s hopes for American videotex services delivered to television sets or dedicated terminals had faded, though several providers (including online newspapers) migrated their services to be available online via personal computers.

Most accounts of videotex history cite several reasons for its difficulties in the US and elsewhere. First, videotex was a top-down phenomenon, depending more on industry and government push than on consumer pull. It tended to be most successful where state agencies and national telecommunications monopolies sponsored and built systems along the lines of other telecommunications services such as the telephone. In the late 1970s, national monopolies were searching for new uses for their rapidly expanding bandwidth, and state industrial policies promoted national champions (e.g. British Telecom, French Télécom, Deutsche Telekom) in international markets for telecommunications and computing equipment and services. Videotex systems were promising on both counts. It is notable, for example, that many American videotex trials employed foreign technologies. Though a consortium of US players developed the North American Presentation Level Protocol Syntax (NAPLPS) protocol in the early 1980s, AT&T lobbied the FCC to accept a modified version of Canadian Telidon technology as the US standard, while CBS advocated the French Antiope system. However, where no state or monopoly interest was willing to underwrite the startup and maintenance costs of such large distributed systems – as in the US – videotex stalled.

Others cite problems with the technology itself, particularly the cost, complexity and relatively unsophisticated display capabilities of specially adapted television sets or dedicated videotex terminals. In a sense, these platforms were 'closed' in that they did not give sub-scribers access to content or services beyond the provider's system. Videotex adapters could add hundreds of dollars to the price of a TV; keypad codes could be arcane and difficult to remember; and (with the exception of the Telidon system) page displays were often limited to a few lines of ragged text and crudely rendered graphics. As more users called up pages, the slower page retrievals became. And many systems that made large initial capital investments got 'locked in' to early technical standards and could not afford to upgrade later.

Furthermore, videotex was introduced in the US at about the same time as personal computers and modems, which provided access to similar rival information services like CompuServe. PCs and modems had the advantage of being a more 'open' platform: users could subscribe to whatever services they chose, and were not restricted to one provider or source of information. Furthermore, almost any computer screen could produce better graphics and more readable text than videotex, even before graphical user interfaces like the Macintosh desktop or its derivative, Windows, became common. Videotex-adapted television sets could hardly compete with PCs in terms of speed, flexibility and power. To some extent, then, videotex enjoyed greater popularity where markets for personal computing had not yet developed. Once PCs and the Internet became widely available, existing videotex sys-tems had to go online to survive, or be replaced by Internet-based services and eventually the World Wide Web.

Another reason for videotex's poor showing may be ideological (Case, 1994). Videotex

evolved during a period dominated by expansive new visions and rhetoric heralding the emerging 'information society', in which information would be the new commodity and communication the new market. Access to information services became a staple of US urban policy in the 1970s, for example, as planners envisioned 'information utilities' that would provide information services to poor and underserved neighbourhoods via cable television technology (Greenberger, 1964; Light, 2003). This faith in the new technologies may have created unrealistic or premature expectations among key players for videotex and similar services. Many believed that the new hybrid technological infrastructure, which combined computing and telecommunications (and gave rise to awkward neologisms like 'compunications' and *télématique*, or 'telemat-ics' in English) would break down institutional and national boundaries, reduce or eliminate the costs of labour, materials and transporta-tion, and deliver information and services to consumers instantly and transparently at a fraction of the previous cost. These new 'infor-mation utilities', including videotex, would cre-ate new markets in information and, indeed, in bandwidth itself (Dordick et al., 1981). Industries were particularly interested in the potential for transaction-based services such as home shop-ping, banking and financial transactions, elec-tronic document delivery, and other on-demand, so-called 'interactive' services (Greenberger, 1985; Institute for the Future, 1970; Tydeman et al., 1982). Such transaction-based services promised new sources of profit for the private sector and a revival for stagnating national economies (Nora and Minc, 1981; Sigel, 1980).

With the benefit of hindsight it seems clear that while videotex delivered via television sets or dedicated terminals may have failed as a particular technological platform, the essen-tially commodified and transactional vision of telematics and information utilities lives on in recent market enthusiasms for e-commerce, electronic publishing, online trading and auctions, and 'end user information services' (Case, 1994). Still, information delivery and commercial transactions have never been as compelling to consumers as the opportunity for interpersonal interaction online. Survey research shows that people use the Internet far more frequently for electronic mail and related services like real-time messaging or chat rooms than for shopping, banking or document retrieval (Pew Internet and American Life Project, 2005). Distinctions have emerged between 'content' uses of new media where every mouse click represents potential revenue (such as shopping; music, video or electronic book downloads; Web browsing; travel booking), and 'community' uses (e-mail, chat, instant messaging) which tend to be less lucrative. The early vision of telematics, focused on information delivery and commercial transactions, was the primary influence on videotex design and implementation. But users seem to have expected more.

DETERMINATION AND CONTINGENCY

The preceding cases illustrate that the new media development process entails design and use, negotiation and consensus, engineering specifications and market demands, channels and content, the material and the social. More generally, these dualities can be recast as a dynamic relationship between determination and contingency. *Determination* is the effort to specify conditions or 'impose coherence' in a situation with the intent of achieving some desired outcome (Schön, 1988, 1990). *Contingency* is the existence of many possible conditions in an uncertain situation. Complete certainty is never fully achieved, so in a sense there is no final design 'solution' for a given technological problem.[4] Rather, designers contend with contingency by making choices from among existing conditions or by creating new ones. In turn, these choices create new conditions and uncertainties that prompt further specifications or choices, and so on. Technology design and development can therefore be relatively 'loose' or 'tight' depending on the prevailing tendency at any given point toward contingency or determination, respectively.

Diffusion and SST can be thought of as having differing profiles in terms of the determination/contingency framework. For example, diffusion might be said to tend more toward determination *vis-à-vis* the origin of technologies, the actors involved, and dynamics and distributive mechanisms, though it leans more toward contingency regarding choice and consequences. SST, on the other hand, seems to align more with contingency on almost all counts, though some scholars (especially actor-network theorists) also recognize that technological change often leads to closure and irreversibility when innovations are widely adopted. Interestingly, frameworks like actor-network theory and sociotechnical paradigms could both be placed near the middle in terms of determination and contingency. They both emphasize the networked interrelationships among individuals, technologies and institutions, and the barriers to innovation brought about by technological 'embeddedness', standardization, network externalities, or prevailing technological regimes ('paradigms').

Moments of Technology Development

Furthermore, the e-mail and videotex cases suggest that determination and contingency are played out at several critical points or 'moments' in development. Moments in this context are not specific points in time, but rather notable or conspicuous elements having the potential to move development in one direction or another. They do not necessarily follow in the linear order that the following list suggests; moments can and frequently do overlap or relate in other ways. Table 12.1 gives examples of how the moments can vary depending on the prevailing tendency toward determination or contingency.

Origin

In the first moment of the development process new ideas are generated and tried out. Origins may be responses to specific problems or situations, or may arise more spontaneously, when an idea is proposed just because it is possible or interesting. Origin is principally a creative moment; it can be intensely active or may take the form of a simple conceptualization. Origins may involve whole

Table 12.1   *Determination versus contingency in moments of new media development*

Moments	Determination ⟷	Contingency
Origin	Institutional sources of innovation Innovation pre-defined by R&D process	Innovation is open, reflexive
Actors	A few controlling interests Human or organizational actors	Many players, no signal interest Institutions, technologies and people can all act, have influence
Dynamics	Slow, stable, organized, linear Dominant groups create barriers to entry Externalities, irreversibility	Rapid, volatile, reversible, disorganized or self-organizing systems
Choice	Few choices	Many choices
Formal properties	Established styles, forms, genres Existing forms constrain new ones	Experimental, recombinant, temporary forms
Distributive mechanisms	Centralized, restricted access, few channels	Decentralized, open access, multiple channels
Consequences	Closure, stability, standardization, barriers to entry, monopoly	Lack of standards, 'churn', proliferating forms and users, competition

teams of people sharing and negotiating ideas, or individuals trying to solve problems in a new way. In the economics of technology, Schumpeter distinguishes between 'invention' and 'innovation' (Freeman, 1991): invention corresponds to the generation of a new concept, while innovation involves its communication or transfer beyond the originator(s).

Actors

The second moment is the *actors* involved in new media development. Actors include anyone who makes choices that affect the subsequent uses or forms of the technology, including professionally trained specialists. Sonnenwald (1993) argues that there are many types of actors involved in design, each with different (sometimes conflicting) interests, requirements and expectations.

Dynamics

The third moment is complex and extends throughout the development process. *Dynamics* involves the movement and momentum of a new technological idea, its expression, and its adoption and use. Development dynamics may be volatile or stable, fast or slow, may move ahead easily or be impeded or encounter resistance, or even be reversed. Technologies may

become standardized (that is, undergo closure), or standards may break down. Dynamics is illustrated by the concept of critical mass in diffusion theory, technological trajectories in the economics of technological change (Dosi, 1982; Nelson and Winter, 1977, 1982), and momentum in SST (Hughes, 1987).

Choice

The fourth moment is closely related to dynamics, and also operates more or less constantly throughout the development process. Contingency is characterized by a wide variety of *choices*, while determination forecloses or limits choice. More 'durable' technologies constrain subsequent choices (Latour, 1991).

Formal Properties

Expressions or physical forms of a technology emerge as it develops. Form may be influenced by ergonomic or aesthetic considerations or by the usability of the technology. In diffusion theory, the *formal properties* of an innovation make it observable by potential adopters. Style or production values can be important aspects of form.

Distributive Mechanisms

The sixth moment involves the means by which new ideas, things or practices spread.

Distributive mechanisms include interpersonal networks, existing media technologies, markets, and organizational or institutional structures. Fairness or equity of distribution is an important consideration (for example, as governed by universal service regulations for telephone service). Distribution is often highly politicized because different actors may have relatively more or less power to influence or benefit from distribution. Access to technology is one outcome of particular patterns of distribution.

Consequences

The final moment involves the effects, 'impacts' or other outcomes of a technology, whether intended or unanticipated. *Consequences* may emerge early in the development process and 'feed forward' to affect later phases, or may not become apparent until the technology is widespread. Consequences affect subsequent development; for example, a successful technology is likely to generate a whole group of imitators or similar works (perhaps creating a genre with particular formal properties). An unsuccessful technology may discourage further experimentation or creative uses of related ideas.

Determination and Contingency in E-mail and Videotex

In retrospect, though e-mail succeeded and the original videotex platform did not, both demonstrate the interrelationship between determination and contingency in the moments of media development. Videotex seems to have been the more determined technology, especially at the outset. Fewer actors were involved, typically in alliances between PTTs and national monopolies, or among corporate media firms. Technical standards were established early, which had the effect of locking in relatively unsophisticated graphics and interfaces, at least in some systems. The first operators had clearly defined markets in mind, though their subscription projections were generally overoptimistic. Consumer resistance slowed the initial momentum of videotex development; operators tried to rekindle interest by reorienting the services from household to business customers, but this strategy was not

much more successful. In France, videotex was more flexible, offering messaging and chat as well as information services, and the state/PTT alliance made much larger initial investments and subsidized the service heavily for nearly a decade. The system was inexpensive for consumers and the number of subscribers grew steadily. But as more information services went online and more households and businesses adopted PCs and modems, videotex lost much of its appeal in France, as it had elsewhere.

E-mail also began as a highly constrained system. The underlying ARPANET infrastructure, including packet switching, was institutionally commissioned, paid for and controlled by ARPA. As with videotex, very few actors were involved at the outset and access to the system was strictly limited, but unlike the sponsors of videotex ARPA provided little institutional 'push' that would move the technology beyond its original base in federally funded computer science research.

In fact, e-mail itself – an unanticipated use of the system that demonstrated users' 'interpretive flexibility' – shifted the dynamic of networked computing toward proliferation and contingency. The ARPANET was transformed by 'user activism' that began with electronic mail (Abbate, 1999: 90). E-mail opened up collaborative possibilities far beyond the file sharing and distributed data processing originally envisioned by ARPA project directors. Perhaps unwittingly, computer scientists with ARPANET access played the role of 'early adopters' in the diffusion sense, modelling the benefits of e-mail for colleagues in computer science and eventually throughout academia. E-mail had immediate intuitive appeal; user 'pull' rather than industry push helped accelerate the trend toward networked computing and 'internetworking' among major institutions. Eventually the same model was reproduced all the way to the desktop with the Internet, PCs, modems (later, broadband) and wireless networks.

Certainly, technical and administrative barriers to networking and e-mail arose at each step in its development and diffusion. It took about 25 years for e-mail to move from DARPA researchers, to computer science at large, to other disciplines in major research universities and large corporate organizations, to smaller universities and colleges, and finally to most American businesses and households. But along the way, networked computing as a medium, including e-mail, transformed expectations about interpersonal communication, written discourse, privacy, workplace life, organizational forms and hierarchies, as well as the access to information and entertainment that videotex was supposed to provide. Today, e-mail is virtually ubiquitous in education, business and government and most households in developed nations, and use is rising around the world.

From an SST perspective, we might say that videotex developers misunderstood potential users and their everyday needs for information. Systems were complex and expensive, and offered information and services that could readily be obtained elsewhere. System sponsors seemed to have a deterministic, 'build it and they will come' faith that the availability of the technology itself would compel subscribers to change their information-seeking habits – and pay for the privilege. There was little opportunity for subscribers to modify or adapt the system for their own purposes, except in France, where impromptu bulletin boards and chat groups developed. The transaction-based platform precluded real interpersonal interaction in most systems. For e-mail, on the other hand, the developers themselves were the original users, and had some latitude to design the system according to their needs and preferences. The system was also 'free' to most individual users in the early stages, in the sense that it was subsidized by large research grants, and later underwritten by the research universities, government and private firms. (Users would later assume more of the costs of connect time, software and hardware.) A system originally intended for file sharing and distributed data processing (transactions) was adapted to permit interpersonal communication. In the process it became, and still is, the 'killer app' of networked computing.

From the diffusion perspective, the roles of system designers and innovators, the influence of opinion leaders on later adopters, the social ties and persuasive interactions among system users, the presence or absence of critical mass, adaptation or reinvention, and the network effects or externalities of system growth are all clear in both cases. The diffusion curve of most videotex

systems never achieved critical mass or 'takeoff', while the curve for e-mail has something of a punctuated equilibrium shape, with alternating phases of growth and stability. Videotex was a relatively stable innovation, while e-mail's features evolved as new groups of users adopted it. For example, the simple text format of e-mail messages remained more or less unchanged until business users added features like document attachments and links to calendars and spreadsheets and a friendlier graphical interface.

CONCLUSION

To conclude, in this chapter I have attempted to provide a general conceptual overview of the development of new media technologies. It is a complex, multilayered process that involves many different groups and their interests, but one way to understand it is to consider shifts between determination and contingency at different moments or steps in the development process. I have focused on two important perspectives on technology and social change that have been widely influential in new media research, to show how they incorporate determination and contingency in their analyses. Diffusion of innovations and social shaping of technology have different disciplinary and philosophical foundations and different orientations toward technology and action. Yet both provide useful tools for observing and describing the technology development process.

I reviewed the development of two media technologies, videotex and electronic mail, to identify instances of determination and contingency in each case. I also briefly compared the two technologies from the viewpoints of diffusion and SST, to demonstrate how the two perspectives might analyse them differently while still incorporating moments of determination and contingency. The cases presented here are necessarily brief; more extensive historical analysis might reveal important details or themes that have been overlooked here. Similarly, the descriptions of diffusion theory and SST would benefit from a more comprehensive literature review highlighting significant theoretical refinements and empirical studies. Readers are encouraged to review the main works cited here for additional background.

However, despite this limited treatment the determination–contingency framework, organized around the moments of technology development, may offer a means for future studies to compare and triangulate theoretical approaches as well as the media technologies themselves.

NOTES

I would like to acknowledge the research and editorial assistance of Marjorie Rauen on the original version of this chapter. Pablo Boczkowski also provided invaluable comments and suggestions, particularly regarding the section on videotex.

1 With worrisome consequences for content regulation and intellectual property rights, as Verhulst points out in the present volume.

2 I thank Donald Case for this insight.

3 For more background about the development and history of videotex, see Case (1994), Mayntz and Schneider (1988), Mosco (1982), Rogers (1986), Schneider (2000), Schneider et al. (1991), and Tydeman et al. (1982). This section draws primarily from these works. Also, see Boczkowski (2004).

4 Though as Latour (1993, 1996) emphasizes, some solutions – we might think of books or broadcast television – may become so durable that they powerfully constrain any subsequent developments

REFERENCES

Abbate, J. (1994) 'The Internet challenge: conflict and compromise in computer networking', in J. Summerton (ed.), *Changing Large Technical Systems*. Boulder, CO: Westview. pp. 193–210.

Abbate, J. (1999) *Inventing the Internet*. Cambridge, MA: MIT Press.

Aitken, H.G.J. (1985) *The Continuous Wave: Technology and American Radio, 1900–1932*. Princeton, NJ: Princeton University Press.

Allen, D. (1983) 'New telecommunications services: network externalities and critical mass', *Telecommunications Policy*, 12 (3): 257–71.

American Management Association (2001) *2001 AMA Survey: Workplace Monitoring and Surveillance*. Available online: http://www.amanet.org/research/pdfs/ems_short2001.pdf

American Management Association (2004) *2004 Workplace E-mail and Instant Messaging Survey*.

Available online: http://www.amaneet.org/research/pdfs/IM_2004_Summary.pdf

Antonelli, C. (ed.) (1991) *The Economics of Information Networks*. Amsterdam: North-Holland.

Bijker, W.E. (1995) *Of Bicycles, Bakelites and Bulbs: Toward a Theory of Sociotechnical Change*. Cambridge, MA: MIT Press.

Bijker, W.E. and Law, J. (eds) (1992) *Shaping Technology/Building Society: Studies in Sociotechnical Change*. Cambridge, MA: MIT Press.

Bijker, W.E., Hughes, T.P. and Pinch, T. (1987) *The Social Construction of Technological Systems*. Cambridge, MA: MIT Press.

Blau, P. (1982) 'Structural sociology and network analysis: an overview', in P.V. Marsden and N. Lin (eds), *Social Structure and Network Analysis*. Beverly Hills, CA: Sage. pp. 273–9.

Bloor, D. (1991) *Knowledge and Social Imagery*, 2nd edn. Chicago, IL: University of Chicago Press.

Bloor, D. (1992) 'Strong programme', in J. Dancy and E. Sosa (eds), *A Companion to Epistemology*, London: Blackwell. p. 494.

Boczkowski, P.J. (1999) 'Mutual shaping of users and technologies in a national virtual community', *Journal of Communication*, 49 (2): 86–108.

Boczkowski, P.J. (2004) *Digitizing the News: Innovation in Online Newspapers*. Cambridge, MA: MIT Press.

Bodet, C., Joram, D. and Lamarche, T. (1991) 'Savoir-faire and telecommunication market structure: cooperation, domination and competition', in C. Antonelli (ed), *The Economics of Information Networks*. Amsterdam: North-Holland. pp. 301–24.

Brown, J.S. and Duguid, P. (1994) 'Borderline issues: social and material aspects of design', *Human–Computer Interaction*, 9: 3–36.

Bucciarelli, L.L. (1994) *Designing Engineers*. Cambridge, MA: MIT Press.

Callon, M. (1986) 'The sociology of an actor-network: the case of the electric vehicle', in M. Callon, J. Law and A. Rip (eds), *Mapping the Dynamics of Science and Technology: Sociology of Science in the Real World*. London: Macmillan. pp. 19–34.

Callon, M., Law, J. and Rip, A. (eds) (1986) *Mapping the Dynamics of Science and Technology: Sociology of Science in the Real World*. London: Macmillan.

Case, D.O. (1994) 'The social shaping of videotex: how information services for the public have evolved', *Journal of the American Society for Information Science*, 45 (7): 483–97.

Ceruzzi, P.E. (1998) *A History of Modern Computing*. Cambridge, MA: MIT Press.

Comer, D. (1983) 'The computer science research network CSNET: a history and status report', *Communications of the ACM*, 26 (10): 747–53.

David, P.A. (1985) 'Clio and the economics of QWERTY', *American Economic Review*, 75 (2): 332–7.

Dierkes, M. and Hoffmann, U. (eds) (1992) *New Technology at the Outset: Social Forces in the Shaping of Technological Innovations*. Frankfurt and New York: Campus.

Dordick, H., Bradley, H. and Nanus, B. (1981) *The Emerging Network Marketplace*. Norwood, NJ: Ablex.

Dosi, G. (1982) 'Technical paradigms and technological trajectories: a suggested interpretation of the determinants and directions of technological change', *Research Policy*, 11: 147.

Dosi, G., Freeman, C., Nelson, R., Silverberg, G. and Soete, L. (eds) (1988) *Technical Change and Economic Theory*. London: Pinter.

Edwards, P.N. (1996) *The Closed World: Computers and the Politics of Discourse in Cold War America*. Cambridge, MA: MIT Press.

Emirbayer, M. and Goodwin, J. (1994) 'Network analysis, culture and the problem of agency', *American Journal of Sociology*, 99 (6): 1411–54.

Fischer, C.S. (1982) *To Dwell Among Friends: Personal Networks in Town and City*. Chicago and London: University of Chicago Press.

Fischer, C.S. (1992) *America Calling: A Social History of the Telephone to 1940*. Berkeley, CA: University of California Press.

Freeman, C. (1991) 'The nature of innovation and the evolution of the productive system', in *Technology and Productivity: The Challenge for Economic Policy*. Proceedings of a conference sponsored by the Technology/Economy Programme, OECD. Paris: Organization for Economic Cooperation and Development. pp. 303–14.

Galambos, L. (1988) 'Looking for the boundaries of technological determinism: a brief history of the US telephone system', in R. Mayntz and T.P. Hughes (eds), *The Development of Large Technical Systems*. Frankfurt and Boulder, CO: Campus and Westview. pp. 135–53.

Garton, L. and Wellman, B. (1995) 'Social impacts of electronic mail in organizations: a review of the research literature', in B.R. Burleson (ed.), *Communication Yearbook 18*. Thousand Oaks, CA: Sage. pp. 434–53.

Greenberger, M. (1964) 'The computers of tomorrow', *Atlantic Monthly*, 213 (5): 63–66.

Greenberger, M. (ed.) (1985) *Electronic Publishing Plus*. White Plains, NY: Knowledge Industry.

Griliches, Z. (1988) *Technology, Education and Productivity*. New York: Basil Blackwell.

Gross, P.R. and Levitt, N. (1994) *Higher Superstition: The Academic Left and Its Quarrels with Science*. Baltimore, MD: Johns Hopkins University Press.

Hamilton, P. (1996) 'Systems theory', in B.S. Turner (ed.), *The Blackwell Companion to Social Theory*. London: Blackwell. pp. 143–70.

Holton, R.J. (1996) 'Classical social theory', in B.S. Turner (ed.), *The Blackwell Companion to Social Theory*. London: Blackwell. pp. 25–52.

Hughes, T.P. (1983) *Networks of Power: Electrification in Western Society, 1880–1930*. Baltimore, MD: Johns Hopkins University Press.

Hughes, T.P. (1986) 'The seamless web: technology science, etcetera, etcetera', *Social Studies of Science*, 16: 281–92.

Hughes, T.P. (1987) 'The evolution of large technical systems', in W.E. Bijker, T.P. Hughes and T. Pinch (eds), *The Social Construction of Technological Systems*. Cambridge, MA: MIT Press. pp. 51–82.

Institute for the Future (1970) *Potential Demand for Two-way Information Services to the Home 1970–1990*. Menlo Park, CA: Institute for the Future.

Jennings, D.M., Landweber, L.H., Fuchs, I.H., Farber, D.J. and Adrion, W.R. (1986) 'Computer networking for scientists', *Science*, 231 (28 February): 943–50.

Katz, M.L. and Shapiro, C. (1986) 'Product compatibility choice in a market with technological progress', *Oxford Economic Papers*, November (supplement): 146–65.

Kling, R. (ed.) (1996) *Computerization and Controversy: Value Conflicts and Social Choices*, 2nd edn. San Diego, CA: Academic.

Kling, R. (1999) 'What is social informatics and why does it matter?', *D-Lib Magazine*, 5 (1). Available online: http://www.dlib.org:80/dlib/january99/kling/01kling.html

Kling, R. and Scacchi, W. (1982) 'The web of computing: computer technology as social organization', *Advances in Computers*, 21: 1–90.

Knie, A. (1992) Yesterday's decisions determine tomorrow's options: the case of the mechanical typewriter', in M. Dierkes and U. Hoffmann (eds), *New Technology at the Outset: Social Forces in the Shaping of Technological Innovations*. Frankfurt and New York: Campus. pp. 161–72.

Knorr, K. (1981) *The Manufacture of Knowledge: An Essay on the Constructivist and Contextual Nature of Science*. Oxford: Pergamon.

Koontz, V. (1976) 'Determinants of individuals' knowledge, attitudes and decisions regarding a health innovation in Maine'. Unpublished doctoral dissertation, University of Michigan, Ann Arbor, MI.

LaPorte, T.R. (ed.) (1991) *Social Responses to Large Technical Systems: Control or Anticipation.* Dordrecht and Boston: Kluwer.

Latour, B. (1991) 'Technology is society made durable', in J. Law (ed.), *A Sociology of Monsters: Essays on Power, Technology and Domination.* London: Routledge. pp. 103–31.

Latour, B. (1993) *We Have Never Been Modern.* New York: Harvester-Wheatsheaf.

Latour, B. (1996) *Aramis, or the Love of Technology.* Cambridge, MA: Harvard University Press.

Latour, B. and Woolgar, S. (1986) *Laboratory Life: The Construction of Scientific Facts*, 2nd edn. Princeton, NJ: Princeton University Press.

Law, J. and Hassard, J. (eds) (1999) *Actor-network Theory and After.* Oxford: Blackwell.

Light, J.S. (2003) *From Warfare to Welfare: Defense Intellectuals and Urban Problems in Cold War America.* Baltimore, MD: Johns Hopkins University Press.

Mackay, H. and Gillespie, G. (1992) 'Extending the social shaping of technology approach: ideology and appropriation', *Social Studies of Science*, 22: 685–716.

MacKenzie, D. (1991) 'Notes toward a sociology of supercomputing', in T.R. LaPorte (ed.), *Social Responses to Large Technical Systems.* Dordrecht: Kluwer. pp. 159–75.

MacKenzie, D. and Wajcman, J. (eds) (1999) *The Social Shaping of Technology*, 2nd edn. Philadelphia, PA and London: Open University Press and Taylor & Francis.

Mahler, A. and Rogers, E.M. (1999) 'The diffusion of interactive communication innovations and the critical mass: the adoption of telecommunications services by German banks', *Telecommunications Policy*, 23 (10–11): 719–40.

Markus, M.L. (1987) 'Toward a "critical mass" theory of interactive media: universal access, interdependence and diffusion', *Communication Research*, 14: 491–511.

Mayntz, R. and Hughes, T.P. (eds) (1988) *The Development of Large Technical Systems.* Boulder, CO: Westview.

Mayntz, R. and Schneider, V. (1988) 'The dynamics of system development in a comparative perspective: interactive videotex in Germany, France and Britain', in R. Mayntz and T.P. Hughes (eds), *The Development of Large Technical Systems.* Boulder, CO: Westview Press. pp. 263–98.

McDermott, J. (1969) 'Technology: the opiate of the masses', *New York Review of Books*, 31 July.

Mitchell, J.C. (1975) 'The concept and use of social networks' (1969), in J.C. Mitchell (ed.), *Social Networks in Urban Situations: Analyses of Personal Relationships in Central African Towns.* Manchester: Manchester University Press, for the Institute for African Studies, University of Zambia. pp. 1–50.

Mosco, V. (1982) *Pushbutton Fantasies: Critical Perspectives on Videotex and Information Technology.* Norwood, NJ: Ablex.

Mumford, L. (1964) *The Myth of the Machine.* Vol. 1: *Technics and Human Development.* New York: Harcourt Brace Jovanovich.

Mumford, L. (1970) *The Myth of the Machine.* Vol. 2: *The Pentagon of Power.* New York: Harcourt Brace Jovanovich.

Nelson, R. and Winter, S. (1977) 'In search of a useful theory of innovation', *Research Policy*, 6 (1): 36–75.

Nelson, R. and Winter, S. (1982) *An Evolutionary Theory of Economic Change.* Cambridge, MA: Harvard University Press.

Newell, A. and Sproull, R.F. (1982) 'Computer networks: Prospects for scientists', *Science*, 215 (12 February): 843–52.

Nora, S. and Minc, A. (1981) *The Computerization of Society.* Cambridge, MA: MIT Press.

Perez, C. and Soete, L. (1988) 'Catching up in technology: entry barriers and windows of opportunity', in G. Dosi, C. Freeman, R. Nelson, G. Silverberg and L. Soete (eds), *Technical Change and Economic Theory.* London and New York: Pinter. pp. 458–79.

Pew Internet and American Life Project (2002) *Email at Work.* Washington, DC: Pew Internet and American Life Project. Available online: http://www.pewinternet.org/pdfs/PIP_Work_Email_Report.pdf

Pew Internet and American Life Project (2005) *Internet Evolution: The Mainstreaming of Online Life.* Available online: http://www.pewinternet.org/pdfs/Internet_Status_2005.pdf

Rammert, W. (1992) 'Research on the generation and development of technology: the state of the art in Germany', in M. Dierkes and U. Hoffmann (eds), *New Technology at the Outset: Social Forces in the Shaping of Technological Innovations.* Frankfurt and New York: Campus. pp. 62–89.

Rice, R.E. (1980) 'The impacts of computer-mediated organizational and interpersonal communication', *Annual Review of Information Science and Technology*, 15: 221–49.

Rice, R.E. and Rogers, E.M. (1980) 'Reinvention in the innovation process', *Knowledge: Creation, Diffusion, Utilization*, 1 (4): 499–514.

Rogers, E.M. (1986) *Communication Technology: the New Media in Society.* New York: Free Press.

Rogers, E.M. (1995) *Diffusion of Innovations*, 4th edn. New York: Free Press.

Rogers, E.M. and Kincaid, D.L. (1981) *Communication Networks: Toward a New Paradigm for Research*. New York: Free Press.

Rosenberg, N. (1982) *Inside the Black Box: Technology and Economics*. New York and Cambridge: Cambridge University Press.

Rydell, R.W. (1993) *World of Fairs*. Chicago, IL: University of Chicago Press.

Schneider, V. (1991) 'The governance of large technical systems: the case of telecommunications', in T.R. LaPorte (ed.), *Responding to Large Technical Systems: Control or Anticipation*. Dordrecht and Boston: Kluwer. pp. 19–42.

Schneider, V. (1994) 'Multinationals in transition: global technical integration and the role of corporate telecommunication networks', in J. Summerton (ed.), *Changing Large Technical Systems*. Boulder, CO: Westview. pp. 71–91.

Schneider, V. (2000) 'Evolution in cyberspace: the adaptation of national videotext systems to the Internet', *The Information Society*, 16 (4): 319–28.

Schneider, V., Charon, T., Graham, J.M., Miles, I. and Vedel, T. (1991) 'The dynamics of videotex development in Britain, France and Germany: a cross-national comparison', *European Journal of Communication*, 6: 187–212.

Schön, D.A. (1988) 'Designing: rules, types and worlds', *Design Studies*, 9 (3): 181–90.

Schön, D.A. (1990) 'The design process', in V.A. Howard (ed.), *Varieties of Thinking: Essays from Harvard's Philosophy of Education Research Center*. New York: Routledge. pp. 110–41.

Sigel, E. (ed.) (1980) *Videotext: The Coming Revolution in Home/Office Information Retrieval*. White Plains, NY: Knowledge Industry.

Slotten, H.R. (1995) 'Radio engineers, the Federal Radio Commission, and the social shaping of broadcast technology: creating "Radio Paradise"', *Technology and Culture*, 36 (4): 950–86.

Sonnenwald, D.H. (1993) 'Communication in design'. Unpublished PhD dissertation, Rutgers University, New Brunswick, NJ.

Star, S.L. (ed.) (1995) *The Cultures of Computing*. Oxford: Blackwell.

Star, S.L. and Griesemer, J.R. (1989) 'Institutional ecology, translations and boundary objects: amateurs and professionals in Berkeley's Museum of Vertebrate Zoology, 1907–1939', *Social Studies of Science*, 19: 387–420.

Star, S.L. and Ruhleder, K. (1996) 'Steps towards an ecology of infrastructure: design and access for large information spaces', *Information Systems Research*, 7 (1): 111–34.

Steinfield, C. (1986) 'Computer-mediated communication systems', *Annual Review of Information Science and Technology*, 21: 167–202.

Suchman, L. (1987) *Plans and Situated Actions: The Problem of Machine–human Communication*. Cambridge: Cambridge University Press.

Suchman, L. (1996) 'Supporting articulation work', in R. Kling (ed.), *Computerization and Controversy: Value Conflicts and Social Choices*, 2nd edn. San Diego, CA: Academic. pp. 407–23.

Suchman, L. and Jordan, B. (1997) 'Computerization and women's knowledge', in P.E. Agre and D. Schuler (eds), *Reinventing Technology, Rediscovering Community*. Greenwich, CT: Ablex. pp. 97–105.

Summerton, J. (1994) *Changing Large Technical Systems*. Boulder, CO: Westview.

Tydeman, J., Lipinski, H., Adler, R., Nyhan, M. and Zwimpfer, L. (1982) *Teletext and Videotex in the United States: Market Potential, Technology, Policy Issues*. New York: McGraw-Hill.

Umble, D.Z. (1992) 'The Amish and the telephone: resistance and reconstruction', in R. Silverstone and E. Hirsch (eds), *Consuming Technologies: Media and Information in Domestic Spaces*. London: Routledge. pp. 183–94.

Valente, T. (1995) *Network Models of the Diffusion of Innovations*. Cresskill, NJ: Hampton.

Wellman, B. (1988) 'Structural analysis: from method and metaphor to theory and substance', in B. Wellman and S.D. Berkowitz (eds), *Social Structures: A Network Approach*. Cambridge: Cambridge University Press. pp. 19–61.

Wellman, B. and Berkowitz, S.D. (1988) 'Introduction: studying social structures', in B. Wellman and S.D. Berkowitz (eds), *Social Structures: A Network Approach*. Cambridge: Cambridge University Press. pp. 1–13.

Williams, R. and Edge, D. (1996) 'The social shaping of technology', *Research Policy*, 25: 865–99.

Winner, L. (1977) *Autonomous Technology: Technics-out-of-control as a Theme in Political Thought*. Cambridge, MA: MIT Press.

Winner, L. (1986) 'Do artifacts have politics?', *in The Whale and the Reactor: A Search for Limits in an Age of High Technology*. Chicago, IL: University of Chicago Press. pp. 19–39.

13

New Media and New Economy Cluster Dynamics

PHILIP COOKE

This chapter focuses on the organizational characteristics of new media businesses. Like other new economy industries such as information and communication technologies (ICT), including varieties of software engineering, and biotechnology, such firms tend to cluster in geographical proximity. They do this for a number of reasons, but the main one seems to be to access 'spillovers'. These are external economies that come from co-location with other like-minded or complementary businesses. Opportunities for joint contracts, sharing of knowhow, and exchange of human or, more collectively, social capital are greater in such settings. New media differ from other new economy clusters in being less likely to agglomerate around universities or research laboratories and more likely to occupy downtown fringe locations where rents may be relatively cheap because industry has vacated space, but access to large customers in film, TV, advertising and publishing is good. Moreover, ambience is important too; thus fashion, funky entertainment and fusion food are likely ingredients in the general scene. But, as is reported next, important features of new media have been changing and there are good reasons for thinking that rapid transitions in forms of new media articulation have become endemic.

Thus in the 1990s the glamorous new technology was multimedia, subsequently known more widely as new media. Today, new media's public prominence has been eclipsed by interest in Internet or dot.com businesses, mobile telephony, iPod, and a revived biotechnology. It is by now well appreciated that a new economy stock may well hold the public eye for a brief period, before investor hypermobility moves to the next 'new new thing' (Lewis, 2000), but for an embryonic sector to, apparently, disappear from view is still slightly shocking. The question that drives this contribution is whether new media retain some intrinsic core identity or have already hypertransmuted into or been absorbed by the Internet and foreseeably into the convergent service delivery medium of the handheld *communicator*. This, of course, is the third-generation mobile or cell phone which in its late second-generation form, such as the Nokia Communicator, already provided telephony, Internet access, musical composition, graphic imaging and e-mail. A Palm device accessed news, music, e-mail, barcode scanning, flight schedules, language translation, expense reports and digicam functions among others. These are clearly varieties of multimedia device. The third generation, in 2005 available on the High Street, provides TV and video services in addition to

Bluetooth capabilities regarding wireless inter-equipment communication, for example the refrigerator tells the mobile phone that it is running short of milk but that the fridge contents can supply ingredients for particular recipes.

Clearly, these functions are new and they are performed by media: so to repeat the question, are they new media? Unquestionably there has been 'morphing' of what, even in conference in 1997 (see for example Braczyk et al., 1999), was painfully being defined as multimedia or new media, into handheld communicator equipment by 2000 and wireless telephony by 2005. But that may not be the whole story. As industries mature, even in a few years, divergences become evident. Thus, whereas specialist banking, financial and stock market information, accessible only by PC on CD-ROM or online in 1997, was accessible on a mobile phone in 2000, advanced computer graphics of the kind now routinely deployed in films like *Star Wars* were probably not. However games deploying comparable pixel densities were, by 2005, commonplace on mobile devices. Internet games firms were part of the dot.com revolution, as were varieties of Internet applications businesses; they had, in many cases, a high market value measured by share price and, having made an initial public offering (IPO), still are often courted and acquired by the likes of Sony, Sega or Nintendo, Nokia, and Microsoft games divisions. By 2000, Web page design, which was considered as the 'bottom-feeder' end of new media, could be performed by anyone with Microsoft Frontpage. By 2005 A4 Desk Flash Website Builders were similarly available.

The texture is complex, not least because much of the nexus of businesses around new media is entrepreneurial, small or very small scale in terms of human capital, but creative and knowledge-driven with even 'virtual firms' being a pronounced feature. Classically, these businesses tend to congregate in geographical clusters, often, as we have noted, where the coffee is good and the street life is vibrant. Crossover interactions between members of social, political or economic networks focused on cultural products with design-intensive content are the lifeblood of such communities. In this sense they are rather like biotechnology firms, clustered near university campuses, that have intellectual power but crave the venture capitalists and large pharmaceutical firms to fund their next contract or milestone. But these do not cohabit spatially, unless the corporate client puts a lookout branch in the cluster. Such small-firm clusters are dynamic, productive and innovative and show remarkable new firm formation and death rates. The two go together: risky businesses operate in clusters because of strength in numbers, or the aforementioned spillover effects. They are an increasingly prominent organizational form as the new economy transcends the old, but as we have seen, their identity can be fleeting.

In what follows, the first section will, reasonably briefly, review the relevant literature on what multimedia and/or new media comprise. Other chapters in this book perform this function at greater length. Nevertheless, it is important to be clear about the focus of *this* contribution, since, as has been argued thus far, the sector is changing and coalescing with some technologies while diverging from others, and it is crucial to understand why and with what effects. Following that, the second section will deal with the interesting question of why industries like new media organize themselves as clusters. These are becoming widespread in new economy sectors, but they were also the spatial form that early capitalism took almost wherever it started, and as Porter (1998) showed for the US, many of those also survive and prosper.

The pivotal part of this section will relate the small-firm clustering phenomenon, where creativity and innovation are pronounced, to overall industry structure, where corporate behemoths like Time-Warner in new media clumsily seek to 'get on board' by acquisition, yet lack the agility and 'absorptive capacity' (Cohen and Levinthal, 1990) to succeed, terminating with their own acquisition by a dot.com firm like America Online (AOL). By 2003, such was the ignominy and so vast the losses incurred ($100 billion) by the merged entity due to AOL's overstating of its advertising revenue that AOL was downgraded to a unit of a division of Time-Warner. On 16 October 'AOL' was removed from the corporate name and within a year all AOL executives had been ousted from senior positions in the now 'repudiated' merged entity (Klein, 2003). Clearly, such new-economy/ old-economy dynamics were interestingly poised at the start of the millennium. Nevertheless, now as then, the predominant industry force remains technological *convergence*.

NEW MEDIA IN TRANSITION

Old media were fairly easy to grasp conceptually: they were products and services that broadcast knowledge, information and entertainment in forms intermediary between the originator and the ultimate consumer of product or service. The 'Gutenberg galaxy', as Marshall McLuhan (1962) called the effect of the invention of the printing press, captures the idea perfectly. The 'word', hitherto accessible only to the priesthood and its interpretations of the source message, became mechanically reproducible as the book, an intermediary object capable of independent, democratic interpretation and use by its consumers. Other communication media such as newspapers, pamphlets and songsheets followed suit. Later, their electronic forms of film, radio, TV and video performed equivalent functions in wider secular fields. So what is new about new media? In one important sense nothing, since CD-ROMs, the Internet, digital databases, computer games content and advanced computer graphics that can simulate anything from tornados to *T. Rex* carry content that informs or entertains as an intermediary between creative talent and consumer. The old, new new thing, to paraphrase Lewis (2000) in respect of new media, was its *convergent* nature. New media involved the capability to have on disk or online a broadcast message that combined still and moving images, text, voice and music as discrete elements of a single product or service. These were made possible because of hardware advances in cabling and routing using upgraded copper or optical fibre, enabling simultaneous transmission of the multiplicity of media – hence multimedia. Clearly, all these media had been previously combinable. Once *The Jazz Singer* had appeared, moving and still images, voice and music were combined on a single medium. The line of trajectory in old media was locked into elaborations and enhancements of these basic tools. But the key to their integration was their property of supporting the *narrative* flow of the product. Coinciding with the more recent hardware enhancements in cabling and routing came the cultural turn against narrative and the rise of the *spatial* consciousness to challenge the *temporal* (Cooke, 1990). The possible and the desirable interacted in the creation of the multimedia product, a classic example of which would be Microsoft's Encarta encyclopaedia.

One of the earlier intellectual contributions to understanding the nature of new media, presented in 1995 and published as Scott (1998), argued that in California new media took the following form. Making their appearance from the mid 1980s in San Francisco, especially Silicon Valley, and Hollywood, Los Angeles, they intersected high technology and cultural industries. For Scott, the industry was organized into four hierarchical levels. At the base was machinery and hardware, notably computing, communication and associated peripherals and components. Resting on this base was programme interfacing software and systems design. Utilizing the software platform were the visual, audio and print media industries at whose intersection were found *multimedia*. Thus Scott's core definition of multimedia or new media exactly replicates ours in that they exist at the point of convergence of traditional or 'old media' and take the form of discrete combinations of voice, text and visual communication. These discrete combinations are then realized as multimedia products and services such as games and entertainment, educational products, business applications and so on. At the product and service end of this chain are two kinds of actor: developers who actually design and make titles, and publishers that market them. The latter sometimes finance the former who tend to be small-medium enterprises (SMEs). Title publishers are both large (e.g. Disney) and SME in scale. Scott concludes that new media emerged in Hollywood as an adjunct to the entertainment, film and music industries with studios such as Fox, Disney, Universal and Time Warner active as publishers and commissioners of multimedia titles. Northern California has a little of this, as with Sony Electronic Publishing, and Dreamworks, but it is strongest in production of the platforms enabling multimedia titles to be produced. In addition, more business multimedia products such as financial and business-related database products (e.g. Dataquest) were developed there.

In their definitive collection on the subject, Braczyk et al. (1999) concur with the definitions discussed so far by saying that 'multimedia' has a narrow and a broader meaning. In the former case it is conceived of as a convergence of several digital media that, interestingly, contain time-sensitive (sound, motion pictures) and time-insensitive (text, graphics) elements used interactively to produce an integrated effect. This is an aspect of the novelty of new media. More broadly, rather as the opening remarks of this contribution emphasized, 'multimedia' can be said to describe the present form taken by information and communications technology (ICT). That is, convergence has almost been achieved, unifying the contributions of content developers, programme and service providers, network operators, server and router suppliers, software and computer, telephony and consumer electronics industries. This elaborates the four-level multimedia value chain identified by Scott (1998). The extent of the then relatively recent technological innovations that made multimedia possible was outlined by Egan and Saxenian (1999). They included: operating systems software at 32 and 64 MB for PCs, audio and video processing on PC, storage growth from CD to DVD, high-resolution and flat-panel displays, colour laser printing, software applications for desktop publishing, image processing and editing for audio and video, interface devices like touch screens, graphic scanners, digital cameras and multimedia projectors, and networking through Internet and WWW accessed through TV, PC and, recently, handheld devices. By 2005,

many of these technologies were embodied in 3G mobile telephony.

So we are clear on the technological convergences that have made new media possible. Now it is time to look at some divergences, even though it is essential to remember that, according to Mansell (2000), the digital economy is fundamentally chaotic, 'devoid of shape, form, edges and geography', in the words of a visionary from British Telecom. Hence, among the divergences there are always coalescences caused by institutional actors such as firms and regulators. One such sphere of coalescence is Hollywood where Scott (1999) observed a 'multimedia and digital visual-effects' industry growing apace. As field leader this obviously had implications for new media and motion picture activities of all kinds. The digital visual-effects element of the couplet arose from digital enhancement through computer graphics applied to conventional media. This encompassed and unified hitherto separate fields of multimedia, animation and special effects into a toolbox routinely used in TV and film and video programming. Scott identified, by 1997, 188 firms doing this kind of multimedia work in Los Angeles, mostly in or near Hollywood.

Another diversion was Internet games, a vast market with abiding growth opportunities. Modern games service providers rely on the fact that up to 80 per cent of games can be played in a multiplayer format on the Internet on a hand-held device or a 'box'. The spectrum of providers runs from the lower end, based on a central server enabling up to 30 to be involved in a system which keeps track of the virtual game world in question, to companies supplying massive multiplayer games based in a 'server farm' capable of serving hundreds of thousands of players, British Telecom's Wireplay and smaller firms like Gameplay were then cases in point. Small startups concentrate on the former segment but are also key in designing and writing code for big games firms in the latter. Advertising to build a customer base is done online and much of the burn rate of startups is explained by the need to advertise. The more widely used games technology, the Sony Playstation 2 or Nintendo Game Boy type with sales of 80 million units has converged with the PC-based multiplayer kind. As Safer (2000) reported, Digital Bridges in early 2000 introduced Wirelessgames.com as a portal delivering multiplayer games to third-generation, wireless application protocol (WAP)-enabled mobile phones. This is a step beyond the large numbers of providers who have developed games playable on the Palm handheld device.

Finally, a further divergence, which, as we have already noted, also comes back to Palms and WAP mobiles, is business information. Despite the leading-edge software to build the global financial nets that were once only the province of currency dealers, but in the dot.com boom, became routinely exploited by day-trading taxi drivers and academics *inter alia*, such systems are characterized by a combination of picosecond speed in monitoring and updating, but a rather dull passivity in service provision. The news cuttings services, while of use, are scarcely interactive and, in consequence, are incapable of supplying the kind of problem-solving advice, tailored to specific need, that is so characteristic of required enterprise support. The dot.com-induced stock market slide after March 2000 cost dearly many such investors and stock option holders who were locked in to swiftly declining paper assets that the popularity of stock markets for non-experts may take a generation to recover.

Curiously, interactivity had been vaunted for decades, since Fowles' *French Lieutenant's Woman*, and in other narrative-oriented entertainment where there is scarcely any market for it. Current cases in point are interactive TV and the cinematically questionable but available interactive ('choose your own plot line and ending') cine-camera developed from the personalized version so successfully deployed in *Blair Witch Project*. But on business information it has yet to surface, leaving global financial markets with relatively unimaginative services in abundance.

Underlining this, Heydebrand (1999) presented a portrait of New York's 'Silicon Alley'. First, New York is home to seven globally

significant multimedia firms, among which Dow Jones and Co. (owners of *Wall Street Journal* and other financial titles) is the leading business information specialist. In London, Pearson Group (owners of *Financial Times* and ft.com) and, particularly, Reuters have comparable functions. Of course, New York's dominant old/new media firms dwarf Dow Jones, particularly Time Warner, Viacom, NBC, CBS and the Hearst Corporation, and these also have new media roles in business and financial information as well as entertainment. Pavlik (1999) noted that in 1997 southern Manhattan had 1106 multimedia firms employing 23,390 while midtown and uptown together had 668 firms employing 25,378. The former, 'Silicon Alley', was, as the numbers signify, the home of the small, creative firm cluster. Most of the multimedia energy of such firms was drawn into the dot.com surge and much of what was temporarily a sector with fleeting identity as multimedia was thus better understood as having morphed into that sphere.

It would be remiss not to pay some attention to the larger entertainment segment of the New York new media industry, where more skills remain in niches around computer graphics, special applications programming and content provision and small firms feed to and from corporate giants such as Time-Warner (TW), for a short time AOL–Time Warner as we have seen. An insider's view of some cultural discontinuities involved in such relationships was supplied by Wolff (1998), whose Wolff New Media (WNM) content business created *NetGuide*. In search of a possible acquisition or at least investment, WNM courted Time-Warner and AOL in the 1990s. The TW New Media Group had recently appointed a new general manager of New Media to join the editor of New Media, an old media journalist who, nevertheless, occupied third position on the headed notepaper. The new appointee replaced an executive whose enthusiasm for new media was such that he announced publicly 'the death of the book', something not guaranteed to please TW shareholders. TW had an Online Steering Committee and a president of Multimedia who outranked the head of the

New Media Group, but knew far less about the subject.

The TW New Media Group was responsible for the company's relationship with AOL who published *Time* on the Internet, for which AOL received free advertising in *Time*. The earnings ratio was at least 1 to 30 in AOL's favour by 1994. The Online Steering Committee was formed to solve the AOL conundrum. TW appointed WNM as a consultant to the Online Steering Group. For the editor of New Media, 'content is king' was the mission statement, to which 'technology is destiny' had recently been added. Hence, 'put *Time* on the Web' became the strategy, despite the obvious evidence that AOL customers had rejected that option substantively. Pathfinder, the vehicle for this, cost TW up to $20 million per year to run on revenues of $2–4 million. Meanwhile WNM started courting AOL, only to find them a firm where the supplicant had to organize the whole corporate interaction process, the exact opposite of the rococo administrative structure of Time-Warner. No result came from the interaction with AOL, whose executives gave every indication of seeking an acquirer as much as WNM, except that in early 2000 the acquired turned out to be Time-Warner and the acquirer AOL. The medium had truly taken over the message.

AOL–Time Warner was the first and maybe last new media conglomerate, merging all the multimedia elements of visual, print and audio media into the ISP-dominated infobahn. Sony, Bertelsmann, Viacom and the rest of the pack also came to terms with this content and communication convergence. As we saw, for AOL–Time Warner it unravelled because of incompatibilities, not least of management style. Klein (2003) reported the detestation of Time-Warner executives for the aggressive, accounts-driven management style that had brought swift growth to AOL's stock market valuation. One Time-Warner executive referred to his AOL counterparts as 'gross creeps', hardly grounds for a happy merger of corporate minds (Klein, 2003: 228). So it is important to recognize the overarching role of large and powerful units of multimedia capital such as Time-Warner, who are, generally speaking, not technologically creative except in making first moves and then aggrandizement. They may not be as intriguing to analyse as the lean and agile startups (which of course included AOL at that time) on whom large corporate actors almost completely depend for new media content. But the creativity to achieve scale without imagination is a subject worthy of study in its own right, yet regrettably perhaps, not one that is able to be pursued here. We have, rather, set the scene by exploring the transmutations of new media and defined the field in the process. The next step is to set that field in a wider context of industry organization and spatial dynamics because, despite the power of the corporate sector, there would be few, even transient, new economy industries without the exploitation, innovation and commercialization capabilities of small, dynamic new business entrants. The next section explores the settings in which such firms prosper.

THE CLUSTER IMPERATIVE IN THE NEW ECONOMY

Clustering is neither an unusual nor a new form of business organization. It was present in the beginning of the industrial age where cotton textiles firms in Britain, France and the USA concentrated in industrial districts, and handgun manufacturers famously clustered in places like Springfield, Massachusetts. They did so to access skilled labour and to pick up as free goods the knowhow that was said to be 'in the air' in such places. For much of the twentieth century the ownership of firms in such districts concentrated so that, for example, the classic auto cluster of Detroit was dominated by the big two producers, Ford and GM, with Chrysler some way behind, and now part of Daimler-Benz's global grouping. But these were once clusters of numerous independent assembly and components supplier firms, and when Japanese competition began to bite in the 1980s the giants began to downsize and externalize production back into supply chains that were by now as much global as local. Simultaneously, new industries such as semi-conductor and computer production grew as new small firms entered production in places like Silicon Valley and Boston (Rogers and Larsen, 1984; Saxenian, 1994), and while the evolutionary trajectories of even these two places have diverged, more such clusters have emerged elsewhere in the world, including the developing world (see, for example, Schmitz and Nadvi, 1999). Fired by the early success of high-technology clusters, many administrations tried to emulate Silicon Valley. Most failed dismally, but one case that stands out as successful and policy-driven is Austin, Texas (see, for instance, Henton et al., 1997) where strong private leadership involving business, government and education in association attracted blue chip firms such as Motorola and IBM as well as high-technology consortia such as Sematech and MCC. It was in the 1970s and 1980s that a soft infrastructure of investors and other knowledge-intensive service providers grew in tandem with a harder incubation infrastructure at the University of Texas, to form an establishment known as IC². From this, what had the look of a branch plant econ-omy became more entrepreneurial as firms like Dell and its suppliers came to prominence through endogenous growth.

Clusters have now become a key mode of economic coordination and focus of govern-ment policies across the world and for a wide variety of industries. The UK IT industry's cluster prospective group Information Age Partnership definition of a cluster as a 'geographical con-centration of interdependent companies and institutions connected by a system of market and non-market links' is a useful starting point, as it captures key elements of competitive *and* collaborative interaction that characterize firm relationships. It also recognizes the impor-tance of *proximity* to those relationships and that important relationships are not limited to those between firms only. It is thus close to Michael Porter's (1998) definition, which is that: 'A cluster is a geographically proximate group of interconnected companies and associ-ated institutions *in a particular field*, linked

by commonalities and complementarities' (emphasis added). This, in turn, underpinned the definition used by the UK Minister of Science for the work of his task force on *biotechnology* clusters, as: 'geographic concentrations of inter-connected companies, specialized suppliers, service providers, firms in related industries and associated institutions (for example uni-versities, standards agencies and trade associa-tions) in particular fields that compete but also cooperate'.

There is nothing wrong with these definitions except that they are all *static*, whereas the key feature of clusters is that they are *dynamic*. Hence we prefer the following also to be taken into account. A cluster displays a shared identity and future vision. It is characterized by 'turbu-lence' as firms spin off, spin out and start up from other firms or institutions. A cluster is an arena of dense and changing vertical input–output linkages, supply chains and horizontal interfirm networks. It is likely to have developed localized, third-party representative governance associations that provide common services but also lobby government for change. A cluster may have caused governments to develop poli-cies to assist cluster development, especially where market failures are present. Over time, clusters can reveal features of emergence, domi-nance and decline. So we come to a preferred definition of a cluster as: 'geographically proxi-mate firms in vertical and horizontal relation-ships, involving a localized enterprise support infrastructure with a shared developmental vision for business growth, based on competi-tion and cooperation in a specific market field'.

Why are clusters more prominent now than hitherto? Why does the hierarchical firm, so pronounced a feature of the mid-twentieth-century corporate landscape, no longer necessar-ily act as the model for economic coordination? There are at least three key reasons for this. First, global competition, initially from Japan and South East Asia, then from the US response to it, caused large corporations to reduce in-house production and administrative overhead while increasing outsourcing and learning, for example, lean production, in order to sur-vive. Second, innovation became a leading competitive weapon and small, knowledge-based firms, often close to universities, were further up the technological learning curve. Ultimately large firms have, in many areas, outsourced even their R&D functions to such entities in a process called 'open innovation' (Chesbrough, 2003). Third, as we have seen in the case of Time-Warner and new media, the intrinsic rigidities of the hierarchical corporate organization meant rapid learning and accommodation to change could not be easily implemented.

In brief, Porter (1998) holds that a number of advantages are derived from clusters, among which are the following. First, *productivity* gains arise from access to early use of better-quality and lower-cost specialized inputs from components or services suppliers in the cluster. Local sourcing can be cheaper because of minimal inventory requirements and transaction costs generally can be lower because of the existence of high-trust relations and the importance of reputation-based trading. Common purchasing can lower costs where external sourcing is necessary. Serendipitous information trading is more likely in contexts where formal or informal face-to-face contact is possible. Complementarities between firms can help joint bidding and scale benefits on contract tenders, or joint marketing of products and services. Access to public goods from research or standards bodies located in proximity can be advantageous.

Second, *innovation* gains come from *proximity* between customers and suppliers where the interaction between the two may lead to innovative specifications and responses. User-led innovation impulses are recognized as crucial to the innovation process and their discovery has led to a better understanding of the interactive rather than linear processes of innovation. Proximity to knowledge centres makes the interaction processes concerning design, testing and prototype development physically easier, especially where much of the necessary knowledge is partly or wholly tacit rather than codified. Localized benchmarking among firms on organizational as well as product and process innovation is facilitated in clusters. Qualified personnel are more easily recruited and are of key importance to knowledge transfer. Informal knowhow trading is easier in clusters than through more distant relationships.

Finally, *new businesses* are more readily formed where better information about innovative potential and market opportunities is locally available. Barriers to entry for new firms can be lower because of a clearer perception of unfulfilled needs, product or service gaps, or anticipated demand. Locally available inputs and skills further reduce barriers to entry. A cluster in itself can be an important initial market. Familiarity with local public, venture capital or business angel funding sources may speed up the investment process and minimize risk premiums for new startups and growing businesses. Clusters attract outside firms and foreign direct investors who perceive benefits from being in a specialized, leading-edge business location. These may also be a further source of corporate spinoff businesses.

Clusters work through networks between a variety of business and other appropriate actors who are familiar with each other's expertise, trustworthiness, reliability and willingness both to share relevant assets (e.g. information or lending a machine or employee if needed) and engage in normal business relationships based on market exchange. Networks can be formal or informal, soft or hard (i.e. contractual, with an agreed project and business plan). In high-technology industry, such linkages are likely to involve research organizations such as universities for knowledge, but also indirectly through spinout firms (Cooke et al., 2000). Aspects of this appear in Figure 13.1, which anatomizes key parts of the Cambridge (UK) IT cluster, showing regular cooperative as well as competitive relationships within the cluster.

A key question for policy is: can clusters be built? This refers to the role of policy on the part of different levels of government. While many correctly cast doubt on the difficulty, if not impossibility, of building clusters from zero, this has not stopped governments trying to do this in the past. Technopoles and the cognate notion of 'technopolis' are cases in point.

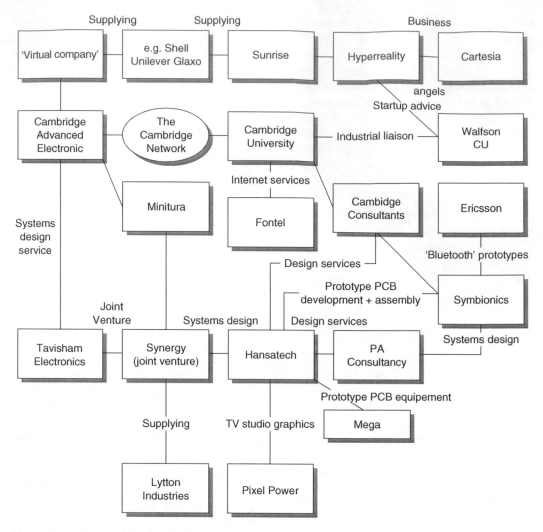

Figure 13.1   *Aspects of the Cambridge IT Cluster*

These are large spaces, sometimes even whole towns or cities, designated by governments as locations for which incentives are available to encourage corporations or public organizations to relocate research and development (R&D) facilities. The aspiration was that these would interact with synergetic growth and innovation effects. France and Japan built 'technopoles' by attracting research branches to co-locate in special zones such as Sophia Antipolis and Tsukuba City. However, most commentators agree these are not clusters. Indeed Japan has abandoned its technopolis programme in favour of a 'clusters' programme since 2001 (Cooke et al., 2004). This is because synergetic interactions scarcely occured despite proximity; most interactions persisted over distance back to corporate headquarters or other corporate divisions elsewhere. There was little evidence of spinoff or other kinds of new firm formation despite this also being a key aspiration. This lack of local linkage denied technopoles the status of clusters. Synergy effects are now understood to be extremely hard to create. But it is now better understood that a 'soft infrastructure' of knowledge-intensive business services ranging from investment, management, legal, patenting and technology transfer to specialist consultancies is a key presence in most successful clusters. These were typically not present in technopoles. Synergies, meaning a surplus or Gestalt effect created by fruitful interaction, can be assisted enormously by the market transactions of such private intermediaries and the supportive actions of grant-giving public ones.

However, where there is something with which to work, especially in creative and knowledge-intensive activity, then policy may enhance cluster formation. Some examples of this include Finnish regional science and technology policy encouraging universities to set up technology parks on university campuses, with Nokia or other research labs acting as customers to multi-media software and computing services supplied by startups. The Technical University at Tampere has generated a small multimedia cluster on its Hermia Technology Park. As Nokia recognized content to be the key to its future profitability with hardware being outsourced to China, it built a number of new R&D laboratories in proximity to behavioural psychology and cognitive neuroscience research centres of universities such as Helsinki, Tampere and Jyväskäla to access new knowledge applicable to games technologies, notably its N-Gage box and 3G mobile telephony solution. In the US, clusters are often promoted at state level through setting up infrastructure, industry associations, grants, tax credits and R&D credits. But there still has to be a knowledge-generating source in research labs or other key firms.

Stimulated by the evident success of Silicon Valley, California in the 1970s and 1980s, many national and regional governments sought to encourage the formation of high-technology industry complexes by earmarking budgets and special high-tech development zones, modelled to some extent on the pattern established by the science park at Stanford University, founded in 1951 (Castells and Hall, 1994). It is well known that Frederick Terman, later Provost and Vice-President at Stanford, was the driving force behind Stanford Industrial Park, as it was officially known, and that among his student entrepreneurs were the founder of Litton Industries, and later Hewlett and Packard, preceded as tenants on the park by Varian and succeeded by Fairchild Semiconductors. Fairchild was the matrix for Intel, National Semiconductors, American Micro Devices and some 40 other US chip manufacturers from 1957, when the 'Shockley eight' began to find their feet.

The science-push emphasis of the story fitted in well with the dominant *linear* model of innovation then at the forefront of understanding of the relationship between scientific progress and the commercialization of products and processes. Clearly also, for what, with hindsight, were the truly radical innovations of semiconductors, namely integrated circuits and microprocessors, technology push was a significant impulse, at least in relation to civilian applications. Even so, the role of the Department of Defense and the National Aeronautics and Space Administration as *users* of miniaturized computers and guidance systems has perhaps been highlighted less than their role as suppliers of large-scale *funding* for the development of microcircuitry. We still know relatively little about the nature and extent of interaction between users and technologists at the early stage of the development of these new technologies, though it has been argued that 67 per cent of the functional source of innovation development for semiconductors was *users* and only 21 per cent *manufacturers* (von Hippel, 1988: 4).

To return to the efforts by policy-makers to model high-tech innovation on developments at Stanford and Silicon Valley, it is clear that most approaches have involved the idea of co-locating research centres and innovation-intensive firms in science and technology parks. In some cases this has involved designating whole cities as science cities or technopoles. Although benefits have been accrued from such plans, there is also in the literature that reviews such developments a frequent sense of disappointment that more has not been achieved. In cases drawn from France and Japan, countries that have arguably proceeded furthest with the *technopolis* policy, a certain absence of *synergies* has been observed among co-located laboratories and firms. Science parks, in themselves, have not always met the expectations of their founders and efforts have been made to learn from early mistakes. Nowadays, in response to the improvement in understanding of innovation as an interactive, possibly systemic process, more attention is paid to the factors that lead to embeddedness among firms and innovation support organizations (Granovetter, 1985). This anthropological idea refers to the institutional and organizational features of community and solidarity, the exercise of 'social capital' (Cooke and Wills, 1999; Putnam, 1993) and the foundations of high-trust, networked types of relationship among firms and organizations. To some extent also, there is emerging recognition that science parks are a valuable element but not the only or main objective of a localized or regionalized innovation strategy. A good deal of research has been conducted which helps understanding of the nature and range of interaction among firms and organizations engaged in innovation (see, for example, Acs, 2000; Braczyk et al., 1998; Cooke and Morgan, 1998; Cooke et al., 2004; de la Mothe and Paquet, 1998; Edquist, 1997) and policy is moving towards a notion of the *regional innovation system* as an important level at which strategic innovation support is appropriate (Cooke, 1992; Cooke et al., 2000; Tödtling and Sedlacek, 1997).

The French and Japanese examples of technopole implantation help us learn how difficult it is to plan clusters. The French were the first to experiment with the idea of technopoles at Grenoble with Meylan-ZIRST (Industrial Zone for Research in Science and Technology). This has concentrated many public and private research laboratories but produced few synergies among smaller or even larger firms locally. Our example is that of Sophia Antipolis, which has eventually succeeded, like Meylan-ZIRST, in attracting government research laboratories and larger private investment but is perceived still to suffer from the relative absence of interactive innovation. Even in Grenoble, Rallet and Torre (1998) noted that despite strong specialization in

health technologies, research and training infrastructures were 'poorly connected' with local industry and industrial cooperation has been for a long time 'considered insufficient'. De Bernardy (1999) also suggested that, to the extent collective learning was present in Rhône-Alpes it was informal, fragile and vulnerable to market pressures.

Sophia Antipolis

Established in 1972 as a personal mission of Pierre Laffitte, co-director of the prestigious Paris École des Mines, Sophia Antipolis started slowly with little interest in the idea from business or the public sector. After 1975 a second launch was aimed at attracting R&D from US firms. Some, such as Digital, came and were joined by French firms Thomson and L'Oréal, and government pharmacological and information technology laboratories followed. By the early 1990s Sophia Antipolis had 14,000 employees with 9000 of them directly engaged in technological activities (Longhi and Quéré, 1993). Among the US firms locating development units to introduce products to the European market were Cardis, Dow and Rockwell (in addition to Digital).

In Longhi and Quéré's (1993) evaluation the following key points were made. First, innovation networks were still marginal in Sophia Antipolis, especially regarding local activities and employment. While Digital and Thomson had organized a local network, as had two pharmacological firms, interacting with production and research skills locally, few dynamic innovations had ensued and learning from local partnerships was minimal. Second, where a few linkages existed they were almost exclusively vertical, never horizontal. Firms were isolated from their parent organizations and feared 'poaching' from other co-located laboratories. Further, active *mistrust* existed between innovative large firms and local research institutions, although not between the latter and local small, innovative firms. The fear of losing proprietary knowhow was behind this mistrust. Third, there was no local labour market. There was almost no

mobility between firms or organizations. In
each case an internal labour market operated.
The risk of information exchange was the main
reason for this absence of labour market mobility. This was the single most obvious instance of
the lack of an innovative network or milieu
culture at Sophia Antipolis.

In terms of learning from this experience, the
following points are of considerable significance.
There were, by 2000, weak signs of innovative
interaction between larger firms seeking, for
example, locally available software services. Some
French firms were being attracted to Sophia
Antipolis by aspects of its critical mass and network potential. More new firms were still needed
to create sufficient critical mass for synergies and
creative innovation. Where external networking
existed it largely remained a vertical, supply-
chain relationship. The public-sector policy
networks were the most significant factor in
potentially building up local innovative networks. Early on, their main focus had been on
'selling square metres'. Thus, Longhi and Quéré
(1993) concluded Sophia Antipolis was only a
qualified and rather one-dimensional economic
success. A more recent paper by Longhi (1999)
underlined the missing preconditions for collective learning in the absence of a science base,
spinoff firms and weak local interactions.
However, some moderation of the position
occurred when the University of Nice moved its
IT departments to Sophia Antipolis in 1986,
helping create a local labour market supply
resource. Global firms were thereafter making
stronger local linkages with startups and research
institutes. Elements of a localized form of systemic innovation began to emerge after 25 years.

Technopoles in Japan

In Japan, a major effort to build a scientific pole
or cluster occurred at roughly the same time
as in France. Tsukuba originated in 1958 as a
satellite science city for Tokyo. Tsukuba met the
criteria regarding infrastructure, location and
transportation later used to judge which cities
would join the technopolis programme. It was
mainly government funded: the Japan Housing
Corporation built housing for nearly 125,000

people and the Ministry of Construction paid
for infrastructure. Laboratories and a science
and technology university were relocated to the
science city. Only in the 1980s did private
industry show interest in the site, following
construction of a motorway to service the
International Science and Technology Expo of
1985. Public investment by 1990 was $1.1
billion. But many national research institutes
(e.g. Inorganic Materials; Disaster Prevention;
High Energy Physics; Health and Hygiene; and
Environment) continued to experience difficulties in developing linkages other than the
vertical ones typical of government agencies.
Hence they did not share facilities or link to
universities or private industry. There was also
a lack of new spinoff firms. Tsukuba was seen as
an isolated island, although in the 1990s more
local conferences and information exchanges
began to occur. But, in general, there was relatively little synergy among organizations.

An evaluation of the Japanese technopolis
programme was reported in Castells and Hall
(1994). They concluded that there had been
failure to achieve the original vision. Some
were dormitory or conventional new towns,
not technopoles. There was a branch-plant
syndrome as decentralized firms mainly conducted routine assembly work for the parent
company. There had been failure to develop
university–industry links; the main links were
with local technical laboratories rather than
universities. Notable was a lack of 'soft infrastructure' consisting of venture capital, R&D
consortia and university research networks.
There had been a failure to relocate R&D laboratories. Before decamping to China, these had
been relocating closer to headquarters than to
factories. Problematic was a lack of interindustry linkages because of the weak R&D and
strong branch-plant characteristics. There was
a lack of spinoff for the same reasons as the
absence of interindustry linkages and universities.
In general, the conclusion made by Castells
and Hall (1994) was that the Japanese technopolis programme had not yet proved itself
successful in terms of interactive innovation.
As we saw, by 2001 the programme had been
closed down.

Neither France nor Japan became leading players in new economy sectors, new media in particular, except for handheld electronic games by Sega and the like (though recall most of the creative work is done by startups in the UK and US). Nonaka and Reinmöller (1998) had an interesting take on this, at least for Japan. They referred to Japan's problem as 'the legacy of learning'. That is, Japan spent so much time and energy on catching up with the West by learning from its practices and seeking to improve upon them in mature sectors, that its economy became locked into old economy activities and its universities and technopoles failed to anticipate any new economy areas. Now there is a frantic effort to relearn and leapfrog as once before, but economic conditions are far less propitious for achieving this than they once were. France also suffers from an overdependence on institutional structures that are state-led and subsidized, a predeliction for mature old economy sectors and a weak base in the new economy. This could be said of the other European big-hitting economies: only the UK has a good presence in new economy business, including new media, while Germany and Italy are adrift in major ways despite strong German media corporations like Kirch and Bertelsmann.

NEW MEDIA CLUSTERS AND THE INDUSTRY TRAJECTORY

We thus do not find much 'new economy' industry, particularly that relating to new media, to be satisfactorily built by public policy from scratch, with the small but interesting exception of the Finnish policy of inducing multimedia firms from technology faculties linked to a proximate and exacting user such as Nokia. More typical are the following five cases in cities varying in size from the global metropolitan to the regional business or administrative capital, where the unifying feature is the overwhelming importance for production of the kind of small firm-dominated clusters described in the preceding

section, connected to large, often global customers, located not in geographic but in functional proximity. Functional proximity means 'virtual space' whereby a customer and supplier may be extremely close in their specific shared interest (in an aspect of new media, for example) but geographically poles apart. Of the two, geographic proximity is the more important from a creativity or innovation capabilities point of view, but of course without finance – especially in new media where there are few public research grants available – there is no demand. So they are conceptually as important as one another, constituting a global capabilities relationship that is fundamental to a given new economy sector. In the largest cities, geographic and functional proximity may coincide (see, for further analysis, Rallet and Torre, 1998).

A good example of the latter case occurs in London, where small, creative new media firms are found in a cluster in Soho and numerous large corporate consumers are found in rather less funky locations in the West End. Soho is interesting in terms of industrial history, having once been London's garment district. Accordingly, comparatively large working spaces were available when these workshops and small factories were no longer viable once scale economies entered the business. The UK film industry has for long been managed and had its distribution arranged from Soho, as to some extent has the recorded music industry. But most famously Soho became one of Europe's leading adult entertainment centres with outstanding jazz and blues clubs, strip joints, and gourmet as well as more affordable restaurants and pubs with artistic clienteles. Much of this economy operated in basements, but in the 1960s into the former clothing workshops upstairs entered the UK software industry, represented by firms like Logica and Hoskyns. The large, relatively open-plan working spaces with attractive iron-frame building construction and cheap rents were ideal for such firms. So unlike SoHo, New York, where such industrial spaces were adaptively reused by artists, helping leapfrog the area into a loft-living cultural space of which one part was new media, Soho, London possessed the fine tilth of multiple cultural forms, including old media, the arts, entertainment and advertising from which multimedia could naturally grow.

As Nachum and Keeble (2000) showed, London has at least 70 per cent of UK employment in media and 90 per cent in music. Of this, Soho captures about 70 per cent and, as they said, 'The entire chain of production – film production and post production, film distribution and sales agents, design, photography, music, advertising – is available in an area of about one square mile' (2000: 11). Soho is also home to foreign media firms as well as those from the UK. Hence multimedia in London has a bias towards traditional media and advertising, growing from the audio, video and print media in the neighbourhood. The main kinds of new media market served involve corporate presentation, entertainment and leisure, particularly Internet games, and advertising and marketing, notably development of Internet websites. In a study by Russ (1998) he shows that London also has subclusters in Covent Garden, Clerkenwell and Shoreditch. The first named is well known as one of Europe's leading urban cultural zones, the ambience of which was reinvigorated when the capital's fruit and vegetable market was adaptively reused for shopping and leisure activities to complement its traditional function as one of the world's leading places for opera. The other two are in London's East End, former industrial and working-class zones; Clerkenwell was once London's clock-making quarter. These locations are selected because they are in cheap rent areas, yet the EC1 postcode is seen as valuable owing to its proximity to central London's huge financial district. Much of the market for these firms is governed by the variety of clients locally available, especially in business services. Although far smaller than the Soho clusters, firms in these mini-clusters congregate for the same reasons, notably that it is useful to be co-located as an insurance against breakdowns of equipment or for subcontracting. Trust in each other is highly valued and accessed as a normal business 'spillover'.

In Heydebrand's (1999) and Pavlik's (1999) studies of multimedia in New York, as we have seen, the entertainment and financial sectors are powerful drivers of the industry with both functional and geographic proximity being key features, albeit, as in London, the precise streetblocks occupied by the corporate giants are somewhat upscale of those of the new media firms themselves. In south Manhattan, especially around SoHo and the iconic 55 Broad Street, where was established the New York Information Technology Center, business, as elsewhere, involved entertainment software, Internet services, CD-ROM title development and website design. Surrounding them functionally and spatially are the advertising, marketing, entertainment, education, publishing and TV, film and video producers and publishers. Heydebrand (1999) saw a three-level structure to the industry with the corporate giants resting on the mass of new media businesses who themselves relate importantly to Silicon Alley's creative and innovative capability as represented particularly strongly by 55 Broad Street. Because the last named is unique to New York, it is more interesting to explore its existence as a public–private intervention than to repeat the locational lineages and rationales of the 1000 plus startups in and around SoHo. That it functions as a cluster with horizontal and vertical networks based on trust, exchange, co-bidding and competition on contracts, subcontracting and knowhow and equipment sharing as in London, is made clear by Heydebrand (1999) and Pavlik (1999) in their accounts.

The development at 55 Broad Street is different in that it is the product of the new economy governance practice of 'associationism' (Cooke and Morgan, 1998). With its first meeting in mid 1997 the New York multimedia innovation network set a mission of developing the city as the global capital of multimedia. It united mayoral and gubernatorial representation, Columbia University's NSF-backed Engineering Research Centre in multimedia, the finance and services community, venture capital, leading multimedia startups, major multimedia companies, arts and culture groups and industry associations. They met in the New York Information Technology Center, 55 Broad Street, brainchild of developer William Rudin, who invested $40 million in superwiring the building as an incubator for multimedia startups. Technologically the building offered, in 1997, turnkey multimedia transmission with satellite access, desktop fibre optics, C5 copper, video conferencing and 100 MB per second Internet bandwidth. There were 72 tenants in 1997, including International Business Machines and many startups in design, reportage, security and research among others. The association, like other cluster governance networks has policies to lobby for tax, equity and rent incentives, business support programmes and expanding incubator opportunities. By 2005 as well as startups it housed the likes of Cap Gemini (software), Nokia (content), Level 3 (communications) and Sun Microsystems (Java mobile devices).

We have already given some attention to Scott's (1998, 1999) studies of Californian multimedia. As we have seen, they are closely linked to the software and peripherals sectors of Silicon Valley, and business and education products, often for San Francisco clients in the north, with the Hollywood entertainment cluster in southern California being the driver of multimedia in Los Angeles. There are many smaller and startup businesses in the clusters, with many of the standard characteristics found generically elsewhere. Geographically, San Francisco's multimedia firms are strung out along Route 101 from south of San Jose to San Mateo and the main concentration in downtown San Francisco, across the Golden Gate bridge to northern Marin County. In Los Angeles, the axis is much less attenuated, concentrated on a line from Burbank through Hollywood to Santa Monica. In California, there are more developers and hardware/ software technicians in the San Francisco area and more entertainment and communication companies in Los Angeles. They also overlap somewhat with pre-existing software and computing clusters, gaining externalities or 'spillovers' from such co-location. Median firm size is small, converging upon nine employees, though it is supplemented with freelancers as required by specific projects; large firms tend to have a more stable labour force profile. Creative workers are rather intensively employed in the industry, at a level approximately equivalent to those employed in technical and business functions together. Firms market products globally but interact in production highly locally. Over half the value of sales is accounted for by inwardly or outwardly subcontracted activities, more than two-thirds of which is local. The San Francisco cluster is more 'associative' (Cooke and Morgan, 1998) in the sense of having developed representative organizations, but real service support is largely private rather than public in origin, except for close association with universities in the Los Angeles cluster.

A second case, of special interest because of its cluster identification and warehouse district location, is that offered by Brail and Gertler (1999) which anatomized the multimedia industry of Toronto, Canada. Underlining the functional division of the industry between developers and publishers by reference to the Canadian Interactive Multimedia Arts and Technologies (IMAT) distinction between *producers* and *publishers*, Brail and Gertler segment the market into four: corporate, education, entertainment, and information/ reference. They speculate that *health* may be developing as a new segment. Interestingly, evidence is advanced of the Ontario Film Development Corporation's view that multimedia, like the film/TV industries, shows increasing *vertical* integration as producers attempt to control distribution channels. However, Brail and Gertler's research evidence suggests this is a misreading of the situation and that most Canadian multimedia firms are independent, small, creative and dualistic (full-timers and freelancers) just as in California.

The Toronto study identified some 300 firms in Ontario (from a Canadian total of some 560), of which 201 (67 per cent) are in metropolitan Toronto. The largest proportion were located near the city centre in former inner-city industrial areas. These displayed flexible workspaces, heritage buildings, proximity to other cultural industries, central business services and clients. Toronto combines two capital functions, corporate/financial and cultural (publishing, film, broadcasting) which acted as magnets for multimedia firms. Research with firms in face-to-face interviews revealed that locational preference was determined by the relational questions noted earlier, flexible and affordable space, and the 'downtown' ambience. Clients were mainly Toronto based but links were developing with the California clusters. Interviewees reported little interfirm information sharing, a competitive ethic, and low-trust relationships at the horizontal level, i.e. between firms of similar size and with similar or complementary assets. Informal knowhow sharing occurs between individuals rather than firms. Confidentiality clauses and secrecy on competitive bid prices are normal even though there are few competitors for contracts. Collaboration among firms occurs but on a strict 'need to know' basis; joint ventures are a favoured mode of collaboration. Finance is precarious, based on venture capital and involving trading of product rights in exchange for funding. High marketing and distribution costs mean firms specialize in customized products, unless they are large, generic producers. Public support for the industry is strong at national, regional and local levels, with funding of projects available from the province of Ontario.

Finally, to show the importance of the link to old media and their re-regulation in the UK, first in stimulating the rise of independent TV programme producers who, second, stimulated directly through spinoff, and indirectly as a market, the formation of multimedia activity, we may look at the case of Cardiff, capital of Wales, one of the UK's four constituent countries. Here we will show both the cluster structure of the industry and the organogram of the wide variety of private and public actors that act as the enterprise support infrastructure for the cluster system,

arranging scholarships and bursaries for different kinds of human capital; representing the industry at Cannes, Venice, Los Angeles and other major festivals; and pump-priming or assisting in small-firm bootstrapping to try to ensure that this small and fledgling industry, dependent mainly on a regional market but pushing to sell more widely, evolves. Cooke and Hughes (1999) provide an account of the industry derived from a survey of 300 firms in multimedia and media, animation, graphics, creative arts and services; 48 (16 per cent) were core multimedia producers (online or offline producers). Of the 145 firms responding to the questionnaire (48 per cent response rate), 28 (19 per cent) were core producers. Of these firms, 17 were specifically set up to produce online and offline products such as CDs composed of film and TV clips for entertainment; CD-interactive musical instrument tutoring; geographical information systems; financial trading CD databases and media business CD databases along with vocational training CDs. A further 11 were providers of Internet services or web page designers. Three of the first group and six of the second are currently located in Cardiff Bay.

In Figure 13.2 the degree of co-location and the known market and non-market interactions between firms are visible. Thus, for obvious reasons, editing firms and the manufacturer of editing equipment interact, but they also cross-connect to the CD-ROM and web design, computer graphics, Internet services and animation firms according to need. Not all firms are located in the main multimedia cluster district in the waterfront area, once the home to the commercial activities of the largest coal-export port in the world; many are dotted around the city of Cardiff. Nor are all firms shown, which would be graphically impossible, so this is a cut across the industry in Cardiff, rather as that of Cambridge was in the previous section. In Figure 13.3 can be seen the rather elaborate associational infrastructure and its functions that underpins the new media and old media industries in Wales.

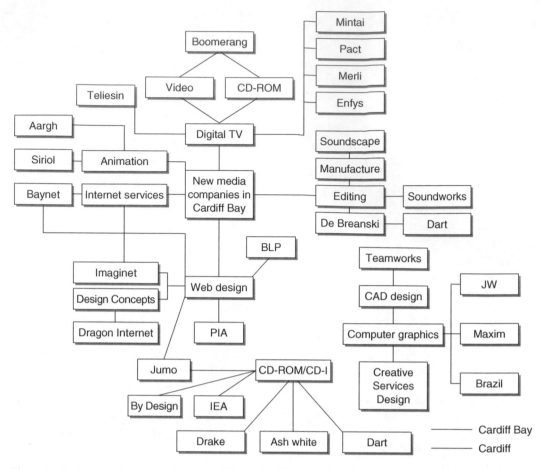

Figure 13.2   *New media companies in Cardiff and Cardiff Bay (selected)*

The relative prominence of this small-scale industry is testified for by the fact that two of its film outputs, *Hedd Wyn* and *Solomon a Gaenor* (both Welsh language titles), and two cartoons received Oscar nominations in the foreign film and animation categories in the 1990s and 2000. Historically, Wales' contribution to Hollywood had been supplying movie stars like Ray Milland (né Reginald Truscott-Jones), Richard Burton (né Richie Jenkins), Anthony Hopkins, Catherine Zeta Jones and Ioan Gruffydd. The promotional activities of an organization like Screen Wales are of some assistance in getting actual feature films before the appropriate assessment panels. However,

more prosaically and of more daily importance are the contracts small media firms get from the three main publishers, BBC, HTV and S4C. Screen Wales also helps them access EU, UK Lottery Film Fund or regional (e.g. the $20 million Wales Film Fund, a public venture capital source) grants and financing through the EU Information Society and Media programmes, or special help from Cardiff's Media City Initiative. So, as in Hollywood, particularly, London, New York and Toronto, but at a smaller scale, new media in Wales are quite closely connected to old media, but developing an identity of their own to some degree before being transmuted, as elsewhere, into Internet

Figure 13.3   *The Cardiff new media cluster*

and other means of communicating online, entertainment, business database, educational, corporate presentation and large- and smaller-scale website design and maintenance.

CONCLUDING REMARKS

Space does not allow for fuller reflection on the movements and transitions that have been registered in this account of the business and spatial dynamics of this burgeoning new industry. In drawing the discussion to a close, three key things stand out. The first of these is that there is a considerable amount of movement, coalescence and divergence but all within an overarching and strong tendency towards technological and even content convergence in new media. Nowadays, all the older media that converged to form new media are available on a 3G mobile phone. They may evolve distinctive forms inherited from the past, like TV, radio and music channels. More likely, they will develop integrated website-like presentational forms with footer text scrolling, video streaming and multiscreening for news and action presentation and music overdubs. This could be seen on some specialist TV channels by 2000, and grew, mainly for monitoring rather than 'absorptive watching' media programming. New media will join traditional media rather than replace it, just as Internet shopping will join 'going to the shops' rather than replacing that activity. There will be more rather than less choice of media experiences.

Second, when we look at the industry dynamics and their economic geography, we find new media to be generically similar to other new economy sectors like IT and biotechnology. These are characterized by small startup firms spinning out from a creative or technologically innovative base, clustering together for reasons of mutual support, knowhow trading, trustful exchange and industry monitoring but, essentially, remaining co-located in the now classical form of the geographic cluster. Firms in such clusters reduce risk by moving into *applications* domains where they use their expertise in new activity markets like client-driven multimedia public relations, event management and conference organization. This is the functionally diversifying but technologically convergent character of the production, or supply of value-added knowledge, side of the equation. Clusters form near knowledge centres like universities, or in new media, where street life is vibrant. Thus far, the new media businesses that have broken free of the hegemony of large old media corporate control are America Online, that ballooned then burst as we saw, and the more specialist businesses like Amazon.com or Yahoo! that have prospered, albeit the latter now integrated into the UK company BT's corporate set-up. These firms grew massively in scale and market capitalization at tremendous speed, without in some cases troubling the accountants to count profits, since there were none. Traditional IT is much more conservative in its business development planning than some of these new

media/Internet types of firm, and perceived as less risky for obvious reasons. They too have displaced behemoths like IBM from pole position in IT, Microsoft and Intel being the key cases in point. Nevertheless, despite the present power of clusters, firms in them still require large corporations as clients and milestone project funders.

Finally, while new economy markets are dynamic, keeping first-mover advantage often reveals market failures. Supporting fledgling new media businesses and whole strands of the industry requires concerted efforts by a range of private and public actors operating associationally. This is well exemplified by the support given to the essentially private 55 Broad Street multimedia scheme, which is looking to the future of New York's position on a global basis. In Cardiff, a smaller-scale activity with roots in a relatively immature independent old media sector gains some valuable infrastructural support, human capital and global promotion from the public and private collaboration system put in place in Wales. In the final analysis, these are necessary but not sufficient to sustain businesses in swiftly changing fields like new media. Markets will dictate survival or annihilation, and markets are increasingly global, but paradoxically, as this contribution has shown, the creative spirits, innovative ideas and social interactions that make new media possible as commercial products are normally clustered in remarkably localized spaces of the new economy.

REFERENCES

Acs, Z. (ed.) (2000) *Regional Innovation, Knowledge and Global Change.* London: Pinter.
Braczyk, H., Cooke, P. and Heidenreich, M. (eds) (1998) *Regional Innovation Systems.* London: UCL Press.
Braczyk, H., Fuchs, G. and Wolf, H. (eds) (1999) *Multimedia and Regional Economic Restructuring.* London: Routledge.
Brail, S. and Gertler, M. (1999) 'The digital regional economy: emergence and evolution of Toronto's multimedia cluster', in H. Braczyk, G. Fuchs and

H. Wolf (eds), *Multimedia and Regional Economic Restructuring*. London: Routledge.

Castells, M. and Hall, P. (1994) *Technopoles of the World*. London: Routledge.

Chesbrough, H. (2003) *Open Innovation*, Boston: Harvard Business School Press.

Cohen, W. and Levinthal, D. (1990) 'Absorptive capacity: a new perspective on learning and innovation', *Administrative Sciences Quarterly*, 35: 128–52.

Cooke, P. (1990) *Back to the Future: Modernity, Postmodernity and Locality*. London: Unwin Hyman.

Cooke, P. (1992) 'Regional innovation systems: competitive regulation in the new Europe', *Geoforum*, 23: 365–82.

Cooke, P. and Hughes, G. (1999) 'Creating a multimedia cluster in Cardiff Bay', in H. Braczyk, G. Fuchs and H. Wolf (eds), *Multimedia and Regional Economic Restructuring*. London: Routledge.

Cooke, P. and Morgan, K. (1998) *The Associational Economy: Firms, Regions and Innovation*. Oxford: Oxford University Press.

Cooke, P. and Wills, D. (1999) 'Small firms, social capital and the enhancement of business performance through innovation programmes', *Small Business Economics*, 13: 219–34.

Cooke, P. Boekholt, P. and Tödtling, F. (2000) *The Governance of Innovation in Europe*. London: Pinter.

Cooke, P., Heidenreich, M. and Braczyk, H. (eds) (2004) *Regional Innovation Systems*. 2nd edn. London: Routledge.

De Bernardy, M. (1999) 'Reactive and proactive local territory: co-operation and community in Grenoble', *Regional Studies*, 33: 343–52.

De la Mothe, J. and Paquet, G. (1998) *Local and Regional Systems of Innovation*. Dordrecht: Kluwer.

Edquist, C. (ed.) (1997) *Systems of Innovation*. London: Pinter.

Egan, E. and Saxenian, A. (1999) 'Becoming digital: sources of localization in the Bay Area multimedia cluster', in H. Braczyk, G. Fuchs and H. Wolf (eds), *Multimedia and Regional Economic Restructuring*. London: Routledge.

Granovetter, M. (1985) 'Economic action and social structure: the problem of embeddedness', *American Journal of Sociology*, 91: 481–510.

Henton, D., Melville, J. and Walesh, K. (1997) *Grassroots Leaders for a New Economy*. San Francisco: Jossey-Bass.

Heydebrand, W. (1999) 'Multimedia networks, globalization and strategies of innovation: the case of Silicon Alley', in H. Braczyk, G. Fuchs and

H. Wolf (eds), *Multimedia and Regional Economic Restructuring*. London: Routledge.

Klein, A. (2003) *Stealing Time: The Collapse of AOL Time-Warner*. London: Simon & Schuster.

Lewis, A. (2000) *The New New Thing*. New York: Norton.

Longhi, C. (1999) 'Networks, collective learning and technology development in innovative high technology regions: the case of Sophia-Antipolis', *Regional Studies*, 33: 333–42.

Longhi, C. and Quéré, M. (1993) 'Innovative networks and the technopolis phenomenon: the case of Sophia-Antipolis', *Environment & Planning C: Government & Policy*, 11: 317–30.

Mansell, R. (2000) 'Knowledge and the Internet: the end of control?'. Sussex University Professorial Inaugural, Falmer, Science Policy Research Unit.

McLuhan, M. (1962) *The Gutenberg Galaxy: The Making of Typographic Man*. Toronto: Toronto University Press.

Nachum, L. and Keeble, D. (2000) 'Foreign and indigenous firms in the media cluster of Central London'. Working Paper no. 154, Cambridge University, Centre for Business Research.

Nonaka, I. and Reinmöller, P. (1998) 'Toward endogenous knowledge creation for Asian economic development', *in Wissenschaftszentrum Berlin Jahrbuch*. Berlin: WZB.

Pavlik, J. (1999) 'Content and economics in the multimedia industry: the case of New York's Silicon Alley', in H. Braczyk, G. Fuchs and H. Wolf (eds), *Multimedia and Regional Economic Restructuring*. London: Routledge.

Porter, M. (1998) *On Competition*. Cambridge, MA: Harvard Business School Press.

Putnam, R. (1993) *Making Democracy Work*. Princeton, NJ: Princeton University Press.

Rallet, A. and Torre, A. (1998) 'On geography and technology: proximity relations in localized innovation networks', in M. Steiner (ed.), *Clusters and Regional Specialization*. London: Pion.

Rogers, E. and Larsen, J. (1984) *Silicon Valley Fever*. New York: Basic.

Russ, A. (1998) 'Multimedia: a new industry in a global city'. Unpublished MSc thesis, Department of Geography, King's College, London.

Safer, S. (2000) 'Get 'em while they're young: America's teens may be leading the handheld revolution', *Red Herring*, 78: 290.

Saxenian, A. (1994) *Regional Advantage: Culture and Competition in Silicon Valley and Route 128*. Cambridge and London: Harvard University Press.

Schmitz, H. and Nadvi, K. (1999) 'Clustering and industrialization: introduction to the special issue', *World Development*, 27: 1503–14.

Scott, A. (1998) 'From Silicon Valley to Hollywood: growth and development of the multimedia industry in California', in H. Braczyk, P. Cooke and M. Heidenreich (eds), *Regional Innovation Systems*. London: UCL Press.

Scott, A. (1999) 'Patterns of employment in southern California's multimedia and digital visual effects industry: the form and logic of an emerging labour market', in H. Braczyk, G. Fuchs and H. Wolf (eds), *Multimedia and Regional Economic Restructuring*. London: Routledge.

Tödtling, F. and Sedlacek, S. (1997) 'Regional economic transformation and the innovation system of Styria', *European Planning Studies*, 5: 43–64.

Von Hippel, E. (1988) *The Sources of Innovation*. Oxford: Oxford University Press.

Wolff, A. (1998) *Burn Rate*. London: Orion.

14

Globalization and the Structure of New Media Industries

TERRY FLEW AND STEPHEN McELHINNEY

GLOBALIZATION AND THE MEDIA

Globalization is a term used to describe, and make sense of, a series of interrelated processes including:

- internationalization of production, trade and finance, with the rise of multinational corporations, reductions in cross-border tariffs upon flows of goods and services, the deregulation of financial markets, and the rise of Internet-based electronic commerce;
- international movements of people (as immigrants, guest workers, refugees, tourists, students and expert advisers), the development of diasporic and emigrant communities, and the increasingly multicultural nature of national societies;
- international communications flows, delivered through telecommunications, information and media technologies such as broadband cable, satellite and the Internet, which facilitate transnational circulation of cultural commodities, texts, images and artifacts;
- global circulation of ideas, ideologies and 'keywords', such as the so-called export of 'Western values', 'fundamentalism', 'the war on terror', democracy, feminism, environmentalism;

- establishment of international regimes in intellectual property which entrench the enforceability of ownership of knowledge and information;
- emergence of local resistance to globalization for domestic political and cultural objectives, by nationalist movements of the political right, progressive and anti-colonialist movements of the left, and extremist religious movements;
- development of international governmental organizations, including regional trading blocs such as the European Union (EU), the North American Free Trade Agreement (NAFTA), the Association of South East Asian Nations (ASEAN) and the Asia–Pacific Economic Cooperation grouping (APEC);
- formation of cultural, professional and standards bodies such as UNESCO, the World Trade Organization, the World Intellectual Property Organization, the European Broadcasting Union, the Asian Broadcasting Union and the International Telecommunication Union;
- the increasing activity of global non-government organizations (NGOs), such as Amnesty International, Greenpeace, Médecins sans Frontières and the Red Cross in domestic and international politics;

- the contested influence of international laws on national policy formation and efforts to sideline multilateral fora (United Nations, World Trade Organization, Kyoto Convention on climate change) where they inhibit national interests;
- the use of overt programs of public relations or 'spin' by governments, multinationals and NGOs aimed at shaping opinion at global, international and local levels.

Developments in communications media have an important role in all of these processes of globalization. The technological forms that are used to communicate messages influence the communicative practice of individuals and institutions, and this in turn influences societies and cultures. Developments in communications media are important in all processes of globalization. There are three dimensions to this centrality of media to globalization. First, media constitute the technologies and service delivery platforms through which international flows are transacted. Second, the media industries are leaders in the push towards global expansion and integration. Finally, the media provide informational content and images of the world through which people seek to make sense of events in distant places. The intersections of these factors can be seen in the universal recognition and astounding levels of public commentary associated with September 11, 'the war on terror', the war in Iraq, the Beslan school massacre in Russia, the Indian Ocean tsunami of December 2004 and other events which affected particular places and communities before becoming 'global' media events.

Manuel Castells (1996, 2000) has provided an important contribution by placing communications media at the centre of the changes that are driving globalization. Castells argues that the period since the late 1970s has seen discontinuous historical and structural change in the economy, society and culture, driven by advances in information and communications technologies (ICTs). Central elements of this information technology paradigm, or *informational society*, include: the pervasive effects of ICTs through all forms of social interaction; the networking logic of systems and social

relationships and the flexibility of these networks; and the convergence of specific technologies into a highly integrated system. As a result, economies have become globally interdependent, with effects felt through entire societies as information and communications establish new forms of relationships 'between economy, state and society in a system of variable geometry' (1996: 1). While there has been an integrated capitalist world economy since the sixteenth century, the current configuration is, for the first time, a global economy 'with the capacity to work as a unit in real time on a planetary scale' (1996: 92).

The role played by communications media in overcoming barriers of space and time should not be seen as being without historical precedent, although the scale, pace and pervasiveness of change are historically unique. From the outset, the growth of media and communications in shaping social and economic life beyond the boundaries of village or immediate community largely corresponds with the rise of literacy. Harold D. Lasswell (1965) saw the roots of media growth in the synchronous programs of mass literacy through universal public schooling and the emergence of markets that stretched beyond local communities. Literacy and international trade links underpinned growth of the commercial press which provided local communities with information on politics, industry, commodities and events in distant locations. The telegraph extended and sped up the movement of this information. James Carey (1992a) has drawn attention to the profound significance of the development of the telegraph in the 1840s, which enabled the rise of the modern, multidivisional corporate enterprise, monopolistic markets and futures exchanges. The telegraph was at the centre of the development of the electrical goods industries, and it restructured everyday language through the impact of 'wire services' upon popular journalism, as it required a new economy of writing style, since payment was by the letter at this time. Most importantly, it meant that the movement of messages was separated from the movement of physical objects, and hence communication separated from transportation, and this 'freed communication from the constraints of geography' (1992a: 204). Associated with this, it changed the way in which communication was thought about, and provided a new model – the transmission model – for conceiving of communication as a social practice. Carey points out that, in this sense, 'the telegraph was not only a new tool of commerce but also a thing to think with, an agency for the alteration of ideas' (1992a: 204).

Media have been given a particularly significant role in globalization debates, because of the particular part that global media are seen as playing in the cultural weakening of the bonds which tie people to nation-states. Ernest Gellner's (1983) analysis of nationalism proposed that culture provides the 'political roof' that links a nation to its people, while Benedict Anderson (1991) drew attention to the historical role of popular print media in enabling the development of the modern nation as an 'imagined community'. From such insights, some have argued that the rise of global broadcast media is leading to an uncoupling between polity and culture within the nation, which is analogous to the uncoupling of polity and economy associated with the rise of multinational corporations and global financial markets. Utilizing the work of Canadian communications historian Harold Innis (1951), Joshua Meyrowitz (1985) and James Carey (1992b) have observed that while print culture was associated with the rise of nationalism, as it promoted continuity over time, decentralization and regional differentiation, broadcast media were space binding, promoting centralization of production, decentralization of dissemination, and international distribution. Drawing upon Anthony Giddens' (1997) interpretation of globalization as a 'consequence of modernity' that involves a 'disembedding' of social relations from local contexts, Chris Barker has described television as simultaneously 'globalized because it is an institution of capitalist modernity' and as 'contributing to the globalization of modernity through the worldwide circulation of images and discourses' (1997: 13). In other words, global media, and global broadcast media in particular, are globalizing in their form as well as their content, and are controlled by corporate interests keen to expand their global market reach. Arjun Appadurai has referred to global mediascapes as one of the five 'landscapes' of global cultural flow – the others being ethnoscapes, technoscapes, financescapes and ideoscapes – which have generated 'fundamental disjunctures between economy, culture and politics' (1990: 296) in all societies over the last 20–30 years.

These views represent conventional starting points for conceptualizing globalization of the media. However, they also reflect perceptions that are rooted in the study of North American or European media discourses. There is equal merit in recognizing that media industries are regulated by national governments, and the markets for information and entertainment are national as well as international. Most nations continue to impose restrictions on ownership and control over electronic media industries and often use quotas or censorship to inhibit the importation of content, although the effectiveness of such rules is challenged by new media (OECD, 1999: 133–4). Economic concerns are not the only motivating factor for regulation. Many governments have extended existing approaches to media regulation to the operation of Internet and other digital forms in ways that minimize political consequences. Singapore, and China have established national firewalls and monitor users (Sussman, 2003; Zittrain and Edelman, 2002), while routine monitoring, surveillance and site blocking is conducted in Saudi Arabia, Burma and the United Arab Emirates, along with Vietnam and Cuba (Kalathil and Boas, 2003).

THE POLITICAL ECONOMY OF GLOBALIZATION: 'STRONG GLOBALIZATION' THEORIES AND THEIR CRITICS

Any listing of the trends and developments associated with globalization raises the issue of whether, as Castells proposes, such developments point to a *qualitative* shift in the pattern of economic, social, political and cultural relations within and between states and societies, or whether they are extensions and intensifications of more long-standing trends, i.e. part of a *quantitative* change. There are also important questions of the relationship between local forms of agency and external structural imperatives. Should globalization be seen as an external force imposing changes upon local and national laws, institutions and policies, or as a set of developments induced primarily by these institutions? Or might globalization be conceived as a joint project between local people seeking access to foreign goods, services and ideas and using them in unique ways that might be likened to 'glocalization' (Robertson, 1994)? While communications technologies such as broadband cable, satellite and the Internet are often presented as forcing nation-states to become more open to globalizing influences, others, such as Linda Weiss in her analysis of the role of the state in East Asian industrialization, have argued that 'globalization must be seen as a politically rather than a technologically induced phenomenon' (1997: 23).

Globalization theories have been developed in the fields of economics, sociology and politics, as well as in media, communications and cultural studies. So-called *strong globalization* theories argue that these developments mark out such a qualitative shift in societies that the analytical and normative categories that guided social analysis in the nineteenth and twentieth centuries, such as the nation-state, society, national economies and national cultures, will be less and less applicable. In economic terms, globalization has been defined by the International Monetary Fund as 'the rapid integration of economies worldwide through trade, financial flows, technology spillovers, information networks, and cross-cultural currents' (1997: 1). The first Director-General of the World Trade Organization, Renato Ruggieri, interpreted this in particularly strong terms when he argued that 'globalization was a reality which overwhelms all others', as did the Australian Foreign Minister, Alexander Downer, when he proposed that 'whether people fear globalization or not, they cannot escape it' (quoted in Flew, 2004a: 179). The pessimistic account of economic globalization presents the spectre of an international 'race to

the bottom' scenario, where the increasingly 'footloose' nature of capital is seen as generating a situation whereby 'capital will be increasingly able to play workers, communities, and nations off against one another as they demand tax, regulation, and wage concessions while threatening to move ... increased mobility of MNCs (multinational corporations) benefits capital while workers and communities lose' (Crotty et al., 1998: 118).

Economists have always recognized the international nature of economic transactions and, at least in the mainstream traditions, have seen international trade and investment as largely positive activities. Yet globalization is perceived as a challenge to mainstream economic theory, since its working premise has been that of an *inter*-national economy, where transactions take place between sovereign nations and economic agents with an identifiable national base. Some economists have cast serious doubts on the empirical and intellectual foundations of 'strong globalization' arguments. Paul Krugman (1997) accuses writers such as Robert Reich of peddling a form of 'pop internationalism' that distorts international trade theory by treating nations as competing entities, analogous to capital and labour. Political economists such as David Gordon (1988) have argued that the statistical evidence presented as proof of economic globalization is misleading, while Andrew Glyn and Bob Sutcliffe (1998) have argued that a focus upon trends in the manufacturing sector is misleading, since the fastest-growing services industry sectors display less international mobility and are less internationally traded than manufactured goods.

In the most extensive critique of economic globalization theories, Paul Hirst and Grahame Thompson (1996) have argued that, while there has been an increase in international economic integration since the 1970s, this is not unique in international economic history since the overall level of international trade and investment in the period from 1890 to 1914 is equal to that of the late 1990s. Like Gordon, and Glyn and Sutcliffe, Hirst and Thompson critique globalization theory on the basis of their belief that it presents an overly pessimistic view of the capacity of nation-states to control the activities of corporations.

Analogous debates about globalization have taken place in sociology and cultural studies. The sociologist John Urry proposed that 'there has been a "Globalization" of economic, social and political relationships that has undermined the coherence, wholeness and unity of individual societies' (1989: 97). In a similar vein, media theorists David Morley and Kevin Robins have argued that, with media globalization, 'audiovisual cultures are ... becoming detached from the symbolic spaces of national culture' (1995: 11). Robertson (1991), Waters (1995) and Shaw (1997) have posed the question of whether a global society has replaced or is superseding discrete national societies as the dominant structuring principle of social relations, with major implications for the methods of sociological analysis. Anthony Smith has expressed concern that such arguments are premised upon an overly rationalistic conception of culture as being in some sense determined by techno-economic structures, and ignoring the 'obstinate fact' that 'national cultures, like all cultures before the modern epoch, are particular, time-bound and expressive ... [and] specific, historical cultures possessing strong emotional connotations for those who share in them' (1991: 178). Stuart Hall (1993) has expressed a similar concern that 'global cosmopolitanism', and a certain blindness to continuities of national cultural experience, are indicative of a certain 'wish-list' element of theories such as liberalism and Marxism, that see nationalism as essentially a transitory and political phenomenon, likely to decline over time as societies become more secular, rational and cosmopolitan.

MEDIA GLOBALIZATION: 'GLOBAL VILLAGE' OR 'CULTURAL IMPERIALISM'?

Media globalization debates can be placed into two camps. Mainstream economists and liberal communications theorists have emphasized the relationship between new technologies and markets, and argued that media globalization promotes opportunities for shared information, borderless communication and global commerce. Further, they believe that global media encourage the spread of liberal democratic ideas and empower citizens worldwide against unjust forms of local authority, by allowing the 'whole world to watch' and witness such injustices. In *The Death of Distance*, Frances Cairncross concluded that: 'Free to explore different points of view, on the Internet or on the thousands of television and radio channels that will eventually become available, people will become less susceptible to propaganda from politicians who seek to stir up conflicts. Bonded together by the invisible strands of global communications, humanity may find that peace and prosperity are fostered by the death of distance' (1998: 279). Not surprisingly, such arguments find favour with the heads of the giant media corporations. Rupert Murdoch (1993) once famously argued that cable and satellite broadcasting had not only 'been a key factor in the spread of freedom' worldwide, but would also 'liberate people from the once-powerful media barons'. This echoes the comments by Ted Turner when launching the 24-hour cable global news service CNN: 'We're gonna take the news and put it on the satellite,' said Turner, 'and then we're gonna beam it down into Russia, and we're gonna bring world peace, and we're gonna get rich in the process! Thank you very much! Good luck!' (quoted in Wark, 1994: 36).

Ironically, while Ted Turner subsequently lost control of CNN, Rupert Murdoch has displayed a chameleon-like ability to operate in diverse political environments, including the United States, Europe, China and India, to expand the reach of the News Corporation into new national markets and audiences. He practices a 'footloose' approach to business that included renouncing his Australian citizenship and moving the incorporation of the News Corporation to the benign business environment of the US state of Delaware in 2004. News Corporation represents the ultimate example of industrial flexibility in the global economy with business units ranging across different media – books, newspapers, magazines, broadcast TV, cable and satellite TV, films, music and the Internet – and across six continents, making it 'the first vertically integrated entertainment-and-communications company of truly global reach' (Shawcross, 1997: 399). Its size, audience reach and influence of its commentators on key political constituencies also encourage affinity with political elites. Since 2001, News Corporation's Fox Network and its leading commentator Bill O'Reilly have been vociferous supporters of US President George W. Bush's 'war on terrorism', invasion and democratization of Iraq and re-election campaign in 2004. The affinity between the Bush administration and the News Corporation was evident in the regulatory support from the Federal Communications Commission for the takeover the largest cable TV network DirecTV. A different hue to the News Corporation has been evident across the Pacific, demonstrated by the dropping of BBC World News from Star-TV's north Asian platforms following expressions of dissatisfaction over critical coverage by the Chinese Government (Atkins, 1995). The approach seems hereditary. After the launch of the News Corporation joint-venture Phoenix TV in China, James Murdoch concurred with official opinion 'that Falun Gong was indeed a dangerous and apocalyptical cult' (Anonymous, 2001). The Murdoch success in forming political alliances with conservative political movements and subsequent media patronage has attracted considerable enmity from a wide range of critics: the former editor of *The Times* in the UK, Harold Evans, who was fired for failing to 'toe the company line' (Evans, 1983), the late British TV scriptwriter Dennis Potter, who named his cancer 'Rupert', and, in 2004, in the documentary *Outfoxed: Rupert Murdoch's War on Journalism* (Greenwald (director), 2004).

For critics of global media, such as political economists and critical communications theorists, the News Corporation's geographic spread and emphasis on distributing sport, entertainment and news globally and creating local versions can be described as an element of *cultural imperialism* or *media imperialism*. The political economy tradition has long drawn attention to the adverse political and cultural implications of the unequal distribution of international communications power and resources, and how they intersect with broader structures of dominance and Western hegemony in the international political economy. The cultural domination approach, associated in particular with North American political economists such as Herbert Schiller (e.g. 1969, 1976, 1989; Nordenstreng and Schiller, 1993) and Edward Herman and Noam Chomsky (1988), as well as theorists of the new world information and communication order such as Kaarle Nordenstreng and Cees Hamelink, has stressed the importance of the internationalization and commercialization of global communications to the status of the United States as the world's dominant capitalist economy. In *Mass Communications and American Empire*, the founding text of this tradition, Herbert Schiller argued that 'Nothing less than the viability of the American industrial economy itself is involved in the movement towards international commercialization of broadcasting' (1969: 95). Linking the study of communications dominance to theories of economic imperialism such as world systems and dependency theories, Schiller defined cultural imperialism in *Communications and Cultural Domination* as 'the sum of processes by which a society is brought into the modern world system and how its dominating stratum is attracted, pressured, forced, and sometimes bribed into shaping social institutions to correspond to, or even promote, the values and structures of the dominating centre of the system' (1976: 9).

Anxieties about the influence of global media on culture and values, as well as their direct political and economic power, were expressed at an international level through the new world information and communication order (NWICO) debate. This debate, which occurred through the United Nations Educational, Scientific and Cultural Organization (UNESCO) from the early 1970s and was led by 'Third World' or so-called 'non-aligned' nations, sought to use UNESCO and other international forums to call for a redistribution of global communications resources to redress international inequalities and enable the development of stronger national and regional communications systems in the developing world. The NWICO debate peaked with the submission of the MacBride Report, *Many Voices, One World*, to the 1980 UNESCO general conference in Belgrade, but declined in the face of hostility from the United States and Britain in particular, who withdrew their funding from UNESCO in 1985 (Gerbner et al., 1994).

In a major contribution to this literature, Edward Herman and Robert McChesney (1997) have outlined in great detail the rise of global media corporations such as News Corporation, Disney and Time-Warner, and shown how their global expansion strategies have been facilitated by national policies of trade liberalization, deregulation of media markets, telecommunications privatization, and the winding-back of funding to national public broadcasters and other non-commercial media and cultural forms. They argue that this expansion has not been primarily the result of technological change or market competition, but is indicative of the extent of transnational corporate influence over national policy-makers and the hegemonic role that has been played by global media in the international dissemination of ideas. For Herman and McChesney, the global media are the 'new missionaries of global capitalism', and their adverse consequences include the spread of individualistic values, displacement of the public sphere, the strengthening of conservative political forces worldwide, and the erosion of local cultures.

Oliver Boyd-Barrett (1998) has distinguished the cultural domination models, based upon neo-Marxist world systems theory, from approaches more directly rooted in Marxist political economy and the Gramscian model of cultural hegemony (see Brewer, 1980 for a discussion of these distinctions). The latter approaches have been critical of the reductive nature of the 'cultural dominance' model and its inadequate treatment of 'local' conditions, lived experience, and the diversity of forms taken by what Annabelle Sreberny-Mohammadi terms 'the many ordinary, everyday ways that life in the South has been affected by the social structures of imperialism' (1997: 51). In particular,

the focus upon conflicts and inequalities between nations in a global state system, and the 'diplomatic' solutions proposed by the NWICO framework, were seen as having the danger of downplaying structures of domination and resistance within nation-states, where the rhetoric of cultural nationalism could be used to promote a conservative and highly regressive national cultural politics (Mattelart et al., 1984).

Two other changes in the dynamics of media globalization were seen as challenging the assumptions of the cultural domination model. First, the process of globalization, and the centrality of communications technologies to this process, meant that models of dependency which assumed direct conflicts with a politically and geographically defined power, and the capacity of the nation-building state to represent mass popular aspirations for 'independence', were becoming less adequate as a way of mapping the relations between economic, political and cultural flows in the world system and their local and national impacts (Canclini, 1986; Martin-Barbero, 1993). Second, the pattern of global media flows has become more complex, as new patterns of audiovisual flow emerged around geolinguistic regions, particularly among Spanish-speaking and Portuguese-speaking communities, and Indian, Chinese and Arabic communities worldwide (Sinclair et al., 1996).

In their analysis of these trends, Sinclair et al. (1996) argue that a 'mid-range' analysis alert to linguistic and cultural differences, as well as regional submarkets, is a necessary corrective to overly global analyses such as theories of cultural or media imperialism. The development of international broadcasting channels to serve particular communities provides an alternative to long-standing concerns about the 'Western' nature of global media and content. The Arabic language news channel *Al-Jazeera* provides one of the more compelling of these non-Western alternatives. Naomi Sakr comments that the emergence of Arabic-language satellite television services has brought a sense of cultural and political identity to the Middle East and acted to raise the international profile of the State of Qatar in the Persian Gulf (Sakr, 2005).

An issue of particular relevance to all critical theories of global media is the relationship between United States hegemony in the global system and the 'soft power' deriving from US media and cultural exports and their impacts upon the culture and values of importing societies. Joseph S. Nye, Jr, Assistant Secretary of Defense for international affairs in the Clinton administration, succinctly defined 'soft power' as the 'ability to achieve desired outcomes in international affairs through attraction rather than coercion. It works by convincing others to follow, or getting them to agree to, norms and institutions that produce the desired behaviour. Soft power can rest upon the appeal of one's ideas or the ability to set the agenda in ways that shape the preferences of others' (quoted in Thussu, 1998: 66–7). Jesus Martin-Barbero has observed that, in assessing the relationship between global media and cultural hegemony in Latin America, 'Much more than the many percent of programmes imported from the United States (including programme formats), what will really affect us will be importing the US model of television' (Martin-Barbero, 1988: 457). Sinclair et al. make a similar observation in critiquing the cultural imperialism theory which, they argue, 'failed to see that, more fundamental than its supposed ideological influence, the legacy of the USA in world television development was in the implantation of its systemic model for television as a medium – the exploitation of entertainment content so as to attract audiences which could then be sold to advertisers' (Sinclair et al., 1996: 9).

STRUCTURES AND SPACES OF THE GLOBAL MEDIA

Alongside debates about flows, audiences and technologies, the global distribution of production and creative activities by media companies invites investigation. Gillian Doyle (2003) points out that media companies have developed structures that allow them great flexibility in the sourcing of content through the formation of joint ventures, production

deals and diagonal mergers that provide synergies between audiovisual commodities held by different corporate entities. These arrangements are best considered through methodology associated with the 'commodity chain' derived from economics to consider industrial activities (Gereffi and Korzeniewicz, 1994). Media activities might be critiqued using a methodology involving the following steps: creative input, development, production, distribution and exhibition. Classic examples of the global spread of these arrangements include Time-Warner's establishment of audiovisual facilities in Australia as a base for production of the *Matrix* trilogy or its subsidiary New Line Cinema's use of locations and personnel in New Zealand to create the *Lord of the Rings* while assembling an ensemble cast of actors from around the world. Doyle (2003) notes that these practices help to reduce the costs and risks associated with production of complex media commodities produced for a global market. The capacity to coordinate this complex industrial activity across time zones and borders has become possible through the utilization of advanced communications and recognition that media content can be exploited across different commodities – a feature film offers spin-offs to games, television programmes and so on. This is particularly evident in new media content produced for children.

MEDIA GLOBALIZATION AND THE ROLE OF TELECOMMUNICATIONS

The transformation of telecommunications through a combination of technological change, regulation, and industrial reconfiguration has spurred a new phase of change in media and communications around the world. These factors have underpinned media globalization and the rise of new media industries and services such as the Internet and increasingly interactive broadcasting platforms. From the outset, the liberalization and privatization programmes begun in the UK during the late 1980s and steadily undertaken throughout

Europe, Latin America, Southern Africa and the Asia–Pacific during the 1990s transformed telecommunications systems from relatively static national utilities charged with the supply of telephone and often postal services to become a dynamic engine of the global economy and communications infrastructure (OECD, 1999).

Liberalization and privatization drew a vast amount of investment capital to the sector for a variety of reasons. First, there was recognition that telecommunications infrastructures would underpin the new economy as distribution and transmission platforms. Second, telecommunications had become an almost ubiquitous utility (primarily in developed economies) via long-standing universal service programmes that had required national telephone utilities to build infrastructures reaching almost every household and business. Third, these infrastructures had been increasingly upgraded to provide digital or high-speed data capability to support wireless, Internet or cable connections. Finally, a new generation of personal communications technologies, including mobile telecommunications (e.g. Bluetooth, Symbian and WAP), was increasingly capable of carrying information and entertainment services that were central to the emerging information economy and associated practices that can be described under the emerging descriptive lexicon of 'e-commerce', 'e-health', 'e-government', 'e-business' and so on (ITU, 2000; OECD, 1999).

An indicator of the importance of telecommunications as a driver of the new economy can be derived from uptake of mobile telephony, including that geared toward the sophisticated interactive information and entertainment services. The International Telecommunication Union (ITU, 2001) has illustrated the growth in the sector with subscribers rising from 11 million in 1990 to an estimated 1.329 billion in 2003, and with more than 250,000 people connecting to new services each day. Likewise, the growth of telecommunications spawned innovative suppliers of new communications technologies that provide the human interface with new media. Increasingly, globalized suppliers including Nokia, Motorola and Ericsson

have created the technologies which have placed new media in our pockets instead of desktops, lounge rooms and offices (see ITU, 2000).

Access to computers, reliable telecommunications infrastructure, and capacities to afford services are market factors inhibiting globalization, although there is considerable evidence that new media and communication technologies are contributing to development in emerging economies and offer means to tackle wider social, health and educational challenges (Melkote and Steeves, 2004). The expanding reach of Internet and mobile telephony into parts of Asia, Africa and Latin America is acting to reconfigure the global experience and use of new media. Figures for Internet access vary greatly. The ITU (2001) estimated that 665 million people would use the Internet in 2003, while the Computer Industry Almanac estimated that more than 1 billion people would have used the Internet by the mid-2000s (Anonymous, 2004). The fastest growth rates for Internet use between 1997 and 2002 were in Asia, the Middle East and Eastern Europe, with China, Brazil, Russia and India emerging as being among the world's largest aggregate Internet-using population (Flew, 2004a: 71–3). Yet, the significant disparities in access and use within and between countries, also known as the *digital divide*, remain. International comparisons of telephone subscribers (mobile and fixed) presented by the ITU demonstrate the stark reality of access: there are 8.65 telephone subscribers per 100 inhabitants across the continent of Africa; 66.62 per 100 in the Americas; 28.52 per 100 across Asia; 96.28 per 100 in Europe and 94.85 in Oceania (ITU, 2004a). Yet these aggregated figures obviously hide disparities between countries: 161.26 lines per 100 people in Hong Kong against 0.85 in Myanmar (ITU, 2004a). Internet hosting presents similar circumstances: 4.22 hosts per 10,000 people in Africa; 2002.47 in the Americas; 50.29 across Asia; 280.95 in Europe and 1053.02 in Oceania. Disparities include 0.01 hosts per 10,000 in Angola compared to 62.25 in South Africa (ITU, 2004b). With the growing importance of Internet and mobile communications as means to access media services, these geographic disparities obviously illustrate the limits to possible participation in emerging media forms like Web logs, forums and file-sharing.

GLOBAL MEDIA AND NATIONAL POLICIES: INFLUENCES AND INTERSECTIONS

There are two important factors which regulate the impact of global media in particular local and national cultures. The first is that of *audiences*. Interpretive approaches, drawing on cultural studies methodologies, have challenged assumptions that global media flows can be identified through measurement of the economic interests of participants. Proponents of these interpretive approaches have pointed to the need to come to terms with the *cultural* meanings that are derived from flows of content and the adoption of media practices, particularly by assessing the relationships with local societies and contexts. Ien Ang has drawn attention to the extent to which 'global media do affect, but cannot control local meanings'; as a result, 'the construction of a "global culture"... should not be conceived as a process of straightforward homogenization', but rather 'local cultures everywhere tend to reproduce themselves ... through the appropriation of global flows of mass-mediated forms and technologies' (1996: 153). At a more empirical level, Michael Tracey (1988) argued that globalization rhetoric disguises the extent to which US TV product has tended to be less popular than local product in almost every country where both are readily available. Tracey also argued that the presence of US imports acts as a trigger to the development of local programming to meet the cultural needs and expectations of local audiences. These findings are supported by Straubhaar (1997), whose empirical analysis of the balance between local and imported programming in various Asian, Latin American, Middle East and Caribbean nations finds that levels of national television programming have been increasing in the majority of these countries in the period from the 1960s to the 1990s. Lent (1993)

also identified a trend for substitution of imports from the US with local content in Thailand.

The issue of 'reterritorialization' has become increasingly possible with new media such as the Internet and the creative use of household information technology and entertainment equipment. One of the fundamental characteristics of the twentieth century was the mass migration of people across the globe. Many of these diasporic communities have sought to remain connected with originating cultures by maintaining links through use of media and communications systems. Miller and Slater's (2000) study of Internet use in Trinidad found that, rather than the Internet being an 'imposed' global technology which 'disrupted' local cultural traditions, the various possibilities of the technology had been taken up in different ways to globally project a 'Trini' identity. In particular, it generated critical linkages between people in Trinidad, the 'Trini diaspora' (e.g. Trinidadian students at North American universities), and wider global communities of interest. Cunningham and Sinclair (2000) illustrate the point with research on the ways that Thai, Vietnamese and Filipino migrants have built communities and remain engaged with home societies with a mixture of old and new media. A variety of mechanisms is used ranging from shopkeepers maintaining videotape libraries, programmes on community radio and television services, websites, and commercial pay-TV services (Cunningham and Sinclair, 2000). Even with ostensibly global media forms, such as Massively Multiplayer Online Games (MMOGs), which also clearly deal in 'fantasy worlds' rather than local cultures, players in Korea prefer local games such as *Lineage* to more North American-based games such as *EverQuest*, for reasons related to language, cultural affinity, and even the time zones in which most of the activity is occurring (Flew and Humphreys, 2004). Such global media flows are illustrative of media globalization, but not of cultural imperialism.

The second major element regulating media globalization, which is *public policy*, and the role it plays in regulating the relationships between global flows and their local impacts within the nation-state. Philip Schlesinger has proposed that national media and cultural policies can be seen as exercises in 'communicative boundary maintenance', out of which emerge distinctive national media cultures, and particular configurations of local and imported media content and styles (1991: 162). This is particularly apparent in broadcasting, where national public broadcasters, national regulatory systems and audience preferences for locally produced material have intersected with economic and technological forces that promote imported programming, and political, cultural and linguistic factors which make particular countries more or less open to imported English-language content from the United States. Countries such as Australia, Brazil, Canada and Mexico, which have always been highly exposed to globalizing cultural influences, have developed 'hybrid' programme forms that negotiate local, national and international cultural markets. Sustained exposure to overseas television programming has been in these instances the trigger for strengthening national production systems, through protectionist cultural policies of *lé défi américain* (Schlesinger, 1991), cosmopolitan programme formats which 'play at being American' (Caughie, 1990), or the fashioning of 'national champions' which can compete in definable global audiovisual markets, such as 'soaps' and *telenovellas* (Moran, 1998; Sinclair et al., 1996).

While national media and communications policies can set limits to the impact of media globalization on national media cultures, such policies can also act as catalysts for globalization. Media policies such as liberalization of media and communications markets are fundamentally shaped by the interaction of domestic politics with global structures and flows, out of which frequently emerge opportunities that become available to local industries. Although corporations based in Europe and North America are most often cited as driving globalization, it is the partnerships and opportunities they offer domestic businesses which often hold the key to market entry. The partnership between the US computer software giant Microsoft and powerful Australian media

conglomerate Publishing & Broadcasting Ltd in building a Web portal called NineMSN, that draws viewers from a range of existing television, print and software businesses to the new media, illustrates this trend (Barr, 2000). The Indian satellite broadcasting system provides another key to conceptualizing media globalization. As a vast and multicultural country, India has attracted foreign investors seeking to establish media and telecommunications businesses. Yet successful entry to the market was not possible until privatization allowed local media and telecommunications interests to develop joint ventures (Mehta, 1998; Thussu, 1999). These commercialized and privatized services could also improve the capacity to reach the various language markets within the country and address political and cultural considerations (Thomas, 1996).

Understanding new media globalization also requires the unpacking of content from the infrastructure that supports production, distribution and exhibition. Establishment of satellite broadcasting systems and telecommunications networks that support the seamless distribution of content is actively supporting the globalization of new media. These mechanisms are being used by local, regional and global businesses to build markets. Several Sino-Thai entrepreneurs have grasped the opportunity to provide the Thai market and regional countries with an alternative to imported programming from either Western countries or Japan. The Thaicom satellite, controlled by the company owned by Thai Prime Minister, Thaksin Shinawatra carries telecommunications services, Internet services and television broadcasts from the five free-to-air Thai-language stations as well as the pay-TV services featuring CNN, BBC World and Nickelodeon to more than 70 million people in Thailand, Laos, Burma, Cambodia and Vietnam (Anon, 1997: 179–93; Thaicom, 2000).

Transnational corporations have long been associated with globalization. Communications and new media systems have supported the expansion of business beyond national markets to a system whereby components are developed, manufactured, assembled and sold far from where corporations exercise control over these activities. Communications technologies and new media are both enabling mechanisms for these practices and businesses in their own right that support the deterritorialization of industrial practices. Some transnational corporations provide communications infrastructures and software that support the activities of other businesses which may also be transnational in nature. More recently, the Internet has provided the platform for businesses to reach consumers or to provide services to other businesses. It has been argued that such arrangements lead to the *disintermediation* of traditional approaches to production, distribution and supply of goods and services. The Internet has allowed consumers to communicate directly with producers of certain types of goods (e.g. books, music and software) and services (e.g. banking, finance, government transactions and information) without the need to use existing channels including retailers. While these trends became increasingly prevalent in the late 1990s, business models remained in flux as these 'convergent service industries' models are tested by traditional and new media, communications and other service industries.

Intellectual property and copyright have become increasingly important factors in the globalization of media and related communications industries. Bettig (1996) notes how copyright provides the means for controlling information and entertainment products and ensuring that they can be exclusively exploited in a particular national market. He also argues that the bulk of the information and entertainment products traded globally are controlled by a handful of corporations based in North America, Europe and Japan. Copyright allows content to be packaged and exploited in different ways across old and new media. For instance, a television programme can be packaged for free-to-air, pay-TV and cable systems. It can be modified and placed on other services and with digital technology re-versioned through inclusion of different sound tracks for multiple markets. At all stages, the copyright owner is able to determine how the content is used and can generate a different pricing schedule for each use. With the establishment of global media markets, copyright is a central issue in

trade negotiations and international relations. US and European software and media industries, in particular, have lobbied for stronger international regimes that require governments to enact laws to protect intellectual property ownership rights that permit the commercial exploitation of content (Drahos with Braithwaite, 2002). As trade in intellectual property becomes an increasingly important sector in the US and European economies, with the growth of new media and related software industries, industry groups including the Business Software Alliance, the Motion Picture Distributors Association of America and the Recording Industry Association of America have sought to launch retaliatory trade actions against countries that do not adequately protect copyright, through organizations such as the World Trade Organization (WTO) and the World Intellectual Property Organization (WIPO) (US Trade Representative, 2000).

The capacity of new media to support the collection, use and storage of vast amounts of personal information by business and governments has underpinned debates on the need to build mechanisms which protect the privacy of individuals using the Internet and other technologies (Garfinkel, 2000; Whitaker, 1999). Use of technologies including cookies and Web bugs to track behaviour across the Web, and the increasing capacity to profile consumers using data gathered from purchases and page accesses, have encouraged the development of international agreements, including the Safe Harbor arrangement between the European Union and United States (see Federal Trade Commission, 2000), to manage the use of and trade in personal information (see Garfinkel, 2000). Both Simon Garfinkel (2000) and Reg Whitaker (1999) also argue that traditional notions of privacy have been curtailed by the development and application of new technologies to the collection and monitoring of personal information by both commercial interests and governments. The Internet and interactive media permit business and government to track and monitor individual behaviour, in ways that would have been previously impossible for even the most authoritarian regime, through the establishment of databases, data-mining techniques, and the application of e-mail monitoring and interception technologies including the 'Carnivore' system utilized by US security agencies. Equally, governments and businesses have sought to adopt technological and procedural measures including Web seals and encryption to protect information they have collected from unauthorized access and use. This sensitivity has been argued to be a factor retarding uptake of e-commerce and other online services promoted by government and business including electronic health, banking and other records (OECD, 2000).

GLOBALIZATION AND POLICY DISCOURSE: FROM DEVELOPMENT COMMUNICATIONS TO THE GLOBAL INFORMATION SOCIETY AND THE CREATIVE INDUSTRIES

One of the ways in which media globalization has influenced national media policies is at the level of dominant policy discourse. Theories of cultural and media imperialism had an analogy with the approach of development communication that emerged from countries in Latin America, Asia and Africa in the 1970s. The approach of *development communication* (Melkote and Steeves, 2004: Chapter 6) was popularized as a means for governments in emerging economies and post-colonial societies to determine which media technologies and approaches they would take to improve the lot of their citizens. The approach encouraged governments to introduce policies that limited foreign control over local industries, emphasized the primacy of the domestic development task, encouraged cultural and information autonomy, valued democratic institutions and offered support for other countries following similar trajectories. Governments of developing countries often placed provision for basic needs above expenditure on advanced communications and media systems, in the belief that raising capital to pay for these infrastructures would drain national budgets, increase levels of foreign debt and require adoption of technologies that were not proven

in local conditions. Moreover, there was recognition that skills to build and operate these systems would not be locally available or could be used for tasks that were more important. Other concerns related to the likelihood that foreign investors would only be interested in providing technologies to profitable customers concentrated in cities, earnings would be repatriated, and governments would lose the capacity to intervene directly in the provision of services.

From the late 1970s, development communication approaches were progressively abandoned as the technological transformation in media and communications industries increased the sophistication and interconnection of media and communications industries. Further, neoliberal economic theories became increasingly influential over national policy formation in both developed and developing countries. In the media and communications sectors, the neoliberal policy agenda could most readily be identified with the trend for countries to privatize national telecommunications monopolies, and to allow the private sector to introduce new television services such as pay-TV, cable and satellite broadcasting. The demise of the new world information and communication order (NWICO) agenda in multilateral forums such as UNESCO in the 1980s marked the symbolic end of development communications as a core element of international media and communications policies. By the 1990s, incorporation of telecommunications and audiovisual policies into the disciplines of the General Agreement on Trade in Services (GATS), with its expectations of progressive trade liberalization and the elimination of differential treatment of domestic and foreign investors, constituted the dominant discursive and policy landscape informing communications policies worldwide.

The concept of 'citizenship', with its political connotations of egalitarianism and nation building being central to most national media policies, was increasingly displaced by the idea that individual interests could be more readily encapsulated in a privately operated, liberalized and market-driven media and communications environment by applying the discourse of 'consumer sovereignty' (Golding and Murdock, 1989; Mosco, 1998). Such arguments appear, at first glance, to readily fit the new media environment of global communications networks, transborder delivery infrastructures, and technologies such as the Internet and digital broadcasting. By contrast, William Melody has argued that much of the literature on the information society 'is either unsupported "blue sky" speculation about future technological and service possibilities, or promotional "hype" by the industries trying to sell the new technologies and potential future services' (1996: 243). Melody sees a critical role for public policy in shaping the development of national information societies, in the context of an emerging global information infrastructure, arguing that 'there will be as many "information societies" as there are societies [and] all countries should not try to charge down a single path emulating the perceived leaders in technological development at any moment in time' (1996: 244). Melody makes the critical point that much discussion about information society policies is focused upon developing the technical infrastructure through which to supply new media and communications services, with considerably less attention paid to developing a society of users of new ICTs, and the sorts of infrastructures that support universal low-cost access to basic information services.

The history of this development trajectory is worth consideration. Armand Mattelart (2003) argues that what came to be popularized as the 'information society' via Daniel Bell's (1973) work and the later configuration of the 'information economy' (Machlup, 1962; Porat, 1977), were deeply ideological projects, sponsored by successive US governments, business and academia, that followed the contours of Cold War rhetoric about emancipating the individual, encouraging political freedom and unlocking private enterprise in ways that supported the formation of a world market. To this end, an array of new communications and computing technologies and methodologies developed in US government and military research facilities from the late 1960s were turned over to commercial interests rather than more socially directed projects while the

OECD began to promote the virtues of an information economy from 1975 (Mattelart, 2003). A consequence of globalization of the media and ICT industries and the opening up of national markets to foreign competition was the establishment of national information policies, in recognition that it would underpin other industrial activities as well as be an important sector in its own right (Northfield, 1999). From the mid 1990s, many countries undertook large-scale programmes to support the transition to the 'information society', often setting up agencies to coordinate activities between governments, the private sector and other relevant stakeholders. While general goals of building advanced telecommunications networks capable of broadband or high-speed Internet were raised and the concept of universal service for all consumers was promoted, national responses naturally varied depending on domestic circumstances. These policies varied from the market-led approaches stressed in Australia, Canada and the European Union, to more state-led and *dirigiste* models, such as the Singaporean 'intelligent island' strategy, Malaysia's multimedia super corridor (MSC) development, and South Korea's 'informatization' policy. Strategies were also developed by local and state governments to attract investment in new media and communications sectors, with iconic North American cities such as New York finding themselves in global 'bidding wars' to retain the head offices of the giant media, entertainment and information technology corporations (Miller et al., 2001; Mosco, 1999).

Information society strategies hit a number of limitations in the late 1990s and early 2000s. The Asian economic downturn of 1997–8 exposed significant problems with 'state capitalist' developmental strategies, and the problems arising from 'picking winners' in the ICT sectors became even more apparent with the downturn of the global information technology sector after the crash of the US NASDAQ stock exchange in April 2001. Moreover, the skill sets associated with IT industries, such as software development, have proved to be able to be acquired from many places, and the capital associated with them to be highly geographically mobile and 'footloose'. As a result, there has been a worldwide outsourcing of such activities to the resurgent economies of China and India, which possess nodes of advanced ICT, large labour forces and comparatively low wages (Rai and Lal, 2000: 226–7).

There has thus been a shift of thinking away from national information society or information economy strategies towards strategies to develop the creative industries, defined more broadly to incorporate the arts, media and intellectual property industries as well as the ICT sector (Cunningham, 2004; Hartley, 2005). This partly reflects a desire for more inclusive and holistic development strategies which harness the creative potential of people more effectively. As British creative industries thinker John Howkins has put it, 'If I was a bit of data, I would be proud of living in an information society. But as a thinking, emotional, creative being – on a good day, anyway – I want something better' (Howkins, 2005: 117). The emergence of creative industries policies, first developed in Britain under the Blair Labour Government in 1998, and since emerging in countries as diverse as Australia, New Zealand, Taiwan, Singapore and Hong Kong SAR, is also reflective of the growing prominence of the digital content or 'copyright' industries as drivers of global economic growth (Flew, 2004a; OECD, 1998; Chapter 6). Creative industries strategies recognize that, in an age of globally mobile capital, commodities and information, it is the 'cultural' or 'software' side of ICTs that can generate distinctive forms of intellectual property, more so than the technologies themselves. It also marks the growing significance attached to cities as distinctive sites of creativity, and the ways in which diverse and original thinkers are attracted to *creative milieux*, or places that generate new experiences and, hence, new ideas (Landry, 2000). In Richard Florida's *The Rise of the Creative Class* (2002) – the best-known application of this thinking – it is culturally vibrant and bohemian cities that are the natural incubators of new ideas, rather than the centres of ICT production and software development. Shalini Venturelli (2005) has interpreted these trends as indicating that culture has now moved from the

margins to the centre of the global information economy:

> Culture can be seen as the key to success in the Information Economy, because for the very first time in the modern age, the ability to create new ideas and new forms of expression forms a valuable resource base of society … Cultural wealth can no longer be regarded in the legacy and industrial terms of our common understanding, as something fixed, inherited, and mass-distributed, but as a measure of the vitality, knowledge, energy, and dynamism in the production of ideas that pervades a given community. As nations enter the Global Information Society, the greater cultural concern should be for forging the right environment (policy, legal, institutional, educational, infrastructure, access etc.) that contributes to this dynamism … The challenge for every nation is not how to prescribe an environment of protection for a received body of art and tradition, but how to construct one of creative explosion and innovation in all areas of the arts and sciences. (2005: 395–6)

The appeal of creative industries strategies, with their emphasis on the value of a broadly defined notion of culture and their commitment to productively harnessing human creativity for wealth-creating purposes, is considerable. In contrast to the information policy strategies of the 1990s, they do not artificially silo-ize information technology development from the arts or media, nor do they draw strict boundaries between commercial and non-commercial developments in the digital media realm. Nonetheless, considered on a global scale, one would wish to make a few cautionary observations. First, the definitional looseness of the term 'creative industries' does require an awareness that it aggregates domains that run from the traditionally subsidized arts to frankly commercial sectors such as advertising and online games; whether the participants in these sectors share the confidence of policy makers in bringing them under the common umbrella of the creative industries, and claiming to devise policies which serve all of their interests, remains to be seen. Moreover, because 'creativity' tends to be seen as a 'good thing', there can be conceptual slipperiness between creative industries and other industries, most notably service industries, where the boundary becomes as much moral as grounded in anything more substantial (Flew, 2004b). Second, for all of the diversity contained in the notion of creativity, there is the danger of creative industries policies adopting a 'cookie-cutter' approach grounded in excessive sameness. Oakley (2004) has expressed concern in the UK context that creative industries strategies too often 'seem hellbent on trying to replicate a single creative industries model', characterized by 'a university, some incubators, and a "creative hub", with or without a café, galleries and fancy shops' (2004: 73). As Oakley notes, such strategies cannot simultaneously work in all places, and it would be better to try and understand and work with local and regional differences rather than apply this model to all places, in the vain hope that, for instance, the British advertising industry may move *en masse* from London to Sheffield or Huddersfield. On an international scale, it would be one thing to observe that Beijing has aspirations to be a creative city, but another to then assume that Richard Florida's emphasis on San Francisco's large gay population as a factor in its creative dynamism will find enthusiastic acceptance with Beijing's local political authorities. Finally, if the creative industries are narrowed down to their more market-specific form of intellectual property – copyrighted culture – we find more familiar patterns of global inequality, with the United States dominating global exports, while developing countries are struggling to direct resources to such sectors when basic human needs are not being met, and where foreign direct investment is often in the lowest-value-adding and most competitive parts of global production networks (United Nations Conference on Trade and Development, 2004).

CONCLUSION

Globalization is a central trend of the late twentieth and early twenty-first centuries. Media and communications technologies, corporations and services have been central features of globalization, both by being part of its structural formation and by transmitting its social, cultural and political consequences across geographic, linguistic and national boundaries. Rather than leading to the demise of nation-states or the homogenization of national cultures, it has involved the dual processes of synchronization of economic and technological infrastructures and the re-emphasis of valued cultural and social differences for domestic political purposes. In practical terms, national governments have responded to global policy discourses promoted by the GATS and the GII by opening national markets to investment and trade across a range of media and communications properties while retaining ownership and control mechanisms that prevent foreign takeover of key industries. In recent years national governments, sensitive to domestic political and economic pressures, have sought to establish new media industries that enable local business to compete with transnational enterprises in local and global markets. Although governments have traditionally intervened in media and communications industries through direct investment, the market liberalization associated with economic globalization has forced sophisticated national regulatory responses. The new media industries have played a central role in these trends, but their capacity to exercise influence independently of supportive arrangements through the negotiating strategies of major economic powers such as the United States, the rules and norms established by multilateral agencies such as the World Trade Organization, and the support of particular national governments, is limited. The 'global information economy' is an unequal one, and one where transnational corporate power is certainly significant and perhaps hegemonic, but its basic contours have similarities with the distribution of power and resources in earlier economic regimes.

REFERENCES

Anderson, Benedict (1991) *Imagined Communities: Reflections on the Origin and Spread of Nationalism*. London: Verso.
Ang Ien (1996) 'Global media/local meaning', in *Living Room Wars: Rethinking Media Audiences*

for a Postmodern World. London: Routledge. pp. 50–61.

Anonymous (1997) 'Thailand', in Alan Baskerville (ed.), *Asian Terrestrial Television*. Thousand Oaks, CA: Baskerville Communications Corporation.

Anonymous (2001) 'Broadcasting in China: unscrambling the signals', *The Economist*, 25 October.

Anonymous (2004) 'Worldwide Internet users will top 1 billion in 2005', *Computer Industry Almanac*. Available online: http://www.c-i-a.com

Appadurai, Arjun (1990) 'Disjuncture and difference in the global cultural economy', in Mike Featherstone (ed.), *Global Culture: Nationalism, Globalization and Modernity*. London: Sage. pp. 295–310.

Atkins, Will (1995) ' "Friendly and useful": Rupert Murdoch and the politics of television in South-East Asia, 1993–95', *Media International Australia*, 75: 54–64.

Barker, Chris (1997) *Global Television: An Introduction*. Oxford: Basil Blackwell.

Barr, Trevor (2000) *newmedia.com.au: The Changing Face of Australia's Media and Communications*. Australia: Allen & Unwin. pp. 20–39.

Bettig, Ronald, V. (1996) *Copyrighting Culture*. Boulder, CO: Westview.

Bell, Daniel (1973) *The Coming of Post-industrial Society: A Venture in Social Forecasting*, New York: Basic Books.

Boyd-Barrett, Oliver (1998) 'Media imperialism reformulated', in *Electronic Empires: Global Media and Local Resistance*. London: Arnold. pp. 157–76.

Brewer, Anthony (1980) *Marxist Theories of Imperialism*. London: Routledge & Kegan Paul.

Cairncross, Frances (1998) *The Death of Distance: How the Communications Revolution Will Change Our Lives*. London: Orion Business.

Canclini, Nestor Garcia (1986) 'Culture and power: the state of research', *Media, Culture & Society*, 10 (4): 467–98.

Carey, James (1992a) 'Space, time and communication', in *Communications as Culture*. New York: Routledge. pp. 142–72.

Carey, James (1992b) 'Technology and ideology: the case of the telegraph', in *Communications as Culture*. New York: Routledge. pp. 201–30.

Castells, Manuel (1996) *The Rise of the Network Society*. Oxford: Blackwell.

Castells, Manuel (2000) 'Information technology and global capitalism', in Will Hutton and Anthony Giddens (eds), *On the Edge: Living with Global Capitalism*. London: Cape.

Caughie, John (1990) 'Playing at being American: games and tactics', in Patricia Mellencamp (ed.),

Logics of Television. Bloomington, IN: Indiana University Press. pp. 44–58.

Crotty, James, Epstein, Gerald and Kelly, Patricia (1998) 'Multinational corporations in the neo-liberal regime', in Dean Baker, Gerald Epstein and Robert Pollin (eds), *Globalization and Progressive Economic Policy*. Cambridge: Cambridge University Press. pp. 117–43.

Cunningham, Stuart (2004) 'The creative industries after cultural policy: a genealogy and some possible preferred futures', *International Journal of Cultural Policy*, 7 (1): 105–16.

Cunningham, Stuart and Sinclair, John (eds) (2000) *Floating Lives: The Media and Asian Diasporas*. Brisbane: University of Queensland Press.

Doyle, Gillian (2003) *Understanding Media Economics*. London: Sage.

Drahos, Peter, with Braithwaite, John (2002) *Information Feudalism: Who Owns the Knowledge Economy*. London: Earthscan Publications.

Evans, Harold (1983) *Good Times, Bad Times*. London: Weidenfeld & Nicolson.

Federal Trade Commission (2000) 'Safe Harbor arrangements'. Available online: http/:www.FTC. gov/privacy/safeharbor/slip.html

Flew, Terry (2004a) *New Media: An Introduction*. 2nd edn. Melbourne: Oxford University Press.

Flew, Terry (2004b) 'Creativity, cultural studies, and services industries', *Communication and Critical/ Cultural Studies*, 1 (2): 176–93.

Flew, Terry and Humphreys, Sal (2004) 'Games: technology, industry, culture', in T. Flew (ed.), *New Media: An Introduction*. 2nd edn. Melbourne: Oxford University Press.

Florida, Richard (2002) *The Rise of the Creative Class*. New York: Basic Books.

Garfinkel, Simon (2000) *Database Nation: The Death of Privacy in the 21st Century*. Cambridge, MA: O'Reilly and Associates.

Gellner, Ernest (1983) *Nations and Nationalism*. Oxford: Basil Blackwell.

Gereffi, Gary and Korzeniewicz, Miguel (1994) *Commodity Chains and Global Capitalism*. Westport, CT: Greenwood Press.

Gerbner, George, Mowlana, Hamid and Nordenstreng, Kaarle (eds) (1994) *The Global Media Debate: Its Rise, Fall, and Renewal*. Norwood, NJ: Ablex.

Giddens, Anthony (1997) 'The globalizing of modernity', in Annabelle Sreberny-Mohammadi, Dwayne Winseck, Jim McKenna and Oliver Boyd-Barrett (eds), *Media in Global Context: A Reader*. London: Arnold. pp. 19–26.

Glyn, Andrew and Sutcliffe, Bob (1998) 'Still underwhelmed: indicators of globalization and their misinterpretation', *Review of Radical Political Economics*, 31 (1): 111–32.

Golding, Peter and Murdock, Graham (1989) 'Information poverty and political inequality: citizenship in the age of privatized communications', *Journal of Communications*, 39 (3): 180–95.

Gordon, David (1988) 'The global economy: new edifice or crumbling foundations?', *New Left Review*, 168: 24–65.

Greenwald, Robert, director (2004) *Outfoxed: Rupert Murdoch's War on Journalism*. Film

Hall, Stuart (1993) 'Culture, community, nation', *Cultural Studies*, 7 (3): 349–63.

Hartley, John (ed.) (2005) *Creative Industries*. Oxford: Blackwell.

Herman, Edward S. and Chomsky, Noam (1988) *Manufacturing Consent: The Political Economy of Mass Media*. New York: Pantheon.

Herman, Edward S. and McChesney, Robert W. (1997) *The Global Media: The New Missionaries of Global Capitalism*. London: Cassell.

Hirst, Paul and Thompson, Grahame (1996) *Globalization in Question*. Cambridge: Polity.

Howkins, John (2005) 'The mayor's commission on creative industries', in J. Hartley (ed.), *Creative Industries*. Oxford: Blackwell. pp. 117–25.

Innis, Harold A. (1951) *The Bias of Communication*. Toronto: University of Toronto Press.

International Monetary Fund (1997) *World Economic Outlook*. Paris: IMF.

ITU (1999) *World Telecommunication Development Report 1999: Mobile Cellular/World Telecommunications Indicators*. International Telecommunication Union, October.

ITU (2000) *Mergers and Alliances 1995–1999: Merger Mania as Telecoms go Multimedia*. International Telecommunication Union. Available online: www.itu.org

ITU (2001) *Key global telecom indicators for the world telecommunication service sector*, Available online: http://www.itu.int/ITU-D/ict/statistics/at_glance/KeyTelecom99.html

ITU (2004a) *World cellular subscribers*, Available online: http://www.itu.int/ITU-D/ict/statistics/at_glance/cellular01.pdf

ITU (2004b) *Information Technology*, Available online: http://www.itu.int/ITU-D/ict/statistics/at_glance/Internet03.pdf

Kalathil, Shanthi and Boas, Taylor C. (2003) *Open Networks, Closed Regimes: The Impact of the Internet on Authoritarian Rule*. Washington, DC: Carnegie Endowment for International Peace.

Krugman, Paul (1997) *Pop Internationalism*. Cambridge, MA: MIT Press.

Landry, Charles (2000) *The Creative City*. London: Earthscan.

Lasswell, Harold, D. (1965) *World Politics and Personal Insecurity*. New York: Free Press.

Lent, John (1993) 'Four conundrums of Third World communication', in K. Nordenstreng and H.I. Schiller (eds), *Beyond National Sovereignty: International Communications in the 1990s*. Norwood, NJ: Ablex.

MacBride, Sean (1980) *Many Voices, One World*. Paris: UNESCO.

Machlup, Fritz (1962) *The Production and Distribution of Knowledge in the United States*, Princeton, NJ: Princeton University Press.

Martin-Barbero, Jesus (1988) 'Communications from culture: the crisis of the national and the emergence of the popular', *Media, Culture & Society*, 10 (4): 447–66.

Martin-Barbero, Jesus (1993) *Communications, Culture and Hegemony: From the Media to Mediations*, trans. E. Fox and R.A. White. London: Sage.

Mattelart, Armand (2003) *The Information Society: An Introduction*. London: Sage.

Mattelart, Armand, Delcourt, Xavier and Mattelart, Michèle (1984) *International Image Markets*. London: Comedia.

Mehta, A. (1998) 'Media regulation in India', *Media Asia*, 25 (2).

Melkote, Srinivas R. and Steeves, Leslie, H. (2004) 'Information and communication technologies for rural development', in Festus Eribo and Charles C. Okigbo (eds), *Development and Communication in Africa*. Oxford: Rowman & Littlefield. pp. 165–73.

Melody, William (1996) 'Towards a framework for designing information society policies', *Telecommunications Policy*, 20 (4): 243–59.

Miller, Daniel and Slater, Don (2000) *The Internet: An Ethnographic Approach*. Oxford: Berg.

Miller, Toby, Govil, Nitin, McMurria, John, and Maxwell, Richard (2001) *Global Hollywood*. London: British Film Institute.

Meyrowitz, Joshua (1985) *No Sense of Place: The Impact of Electronic Media on Social Behaviour*. New York: Oxford University Press.

Moran, Albert (1998) *Copycat TV: Globalization, Programme Formats and Cultural Identity*. Luton: University of Luton Press.

Morley, David and Robins, Kevin (1995) *Spaces of Identity: Global Media, Electronic Landscapes and Cultural Boundaries*. London: Routledge.

Mosco, Vincent (1998) 'Political economy, communication, and labor', in G. Sussman and J.A. Lent (eds), *Global Productions: Labor in the*

Making of the 'Information Society'. Cresskill, NJ: Hampton.

Mosco, Vincent (1999) 'New York.com: a political economy of the "informational" city" ', *Journal of Media Economics*, 12 (2): 103–16.

Murdoch, Rupert (1993) Address given at the launch of New World Communications, London, September.

Nordenstreng, Kaarle and Schiller, Herbert I. (eds) (1993) *Beyond National Sovereignty: International Communications in the 1990s*. Norwood, NJ: Ablex.

Northfield, Dianne (1999) *The Information Policy Maze: Global Challenges – National Responses*. Melbourne: Centre for International Research into Communications and Information Technologies (CIRCIT).

Oakley, Kate (2004) 'Not so cool Britannia: the role of the creative industries in economic development', *International Journal of Cultural Studies*, 7 (1): 67–77.

OECD (1997) *Towards a Global Information Society: Global Information Infrastructure/Global Information Society: Policy Requirements*. Paris: Organization for Economic Cooperation and Development.

OECD (1998) *Content as a New Growth Industry*. Paris: Organization for Economic Cooperation and Development.

OECD (1999) *Communications Outlook 1999*. Paris: Organization for Economic Cooperation and Development.

OECD (2000) *OECD Privacy Guidelines*. Available online: http://www.cs3-hq.oecd.org/scripts/pwv3/pwhome/htm

Porat, Marc U. (1977) *The Information Economy: Sources and Methods for Measuring the Primary Information Sector*. Washington, DC: Department of Commerce; Office of Telecommunications.

Rai, L.P. and Lal, K. (2000) 'Indicators of the information revolution', *Technology in Society*, 22: 221–35.

Reich, Robert (1992) *The Work of Nations*. New York: Vintage.

Robertson, Roland (1991) 'Mapping the global condition: globalization as the central concept', in Mike Featherstone (ed.), *Global Culture: Nationalism, Globalization and Modernity*. London: Sage. pp. 15–30.

Robertson, Roland (1994) 'Globalization or Glocalization', *The Journal of International Communication*, (1) 1, June.

Sakr, Naomi (2005) 'Maverick or model? Al-Jazeera's impact on Arab satellite television', in Jean Chalaby (ed.), *Transnational Television Worldwide*. London: I.B. Tauris. pp. 66–95.

Schiller, Herbert I. (1969) *Mass Communications and American Empire*. New York: Kelley.

Schiller, Herbert I. (1976) *Communications and Cultural Domination*. New York: International Arts and Science Press.

Schiller, Herbert I. (1989) 'Not yet the post-imperialist era', *Critical Studies in Mass Communication*, 8: 13–28.

Schlesinger, Philip (1991) 'On national identity. I: Cultural politics and the mediologists', in *Media, State and Nation: Political Violence and Collective Identities*. London: Sage. pp. 139–51.

Shaw, Martin (1997) 'The theoretical challenge of global society', in Annabelle Sreberny-Mohammadi, Dwayne Winseck, Jim McKenna and Oliver Boyd-Barrett (eds), *Media in Global Context: A Reader*. London: Arnold. pp. 27–36.

Shawcross, William (1997) *Murdoch: The Making of a Media Empire*. New York: Touchstone.

Sinclair, John (1997) 'The business of international broadcasting: cultural bridges and barriers', *Asian Journal of Communication*, 7 (1): 137–55.

Sinclair, John, Jacka, Elizabeth and Cunningham, Stuart (1996) 'Peripheral vision', in John Sinclair, Elizabeth Jacka and Stuart Cunningham (eds), *New Patterns in Global Television: Peripheral Vision*. Oxford: Oxford University Press.

Smith, Anthony D. (1991) 'Towards a global culture?', in Mike Featherstone (ed.), *Global Culture: Nationalism, Globalization and Modernity*. London: Sage. pp. 171–92.

Sreberny-Mohammadi, Annabelle (1997) 'The many cultural faces of imperialism', in *Beyond Cultural Imperialism: Globalization, Communication and the New International Order*. London: Sage. pp. 49–68.

Straubhaar, Joseph D. (1997) 'Distinguishing the global, regional and national levels of world television', in Annabelle Sreberny-Mohammadi, Dwayne Winseck, Jim McKenna and Oliver Boyd-Barrett (eds), *Media in Global Context: A Reader*. London: Arnold. pp. 284–98.

Sussman, Gerald (1997) *Communication, Technology, and Politics in the Information Age*. Thousand Oaks, CA: Sage.

Sussman, Gerald (2003) 'The Tao of Singapore's Internet politics', *Journal of International Communication*, 9 (1): 35–51.

Thaicom (2000) 'Satellite services'. Available online: www.thaicom.net

Thomas, Amos Owen (1996) 'Global-diasporic and subnational-ethnic: audiences for satellite television in South Asia', *Journal of International Communication*, 3 (2): 61–75.

Thussu, Daya Kishan (1998) 'Infotainment international: a view from the South', in *Electronic Empires: Global Media and Local Resistance*. London: Arnold. pp. 63–82.

Thussu, Daya Kishan (1999) 'Privatizing the airwaves: the impact of globalization on broadcasting in India', *Media, Culture & Society*, 21: 125–31.

Tomlinson, John (1997) *Globalization and Culture*. Cambridge: Polity.

Tracey, Michael (1988) 'Popular culture and the economics of global television', *Intermedia*, 16 (2): 9–24.

United Nations Conference on Trade and Development (2004) 'Creative industries and development', UNCTAD *Eleventh Session*, São Paulo, Brazil, 13–18 June. Available online: www.unctad.org/en/docs/tdxibpd13_en.pdf

Urry, John (1989) 'The end of organised capitalism', in Stuart Hall and Martin Jacques (eds), *New Times: The Changing Face of Politics in the 1990s*. London: Lawrence & Wishart. pp. 94–102.

US Trade Representative (2000) 'Special 301 Report'. Available online: www.ustr.gov

Venturelli, Shalini (2005) 'Culture and the creative economy in the information age', in J. Hartley (ed.), *Creative Industries*. Oxford: Blackwell. pp. 391–8.

Wark, McKenzie (1994) *Virtual Geography: Living with Global Media Events*. Bloomington, IN: Indiana University Press.

Waters, Malcolm (1995) *Globalization*. London: Routledge.

Weber, Ian G. (1995) 'The moral market: social vision and corporate strategy in Murdoch's rhetoric', *Media International Australia*, 77: 45–53.

Weiss, Linda (1997) 'Globalization and the myth of the powerless state', *New Left Review*, 225: 3–27.

Whitaker, Reg (1999) *The End of Privacy*. New York: New Press.

Zittrain, Jonathan and Edelman, Benjamin (2002) 'Empirical analysis of Internet filtering in China', Berkman Center for Internet & Society, Harvard Law School. Available online: http://cyber.law.harvard.edu/filtering/china

15

Universal Access to the New Information Infrastructure

HEATHER E. HUDSON

Technological innovation and the transition to a global digital economy have focused new attention on the importance of access for all to telecommunications facilities and services. 'Universal service', meaning access to basic telephone service for all, remains the primary objective. However, the emergence of the Internet is forcing policy-makers to rethink this concept, in terms of both what services should be universally available, and whether 'access' is a more appropriate goal for so-called 'advanced services'. This chapter examines the availability of telecommunications and information services access in industrialized and developing countries, the changing goals and definitions of universal service, and the strategies being implemented to extend access to various levels of service, particularly in rural and disadvantaged areas.

OVERVIEW

Background

The term 'universal service' originated not as a public policy goal, but as an industrial strategy. Theodore Vail, the early visionary head of AT&T, coined the term to mean the delivery of all telephone services through one network, the Bell system (Mueller, 1997). Vail was later willing to submit to government regulation to achieve his goal: a single, unified carrier providing both local and long-distance service throughout the country. However, by 1920, only 35 per cent of American households had a telephone (Crandall and Waverman, 2000). The Communications Act of 1934, which established the Federal Communications Commission, made no specific reference to universal service, although it did invoke 'the public interest' and stated that its purpose was 'to make available, so far as possible to all people of the United States, a rapid, efficient, nationwide … communications service with adequate facilities at reasonable charges'. Over the next 40 years, various methods were adopted to apportion the costs of providing telephone service among various elements in the network, which generally resulted in keeping local service prices low through cross-subsidies from long-distance and other services.

The term 'universal service' was reintroduced in 1975 in testimony by AT&T consultant (and former adviser to President Lyndon Johnson), Eugene Rostow, who sought to ward off competition from MCI and other new long-distance competitors, and to resist the efforts of the Department of Justice to break up AT&T: 'In this struggle, the concept of universal service was redefined in a way that linked it to the practices of regulated monopoly' (Mueller, 1997). While AT&T eventually lost the argument that the way to keep local rates low and affordable was to prevent competition, a system of access charges was implemented so that all carriers would contribute to the costs of providing universal service.

Changing Concepts of Universal Service

The concept of universal service today is 'virtually synonymous with government policies designed to promote the affordability of telephone service and access to the network' (Mueller, 1997). In the US, targeted subsidies to ensure affordable access to a basic telephone service are available for low-income households, regardless of where they are located, as well as for telephone companies providing service in high-cost rural and remote areas, with the result that the price of service is lowered for all households, regardless of income. The Telecommunications Act of 1996 adds two new categories: identifying (but not defining) 'advanced services' that should be universally available; and specifying institutions (namely schools, libraries and rural health centres) rather than households as the means through which these services should be made accessible.

Many other countries have some form of universal service policy, which aims to ensure access to at least basic telephone services throughout the society, including low-income, isolated and disadvantaged residents.[1] In developing countries, such policies are generally formulated as goals to extend access to unserved populations or regions.

THE CURRENT CONTEXT

The concept of universal access must be viewed in a context of changing economic, technological and policy environments. Three major trends driving these changes are the rapid introduction of new technologies and services; the restructuring of the telecommunications sector; and globalization of economies and of communications. Together these developments are changing not only the world of telecommunications, but the ways people work, learn and interact. As noted elsewhere in this volume (see Chapter 18), economic activity is becoming increasingly information intensive, as the costs of information processing and transmission decline. Producers and consumers are becoming part of a globalized economy where national boundaries and time zones are becoming irrelevant. This transition to a so-called 'new economy' is being driven largely by the exploitation of the Internet, which in turn is made possible by changes in technology and communications policies.

Key technological trends that are driving the proliferation of new information and telecommunications services include the following:

- *Digitization*   Telecommunications networks are becoming totally digital, so that any type of information, including voice and video, may be sent as a stream of bits. Digital compression allows more efficient use of bandwidth so that customers may have more choices (such as compressed satellite television channels) and/or lower costs, such as use of compressed video for distance education and compressed voice for Internet telephony.
- *Capacity*   New technologies such as optical fibre have enormous capacity to carry information, and can be used for services ranging from entertainment and distance education to transmission of highly detailed images for remote medical diagnosis. Satellites and some terrestrial wireless technologies also offer a tremendous increase in availability of bandwidth.
- *Convergence*   The convergence of telecommunications, data processing and imaging technologies is ushering in the era of multimedia, in which voice, data and images may be combined according to the needs of users, and distinctions between the traditional sectors of telecommunications, information

processing and broadcasting are increasingly arbitrary and perhaps irrelevant.

- *Ubiquity* Advances in wireless technology such as cellular networks, personal communications systems (PCS) and rural radio subscriber systems offer affordable means of reaching rural customers and urban areas without infrastructure in developing countries. Low-cost wireless services may also replace wireline in industrialized countries as the primary means of personal access.

The policy environment is also changing dramatically, with increasing emphasis on private-sector ownership and market-driven competition. Major models of ownership and structure in the telecommunications sector include the following.

Ownership

- *Government-owned and operated utilities* In most countries (with the notable exceptions of the United States and much of Canada), telephone service was initially established as an offshoot of the postal service, through a government-owned entity often known as the PTT (post, telephone and telegraph). Typically, revenues from telecommunications services may be used to subsidize the postal service, or to contribute to the national treasury. Many countries also have separately managed military telecommunications networks; in China, the army as well as other government departments operate public telecommunications networks.
- *Autonomous public-sector corporations* For countries with government-owned telecommunications operators, the first step for creating incentives to improve efficiency and innovation in the telecommunications sector is to create an autonomous organization operated on business principles. This is often seen as an intermediate step between a PTT structure and some form of privatization.
- *Privatized corporations* Privatization models range from minor investments by private companies, to joint ventures between private carriers and governments, to full

privatization without any government stake or with a small government 'golden share'. Telecommunications carriers in industrialized countries are generally now partially or fully privatized.

Structure

- *Monopoly* Most countries began with a national monopoly model, which has gradually been opened to competition. Many maintain some level of monopoly, for example in the local loop, but alternative providers using wireless and fibre are also beginning to challenge the assumption of natural monopoly in the local loop.
- *Open entry for unserved areas* An intermediate step between national monopoly and competition is a policy of open entry for unserved areas. For example, in the US, Finland, Hungary and Poland, small companies or cooperatives were formed to provide services in areas ignored by the national monopoly carrier.
- *Competition* Competition can range from terminal equipment (now commonly competitive almost everywhere) to new services such as cellular telephony, to value-added services such as Internet access, to full competition in all network services. Hong Kong has perhaps the most competitive environment, with full local competition; many other countries such as the United Kingdom, the United States, Canada, Australia and Japan have authorized local competition, but have little actual competition at the local level.
- *Consolidation* Industrialized countries are now witnessing consolidation among competitors that seek economies of scale or scope, by buying either similar companies (such as the acquisitions by SBC of Pacific Bell and Ameritech, and by Bell Atlantic of NYNEX) or companies that provide new means of accessing customers, such as wireless networks and cable television systems. US examples include AT&T's acquisition of McCaw Wireless and TCI cable television, and Verizon (formed by the merger of Bell Atlantic with GTE).

The ownership and structure of telecommunications networks may influence goals and strategies for universal service. For example, government-owned monopolies may heavily cross-subsidize local and domestic services to extend access; in a competitive environment, dominant carriers (which are likely to be at least partially government owned) may have a special obligation to provide service in areas deemed to be unprofitable. In a fully competitive environment, efforts to ensure universal service must be based on competitively neutral policies such as incentives available to all carriers or explicitly targeted subsidies (see below).

THE IMPORTANCE OF ACCESS TO INFORMATION

The theoretical underpinning of research on the impact of information and communications technologies in general is that information is critical to the social and economic activities that comprise the development process. Much of the research to date on the socioeconomic effects of new communication technologies has examined the role of information networking through telecommunications. Access to information is critical to development; thus information and communication technologies (ICTs) as a means of sharing information are not simply a connection between people, but a link in the chain of the development process itself. Information is obviously central to activities that have come to be known as the 'information sector' including education and research, media and publishing, information equipment and software, and information-intensive services such as financial services, consulting and trade. But information is also critical to other economic activities ranging from manufacturing to agriculture and resource extraction, for management, logistics, marketing and other functions. Information is also important to the delivery of health care and public services (Hudson, 1984, 1995; Saunders et al., 1994).

For individuals, access to information can have personal, social and economic functions, often accomplished using the same devices. An individual can summon help in an emergency via telephone; she may stay in touch with friends and family members and arrange appointments by telephone or e-mail; and she may find the Internet a more efficient means of tracking down consumer information on products and services than the mass media. Entrepreneurial sole proprietors, ranging from programmers and consultants to small farmers and craftspeople, can set up global storefronts on the Internet.

In general, the ability to access and share information can contribute to the development process by improving:

- *efficiency*, or the ratio of output to cost (for example, through use of just-in-time manufacturing and inventory systems, through use of information on weather and soil content to improve agricultural yields);
- *effectiveness*, or the quality of products and services (such as improving health care through telemedicine);
- *reach*, or the ability to contact new customers or clients (for example, craftspeople reaching global markets on the Internet; educators reaching students at work or at home);
- *equity*, or the distribution of development benefits throughout the society (such as to rural and remote areas, to minorities and disabled populations) (Hudson, 1997a).

It is the importance of communication to socioeconomic development and equity that has been the foundation of the 'public interest' concerns in telecommunications, and the concept of universal service as a means of providing accessible and affordable communications throughout the society.

INFORMATION GAPS

In industrialized countries and other high-income countries, telephone service is almost universally available through fixed lines and increasingly through wireless networks. Ownership of computers is widespread, and use of the Internet is increasing dramatically. In the US, about 95.5 per cent of households have telephones, while 56.5 per cent have personal computers and 50.5 per cent have Internet access (Federal Communications Commission, 2004). However, despite growth in access overall, there is a widening gap between high- and low-income households. Urban households with incomes of $75,000 and higher are more than 20 times as likely to have access to the Internet than rural households at the lowest income levels, and more than nine times as likely to have a computer at home (McConnaughey et al., 1999). Blacks, Hispanics and native American populations now lag further behind whites and Asian Americans in computer ownership and online access (see Winseck, and Gandy, in this volume).

In the rural US, there has been significant progress in access to basic telecommunications. Distance no longer accounts for difference in household access to a telephone; income levels are now a better predictor. Yet the gap in access to the Internet persists. Regardless of income level, Americans living in rural areas are lagging behind in Internet access; at the lowest income levels, those in urban areas are more than twice as likely to have Internet access as rural Americans with similar incomes.[2] Those who are connected typically pay more than their urban counterparts for Internet access. Disparities in Internet access are found in the Canadian north and the Australian outback, and in rural and disadvantaged parts of Europe.

However, this so-called 'digital divide' is much more pronounced in developing countries, where access to information and communications technologies (ICTs) remains much more limited. In its *Statement on Universal Access to Basic Communication and Information Services* of April 1997, the United Nations Administrative Committee on Coordination noted the following:

The information and technology gap and related inequities between industrialized and developing nations are widening: a new type of poverty – information poverty – looms. Most developing countries, especially the Least Developed Countries (LDCs), are not sharing in the communications revolution, since they lack:

- affordable access to core information resources, cutting-edge technology and to sophisticated telecommunications systems and infrastructure;
- the capacity to build, operate, manage and service the technologies involved;
- policies that promote equitable public participation in the information society as both producers and consumers of information and knowledge; and
- a work force trained to develop, maintain and provide the value-added products and services required by the information economy. (ITU, 1998: 10)

More than 85 per cent of the world's Internet users are in developed countries, which account for only about 22 per cent of the world's population.[3] Of course, Internet access requires both communications links and information technologies, particularly personal computers or networked computer terminals. While there is still much less access to telecommunications in developing countries than in industrialized countries, at present, the gap in access to computers is much greater than the gap in access to telephone lines or telephones. High-income countries had more than 14 times as many telephone lines per 100 population as African countries, but 35 times as many computers and more than 300 times as many Internet users per 100 population (Table 15.1).

Typically, a high percentage of developing country residents live in rural areas (as much as 80 per cent of the population in the least-developed countries), where access to communication networks is much more limited than in urban areas (Table 15.2). It should be noted that Table 15.2 overestimates rural access because the 'rest of country' includes everything except the largest city. Also, facilities are not likely to be evenly distributed throughout the country, so that in poorer nations there may be many rural settlements without any communications infrastructure.

Internet Access Indicators

Table 15.1   *Internet access by region*

Region	Main tel. lines 100 pop.	PCs/100	Internet users 100
Africa	2.7	1.3	0.03
Americas	34.8	29.0	14.5
Asia	11.7	4.6	0.4
Europe	36.6	21.4	2.3
Oceania	39.1	42.4	9.7
World	17.1	10.2	9.9

Source: Derived from ITU (2004).

ACCESS PARAMETERS

Access versus Service

The terms 'universal access' and 'universal service' are sometimes used interchangeably, although access is becoming the more common term. The distinction is between services that are delivered to all users, and access to a variety of services that may be provided to individual users, households, community facilities, institutions and workplaces, etc. However, it is also necessary to consider access to the technologies connected to these networks that make possible information access and processing, particularly when considering access to the Internet. Typically, end-user equipment would include personal computers with sufficient speed and capacity to process data from the World Wide Web (or networked terminals with central access to sufficient capacity), and access to value-added services such as Internet service providers (ISPs).

Access is thus a broader concept than service, and involves the following components.

- *Infrastructure*   Reach of networks and services, for example to rural areas, low-income populations in inner cities; available bandwidth (such as broadband capacity for high-speed Internet access).
- *Range of services*   For example, basic voice service (plain old telephone service or 'POTS'), value-added services such as ISPs.
- *Affordability*   Pricing of installation, monthly service, usage by time or volume, etc.
- *Reliability*   Quality of service, as shown by extent of outages, breakdowns, circuit blockage, circuits degraded by noise or echoes, etc.

Another important component of access is specification of the entitities to whom telecommunications services should be accessible. Users may be considered in several categories.

- *Public*   Geographic, i.e. urban/rural, regional; demographic, i.e. disadvantaged people such as low-income groups, the disabled, ethnic or other minorities.
- *Commercial enterprises*   Large and small businesses, entrepreneurs; critical sectors, i.e. agriculture, transportation, manufacturing, tourism, etc.
- *Public services*   Health care, education, other government/public services, etc.; non-profit and non-governmental organizations (NGOs).

Universal Access: A Moving Target

Universal access should be considered a dynamic concept with a set of moving targets.

Table 15.2   *Access to telecommunications*

Country Income classification	Teledensity (telephone lines per 100)		
	National	Urban	Rest of country
High	46.0	52.9	43.8
Upper middle	13.7	25.7	11.5
Lower middle	9.7	22.1	7.2
Low	2.5	6.5	2.3

Source: Derived from ITU (1998).

Rapid technological change dictates that the definitions of basic and 'advanced' or 'enhanced' services will change over time, while the unit of analysis for accessibility may be the household, the municipality, or even institutions such as schools and health centres. Thus, for example, a multi-tiered definition of access could be proposed, identifying requirements within households, within communities and for education and social service providers. For example:

- *level one* community access, for example through kiosks, libraries, post offices, community centres, telecentres;
- *level two* institutional access through schools, hospitals, clinics;
- *level three* household access.

Economic and demographic diversity in inner cities, impoverished rural areas, and developing countries will require a variety of goals for information infrastructure. In North America and Europe, the goal has been to provide basic telephone service to every household, with the assumption that businesses and organizations could all afford access to at least this grade of service. However, for Internet access, the US is applying community and institutional access models. As noted earlier, the US Telecommunications Act of 1996 specifies that 'advanced services' should be provided at a discount to schools, libraries and rural health centres. 'Advanced services' are currently interpreted as Internet access. In the future, it is likely that advanced services will be redefined, perhaps to include access to new generations of services available through the Internet or its successors. It should also be noted that industrialized countries such as the US and Canada have extended the concept of basic service beyond quality adequate for voice to include single-party service, and circuits capable of supporting the capacity of current modems, with the assumption that people will want to communicate electronically from their homes.[4] These criteria are also likely to be revised over time to keep pace with the demands of the information economy.

Developing countries generally use community access criteria: China, India, Mexico, Nepal and Thailand, for example, aim for at least one telephone per village or settlement. Other developing countries set targets of public telephones within a radius of a few kilometres in rural areas (ITU, 1998: 69). The ITU's Maitland Commission called for a telephone within an hour's walk throughout the developing world.

The Danger of Electronic Islands and Ghettos

National goals of interoperability and open standards are needed to ensure that users are not left on 'electronic islands' because their service provider is not interconnected with other networks. An analogy would be the early stages of commercial e-mail, when each e-mail service was autonomous, so that communication between subscribers to different services was impossible or at least very cumbersome.

There is still a danger of creating electronic ghettos – low-profit regions such as inner cities and rural areas – that carriers and service providers may have little incentive to serve or upgrade. For example, large US telephone companies have been reluctant to upgrade their networks in rural areas by adding technologies such as signalling system 7 (SS7), integrated services digital network (ISDN) and digital subscriber line (DSL). Ironically, customers of some rural telephone companies that have invested in new facilities may gain little benefit if the connecting long-distance carriers do not offer similar services.

TECHNOLOGICAL TRENDS

Demand for Internet access has created a market for higher-speed communication than is typically available over a dialup telephone line. The least-cost solution in areas with communications infrastructure is to upgrade these facilities, for example to offer DSL over existing telephone lines or cable modems for access over cable television networks. Where population density is high and funds are available, optical fibre is being provided to the end user (for example, in Singapore and in new subdivisions in industrialized countries). However, high-capacity wireless networks may offer a lower-cost solution than optical fibre to provide high-speed networking.

In the past, there have been few incentives for carriers to provide access to low-income customers such as disadvantaged minorities and inner-city residents who are presumed to have limited demand for new services, and rural and remote regions where the cost of extending or upgrading facilities and services is assumed to be higher than expected revenues. However, technological innovations, many of which were initially designed for other applications, are now creating opportunities to reduce costs and/or increase revenues among these populations. As noted earlier, high-capacity wireless may be a less expensive means of providing or upgrading access in urban areas. Wireless also has enormous potential in rural areas where the cost of installing cable or fibre is much higher. Satellite systems may also be used in rural areas for basic telephony (generally through a local network connected to a community satellite terminal) or for Internet access (which could also be through an individual VSAT – a very small aperture terminal). More information on these technologies and their implications for improving access is provided in the Appendix at the end of this chapter.

There are several significant implications of these technological trends, particularly for rural and developing regions.

- *Distance is no longer a barrier to accessing information* Technologies are available that can provide interactive voice, data and multimedia services virtually anywhere.
- *Costs of providing services are declining* Satellite transmission costs are independent of distance; transmission costs using other technologies have also declined dramatically. Thus communications services can be priced not according to distance, which penalizes rural and remote users, but per unit of information (message, bit) or unit of time.

- *The potential for competition is increasing* Lower costs make rural/remote areas more attractive. New competitors can offer multiple technological solutions, including wireless, satellite, copper, cable and others described above.

In addition, it is no longer technically or economically necessary to set rural benchmarks lower than urban benchmarks for access – both to basic telecommunications and to the Internet. The US Telecommunications Act of 1996 requires that rural services and prices are to be *reasonably comparable* to those in urban areas. This standard rejects the assumption that 'something is better than nothing' in rural areas because minimal service was all that was either technically feasible or economically justifiable. However, as noted earlier, advances in technologies such as terrestrial wireless and satellite systems can now provide higher quality at lower cost in rural areas. The implications of these changes in policy and technology are particularly critical in enabling rural residents to participate in the digital economy.

While the US and other industrialized countries must upgrade outdated wireline networks and analogue exchanges in rural areas, developing countries can leapfrog old technologies and install fully digital wireless networks. Thus developing country regulators can also adopt rural comparability standards to avoid penalizing rural services and businesses in access to information services. For example, in the Philippines, after extensive discussion, both government and industry representatives agreed on rural benchmarks including digital switching, single-party service, and line quality sufficient for facsimile and data communications.[5]

UNDERSTANDING DEMAND FOR COMMUNICATION SERVICES

Lack of understanding of demand for telecommunications services (i.e. the need for the service and ability to pay) creates problems in designing universal service policy. For example,

Table 15.3   *Access to telephones v TV sets per household*

Country income classification	Telephone lines per household	TV sets per household	Ratio TV sets/telephone lines
High	96.1	97.1	1.01
Upper middle	59.0	92.6	1.60
Lower middle	49.4	89.4	1.80
Low	8.2	35.2	4.30

Source: Derived from ITU (2004).

'low-income' households in industrialized countries may be able to pay for the cost of monthly telephone service subscriptions, which are likely to cost less than other utilities and than entertainment, including cable television (Crandall and Waverman, 2000). Thus, it may not be necessary to provide a subsidy for service to most low-income households. However, utilization of the network (for long-distance or measured rate calls) which subscribers need to maintain contact for family or work may be much more expensive. Some consumer representatives have advocated a policy of providing a live telephone connection in all dwellings which could be used for emergencies. Other possibilities include blocks on the line to prevent unauthorized use for other than local calls, and prepaid service in the form of a rechargeable account or smart card that allows calling only up to the limit of funds on the card or in the account.

Communications service providers may also be reluctant to extend services to poorer populations who are assumed to have insufficient demand to cover the cost of providing the services and necessary infrastructure. Certainly, household income may be the best indicator of both willingness and ability to pay for communication services. Typically higher-income populations are better educated, and are thus likely to have not only the money but also the skills to use new technologies and services.

However, indicators other than population and household income may be better predictors of demand for communication services. One study estimates that rural users in developing countries are able collectively to pay 1 to 1.5 per cent of their gross *community* income for telecommunications services (Kayani and Dymond, 1997: xviii). The ITU uses an estimate of 5 per cent of *household* income as an

affordability threshold. To generate revenues to cover capital and operating costs of the network, the average household income required would be $2060; for a more efficiently run network, it would be $1340 (ITU, 1998: 35). Using the higher estimate, 20 per cent of households in low-income countries could afford a telephone; in lower-middle-income countries the range could be from 40 to 80 per cent; while in upper-middle-income countries such as Eastern Europe, more than 80 per cent of households could afford telephone services (1998: 37).[6]

Just as income may not fully explain demand for information technologies and services, lack of access to telephone services cannot necessarily be attributed to lack of demand or purchasing power. For example, in many developing countries, television sets are much more prevalent than telephones. In industrialized countries, both TV sets and telephone lines are almost universally available. However, in lower-middle-income countries there are almost twice as many TV sets as telephone lines, while in low-income countries there are more than four times as many TV sets as telephone lines (see Table 15.3). It appears that where television is available, a significant percentage of families will find the money to buy TV sets. Thus, even in the poorest countries, there may be much more disposable income available than per capita GDP data would indicate, and there may be significant demand for other information services.

Other approaches may also be used to gauge demand for information services. For example, the presence of video shops indicates significant disposable income available for television sets, video cassette players and cassette rentals. Telephone service resellers (such as in Indonesia, Senegal and Bangladesh), local cable television operators (common in India) and small satellite dishes on rural homesteads and urban flats (common in Eastern Europe and many Asian countries) also signal demand and ability to pay for information services.

A conclusion that can be drawn from the above analysis is that changing the policy environment to create incentives to serve previously ignored populations may significantly increase access among these groups. Incentives are some of the innovative strategies that have been adopted to provide community access to telecommunications, and more recently to the Internet, which are summarized in the next section.

POLICIES AND STRATEGIES TO INCREASE ACCESS

Community Access Requirements

Some countries such as Chile and Mexico have mandated requirements for operators to install payphones in rural communities; South Africa has also required its wireless operators to install fixed rural payphones. Franchised payphones have been introduced in Indonesia, India, Bangladesh and other countries in order to involve entrepreneurs where the operator is still government owned. Indonesia's franchised call offices, known as wartels (*warung telekomunikasi*), operated by small entrepreneurs, generate more than $9000 per line, about ten times more than Telkom's average revenue per line (ITU, 1998: 77). Franchised telephone booths operate in several francophone African countries; in Senegal, phone shops known locally as telecentres average four times the revenue of those operated by the national carrier (1998: 77–8). In Bangladesh, Grameen Phone has rented cell phones to rural women who provide portable payphone service to their communities. Such examples of simple resale can create incentives to meet pent-up demand even if network competition has not yet been introduced.

Telecentres and other public facilities can provide access to e-mail, which is much faster than the postal service and cheaper than facsimile transmission. For example, a message of 2000 words takes 10 minutes to read over a telephone; 2 minutes to send by fax; and about 4 seconds to transmit via a 28.8 kbps modem (M. Hegener, quoted in ITU, 1998: 80). Such services can be valuable even for illiterates. For example, a Member of Parliament from Uganda stated that his father sent many telegrams during his lifetime, but could neither read nor write. Local scribes wrote down his messages. Similarly, 'information brokers' ranging from librarians to cybercafé staff can help people with limited education to send and access electronic information.

Virtually every major city in the developing world now has cybercafés or privately operated telecentres equipped with personal computers linked to the Internet. The African Communications Group plans wireless kiosks for Internet access, with web pages enabling artisans, farmers and other small entrepreneurs to set up shop in the global marketplace (Petzinger, 1998: B1). Initiatives to provide public Internet access through community telecentres are being supported by several development agencies including the International Telecommunication Union (ITU), UNESCO, United Nations Development Programme (UNDP), Canada's International Development Research Centre (IDRC), and the US Agency for International Development (USAID). South Africa is also supporting the installation of telecentres equipped with phone lines, facsimile and computers with Internet access through a universal service fund; South Africa now plans to provide Internet access to government information and electronic commerce services through post offices. Many other countries are extending public access to the Internet through telecentres, libraries, post offices and kiosks.

Access to telephones through booths, kiosks and telecentres can be coupled with electronic messaging to provide a 'virtual telephone service'. TeleBahia in north-eastern Brazil offers a virtual service for small businesses without individual telephones. These customers rent a voice mailbox for a monthly fee and check their messages from a payphone, providing a means for clients to contact them. African Communications Group[7] is setting up wireless public payphones and providing voice mail accounts and pagers that announce incoming messages. The recipient calls back or leaves a voice mail message using a phone card; the service is priced for people making $200 per month (Petzinger, 1998: B1). Similar systems are used for migrant farm workers in California to enable them to stay in touch with their families, and in homeless shelters to enable job seekers to be contacted by employers.

Service Obligations

Many countries include a universal service obligation (USO) as a condition of the licence. The cost of USOs may vary depending on geography and population density. British Telecom's universal service obligation costs just 1 per cent of its total revenue base (Oftel, 1994; quoted in Kayani and Dymond, 1997: 53). Latin American countries with USOs include Argentina, Chile, Mexico, Peru and Venezuela. In Mexico, the privatized monopoly operator TelMex was to provide service to all communities with at least 500 population by the year 2000. In the Philippines, local exchange obligations are bundled with cellular and international gateway licences; licensees were required to install up to 300,000 access lines in previously unserved areas within three years (Hudson, 1997b).

Some countries use a 'carrier of last resort' model which has the obligation to provide service if no other carrier has done so. Typically, the dominant carrier bears this obligation and is entitled to a subsidy to provide the service. However, this approach can be flawed if it provides no incentive for the carrier with the USO to use the most appropriate and inexpensive technology and to operate efficiently. It can also serve as a justification for the dominant carrier to be protected from competition because it has additional costs and obligations not required of new competitors.

However, rather than designating a single carrier of last resort, some countries are introducing bidding schemes for rural subsidies. In Chile, a development fund was established in 1994 to increase access for the approximately 10 per cent of the population in communities

without telephone access. The regulator estimated the required subsidies, distinguishing between commercially viable and commercially unviable, and put them out to competitive tender. There were 62 bids for 42 of the 46 projects. Surprisingly, 16 projects were awarded to bids of zero subsidy; as a result of preparing for the bidding process, operators were able to document demand and willingness to pay in many communities. Once completed, these projects will provide service to about 460,000 people, about one-third of the Chilean population without access (ITU, 1998: 79). Peru is introducing a similar programme.

Subsidies

A variety of schemes can be used to subsidize carriers that serve regions where revenues would apparently not cover costs. Subsidies may be paired with USOs to compensate the carrier with the obligation to serve. The traditional means of ensuring provision of service to unprofitable areas or customers has been through cross-subsidies, such as from international or interexchange to local services. However, technological changes and the liberalization of the telecommunications sector now make it impracticable to rely on internal cross-subsidies. For example, customers may bypass high-priced services using so-called 'callback'[8] services or Internet telephony.

In a competitive environment, cross-subsidies cannot be maintained. Carriers that have relied on revenues from one service to subsidize another now face competitors who can underprice them on individual services. Also, new entrants cannot survive if their competitors are subsidized. Therefore, if subsidies are required, they must be made explicit and targeted at specific classes of customers or locations such as the following.

- *High-cost areas* Carriers may be subsidized to serve locations that are isolated and/or have very low population density so that they are significantly more expensive to serve than other locations. This approach is used in the US and has recently been mandated in Canada.

- *Disadvantaged areas or customers* Subsidies may target economically disadvantaged areas or groups that could not afford typical prices for installation and usage, or where demand for service is significantly lower than average. Some carriers may offer interest-free loans or extended payment periods to assist new subscribers to connect to the network. In the US, the Lifeline programme subsidizes basic monthly service charges for low-income subscribers. The subsidy funds come from a combination of carrier contributions and surcharges on subscriber bills. Some 4.4 million households receive Lifeline assistance. Also in the US, the Linkup programme subsidizes connection to the network for low-income households.

- *Route averaging* Some countries including Australia, Canada, the United Kingdom and the United States require that rates be averaged so that all customers pay uniform distance charges, regardless of location. Thus, for example, the rate per minute between Sydney and Melbourne would be the same as the rate over an equal distance in the Australian outback, where costs are much higher. Such policies can bridge the digital divide by reducing rural access costs.

Funding Universal Service

Funds for subsidies may be generated from several sources such as contributions required from all carriers: for example, a percentage of revenues, a tax on revenues or a surcharge on customer bills. Subsidies may also come from general tax revenues or other government sources.

- *Transfers among carriers* Some countries with many carriers rely on settlement and repayment pooling schemes among operators to transfer payments to carriers with high operating costs. For example, the US Universal Service Fund is mandated by the Federal Communications Commission (FCC) but administered by the carriers through the National Exchange Carriers Association (NECA), and transfers funds to subsidize access lines to carriers whose costs are above 115 per cent of the national average.[9]

- *Government-financed funds* In Poland, over 7885 localities were connected between 1992 and 1996 with funding of US$20 million from the state budget (ITU, 1998: 78). In 1994, Peru established a rural telecommunications investment fund, FITEL (Fondo de Inversion de Telecomunicaciones), which is financed by a 1 per cent tax on revenues of all telecommunications providers, ranging from the country's newly privatized monopoly operator Telefonica/ENTEL to cable TV operators. Since established, it has generated an average of US$450,000 per month, growing by US$12 million annually (1998: 79). Private-sector operators may apply to FITEL for financing (Kayani and Dymond, 1999: 63–4).

Licensing Rural Operators

Some countries grant monopoly franchises to rural operators. For example, Bangladesh has licensed two rural monopoly operators; they are allowed to prioritize the most financially attractive customers and charge a substantial up-front subscriber connection fee. The Bangladesh Rural Telecommunications Authority (BRTA) is profitable, even though it has to provide at least one public call office (PCO) in each village that requests one (Kayani and Dymond, 1997: 18).

However, other countries are opening up rural areas to competition as part of national liberalization policies. Argentina allows rural operators to compete with the two privatized monopolies, Telecom and Telefonica. Some 135 rural cooperatives have been formed to provide telecommunications services in communities with fewer than 300 people (1997: 18). Finland's association of telephone companies has created several jointly owned entities that provide a range of rural, local and long-distance services in their concession areas, in competition with the national operator (1997: 19). In Alaska, a second carrier, GCI, competes with AT&T Alascom to provide long-distance services in rural and remote areas. This competition has benefited Alaskan schools in gaining access to the Internet. GCI has assisted school districts in applying for E-rate subsidies for Internet access, apparently viewing this initiative as a win–win opportunity for both schools and the telephone company.

Although in most countries a single carrier provides both local and long-distance services, it is also possible to delineate territories that can be served by local entities. In the US, the model of rural cooperatives fostered through the Rural Utilities Service (formerly Rural Electrification Administration) has been used to bring telephone service to areas ignored by the large carriers. As noted earlier, wireless technologies could change the economics of providing rural services, making rural franchises much more attractive to investors. As a result of availability of funds from the RUS for upgrading networks, rural cooperatives in the US typically provide more modern facilities and better Internet access than provided by large telephone companies serving rural areas.

Third parties may also be permitted to lease capacity in bulk and resell it in units of bandwidth and/or time appropriate for business customers and other major users. This approach may be suitable where some excess network capacity exists (e.g. between major cities or on domestic or regional satellites). Resale is one of the simplest ways to introduce some competition and lower rates for users, but is not legal in many developing countries, even where some excess capacity exists in backbone networks.

CURRENT AND FUTURE TRENDS

Understanding Trends in Access

Research is needed to determine which underlying factors are the best explanations of variations in access. For example, in the US, attention is frequently focused on ethnicity and rurality, e.g. access by blacks, Hispanics and native Americans, and on disparities between urban and rural residents. However, other factors such as income and education (often highly correlated) may influence access. Similar analysis in other countries may reveal underlying factors that form barriers to access. As definitions of access change to include

computers and Internet connectivity as well as a telephone service, we could expect that education would be an increasingly important predictor of access, since better-educated people would tend to have better technical skills and greater perceived need for use of computers and online services.

Other industrialized countries show trends broadly similar to those in the US, with access greater among those with higher incomes and more education, and somewhat greater in urban than in rural areas. However, the percentage of the population with Internet access at home or at work is more than twice as high in the US, Canada, the Nordic countries and Australia as in the United Kingdom, and more than three times higher than in Germany, Japan and France (ITU, 1999a: 22). It would be useful to learn what enabling or inhibiting factors are contributing to these disparities.

Studies of outliers and anomalies could also improve our understanding of trends in access to new services and their implications. For example, why are the Scandinavian countries (Finland, Sweden, Norway, Denmark) in the top ten countries in Internet hosts per 1000 population, and what impact is this high level of Internet access likely to have on their economies? Does the fact that Israel, Ireland and Taiwan have more Internet hosts per 1000 population than France and Japan indicate future trends in economic growth, or is it a short-term artifact of national policies? Are middle-income countries such as Egypt and Jordan, which have better Internet access than other economically similar countries, likely to reap greater economic benefits than countries with below-average access such as Tunisia and Algeria? Among the 'Asian tigers', does the greater Internet access of Singapore, Hong Kong and Taiwan give them an advantage over South Korea, Malaysia and Thailand (1999a: 22, 38)?

From Access to Use

Beyond access, it will be important to understand what factors influence use of information services once they are accessible, either through individual ownership and connectivity or via public sites such as schools and libraries. Are there other factors such as computer use at school that are likely to encourage access? Are there strategies such as community access or training that could increase utilization? Among youth, are there specific factors such as exposure at an early age that appear preconditions for later use? Among adults, are there information-seeking behaviours or social norms that may influence use of ICTs? For example, in some cultures, women may be discouraged from using technology; also, older or less educated people may feel more comfortable using an 'information broker' such as a librarian, social worker or extension agent to find information they need or to contact others electronically.[10] Anecdotal evidence from projects such as SeniorNet in the US and telecentres in developing countries indicates that such resource people can be very important as facilitators, especially at early stages in using the Internet among some populations such as senior citizens and women. For example, at telecentres with local facilitators in Mali, Uganda and Mozambique, from 30 to 45 per cent of the users are women, despite the fact that women typically have less education and exposure totechnology than men in these societies.[11]

CONCLUSION

The concept of universal service continues to evolve, both in terms of services that should be universally included and in our understanding of access – meaning that the services are available, affordable and reliable. This chapter has shown how innovative technologies, strategies and policies can help to increase access to communication services. However, it is important to note that more than access will likely be necessary to achieve significant benefits. A workforce with sufficient general education and specialized training as well as an institutional environment that fosters innovation and productivity are likely to be critical factors. Effective applications of these facilities may require training, mentoring and, in some cases, facilitation through intermediaries. Sustainability will

continue to be a concern, particularly in maintaining non-commercial forms of access such as through schools and libraries, and non-profit community access centres.

APPENDIX: TECHNOLOGIES AND SERVICES FOR EXTENDING ACCESS

The following are key technologies that offer new or lower-cost access to information and telecommunication services:

Wireline

Digital Subscriber Line (DSL)

This technology offers increased capacity, suitable for Internet access, over existing copper wire, making it an attractive option for upgrading Internet access in urban areas where telephone lines are already installed (its range is too limited for rural areas). However, it should be noted that copper wire is prone to theft in some countries: Telkom South Africa reported more than 4000 incidents of cable theft in 1996, at an estimated cost of R230 million (about US$50 million) (ITU, 1998: 60).

Interactive Cable Systems

Coaxial cable installed to deliver cable television can also be upgraded to provide telephony and Internet access. Cable modems provide faster transmission than DSL; however, older cable systems are not optimally configured for inter-activity, and quality of service may be inferior to that provided by telephone companies.

Hybrid Fibre/Coax (HFC)

A combination of optical fibre and coaxial cable can provide broadband services such as TV and high-speed Internet access as well as telephony; this combination is cheaper than installing fibre all the way to the customer premises. Unlike most cable systems, HFC allows two-way communication. The fibre runs from a central switch to a neighbourhood node; coax links the node to the end user such as the subscriber's home or business. HFC is found in many industrialized countries; developing countries with HFC projects include Chile, China, India, South Korea and Malaysia (1998: 57).

Optical Fibre

Optical fibre is commonly found in links between switches, terrestrial backbone networks and submarine cables. Fibre is being installed in new towns and subdivisions in industrialized countries, but the cost of upgrading existing local loops to fibre is very high. However, Singapore has provided fibre to end users, and Japan is committed to upgrading local loops to optical fibre throughout the country.

Terrestrial Wireless

Cellular

Cellular technology, originally designed for mobile services (such as communication from vehicles), is now being introduced for personal communications using small portable handsets. Wireless personal communications are almost ubiquitous in Scandinavia, Japan and Hong Kong, and are proliferating very rapidly in other industrialized and emerging economies. In developing countries without sufficient wireline infrastructure, wireless personal networks can provide a primary service. In China, there are more than 70 million wireless customers; other developing countries where wireless is used as a primary service include Colombia, Lebanon, Malaysia, the Philippines, Sri Lanka, South Africa, Uganda, Venezuela and Thailand (ITU, 1998: 49).

Wireless Local Loop (WLL)

Wireless local loop systems can be used to extend local telephone services to rural customers without laying cable or stringing copper wire. WLL costs have declined, making it competitive with copper; wireless allows faster roll-out to customers than extending wire or cable, so that revenue can be generated more quickly; it also has a lower ratio of fixed to incremental

costs than copper, making it easy to add more customers and serve transient populations. Wireless is also less vulnerable than copper wire or cable to accidental damage or vandalism. Examples of countries with WLL projects include Bolivia, Czech Republic, Hungary, Indonesia and Sri Lanka (ITU, 1998: 53).

Cordless

Short-range cordless extensions can provide the link from wireless outstations to subscriber premises; the DECT (digital European cordless telephone) technology standard will also allow the base station to act as a wireless PBX (Kayani and Dymond, 1997: 48). For example, DECT has been used in South Africa for the link to rural subscribers.[12]

Wireless Payphones

Cellular installations can be used to provide fixed public payphones. For example, new cellular operators in South Africa were required to install 30,000 wireless payphones within five years as a condition of the licence. By March 1997, almost 15,000 wireless payphones had been installed (ITU, 1998: 50). Alternatively, a cellular subscriber may resell access. Entrepreneurs in Bangladesh offer payphone service using cell phones leased from Grameen Phone, which they carry by bicycle to various neighbourhoods.

Multi-access Radio

Time division multiple access (TDMA) radio systems are a means of providing wireless rural telephony. They typically have 30–60 trunks and can accommodate 500–1000 subscribers. Their range can be extended using multiple repeaters (Kayani and Dymond, 1999: 27).

WiFi

Wireless fidelity (WiFi) refers to a set of standards known as IEEE 802.11 which are used for wireless communications over short distances. WiFi can be used for networks in the home or business, but also to cover a campus or a village. WiFi is now built into most laptop computers.

Satellite Technologies

Very Small Aperture Terminals (VSATs)

Small satellite earth stations operating with geosynchronous earth orbiting (GEO) satellites can be used for interactive voice and data, as well as for broadcasting of data, audio and video. Remote villages in Alaska and the Canadian Arctic use satellites for telephone service, Internet access and broadcast reception. VSATs may also offer affordable access for business networks: banks in remote areas of Brazil are linked via VSATs; the National Stock Exchange of India links brokers with rooftop VSATs.

Demand Assignment Multiple Access (DAMA)

In GEO satellite systems, instead of assigning dedicated circuits to each location, DAMA allows the terminal to access the satellite only on demand and eliminates double hops between rural locations served by the same system. The system is very cost-effective because satellite transponder expense is reduced to a fraction of that associated with a fixed-assigned system for the same amount of traffic. Also, digital DAMA systems provide higher bandwidth capabilities at much lower cost than analogue. DAMA is used to reduce costs of village telephone service in Alaska, and is now used in other satellite dialup networks.

Global Mobile Personal Communications Systems (GMPCS)

Using low earth orbiting (LEO) satellites, these systems – such as Globalstar, Iridium and ICO – can provide voice and low-speed (typically 2400 to 9600 kbps) data virtually anywhere, using portable satellite phones. However, the price per minute for these services may be much higher than national terrestrial services, and the first generation of LEOs has very limited bandwidth.

Internet via Satellite

Internet gateways can be accessed via geostationary satellites. For example, MagicNet (an ISP in Mongolia) and some African ISPs access the Internet in the US via PanAmSat, and residents of the Canadian Arctic use the Anik satellite system, while Alaskan villagers use US domestic satellites. However, these systems are not optimized for Internet use, and may therefore be quite expensive. Several improvements in using GEOs are becoming available.

- *Optimized interactive access via VSAT*: Several companies are developing protocols for fully interactive Internet access via satellite, that should be much more efficient than current systems.[13]
- *Hybrid systems*: This approach uses a VSAT as a downlink from the ISP, but provides upstream connectivity over existing telephone lines. Some rural schools in the US are using hybrids for Internet access.
- *High-bandwidth LEOs*: Future LEO systems are being planned to provide bandwidth on demand. Future constellations of LEO satellites may provide another means of Internet access via satellite (Hudson, 1998a).
- *Data broadcasting*: Satellites designed for digital audio broadcasting (such as Worldspace) can also be used to broadcast web pages to small receivers. Users would not have a fully interactive service, but could receive regular downloads of specified pages addressed to their receivers.

Digital Services

Compressed Voice

Compression algorithms can be used to 'compress' digital voice signals, so that eight or more conversations can be carried on a single 64 kbps voice channel, thus significantly reducing transmission costs.

Internet Telephony (Voice over IP)

Some carriers are beginning to offer dialup access to Internet telephony. The advantage of using Internet protocols for voice as well as data is that transmission costs are much lower than over circuit-switched telephony networks. IP telephony generally requires broadband access.

Compressed Video

Compressed digital video can be used to transmit motion video over as few as two telephone lines (128 kbps), offering the possibility of low-cost video conferencing for distance education and training. Interactive low-resolution video can also now be delivered over the Internet.

Smart Cards

Prepaid phone cards, widely available in Europe and Japan, have been introduced in developing countries to eliminate the need for coin phones (which require coin collection and may be subject to pilferage and vandalism). Cellular operators have now extended this concept to offer prepaid cellular service using rechargeable smart cards, so that telephone service is now available to customers without credit histories or even bank accounts. In South Africa, Vodacom sold more than 300,000 prepaid starter packs and one million recharge vouchers for cellular use in 1997 (ITU, 1998: 44). In Uganda, within one year of licensing a second cellular operator, aggressive marketing of a prepaid service and attractive pricing have resulted in there being more cellular customers than fixed lines in the country. For most of the new subscribers, their cell phone is their first and only telephone.[14]

NOTES

1 For a comparison of universal service in the United States, Canada and the United Kingdom, see Crandall and Waverman (2000).

2 Fact sheet: 'Rural areas magnify "digital divide"'. Available online: www.ntia.doc.gov/ntiahome/digitaldivide/factsheets/rural.htm

3 It should be noted that Japan and Australia are included in the Asia and Oceania categories in Table 15.1; the estimate in the text includes them with industrialized countries of Europe and North America.

4 See www.crtc.gc.ca

5 Meeting at Department of Transport and Communications attended by the author, Manila, January 1998.

6 It should be noted that this calculation appears to assume even distribution of income throughout the society at higher income levels, which is not necessarily true.

7 Africa Communications Group is to be known as Adesemi Communications International.

8 The simplest form of callback involves a caller in an area where tariffs are high asking the other party to call back using cheaper rates from their location. Simple examples include a traveller using a hotel's payphone to call home and asking family members to call back to her room, rather than paying the hotel's high charges. Now callers in high-cost areas (typically developing countries) can set up an account with a callback company and then call a special number, hang up and wait for the return call from the cheaper jurisdiction. The company can identify the caller without even answering the call, and can set up the call between the two parties using its own software.

9 See www.neca.org, and information on the Universal Service Fund on the FCC's website: www.fcc.gov

10 For example, peasant farmers in Ecuador found out how to eliminate a pest that was destroying their potato crop through the assistance of a fieldworker who posted their question on several Internet newsgroups (personal communication, October 1999).

11 Heather E. Hudson, field research and unpublished reports, 1999. (See also Hudson, 2003, 2004a, 2004b)

12 It should be noted that a disadvantage of all these wireless technologies is limited bandwidth. While they can be used for e-mail, they do not provide sufficient capacity for accessing the World Wide Web at present. However, a new protocol known as WAP (wireless application protocol), developed to enable cellphone users to access the Web, may also make it possible to access text on the Web using very limited bandwidth.

13 See www.alohanet.com; also *The Red Herring*, 29 September 1998. Available online: www.redherring.com/mag/issue59/limit/html

14 Personal interview, Uganda Communications Commission, Kampala, November 1999.

REFERENCES

Anderson, Robert H. et al. (1995) *Universal Access to E-Mail: Feasibility and Social Implications.* Washington, DC: RAND.

Aufderheide, Patricia (1987) 'A universal service: telephone policy in the public interest', *Journal of Communication*, 37 (1): 81–96.

Aufderheide, Patricia (1999) *Communications Policy and the Public Interest: The Telecommunications Act of 1996.* New York: Guilford.

Crandall, Robert W. and Waverman, Leonard (2000) *Who Pays for Universal Service?* Washington, DC: Brookings Institution.

Cronin, Francis J., Colleran, Elisabeth K., Herbert, Paul L. and Lewitzky, Steven (1993) 'Telecommunications and growth: the contribution of telecommunications infrastructure investment to aggregate and sectoral productivity', *Telecommunications Policy*, 17 (9): 677–90.

Cronin, Francis J., Parker, Edwin B., Colleran, Elisabeth K. and Gold, Mark A. (1993) 'Telecommunications infrastructure and economic development', *Telecommunications Policy*, 17 (6): 415–30.

Duestenberg, Thomas J. and Gordon, Kenneth (1997) *Competition and Deregulation in Telecommunications: The Case for a New Paradigm*. Indianapolis: Hudson Institute.

European Union (1993) *Communication on Developing the Universal Service for Telecommunications in a Competitive Environment*. COM 93/543. Brussels, 15 November.

European Union (1996) *Communication on Universal Service for Telecommunications in the Perspective of a Fully Liberalised Environment*. COM 96/73 final. Brussels, 13 March.

Federal Communications Commission (2004) *Trends in Telephone Service*. Washington, DC: Federal Communications Commission.

Hardy, Andrew P. (1980) 'The role of the telephone in economic development', *Telecommunications Policy*, 4 (4): 278–86.

Henry, David et al. (1999) *The Emerging Digital Economy II*. Washington, DC: US Department of Commerce.

Hobbs, Vicki M. and Blodgett, John (1999) 'The rural differential: an analysis of population demographics in areas served by rural telephone companies'. Paper presented at the Telecommunications Policy Research Conference, September. See also www.rupri.org

Hudson, Heather E. (1990) *Communication Satellites: Their Development and Impact*. New York: Free Press.

Hudson, Heather E. (1995) *Economic and Social Benefits of Rural Telecommunications: A Report to the World Bank*. Washington, DC: World Bank.

Hudson, Heather E. (1997a) *Global Connections: International Telecommunications Infrastructure and Policy*. New York: Wiley.

Hudson, Heather E. (1997b) 'Converging technologies and changing realities: toward universal access to telecommunications in the developing world', in *Telecom Reform: Principles, Policies, and Regulatory Practices*. Lyngby: Technical University of Denmark.

Hudson, Heather E. (1998a) 'The significance of telecommunications for Canadian rural development'. Testimony on behalf of the Public Interest Advocacy Centre and others, Canadian Radio, Television and Telecommunications Commission Hearing on Telecom Public Notice CRTC 97–42, Service to High-Cost Serving Areas.

Hudson, Heather E. (2003) 'Bridging the broadband divide: strategies for rural and developing regions'. Proceedings of the ITU Telecom Forum, ITU Telecom World 2003, Geneva: International Telecommunication Union.

Hudson, Heather E. (2004a) 'Investing in infrastructure: increasing Internet access in the developing world'. Proceedings of the Telecommunications Policy Research Conference.

Hudson, Heather E. (2004b) 'Universal service: what have we learned from the E-rate?', *Telecommunications Policy*, 28 (3–4): 309–21.

Hundt, Reed E. (2000) *You Say You Want a Revolution: A Story of Information Age Politics*. New Haven, CT: Yale University Press.

ITU (1998) *World Telecommunication Development Report 1998*. Geneva: International Telecommunication Union.

ITU (1999a) *Challenges to the Network: Internet for Development*. Geneva: International Telecommunication Union, October.

ITU (1999b) *World Telecommunication Development Report 1999*. Geneva: International Telecommunication Union.

ITU (2004) *World Telecommunication Indicators Database*, 8th edn. Geneva: International Telecommunication Union.

Kayani, Rogati and Dymond, Andrew (1997) *Options for Rural Telecommunications Development*. Washington, DC: World Bank.

Maitland Commission (1984) *The Missing Link*. International Commission for Worldwide Telecommunications Development. Geneva: International Telecommunication Union, December.

Margherio, Lynn et al. (1998) *The Emerging Digital Economy*. Washington, DC: US Department of Commerce.

Mueller, Milton (1997) *Universal Service: Competition, Interconnection, and Monopoly in the Making of the American Telephone System*. Cambridge, MA: MIT Press.

Mueller, Milton and Schement, Jorge Reina (1996) 'A universal service from the ground up: a study of telephone penetration in Camden, New Jersey', *The Information Society*, 12: 273–92.

National Telecommunications and Information Administration (1994) *20/20 Visions*. Washington, DC: US Department of Commerce.

National Telecommunications and Information Administration (2004) *A Nation Online: Entering the Broadband Age*. Washington, DC: US Department of Commerce.

National Telecommunications and Information Administration (1997) *Falling through the Net: Defining the Digital Divide.* Washington, DC: US Department of Commerce.

O'Siochru, Sean (1996) *Telecommunications and Universal Service: International Experience in the Context of South African Telecommunications Reform.* Ottawa: International Development Research Centre.

OFTEL (1994) *A Framework for Effective Competition.* London: Office of Telecommunications.

Parker, Edwin B. and Hudson, Heather E. (1995) *Electronic Byways: State Policies for Rural Development through Telecommunications,* 2nd edn. Washington, DC: Aspen Institute.

Parker, Edwin B., Hudson, Heather E., Dillman, Don A. and Roscoe, Andrew D. (1989) *Rural America in the Information Age: Telecommunications Policy for Rural Development.* Lanham, MD: University Press of America.

Petzinger, Thomas, Jr (1998) 'Monique Maddy uses wireless payphones to battle poverty', *Wall Street Journal,* 25 September: B1.

Saunders, Robert, Warford, Jeremy and Wellenius, Bjorn (1994) *Telecommunications and Economic Development,* 2nd edn. Baltimore, MD: Johns Hopkins University Press.

Schement, Jorge Reina (1995) 'Beyond universal service: characteristics of Americans without telephones', *Telecommunications Policy,* 19: 477–85.

Telecommunications Act of 1996 (1996) United States Congress. Public Law 104-104, 8 February.

World Information Technology and Services Alliance (1998) *Digital Planet: The Global Information Economy.* Washington, DC: WITSA.

WEBSITES

Alaska Public Utilities Commission: www.state.ak.us/local/akpages/COMMERCE/apuc.htm

Aloha Networks: www.alohanet.com

Canadian Radio Television and Telecommunications Commission (CRTC): www.crtc.gc.ca

Department of Commerce: www.ecommerce.gov/ece

Federal Communications Commission: www.fcc.gov

General Communications Inc. (GCI): www.gci.com

National Computer Board of Singapore: www.ncb.gov.sg

National Exchange Carriers Association: www.neca.org

National Telecommunications and Information Administration: www.ntia.doc.gov

Rural Utilities Service: *The Red Herring:* www.redherring.com

Vitacom, Inc.: www.vitacom.com

Part Three

New Media, Institutions and Governance

16

The Regulation of Digital Content

STEFAAN G. VERHULST

Much discussion about the digitalization of content and the consequent convergence of broadcasting, telecommunications and IT suggests that digitalization challenges existing communications regulation (Gillett and Vogelsang, 1999; Verhulst and Marsden, 1999; Verhulst and Sandvig, 2004; Verhulst et al., 1999). In recent years, familiar and traditional regulatory models have been increasingly questioned and challenged (Hitchens, 1997). This chapter starts from the assumption that the search for appropriate regulatory and policy responses necessary as a result of the policy vacuum created by new technologies is leading to a 'paradigm shift', in Thomas Kuhn's traditional sense of the word.[1] Kuhn describes the uncertainty and chaotic process of changing from one world view to another that occurs during a paradigm shift. In his conception, as the new paradigm emerges, it subsumes the previous paradigm and replaces it with one that answers more questions and encompasses more of the consensus of the community.[2] This chapter demonstrates the ongoing – yet still incomplete – paradigm shift in content regulation, and observes that the existing laws that serve as the regulatory framework to control content are coming under increasing scrutiny.

In response to this scrutiny, scholars, governments and industry worldwide have been searching for a new regulatory paradigm

(Longstaff, 2000). The European Commission released its Green Paper on the regulatory implications of convergence as early as December 1997, consultations were finalized late 1999, and consequent Directives were drafted in 2000. Similarly, in March 1998, the Organization for Economic Cooperation and Development (OECD) hosted a Roundtable on Communications Convergence. The United Kingdom Green Paper on convergence followed in July 1998 and a White Paper was released at the end of 2000. During the same period a number of other European countries, the USA, Canada and Australia conducted reviews and consultations on the most appropriate regulatory regime for the introduction of digital television. Japan announced a review of the impact of convergence on communication regulations and the Productivity Commission in Australia published the results of its review of broadcasting regulation in early 2000. As late as November 2004, however, the European Commission released a paper on 'Challenges for the European Information Society beyond 2005', suggesting the extent to which the new paradigm was still evolving across jurisdictions. Similarly, in the United States, at the outset of the debate to reconsider the Telecommunications Act, widespread disagreement existed even in early 2005 regarding the desirability of a common legal framework that could be applied both to cable and telecoms; meanwhile, in Australia, debate continues over proposed laws to regulate digital content.

All these efforts indicate the search for a new paradigm of regulation. Just as importantly, they also indicate that, despite the debate about the diminishing role of regulation in a converged world, the proposed new paradigm is more one of re-regulation and self-regulation than deregulation (Majone, 1990; Prosser, 1997: Chapter 10). Although the rhetoric of the early and mid 1990s would have had us believe that regulation – in whatever form or shape – was headed towards obsolescence, recent developments have made clear that the newly emerging paradigm will be somewhat more complicated, combining elements of traditional regulation (including by the state) with new models of self- and co-regulation. Indeed, although this chapter spends a considerable portion of time discussing some of the forces undermining the traditional paradigm, it performs the equally important task of showing that early assumptions about the new paradigm were somewhat flawed. The collapse of the dot.com boom, the telecommunications meltdown of the late 1990s and the rise of spam and other forms of pollution – all of these developments have introduced a note of uncertainty into the once-confident march towards deregulation (Baird, 2003; Baird and Verhulst, 2004).

This does not mean that the paradigm shift will not occur. It simply means that the shift, as and when it happens, is expected to be evolutionary rather than revolutionary (Kohl, 1994). Television services will merge further with online services only when telecommunication networks are sufficiently advanced;[3] state regulation will give way to new models of regulation only when concerns over content pollution, legitimacy, security and civil liberties are adequately addressed. Uncertainty over the speed of change makes it difficult for governments and policy-makers to determine the priority that should be given to reform. Doing nothing may retard market developments. Moving too soon may mean that decisions are made with too little information. It is within this uncertain and shifting landscape that this essay attempts to outline some of the forces undermining the traditional paradigm, and similarly to present some of the parameters of an emerging new paradigm of self-regulation.

In discussing these issues, two points about the nature of the new media landscape should be kept in mind. First, there remain strong geographical differences in thinking about regulation. Commercial television regulation in Europe and the US is historically divergent, and as a result the debate about a possible paradigm shift is different. In Europe, the overriding political importance ascribed to the medium resulted in strict prior regulation of both content and structure. In the US, First Amendment protection of free speech has led to an artificial obsession with exclusively structural controls, though government has contrived to ensure similar outcomes to those in Europe.

Second, and partly as a result of the evolutionary character of the search for a new paradigm, there persist two distinct service categories and regulatory responses within the new communications platforms. The first are TV-type services that require broadband (high bandwidth) delivered to the home. The second are online Internet-type services that require interactivity and medium bandwidth delivered to the home. Differences between the TV-type approach and the online interactive Internet-type approach can be noticed in the functions of the applications such as entertainment and shopping versus communication and information, the target users such as consumers at home and special interest groups, and data types such as audio/video versus text/programmes. Differences can also be noticed in the terminal devices, such as the differences between low-resolution TV sets and PC, in the geographic scope such as between national, regional and global, and between distribution that is terrestrial, over cable or over the telephone.

Access ethics that determine whether the system will be closed, open or universal, economic orientation that governs whether information is shared or sold, and the rollout schedule that shows the maturity level of the situation, also illustrate differences between the TV-type approaches and the online Internet-type approaches (Press, 1994). The differences are slowly disappearing as convergence is becoming more and more real. However, they remain important for policy-makers – not least because the divergent policy and regulatory perspectives (not to mention rivalry) which the broadcasting and telecommunications regulators, even within converged regulatory bodies, bring to the task make choosing or designing regulatory tools suitable for convergence extremely difficult.

Both these trends are important to consider because they demonstrate the uneven and complicated field within which new paradigms of regulation are emerging. As we argue throughout this essay, there can be no single definition of self-regulation, nor indeed of any other form of regulation. Instead, self-regulation must be seen as a multifarious and multistranded process that means different things in different contexts; in addition, as we discuss, it includes multiple actors, from all sectors of society (Baird and Verhulst, 2004).

Within those parameters, this chapter aims to outline the so-called paradigm shift in traditional means of controlling content, often labelled 'negative regulation'[4] (Waverman, 2000). Digitalization clearly affects all areas of communications policy, and all sectoral regulations involved, yet this chapter will mainly focus on audiovisual content as the area where content policies and regulations are most heavily concentrated (Jassem, 1999: 31–49). The chapter begins by discussing the forces and assumptions leading towards a paradigm shift; these include the loss of scarcity, the process of disintermediation, and more generally the process of convergence. The chapter then reviews the role self-regulation can play as an alternative paradigm to government or command-and-control regulation. Finally, the chapter concludes by evaluating the assumptions that are associated with the new paradigm.

One further theoretical reflection should be made at the outset. There is an assumption implicit in the notion of a paradigm shift called 'technological determinism' that concerns the causal relationship between technological developments and social impact or change. This technological determinism is of course not new.[5] Indeed, within several theories of social evolution, technological innovations are regarded as the most important determinants of societal change (Bell, 1973; Kahn and Wiener, 1967; Kerr, 1983). Yet, causal theories vary in the degree of determinism they reflect, although those expounding them seldom make this explicit. Critics have sometimes made a distinction between 'hard' and 'soft' technological determinism, the latter allowing somewhat more scope for human control and cultural variation (Chandler, 1995).

In their definitions, strong or hard technological determinism is the extreme stance that a particular communication technology is either a sufficient condition (sole cause) or at least a necessary condition (requiring additional preconditions) for determining social organization and development. Either way, certain consequences are seen as inevitable or at least highly probable.

Weak or soft technological determinism, more widely accepted by scholars, claims that the presence of a particular communication technology is an enabling or facilitating factor leading to potential opportunities which may or may not be taken up in particular societies or periods. Its absence may also be a constraint to development. Within that context, Ithiel de Sola Pool declared that 'Technology shapes the structure of the battle but not every outcome' (Finnegan et al., 1987: 32). Other 'factors' are also involved, and 'technoeconomic determinism' is sometimes associated with this stance. The 'weak case' is less tidy and less generic than the 'strong case' but it is more in accord with the available evidence. This chapter adopts an intermediate position in this debate of technological determinism versus social choice, acknowledging the importance of technological innovation but without ignoring the impact of other political, economic, legal and cultural variables.

THE UNDERPINNINGS OF THE PARADIGM SHIFT

Digitalization and Convergence

At the heart of the paradigm shift lies digitalization, whereby all forms of data such as alphanumeric text, graphics, still and moving pictures, and sounds are translated into 0s and 1s or digital bits.[6] This then enables controlled storage in large volume, easy manipulation and display of these data, and quick transmission without loss of quality in an integrated bit stream on a common channel (Garnham, 1994: 10). This common digital environment is driving the convergence that is taking place at all levels of the value chain (Drucker and Gumpert, 2000; Verhulst et al., 1996: 4–6).

Convergence of the content of media or of media forms allows for the integration of the different kinds of information. The strict demarcation between different media becomes blurred (Cable and Distler, 1995: 2). Negroponte describes this state as 'mediumlessness' (1995: 71). Different content that had previously been carried by different physical media might be carried by a single medium like a CD-ROM. On the other hand, content that had previously been carried by a single medium may be distributed through several different physical media such as electronic newspapers (Institute for Information Studies, 1995: xiii).

As a result of digitalization of content, almost every message can be transported from point A to any point B in any physical way. The movement from a single-purpose network or transmission mode towards multipurpose networks is the result (Ducey, 1995: 3). This is called convergence of delivery channels.

Digital content requires a display terminal (desktop) and a decoder (set-top) (Garnham, 1994: 10). As stated in the World Telecommunication Development Report in 1995, there are essentially three user devices for accessing new communications services: the mobile telephone, the personal computer and the television (International Telecommunication Union, 1995). The concept of either PCTV (a PC with the ability to receive television signals) or a television with microprocessor technology for receiving digitally encoded data via phone lines has prompted the idea of a combined interactive platform designed to suit all needs (Dataquest, 1995). This idea is called convergence of customer interfaces. Besides this battle for the desktop, there is also a much more significant battle for the so-called middleware

such as the set-top box or conditional access decoder, application programme interface and electronic programme guides. Electronic programme guides are a key issue in the regulatory questions discussed below.

Digitalization has led to the convergence of industries and markets, the creation of a new media consumption environment and hence a fundamentally different regulatory context.

Regulatory Context

Shift in Scarcities and Intermediaries

Digitalization and convergence drastically change the foundation upon which the traditional regulatory broadcasting regime is based. The analogue model was characterized by scarcity of frequencies and few intermediaries, a one-to-many flow of information, distinctive industry sectors, linear programming, a mediated consumption environment and national boundaries. All this created the shared perception that broadcasting was pervasive and invasive in society and that television content needed to be controlled in a structural and restrictive or negative manner to ensure that public policy goals such as quality, diversity, impartiality and fairness were met.[7] The rise of digital television and the Internet has confounded, if not totally eliminated, these traditional understandings of 'television' and broadcasting regulation (Owen, 1999). Table 16.1 outlines the foundation behind regulation for the analogue and digital models.

As shown in Table 16.1 the debate about digital content is based on the assumption that there is abundance, as opposed to scarcity in the analogue model, and that there are new and different mediation processes in the digital environment that are not present in the analogue environment. As part of the latter assumption, disintermediation and individual involvement cause traditional mediators to become obsolete.

To an extent, these assumptions are accurate. The flow of information has widened and the number of channels available has steadily grown as digitalization and cheaper content production have made more data publicly available.

Table 16.1   *Regulatory context*

Analogue model	Digital model
Scarcity and few players (duopoly)	Abundant players (branding)
One-to-many	Many-to-many
Distinctive sectors	Convergence of sectors
Linear programming	Non-linear programming (on demand)
Mediated consumption environment	Disintermediation and individual consumption environment
National boundaries	Transnational and global

Three related technological/commercial 'laws' have heavily influenced these and other assumptions about content and network abundance: Moore's law, Metcalfe's law and the more recent Gilder's law.

Moore's law is based on the observation that the maximum processing power of a microchip, at a given price, doubles roughly every 18 months.[8] That means computer power increases at an explosive rate, and conversely the price of a given level of computing power decreases at the same dramatic rate.

Metcalfe's law, on the other hand, describes a technological and economic force that pushes the growth of the Internet. As a network grows, the utility of being connected to that network grows even more. Thus Metcalfe's law says that the value of a network is equivalent to the square of the number of nodes.[9]

Gilder's law, finally, says that bandwidth will rise at a rate three times the rate at which processing power is increasing, or three times the rate of Moore's law (Gilder, 2000). In other words, with processing power doubling every 18 months, bandwidth will double every 6 months.

These three 'laws' drive the 'abundance' determinism associated with digital technology; yet the question remains, which we will address further, whether these 'laws' can also be applied to content. In addition, so-called 'disintermediation' is the development of new content producers, the ability of users to link to information without any indirect barrier or mediation, and the ability to obtain non-linear access to programming that ranges from on demand to interactivity.[10] It is assumed that within this new digital setting, the locus of power has shifted from the service or content provider to the user, creating a many-to-many communications environment (Berman and Weitzner, 1995). The significance of the 'old

intermediaries', who mediated the flow of information from the top to the bottom, has decreased and the new digital services are global, recognizing no national boundaries.

In addition, a further challenge to traditional forms of state-led regulation is the rise of globalization. In the new context, governments do not have the comfort of being able to consider the issues simply within the confines of their territorial four walls. Not only do those concerned have to contend with the impact of these technological developments, but they also have to recognize that these technological advances will not respect traditional jurisdictional boundaries. Among the most famous examples of this phenomenon occurred in 2000, when the French government, invoking its hate speech laws, attempted to block access to certain neo-Nazi items for sale on the Yahoo! Site. The ensuing case raised difficult questions about conflicts between US and French hate speech laws. More generally, the case illustrated the difficulty of regulating across borders in an age of global information flows. Such flows have contributed tremendously to the claimed end-of-scarcity and increased the pervasiveness of the content. These developments are at the heart of challenges to the current basis for regulation.[11]

Shift in Information Flows

Another way of representing the paradigm shift of content structures has been suggested by Bordewijk and van Kaam (1982), who developed a framework to identify the main forms of 'information traffic'. According to them, the two main features of communication flows are: (1) storage and access to information and (2) use of information in the context of control of time and choice. Cross-tabulating both according

Table 16.2   *Information flows*

Central information store	Individual information store	
Central control of time and subject	Allocution	Registration
Individual control of time and subject	Consultation	Conversation

to whether they are central or individual depicts a set of four categories of content flow. Table 16.2 demonstrates this cross-tabulation. The four categories in the table can be explained as follows:

- *Allocution* is the simultaneous transmission of a centrally constituted 'offer' of information intended for immediate attention, according to a centrally determined time scheme such as in traditional broadcasting.
- *Conversation* is an exchange between individuals of content already available to them, according to a mutually convenient time scheme such as over the telephone.
- *Consultation* is the selective consultation by individual participants of a central store of information at times determined by each individual such as when individuals use the library or newspapers.
- *Registration* is the collection of information available to, or about, individual participants, according to a centrally determined choice of subject and time in a central storage area or 'store'. This is a long-established element in many organizations for record-keeping, control, and surveillance.

The difference between a central and an individual information store is also analogous to that between a mass media organization and a single audience member. It can correspond to the difference between information-rich individuals and those who are information poor. The difference between central and individual control of access also relates to that between constraint and freedom and between low and high communication potential. One other use of the scheme, according to van Dijk (1994: 119), is to note that the top row entries, allocution and registration, are associated with a need for government regulation, and the bottom row, consultation and conversation, with absence of interference.

Briefly, the earlier paradigm governing content regulation was based upon an allocution model. In contrast, digital content allows for an increase in the possibilities for consultation such as in interactive TV, for conversation such as over e-mail, and for registration such as through subscription-based content. This suggests a shift from allocution to the other cells of the model. It also indicates a general empowerment of the individual to gain information and a reduction in the dominance of centralized public sources or intermediaries, as indicated above.[12] New technologies like instant messaging and P2P file-sharing systems have only hastened these processes. To a significant extent, it is now possible for individual information stores to develop so that much more extensive 'conversation' patterns could reduce dependence on, and hence influence, central information stores (McQuail, 1986).

Andrew Shapiro makes a similar observation with regard to the Internet in his book *The Control Revolution* (1999). He convincingly shows how the Internet purports to radically expand control over personal connections with the world. According to Shapiro, the Internet drastically increases our individual ability to make and affect choices about how we take in news and other information, how we engage each other in social interactions, education, work and political life, and how we make decisions about allocating collective resources.[13] As such, the shift challenges the invasiveness, publicness and influence that have been attributed to traditional broadcasting and which will be discussed at length later.

THE REGULATORY PARADIGM SHIFT

Rationales Behind Content Regulation

Why, and how, do these developments challenge existing patterns of regulation? In order to answer this question, we need to understand some of the rationales that traditionally underpin regulation.

First, it is essential to understand that the starting point for every regulatory intervention and reform must be the policy objective, not the means of achievement. In other words, the need and rationale for the changes in rules and techniques must be identified before all other considerations; we must be guided by ends, not means. Justifications for intervention often arise from an alleged inability of the market-place to deal with particular structural problems. Among the concerns listed by Hoffman-Riem (1996) are 'pluralism, diversity, fairness, and impartiality; social responsibility; mainte-nance of high quality programming and of cultural and linguistic identity; coverage of important events; protection against abuse of market power; strengthening national and regional industries; protection of consumers; and maintenance of standards in matters of violence, sex, taste and decency'. Other ratio-nales are often brought up in political debate over media and content regulation and the details of a programme frequently only reflect political force.[14]

In the prior paradigm, where there was a scarcity of channels that were viewed mainly by families or in semi-public settings, it was justified for democratically accountable public institutions to intervene and regulate what was seen. The rationale for intervention hinged on liberal democratic notions of the particular importance of media and notions of market failure and harm to individuals, particularly children. Former European Commissioner for Audiovisual Policy, Marcelino Oreja (1999), summarized these notions and rationales from a European perspective:

> The starting point is, of course, to recognize the crucial role that media play in our society. The role of the media goes much further than simply providing information about events and issues; media also play a formative role in society. That is, they are largely responsible for form-ing the concepts, belief systems and even the languages – visual and symbolic as well as verbal – which citizens use to make sense of, and to interpret the world in which they live … There are a certain number of public inter-est objectives which should be preserved in our soci-eties, and which have a European dimension. In my

opinion, these could be summarized as follows: ensuring plurality of ownership; ensuring fair and effective com-petition; ensuring diversity of content; protecting indi-vidual rights to privacy, free speech, etc.; protecting intellectual property rights; maximizing individual con-sumer choice and access to information; and, very importantly, ensuring a high level of protection of minors and human dignity.

In addition, content regulation of broadcasting was seen as justified because of the particular features of broadcast content, which distinguish it from other media such as telephones and the press. These include pervasiveness, invasiveness, publicness and influence (Tambini and Verhulst, 2000).

- *Pervasiveness*: Since terrestrial transmitters can carry only a limited number of channels, and the broadcasting spectrum provides only a limited space for programming, each programme has been perceived as pervasive. It has therefore been imperative from the outset to ensure that terrestrial broadcasting channels reflect the opinions, taste and culture of as many different people as possi-ble, often through a public broadcasting system or public service obligations.[15] In addition, in the 1980s, media policies were developed to ensure that political, ethnic and other minorities had more presence on tele-vision. These policies were justified because of the pervasiveness of the medium of TV, and of the scarce range of available channels.
- *Invasiveness*: Content is more invasive if users do not know what content they are about to receive or do not actively choose it. As opposed to traditional broadcasting, content accessed in books and via the Internet is more likely to be deliberately chosen. The lack of control over the prod-ucts offered by broadcast media has justified setting up a legal regime specific to them in order to protect the listener or viewer (Poulet and Lamouline, 1995: 36). When content is invasive, central negative content controls may apply. New forms of delivery, such as encrypted narrowcasting, where adult users have a high degree of choice and control, are generally subject to less regula-tion than free-to-air television (Department of Culture, Media and Sport, 1999: 1.14).

- *Publicness*: All societies have taboos that are crucial for monitoring social cohesion and individuals' sense of trust and community. Taboos exclude certain topics from 'public' communication and, conversely, public communication is reserved for topics and content that are considered part of the public domain and of a specific value. Broadcast media are considered one of the key places where societies think about and discuss crucial issues about survival and purpose. The contents they carry constitute a large part of what individuals have in common and provide key reference points in broader political and cultural debates.

- *Influence*: Broadcasts have sometimes been accredited with the ability to directly influence revolutions and bring down governments but can also have a subtler agenda-setting influence as they determine the focus of public political debate each day. The high degree of influence of broadcast content warrants close public regulation of potential abuses and makes it imperative to develop the means to ensure that content is not used in a manipulative way. Where there are very few dominant sources of information, or just a handful of television channels, their influence can be of paramount importance in forming public opinion. It is justified to ensure that such content is neither harmful nor undemocratic, and that it promotes publicly shared values, rather than those of a powerful minority.

Digitalization challenges these justifications on many fronts. As a result of convergence, it is claimed that the pervasiveness, invasiveness, publicness and influence of content decrease or even disappear. However, such claims must be taken with due consideration, and with a certain dose of scepticism. Indeed, the European Green Paper on Convergence displayed a contrarian perspective on this issue:

> The fundamental objectives underpinning regulation in the Member States are not undermined by convergence ... Nevertheless the nature and characteristics of convergence as well as the perceived need of industry actors for regulatory intervention to be limited and closely targeted, should lead public authorities at both a national and a European level to re-examine the role and weight of regulation in a converging marketplace. (European Commission, 1997)

This is not to say that digitalization, disintermediation and the end-of-scarcity are not ushering in dramatic changes. Of course they are. But such scepticism is an indication that public interest objectives cannot be considered altogether irrelevant or invalid as a result of technological change. As we have discussed, technological change remains an uneven and uncertain process. Moreover, it is important to point out that many of the assumptions made in the early and mid-1990s have proven at best hasty, and perhaps even false. For example, early hopes for disintermediation have given way to more realistic analyses of reintermediation (Hammer, 2000; Shapiro, 1998). While it is true that some old intermediaries have fallen by the wayside, often these have simply been replaced by new intermediaries (for example, search engines and walled gardens like AOL). One of the effects of reintermediation has also been to maintain (or reintroduce a certain element of) scarcity: new forms of control have emerged in the digital realm, and these forms of control once again determine access. The fact that such forms of control are often intertwined with economic or political control only complicates the picture.

All of this suggests that any new paradigm of regulation must remain realistic about the technical and socioeconomic landscape within which it emerges. While changes have been dramatic, the envisioned 'telecosm' (in George Gilder's (2000) famous phrase which captured the breathlessness of the 1990s) is yet to emerge. This suggests that where features of pervasiveness, invasiveness, publicness and influence remain, content regulations may continue to apply (albeit in a perhaps different form); in other places, a new paradigm may indeed be necessary. To meet the requirements of this complicated, and layered, landscape, it is suggested that a functional approach is needed, one which does not depend solely on technology or forms of delivery, but which recognizes the

Table 16.3 *Regulatory mechanism*

Traditional means of content control	Paradigm shift: digital ecology
1 Government regulation through:	1 Self-regulation through:
• licensing systems (programme code) • programme scheduling (watershed) • physical bottlenecks (broadcasting responsibility) • statutory complaints mechanism	• codes of conduct • green/red listing (pool) • technical bottlenecks (parent empowerment) • hotlines
2 Single institutional approach (monopoly)	2 Plural/competing approaches
3 Sector-specific rules	3 Content/convey distinction
4 Media ownership rules (diversity/pluralism)	4 Access and bottleneck regulation

particular nature of the content and the character of the audience receiving it. It is this recognition that has led to the call for a shift towards a self-regulatory approach. Such an approach, it is felt, offers the promise of a more 'sensitive' and flexible form of regulation. In the next section, we discuss some features of that approach.

Shift in Regulatory Mechanism

Because analogue television was considered as more pervasive, invasive and influential within society than any other medium, the call for and development of stronger government regulation were justified. Broadcasting regulation was and is based upon a licensing system with guidelines restricting what kinds of content and advertisements can be broadcast, specific programme schedules or watershed policies, classification of programmes developed by a single institution, and consequent acoustic or visual announcement of programmes.

Broadcasters, as a rule, took their responsibility toward programming content very seriously, and have been keenly aware of the expectations of their audiences, who could complain to statutory bodies in case of offence. Moreover, analogue television was controlled nationally and audiovisual policies were in many cases nationalistic. Finally, access rules and mechanisms ranging across ownership rules, must-carry rules, listed events and even public service broadcasting monopolies all helped to ensure that broadcasters fulfilled the envisioned roles.

Clearly, these approaches, originally established for terrestrially based mass audience channels, have become much more difficult to

maintain as the sources of programming have multiplied and new technologies have made the prospect of regulation far more unmanageable. Because of converging technologies, it is also increasingly difficult to differentiate between 'telecommunications' and 'broadcasting'. The spread of broadband, for example, means that it is now possible to view television programs over DSL-enhanced telephone lines. New mechanisms and paradigms appropriate for a changing multichannel, digital and online environment need to be considered. Table 16.3 provides a review of the traditional methods used to control broadcasting content compared with the new methods now being developed for controlling content in the online converged environment.

Self-regulation plays an overarching role in this search for adequate solutions. It involves many regulatory subjects, including domain names, standard setting of conditional access systems, open access and e-commerce. However, most of the public concern and debate concerning self-regulation has focused on illegal and harmful content, the scope of this chapter. Indeed, given the deluge of spam, viruses and other forms of so-called 'pollution', the concern has only increased in recent years.

This concern has prompted substantial and public industrial response. However, given the complexity of the new services (different platforms with different communications capacities) no single approach, relying on one form or one set of actors, can provide a solution to content concerns in the changing and shifting environment that is the Internet. The development of a self-regulatory regime for digital services will be comprised of multiple

Table 16.4   *Paradigm of society*

Characteristics of social interaction			Realms of social order	
	Technology	Economy	Civic institutions	Polity
Modalities of regulation	Architecture	Market	Norm	Law
Enforcement agent	None	Seller/buyer	Peers	Police/courts
Timing of constraint	Before	During	Before/after	After
Nature of constraint	Physical	Money	Opprobrium	Sanction
Basis of relationships	Structure/flow	Production	Experience	Power
Basis of participation	Inhabitant	Producer/consumer	Member	Citizen
Primary institutions	Place/space Internet	Enterprise Union	Family/Church	State Media

complementary actions, tools and mechanisms. At least four main strands have been suggested and recommended:[16]

- Codes of conduct should be adopted to ensure that Internet content and service providers act in accord with the law and with principles of social responsibility.
- There should be comprehensive use of rating/filtering technology and green/red lists.
- Content response and complaints systems such as hotlines must be made available to users.
- Success requires awareness among users of the means to filter and block content, their power to redress complaints, and the level of conduct that is promised by the industry.

It has been argued that the most distinct of these means for enhancing protection and free speech is the use of filtering and blocking mechanisms, using plural and often competing rating systems. This is not to say that legal controls or codes of conduct are unimportant, but rather that the shift from 'hard law to software' can clearly be considered as an empowerment and improvement of users' choice. Hence the major response to the call for self-regulation involves processes that promote filtering and rating systems.

Shift from Law to Technology

Lawrence Lessig in his book *Code and Other Laws of Cyberspace* (1999) has also made an analysis of the paradigm shift from 'hard law to software'. He challenges the myth that cyberspace is incapable of regulation, and argues that our notions of liberty and rules are undergoing a transformation as we are forced to make value choices not previously confronted in constitutional theory. According to Lessig, social order is created by human activity in four realms – technology, economy, civic institutions and the polity. Table 16.4 outlines these realms. Social order emerges because human activity is routinized or regulated in each of these realms. Lessig defines the 'modalities of regulation' in each realm – architecture, the market, norms and laws – by the nature and timing of constraints and the enforcement agents (1999: 235–7). Sociologically, many other aspects of social order can be added in each realm. Central in the discussion below are the institutions through which activity is channelled and the nature of relationships, identity and participation in each.

Using the terminology in Table 16.4, Lessig suggests that the very architecture of cyberspace allows profound control of information flows. Technical rules and protocols are themselves critical regulators of cyberspace. In these terms, the 'code' becomes the constitution for cyberspace. At the same time, Lessig points out that 'code' is not the sole regulator of behaviour in cyberspace. Social norms form an important aspect of control in cyberspace, whether those norms are formed locally or remotely. Similarly, market regulation (such as pricing and terms of service) has a powerful and central constraining effect on behaviour in cyberspace. Finally, Lessig indicates that law is still present in the equation. Indeed, he argues that law may regulate the architecture itself, or change behavioural norms.

Lessig's discussion of modalities of regulation is not simply descriptive, but proscriptive. First, he argues that open code, as opposed to proprietary code, reduces the capacity of government to impose requirements on citizens. At the same time, while open code might make it harder for government to control the myriad of software developers around the world, it can also facilitate the capability of government to impose particular software modules for products sold in its territory. Second, as the Internet moves into a commercial phase, the emerging paradigm requires urgent measures to preserve the Internet's openness. Lessig's concern in the discussion of cyberspace is that in the face of a powerful technology, there is a tendency to passively accept the technological edicts of the code writers, rather than assert control over the definitions and development of society:

> We will treat code-based environmental disasters – like Y2K, like the loss of privacy, like the censorship of filters, like the disappearance of an intellectual commons – as if they were produced by gods, not by Man. We will watch as important aspects of privacy and free speech are erased by the emerging architecture of the panopticon, and we will speak, like modern Jeffersons, about nature making it so – forgetting that here, we are nature. We will in many domains of our social life come to see the Net as the product of something alien – something we cannot direct because we cannot direct anything. Something instead that we must simply accept, as it invades and transforms our lives. (1999: 233)

Lessig goes on to issue a call to arms (1999: 58–9). The animus for the call is a fear that the dictates of the code writers, driven by commercial interests, will be corrosive of fundamental values in our society such as justice, equality and democracy (1999: 15, 206, 209). He stresses the need to act to preserve key values and policy objectives on the Internet.

These legal, market and technological analyses suggest that there is a close nexus between technology and the economic and legal structure and that these spheres are driving changes through the remainder of society. As Manuel Castells argues in his book *The Rise of the Network Society* (1996), technology deployment, economic activity, social interaction and political institutions, within broad limits, can be directed toward specific goals:

> Yet, if society does not determine technology, it can, mainly through the state, suffocate its development. Or alternatively, again mainly by state intervention, it can embark on an accelerated process of technological modernization able to change the fate of economies, military power, and social well being in a few years. Indeed, the ability or inability of societies to master technology, and particularly technologies that are strategically decisive in each historical period, largely shapes their destiny, to the point where we could say that while technology *per se* does not determine historical evolution and social change, technology (or the lack of it) embodies the capacity of societies to transform themselves, as well as the uses to which societies, always in a conflictive process, decide to put their technological potential. (1996: 7)

These concerns involve values that are very much at the heart of the debate over the definition of self-governance. They suggest that any adequate form of governance must comprise what Yochai Benkler (2000), whose analysis also informs Lessig's, calls several 'layers'. Code (or software) is one important layer at which control and governance can be effected; hardware or infrastructure represents another layer. But an equally important layer, as both Lessig and Benkler make clear, is that of the state – although the role of government may be reduced or modified, it cannot be eliminated in a comprehensive and multilayered analysis of governance in the digital age. In the next section, we consider in greater detail the role of the state in self-regulatory mechanisms.

THE PARADIGM SHIFT REVIEWED

The Concept and Definition of Self-regulation

Despite almost a decade of writing and theorizing about self-regulation, the concept often remains somewhat vague. The initial problem inherent in every approach to self-regulation therefore lies with definition. There is no single definition for self-regulation that is entirely satisfactory, nor should there be. Self-regulation on the Internet evolves as the nature of the Internet alters. Different profiles of self-regulation emerge that adjust to the varying regulated aspects of the Internet. Self-regulation has and will continue to have different meanings from sector to sector and from state to state. Furthermore, whatever its implications or suggestions, self-regulation is almost always a misnomer. It hardly ever exists without some relationship to the state – a relationship that itself varies greatly. The meaning of self-regulation shifts depending upon the extent of government coercion or involvement and upon accurate public perceptions of the relationship of private sector and state.

Despite these and similar complexities, governments, industries and users employ the term 'self-regulation' frequently, almost indiscriminately. It is assumed to have a predetermined meaning when it does not. A study of self-regulation in the media sector and European Community law noted that 'the term "self-regulation" is often used as a matter of course, as if it were (1) a specific and defined term, and (2) an equally specific and defined regulatory practice. Yet in general, this is not the case' (Ukrow, 1999: 11). From the outset, then, in order to manage social concerns connected to the new technology there needs to be an exploration of self-regulation's variety of meanings and the implications of each meaning:

> Larry Irving, former US Assistant Secretary of Commerce, observed: At one end of the spectrum, the term is used quite narrowly, to refer only to those instances where the government has formally delegated the power to regulate, as in the delegation of securities industry oversight to the stock exchanges. At the other end of the spectrum, the term is used when the private sector perceives the need to regulate itself for whatever reason – to respond to consumer demand, to carry out its ethical beliefs, to enhance industry reputations, or to level the market playing field – and does so.[17]

Even here, the range of variable meanings emerges. Because 'self-regulation' is thought to exist when private entities have been commanded to act or become the delegates of state power, the intertwining of state and private industry is implicitly recognized, although the 'governmental nature of self-regulation' may differ across sectors (Baldwin and Cave, 1999: 125). Questions remain over the propriety and clarity of delegation, the circumstances under which state functions can or ought to be carried out by private groups, and the division of power and responsibility between the state and private groups.

On the other hand, as Secretary Irving suggests, the private sector 'perceives the need to regulate itself'. The source of that need is often the threat of public regulation, a societal

demand for increased responsibility by the private sector, or economic factors. Other variables may include the extent of the role played by self-regulators, the degree of binding legal force attached to self-regulatory rules, and their coverage of an industrial sector (1999: 126). These areas of indeterminacy are grounds for a statement in a recent bibliography on self-regulation on the Internet prepared for the OECD: 'While there is broad consensus that self-regulation of the Internet is critical to its future growth, there is little consensus about how to achieve or implement a self-regulatory regime' (Gidari, 1998).

The 'Self' of Internet Self-regulation

In addition to the confusion over how to define self-regulation, determining what ought to be included in the 'self' of self-regulation in the context of digital content is also a complex question. A cornucopia of institutions partakes of self-regulatory characteristics. Voluntary institutions generated by the Internet and not by government are the very backbone of efforts to deal with harmful content.[18] In many discussions, governments have failed to recognize that the Internet industry is not monolithic and that there is no single 'industry' that speaks for the whole of the Internet (Gidari, 1998). Moreover, the fact that the Internet is relatively young and still in a rapid growth stage also means that in many cases effective cooperative action such as the creation of industry associations is also in its early stages. One interesting example of such cooperation is the pan-European Association of the Internet Service Providers' Associations (EuroISPA) of some EU member states.[19]

The definition of 'self' cannot be divided between different sectors of the industry that form cohesive communities either. Indeed, it has been suggested that self-regulation operates more effectively when it involves interrelated levels of the industry, which often do not form one coherent body. For example, Boddewyn's (1989) study of the advertising industry found that self-regulatory systems were strengthened when they included distribution systems such as television networks. Many of the Internet self-regulatory bodies contain representatives from different sectors of the industry. For example, in Australia, Internet Industry Association Australia (IIA) has a membership that includes telecom carriers, content creators and hardware developers.[20] In contrast, the self-regulatory organizations in the United Kingdom tend to have a narrower membership, with the Internet Service Providers' Association (ISPA) and the London Internet Exchange (LINX) the two leading ISP groups, whose memberships are restricted to providers.[21]

There is also an increasing social demand for breadth in the definition of 'self' for self-regulation on the Internet. If the function of self-regulation is to minimize harmful and illegal conduct on the Internet, particularly as it affects young people, then it must become more, rather than less, extensive. Albert Gidari (1998), Executive Director of the Internet Law and Policy Forum, has stated that often the 'self' in self-regulation too narrowly focuses only on the business sector. A narrow conception of self-regulation places too much of the burden on industry to solve the legal and policy issues when other participants such as stakeholders and administrators could contribute to the overall self-regulatory regime.

In particular, there is increasing recognition that civil society, in the form of non-profit actors and consumer groups, can play a critical role in self-regulation. Among the most famous of such groups is the US-based TRUSTe initiative, which has taken the lead in certifying websites' privacy policies. ICANN, the non-profit body responsible for managing the domain name system (DNS), is another notable example. Such groups play an important role in negotiating between the state and business. As non-partisan actors, trusted by the public, they can plan an intermediary role, facilitating the emergence of governance initiatives that satisfy all stakeholders.

The role of non-state actors suggests the extent to which self-regulation is increasingly seen as a multisectoral process. Because of this, a wide variety of self-regulating communities or mediating institutions is likely to come into existence. Moreover, competing self-regulatory

regimes may emerge within any given sector. Resulting patterns and institutions of self-regulation will differ geographically. Each state has different social demands, different constitutional structures, and different traditions of industry–government cooperation in the fields of media and speech. One study of self-regulation and self-generation of standards that compared the experiences in Canada and the United States demonstrated marked differences in the scope of cooperation with the government, shared standards, and the notion of self-regulation as a social and collaborative act (McDowell and Maitland, 1998).

When it comes to content regulation, differences in self-regulation, state to state, will also turn on the speech traditions in each society and the way that each conceptualizes the Internet and digital content. Where the Internet is perceived as derived or related to telephony, self-regulatory practices and standards that have emerged in telecommunications may predominate. In the United States, partly because of the First Amendment tradition, self-regulation is distinctively a form of avoidance of, confrontation with, and studied separation from government. However, a comparative overview of self-regulatory systems in the media in all EU member states identified clear differences in meaning and structure of the self-regulatory systems (Brohmer and Ukrow, 1999).

Costs and Benefits of Self-regulation

It is generally suggested that the professed advantages of self-regulation over governmental regulation include efficiency, increased flexibility, increased incentives for compliance, reduced cost, and minimized government intrusion in the speech field (Price and Verhulst, 2000). However, when considering these self-regulatory attempts as an effective alternative to government regulation, five considerations must be weighed (see Table 16.5).

First, self-regulation ought to be perceived as a paradigm different from deregulation or non-regulation. Deregulation directly aims at removing any regulation perceived to be

Table 16.5   *Self-regulation*

Advantages of self-regulation over governmental regulation	Considerations and challenges for self-regulation
<ul><li>Increased efficiency</li><li>Increased flexibility</li><li>Increased incentives for compliance</li><li>Transnational scope</li><li>Increased expertise</li><li>Reduced cost</li><li>Minimized government intrusion in the speech field</li></ul>	<ul><li>It is almost always a misnomer and government involvement usually continues</li><li>The paradigm is different from deregulation or non-regulation</li><li>It involves significant regulatory costs</li><li>Self-regulation requires active consumer and citizen consultation (corporatist)</li><li>Strong and committed support or social responsibility from all parties is necessary; free-riders should be considered</li><li>A balance between the carrot and the stick may improve effectiveness</li></ul>

excessive and hindering market forces. Self-regulation, as an ideology or approach to management, does not aim primarily to dismantle or dispense with a framework for private activity.

Second, self-regulation involves a dialogue between government and a business association. The form of the dialogue depends on the situation of each party at the beginning of discourse. This may differ across sectors, across countries and in time. As a result, self-regulation has and will continue to have different meanings in different contexts. It is clear, then, that whatever its implication or suggestion, self-regulation is almost always a misnomer. Self-regulation rarely exists without some relationship to the state.

That relationship may vary greatly, but it has become increasingly clear that it is central to the concept of self-regulation. States play a key role in limiting corporate abuses, and in ensuring that certain public-interest objectives are met. In addition, given the transnational nature of many issues under consideration, intergovernmental coordination is clearly required. Of course none of this implies a return to command-and-control regulation, but it does suggest a continued role for the state despite changes in technology and ideology. Third, it is naïve to suggest, as is done continually, that self-regulation does not itself involve significant regulatory costs. For any system, regulatory or self-regulatory, costs are determined by a combination of the policy goals they envisage and the structures and dynamics of the economic and social activities they regulate. Monitoring and evaluative costs otherwise assumed by governments may be

incurred directly by individual companies or indirectly by industry associations that will also generate significant amounts of third-party costs associated with governmental compliance procedures.

Fourth, self-regulation can quickly become moribund without strong and committed support for its development, implementation and enforcement. The very nature of a voluntary system potentially creates a 'free-rider problem', where some actors expend significant resources on the development, monitoring and implementation of codes and standards while others ignore their existence. To be a living and working instrument, a code of conduct or its equivalent must, in practice, be implemented with the agreement of the industry sector to which it is applied.

Fifth, effective self-regulation requires active consumer and citizen consultation based upon shared responsibility at all stages of development and implementation. Without user involvement, a self-regulatory mechanism will not accurately reflect user needs, will not be effective in delivering the standards it promotes, and will not create confidence.

Self-regulatory Mechanism

As we have just seen, self-regulation is a complicated, and often ill-defined, concept. Various challenges to its implementation exist. Nonetheless, despite some of the conceptual vagueness, certain processes and systems have emerged as common mechanisms for effecting self-regulation. In this section, we discuss some of these mechanisms.

In considering these various mechanisms, it is essential to keep in mind the multisectoral nature of self-regulation (which we discussed above). This multisectoral nature highlights the importance of participatory issues: it suggests that any framework or mechanism for self-regulation must be designed in such a way to maintain equal access for all groups and sectors of society. In particular, smaller consumer groups, which are vital to ensuring citizens' rights, often find it difficult to get heard amidst the din of large corporations and governments. In addition, given the increasingly global nature of many issues dealt with by self-regulation, it is essential to ensure representation from developing countries, which may lack the technical or financial capacity to take part in discussions. Indeed, such exclusion (whether perceived or real) has been one of the chief complaints against ICANN, which to this date represents one of the most striking efforts at self-regulation. Each of the following mechanisms, therefore, should take such participatory issues into consideration. They must be designed in such a way to facilitate truly multisectoral participation.

Codes of Conduct

Codes of practice or good conduct embody, at times, mutual obligations by competing actors, for example, in the form of agreements, that require each of them to take certain actions to restrict content that would give any one of them a temporary competitive advantage. Codes provide an indication of the nature of the self-regulatory authority, including whether or not it will impose sanctions for breaches of the code, and upon whom. Codes are often the instrument for the generation or refinement of norms. In the Internet setting, norms negotiated between the industry and government authority are codified to produce the rules.

There are a number of industry initiatives under way directed at developing codes of conduct, and a number of national governments specifically endorse codes as a front-line mechanism for addressing content issues (Blinderman et al., 2000). However, a level of compliance needs to be ensured. Users, both industry and consumers, need guidance with regard to the content of these codes and an impartial arbiter needs to have an appropriate redress mechanism – variables often absent in current initiatives.

Rating and Filtering

As indicated earlier, rating and filtering techniques may offer the best solution to empower parents in controlling the content they deem to be suitable or unsuitable. Developing rating systems is always difficult. However, within an Internet and converged communications setting the following additional challenges can be observed:

- How can sufficient coverage of websites be reached to encourage the use of rating and blocking software?
- How can varieties of rating software be made available to all who want to use them?
- How can the cultural bias (many are US-centric) of existing rating systems be overcome?
- How can an internationally acceptable system be developed that allows national differences?
- How can such systems be made easy to use for content providers and for parents alike?
- How can accuracy, objectivity and consistency of ratings be ensured?

Many initiatives have been developed in response to these questions. Internet Content Rating for Europe (INCORE) and the EU Internet Action Plan have examined guidelines for developing self-rating systems that are appropriate for European cultural and linguistic specifics and are also suitable for global requirements. At the national level, Germany, via the Secorvo Jugendshutz study, and the UK, through the Internet Watch Foundation, have considered the adaptation of US ratings systems to their specific value systems.

Several US-based awareness campaigns such as GetNetWise and NetParents have developed with the goal of highlighting the functioning

Table 16.6　*Self-regulator mechanisms for a digital age*

Ideal	Reality: key challenges
Codes of conduct 'Reflects industry morality'	• Level of compliance/awareness • User guidance • Impartiality of arbiter • Appropriate redress
Rating and filtering 'Golden fleece of parental empowerment'	• Volume of content • Different transmission paths • Objectivity and plurality • Ease of use/access for all parties • Awareness and literacy
Zoning 'Safe playground'	• Underinclusive/overrestrictive • Transparency • Property rights and access
Hotlines 'Concern response system'	• Awareness • Transparency • Expertise • Public/private partnership

of filter systems. Since most websites are not currently rated, most software provides users with the option of blocking sites that do not contain Platform for Internet Content Selection (PICS) ratings. However, this choice may be appropriate for some, but it severely restricts the available options. By blocking most of the web (including possibly some sites designed for younger users), this approach presents children with a severely restricted view of the world.

Zoning

Zoning, or the development of green and red lists, is often considered a more effective manner for creating a 'safe playground'. There are, however, several problems with filtering based on lists of sites to be blocked.

First, both green and red lists are always underinclusive and incomplete. Owing to the decentralized nature of the Internet, it is practically impossible to search all Internet sites for 'objectionable' or 'acceptable' material. Furthermore, since new websites are constantly appearing, even regular updates from the software vendor will not block out all adult websites. Each updated list will be obsolete as soon as it is released, as any site that appears after the update will not be on the list, and will not be blocked.

The volatility of individual sites is yet another potential cause of trouble. Adult material might be added to or removed from a site soon after the site is added to or removed from a list of blocked sites.

There is a general lack of transparency concerning the criteria used by list developers. This obscurity is compounded by practices used to protect lists of blocked sites. Vendors often consider these lists to be proprietary intellectual property, which they protect through encryption. Encryption renders the lists incomprehensible to end users. Companies such as Cyberpatrol have vigorously fought organizations that published Cyberpatrol's lists of blocked sites and programs that would break the encryption. Peacefire.org was one such organization that posted a program that enabled users to access the list developed by CyberPatrol. CyberPatrol challenged the posting in court, claiming copyright violation.[22]

Hotlines

Finally, hotlines have been suggested as an appropriate content concern response system for a decentralized and global environment such as the Internet. However, as Burkert (2000) has indicated, the quality, rules, procedures and organizational contexts of these hotlines play an important role in the acceptance,

Table 16.7 *New challenges*

Regulatory paradigm	New challenges
Disintermediation	Reintermediation
Abundance	New scarcities
User empowerment	Sender power
Open access	Closed offering
Civic sphere	Commercial sphere

functioning and effectiveness of content concern response systems. Hotlines need to establish efficient communications systems, with availability, reliability and transparency as the main qualitative requirements.

Table 16.6 outlines the challenges in instituting codes of conduct, rating and filtering, zoning, and hotlines as effective self-regulatory mechanisms. This is juxtaposed with the ideal of each mechanism, to summarize this section.

CONCLUDING REMARKS: NEW SCARCITIES AND NEW INTERMEDIARIES

The current regulatory paradigm shift for digital content, as outlined and reviewed earlier, is based upon assumptions of disintermediation and loss of scarcity, which in themselves decrease the pervasiveness, invasiveness, publicness and influence of content. Yet a critical analysis, such as we have begun in this chapter, may indicate that some of these assumptions are incomplete, and are based upon limited notions of access, scarcity and mediation. Indeed, as already mentioned, a subtler phenomenon of reintermediation is emerging, and in many ways it creates new (artificial) scarcities (Mansell, 1999: 155–81).

The process of reintermediation is initiated by several elements. One of the dilemmas posed by the increasing flow of information is that too much information paralyses and enervates. The abundance of content has led to a call for and the creation of new types of mediation and hence new intermediaries that can:

- search and navigate in the wealth of information for the right match of information needed;
- warn or even filter and block information that is unwanted or considered harmful;

- contextualize or give information about information through so-called metadata;
- integrate and decode different streams of information;
- customize the reception and consumption of services and information; and
- verify or authenticate the source, the user, and whether payment has been received (Firestone, 1994–5).

These requirements have caused the emergence of new intermediaries in the form of electronic programme guides, portals, search engines, walled gardens, filters, push technology, billing software and intelligent agents. It is predicted that many of these components will be combined within new middleware such as the Multimedia Home Platform to be developed by the Digital Video Broadcasting Group.[23] Table 16.7 delineates the new challenges in the Internet environment against the previous assumptions about that environment.

These new communications network intermediaries do not work, however, in a user-neutral way. The selection, evaluation and functions are to a large extent determined by the creators of the gateway (Hargittai, 2000: 233–53). They decide how much information there will be, what form it will take, in what package or bundle, at what price, and whether there will be choice and access at all. Ultimately, content producers and distributors are not interested only in providing full and free access for users; they are interested in attracting an audience for their portals, packages and developed services, linked with advertising or subscription revenue.

Moreover, there are many ways that intermediaries can influence users' communication patterns. Representation and placement of the information or programming that 'match' the need allow for promotion of or discrimination against some services. The design of the navigation device by intermediaries can influence choice and access (Introna and Nissenbaum, 2000: 1–17). Stand-alone filter systems limit users to decisions made by the software vendor. Moreover, to customize the service, intermediaries also collect valuable information about users and their communication patterns, with risks of privacy intrusions. The danger here is that new and artificial scarcities are created: access to information will vary according to the portal and gateway that are used and whether the users can afford specific subscription fees.

It is essential that the emerging new paradigm of regulation consider some of these issues, and question some of the assumptions leading to the erosion of the previous paradigm. Change is certainly required, but it must be based on a realistic evaluation of the technical landscape, and on an understanding that old scarcities may be giving way to new ones. Access remains a key issue, and participation must remain on the top of the agenda for any new regulatory framework. If such considerations are absent, we face the very real threat of information exiles – a prospect that is likely to pose a significantly larger challenge for regulators than those they already currently confront.

NOTES

The author is grateful to the Markle Foundation for a visiting scholarship in the autumn of 2000 at their New York headquarters that enabled further review of the paradigm shift. The chapter reflects also the content of two seminars held at the Markle Foundation.

1 In his groundbreaking book, Kuhn (1970) argued that 'paradigms', or conceptual world views, that consist of formal theories, classic experiments and trusted methods, define scientific research and thought. Scientists typically accept a prevailing paradigm and try to extend its scope by refining theories, explaining puzzling data, and establishing more precise measures of standards and phenomena. Eventually, however, their efforts may generate insoluble theoretical problems or experimental anomalies that expose a paradigm's inadequacies or contradict it altogether. This accumulation of difficulties triggers a crisis that can only be resolved by an intellectual revolution that replaces an old paradigm with a new one. Kuhn's book revolutionized the history and philosophy of science, and his concept of paradigm shifts was extended to such disciplines as political science, economics, sociology and even law.

2 A more recent and perhaps more 'business management' version of the paradigm concept is offered by Joel Barker (1993). It states that 'a paradigm is a set of rules and regulations that: (i) defines boundaries; and (ii) tells you what to do to be successful within those boundaries' (1993: 14).

3 This is expected to be evolutionary since all parts of the value chain (content, packaging, distribution and customer interface) cannot easily develop simultaneously; the technology required for advanced networks is either not fully developed or remains too expensive to be commercially viable; most of the interactive TV services that a switched broadband network would support are very similar to existing and developing broadcast services. Thus a huge incremental expense would have to be supported by a relatively small range of new services; evolutionary development is more appropriate to the expected nature of consumer demand. For a further discussion see Jamieson (1995: 11).

4 As opposed to 'positive regulation' which includes universal service provisions, state aid, etc.

5 The American sociologist and economist Thorstein Veblen (1857–1929) apparently coined the term 'technological determinism' (Ellul, 1990).

6 In addition to digitalization, there are some other common key technological advances such as compression, optical fibre and extended switching (Negroponte, 1995: 12).

7 These public policy goals are generally based upon the view that broadcasting is a means of communicative self-development and important to the functioning of a democratic society. For a detailed analysis of the rationales behind broadcasting regulation see Hoffman-Riem (1996: 297).

8 For a critical analysis of the value of Moore's law for other technologies see Coffman and Odlyzko (2001).

9 The 'law' postulates that if n people are in a network, the value of the overall network is n^2, given the myriad new connections that can be made to the nth participant. A simple example is that of a fax machine that becomes more useful the more people are connected to it.

10 Disintermediation may also be achieved by the removal of intermediaries from the industry value chain (Moore, 1996).

11 Charles Firestone (1993) has also indicated that at each level of the communications process, production, distribution and reception, there have been two paradigmatic stages of regulation, one of scarcity and one of apparent abundance and competition. At the scarcity stage, usually obtained after an initial period of skirmishing among pioneers for position, the regulation has taken the general form of governmental intervention in order to promote the broader public interest. At the abundant or competitive stage, which overlaps the earlier stage, there has been a reversal, a deregulation to promote greater efficiency. In each case, the paradigm is a regulatory religion, at times demanding faith on the part of the believers.

12 However, what is available for consultation in central stores can still be centrally determined and much will depend on how diverse the central stores are in content and management. Furthermore, in other interpretations the 'registration' pattern may significantly increase the potential for central control through surveillance of information and information-related activities, which may often be politically sensitive.

13 Paradoxically, however, the Internet often becomes a tool to segregate us hermetically from unwanted but sometimes invaluable experiences.

14 For a US account see Corn-Revere (1997). For a more European and UK-oriented discussion see Feintuck (1999).

15 This was particularly pronounced in the US by the famous case *Red Lion Broadcasting Co. v. FCC* (1969), in which the Supreme Court upheld the FCC's 'fairness doctrine', which required licensees to cover controversial issues of public importance and provide a reasonable opportunity for the presentation of opposing points of view. The Court explained that in order to avoid interference on the airwaves, a government agency must limit the number of broadcast speakers. Because only a lucky few can be licensed to broadcast, the government can require those few to act as trustees or fiduciaries on behalf of the larger excluded community, and obligate them to present views, representative of the community, that otherwise would have no broadcasting outlet.

16 The European Internet Action Plan lists these ways as crucial to create a 'safer' Internet environment. See Decision no. 276/1999/EC of the European Parliament and of the Council of 25 January 1999 adopting a Multiannual Community Action Plan promoting safer use of the Internet by combating illegal and harmful content on global networks.

17 Quote by Larry Irving obtained when he was introducing a collection of papers analysing the prospects of self-regulation for protecting privacy (National Telecommunications Information Administration, 1997).

18 However, the history of a voluntary association such as the Internet Corporation for Assigned Names and Numbers (ICANN) indicates how seeming autonomy begins with government encouragement. See http://www.icann.org

19 To learn more about EuroISPA see http://www.euroispa.org/index.html

20 For information about Internet Access Australia see http://www.iia.net.au

21 For information about ISPA UK see http://www.ispa.org.uk and for the London Internet Exchange Ltd see http://www.linx.net

22 After the case was initially lost, a federal appeals court in the US allowed the American Civil Liberties Union (ACLU) to recommend that peacefire.org along with two other clients exercise their First Amendment rights and continue to post the lists. In addition, the recent copyright law regulations passed by the Library of Congress in October 2000 exempt '"reverse engineering" of or unauthorized access to filtering software in order to expose the list of blocked sites' from the law. For further information about the case see ACLU press releases entitled: 'Censorware copyright controversy leaves clients, consumers in the dark, ACLU says', Tuesday 28 March 2000, and 'ACLU gives clients green light to post blocking software code', Tuesday 31 October 2000. They are available at http://www.aclu.org/news/2000/n032800b.html and http://www.aclu.org/news/2000/n103100.html, respectively. Even in light of these events, the considerations behind protecting their lists remain substantial for the companies developing them.

23 See http://www.dvb.ch

REFERENCES

Baird, Zoë (2003) 'Promoting innovation to prevent the Internet from becoming a wasteland', *Federal Communications Law Journal*, 55: 441.

Baird, Zoë and Verhulst, Stefaan (2004) 'A new model for global Internet governance', in *Governance in the 21st Century: The Partnership Principle*. Frankfurt and Main: Alfred Herrhausen Society for International Dialogue.

Baldwin, R. and Cave, M. (1999) *Understanding Regulation*. Oxford: Oxford University Press.

Barker, J.A. (1993) *Discovering the Future: The Business of Paradigms*. New York: Harper Business.

Bell, D. (1973) *The Coming of Post-industrial Society: A Venture in Social Forecasting*, reprinted 1976. London: Heinemann Educational.

Benkler, Yochai (2000) 'From consumers to users: shifting the deeper structures of regulation towards sustainable commons and user access', *Federal Communications Law Journal*, 52 (3): 561.

Berman, J. and Weitzner, D.J. (1995) 'Abundance and user control: renewing the democractic heart of the First Amendment in the age of interactive media', *The Yale Law Journal*, 104 (7): 1619–31.

Blinderman, E., Price, M. and Verhulst, S. (2000) *Codes of Conduct and Other Self-regulatory Documents: Emerging Patterns of Norm Formulation and Enforcement on the Internet*. Gutersloh: Bertelsmann Foundation.

Boddewyn, J.J. (1989) *Advertising Self-regulation and Outside Participation: A Multinational Comparison*. New York: Quorum.

Bordewijk, J.L. and van Kaam, B. (1982) *Allocutie: Enkele gedachten over communicatievrijheid in een bekabeld land*. Baarn: Bosch & Keunig.

Brohmer, J. and Ukrow, J. (1999) *Die Selbstkontrolle in Medienberich in Europa: Eine Rechtsvengleichende Untersuchung*. Saarbrüken: EMR.

Burkert, H. (2000) 'The issue of hotlines', in J. Waltermann and M. Machill (eds), *Protecting Our Children on the Internet: Towards a New Culture of Responsibility*. Gutersloh: Bertelsmann Foundation.

Cable, V. and Distler, C. (1995) *Global Superhighways: The Future of International Telecommunications Policy*. London: Royal Institute of International Affairs.

Castells, M. (1996) *The Rise of the Network Society*. Oxford: Blackwell.

Chandler, D. (1995) 'Technological or media determinism'. Available online at the Media and

Communications Studies site: http://www.aber. ac.uk/media/Documents/tecdet/tecdet.html

Coffman, K.G. and Odlyzko, A.M. (2001) 'Internet growth: is there a "Moore's law" for data traffic?', in J. Abello, P.M. Pardalos and M.G.C. Resende (eds), *Handbook of Massive Data Sets*. The Hague: Kluwer.

Corn-Revere, R. (ed.) (1997) *Rationales and Rationalizations: Regulating the Electronic Media*. Washington, DC: Media Institute.

Dataquest (1995) 'The war for the interactive platform of the future: TV versus PC'. Available online: http://www.dataquest.com

Department of Culture, Media and Sport (1999) *Regulating Communications: The Way Ahead: Results of Consultation Paper*. London: Department of Culture, Media and Sport.

Ducey, R.V. (1995) *A New Digital Marketplace in Information and Entertainment Services: Organizing around Connectivity and Interoperability*. Washington, DC: National Association of Broadcasters.

Drucker, Susan and Gumpert, Gary (2000) 'The emergence of convergence', *The Public*, 7 (4): 37.

Ellul, J. (1990) *The Technological Bluff*. Grand Rapids, MI: Eerdmans.

European Commission (1997) *Green Paper on the Convergence of the Telecommunications, Media and Information Technology Sectors and the Implications for Regulation: Towards an Information Society Approach*. Com (97) 623.

European Commission (2004) *The Future Of European Regulatory Audiovisual Policy*. Com (2003) 784 final.

Feintuck, M. (1999) *Media Regulation, the Public Interest and the Law*. Edinburgh: Edinburgh University Press.

Finnegan, R. Salaman, G. and Thompson, K. (eds) (1987) *Information Technology: Social Issues*. London: Hodder & Stoughton/Open University.

Firestone, C. (1993) 'The search for the holy paradigm: regulating the information infrastructure'. Presented at the Conference on the Changing Nature of Information Infrastructure, Washington, DC, 12 October.

Firestone, C. (1994–5) 'Digital culture and civil society: a new role for intermediaries?', *Intermedia*, 22 (6).

Garnham, N. (1994) 'What is multimedia?', in *Legal Aspects of Multimedia and GIS*. Lisbon 27/28 Legal Advisory Board Conference (DG XIII), October.

Gidari, A. (1998) 'Observations on the state of self-regulation of the Internet'. The Ministerial Conference of the OCED, 'A borderless world: realizing the potential for global electronic commerce'. Ottawa, Canada: Internet Law and Policy Forum.

Gilder, G. (2000) *Telecosm: How Infinite Bandwidth Will Revolutionize Our World*. New York: Free Press.

Gillett, S.E. and Vogelsang, I. (eds) (1999) *Competition, Regulation and Convergence*. Hillsdale, NJ: Erlbaum.

Hammer, Michael (2000, 2002) 'The myth of disinter-mediation', *Information Week Online*, 12 March.

Hargittai, E. (2000) 'Open portals or closed gates? Channeling content on the World Wide Web', *Poetic*, 27 (4): 233–53.

Hitchens, L. (1997) 'Introduction to the special feature on Communications Regulation – New Patterns and Problems', *Journal of Information, Law and Technology (JILT)*, 3. Available online: http://elj. warwick.ac.uk/jilt/issue/1997_3/hitchen.htm

Hoffman-Riem, W. (1996) *Regulating Media: The Licensing and Supervision of Broadcasting in Six Countries*. New York: Guilford.

Institute for Information Studies (1995) 'Crossroads on the information highway: convergence and diversity in communications technologies', *Annual Review of the Institute for Information Studies*. Washington, DC: The Aspen Institute.

International Telecommunication Union (1995) *World Telecommunication Development Report 1995*. Geneva: ITU. Available online: http://www.itu.int/ti/wtdr95

Introna, L. and Nissenbaum, H. (2000) 'Shaping the Web: why the politics of search engines matters', *The Information Society*, 16 (3): 169–85.

Jamieson, J. (1995) *Convergence and the New Media: A Roadmap*. London: Institute for Public Policy Research.

Jassem, H. (1999) 'Different strokes for different folks: the intersection of regulatory principles and technology', in S.J. Drucker and G. Gumpert (eds), *RealLaw @ Virtual Space: Regulation in Cyberspace*. New Jersey: Hampton.

Kahn, H. and Wiener, A.J. (1967) *The Year 2000*. New York: Macmillan.

Kerr, C. (1983) *The Future of Industrial Societies: Convergence or Continuing Diversity?* Cambridge, MA: Harvard University Press.

Kohl, Uta (1994) 'Legal reasoning and legal change in the age of the Internet: why the ground rules are still valid', *International Journal of Law and Information Technology*, 7 (2): 123.

Kuhn, T. (1970) *The Structure of Scientific Revolutions*, 2nd edn. Chicago: University of Chicago Press.

Lessig, L. (1999) *Code and Other Laws of Cyberspace*. New York: Basic.

Longstaff, P.H. (2000) New Ways to Think about the Visions Called 'Convergence': A Guide for Business and Public Policy. Program on Information Resources Policy, Harvard, July.

Majone, Giandomenico (1990) *Deregulation or Reregulation? Regulatory Reform in Europe and the United States*. London: Francis Pinter.

Mansell, R. (1999) 'New media competition and access: the scarcity–abundance dialectic', *New Media & Society*, 1 (2): 155–82.

McDowell, S.D. and Maitland, C. (1998) 'Developing television ratings in Canada and the United States: the perils and promises of self-regulation', in M.E. Price (ed.), *The V-chip Debate*. New York: Erlbaum.

McQuail, D. (1986) 'Is media theory adequate to the challenge of new communications technologies?', in M. Ferguson (ed.), *New Communication Technologies and the Public Interest*. London: Sage. pp. 1–18.

Moore, C. (1996) 'Disintermediation: communications technologies are having some impact', in *Dataquest Interactive: Ask the Analyst*, 19 March.

National Telecommunications and Information Administration (1997) 'Privacy and Self-regulation in the Information Age', Introduction. Available online: http://www.ntia.doc.gov/reports/privacy_rpt.htm

Negroponte, N. (1995) *Being Digital*. London: Hodder & Stoughton.

Oreja, M. (1999) Seminar on 'Self-regulation in the media'. Jointly organized by the German Presidency of the European Union and the European Commission.

Owen, B. (1999) *The Internet Challenge to Television*. Cambridge, MA: Harvard University Press.

Poulet, Y. and Lamouline, C. (1995) *From Information Superhighways to 'Electronic Democracy': The Impact of Information and Communication Technology on Individual Liberties*. Strasburg: Council of Europe, 4 December.

Press, L. (1994) 'Two cultures, the Internet and interactive TV'. Les autoroutes électroniques: usages, droît et promesses, 13 May. Available online: http://www.droit.umontreal.ca/CDRP/Conferences/AE/index_fr.html

Price, M. and Verhulst, S. (2000) 'The concept of self-regulation and the Internet', in J. Waltermann and M. Machill (eds), *Protecting Our Children on the Internet: Towards a New Culture of Responsibility*. Gutersloh: Bertelsmann Foundation.

Prosser, T. (1997) *Law and the Regulators*. Oxford: Clarendon.

Shapiro, A.L. (1998) 'Digital middlemen and the architecture of electronic commerce', *Ohio Northern Law Review*, 24: 795.

Shapiro, A.L. (1999) *The Control Revolution: How the Internet Is Putting Individuals in Charge and Changing the World We Know*. New York: Public Affairs.

Tambini, D. and Verhulst, S. (2000) 'The transition to digital and content regulation', in D. Tambini (ed.), *Communications Reform*. London: Institute for Public Policy Research.

Ukrow, J. (1999) *Self-regulation in the Media Sector and European Community Law*. Saarbrücken: EMR.

Van Dijk, J. (1994) *De netwerkmaatschappij: Sociale aspecten van nieuwe media*. Houten/Zaventem: Bohn Stafleu Vam Loghum.

Verhulst, S. and Marsden, C. (1999) *Convergence in Digital Television Regulation*. London: Blackstone.

Verhulst, S., Goldberg, D. and Prosser, T. (1996) *The Impact of New Communications Technologies on Concentration and Pluralism*. Strasburg: Council of Europe.

Verhulst, S., Goldberg, D. and Prosser, T. (1999) *Regulating the Changing Media*. Oxford: Clarendon.

Verhulst, S. and Sandvig, C. (2004) 'The Internet and public policy in comparative perspective', in M. Price and H. Nissenbaum (eds), *The Academy and the Internet*. New York: Peter Lang.

Waverman, L. (2000) *Broadcasting Policy Hits the Internet*, 22 May. Available online at the Global Internet Project: http://www.gip.org under 'publications' and category 'governance'.

17

From Hierarchies to Network Firms

FRANÇOIS BAR WITH CAROLINE SIMARD

Over the past quarter-century, organizations' growing reliance upon networking technologies has brought about a deep transformation of economic activities. Information networks, once considered merely a utility like water or natural gas systems, moved centre stage during that period to become strategic infrastructures. From a technological standpoint, digital convergence was the fundamental enabler of this transition. Telecommunications and computing became more alike: networks were built upon digital technologies and increasingly served to interconnect computers, while computers relied ever more upon networks to support their basic operations. Software, at the heart of the resulting digital networks, made it possible to create new communication applications for individuals or organizations to collaborate and compete. Software also came to define network configuration – the set of rules determining who can communicate with whom, to do what and under which conditions – so that ownership of the underlying hardware alone no longer guaranteed control of the network's uses. The result was a fast-evolving, software-defined, indispensable, and increasingly capable information infrastructure: the 'new media' of much economic activity, our focus in this chapter.

While the information networks born of digital convergence spread through all economic sectors in developed countries, their deployment and implementation have taken many forms. A range of factors, such as the nature of pre-existing economic arrangements, the state of the national communication infrastructure, or national telecom policy, have influenced and shaped the deployment of intra- and inter-organizational networks. As a result, while the new media share a common technological lineage, they have been put to a variety of uses in organizations, with diverse consequences. For example, digital networks have been used at times to reinforce central coordination and at others to enable decentralized power; to buttress existing organizations or to invent new ones; to strengthen long-term, stable economic partnerships or to support fluid, fast-changing virtual teams.

At the individual level, new media networks permit new work arrangements overcoming time and space constraints (Morton, 1991; Sproull and Kiesler, 1991; Wigand, 1997), allowing firms to cut costs associated with coordinating dispersed geographical facilities. These network-enabled work arrangements are said to result in increased job satisfaction and empowerment (Malone, 2004; Sproull and Kiesler, 1991), and provide access to a wider pool of potential employees, unlimited by geographical constraints (Cash et al., 1994).

At the firm level, new media networks make multiple kinds of reorganization possible.

They are said to yield faster response time to market changes (Lucas, 1996), better maintenance and access to organizational memory (Morton, 1991), improved leverage of organizational knowledge (Carayannis, 1998; Finholt et al., 2002), speedier and more efficient information flows, better coordination of group communication, greater employee participation, rapid scheduling, efficient task assignment and reporting, enhanced communication across hierarchical levels, and enhanced coordination of communication within dispersed groups (Sproull and Kiesler, 1991). They also help improve dispersed employees' organizational commitment by acting as a 'window on the corporation' and enabling better socialization of new organizational members.

In addition to improving existing organizations, the new media networks are said to permit entirely new organizational forms. First among such IT-enabled organizational forms is the networked organization where all participants are linked (Rockart and Short, 1991) and the organization flexibly reorganizes itself around each new task (Baker, 1992). Networks also play a crucial role in the establishment and maintenance of internal and external linkages, transforming hierarchies and markets. The network organization thus extends beyond the boundaries of individual firms to form a wider network of multiple organizations (Malone and Laubacher, 1998), increasing interdependence within industries (Rockart and Short, 1991). This state of increased communication between suppliers, distributors and business partners (Cash et al., 1994; Lucas, 1996) supports improved interorganizational arrangements such as strategic networks and the Japanese *keiretsu*, and timely cooperation forms such as joint ventures and consortia (Wigand, 1997). At the extreme, the network model leads to virtual organizations (Davidow and Malone, 1992; Malone, 2004), composed of a set of loosely coupled, self-organizing networked individuals in geographically dispersed locations. New media would thus usher in an 'e-lance' economy (Malone, 2004; Malone and Laubacher, 1998), where individuals or autonomous groups come together around specific projects.

The present survey of the new media impact on industrial organization is structured in three sections. It begins with a review of the economic hopes that were pinned on the technology, in particular on its potential to increase productivity. It then examines how the impact of new media on industrial organization has been analysed, through their impact on two organizational archetypes – markets and hierarchies – and their enabling of an alternative, the network organization. The final section looks at how this analysis fits with the facts in a few emblematic case studies.

NEW MEDIA AND ECONOMIC PROMISES

The convergence of computing and telecommunications into new communication media became clear in the mid 1970s. Observers coined new terms to describe this emerging information infrastructure, such as the French *télématique* (Nora and Minc, 1978) or its less euphonic English cousin 'compunications' (Oettinger and Weinhaus, 1979). The new networks promised to create a foundation for the emerging information economy (Porat and Rubin, 1977), an economic system that would rely increasingly on information-based processes as part of production and exchange activities. In this 'post-industrial' society (Bell, 1973), agriculture and manufacturing would no longer be the basis for economic power. Instead, knowledge workers would make the greater contribution to value creation. As a result, the new media network infrastructure would become the essential backbone of economic activity and control (Beniger, 1986). It would thus usher in new ways to organize economic and social life, leading to the emergence of the information economy (Porat and Rubin, 1977) and the network society (Castells, 1998).

One crucial expectation in these formative years was that reorganizing the economy around information technology and networks would yield tremendous productivity increases, which would more than justify the investments required. Yet, throughout the early years of technology deployment, productivity gains proved elusive, prompting economist Robert Solow's (1987) quip that 'You can see the computer age everywhere but in the productivity statistics', the so-called *productivity paradox* (Brynjolfsson, 1993; David, 1990). In part, the sweeping claims inspired by information technology resulted from a propensity 'to suffer from a kind of "telescopic vision": the possible future appears both closer at hand and more vivid than the necessary intervening, temporally more proximate events on the path leading to that destination' (David, 1989: 5). Three broad categories of explanations have been offered to explain that situation: mismeasurement of real output growth, poor understanding of the true benefits of computers, and underestimation of the learning and adaptation required (David, 2000).

Brynjolfsson (1993) points out prevalent measurement errors in the formulation of the paradox. Productivity statistics do not account for the type of productivity gains that result from information technology deployment, such as increased quality, speed and responsiveness, and increased business scope. Increased scope in particular is problematic because it reduces economies of scale and often appears as a decrease in productivity despite the business's increased value to customers. Hitt and Brynjolfsson (1996) suggest that three questions should be asked: whether IT has increased productivity, whether it has improved business profitability, and whether it has created value for consumers. When separating these questions, they find that IT investment increased production output, failed to increase profitability, and significantly increased consumer value. Increased productivity leads to increased competition, which in turn leads to lower profitability. Productivity gains can also be achieved through Furthermore, some of the benefits of computing that may impact firm growth are intangible, such as employee satisfaction and increased consumer and investor confidence (Brynjolfsson et al., 2002). In more recent research, the authors find that the long-term benefits of computerization are much greater than the short-term impact on productivity (Brynjolfsson and Hitt, 2003).

Further, information technology alone doesn't guarantee productivity gains. Indeed, organizations can worsen their productivity if they simply deploy computer networks to automate old processes (Brown and Hagel, 2003; Brynjolfsson and Hitt, 1998; David, 1990). Once new organizational processes and skilled labour are combined with IT, productivity gains become apparent (Bresnahan et al., 2002). A more realistic view of IT's benefits is to recognize that technology is just one element, not a single determinant, of the thorough business transformation required to improve productivity (Brynjolfsson and Hitt, 1998). In addition, the new media constitute a complex interrelated system. Benefits in one part of that system often require compatibility and standardization with deployments in other parts of the system as well as previous systems deployments, and the overall infrastructure is highly dependent on network externalities (David, 1990). New media systems also require the presence of complementary assets, such as trained users, to be used effectively. As a result, 'the emergence of a new techno-economic regime based on computer and communications innovations will be a protracted and historically contingent affair' (1990: 356).

As the new media networks emerged, the traditional Fordist firm and the interorganization coordination mechanisms that went along with it began reaching their limits (Cohen and Zysman, 1987). Organizations required greater flexibility, both static and dynamic, to adjust to new competitive environments (Coriat, 1994). This prompted the emergence of new organizational forms, made possible by network technologies (Antonelli, 1992; Piore and Sabel, 1984). Overall, however, the emergence of the network society is not simply driven by the deployment of a new media infrastructure. Rather, it represents a broader transformation, made possible by the development of new ways to organize production and exchange activities. In this reorganization, the new media are a critically important element, but only one element. They support change as they enable the design and implementation of new organizational forms and permit a rearticulation of production processes. They also suggest further change, as the digital network's increasing flexibility lets end users experiment directly with diverse communication configurations and the organizational arrangements they imply (Bar, 1990). In the end, the key to overcoming the productivity paradox resides in the ability to reorganize around the new media. The other chapters in this part explore this reorganization process within work groups and firms. We focus here on the broader reorganization of interactions between these entities and its implications for industrial organization.

UNDERSTANDING THE IMPACT OF NEW MEDIA ON INDUSTRIAL ORGANIZATION

An understanding of the impact of new media on the organization of economic activity starts with the fundamental theory that explores the reasons behind specific patterns of economic organization: transaction cost economics (TCE). Oliver Williamson (1975) formulated transaction cost theory, building on the work of Coase (1937), to identify the most efficient governance structure according to the varying nature of transactions between firms. He identified two extreme forms of organizations: markets and hierarchies. Markets provide a decentralized, self-governing structure within which firms can find partners and negotiate specific transactions, allowing for fluid changes in patterns of economic interaction. Hierarchies, by contrast, represent rigid, centrally governed structures within which economic actors interact in a stable and predictable fashion. According to transaction cost economics, the relative costs of setting up transactions between actors within these two extreme organizational structures leads to the choice of one over the other. Because digital networks increasingly support these interactions, they can affect the relative cost of market and hierarchical transactions, thereby resulting in changes in previous industrial organization.

Transaction cost theory is based on two key assumptions: bounded rationality and opportunism (Williamson, 1996). Actors engaged in transactions are rationally bounded and are therefore unable to process large amounts of information and consider all the alternative choices, leading to satisficing behaviour, or opting for a 'good enough' action (Simon, 1957). Applied to TCE, this means that 'all complex contracts are unavoidably incomplete' (Williamson, 1996: 37), with the risk that extra transaction costs can occur down the road because of missing information. Thus, a major purpose of organizing is the attempt to compensate for bounded rationality and to reduce opportunistic behaviour among the involved actors, establishing the relative stability necessary for long-term planning.

Hierarchies offer lower transaction costs, reduce opportunistic behaviour and mitigate the downsides of bounded rationality through a higher degree of administrative control (Williamson, 1975). Indeed, it is easier to resolve disputes internally and therefore transactions contracts can be left more incomplete than in the case of markets (Williamson, 1996). Markets by contrast, organized around spot contracts, reduce transaction costs in the case of products of a low degree of specificity, whereas hierarchies are appropriate for highly specific products (Williamson, 1975, 1996). When complexity, uncertainty and specificity increase, more information processing is needed. Hierarchies and centralized communication structures are more suited to the processing of such complex information.

Obviously, most of these transaction costs result from the acquisition, processing and transmission of information about products, production and work processes, or about the qualifications of economic partners. Therefore, because new media precisely aim at transforming information activities, they can be expected to have significant effects on these costs. Thus, transaction cost economics has been applied to understand the impacts of new media on economic organization. But if digital networks clearly have the potential to improve the functioning of both hierarchies and markets, their ultimate impact on economic organization is more controversial: will the new media result in more hierarchies, more markets, or new organizational forms?

Better Hierarchies

One effect of digital network technology on economic organization has been to promote the creation of 'electronic hierarchies' (Malone et al., 1987). Digital networks allow tighter coordination between organizations within the same value chain, leading to greater vertical integration (Clemons and Kleindorfer, 1992). This integration may be virtual (realized simply through tight interorganizational information networks), or formalized through corporate structures or cross-ownership. In either case, this leads to hierarchies where buyers work with stable, predetermined suppliers (Malone et al., 1987). Some analysts have described the electronic hierarchy as an 'electronic monopoly', reflecting the exclusive buying relationship established with a supplier (Chodhury, 1997). For example, Clemons and Row (1992) report the quasi-vertical integration enabled by network technology between Procter & Gamble and Wal-Mart. In this electronic hierarchy, P&G has electronic access to all sales data, and is able to deliver inventory to Wal-Mart as needed, enabling Wal-Mart to avoid the cost of holding inventory and order processing.

This is an example of what Malone et al. call the 'electronic integration effect' of the new media, where companies articulate tightly coupled processes around information networks. The electronic integration effect is most typically produced in electronic hierarchies (Malone et al., 1987). Indeed, it permits a level of integration that is not possible with other interorganizational networks, enabling the optimization of the integration of the total value chain (Chodhury, 1997). The supplier, through this exclusive relationship, is able to collect a significant amount of information about the buyer's needs and integrate its processes to those of the buyer to better meet those needs. However, the buyer loses the potential advantage of being able to scan the market for the better offer, which is characteristic of the market form of network governance (Chodhury, 1997).

More Perfect Markets

The same digital networks can also serve to build electronic markets. These 'e-markets' are

also said to lead to the elimination of intermediaries, acting as electronic brokers that put buyers in direct communication with sellers (Malone et al., 1987). The resulting disintermediation, combined with more intense, 'friction-free' price competition, could lead to more perfect markets (Bakos, 1996). However, as some analysts have speculated, while existing intermediaries may be eliminated or forced to adapt, new types of electronic intermediaries will emerge. Bakos (1998) foresees the emergence of intermediaries that will match buyers and sellers, provide product and customer information to interested parties, and manage physical delivery and payment functions.

Indeed, network technology has the potential to lead to an economy organized around constantly emerging electronic markets (Benjamin and Wigand, 1995; Keen, 1981; Malone et al., 1987). Malone et al. have formulated the 'electronic markets hypothesis', arguing that in addition to reducing production costs, IT will reduce coordination costs usually associated with markets. In that view, an electronic market is a multilateral interorganizational information system that, because of the scalability of the new media, can link a potentially unlimited number of buyers and suppliers (Choudhury et al., 1998). Hence, the digital network serves the function of market (Benjamin and Wigand, 1995). The network itself becomes the marketplace (Bar, 2001). This form offers price competition advantages, while offering little opportunity for electronic integration between buyer and supplier, since they engage in constantly reconfigured spot transactions rather than long-term relationships (Chodhury, 1997).

A firm will set up or join an electronic market if it assumes that the profits to be realized from a large volume of potential buyers are greater than the potential loss caused by lowering prices due to increased competition (Benjamin and Wigand, 1995). Malone et al. (1987) suggest that digital networks lead to an 'electronic brokerage effect', where electronic markets can act as brokers, resulting in an increase of possible quality alternative suppliers and buyers and a decrease in the cost of the selection process (Bakos, 1998; Benjamin and Wigand, 1995; Malone et al., 1987). This will potentially have the effect of eliminating intermediaries between the manufacturer and the buyer (disintermediation), as the information superhighway will enable direct market contact between manufacturer and consumers (Benjamin and Wigand, 1995). Besides the reduction of coordination costs, the emergence of markets will result from IT's ability to simplify complex product descriptions for highly complex products that were usually traded through hierarchies.

While traditional intermediaries between manufacturers and sellers are disappearing, there is a significant cost to consumers in the electronic marketplace of acquiring all the information necessary to identify sellers and compare prices. Hence, new intermediaries are emerging. The number of firms that have positioned themselves as the intermediaries of electronic markets have grown substantially in recent years. Auction giant EBay, Amazon.com, Yahoo!, and Shopping.com are such firms positioning themselves as intermediaries where individual sellers and buyers meet and exchange goods. These intermediaries enable sellers of all sizes to access immense pools of consumers. These firms have found that profit-making in the electronic marketplace is more readily achieved by acting as the meeting place of a community of sellers and buyers rather than holding inventory themselves (Leschly et al., 2002; Yin, 2004).

Beyond Hierarchies and Markets: Network Organizations

As new media transform traditional markets and hierarchies, pure examples of these two forms become more elusive. Indeed, hierarchical organizations increasingly rely on network-based, market-like processes to coordinate the work of their employees and work groups, or to conduct business with the clients, suppliers and subcontractors that constitute their extended hierarchy. Likewise, many network-based markets depend on features traditionally associated with hierarchical organizations,

combining the market's arm's-length dealings with tighter longer-term relationships among market partners, including for example the pre-qualification of buyers and sellers who become part of the market's inner circle, or the establishment of a hierarchy of markets for the governance of subtasks. Confronted with such evolution, transaction cost economics tends to view these new organizational forms as hybrids of market and hierarchy.

However, others argue that we are witnessing not simply the combination of traditional markets and hierarchies, but the emergence of a distinctly new form of economic governance, the network organization (Antonelli, 1992; Jarillo, 1988). Because networks allow a distinct form of economic governance, transaction cost economics and its focus on dyadic relationships (Williamson, 1996) is ill-suited to the study of network organizations (Powell, 1990). The main distinction they identify between the new network form and the traditional markets and hierarchies is the nature of relationships between actors. In a network, independent actors cooperate on a long-term basis, and the relationship is based on trust and goodwill. In a hierarchy, relations can be long term, but a specific authority is identified as having the ability to resolve arising disputes. In a market, relationships are episodic, and last only for the duration of a specific transaction (Poldony and Page, 1998).

Network organizations existed before the emergence of the new media (such as, for example, in northern Italy's textile industry: Piore and Sabel, 1984). Digital networks, however, have proven essential to the more widespread adoption of new network forms of organizations. Castells suggests that digital networks favour a distinct form of organization, the network enterprise, which he defines as 'that specific form of enterprise whose system of means is constituted by the intersection of segments of autonomous systems of goals' (1998: 171). This organizational form is characterized by long-term exchange relations, but with the absence of an ultimate authority to arbitrate possible disputes (Poldony and Page, 1998). By reducing transaction costs (Ciborra, 1983; Jarillo, 1988), and more specifically coordination costs, digital networks 'can facilitate the development of stable, tightly coupled relationships among firms' (Clemons and Kleindorfer, 1992: 10). Involved in a network relationship based on long-term trust, a firm does not have to worry about opportunistic behaviour on the part of other firms in its network. The use of network technology to support the network form can further reduce transaction costs through a fast and tight coupling of the participating firm's processes.

Various strands of the literature analysing new media's impact on industrial organization tend to adopt a deterministic approach. Extrapolating from the characteristics of the new media technology they investigate, they predict corresponding characteristics of the organizations that use them. Individually, when looking at particular economic sectors or at specific organizational arrangements, these studies have assessed how the new communication technologies affect the prior balance between market and hierarchy, or promote the development of new network forms of organizations. They diverge in their assessments, some concluding that new media result in better hierarchies, some finding that new media lead to greater reliance on market processes, others showing that new media bring about entirely new organizational forms. Taken together, however, they offer a different picture. They show that new media technologies do not determine organizational form, but can in fact support a variety of different approaches to reorganization. They suggest that the resulting organizational form will be determined less by new media technology than by other characteristics of the firm's internal processes and external competitive environment. In fact, in several industries, similar communications technologies have supported different organizational outcomes in different periods, as in the cases explored below.

CASE STUDIES

This section reviews some of the classic case studies of the establishment of new media networks between economic entities and their effect on the resulting economic organization. We review some of the literature on electronic data interchange (EDI), airline computerized reservation systems, and strategic information systems. These show how similar new media systems and technologies, deployed in various circumstances or at different times, entail different organizational implications. The important variables include the competitive environment within which they are deployed, and the relative positions of the actors engaged in network-mediated interaction.

Better Hierarchies? Electronic Data Interchange

Electronic data interchange (EDI) systems were one of the earliest new media technologies aimed at enhancing interorganization interactions. First deployed in the mid 1970s, their main purpose was to facilitate the exchange of formatted information between firms (rather than free-form communication). EDI technology has diffused in certain industries and its adoption is no longer limited to large companies (Jackson and Sloane, 2003; Lee et al., 2005). Once two business partners agree to use a common EDI standard, they can electronically exchange highly specified messages such as parts orders, invoices or payments. The EDI standards define precise formats for data fields containing codified information including parts numbers, prices, quantities, delivery locations, shipment times or account numbers. EDI systems have made possible the automation and standardization of interorganizational communication networks (Brousseau, 1994).

The initial development of EDI standards was a laborious process, requiring painstaking definition of the information required for many diverse transactions. As a result, EDI was initially aimed at improving existing bilateral or multilateral business relationships between buyers and sellers engaged in sustained, long-term relationships. Sets of EDI standards emerged in individual industries, most notably manufacturing (principally automotive), retail and distribution (including transportation), and banking. The high specificity of interactions between members of the related value chains made them good candidates for that technology. Early EDI deployments thus aimed to rationalize existing supply chains and impose on them a coherent governance. In so doing, EDI implementations were not meant to stop at the strict automation of individual economic relationships, but intended to reorganize broad cross-firm production and exchange processes within existing supply chains. Their goal was to create an extended hierarchy that reached beyond individual firms to include their long-term business partners. A variety of EDI standards emerged in different industry sectors, each associated with the articulation of a particular electronic hierarchy.

Over time, however, a different analysis of EDI networks would emerge. EDI systems, like all communication technologies, arc associated with strong network externalities (Katz and Shapiro, 1985). Therefore, companies within one industry have economic incentives to adopt common standards in order to be able to do business with each other electronically. As a result, one would expect the different EDI standards to merge, at least within industries, creating conditions for the support of a more fluid organizational structure. Common EDI standards would enable the rapid establishment of bilateral electronic dyads or their swift dissolution, where a buyer or seller uses EDI technology to sustain links with a selected number of sellers or buyers (Chodhury, 1997). Rather than supporting extended hierarchies, EDI would then enable network forms of economic organization and could even, in extreme cases, support electronic markets.

In reality, a variety of configurations emerged in different industries, in different countries and at different times. For example in the North American automotive manufacturing industry, EDI standardization was driven primarily by the large auto-makers. Industry-wide standardization efforts were limited as each promoted a distinct EDI implementation, partly for strategic reasons (to better control their respective supply chains) and partly for lack of traditions or policies encouraging coordination. While each auto-maker was able to force its preferred system on its parts suppliers, individual suppliers who sold to multiple auto-makers had to support multiple EDI standards and incur the related costs. The result was a series of Balkanized electronic hierarchies (Bar, 1990, 1995). By contrast in the European auto industry, a combination of policy incentives for coordination, stronger industry institutions and the greater relative strength of parts suppliers led to much greater industry-wide standardization, supporting an arrangement closer to the network form of organization (Brousseau, 1996).

These examples show how one technology, EDI, can be implemented in very different ways and lead to remarkably different organizational results. Brousseau (1994) further points out that organizational stability will also play an important role in the implementation of such technologies. In particular, EDI is unlikely to be successfully implemented in highly certain environments (because it would then be obsolete) or highly uncertain environments (because EDI implementation assumes some knowledge of what future communication needs will be) (1994: 337). In industries where the environment is uncertain and the business relationships must remain flexible, highly standardized EDI implementation could become detrimental by reducing network flexibility. In a case study of EDI implementation in Singapore, Teo et al. (1997) have shown that network technology can lead to a transformation of organizational structure, business networks, business scope and competitiveness. Hence, the real benefits of EDI systems reside not in the technology itself but in the restructuring of business processes and the establishment of new network partnerships (Gottardi and Bolisani, 1996). It remains to be seen whether EDI will eventually be uprooted by Internet-based interorganizational systems (Soliman and Janz, 2004).

Better Markets? Airline Computerized Reservation Systems

The airline industry provides another interesting illustration of the new media's consequences for the organization of economic activity. Successive waves of digital network deployment have led the organization of airline reservations from hierarchy, to biased market, to less biased market, to a network organization around Internet-based systems and disintermediation. With the deployment of the first computerized reservation systems (CRSs), American Airlines' SABRE in particular, airlines controlled an electronic hierarchy that extended to travel agencies. In time, that system became more open to competing airlines and other travel service providers and came to resemble more closely an electronic market, within which travel agents could access offers from all suppliers on an equal footing. The Internet pushed the industry closer to a perfect market, where travellers are in direct contact with airlines, negotiating for prices and conditions within a more perfect market.

A closer look at airline reservation systems shows that network technology didn't drive that transition alone. Airlines encouraged the shift from hierarchy to market, hoping for greater profits by ensuring that their reservation system offered tickets from all airlines, thus making it more attractive to the customer (Dang-Nguyen, 1996). However, research suggests that even organizations which possess significant market share can suffer profit losses when joining an electronic market. Indeed, the price reductions forced on them by competitive markets reduce their profit margins, such as has been the case for the airline carriers who joined SABRE and APOLLO (American and United's respective CRSs). Here as in other cases, however, the critical mass of other joiners leaves little choice to an organization but to join the electronic market. Even dominant players such as United and American reportedly suffered a loss as a result of having to share SABRE and APOLLO with other suppliers (Benjamin and Wigand, 1995).

Competitive incentives and the pursuit of critical mass did not alone result in the creation of a (more) open market for airline reservations. Government policy provided additional inducement, when the Department of Justice's antitrust department showed that the hierarchical airline reservation systems such as the first-generation SABRE were biased toward their owner airline company (Dang-Nguyen, 1996). Overall, this evolution suggests that networking technology, while it creates opportunities for reorganization, doesn't alone determine the economic organization of a particular activity: depending on the strategic priorities of the dominant participants, and on external factors such as antitrust policy, the application of new media can lead to tighter hierarchy as well as a more perfect market as it did in the airlines case.

American Airlines generated revenues by selling their system and know-how to other companies spanning numerous industries, while still hoping to be the best at using the information strategically (Hopper, 1990). This is consistent with the proposition that in an electronic market, the profits of the market-maker and network designer will remain higher than those of other companies participating in the market (Benjamin and Wigand, 1995); the network maker benefits from 'co-specialized assets' giving it the ability to appropriate more benefits from the electronic market (Duliba et al., 2001). SABRE became an 'electronic travel supermarket', a 'computerized middleman' (Hopper, 1990), linking suppliers and buyers of the travel and tourism industry through network technology. Benjamin and Wigand (1995) argue that policy-makers must set guidelines to regulate electronic organizations to ensure that a market-maker refrains from creating network bias in favour of a specific supplier (as was the case with SABRE).

SABRE and APOLLO have been replaced by the Internet as the electronic marketplace. The Internet has led to further disintermediation in the airline industry and a more perfect market, eliminating the role of the travel agent as airlines sell directly to consumers on websites. While some intermediaries have disappeared, new ones have emerged as new companies position themselves in the marketplace for a wider array of services. Hence, while users can buy airline tickets directly from the airlines' websites, they also enjoy the benefits of lower search costs associated with centralizing their travel purchases within a single intermediary. Travelocity.com, Expedia.com and other sites that offer not only airline reservations but also hotel, car and other services, have emerged as the new middle-men of the travel industry.

Strategic Use of Information Technology

An important aspect of the story becomes apparent through these various examples. When companies deploy new media infrastructure and applications, they will strive to enhance their own strategic position. In some cases, this may motivate them to sponsor a sweeping rearticulation of their supply chain or a reorganization of the marketplaces they participate in. In other cases, they may encourage the formation of alliances to foster the deployment of standardized systems. Or they may choose instead to pursue isolated, proprietary technologies precisely because such lack of interoperability creates entry barriers for their competitors. In the end, their strategic response to the particular competitive challenges they face, more than intrinsic characteristics of the new media technologies they choose to deploy, will determine the organizational consequences.

There are many examples of these strategic uses of information technologies. Companies have used information systems strategically to gain information from markets and gain a competitive advantage over other firms in the market, shifting the competitive position of organizations within industries. Cash and Konsynski (1985) give the example of an automotive manufacturer who uses network technology to scan the market for the lowest possible bid for a product, thus increasing the market position of the manufacturer by driving down prices. Clemons et al. (1996) provide several cases of dominant firms losing their most profitable customers to aggressive new entrants relying on IT. Indeed, flexible new entrants rely on IT to get information from the market, to identify and target the most profitable customers of an industry.

By providing lower costs and more effective distribution channels to customers through the use of IT, these new entrants are 'cream-skimming', attracting the most profitable customers away from established firms (Clemons et al., 1996). For example, Clemons and Weber (1994) cite the example of new entrants in the airline industry who threaten the market shares of American Airlines and United Airlines, by gathering information from the marketplace, identifying the most profitable customers, and offering them lower-cost, specific point-to-point services on the most travelled routes. Indeed, digital networks dramatically reduce the cost of capturing, storing and analysing information from the marketplace. Hence, using interorganizational networks, the Inter-Continental Hotel chain is able to target its most profitable customers by capturing very detailed information on their needs and wants and sharing it within network hotels. The Inter-Continental profitable customer will therefore obtain highly catered service, whether staying in New York or London (Clemons and Weber, 1994). Similarly, following the deregulation of the London Stock Exchange, Barclays de Zoete Wedd securities firm reacted to increased competitive pressure by using an information system named Beatrice which enabled it to identify, rank and project the growth potential of its most profitable customers. The firm was then able to target the most profitable customers and offer them new tailored services, while dropping less profitable customers (Clemons and Weber, 1990, 1994). Another possible strategy is price discrimination, in which different customers are charged different prices (Bakos, 1998). Hence, an organization can ask more from the less profitable customer, while lowering prices for the most desirable customer, and increasing profits.

This process is not necessarily at the expense of the customer since it enables organizations to serve customers that would otherwise be priced out of the market (Bakos, 1998). This is another example of digital networks being used for competitive advantage, moving from a 'one size fits all' strategy to a tailored, market segmentation strategy (Clemons and Weber, 1994). With digital networks becoming increasingly ubiquitous, organizations are becoming less system builders than system architects, trying to gain competitive advantage from existing network structures rather than building one anew. The goal for organizations then becomes to outsmart each other in using the information network strategically (Hopper, 1990).

CONCLUSION

Our overview of the new media's impact on industrial organization shows that a diversity of outcomes can be expected. The application of digital networking technologies to economic processes of production and exchange, under different circumstances, has served to support and improve hierarchies, markets or new network forms of organization. In the effort to understand the mechanisms at work, one characteristic of new media networks is fundamental. Because the new media are built upon digital technologies, their architecture and the applications they support are defined in software. Control over their configuration is therefore flexibly separable from ownership of the underlying network infrastructure. This creates opportunities for the many actors using these networks to shape them in ways that further their competitive goals.

For the organizations involved, this ultimately boils down to an essential challenge: their ability to create relative advantage through the combination of economies of scale and economies of scope, reconciling standardized processes with rapidly changing, differentiated products and services. The resulting economic regime, which some have called 'mass variety' (Coriat, 1993), combines the search for static flexibility through adaptation to short-term market variations with the more enduring benefits stemming from dynamic flexibility. Meeting this challenge requires smart choices of technologies and work organization methods. The production systems developed around new media play an essential role in promoting better production and exchange processes, the only way to improve overall productivity, and greater flexibility in programming and reprogramming these processes.

However, new media do not dictate the outcome, nor is their implementation preordained by the technology's characteristics. Rather, they serve to suggest, supplement and support a sweeping organizational transformation of production and exchange activities, from product and service design to production methods, from marketing techniques to exchange mechanisms. For the organizations involved, this is precisely what makes the new media 'strategic'.

REFERENCES

Antonelli, C. (1992) 'Information economics and industrial organization', *Human Systems Management*, 53–60.

Baker, W.E. (1992) 'The network organization in theory and practice', in N.N.R.G. Eccles (ed.), *Networks and Organizations*. Boston: Harvard Business School Press. pp. 397–429.

Bakos, Y.J. (1996) 'Reducing buyer search costs: implications for electronic marketplaces', *Management Science*, 43 (12): 1676–92.

Bakos, Y.J. (1998) 'The emerging role of electronic marketplaces on the Internet', *Communications of the ACM*, 41 (8): 35–42.

Bar, F. (1990) 'Configuring the telecommunications infrastructure for the computer age: the economics of network control'. Working Paper 43, Berkeley Roundtable on the International Economy, University of California Berkeley Institute of International Studies.

Bar, F. (1995) 'Intelligent manufacturing in the global information economy', in W. Drake (ed.), *The New Information Infrastructure: Strategies for U.S. Policy*. New York: 20th Century Fund. pp. 55–74.

Bar, F. (2001) 'The construction of marketplace architecture', in *Tracking a Transformation: E-commerce and the Terms of Competition in Industries*. The BRIE-IGCC E-conomy Project Task Force on the Internet (eds), Washington, DC: Brookings Institution Press.

Bell, D. (1973) *The Coming of Post-industrial Society: A Venture in Social Forecasting*. New York: Basic.

Beniger, J.R. (1986) *The Control Revolution: Technological and Economic Origins of the Information Society*. Cambridge, MA: Harvard University Press.

Benjamin, R. and Wigand, R. (1995) 'Electronic markets and virtual value chains on the information superhighway', *Sloan Management Review*, 36 (2): 62.

Brousseau, E. (1994) 'EDI and inter-firm relationships', *Information Economics & Policy*, 6 (3, 4): 319–47.

Brousseau, E. (1996) 'Intermédiation par les réseaux: quelles institutions?', in E. Brousseau, P. Petit and D. Phan (eds), *Mutations des télécommunications, des industries et des marches*. Paris: Economica. pp. 171–229.

Bresnahan, T., Brynjolfsson, E. and Hitt, L. (2002) 'Information technology, workplace organization, and the demand for skilled labor: firm-level evidence', *Quarterly Journal of Economics*, 117: 339–76.

Brown, J.S. and Hagel, J., III (2003) 'Does IT matter? An HBR debate', *Harvard Business Review*, June 2003: 2–4.

Brynjolfsson, E. (1993) 'The productivity paradox of information technology', *Communications of the ACM*, 36 (12): 67–77.

Brynjolfsson, E. and Hitt, L.M. (1998) 'Beyond the productivity paradox: computers are the catalyst for bigger changes', *Communications of the ACM*, 41 (8): 49–55.

Brynjolfsson, E. and Hitt, L. (2003) 'Computing productivity: firm-level evidence', *Review of Economics and Statistics*, 85 (4): 793–808.

Brynjolfsson, Erik, Hitt, Lorin M. and Shinkyu, Yang (2002) 'Intangible assets: computers and organizational capital', *Brookings Papers on Economic Activity*: Macroeconomics (1): 137–99.

Carayannis, E.G. (1998) 'The strategic management of technological learning in project/program management: the role of extranets, intranets, and intelligent agents in knowledge generation, diffusion, and leveraging', *Technovation*, 18 (11): 697–703.

Cash, J.I., Jr, and Kosynski, B.R. (1985) 'IS redraws competitive boundaries', *Harvard Business Review*, 63 (2): 134–42.

Cash, J.I., Jr, Eccles, R.G., Nohria, N. and Nolan, R. (1994) *Building the Information-age Organization: Structure, Control, and Information Technologies*. Boston: Irwin.

Castells, M. (1998) *The Rise of the Network Society*. Cambridge, MA: Blackwell.

Chodhury, V. (1997) 'Strategic choices in the development of interorganizational information systems', *Information Systems Research*, 8 (1): 1–24.

Chodhury, V., Hartzel, K.S. and Kosynski, B.R. (1998) 'Uses and consequences of electronic markets: an empirical investigation in the aircraft parts industry', *MIS Quarterly*, 22 (4): 471–507.

Ciborra, C.U. (1983) 'Markets, bureaucracies and groups in the information society: an institutional appraisal of the impacts of information technology', *Information Economics and Policy*, 1: 145–60.

Clemons, E.K. and Kleindorfer, P.R. (1992) 'An economic analysis of interorganizational information technology', *Decision Support Systems*, 8: 431–46.

Clemons, E.K. and Row, M.C. (1992) 'Information technology and industrial cooperation: the changing economics of coordination and ownership', *Journal of Management Information Systems*, 9 (2): 9.

Clemons, E.K. and Weber, B.W. (1990) 'London's big bang: a case study of information technology, competitive impact, and organizational change', *Journal of Management Information Systems*, 6 (4): 41–59.

Clemons, E.K. and Weber, B.W. (1994) 'Segmentation, differentiation, and flexible pricing: experiences with information technology and segment-tailored strategies', *Journal of Management of Information Systems*, 11 (2): 9.

Clemons, E.K., Croson, D.C. and Weber, B.W. (1996) 'Market dominance as a precursor of a firm's failure: emerging technologies and the competitive advantage of new entrants', *Journal of Management Information Systems*, 13 (2): 59–75.

Coase, R.H. (1937) 'The nature of the firm', *Economica*, 4: 386–405.

Cohen, S.S. and Zysman, J. (1987) *Manufacturing Matters: The Myth of the Post-industrial Economy*. New York: Basic.

Coriat, B. (1993) *Globalization, Variety and Mass Production: The Metamorphosis of Mass Production in the New Competitive Age*. Paris: CREI, Université Paris XIII.

Coriat, B. (1994) *L'Atelier et le robot: essai sur le fordisme et la production de masse à l'âge de l'électronique*. Mesnil-sur-l'Estrée: Firmin-Didot for C. Bourgeois.

Dang-Nguyen, G. (1996) 'Les systèmes de réservation aerienne et l'économie des réseaux', in E. Brousseau, P. Petit and D. Phan (eds), *Mutations des télécommunications, des industries et des marches*. Paris: Economica. pp. 231–62.

David, P.A. (1989) 'Computer and dynamo: the modern productivity paradox in a not-too-distant mirror'. CEPR Publication 172, Stanford University, Stanford, CA.

David, P.A. (1990) 'The dynamo and the computer: an historical perspective on the modern productivity paradox', *The American Economic Review*, Papers and Proceedings of the Annual Meeting of the American Economic Association, May, 80 (2): 355–61.

David, P.A. (2000) 'Understanding digital technology's evolutions and the path of measured productivity growth: present and future in the mirror of the past', in E. Brynjolfsson and B. Kahin (eds), *Understanding the Digital Economy*. Cambridge, MA: MIT Press.

Davidow, W.H. and Malone, M.S. (1992) *The Virtual Corporation: Structuring and Re-vitalizing the Corporation for the 21st century*. New York: HarperCollins.

Duliba, K.A., Kauffman, R.J. and Lucas, H.C. (2001) 'Appropriating value from computerized reservation system ownership in the airline industry', *Organization Science*, 12 (6): 702–28.

Finholt, T., Sproull, L. and Kiesler, S. (2002) 'Outsiders on the inside: sharing know-how across space and time', in P. Hinds and S. Kiesler, *Distributed Work*, Cambridge, MA: MIT press.

Gottardi, G. and Bolisani, E. (1996) 'A critical perspective on information technology management: the case of electronic data interchange', *International Journal of Technology Management*, 12 (4): 369–90.

Hitt, L.M. and Brynjolfsson, E. (1996) 'Productivity, business profitability, and consumer surpluses: three different measures of information technology value', *MIS Quarterly*, 20 (2): 121.

Hopper, M.D. (1990) 'Rattling SABRE – new ways to compete on information', *Harvard Business Review*, May–June: 118–25.

Jackson, M. and Sloane, A. (2003) 'Modelling information and communication technology in business: A case study in electronic data interchange (EDI)', *Business Process Management Journal*, 9 (1): 81–113.

Jarillo, J.C. (1988) 'On strategic networks', *Strategic Management Journal*, 9: 3–41.

Katz, M.L. and Shapiro, C. (1985) 'Network externalities, competition, and compatibility', *The American Economic Review*, 75 (3): 424–40.

Keen, P.G.W. (1981) 'Communications in the 21st century: telecommunications and business policy', *Organizational Dynamics*, 10 (2): 54–67.

Lee, S., Lee, K. and Kang, I.W. (2005) 'Efficiency analysis of controls in EDI applications', *Information & Management*, 42 (3): 425.

Leschly, S., Roberts, M.J., Sahlman, W.A. and Thedinga, T. (2002) 'Amazon.com', *Harvard Business Review*, Case Study.

Lucas, H.C., Jr (1996) *The T-form Organization*. San Francisco: Jossey-Bass.

Malone, T.W. (2004) *The Future of Work: How the New Order of Business Will Shape Your Organization, Your Management Style, and Your Life*. Cambridge, MA: Harvard Business School Press.

Malone, T.W. and Laubacher, R.J. (1998) 'The dawn of the e-lance economy', *Harvard Business Review*, Sept.–Oct.: 145–52.

Malone, T.W., Yates, J. and Benjamin, R.I. (1987) 'Electronic markets and electronic hierarchies', *Communications of the ACM*, 30 (6): 484–97.

Morton, M.S.S. (1991) 'Introduction', in M.S.S. Morton (ed.), *The Corporation of the 1990s: Information Technology and Organizational Transformation*. New York: Oxford University Press.

Nora, S. and Minc, A. (1978) *L'informatisation de la société: rapport à M. le Président de la République*. Paris: La Documentation Française.

Oettinger, A.G. and Weinhaus, C.L. (1979) 'National stakes in the compunications revolution: jurisdictional cost separations'. Working Paper w-79-2, Harvard University Program on Information Resources Policy, Harvard University, Cambridge, MA.

Piore, M.J. and Sabel, C.F. (1984) *The Second Industrial Divide: Possibilities for Prosperity*. New York: Basic.

Poldony, J.M. and Page, K.L. (1998) 'Network forms of organization', *Annual Review of Sociology*, 24: 57–76.

Porat, M.U. and Rubin, M.R. (1977) *The Information Economy*. Washington, DC: US Government Printing Office.

Powell, W.W. (1990) 'Neither market nor hierarchy: network forms of organization', in B.M. Staw and L.L. Cummings (eds), *Research in Organizational Behavior*, vol. 12. Greenwich, CT: JAI. pp. 295–336.

Rockart, J.F. and Short, J.E. (1991) 'The networked organization and the management of interdependence', in M.S.S. Morton (ed.), *The Corporation of the 1990s: Information Technology and Organizational Transformation*. New York: Oxford University Press. pp. 189–219.

Simon, H. (1957) *Models of the Man*. New York: Wiley.

Soliman, K.S. and Janz, B.D. (2004) 'An exploratory study to identify the critical factors affecting the decision to establish Internet-based interorganizational information systems', *Information and Management*, 41 (6): 697.

Solow, R.M. (1987) 'We'd better watch out', *New York Review of Books*, 12 July: 36.

Sproull, L. and Kiesler, S. (1991) *Connections: New Ways of Working in the Networked Organization*. Cambridge, MA: MIT Press.

Teo, H., Tan, B.C.Y. and Wei, K. (1997) 'Organizational transformation with electronic data interchange: the case of TradeNet in Singapore', *Journal of Management Information Systems*, 13 (4): 139–65.

Wigand, R. (1997) 'Electronic commerce: definition, theory and context', *Information Society*, 13 (1): 1–16.

Wigand, R., Picot, A. and Reichwald, R. (1997) *Information, Organization, and Management: Expanding Markets and Corporate Boundaries*. New York: Wiley.

Williamson, O.E. (1975) *Markets and Hierarchies, Analysis and Antitrust Implications: A Study in the Economics of Internal Organization*. New York: Free Press.

Williamson, O.E. (1996) *The Mechanism of Governance*. New York: Oxford University Press.

Yin, P.L. (2004) 'Online auction markets', *Harvard Business Review*, Note, August 23, 2004.

18

New Media and the Economics of Information

DON LAMBERTON

The economics of information is not a tidy, separate small part of economics for some reason of special interest in media matters. The information perspective is a significant challenge to the whole corpus of economics, with destructive implications for mainstream economic theory and its analytical and policy outcomes, yet holding great potential for new theory, new approaches to organization, and new solutions to decision and policy problems. Information, which includes knowledge or 'information of indefinite tenure' (Machlup, 1982: 9), is multifaceted: a resource, a commodity, a perception of pattern, a constitutive force in society (Braman, 1989). It is central to the making of decisions by consumers, business and governments and so plays a key role in the way the economic system works.

For the most part, the economy is envisaged or modelled as predominantly a market system in which business and households are the basic sectors.[1] The business sector employs workers and makes the decisions to invest in plant and equipment that enable the production of goods and services. Purchasing power flows from business to households in the form of wages, rent, interest and dividends that fund household spending. More reality is achieved in the model by adding government, financial institutions and the rest of the world. Business subdivides into industries, each of which produces some widely identified good or service: wheat, beer, motor cars, food, chemicals, computers, software, media. These goods and services are purchased by households, governments and other firms or by the rest of the world. Such market systems function within a wider social framework and require elaborate, durable and costly institutions.

Industrial change is pervasive (Mokyr, 2002) A complete catalogue would be very lengthy; major items would be new products and services, new technologies, new forms of organization, new policy initiatives including regulatory changes, new institutions, new standards, innovation, substitution of new for old, demand shifts, cost reductions and cost increases, outsourcing, downsizing, restructuring, mergers, takeovers, alliances, new images, new theories. It is important to appreciate that from an industrial change perspective, media and multimedia have some special characteristics but share basic involvement in information activities with industry at large. Much recent debate has focused on what has been regarded as special, whereas this chapter seeks to restore the balance. A review (Wildman, 1998) of media and multimedia listed the following research matters: advances in IT, revised regulatory philosophy, economies of scope and scale, programme choice, the public good character of media content, advertising, multimedia as integration for delivery by a single medium of different types of content, despecialization of transmission technologies, and integrated packages of media and tele-communications services. It is hoped that this chapter will provide a framework for analysis of the role of information in industrial change that extends beyond the media context.

AN INFORMATION PERSPECTIVE

The economics of information looks through the economist's lens at the information activities in all parts and all processes of the economy. It would be easy to assume that an economics of information is now being created in response to recent changes: computerization, satellites, mobile phones, ATMs and the like (Shapiro and Varian, 1999). These developments have spawned a naming flurry with a surfeit of adjectives: new, information, knowledge based, digital, online, Internet, attention (because information consumes the scarce resource of attention), administrative, nude (transparent and exposed), Cisco (in the image of the giant networking equipment firm). Each in its own way attempts to highlight the feature perceived as central to the contemporary economy; and each runs the risk of overemphasizing some part of the new at the expense of the old. Consider, for example, the online version which sees online business activity as a separate *economy* and makes comparison with national economies. Online activity is not a separate economy, nor are NASDAQ businesses as a group. They are part of a larger whole, using and building upon the labour force, the knowledge base, public assets, the legal framework, other institutions, and the entire social capital of the society.

Nor is the information economy new. A perceptive 1960 paper by Richard Meier speculated about 'probably the most significant category of developments in natural science,

engineering and psychology over the last decade. *Information theory* and *information technology* are', he said, 'bringing about striking changes in the organization of production and, through their influences upon institutions and professions, have been adding to our understanding of the properties of economic growth' (1960: 98). The following year, Stigler saw information as still in 'a slum dwelling in the town of economics' but with prospects of moving to a better location (1961: 61); and only one year later Fritz Machlup's (1962) major empirical effort delineated in rich detail for the first time the dimensions of the US knowledge-based economy in which knowledge production and distribution accounted for 29 per cent of GNP.

A reviewer of Machlup's book judged it to contain enough dynamite to blast traditional economics into orbit (Boulding, 1963: 36). His judgement was correct but – changing the metaphor – economists rolled with the punches, took on board some of the questions and some of the jargon, and evaded the need to get down to the fundamentals. With the millennium approaching, a leading practitioner of the economics of information could state that 'standard economic theory has little to say about the efficiency of the knowledge based economy' (Stiglitz, 1999: 19, n. 14).[2]

It is important to consider why the economics discipline has been unable or unwilling to change. Of course, the pressure can be seen either as a problem in keeping up with industrial change – the change from economies dominated by steel, manufacturing, chemicals, textiles and shipping to a world in which the most important firms are in telecommunications, computers, software, education and tourism; from the days of US Steel and DuPont to the emergence of global firms like Microsoft and Cisco – or an internal matter of obsolescence of the discipline. Economics Nobel winner Kenneth Arrow (1974) has mounted a good case for all successful organizations being subject to organizational obsolescence or lock-in. This is inherent, he argues, in the economic characteristics of information: 'the combination of uncertainty, indivisibility, and capital intensity associated with information channels

and their use imply (a) that the actual structure
and behaviour of an organization may depend
heavily upon random events, in other words
on history, and (b) the very pursuit of efficiency
may lead to rigidity and unresponsiveness to
further change' (1974: 49). If the economics
discipline itself is viewed as an organization,
rigidity and unresponsiveness are only to be
expected.

This critique is strengthened by the likelihood of distorted images. Cost considerations
plus management practices leave the analyst
dependent upon incomplete, inappropriate
and outdated statistics collected by national
and international agencies. Even if the data did
not suffer from these deficiencies, it is likely
the analyst is wearing faulty lenses. Having
studied two provincial towns, one in South
East Asia and one in North Africa, every now
and again over four decades, anthropologist
Clifford Geertz (1995) posed the question
of how the goings-on in those towns had
changed. He had telling words about what
actually takes place in this attempt to provide
answers and the implications for objectivity
and science.

> Floundering through mere happenings and then con-
> cocting accounts of how they hang together is what
> knowledge and illusion alike consist in. The accounts
> are concocted out of available notions, cultural equip-
> ment ready to hand. But like any equipment it is
> brought to the task; value added, not extracted. If objec-
> tivity, rightness, and science are to be had it is not by
> pretending they run free of the exertions which make or
> unmake them. (1995: 3)

These cautions have special application to
attempts to make sense of industrial change in
the information economy. Uncertainty is the
complement of knowledge; information activities constitute the major claim on resources;
and the limitations of the information and
information handling capabilities of each individual create social interdependence.

MARKET AND TECHNOLOGY BIASES

Two elements of bias have to be emphasized.
First, there is the tyranny of the market.
Economics has been reluctant to become

involved in the study of what happens inside
organizations (Simon, 1991); it did not take an
active interest in either psychology or organization science and it tried to keep aloof from
management and marketing. This situation is
changing; and while there is some deliberate
and systematic crossing of borders (Boisot and
Canals, 2004; Crampton, 2003; Dow and Earl,
1999; Droege, 1997; Eliasson, forthcoming;
Hodgson, 1999; Lamberton, 1996a, forthcoming; Lazaric and Lorenz, 1998; Macdonald,
1998; Macdonald and Nightingale, 1999), there
are still major deficiencies in theoretical and
empirical research and official statistical collections. There were major consequences for economic theory because it had taken 'on a
character belonging to the manipulable, calcu-
lable, external world of things, not the world of
the conscious mind in its eternal stations on the
edge of the void of time, the conscious mind
whose being consists precisely in the endless
gaining of knowledge' (Shackle, 1972: 3).

'Things' could easily include plant and
machinery and buildings but could not cope
with intangible assets. An important consequence is that an economic statistic that is crucial for the economic modelling and storytelling,
investment, excludes the very things that are
thought to be of increasing importance in the
information economy. The old questions such as
'What is investment?', 'What is capital?' have
come to the surface again. Should expenditure
on information be treated as investment? Is
information capital? Like other forms of capital,
information is structured (Lamberton, 1999);
its parts complement each other, imposing
sequences or lags, and there are interactions with
other 'assets'. For example, a reputation for consistent behaviour can reduce information costs.
It is now recognized that significant elements of
investment – education, R&D, computers, software, organizational capital, institution building –
ought to be included on a systematic basis
(Kirova and Lipsey, 1998; Webster 1999).

Because 'things' were easier to handle, the
second bias – a sharp focus on technology in a
hardware sense – shaped efforts to make sense
of the information revolution by focusing on
information and communication technologies
(ICT) rather than information. Machlup's

(1962) pioneering work and later research had adopted a wide coverage and, by capturing both the information activities that happened in markets and those that happened inside organizations, had sought to deal in a comprehensive way with the role of information. This led to the development of concepts of both a primary information sector for goods and services sold on established markets, and a secondary information sector to record the value added of information activities used in producing non-information goods and services. Some influential reports adopted a different approach. For example, Miles and associates (1990) emphasized the convergence of computing and communications. Some process was leading to the convergence and, to the extent computers and telecommunications had been transformed by that process, they were said to be the core of IT. Because that process was facilitating transformations in the whole economy – the information economy – they believed the interesting issue was the extent to which products and services were ICT intensive. As a final step, the factor promoting convergence was identified: the microelectronics revolution.

The process of informatization was, from this perspective, to be seen as the progressive application of information and communication technologies. Official documents acquired an ITEC (Information Technology, Electronics and Communications) label. A United Kingdom Green Paper (Hawkins et al., 1997), for example, was given a quite specific title: *Mapping and Measuring the ITEC Sector in the United Kingdom*. There was scant recognition of the profound role of information as explored, on an interdisciplinary basis, in a major conference in the 1980s (Machlup and Mansfield, 1983). Historical research could, of course, exercise a corrective influence. Is it reasonable to assume that the information economy began with microelectronics? Organizational development is reported to have been the main form of technological progress during the eighteenth century (Groenewegen, 1977). Changes that led to the growth of clerical occupations to such an extent that they became the dominant occupational group (Schement and Curtis, 1995: 71–101) suggest an earlier date for the onset of the information revolution. What of a future in which it is conceivable that electronics might merge with or be supplanted by biotechnology?

What lies behind this promotion of ITEC primacy which was accorded priority status in growth and development plans and has a great deal to do with the observed patterns of industrial change? Governments and those responsible for policy rhetoric have had a key role. But as Mathias warned, 'Some present day governments ... like some economic historians and contemporary tourists, have been too impressed by dramatic instances of the latest technology when making judgments about the sources of productivity' (1983: 18). A cursory study of economic history shows how these iconic industries rise and fall, for example, steel, textiles, motor vehicles, aerospace and, recently, the more general 'high-tech' category. Of course, some new industries may prove long-lasting because they reach to fundamental aspects of the human experience. The genome project may be a good illustration. The decoding and dissemination of the human genome fits into 'a vastly larger landscape of legal, ethical and political issues', is 'certainly part of the information economy', and 'probably has more far-reaching implications for the human species than any other aspect of the "information revolution"' (Tyler, 1999: 518).

As implied earlier, the tyranny of the market has complemented the technological determinism. A strong case can be made (Simon, 1991) for viewing the economy, not as a market system, but as an organizational economy, with market relations among organizations. Those promoting the ITEC view seem unwilling to recognize that the market, with its imperfections, is 'the largest and most effective information system in existence' (Machlup, 1979: 113). It seems a reasonable approach to say that when bureaucracy, both private and public, is combined with the market the resulting aggregate is the information economy. The primary and secondary information sector concepts emerged from attempts, working with very limited statistical data, to show that such an economy functioned through the combined roles of market and administrative decision. Analysis of the linkages within and between industry sectors and between information and non-information sectors involved a great deal more than the information component that Miles et al. conceded had been a feature of all societies. A solution to these difficulties is to treat bureaucracy or organization generally as technology.[3]

The notion that markets can always, in principle, deliver better outcomes than states and the law, i.e. neoliberal economic rationalism, as a basis for economic policy with respect to industrial change, has distinct weaknesses. First, as mentioned earlier, mainstream economics of the non-information economics variety has little to say about the efficiency of the information economy. Second, the private enterprise component makes rather simplistic assumptions about administrative efficiency, responsiveness and innovativeness (Nelson, 1981: 60). These assumptions are in effect judgements about information processes which have been subjected to research. While that research (Grigorovici et al., 2004; Macdonald, 1996, 1998; Macdonald and Nightingale, 1999) has not managed to provide simple models of industrial change, it has established the complexity involved and effectively undermined the sweeping claims of the privatization approach.[4] This is an important stage in the development of ideas about industrial development because it challenges the strong presumption that has held sway ever since Adam Smith's *Wealth of Nations*, that the industrialist knows best how to conduct his own business.

ECONOMIC CHARACTERISTICS OF INFORMATION

Asking questions about efficiency in the modern information economy raises issues, not just about IT and telecommunications, but about capabilities (Loasby, 1998), information stocks, organizational capital and learning. This is a far cry from the old economics with its firms that were given units of coordinating ability, reading best practice resource combinations from a recipe book (see Lamberton, 1965), and it

points to the policy vacuum that has been created by the information revolution. For example, should policy address not only education in school but also education of industrialists (Pandit et al., 1997)? And if the effectiveness of such 'messages' depends upon the state of readiness of the recipients, is monitoring of learning and performance desirable? Some will respond by invoking the economic rationalist market view but there are quite fundamental difficulties. Information can be a commodity, as is readily apparent from the wide range of information industries, but only to a limited extent (Arrow, 1984: 142). Therefore, it is not permissible to simply treat information as the $n+1$th commodity and then proceed with the analysis as if nothing else had changed. A market system with information elements cannot lead to the traditional efficient allocation of resources. First, information is indivisible in use: the same information is not bought twice in ordinary circumstances; and 'how to' information about production is independent of the scale of production. Therefore, it pays a business planning large-scale operations to buy better information than a small firm. A consequence is that information creates economies of scale throughout the economy and this causes a departure from what is expected of the competitive economy. It seems reasonable to think that the more information-intensive the economy as a whole, the greater the likelihood that this is a significant departure.

Second, information is inappropriable. The possessor does not lose information when it is transmitted. Also, the cost of transmitting information is normally much lower than the initial cost of production. Add to this the facts that information has the characteristics of a public good[5] and that intellectual property rights cannot give absolute security of benefits. The consequence of this combination of circumstances is that investment in uncertain activities like R&D will be less than optimal from a social point of view.

This general viewpoint, shaped by Arrow's classic 1962 paper, was welcomed by vested interests because it justified subsidization of those activities. Politically, it was welcomed in a Cold War setting. Industry stood to benefit, as did both universities and research centres and their employees. Thinking based on this modelling of the process of R&D, innovation and development has remained a powerful influence. There are, however, several flaws in the modelling.

The Arrovian analysis tends to be somewhat supply based. For example, looking to the demand side, it is apparent that there is often no public ready and eager to utilize information. This emerges on closer scrutiny of the characteristics of information. Arrow, in his original analysis, was aware of this (Lamberton, 1999) and he acknowledged:

- difficulties arose in defining an item of information and differentiating it from other items;
- information purchases were often made largely in ignorance of their value;
- some generators of information had advantages of special knowledge and skills;
- intellectual property rights could never provide complete protection;
- information items in use are interdependent.

These qualifications to the reasoning seem to have slipped out of sight in subsequent debate and policy formulations. It is therefore necessary to resurrect the complexity of information structures, the continuous nature of information processes, and the time dimensions involved. Two comments serve this purpose. First, 'Knowledge is not a pile of homogeneous material, but a complex structure of heterogeneous thoughts, each available at zero marginal cost but usable only together with resources available only at positive and often very high cost' (Machlup, 1982: 10). Second, there is need for modelling of the economy, or of its parts, 'in which information is continuously being collected and processed and in which decisions, based on that information, are continuously being made' (Stiglitz, 1985: 23).

Considerations of structure and flow provide scope for strategic behaviour and modify conclusions about divisibility and appropriability. The scope of indivisibilities may be extended and appropriability may be enhanced. There may then be opportunities for organizational experiment, e.g. alliances. The scope of

competition may well be diminished. From an analytical perspective, there is a shift from modelling of optimizing to study of historical processes. Sequences of experiment, learning, decision and innovation become important. This shift has major implications for management, innovation and policy and the industrial change they generate. Information in its diverse combinations of characteristics, structured forms and sequences contrasts sharply with information as an all-purpose lubricant in the economic system.

RESEARCH

The scope of research in the economics of information is so wide that this context permits only a highly selective coverage under each of the topics selected. A short summary is given along with appropriate and up-to-date references to permit fuller exploration.

Property Rights

Intellectual property 'is a broad term that is used to describe the wide range of rights that are conferred by the legal system in relation to discrete items of information that have resulted from some form of human intellectual activity' (Ricketson, 1992: 54), such as inventions, scientific discoveries, literary and artistic works, trademarks, industrial designs. Traditional categories devised centuries ago have been found inadequate. 'Patents' and 'copyright' became overloaded but provision had to be made for items as diverse as integrated circuits, software, plant varieties, genetic materials, personal images, cultural works, business methods, and surgical techniques. This has been achieved through wider interpretations of the old categories or through new, specific pieces of legislation, e.g. for plant varieties.

The importance of economic considerations has been widely acknowledged (Drahos, 1998, 2000; Lamberton, 1994). However, the definition quoted above is a lawyer's definition and it ignores the impossibility of items of information being discrete. Their complementarity is what gives them meaning and economic significance; and those complementarities build sequences and create lags that affect choices. There are legal disputes over property rights where, for example, it has been argued that a sculpture might have been created as a 'response' to a photograph. This points to wide-ranging possibilities of complex learning and response in the production and dissemination of information (Towse, 2001).

Industrial change in a knowledge-based economy is leading to growing tension between the system of legal relations and economic determinants. Continuation of this trend seems highly probable if economic activity becomes even more information intensive. 'Information is the basis of production, production is carried on in discrete legal entities, and yet information is a fugitive resource, with limited property rights' (Arrow, 1996: 651). Several consequences are already apparent. First, legal activity is increased. A good illustration is the use of meta-tags, one of the associational tools essential to the operation of the World Wide Web. Their function as indices of websites which search engines read and rely upon in looking for appropriate content in response to queries submitted to them generated controversies as meta-tag use impacts on the property rights of website owners (Ramiscal, 2000). Second, costs are raised in the settling and anticipation of legal conflicts. Markets for protective strategies and technologies are fostered, both domestically and internationally; and impetus is given to attempts to further develop protective technologies. Other consequences will include: internal efforts by firms to improve their assessment of the value of information assets; business efforts to cope with intellectual property problems by forming alliances; and calls for an expanded role on the part of governments and international organizations.

A related element in the industrial change process is the establishment of standards among those having an economic incentive to be concerned with the technical basis of product networks (Temple and Williams, 2002; Todd, 2004). Where the numbers involved are large, there are coordination problems. Some

become locked into their alternative, and knowledge of alternatives may be imperfect. Diversity may undermine very real long-run opportunities for better systems. A firm's business strategy often aims to have its alternative adopted as the industry standard – and such dominance is a regulatory matter. Various outcomes for innovation emerge: on the one hand, there can be encouragement of R&D and improvement of goods and services, or, on the other hand, the activities can be made more rigid and can hinder innovation. The outcomes in particular circumstances will depend upon 'the market structure, chance historical events, and the costs of technical alternatives' (Greenstein, 1992). As in the case of intellectual property rights, better understanding of these alternative outcomes might come from adoption of an information perspective with special attention to learning.

Market Structure

Industrial economics and industrial organization research has adopted market structure as a major focus of analysis. Sutton (1998) synthesizes the two major approaches in terms of (1) industry characteristics and (2) evolution of the size distribution of firms in a 'typical' industry. He provides systematic statistical evidence and detailed case studies, gives attention to both the telecommunications and computer industries, and treats the issues and analysis so comprehensively as to be an effective antidote to the excessive hype and wild projections of the development of information-related industries of recent times.

For decades, market structure research has been dominated by the seemingly simple notion of barriers to new competition. Sutton explains that 'a proper understanding of market structure requires a meshing of two ideas: strategic interaction between groups of close substitute products and (approximate) independence across clusters of such products' (1998: 495). His analysis builds on the old idea of a gap in the chain of substitutes using three principles: first, firms do not pursue loss-making strategies; second, if a profitable opportunity exists, some firm will take it; and, third, in markets consisting of independent submarkets, a 'symmetry' principle excludes the possibility that a firm enjoy some advantage over its rivals in entering a submarket by virtue of earlier experience in other submarkets. His objective is to limit the number of outcomes that could be expected to show up in empirical data. He acknowledges real-world complexity: 'Any adequate story of why, within the limits set by these few constraints, structure takes this form or that, must come to grips with the influence of history. If we track down, industry by industry, the events that caused things to go one way or another, we rapidly find ourselves immersed in the historian's domain of accident and personality' (1998: xv). The choice is posed as between richer theory and statistical regularity.

Has there been some major omission in this approach? The information perspective would seem to be a candidate. Each of Sutton's principles turns on what assumptions are made about what firms know. The first two imply knowledge of future losses and profits; and the symmetry principle denies the role of the informational asymmetries flowing from prior experience. In the knowledge-based economy, information costs loom large in the costs structures of firms (Eliasson et al., 1990). Should not these information mechanisms somehow be made part of the central analysis rather than be tucked away in the residual 'domain of accident and personality'? Information is a resource, albeit intangible; and changes in information costs and information technology shape organizational forms and the expectations of decision-makers. Of course, this change would have other consequences. It would require an even more complicated picture of the market, theory that is only now beginning to be built, and propositions that do not fit easily with conventional industry data.

The information perspective must be integral to industrial change. Just as it has been recognized that there is no catalogue of alternative technologies, so too there is awareness that firms find or create their profitable opportunities. They are obliged to learn and to seek comparative advantage through learning. Those processes seem so important in the knowledge-based economy that they ought to be part of the search for statistical regularity and not treated as exceptions.

The firm as the unit would seem to warrant further consideration. Some industries, especially information-intensive ones, show a marked tendency to resort to alliances, e.g. telecommunications, basic research and airlines. The alliances development lacks good theory. In this context, it seems clear that the firm is not a clearly defined entity and changes in organizational form have implications for the modelling of market structure.

Demand Studies

The major concern about demand studies relevant to the information economy is that they relate to demand for IT, access, advertising but only indirectly to information itself. Telecommunication has received a good deal of attention. Here the classic work is Taylor's *Telecommunications Demand in Theory and Practice* (1994), complemented by a Special Issue of *Information Economics and Policy* (1989) and more recently by Loomis and Taylor's *The Future of the Telecommunications Industry: Forecasting and Demand Analysis* (1999). These studies suffer from the limitation that they are very largely based on North American data and there is need for similar studies in other economic and social conditions, with different patterns of consumption, different income levels, different regulatory arrangements, and generally different stages of technological development (e.g. Das and Srinivasan, 1999; Karikari and Gyimah-Brempong, 1999).

Topics that have been clarified include residential access, business demand, price and income elasticities, cross-price elasticities between services, and demand for custom-calling features. Externalities had been seen as important for toll-to-local subsidy reasons but now attention has been given to the ways in which calls 'give rise to further calls, quite independently of price and income' in a process labelled 'the dynamics of information exchange' (Taylor, 1994: 259). This marks an all-too-rare event when the narrower 'telecom economics' is brought into an analytical partnership with the wider economics of information.

Research priorities were: business demand, residential cross-price elasticities, the relationship between telecommunications and other goods and services in household budgets, the dynamics of information exchange, and firm-specific elasticities (as monopoly suppliers have been replaced by duopoly or oligopoly). As Taylor saw the research agenda:

> The challenge for demand analysis in the telephone companies … is to forge links with marketing departments and to become integrated into company budgeting and forecasting processes. Applied demand analysis has a strategic role to play in a competitive environment, ranging from the conventional types of elasticity estimation in traditional markets to the identification of new markets. The possibilities are vast. It only requires imagination, hard work – and some humility – on the part of economists and demand analysts. (1994: 270)

Such research has been hampered by the deregulation and restructuring of telecommunications, and reflects both a high degree of specialization and business interests. The most productive research might prove to be on the dynamics of information exchange theme. For example, how do communities of interest form (1994: 268, n. 19)? Worthwhile questions include: how do such communities cohere and disintegrate? how are new information goods and services adopted? How do calls create need for further calls? How are business (and more generally organizational) needs for information shaped and managed? Findings from such research might throw some light upon a wide range of phenomena and processes, e.g. changing urban patterns of cooperation and conflict; intercountry relationships; and the formation of regional patterns (Madden, 1999).

Two further topics serve to illustrate the potential of demand studies. First, a RAND report addresses the question, 'What are the opportunities for and the obstacles to increased use of the Internet and electronic mail to facilitate communication between government agencies and the citizen clients?' (Neu et al., 1999: iii). The communication envisaged is citizen–government personal communication rather than the downloading of forms. Surveys indicated that such usage had barely begun.

Security issues loomed large. Trends were reported as 'not encouraging … [and] many gaps in the availability of a computer at home were major in both [1993 and 1997] and had *widened* in the four-year interval' (1999: xxi). Operational concerns were acknowledged but the Internet was nevertheless judged appropriate for the purpose, allowing improved service. The conclusion was an expression of faith: 'Citizens will eventually insist on communication with government agencies by e-mail' (1999: xxiii).

It may seem reasonable to ask why, if large numbers of interactive transactions are taking place on the Internet, there is no demand for citizen–government communication. However, nearly half the US population did not then have the necessary access, and operation of a dual system would add to cost. Even if security problems were all solved, the nature of the communication involved may present major difficulties. The full costs have not been assessed, especially in respect of legal aspects, and citizens may well want and feel entitled to time to reflect. At the heart of the report's optimism is a failure to appreciate that homogeneous goods account for the bulk of trade on the Internet. Even lowering of cost and provision of facilities may not offset the consequences of intermittent communication about diverse, specific matters. Not even the hoped-for extension of agent technology (Vulkan, 1999) will present an immediate solution to these content difficulties.

A second topic points to the barriers to demand for information in a developing country context, where 'downloading' proves inappropriate (Stiglitz, 1999: 4). This is a major issue for development policy and programmes:

> Logic dictates that information is an essential resource for the social and economic development of Third World countries, but how can this be demonstrated? How tangible is the linkage between information investments and the achievement of specific development goals? The limited status accorded to information in most developing countries suggests that its potential value is not self-evident. (Menou, 1993: ix)

It is a valid response by those accountable for policies and decisions, when faced with reports of growing numbers of computers, telephone lines and databases, to ask, 'So what?'

A research programme of the International Development Research Centre (IRDC) in Canada (McConnell, 1995; Menou, 1993) has pursued case studies of the impact of *information* in different geographical and information environments (e.g. Africa, Asia, the Caribbean and Latin America). There are lessons to be learned here as a similar approach is needed in many other situations. The real issues arise from the limitations of the resources and capabilities available and the perceptions of the value of information; and these issues cannot be addressed if the focus is on IT in a narrow sense. A wide range of outcomes between the extremes of stagnation and information cascades[6] (Geroski, 2000) is possible.

The IT Productivity Paradox

The IT productivity paradox has been debated for a long time and is not resolved: the ubiquitous computer is seen as a source of great productivity gains and profits, bringing a golden age of growth, and yet it remains difficult to detect the impact. Some observers highlight technical support, new software and retraining, concluding there are substantial hidden costs. Others point to such indicators as the massive outlays on new IT, stock market booms in new technology stocks, business and policy hype, and IT skill shortages in developed and undeveloped countries alike. They offer various explanations, e.g. the measurements are defective; the payoff is still in the pipeline. Care has to be taken to sort out the elements of truth in both sides of the argument.

Is there an authoritative evaluation? US research by leading productivity analysts reports that

> computer-related gains, large returns to the production and use of computers, and network effects are fundamentally changing the US economy. However, they are not ushering in a period of faster growth of output and total factor productivity. Rather, returns to investment in IT equipment have been successfully internalized by computer producers and computer users. These economic agents are reaping extraordinary rewards for mobilizing investment resources and restructuring economic activities. The rewards are large because of the swift pace of technical change and the rapid deployment of IT equipment through substitution, not because of

spillovers to third parties standing on the sidelines of the computer revolution. (Jorgenson and Stiroh, 1999: 114)

A companion study puts this into historical perspective:

> Much of what we are seeing now is 'second order', for example the VCR which combines TV and movies but does not have the fundamental impact of either, and much of the use of the Internet which substitutes one form of entertainment for another. Enthusiasts might note that the computer has not created the paperless office, but rather a duplication of electronic activities, all of which generate paper. (Gordon, 1999: 127)

Much in these debates has to be discounted heavily. Stock market valuations of new technology stock are notoriously optimistic and, like the business 'strategies' that inspire them, overly influenced by technological possibilities that take little account of social and economic conditions that affect outcomes.

The Jorgenson and Stiroh analysis emphasizes substitution of IT for other types of capital and labour: 'the massive substitution towards computers in both business and household sectors as the price of computers fell dramatically in the 1980s and 1990s' (1999: 109). The technical change residual in their analysis is the growth spillover after allowing for the growth of all other inputs, including IT equipment – also labelled the growth of total factor productivity. Contrary to the expectations of what they call a Computer Cargo Cult among economists and economic historians, there has been no flood of spillovers after the deployment of IT equipment: 'the story of the computer revolution is one of relatively swift price declines, huge investment in IT equipment, and rapid substitution of this equipment for other inputs' (1999: 110).

Some parts of this analysis can be challenged. The knowledge-based economy calls for a wider definition of measured investment. Education and learning are not to be measured only in terms of schools and universities, as business, official agencies and households are engaged in a continuous process of learning. Knowledge production should take in both R&D and other expenditures that achieve the same ends. Surely software qualifies for inclusion? What of organizational capital and institution building? In separating out expenditure on computers, it seems desirable to take account of the pervasive nature of computers. Jorgenson and Stiroh concede that they

> have substantially understated the impact of IT equipment, since we have focused specifically on computers and do not include closely related high-technology products. For example, much telecommunications gear is indistinguishable from IT equipment. Also, computers and semiconductors are now routinely embedded in automobiles and machinery, but we exclude these intermediate inputs from the aggregate production function. (1999: 113)

But just as computers find their way to distant places through processes of change, so too do changes in knowledge, organizational form, new behaviour patterns, new languages and new capabilities. How do these figure in the measured growth of inputs and TFP calculations (Lee et al., 2000; Preissl, 1997; Shin, 2000)?

There is a view that the modern human capacity emerged with *H. sapiens* and that the crucial innovation may have been the invention of language.

> For language is not simply the medium by which we express our ideas and experiences to each other. Rather it is fundamental to the thought process itself. It involves categorizing and naming objects and sensations in the outer and inner worlds and making associations between resulting mental symbols. It is, in effect, impossible for us to conceive of thought (as we are familiar with it) in the absence of language, and it is the ability to form mental symbols that is the fount of our creativity, for only once we create such symbols can we recombine them and ask such questions as 'What if …?' (Tattersall and Matternes, 2000: 44)

Suppose 'computerization' as it progresses involves a change equally fundamental. What might be the social and economic manifestations?

Two matters would seem to be related to this query. The first is coordination – a concept not by any means fully explored in economics but one that has loomed larger since the development of the economics of information. In many applications, IT effects coordination and this leads to substitution of equipment for labour. As the perceived cost of coordination declines, more coordination is put into use. Given more time, potential for infrastructure changes in not only equipment but also organization is detected, and internal reorganization and industry restructuring take place in

ways deemed appropriate to the coordination capabilities. Perhaps there is a case for asking whether some of the technological change is demand induced. It would be necessary to include abstract improvements such as organizational and attitudinal changes under the technological change heading.

These thoughts can be brought to bear on the impact of new media. Dudley (1999) asks the question: what has been the relationship, if any, between Europe's communications technology and its rate of economic growth over the past millennium? In the tradition of Innis, his analysis is framed in terms of relative changes in decoding, transmission and storage information costs. This permits a plausible account of history through changes in technology and capabilities – an account that makes use of the characteristics of languages and changes in relative component costs. It points to the possibility that the productivity failure reported by Jorgenson and Stiroh occurred because the new technologies were not yet sufficiently cost-effective to displace those whose positions of strength were established in the previous cycle of cost changes. If so, the Computer Cargo Cult adherents can take heart.

Information and Organization

Organizational change issues have been raised under other headings. One topic, already mentioned, will expose some of the issues involved. The firm, no longer a mathematical point as it was in classical economic theory, is now an imperfect network of information flows. The information it requires comes from outside sources as well as being generated internally. Just as the firm's product was made a variable by the development of monopolistic and imperfect competition theory, so the organization has been made a variable through the development of the economics of information.

This has opened up a great new territory for management, for those seeking to provide management services and for disciplines like management studies and organization science. Much of the literature reflects preoccupation with the new technologies and their possibilities. The prime purpose of obtaining information remains control, but a great deal of management effort in the new economy assumes that there are known ways of collating information and achieving control. Information can be identified, obtained, put to use, and stored away until the next time it is needed. This is an industrial model of information utilization, e.g. data warehousing, but for the most part lacking in cost analysis. Psuedo-measurement has generated strange units and calculations. One encounters references to 'shelf-kilometres' of documents; and, in a strange mix of ingenuity and ingenuousness, one study of the productivity of space telescopes conjures up the number of research papers using observations from a particular station per square metre of telescope lens (Trimble, 1996: 237–46)! Tacit knowledge is defined as what cannot be articulated, but this has not prevented plans to create electronic databases of tacit knowledge. While all this reflects some sense of the value and importance of information, there is a failure to address the real management issues. What information is needed? Is it obtainable within the organization? What are the likely external sources? Do internal and external flows mix easily? What costs are involved? What skills are required? If organizational obsolescence is taken to be a normal experience because of the economic characteristics of information, are there remedies?[6]

A belief that the needed information can be obtained and applied seems often to serve as a barrier to good management.

> [A]dvocates of change ... encourage change as they acknowledge information, as something contained within a system ... This is change which is sufficiently ordered to be studied, to be modelled, to be learnt and taught, to fit into existing policy and strategy ... This is the change of mission statements and vision statements. (Macdonald, 1998: 283)

The simple, inescapable truth is that managers do not face 'an endless examination in arithmetic', nor is there 'an algebra of business which only needs to be supplied with a sufficiency of information to guarantee success' (Shackle, 1968: 3). New technology can do much to create, store and make available information but it cannot ensure such a sufficiency. The new managerialism that focuses on

control and performance is responding to the inappropriateness of time worked as a measure but has confidence that the relevant activities can be measured. 'There is little consideration for the intangible, the unmeasurable, the indirect, the long term; flexibility is sacrificed to technical efficiency. Rather than reconciling themselves with living with uncertainty, managers are provided with the comfortable delusion that method will eliminate uncertainty' (Macdonald, 2002).

Space does not permit exploration of the entire management empire, but one industrial change can illustrate the relevance of the economics of information. Alliances between firms have become more prominent, e.g. in telecommunications, airlines and media. In the case of telecommunications, by the 1990s, well over 50 per cent of all international phone calls were handled by the four major alliances. Globalization has created pressures to expand, but why has this been done through alliances rather than by mergers and takeovers? To date there are no adequate theories of alliances and there has been an inclination to attribute their growth to deregulation, including a more permissive antitrust policy towards interfirm collaboration, e.g. in respect to basic research. If, however, alliances are entered into both to fill the gaps left by deregulation and to effect information sharing and coordination, then this latter influence obviously falls within the economics of information. In so far as a new organizational form is involved, this is to be shared with organization science and management (Engelbrecht, 1997: 19–42; Noam and Singhal, 1996).

Some sense of the complexity of administrative and institutional processes emerges from an examination of the potentially productive but sadly neglected role of the subversive, not the machine-breaking Luddite, dobber or whistleblower, but the thinking person who persists in asking 'Why?' and challenges orthodoxy, whether it be in the boardroom, on the factory floor, in interdepartmental meetings, or in the community at large. In contrast to most of the other resources that have to be used with information, the services of the subversive may well be low cost but highly productive.

A market element in the provision of additional information precludes genuine dissent. Life is easier and the pay better in a climate of consensus. The consequence is that there is failure to address the unwillingness or inability of executives to consider what they deem irrelevant – or threatening – once their organizations have become obsolete or are victims of lock-in. The economical use of information supposedly effected by the market system may not really be a virtue; executives may be using as much information as they are capable of or willing to use, in which case there is little to be gained from pressing upon them the services of more and more knowledge officers, gatekeepers, mentors, part-time board members and consultants. What is needed are 'reality instructors' – an invention of novelist Saul Bellow – and some way of ensuring that their message is heard and understood. Meantime, a company float with dissent as its chief or only product would not be looked upon with favour in the stock market. Can new organizational design influence the demand side and achieve optimum use of information? Possibly, but it will require keeping clear of technological fundamentalism, plus both thoroughgoing innovation in organizational design and the backing of new social sanctions.

Economics of Language

If language is fundamental to the thought process itself, there ought to be an economics of language in the knowledge-based economy (Lamberton, 1998, 2002b; Snow, 1998: 159–72). It seems a logical extension of concern with information. One of the pioneering papers expressed the belief that enquiring into language and communication systems was dealing with 'the essential stuff of economics' and hoped there would be 'a future economics of the most developed and most fully studied system of communication within human organizations: the language, spoken or written' (Marschak, 1965: 523).

As noted in discussing the IT productivity paradox, machine languages may play a similar role to that of natural languages. Researchers should be alive to the potential for machine languages to affect and effect mental symbols and influence organization (Pelikan, 1969: 625–31; Ryan, 1993).

Economic Development

The great bulk of literature dealing with communications and development focuses on telecommunications and IT equipment. This technological infrastructure has had attributed to it almost magical powers. But do telecommunications and equipment investment promote economic development, or does economic development create the demand for more telecommunications services? A strong case can be made (see 'Demand studies' earlier) for approaching this question from a different perspective and asking what is the role of information in the development process. Information capabilities are such that a telecommunications infrastructure is not an information infrastructure (Lamberton, 1996b: 31–8).

Attention should focus on the perceptions, aspirations and policies of industries and governments in their choice of technologies and patterns of socioeconomic development. What factors shape the perceptions of prospects? First, there are cost expectations – e.g. specific costs of modernization of old networks and provision of new networks; costs of infrastructure to make the system as a whole work – and these can be interpreted narrowly as information infrastructure, or much more widely, recognizing that the demand for telecommunications is very largely a derived demand and so a function of the entire process of economic growth. Second, there are some quite deep-seated notions. The causality notion may be the most important. Are telecommunications the linchpin – the 'driver' that leads development? Another notion is globalization; and here it may be that there has been global thinking to excess and too little heard about regionalization (Madden, 1999). Convergence is a third notion. Many studies fail to define this basic concept and list so many paradigms that convergence lacks useful meaning as all these elements are said to be fusing together. For example, communications, information, entertainment, publishing, retailing, financial services, information and Internet paradigms have been proclaimed (Adler, 1995). Then there is coordination, which raises the question whether the market can provide all that is needed. So the building of the infrastructure that is needed for an effective information economy requires organization and institutions as well as markets and technology.

Telephone lines without conversations and data flows do little to generate development. Investment, growth of income and cultural change may do much more, creating, in due course, greater demand for communications. In this way the potential of information as 'a powerful and reusable resource for development' (McConnell, 1995: 2) may be realized.

Policy

Why is it that standard economic theory has little to say about the efficiency of the knowledge-based economy? (See the introduction paragraphs to this chapter.) This can be answered on several levels. If all decision-makers are well informed and new information flow can be ignored, efficient outcomes can be defined. But once the insufficiency of information is admitted, there are problems. As Fritz Machlup suggested, the aim can be 'to act intelligently, with full consideration of the pertinent knowledge at hand and of the pertinent knowledge available at reasonable cost'. This is not the same as seeking 'optimization in making use of the totality of knowledge' and 'requires little argumentation'. Taking cost-effective action falls short of being Pareto efficient. The latter, however, 'invites speculations that may again widen the focus to include choices among alternative actions on different fronts, actions for which different batches of knowledge are used; in this case, we may easily slip again into the sea of undecidability' (1982: 10).

The traditional justifications for intervention in market outcomes are externalities, informational asymmetry and increasing returns. Information phenomena are the trouble spots in economics so it is not altogether

unexpected that each of these justifications proves to have informational aspects. It has long been argued that information is very largely a public good. The second justification needs no comment. As for increasing returns, as Samuelson reasoned long ago, they are 'the prime case of deviations from perfect competition … Universal constant returns to scale (in everything, including effective acquisition and communication of knowledge) is practically certain to convert *laissez-faire* or free enterprise into perfect competition' (1967: 117). These hopes are dashed in the knowledge-based economy where the importance of information ensures there are pervasive economies of scale.

Taken together, these considerations are a powerful critique of policy approaches based on mainstream economics. However, awareness of these difficulties has yet to be reflected in policy action – and, for that matter, in much of the modelling and analysis of both researchers and consultants. Both new policy initiatives and modification of existing policies are needed. For example, the focus should shift from short-term allocative efficiency to 'a set of long-term policies aimed at enhancing the knowledge base … through increased investment in the knowledge infrastructure, the knowledge distribution system, and the human knowledge component (human resources, education, training and organisational change)' (Soete, 1996: 387). An excellent illustration of the need for modification arises in the regulatory area. Given the characteristics of information and the new technological capabilities, the knowledge-based economy affords 'greater scope for the suppression of competition' (Stiglitz, 1999: 8). A consistent approach needs to be developed in intellectual property systems where administrative simplicity has hampered efforts to 'fine tune' the term and strength of the rights by taking account of the diversity of inventions and innovations.

In summary, the knowledge-based economy offers opportunity for an enhanced public role in the provision of information, 'invention' of new institutions, establishment of systems of remuneration more appropriate to 'information work', and many ways of effecting greater coordination. This last is a matter for macro- as well as microeconomic policy (Earl, 1998: 331–42).

Distorted Images

There is perennial complaint that official statistics provide distorted images of what is happening in the economy. Costs, administrative inertia and outdated lenses result in a failure to catch up with the industrial and social change that is taking place. The most familiar problem is highlighted by 'shadow' economy studies showing that quite a large part of conventionally defined activity is not captured in official statistics and suggesting that their scope should be extended to take in some elements of non-market activity.

Decisions have to be made about what is important in understanding events in the economy. The emerging focus on the role of knowledge is creating major problems for those responsible for official collections. How is knowledge to be measured? Must all knowledge be measured or just new knowledge? Is new knowledge to be captured in R&D or are there other components that are also important? What should be included in investment – both in knowledge itself and in effecting change (Kirova and Lipsey, 1998)?

A new social accounting is needed, with 'a new paradigm: new models, new variables. This will mean new measures … New approaches, perhaps grounded in other disciplines [than economics], must be developed to quantify knowledge variables like firm learning, know-how, adaptation' (Carter, 1996: 67). All this flows from recognition not just that economic theory, research and policy have to catch up with contemporary conditions but that the failure of the discipline to devise a central role for knowledge has always been a fundamental flaw.

WHAT IS NOT KNOWN

Perhaps Geertz-style narratives will always need to be rewritten; perhaps Shackle's 'endless

gaining of knowledge' implies that the tenure of all knowledge expires because the lenses being used are changed as new conceptual frameworks are imagined. This may be an uncomfortable thought for those dominating present academic gatherings, just as contemplating the demise of dominant firms or governments in office makes business leaders and ministers uneasy. Such contemplations link to the unwillingness of governments and industry to support the more challenging social science research.

In terms of research, there is a need to ask what 'not known' implies. Does not listing items in this category imply some knowledge about them? It might be useful here to invoke two categories. First, there are questions sufficiently well defined to be outlined in research funding proposals and acceptable to research councils because they fall within the current paradigms, fads and fashions.[7] The researchers became the prey of endorsed questions. Second, there are confessions of ignorance and expressions of hope and willingness to search for central questions that challenge orthodoxy; to search for new lenses through which to view the economy. Fritz Machlup did so with his 1962 book *The Production and Distribution of Knowledge in the United States*, and it has been widely acknowledged that the impact has been profound even if somewhat less than Kenneth Boulding had hoped.

This overview of the contribution that the economics of information is making to the study of industrial change has been cast in terms of two 'econ' tribes: mainstream economics and the economics of information. A more comprehensive effort to cope with the complexity of the real-world processes of change must acknowledge the many other tribes and disciplines and will require multi-tribal and interdisciplinary work. The shaping of an information science or information studies needs to take guidance from the existing limited understanding of the relationships between the economy in the mainstream sense and the meshing of conventions, knowledge, culture and institutions that makes up society. Hopefully, the joint ventures, alliances and possible mergers among the econ tribes would reflect similar senses of direction in multidisciplinary research, so yielding questions for the second, challenging category. This chapter ends with some speculations about some such potential lines of enquiry.

It has been argued that 'there is a *prima facie* case for regarding the evolution of economic systems as an entropic phenomenon but with information rather than energy providing the main propagating role' (Clark, 1991: 102). Hodgson responded, stressing the difficulty: 'Although tantalizing, this suggestion must overcome the difficult problem of the definition of "information" and the distinction between different types of information or knowledge' (1993: 300, n. 8). The primary information and secondary information sector approach was an attempt to structure the complex information activities and was modified so that it fits into an input–output framework (Stäglin, 1989). The next stage might be to shift the focus to the demand side; to seek out the mix of characteristics that underlies the demands depicted in such modelling and their relationships with the capabilities and resources of the information users and the constraints on their decisions. For example, attention is now said to be one of the scarce resources. It is not enough to recognize that information is multifaceted; a richer taxonomy is needed (Lamberton, 1999).

The recent focus on telepistemology, the study of knowledge acquired at a distance by means of e.g. the telephone, television and now the Internet, hints at the potential but also shows the difficulties involved. Leo Marx comments on a recent book: 'As the electronic revolution gains momentum, the boundary between humanity's manufactured andits flesh-and-blood bodily experience is rapidly shifting … All the contributors recognize its extent and its import, but most of them … reject the popular delusion that the boundary is about to be erased' (Goldberg, 2000: blurb). Economists studying the demand for Internet services, management experts trying to devise optimal business organizations and all those concerned, especially policy-makers, about the messy philosophical and social problems should pay heed.

Given such awareness, study of the ongoing processes of information provision, learning, decision, organizational change and growth – in short, industrial change – has potential for collaboration. Can, for example, current initiatives in the economics of information (Lamberton, 1998) come together with related efforts in organizational science (Brousseau, 2000; Ciborra and associates, 2000; Macdonald, 1998; Nonaka et al., 1998; Oniki, 1999), evolutionary economics (Eliasson and Taymaz, 2000), cognitive economics (Paquet, 1999) and endogeneous growth theory (Adams, 2000; Engelbrecht, 1999; Romer, 1986)? The complexities become even greater if the spatial dimension is accorded the importance it probably deserves (Droege, 1997; Gaspar and Glaeser, 1998; Wilson and Corey, 2000). But where is the funding organization to provide the support for what could be a momentous occasion?

The potential outcomes have major implications for policy (*The Economist*, 2000). Increasingly in the knowledge-based economy, conventional thought about efficient choices is proving inadequate to the task. There is reason to reject the policy of 'trust the market' on knowledge issues. This may initiate, on the one hand, the pendulum swing back towards intervention; and on the other, a return to mercantilistic initiatives and reliance upon 'trickle-down' to the key issue, poverty. The information revolution has not and will not in some miraculous way eliminate the scarcities and inequities that characterize society and its industrial organization.

FUTURE DEVELOPMENTS

The future will bring more new media and more industrial change but will it bring an appropriate new economics? As the economics of information, broadly interpreted, embraces most of the major changes in both economic theory and policy over the last three or four decades, there might seem to be some cause for optimism but the opposing pressures are powerful. As Martin Shubik reasoned, 'The rational utilitarian man, the Invisible Hand, and the democratic vote may be regarded as a trinity for economics and political faith in a free-enterprise democracy' (1967, in Lamberton, 1971: 357).

Cyberspace is no mere virtual reality but a rich geography of practices and power relations (Crampton, 2003). The Internet is not inherently democratic. Kalathil and Boas (2003) have examined the full range of Internet use under eight authoritarian regimes: China, Cuba, Singapore, Vietnam, Burma, United Arab Emirates, Saudi Arabia and Egypt. As Jennifer Windsor of Freedom House says on Kalathil and Boas' book's cover, 'the Internet is by no means a guaranteed "silver-bullet" in eluding, and indeed defeating, the control of authoritarian rulers'.

However, the economics of information has failed to tackle some core issues. Its analysis and basic assumptions still reflect the Shubik trinity. In ways that have suited the powerful, the key to the future was deemed to be access – to new technology. What was neglected were the capabilities which required so much more than a typewriter, a telephone, or a computer. They required knowledge, incentives, skills to make the access effective, and above all time to learn. Capital was much more than land, buildings and machines.

This complexity favoured and generated coalitions: as investors, business alliances, and government. The Galbraithian military–industrial complex is well-known but the pervasiveness of such coalitions is not fully appreciated. Haber et al. (2003) present a fascinating account of Mexican experience, concluding that property rights are not a public good but are enforced selectively as private goods, with the payoffs shared by the participating groups and government. Going digital does not ensure democratic processes nor does access to technology and the entire information resources of nations ensure changes in income distribution.

In such situations information sharing is very much in vogue (Helmstadter, 2003). The playing field is far from level. While focusing on access, researchers have neglected the participants' capabilities of using information. These capabilities are the product of education and past experience. They fit with mindsets which override tidy optimization calculations (Lamberton, forthcoming).

To speak of assumptions would suggest reasoning which could be revised, but mindsets are less flexible. Business schools foster the myth of the entrepreneur floating from one venture to the another in a world of optimization. The reality may be a lack of imagination and tunnel vision that makes information collecting and its interpretation ever more selective. These paths lead eventually to the decline of empires, the fall of governments, business failures and inward-looking research.

These patterns have long been recognized. Adam Smith wrote about the prejudices of education. We often overlook that schools of thought do seem to outlive their usefulness. Nevertheless, we fail to recognize that mindsets are part of our capabilities – initially productive of creativity and innovation but later a restraining influence. We tend to assume they are tamed, managed and retired through education. We neglect their time dimensions and we neglect the ways in which they are helped and hindered by the very division of labour with its specialization that we believe fundamental to productivity and growth.

For both analysis and policy purposes we need to probe more deeply and disaggregate more minutely. Curiously, the Lessig message (2001) with the added 'Remix Me' refrain seems to have much in common with Hofstadter who wrote that 'metaknowledge and knowledge are simmering together in a singuler stew, totally fused and flavouring each other richly' (1986: 538). Each of us comprehends some part of this 'stew' and comes to the table with individual capabilities and mindsets. These are tools and resources with both limitations and potentials, fashioned basically by the division of labour and the education system.

NOTES

This chapter builds on and extends Lamberton (1971, 1984, 1996a, 1997, 2002a, 2002b). See also Macdonald and Nightingale (1999). Perhaps an explanatory note on 'economics' is permissible. In the context of media and communication literature, one meets frequently the claim that information has been commoditized. Those making this claim should ponder carefully the extent to which major contributors have, as has been done in this chapter, laid stress on the fact that information can be a commodity but only to a limited extent. Similarly, there is an almost standard claim that information for the economist, perhaps defined as what reduces uncertainty, is devoid of content. This is more or less true of the Shannon treatment but that was an engineering approach. Utility and even profit can be interpreted to include not only money gains but also other satisfactions: consumption, power, bequests or interesting challenges. Therefore, the criticism holds for 'information as oil' but it loses its force when the richer concepts of information as structured capital, as resource, as commodity, as perception of pattern and as a constitutive force in society are adopted. Finally, it should be added that economics does not speak with one voice: it is 'made up of a variety of sub-field specialists, different generations with different kinds of training, persons of greatly varying ideological preferences, individuals with markedly different perceptions regarding appropriate methodological choices, and a lot of Indians and a lot of would-be chiefs ... what interests one segment of the profession bores another' (Perlman, 1981: 4).

1 'The concept of a more or less freely functioning market system has been central to economic theory during the last three hundred years of its development' (Vickers, 1995: v). This defines and limits mainstream economics which appears as 'trust the market', 'small government' and economic rationalism. It emphasizes production rather than consumption, judges progress in terms of economic growth, and avoids matters of both institutions and internal organization. The counterview in terms of the tyranny of the market has come increasingly to base its critique on the mostly implicit assumptions about the role of information (Lamberton, 1996a; Middleton, 1998; North, 1990; Stiglitz, 1994; Thurow, 1983; Vickers, 1995; Vines and Stevenson, 1991).

2 An allocation of resources is (Pareto) efficient if no one can be made better off without someone else being made worse off. Major new works, for example Jones (2003) still endeavour to approach analysis of the knowledge economy from a neoclassical perspective.

3 Schement and Curtis advocate such an approach: 'bureaucracy ... is itself an information technology' (1995: 230).

4 Grigorovici et al. (2004) acknowledge the significant paper by Michel Menou (1985). See also Menou (1993) with his call for research into the *use* of information rather than expenditure on ICT. For a new, disaggregated approach to the effects of liberalization on the composition of R&D activity, see Calderini and Garrone (2001).

5 A public good is characterized by non-rivalrous consumption (the marginal costs of providing it to an additional person are zero) and non-excludability (the costs of excluding an individual from consumption are prohibitively high).

6 Nightingale (2003) has posed important questions about reliance upon the tacit vs codified dichotomy.

7 For literature on these as economic phenomena see Bikchandani et al. (1998) and Anderson and Holt (1997).

REFERENCES

Adams, J.D. (2000) 'Endogenous R&D spillovers and industrial research productivity'. Working Paper 7484. New York: National Bureau of Economic Research.

Adler, R.P. (1995) 'Introduction', in Institute for Information Studies, *Crossroads on the Information Highway: Convergence and Diversity in Communications Technologies*. Queenstown, MD: Institute for Information Studies.

Anderson, L.R. and Holt, C.A. (1997) 'Information cascades in the laboratory', *American Economic Review*, 87 (2): 847–62.

Arnott, R., Greenwald, B., Kanbur, R. and Nalebuff, B. (eds), *Economics for an Imperfect World: Essays in Honor of Joseph E. Stiglitz*. Cambridge, MA: MIT Press.

Arrow, K.J. (1962) 'Economic welfare and the allocation of resources for invention', reprinted in D.M. Lamberton (ed.) (1996), *The Economics of Communication and Information*. Cheltenham: Elgar. pp. 227–43.

Arrow, K.J. (1974) *The Limits of Organization*. New York: Norton.

Arrow, K.J. (1984) *Collected Papers of Kenneth J. Arrow: The Economics of Information* Vol. 4. Oxford: Blackwell.

Arrow, K.J. (1996) 'Technical information and industrial structure', *Industrial and Corporate Change*, 5: 645–52.

Bikchandani, S., Hirshleifer, D. and Welch, I. (1998) 'Learning from behavior of others: conformity, fads, and informational cascades', *Journal of Economic Perspectives*, 12 (3): 151–70.

Boisot, M. and Canals, A. (2004) 'Data, information and knowledge: have we got it right?', *Journal of Evolutionary Economics*, 14: 43–67.

Boulding, K.E. (1963) 'The knowledge industry. Review of Fritz Machlup, The Production and Distribution of Knowledge in the United States', *Challenge*, 11 (8): 36–8.

Braman, S. (1989) 'Defining information: an approach for policymakers', reprinted in D.M. Lamberton (ed.) (1996), *The Economics of Communication and Information*. Cheltenham: Elgar. pp. 3–12.

Brousseau, E. (2000) 'What institutions to organize electronic commerce? Private institutions and the organization of markets', *Economics of Innovation and New Technology*, 9 (3): 245–73.

Calderini, M. and Garrone, P. (2001) 'Liberalisation, industry turmoil and the balance of R&D activities', *Information Economics and Policy*, 13 (2): 199–230.

Carter, A.P. (1996) 'Measuring the performance of a knowledge-based economy', in OECD Documents, *Employment and Growth in the Knowledged-based Economy*. Paris: OECD. pp. 61–8.

Ciborra, C.U. and associates (2000) *From Control to Drift: The Dynamics of Corporate Information Infrastructures*. Oxford: Oxford University Press.

Clark, N.G. (1991) 'Organisation and information in the evolution of information systems', in P.P. Saviotti and J.S. Metcalfe (eds), *Evolutionary Theories of Economic and Technological Change: Present States and Future Prospects*. Reading, MA: Harwood. pp. 88–107.

Crampton, J.W. (2003) *The Political Mapping of Cyberspace*. Edinburgh: Edinburgh University Press.

Das, P. and Srinivasan, S.J. (1999) 'Demand for telephone usage in India', *Information Economics and Policy*, 11 (2): 177–94.

Dow, S.C. and Earl, P.E. (eds) (1999) *Economic Organization and Economic Knowledge: Essays in Honour of Brian J. Loasby*. Cheltenham: Elgar.

Drahos, P. (ed.) (1998) 'Trade and intellectual property', *Prometheus*, 16 (3) (special issue).

Drahos, P. (ed.) (2000) *Intellectual Property*. Aldershot: Ashgate.

Droege, P. (ed.) (1997) *Intelligent Environments: Spatial Aspects of the Information Revolution*. Amsterdam: North-Holland.

Dudley, L. (1999) 'Communications and economic growth', *European Economic Review*, 43: 595–619.

Earl, P.E. (1998) 'Information, coordination and macroeconomics', *Information Economics and Policy*, 10 (3): 331–42.

Eliasson, G. (forthcoming) 'The nature of economic change and management in a new knowledge based economy', *Information Economics and Policy*.

Eliasson, G. and Taymaz, E. (2000) 'Institutions, entrepreneurship, economic flexibility and growth: experiments on an evolutionary micro-to-macro model', in U. Canter, H. Hanusch and S. Klepper (eds), *Economic Evolution, Learning, and Complexity*. Heidelberg: Physica. pp. 265–86.

Eliasson, G., Folster, S., Lindberg, T., Pousette, T. and Taymaz, E. (1990) *The Knowledge-based Economy*. Stockholm: Industrial Institute for Economic and Social Research.

Engelbrecht, H.-J. (1997) 'The international economy: knowledge flows and information activities', in D.M. Lamberton (ed.), *The New Research Frontiers of Communications Policy*. Amsterdam: North-Holland. pp. 19–42.

Engelbrecht, H.-J. (1999) 'International knowledge spillovers, absorptive capacity and productivity in OECD countries', in S. Macdonald and J. Nightingale (eds), *Information and Organization: A Tribute to the Work of Don Lamberton*. Amsterdam: North-Holland. pp. 46–85.

Gaspar, J. and Glaeser, E.L. (1998) 'Information technology and the future of cities', *Journal of Urban Economics*, 43: 136–56.

Geertz, C. (1995) *After the Fact: Two Countries, Four Decades, One Anthropologist*. Cambridge, MA: Harvard University Press.

Geroski, P.A. (2000) 'Models of technology diffusion', *Research Policy*, 29 (4–5): 603–25.

Goldberg, K. (ed.) (2000) *The Robot in the Garden: Telerobotics and Telepistemology in the Age of the Internet*. Cambridge, MA: MIT Press.

Gordon, R.J. (1999) 'US economic growth since 1870: one big wave?', *American Economic Review*, 89 (2): 123–8.

Greenstein, S.M. (1992) 'Invisible hands and visible advisors: an economic interpretation of standardization', *Journal of the American Society for Information Science*, 43 (8): 538–49.

Grigorovici, D.M., Schement, J.R. and Taylor, R.D. (2004) 'Weighing the intangible: towards a theory-based framework for information society indices', in E. Bohlin, S.L. Levin, N. Sung and C.-H. Yoon, *Global Economy and Digital Society*. Amsterdam: Elsevier, pp. 169–99.

Groenewegen, P.D. (1977) 'Adam Smith and the division of labour', *Australian Economic Papers*, 16: 161–74.

Haber, S., Razo, A. and Maurer, N. (2003) *The Politics of Property Rights*. Cambridge: Cambridge University Press.

Hawkins, R.W., Mansell, R.E. and Steinmueller, W.E. (1997) *Mapping and Measuring the Information Technology, Electronics and Communications Sector in the United Kingdom*. Brighton: SPRU, University of Sussex.

Helmstadter, E. (ed.) (2003) *The Economics of Information Sharing: A New Institutionalist Approach*. Cheltenham: Elgar.

Hodgson, G.M. (1993) *Economics and Evolution: Bringing Life Back into Economics*. Cambridge: Polity.

Hodgson, G.M. (1999) *Economics and Utopia: Why the Learning Economy Is Not the End of History*. London: Routledge.

Hofstadter, D.R. (1986) *Metemagical Themes: Questing for the Essence of Mind and Pattern*. New York: Bantam.

Jones, D.C. (ed.) (2003) *New Economy Handbook*. Amsterdam: Elsevier.

Jorgenson, D.W. and Stiroh, K.J. (1999) 'Information technology and growth', *American Economic Review*, 89 (2): 109–15.

Kalathil, S. and Boas, T.C. (2003) *Open Networks, Closed Regimes: The Impact of the Internet on Authoritarian Rule.* Washington, DC: Carnegie Endowment to International Peace.

Karikari, J.A. and Gyimah-Brempomg, K. (1999) 'Demand for international telephone services between US and Africa', *Information Economics and Policy*, 11 (4): 407–35.

Kirova, M. and Lipsey, R. (1998) 'Measuring real investment: trends in the United States and international comparisons'. Working Paper 6404, National Bureau of Economic Research, New York.

Lamberton, D.M. (1965) *The Theory of Profit.* Oxford: Blackwell.

Lamberton, D.M. (ed.) (1971) *The Economics of Information and Knowledge.* Harmondsworth: Penguin.

Lamberton, D.M. (1984) 'The economics of information and organization', in M.E. Williams (ed.), *Annual Review of Information Science and Technology (ARIST)*, vol. 19. Knowledge Industries Publicationsfor American Society for Information Science. pp. 3–30.

Lamberton, D.M. (1994) 'Intellectual property and innovation', in M. Dodgson and R. Rothwell (eds) *Handbook of Industrial Innovation.* Aldershot: Elgar. pp. 301–10.

Lamberton, D.M. (ed.) (1996a) *The Economics of Communication and Information.* Cheltenham: Elgar.

Lamberton, D.M. (1996b) 'A telecommunications infrastructure is not an information infrastructure', *Prometheus*, 14 (1): 31–8.

Lamberton, D.M. (ed.) (1997) *The New Research Frontiers of Communications Policy.* Amsterdam: North-Holland.

Lamberton, D.M. (1998) 'Language and critical mass'. Paper presented at the 12th Biennial International Telecommunications Society Conference, Stockholm.

Lamberton, D.M. (1999) 'Information: pieces, batches or flows?', in S.C. Dow and P.E. Earl (eds), *Economic Organization and Economic Knowledge: Essays in Humour of Brian J. Loasby.* Cheltenham: Elgar. pp. 209–24.

Lamberton, D.M. (ed.) (2002a) *Managing the Global: Globalization, Employment and Quality of Life.* London: I.B. Tauris and The Toda Institute for Global Peace and Policy Research.

Lamberton, D.M. (ed.) (2002b) *The Economics of Language.* Cheltenham: Elgar.

Lamberton, D.M. (forthcoming), 'Information sharing', in D. Rooney, G. Hearn and A. Ninan (eds), *Knowledge Economy Handbook.* Cheltenham: Elgar.

Lazaric, N. and Lorenz, E. (eds) (1998) *Trust and Economic Learning.* Cheltenham: Elgar.

Lee, C.-H., Sophie, Barua A. and Whinston, A.B. (2000) 'The complementarity of mass customization and electronic commerce', *Economics of Innovation and New Technology*, 9 (2): 81–109.

Lessig, L. (2001), *The Future of Ideas: The Fate of the Commons in a Connected World.* New York: Random House.

Loasby, B.J. (1998) 'The organization of capabilities', *Journal of Economic Behavior & Organization*, 35: 139–60.

Loomis, D.G. and Taylor, L.D. (eds) (1999) *The Future of the Telecommunications Industry: Forecasting and Demand Analysis.* Dordrecht: Kluwer.

Macdonald, S. (ed.) (1996) 'Informal information flow', *International Journal of Technology Management*, 11 (1–2) (special issue).

Macdonald, S. (1998) *Information for Innovation: Managing Change from an Information Perspective.* Oxford: Oxford University Press.

Macdonald, S. (2002) 'Managing with method: information in policy and strategy for innovation', in D.M. Lamberton (ed.) *Managing the Global: Globalization, Employment and Quality of Life.* London: I.B. Tauris and The Toda Institute for Global Peace and Policy Research. pp. 209–22.

Macdonald, S. and Nightingale, J. (eds) (1999) *Information and Organization: A Tribute to the Work of Don Lamberton.* Amsterdam: North-Holland.

Machlup, F. (1962) *The Production and Distribution of Knowledge in the United States.* Princeton, NJ: Princeton University Press.

Machlup, F. (1979) 'An economist's reflections on an Institute for the Advanced Study of Information Science', *Journal of the American Society for Information Science*, 30 (2): 111–13.

Machlup, F. (1982) 'Optimum utilization of knowledge', *Society, Knowledge, Information, and Decisions*, 20 (1): 8–10.

Machlup, F. and Mansfield, U. (eds) (1983) *The Study of Information: Interdisciplinary Messages.* New York: Wiley.

Madden, G. (1999) 'Asia–Pacific information flows and trade', in S. Macdonald and J. Nightingale (eds), *Information and Organization: A Tribute to the work of Don Lamberton.* Amsterdam: North-Holland. pp. 393–406.

Marschak, J. (1965), 'Economics of language', reprinted in D.M. Lamberton (ed.) (1971), *Economics of Information and Knowledge.* Harmondsworth: Penguin. pp. 37–58.

Mathias, P. (1983) 'The machine: icon of economic growth', in S. Macdonald, D.M. Lamberton and

T. Mandeville (eds), *The Trouble with Technology: Explorations in the Process of Technological Change.* London: Pinter.

McConnell, P. (ed.) (1995) *Making a Difference: Measuring the Impact of Information on Development.* Ottawa: International Development Research Centre.

Meier, R.L. (1960) 'Information, resource use and economic growth', in J.J. Spengler (ed.), *Natural Resources and Economic Growth.* Ann Arbor, MI: Resources for the Future, Inc. and Social Sciences Research Council.

Menou, M. (1985) 'An information system for decision support in national information policy-making and planning', *Information Processing & Management,* 21 (4): 321–61.

Menou, M. (ed.) (1993) *The Impact of Information on Development.* Ottawa: International Development Research Centre.

Middleton, R. (1998) *Charlatans or Saviours? Economists and the British Economy from Marshall to Meade.* Cheltenham: Elgar.

Miles, I. and associates (1990) *Mapping and Measuring the Information Economy.* London: British Library Board.

Mokyr, J. (2002) *The Gifts of Athena: Historical Origins of the Knowledge Economy.* Princeton, NJ: Princeton University Press.

Nelson, R.R. (1981) 'Assessing private enterprise: an exegesis of tangled doctrine', reprinted in D.M. Lamberton (ed.) (1996), *The Economics of Communication and Information.* Cheltenham: Elgar. pp. 59–77.

Neu, C.R., Anderson, R.H. and Bikson, T.K. (1999) *Sending Your Government a Message: E-mail Communication between Citizens and Government.* Santa Monica, CA: RAND Science and Technology.

Nightingale, P. (2003) 'If Nelson and Winter are only half right about tacit knowledge, which half? A Searlean critique of codification', *Industrial and Corporate Change,* 12 (2): 149–83.

Noam, E. and Singhal, A. (1996) 'Supra-national regulation for supra-national telecommunications carriers?' *Telecommunications Policy,* 20 (10): 769–87.

Nonaka, I., Ray, T. and Umemoto, K. (1998) 'Japanese organizational knowledge creation in Anglo-American environments', *Prometheus,* 16 (4): 421–39.

North, D.C. (1990) *Institutions, Institutional Change and Economic Performance.* New York: Cambridge University Press.

Oniki, H. (1999) 'On the informational structure and functioning of Japanese organisations: a comparison with Western organisations', in S. Macdonald and J. Nightingale (eds), *Information and Organization: A Tribute to the Work of Don Lamberton.* Amsterdam: North-Holland. pp. 197–214.

Pandit, N., Swann, G.M.P. and Watts, T. (1997) 'HTSF marketing and customer education: a role for a technology awareness programme?', *Prometheus,* 15 (3), 293–308.

Paquet, G. (1999) 'Lamberton's road to cognitive economics', in S. Macdonald and J. Nightingale (eds), *Information and Organization: A Tribute to the Work of Don Lamberton.* Amsterdam: North-Holland. pp. 63–79.

Pelikan, P. (1969) 'Language for a limiting factor for centralization', *American Economic Review,* 59 (4): 625–31.

Perlman, M. (1981) 'Editor's note', *Journal of Economic Literature,* 19 (1): 1–4.

Preissl, B. (1997) 'Information technology: a critical perspective on its economic effects', *Prometheus,* 15 (1): 5–25.

Ramiscal, N.G. (2000) 'The nature and functions of meta-tags: covert infringement of trademarks and other issues', *Prometheus,* 18 (1): 39–57.

Ricketson, S. (1992) 'New wine into old bottles: technological change and intellectual property rights', *Prometheus,* 10 (1): 53–82.

Romer, P.M. (1986) 'Increasing returns and long-run growth', *Journal of Political Economy,* 94 (5): 1002–37.

Ryan, J.P. (1993) 'Machine translation: matching reality to expectations', in S. Nirenburg (ed.), *Progress in Machine Translation.* Amsterdam: IOS.

Samuelson, P.A. (1967) 'The monopolistic competition revolution', in R.E. Kuenne (ed.), *Monopolistic Competition Theory: Essays in Honor of Edward H. Chamberlin.* New York: Wiley. pp. 105–38.

Schement, J.R. and Curtis, T. (1995) *Tendencies and Tensions in the Information Age: The Production and Distribution of Information in the United States.* New Brunswick, NJ: Transaction.

Shackle, G.L.S. (1968) 'Policy, poetry, and success', in G.L.S. Shackle (ed.), *On the Nature of Business Success.* Liverpool: Liverpool University Press. pp. 3–18.

Shackle, G.L.S. (1972) *Epistemics and Economics: A Critique of Economic Doctrines.* Cambridge: Cambridge University Press.

Shapiro, C. and Varian, H.R. (1999) *Information Rules: A Strategic Guide to the Network Economy.* Boston: Harvard Business School Press.

Shin, I. (2000) 'Use of informational network and organizational productivity: firm-level evidence in Korea', *Economics of Innovation and New Technology,* 9 (5): 447–63.

Shubik, M. (1971), 'Information, rationality, and free choice in a future democratic society', in D.M. Lamberton (ed.), *Economics of Information and Knowledge*. Harmondsworth: Penguin.

Simon, H.A. (1991) 'Organization and markets', *Journal of Economic Perspectives*, 5 (2): 25–44.

Snow, M.S. (1998) 'Economic, statistical, and linguistic factors affecting success on the test of English as a foreign language (TOEFL)', *Information Economics and Policy*, 10 (2): 159–72.

Soete, L. (1996) 'Globalisation, employment and the knowledge-based economy', in OECD Documents, *Employment and Growth in the Knowledge-based Economy*. Paris: OECD. pp. 383–7.

Stäglin, R. (1989) 'Towards an input–output subsystem for the information sector', reprinted in D.M. Lamberton (ed.) (1996), *The Economics of Communication and Information*. Cheltenham: Elgar. pp. 114–27.

Stigler, G.J. (1961) 'The economics of information', reprinted in D.M. Lamberton (ed.) (1971), *The Economics of Information and Knowledge*. Cheltenham: Elgar. pp. 61–82.

Stiglitz, J.E. (1985) 'Information and economic analysis: a perspective', *Economic Journal*, supplement, 95: 21–41.

Stiglitz, J.E. (1994) *Whither Socialism?* Cambridge, MA: MIT Press.

Stiglitz, J.E. (1999) 'Public policy for a knowledge economy' (speeches). Available online: www.worldbank.org

Sutton, J. (1998) *Technology and Market Structure: Theory and History*. Cambridge, MA: MIT Press.

Tattersall, I. and Matternes, J.H. (2000) 'Once we were not alone', *Scientific American*, 282 (1): 38–44.

Taylor, L.D. (ed.) (1989) 'Telecommunications demand modeling', *Information Economics and Policy*, 3 (4) (special issue).

Taylor, L.D. (1994) *Telecommunications Demand in Theory and Practice*. Dordrecht: Kluwer.

Temple, P. and Williams, G. (2002) 'Infra-technology and economic performance: evidence from the United Kingdom measurement infrastructure', *Information Economics and Policy*, 14 (4): 435–52.

The Economist (2000) 'A survey of the new economy', 23 September: 1–40.

Thurow, L.C. (1983) *Dangerous Current: The State of Economics*. New York: Oxford University Press.

Todd, J. (2004) *For Good Measure: The Making of Australia's Measurement System*. Drow's Nest: Allen & Unwin.

Towse, R. (2001) *Creativity, Incentive and Reward: An Economic Analysis of Copyright and Culture in the Information Age*. Cheltenham: Elgar.

Trimble, V. (1996) 'Productivity and impact of large optical telescopes', *Scientometrics*, 36 (2): 237–46.

Tyler, M. (1999) 'Review of Lamberton (ed.), *Communication and Trade*' *Telecommunications Policy*, 23: 717–18.

Vickers, D. (1995) *The Tyranny of the Market: A Critique of Theoretical Foundations*. Ann Arbor, MI: University of Michigan Press.

Vines, D. and Stevenson, A. (1991) *Information, Strategy and Public Policy*. Oxford: Blackwell.

Vulkan, N. (1999) 'Economic implications of agent technology and e-commerce', *Economic Journal*, 109: F67–90.

Webster, E. (1999) *The Economics of Intangible Investment*. Cheltenham: Elgar.

Wildman, S.S. (1998) 'Media and multimedia: the challenge for policy and economic analysis', *Information Economics and Policy*, 10 (1): 1–7.

Wilson, M.I. and Corey, E. (eds) (2000) *Information Tectonics: Space, Place and Technology in an Electronic Age*. New York: Wiley.

19

New Media and Trade Policy

ANDERS HENTEN AND KNUD ERIK SKOUBY

This chapter is concerned with trade and industry policy aspects of information society concepts and policies. Two sets of concepts are thus the focus of attention: 'information society' and 'trade and industry policy'. Whereas information society questions are widely discussed in this *Handbook* and will not be subject to any extensive deliberation here, it should be noted that the information society concepts are seldom defined or explicitly discussed, and that this applies not only to information society visions of governments, companies, etc., but also to more academic expositions.[1] Although this is regrettable, we will not here venture into a definition exercise regarding the information society concept but use the term in the same manner as it is mostly used, as a framework or template for discussions regarding the changes in society that are related to the increasing production and usage of information and communication technologies and services.

With respect to the other concept, 'trade and industry policy', the delimitation of the area corresponds to what, for instance, the Department of Trade and Industry in the UK and the Department of Commerce in the US deal with, namely the establishment and development of favourable framework conditions for business development in both the production and distribution fields. Trade does not necessarily denote international relations.

However, in our exposé, we pay special attention to the international aspects of trade and industry policy developments as the internationalization (or globalization) of the economy increasingly is related to the opportunities offered by information and communication technologies.

Elsewhere in the *Handbook*, other aspects of information society developments are dealt with, including implications for the development of democratic procedures, access to information, etc. Some of these subjects are more or less related to the issue of trade and industry policy. They have a bearing on trade and industry developments, and trade and industry policy cannot be isolated from other policy areas. This is often reflected in information society visions of governments where trade and industry policy initiatives are seen as part of a more encompassing strategy comprising both 'harder' matters concerning economic development and 'softer' issues regarding democracy, education, universal access, etc. In this chapter, however, we seek to concentrate on matters that are at the core of trade and industry policy questions, and other matters will only be dealt with if closely related to this subject.

The chapter first discusses more thoroughly the subject matter of the trade and industry policy aspects of information society concepts and policies. After that, the academic origins of the debates on information society developments are briefly traced. This is followed by a review of trends in economics and other social science research that have keenly affected information society discussions in the political establishment. We then concentrate on the information and communication equipment and service-producing sectors themselves, and deal with internationalization aspects. A presentation is given of the main trends in the information society visions and plans that have cropped up since the beginning of the 1990s, and is followed by the summary and conclusion.

The idea and aim of the chapter are thus to review important academic trends and sources in the area of trade and industry policy aspects of information society discussions, and to relate these to the host of information society visions and policy declarations that have been issued by governments and other public authorities since the beginning of the 1990s.

A somewhat reassuring conclusion for the world of academia is that academic analyses seem to have had a visible impact on discussions among political decision-makers in this area. There is not a large gulf between academic analyses and the discussions taking place on the political scene. However, this may be an expression of a lack of sophistication on the part of the academic analyses of the societal changes related to the developments that have been dubbed 'information society', 'knowledge society' and 'network society'.

The main issue of the chapter is to examine the continued need for and existence of national trade and industry policies in the present information society settings characterized by fast technological developments in the information and communication technology fields, internationalization of the economy and a prominent position for liberal policies and ideology.

In trade and industry policies these developments have resulted in a turn away from direct forms of state interventionism towards more indirect forms of framework regulation. But they have not resulted in abolition of the need for or existence of national trade and industry policies as such. Where formerly trade and industry policies were concentrated on regulating more closed national markets and on

supporting spearhead industries internationally, the policies of today focus more broadly on situating the national economies as advantageously as possible in the international economy.

This development is reflected in the great number of information society visions and plans that public authorities all over the world have been issuing during the past decade. Although it would seem to be a paradox that a liberalization of the national economies is followed by so much state planning, the reason is exactly the increasing internationalization of the economy that sets the need for new national trade and industry policies. However, these trade and industry policies are often not very specific but consist of broader vision statements, a fundamental belief that market forces will ultimately realize the visions, and an external framework regulation of the markets.

Trade and industry policies all over the world have much that is similar, but there are, of course, also many differences: policies in Europe, for instance, to a greater extent than US policies, are stretched between wealth and welfare policies. In spite of such differences, the chapter mainly deals with policy developments in Europe as these clearly illustrate the general trend from state interventionism to external regulation.

SUBJECT MATTER

In general terms, at present, the two most important areas of interest in the discussions of information societies are information and communication technologies and services, and internationalization/globalization – according not only to the information society visions and plans of public authorities but also to more theoretical analyses. ICTs and internationalization are the recurrent themes in most discussions of the matter.

Internationalization is the subject of a separate section in this chapter, where different approaches to the analysis of the internationalization of the economy are put forward, as well as different attitudes to the desirability of this development. There are, however, analysts who claim that the importance ascribed to internationalization is exaggerated and not based on well-documented facts. This applies, for instance, to Paul Krugman (1997) who has argued sharply against tendencies to pay too much attention to the importance of internationalization for the US economy. It also applies, for example, to Paul Bairoch (1996) who has analysed indicators of the degree of internationalization over a long period stretching back to the late nineteenth century, and who shows that internationalization was as developed at the beginning of the twentieth century as it was at the beginning of the 1990s. It furthermore applies to Paul Hirst and Grahame Thompson in their book *Globalization in Question* (1996). But apart from such 'dissenting' views, there is an overwhelming focus on internationalization as an important trend in trade and industry developments today.

ICTs are, obviously, of central importance, and there are (at least) two sides to this importance. One side is related to the production of information and communication technologies and services. The other side has to do with the implications of the usage of these technologies and services in other societal connections – where the usage in other business areas is the other half of the issue in this chapter.

In a way, the focus of attention with respect to ICTs has changed, moving to and fro during the past 40 years or so. In the first period, in the 1960s and 1970s, there was a strong interest in the usage of information technologies for the purpose of automating industrial production. However, as we shall see in the following section on the origins of the discussions on information societies, there was, at the same time, an interest in information-processing occupations. In the following period, the focus of attention shifted more to the production of information and communication technologies and services. This was clearly the case in the European Community where big research programmes were launched, with first and foremost the Research in Advanced Communications in Europe (RACE) programme in the telecommunications field, demonstrating the interest in promoting the ICT sector in Europe by way of joint research initiatives.

Although this interest in promoting ICT production is still important, research interest gradually shifted back to the usage side during the 1990s. In the European Union, this shift is partly reflected in the changing focus of the telecommunications-oriented research programmes, from Advanced Communication Technologies and Services (ACTS) to Information Society Technologies (IST) today, where the title in itself illustrates both the central importance that the European Community attaches to information and communication technologies in the building of information societies, and the preferred framework and direction of information technology developments, namely their ability to support information society developments. But it is even more clearly reflected in the many information and network society vision statements by EU institutions or public authorities in individual member states.

However, lately one could claim that the centre of attention is returning to the production of information and communication products – however, this time with an emphasis on the production of services and content. There is a rising discussion concerning a new network economy, which encompasses 'old physical' production areas if they adopt the new ways of trading and interacting electronically, but mostly deals with the production of information or knowledge content and goods and services that are related to networked technologies and services.[2]

Of course, this kind of overall characterization of research and discussion themes risks suppressing other important development trends. All along there have been analyses and debates regarding both the development of information and communication technologies and services and their implications for other production fields. However, the shifts in focus between the production of ICTs and the usage of ICTs still illustrate important development trends in the discussions, especially with respect to the shift in emphasis from the production side in the 1980s towards the implication side since the 1990s. This is very clear, at present, as the implication side is very much where the discussion is today.

There are, however, two important themes to be added to the issues of internationalization and ICTs in the characterization of central questions concerning trade and industry policy aspects of information society developments. The first one is services and their increasingly dominant position in the economy. Services constitute around 60–70 per cent of national GDP and occupations in developed economies. In developing countries, the picture is more mixed. However, services in developing countries also constitute the largest share of registered production.

It is, however, far from all services that are of interest in relation to the information society theme. Most services are 'old-fashioned' person-to-person services or services dealing with physical goods as, for instance, many repair services. However, information- and knowledge-intensive services constitute a growing share of services in total, and these services can, to different degrees, be entered on electronic media and transported on communication networks. There is, therefore, a special synergy between ICTs and information-intensive services, and services do play a special role in the development of information societies. This should be and often is reflected in trade and industry policy developments.

The second theme is liberalization. Since the beginning of the 1980s, a wave of liberalization has dominated politics and ideology, not only in the US, Europe and Japan but in almost every region of the world. It has strongly affected the communication areas as the societal organization of both telecommunications and broadcasting has been changed considerably. But it has also more generally affected the whole manner in which trade and industry policies are conducted. Liberalization and its many consequences with respect to new regulatory provisions are an important part of information society programmes. Liberalization of telecommunications and broadcasting are perhaps the most important results of the whole surge towards 'information societies'.

ORIGINS

Although debates on information, knowledge or network societies are most often seen as something new, they actually go back more than 40 years and even further if, for instance, some of the discussions on the importance of knowledge and the growth of services are included. We will, however, confine ourselves to the contributions that are directly linked to the present understanding of information society developments with a bearing on trade and industry policy.

The 'information society' concept itself can be traced back to the first half of the 1960s. A group of researchers from Napier University in Scotland have done a thorough investigation in this field, discussing the different possible origins of the concept and concluding that 'the lion's share of the credit for inventing the "information society"' must be assigned to the editorial staff of the Japanese journal *Haso Asahi* which ran a number of articles with titles including the words 'information society' from 1964 onwards (Duff et al., 1996: 119).

In the US, the term 'information society' was not used until 1970 where it first appeared in the discussions of the American Society for Information Science (1996: 118). However, the origins on the content side rather than the actual words are most often ascribed to the American economist Fritz Machlup, whose work *The Production and Distribution of Knowledge in the United States* was published in 1962. But as pointed out by Duff et al. (1996: 118), Machlup's book is concerned with the 'knowledge industry', not with the 'information society'.

Nevertheless, seen from our perspective in this chapter, Machlup's book constitutes an important starting point for the development of the conception and understanding of the trade and industry implications of the development of knowledge/information societies. He developed a foundation for analyses of the 'information economy' and documented the importance of knowledge production and distribution in a society that, at that time, was conceived as an industrial society.

Later, when this development had moved much further, Machlup's work was followed by a great many other 'measurements' of the information economy. The work led by Marc Uri Porat and resulting in the publication *The Information Economy: Definition and*

Measurement (1977) was the most prominent example. While Machlup operated with a definition of knowledge production that centred on sectors producing what he saw as knowledge products, the team led by Porat included two information sectors, the primary and the secondary, where the primary sector is comprised of companies that produce information goods and services and the secondary includes all information services for internal use in public institutions and private companies. On this basis, it was concluded that, in 1967, 53 per cent of all labour income in the US could be ascribed to information work of different kinds (1977, vol. I: 8).

Another often-cited originator of information society analyses is Daniel Bell, who published *The Coming of Post-industrial Society* in 1973. Although the term 'post-industrial society' cannot unequivocally be equated with the term 'information society', this book has since been seen as the foundation for subsequent theories concerning the information society concept – even though Bell was not too confident about the concept 'information society' himself (see, for instance, Duff, 1998). In his book, Bell analyses different aspects of what is now often summarized by the term 'information society': the composition of the workforce, the importance of information and knowledge in society, and the development of computer and communication technologies – all of which are issues that are still central to the discussions on information society developments.

The last origin to be dealt with here, even though many others might deserve mentioning, is the book by Peter Drucker, *The Age of Discontinuity* (1969/1994). Even in 1969 Drucker was writing about the new 'knowledge technologies'. He also analysed what he called the development 'from international to world economy' (77–168) – a theme that is today vital in many analyses of the changing world economic conditions under the headline of 'globalization'. Last but not least, he stated that the economy could best be described as a 'knowledge economy', thus preceding the many subsequent claims for a knowledge economy by a couple of decades.

THEORIES OF INDUSTRIAL CHANGE

This section reviews trends in the theories of industrial and economic change that clearly have affected thinking on trade and industry policy among political and administrative decision-makers. It is, of course, conceivable that more popular writings, as for instance the works of Alvin Toffler (1980), John Naisbitt (1982) or Nicholas Negroponte (1995), have had a greater and more direct impact on decision-makers. However, here we concentrate on the more academic contributions.

The theoretical contributions that we have chosen are the so-called regulation school, theories on flexible specialization, and theories on changes in the technoeconomic paradigms. There are many common threads in these theories. They all focus on industrial and economic change and they all have a kind of holistic approach[3] to change, integrating different aspects of the societal complex – not just the economic aspect. In the same vein, the writings of Manuel Castells should be mentioned. His monumental work on *The Rise of the Network Society* (1996) and the two works on *The Power of Identity (The Information Age)* (1997) and *End of Millenium* (1998) constitute a holistic analysis of global developments leading to the present network and information society developments.

It could be argued, and with good reason, that by far the most influential trend in trade and industrial policy in the past 20 years has been liberalism and, with respect to economic theory, a return to neoclassical economics. This trend has had a strong impact both on theoretical thinking and on practical policies. However, we have in this section chosen to look at theories that take alternative approaches although they do not exclude the trend of liberalism (discussed later). Liberal thoughts can be incorporated and are often part of the theoretical complexes.

The *regulation school* clearly has – in its intention at any rate – a focus on the totality of societal formation. It is interested in the relationship between production, consumption and political intervention and it also examines the social struggles that lie behind the actual organization of the economy and the political sphere. The two most important concepts are 'accumulation regime' and 'mode of regulation' – where the first denotes conditions in the production sphere with an emphasis on the relations between capital and labour and capital growth, and the second deals with political organization and intervention. The interesting thing is to study how these two spheres relate to one another.

The regulation school is often called the French school of regulation, as some of the more prominent proponents are French: Michel Aglietta (1979), Alain Lipietz (1987) and Robert Boyer (1990). The regulation school clearly had its roots in a Marxist discourse on production relations, but has contributed to a much broader trend trying to explain the reasons for the economic (and political) crisis that began in the 1970s and the subsequent changes in the economic and political system. The emphasis has been on explaining how the accumulation regime and the mode of regulation were constructed in the post-World War II period, why and how this system has been breaking down, and in what direction the economic and political system is developing today.

The period from the end of World War II to the beginning of the 1970s is seen as a relatively stable period with steady economic growth. The period is called the Fordist period,[4] after Henry Ford as the paradigmatic representative of both mass production and relative welfare for workers. The Ford Corporation, when it really took off, paid higher wages to its employees than the average production site. This created a more stable labour force and also allowed for higher consumption by the employees. The paradigmatic system is thus based on a relationship and adaptation between mass production and mass consumption. The question is how such a system is created and what holds it together.

Part of the answer is that it is created in and by the social struggles between the classes and that it is held together, among other things, by the political governance of the state. There is a strong focus on the role of the state in the

theories of the regulation school – which is obvious from its name. Markets are not seen as functioning independently of the political governance system. Markets are, to a large extent, politically constructed or, at least, held together by political regulation or intervention, and the founding economic theories of the Fordist period were much inspired by the writings of John Maynard Keynes who had, *inter alia*, emphasized the importance of stabilizing demand in order to avoid the worst fluctuations of the market.

However, this system gradually broke down during the 1970s and 1980s, triggered by the so-called oil crises of the 1970s. The period that followed was called the post-Fordist epoch by the regulation school, and the main questions being what caused this dissolution and what are the bases of a new period of economic growth.

The main reason for the dissolution of the Fordist period dealt with by the theories of post-Fordism is the increasing globalization of economic, political and ideological conditions. Another important reason is that there are limits to the positive relationship between production and consumption. Higher wages do facilitate more consumption and, therefore, increased production. But higher wages also cut down on the profits of investment, and consequently means were developed to undercut the strongholds of labour, comprising direct attacks on trade unions and changes in the organization of production.

Regarding globalization, the reason that these processes are so important to the regulation school is that production (and consumption) in the Fordist system, basically, is nationally oriented. With increasing globalization, national relations between production and consumption fall apart, there is increased international competition putting pressure on social contracts between capital and labour, and the role of the state is changed. This last point has, in the general debate, often been interpreted as a diminishing role for the state. However, proponents of the regulation school have been more inclined to see it as a new role for the nation-state. In the increasingly global marketplaces, nations tend to compete for production to be located in their country, competing on establishing the most favourable conditions for investment. But this does not necessarily mean bad conditions for employees and people in general. A new role for the nation-state is to develop conditions with highly qualified labour power, efficient infrastructures, etc. This line of thought has, for instance, been taken by Robert Boyer and Daniel Drache (1996).

But what is the relevance of all this to trade and industry policy in an information society context? There is not much emphasis on the role of information or of information and communication technologies in the regulation school. However, the reason that it is interesting is the description of the post-Fordist epoch with its new, more flexible production structures, its more global production structures, and its emphasis on new roles for the nation-state: all of these issues are central in today's information society discussion.

The *flexible specialization* theory, which is the second theoretical trend to be presented here, can be interpreted as a variation of the theory of post-Fordism, which, as described, also underlines the importance of flexible work processes in the new era. However, the strength of the flexible specialization theoretical branch is that it sheds light and concentrates specifically on production structures, whereas the regulation school is more concerned with the relations between production and political regulation.

The primary proponents of the theory of flexible specialization are Michael Piore and Charles Sabel with their book *The Second Industrial Divide* (1984). But many others have followed, and there is a whole branch of analyses based on the concept of flexible specialization.

Piore and Sabel (1984) explicitly reject the explanation for the economic crises of the 1970s which proposes that state regulation limits the initiatives of entrepreneurs. They also reject the idea that the oil crises have any significant importance. None of these rejections, however, is directed against proponents of the school of regulation, as they do not see the oil crises as anything else than triggering events, and as they have focused not on the limitations that national states might have put on private

initiative, but on the changing role that the national state has had to adopt in the face of globalization. However, these rejections show that Piore and Sabel's theory of flexible specialization is focused on the inner working of production and that the reasons for the breakdown of the former system must be found in the structures of production themselves.

Piore and Sabel point at cycles of production where new uses of labour and machines are followed by periods of expansion, but which culminate in crises signalling the limits of these arrangements (1984: 4). According to the authors, there are two kinds of crises: one where the existing match between production and consumption falls apart, and the other where the type of technology chosen and the production structures around it reach their limits of expansion (1984: 4–5).

This second kind of crisis is the one that interests Piore and Sabel the most. They describe situations in which different technology paths are possible as 'industrial divides'. The first great industrial divide took place at the beginning of the nineteenth century, when the dominant mode of production chosen was mass production instead of flexible craft production. Today, we face a second industrial divide, as the mass production system has entered crisis and it is once again possible to choose a new path where craft-based flexible production methods constitute a feasible possibility.

The words 'choose/chosen' are well considered by Piore and Sabel, as they believe that there is no one 'natural' path of production structures but that production structures are social constructs. The authors propose that a structure of flexible specialization is the best 'choice' in the present situation.

The relevance of this theory for our discussion of trade and industry policy with regard to information society developments is once again the emphasis on new production structures and the possibilities in these more flexible systems. One would think that ICTs would have a prominent place in such systems as they allow for a better coordination of, for instance, networks of companies. And computer technology is also dealt with in the book, representing new and more flexible work tools instead of special-purpose machines used in the production of standardized mass production items. However, ICT is seen not as *the* vital technology in the development of flexible production structures, but as one important element among others (1984: 262).

The third and last of the theories that will be presented in this section is the so-called theory of *technoeconomic paradigms*. The most outstanding representatives of this theoretical trend are Christopher Freeman and Luc Soete (1982) and Giovanni Dosi (1984). Many of the thoughts in this theoretical trend are similar to those presented in the paragraphs on the regulation school and on flexible specialization. However, the theory of technoeconomic paradigms is characterized by a keener concentration on technology – especially technological innovation. It is, therefore, also often subsumed under the broader term 'innovation economics'.[5]

Technology has often not played any central role in economic theory, although there are some prominent exceptions: Adam Smith (partly), Karl Marx and Joseph Schumpeter. Mostly technology has been seen as an exogenous factor not to be dealt with more extensively. But in the theory of technoeconomic paradigms, technology is assigned a central role and is made the object of thorough analysis.

Four different kinds of innovation are depicted: (1) incremental innovations, which are the day-to-day improvements in existing production and marketing activities; (2) radical innovations, which are the results of more committed research and development activities which may result in wholly new products, but normally are confined to individual production sectors; (3) innovations of technological systems that are more fundamental innovations affecting a number of sectors; (4) changes in the technoeconomic paradigm, which affect the whole production system and constitute the basis for new production paradigms.

The understanding of the term 'paradigm' is borrowed from the philosopher Thomas Kuhn, whose book *The Structure of Scientific Revolutions* (1962) analysed the developments in science as structured by paradigmatic ideas changing over time. In the theory of technoeconomic paradigms this understanding is transferred to the field of production where succeeding technoeconomic paradigms are seen as based on different technologies and associated organizations of production.

The first paradigm or wave in the industrial era from 1780 to 1840 was the time of the industrial revolution. The key products were textiles and the energy systems were based on water power. A second paradigm revolved around iron and coal production and energy systems built on steam power, etc. Since the late twentieth century, a new technoeconomic paradigm has been under way, based on microelectronics and computer networks. ICTs are thus the central technologies in this new wave, illustrated by the fact that ICTs are used in practically all production areas. ICTs are the pervasive and generic technologies of our time.

Such thoughts are not entirely new as they are based on the works of Joseph Schumpeter, especially his book *Business Cycles* (1939), and before him Kondratieff (1925) and his theory of long waves in economic life. However, the proponents of the theory of technoeconomic paradigms have combined the thoughts of Schumpeter with Kuhn's theory of successive paradigms and have used these theoretical tools to examine the vital importance of ICTs today, and the many implications that these developments have on economic and social developments. There is no doubt that these thoughts have had a significant impact on the understanding of information society developments among political and administrative decision-makers.

THE ICT SECTOR

The sector comprised of information, communication and telecommunication activities, the ICT sector, has emerged as one of the most dynamic conglomerates of economic activities among industrialized countries and increasingly also among developing countries. The use of computing and communication technologies is transforming the way we produce, consume and accumulate wealth. It is generally acknowledged that a thorough restructuring is evolving and this has often been described under the headings of convergence or, at a point of time, 'new economy', indicating that economics rooted in the ICT sector is based on new relations, rules and models of accumulation. However, it is not clear to what extent something is new from a theoretical point of view. This has partly to do with the fact that ICT is a troublesome area for the analyst. The activities of the sector unfold in three distinctly different areas or dimensions:

1   as a generic technology that is applied in most economic activities;
2   as an industry producing the equipment and software support for the generic technology;
3   as a broad and fast-growing service industry using the technology, equipment and software support mentioned earlier.

It is the combined effects of the three areas that give the ICT sector its vast potential. The background is that computing was 'just' part of the array of new technologies that resulted from the war effort and formed the material basis for the Fordist boom, first in the US and then gradually in the rest of the Western world. After four shifts of generation in computing, the fifth generation unexpectedly took the form of a rapid integration of computing and communications in the 1980s (Eliasson, 1998). This again was based on two developments. One is the introduction of personal computers. The other is the breakup of the Bell/AT&T system.

During the 1980s, personal computers were steadily adopted by businesses. By 1990, they began to enter the home and the microprocessor became embedded in tools, products for the home, cars, etc. By 2005, the power of computer chips is still being doubled roughly every 18 months (Moore's law), and increasingly pervasive computing is a reality as almost everything comes with a small, cheap chip. But it is in the combination with telecommunications, related to the Internet and mobile services, that the biggest potentials are emerging.

The trajectory of telecommunications parallels the computing development but is, to a large extent, rooted in organizational/institutional developments. The breakup of AT&T

initiated in 1982 resulted immediately in heavy entrepreneurial activity in the US as companies like MCI and Sprint raced to build nationwide fibre-optic networks. But it also initiated a global liberalization drive propelled in Europe by the European Commission from 1987 onwards. The call for liberalization in Europe was really articulated by the issue of the Green Paper of 1987 that aimed to make the European telecommunication market become one market like its rivals in the US and Japan. Further, the ambition was to create a competitive market with its alleged virtues of lower prices and faster service and technology development. By 1 January 1998, telecommunication markets including infrastructure provision and telephony had opened up for competition in the majority of countries in the European Union and the European Economic Area. Telecommunication markets were liberalized, and this was further confirmed by a new 'regulatory package' (2002) aiming at harmonizing also the implementation of rules on the national markets.

Now, competition as an organizing principle may mean very different things. The most important dimension of the discussion concerns the differences between proponents of pure competition in the form of *laissez-faire*, where the market is just liberalized without any further regulation (advocated by incumbent operators), and types of regulated competition where an asymmetric regulation is established in order to open the market for new providers.

The pure competitive situation presupposes non-violation of the traditional full competition assumptions: no dominant supplier, no barriers to entry, transparent pricing, etc. None of these assumptions was initially or is today fulfilled on the telecommunication markets, with incumbent operators still having a dominant market share and controlling the delivery channels – the networks. These severe market failures call for regulation to ensure, for example, non-discriminatory access to networks, transparent pricing, etc. Hardly anyone disputes that this type of regulation is needed, and the liberalization that has been under development in the EU for the last 15 years has been liberalization in the sense that regulations aim at advancing competition. Such a liberalization of markets does not, however, in itself lead to a situation where new competitors can obtain considerable market shares and compete with the incumbent operators on an equal footing. The former national monopolies have far too dominant positions in existing markets for this to develop.[6]

Even if it seems that the liberalization of telecommunication markets has not led to anything resembling a fully competitive market, and instead of legal monopolies we now have the old incumbents as quasi-monopolies with competition at the fringes, the liberalization of telecommunications has, nevertheless, played a dominating role in ICT developments. What began as fringes open for competition outside the focus of the traditional operators has developed into some of the most dynamic areas: the Internet, international communication, mobile and value added.

The symbiotic relationship that developed between the computer and telecommunication technology sectors led to major economic growth, first in the US from the beginning of the 1990s, and a few years later in Europe as well. Generally attributed to the explosive growth of the Internet, there was traditional economic growth effects as direct job creation, and traditional side-effects as exponential growth in hardware and infrastructure companies. Building the new information infrastructure emerged as one of the great global businesses with seemingly unlimited growth potentials. But in 2000, the bubble bursted, and activity, employment and share prices fell back. Five years later, the sector is reinstalled as a growth sector – on a lower and more realistic level but again with the most dynamic immediate economic impact is related to the third part of the converging ICT sector, the content-producing communication and mass communication industry. The ICT-related media industry is growing very fast to be ready to take advantage of the network's capabilities such as interactivity and individual customization (e.g. video on demand). The Internet has consolidated its status as the likely future medium, and the old television networks are engaged in

a struggle with newcomers such as Disney and Microsoft for the dominance of digital TV. The empirical evidence of this is unfolding as mergers, fights for future markets, etc., but the field of convergence is still new as an academic discipline and the related social science research is still in its infancy. As a tendency, two points of view can be seen. One is the conventional view on convergence, in the sense that this is seen as an important driver for technological and economic development (Baldwin et al., 1996). Another point of view is more critical towards these possibilities in convergence owing to, for example, inherent differences among the traditional sectors involved with respect to technologies, organization and other structures (Garnham, 1996).

One effect of the emerging convergence, the liberalization and internationalization in the ICT areas, is that standards developments increasingly become an important issue. In a network, environment standards and interoperability are crucial. In the old regime with monopoly operators, standardization was dealt with in official or semi-official institutions such as the ITU with its subcommittees. In a market-driven environment this is no longer sufficient, and as a result standardization research is a fast-growing area that is acquiring great importance. Compatibility is a central theme and has been elaborated, for example, by Paul Allen (1995) and Stanley Besen (1995).

Statistically, the development of the ICT sector can be illustrated in different ways. As mentioned earlier, the sector is one of the most dynamic ones as the growth contribution of the sector is far greater than its share of GDP. Following the earlier discussion, the direct growth contribution from the US ICT sector during the 1990s has been estimated at about 15 per cent (OECD, 1999), whereas the total growth contribution of the sector has been estimated at 25–30 per cent (US Department of Commerce, 1999). This compares with a sector share of GDP of 8 per cent (US Department of Commerce, 1999). Furthermore, the development of the ICT sector in the emerging network economy has led to increasing productivity and competition and lower inflation. These effects are so far distinguishable especially in the US,[7] but are increasingly felt in Europe and even in developing countries. In Europe, the contribution of ICT investments to GDP generally doubled when comparing 1990–1995 with 1995–2002 (OECD, 2004). One of the strongest indirect economic effects is seen in the service industries where ICTs create the possibilities for new divisions of labour and new tendencies in internationalization. Traditionally, most services have to be consumed where and when they are produced, as they cannot be transported. Once information-intensive services are detached from human beings and stored on electronic media, they can be transferred on telecommunication lines and traded across borders. Other services also experience an increased tradability when the acts of contacting and contracting become easier with new ICTs.

The emergence of ICTs as the pervasive and generic technologies in the global economy makes it difficult today to see these technologies just 'as one important element among others' (Piore and Sabel, 1984: 262). The convergence of computing, telecommunications and mass media as a phenomenon associated with the development of ICTs has introduced 'placelessness' in production, i.e. geographical localization is becoming less important. That placelessness is gaining importance especially in the production of services has been argued from a theoretical point of view (UN, 1994) and can be observed in, for example, the development of Bangalore, where a region in a developing country has emerged as a vital partner in the international production of software. First its role was as a supplier of cheap, basic coding jobs and then increasingly it has become an innovative environment for the development of sophisticated products. This is, however, no longer a unique example. Increasingly, there is evidence that ICTs enable the participation of developing countries in the international division of labour at an advanced level. During the last few years a small but growing indigenous software industry directed towards both the home market and the international market has emerged in West Africa and is increasingly seen as a possible avenue for participation in the global information society (Wayo Seini et al., 1998).

INTERNATIONALIZATION

Alongside the development of ICTs, internationalization is often depicted as the most important fundamental feature of information society developments. But why is this, and how does the importance of internationalization manifest itself? These questions are briefly dealt with at the beginning of this section, after which the discussion concentrates on developments in theories of internationalization with special interest for trade and industry policies.

The overall importance of internationalization is related to the implications that it has for the productive structures in different countries, based on competition from producers from other countries (import and settlement), and to the new possibilities for expansion (export and settlement) and political governance: compare the discussions of the above-mentioned regulation school. This applies broadly to all industries (but not to the same extent), including the sectors that produce information and communication goods and services. On the other hand, ICTs have strong implications for the possibilities for trading and producing internationally because ICTs improve communications both between trading partners and inside transnational corporations. There is thus an affinity between questions of internationalization and questions of trade and industry policies in an information society context.

At the beginning of the chapter, the extent of the importance of internationalization was briefly discussed. Paul Krugman, Paul Bairoch, and Paul Hirst and Grahame Thompson were mentioned as examples of researchers who have advanced the view that too much emphasis can be attached to the phenomenon of internationalization. The reason for this view may be that in some expositions, if not all, far too many developments are attributed to internationalization.[8] After a good number of years spent attracting attention to the questions of internationalization,[9] it may seem to some economists that everything in public debates, apparently, can be explained by reference to the developments of internationalization and that this requires some measure of correction. Examples of writings that either favour or condemn internationalization, i.e. see it as either a great advantage or a threat, are Martin Wolf's *Why Globalization Works* (2004), Jagdish Bhagwati's *In Defence of Globalization* (2004) (benefit), Noami Klein's *No Logo* (2000) and George Monbiot's *The Age of Consent* (2003) (threat). However, in spite of such differences in view, there is general agreement that internationalization is extremely important and has vast implications, not only for trade and industry development but also for society at large.

Theories of internationalization deal with many subjects, and it is impossible to do them justice in such a short space. However, the theme can be subdivided into two categories, namely trade and foreign establishment (settlement). Most often, these two subjects are treated separately, and in this section we concentrate on the discussions that take trade as their point of departure, not because foreign establishment is uninteresting – quite the contrary – but because trade discussions constitute the classical point of departure in theories of internationalization and because most of the themes that are interesting in an information society trade and policy discussion context can be approached via the trade debates.

Classical trade theory builds on David Ricardo's *The Principles of Political Economy and Taxation* (1817/1947) where the theory of comparative advantages was first expounded. In fact, Adam Smith in his book *The Wealth of Nations* (1776/1947) had already paved the way for a theory of absolute advantages. These two trends in the theoretical work regarding trade have continued to exist ever since. They do not necessarily exclude each other, but they emphasize different aspects of the determinants of trade. The theory of comparative advantages focuses on the determinants of international specialization, while the theory of absolute advantages focuses on economic power relations between countries. The theory of comparative advantages has had a dominant position ever since Ricardo, but there have also been other trends relating to different kinds of industrial policies, e.g. concerning the protection of infant industries and for the past 20–30 years

concerning 'strategic trade policies', and even theories of absolute advantages. Also, innovation systems approaches constitute implicit criticisms of a pure comparative advantage approach.

The theory of comparative advantages clearly has some explanatory power in relation to trade between countries with different endowments. But the strongest reason for the persistence of the dominant position of this theory in international economic relations is probably that it supports the normative claim for the advantages of free trade. However, the assumptions on which the theory builds are not only very strict but in many ways highly unrealistic.[10]

In relation to our discussion, we will only mention three assumptions that are clearly unrealistic: that both product markets and factor markets are assumed to be perfectly competitive; that all factors of production are perfectly mobile within countries but immobile between countries; and that different countries enjoy equal access to the same body of technological knowledge. The first assumption applies generally in traditional neoclassical economics, but is no more realistic in international relations than in national circumstances. One of the implications is that there are production areas where economic rents (extra profit and/or extra high wages) are appropriated, and not only on a short-term basis. The second assumption regarding immobility of production factors is notoriously not true: international investment is gaining increasing importance. The third assumption concerning technical knowledge cannot be subscribed to either: this is one of the differences between countries that has a growing importance today.

The second assumption is the one that has attracted most attention in broader public discussions on international economic relations. Where internationalization formerly, to a larger extent, consisted of trade between countries, international investment and settlement in foreign countries is gaining increasing importance. The extent to which this is true can be discussed and is discussed, but international investments are important and have a growing importance. On a world political level, this is reflected in the negotiations in the World Trade Organization (WTO) where not only traditional trade questions are raised, and in the attempt by the Organization for Economic Cooperation and Development (OECD) to establish a multilateral agreement on investment (MAI). It is also reflected in the increasing internationalization of services, where modes of internationalization other than traditional trade are of central importance.

Such developments and observations have led to a discussion of whether the term 'globalization' is more appropriate than the term 'internationalization', as the word 'internationalization' in itself denotes relations between (inter) nations while globalization, ostensibly, better expresses a situation where national borders are becoming less important in economic activities. We see the advantages of the term 'globalization' if internationalization is understood as describing merely traditional trade relations between countries. However, in both trade relations and international investment, there are still large national interests and one should not underestimate the importance of nation-state initiatives. As we shall see in the following, a continued role for the nation-state in international trade and industry policies can even be envisioned and defended.

The first and third assumptions regarding the theory of comparative advantages have been widely discussed in academic work. The question is whether, or to what extent, the theory of comparative advantages is the best way to analyse the positions of strengths and weaknesses of countries in different production areas and whether, or to what extent, the proposition of free trade advantages for all can be supported. The obvious fact is that different countries have different possibilities for access to technological knowledge and technologies. Furthermore, there are clearly production areas where rent is appropriated and where, for instance, higher wages cannot be explained by labour power with higher competencies.

These facts have been analysed and crystallized in theories regarding strategic trade policies (see e.g. Paul Krugman, 1986), competitive advantages (e.g. Michael Porter, 1990), absolute advantages (e.g. Giovanni Dosi et al.,

1990) and national innovation systems (e.g. Lundvall (1992). The argument in 'strategic trade policies' is that, as some sectors produce higher rents and as technological innovations play an important role in the differences between companies and countries, one cannot rely on some automatic comparative advantage to create the best of all economic worlds. Strategic policy moves can be appropriate. The term 'competitive advantages' points in the same direction. Instead of more static comparative advantages, based on, for example, natural endowments, more dynamic competitive advantages are the foundations of the distribution of production. And, in the theory of absolute advantages, this argument is taken even further, claiming that some countries may have an overall advantage, covering almost all sectors, and that they will not move all their production into the sectors where their advantages are the best because this is not realistic, and because they are also highly competitive in the sectors where their advantages are the smallest. With ICTs, this situation is very feasible as ICTs are used in all sectors and, therefore, affect the competitiveness of all sectors in the countries that are advanced in the use of these technologies.

The conclusion of all this, in our case dealing with trade and industry policies, is that national and/or regional trade and industry policies are not becoming less relevant than they were in less internationalized phases. In a world where comparative advantages are the dominant mechanisms of distribution of production, there is not a great need for policy intervention, as wealth will automatically be optimized in all countries. However, if strategic moves are necessary and if competitive and even absolute advantages can be created, this calls for appropriate policies to be applied. However, as we shall see in the following section, it also calls for very much the same policies in all countries as they respond to similar mechanisms and priorities.

An open question in continuation of this is whether all countries really face similar situations. Do the poorer countries face issues similar to those faced by the richer countries? The degree of internationalization is, for instance, much lower in poor countries compared with rich countries. By far the largest share of international trade and international investments take place between the US, Europe and the richer countries in Asia. The whole African continent seems practically exempt from international economic relations if one examines international trade and investment on an overall scale, for example, the percentage of international trade in which African countries are involved. However, seen from the perspective of these national economies, international economic relations play an important role and most of the policy discussions follow the same lines as in the richer countries. This partly reflects a policy import from richer countries but also reflects the fact that many of the questions that poorer countries face are not fundamentally different from those faced by richer countries.

POLICY VISIONS

Following the arguments in the sections above, there is general agreement that technological, economic and political developments together constitute the drivers in an increasing internationalization of the economic system. In this relation it is, however, also interesting to analyse to what extent it is possible to conduct national/regional policies. The question is multifaceted and was initially dealt with in research during the 1990s (e.g. Hirst and Zeitlin, 1992). As an immediate empirical observation, a surprising global coordination and timing of plans and visions for the information society can be seen. In 1993 the US government published *The National Information Infrastructure: Agenda Action*; the same year, the European Commission published its White Paper, *Growth, Competitiveness and Employment*; and in 1994 the Japanese government released *Reforms toward the Intellectual Creative Society of the 21st Century*. These were followed during 1994 and 1995 by plans and strategies issued by many countries in Europe. This applies, for example, to the UK and France and to the Netherlands, Sweden and Denmark.

In other parts of the world, Singapore, South Korea, Canada and Australia published national plans during these years. And so did some developing countries in Asia, such as Malaysia, Thailand and the Philippines. Additionally, a G7 meeting in Brussels addressed the question in February 1995, and a Global Information Infrastructure Commission has been set up on the basis of a private initiative.

It is remarkable that so many countries and international institutions, at the same time, elaborate plans and programmes for the exploitation of the potentials of the emerging new information and communication technologies. Not since the construction of the railway system has a similar common international interest and enthusiasm for a technology and its possibilities been shown. Another analogy to this development comes easily to mind. As in the case of the railways, the electronic communication systems are only really useful when they are connected and developed more or less on the same level. It may be possible for a large country like the US to make some progress in ICTs alone. However, for smaller European countries, the advancement of one country very heavily depends on the advancement of other countries. The simultaneous drawing up of information society plans might be seen as an implicit understanding of this and, to a great extent, all of these strategy statements and plans build on the ideas and thoughts in the theoretical literature described earlier.

However, a closer analysis clearly reveals that these first-generation plans/visions hardly represent social planning in a strict sense, owing to two sets of assumptions. The basic problems in planning for a national information society are simply assumed away in the plans presented. The general assumptions are that the information society is emerging as a matter of fact, and attention can then be turned to the support of existing economic-political interests and problems. The second set of underlying assumptions is in reality that the market is taking care of the development of new services, technologies and structures. What seemed to be a global planning exercise was partly a demonstration of the general acceptance of the neoliberal policy vision.

Following the major reorganization of the telecommunication sector in most EU countries, the EU Commission and the member countries have, since the mid 1990s, been engaged in a second wave of information society plans. Where the first wave of plans emphasized liberalization of telecommunications and information technology development, the second wave has focused more on social aspects of information society developments.[11] This understanding is, to a large extent, well founded – especially if the first wave is seen as being represented by the Bangemann Report and the Action Plan of 1994 (European Commission, 1994). However, the shift has to be seen against a changed socioeconomic setting.

The first initiative of the European Commission in its information society planning of the 1990s was the White Paper *Growth, Competitiveness and Employment* of 1993. This was prepared by the Commission under the chairmanship of the former French Socialist Minister of Finance, Jacques Delors, and clearly bears the hallmark of a social democratic concern for job creation and equal opportunity combined with a focus on Europe's competitiveness in an increasingly internationalizing world economy. This broadly focused White Paper was followed by the Bangemann Report in 1994 on the basis of an initiative by the Council. Martin Bangemann is a former German FDP (liberal) minister, and the emphasis in the report, and the Action Plan that built on it, is much more on the issues of liberalization of telecommunications and the primacy of the private sector in the development of an information society.

In 1995, the European Commission initiated a high-level expert group (HLEG), and an Information Society Forum (ISF) was established to analyse 'the social aspects of the information society', as the HLEG (1997) puts it in its final policy report. As a justification for this focus, the HLEG wrote: 'Until that time, the debate on the emerging information society had been dominated by issues relating to the technological and infrastructure challenges and the regulatory economic environment' (1997: 14). There was, therefore, a perceived need for refocusing on the social dimensions

of the 'European model' in line with the White Paper (HLEG, 1997: 17). This trend was further pursued in *eEurope – An Information Society for All* (Commission of the European Communities, 2002) – a plan adopted by the European Council in 2000 and updated in 2002.

The development in EU information society policy can thus be seen as having changed from a technology- and market-oriented focus to a broader social concern. One of the reasons for this priority is clearly that the development of the basic infrastructure through the liberalization of telecommunication has developed in a satisfactory way – seen from the point of view of the Commission. But even if other issues in other contexts may be given priority, the second-generation visions clearly cover a broader area than the first-generation visions. This has not, however, changed the clear neoliberal basis for the visions – a feature that is almost universal even in the present emerging plans/visions from former planned economies in developing countries, where Ghana's vision 'Ghana 2020' can be mentioned as a specific example.

SUMMARY AND CONCLUSION

The most conspicuous developments that have taken place through the last two to three decades with respect to trade and industry policy trends in an information society context can be summarized in the following way. On the technological side, information and communication technologies and services have developed and expanded vastly, and the processes of digitalization have allowed for new technological possibilities to be explored, among them a beginning convergence between formerly separate information and communication sectors. On the economic side, economies have internationalized to an increasing degree, and especially the growing internationalization of production processes (epitomized in the term 'globalization') and the beginning internationalization of services is seen as important. On the political (and ideological) side, liberalism has changed the political climate considerably and has had a clear impact on the societal organization of, for example, electronic communication areas. And other important development trends and features could be mentioned, such as the ever increasing importance of services in the economies, the growth in information processing occupations, the role of information and knowledge in society, new and more flexible work processes and organizations, and changes in the role of national states.

These developments are reflected in economic and social science research and have greatly impacted on the trade and industrial policies implemented by public authorities. With respect to economic and social science theories with influence on information society visions of public authorities, at least four different trends (or areas of research) deserve mentioning here.

The first is concerned with the liberalization of the different communication sectors. Two of these sectors, telecommunications and broadcasting, were formerly in state monopoly or very strictly regulated. However, over the past 20 years this has changed, which clearly has been reflected in economic and social science research where a great deal of work has been done regarding the implications of liberalization.

The second research area is concerned with trends in the internationalization/globalization processes in the economic (and other) sphere(s). This area of research can hardly be drawn together in just one or a few trends. Many different processes are examined, though there is a dominant interest in international investment and the globalization of production structures.

The third deals with evolutionary (and revolutionary) developments in the economy and the importance of technological change. The theories examined in this chapter, to a large extent, are part of these areas of interest – although they also touch upon internationalization and state regulation. It is a broad category encompassing research interested in the technology side of production (innovation economics) and the evolutionary processes in the economy (evolutionary economics).

The fourth theoretical trend is interested in institutional aspects of the economy. This trend has not explicitly been dealt with in this chapter, but plays an important role in the discussions concerning flexible production and the importance and implications of electronic communications in production and distribution.

The influence of these theoretical trends on the discussions and decisions taken at a broader societal level, e.g. among decision-makers on the political scene, has been discussed in the course of this chapter and the evaluation expressed has been that there clearly is a connection between the academic world and the world of economic and political decisions in this area. However, a modification of this evaluation could be made. As much as it is a question of academic research influencing political discussions, one could claim that both 'worlds' have been under the influence of the significant changes that have taken place during the past two to three decades. Still, the overall evaluation is that discussions and concepts that have been crystallized in academic research have had a relatively strong influence on broader political debates and decisions in this area.

In a sense, it is strange that, since the beginning of the 1990s, there has been a surge of information and network society visions and plans issued by public authorities. Often, one of the common understandings is that with the many changes in the economic and political systems, state planning is *passé*. However, there has probably never been so much political planning as has been witnessed in relation to all the information society vision statements in the last decade.

But the content of these plans has changed considerably compared with former political interventions. This change has often been described as a turn away from direct state interventionism towards an emphasis on the creation of framework conditions for economic activity. This development can, for instance, be seen in telecommunications where direct control via ownership of operators is relinquished and indirect regulation is implemented.

The background for this development is multifaceted. However, the development towards framework regulation fits in well with the increasing internationalization where public authorities aim at creating the best possible framework conditions for businesses in an international competitive environment; note, for example, the discussions of the regulation school on the changes in the role of the state.

Analyses show that the trade and industry policies relevant to the information society, implemented in the different countries, are to a large extent similar. The reason is partly that policy directions in one country inspire other countries – and for the poorer countries also there is external pressure from transnational corporations, richer countries and international organizations. However, it is also a result of the competition to become a prime site for production of different kinds in the international divisions of labour. Dynamic competitive advantages are increasingly important compared with more static comparative advantages. This has led to internationalization not only of production but also of trade and industry policies.

There are, nevertheless, differences in the policies. This applies, to some extent, to the priority given to the combination of 'harder' trade and industry policy measures and 'softer' areas like culture, education, etc., although most information/ network society visions today include such areas. But more fundamentally, it applies to the perspective in which trade and industry policies are seen. In Europe, there is a tendency to consider the creation of wealth and welfare as two aspects that should not be separated. In the US, there is a focus on wealth creation, and welfare is considered a byproduct. This is, of course, partly a reflection of the fact that social democratic governments dominate the European Union at present. But it is also a more basic difference, based on the differences in positions of strength of the social classes in the various areas.

NOTES

1 However, in this volume Frank Webster's contribution discusses the information society concepts, which are more comprehensively examined in Webster (1995).

2 Shapiro and Varian (1999) can be seen as an example of such an emphasis on information and knowledge content and networked communication goods and services.

3 This is the expression used by Webster (1995) when examining the regulation school.

4 With inspiration from the writings of Antonio Gramsci (1971).

5 Basic works in the tradition of innovation economics are Rosenberg (1982) and Nelson and Winter (1982).

6 A vast amount of research has been done in the field of telecommunication liberalization and regulation. For a comprehensive overview, see Melody (1997).

7 The US Department of Commerce (1999) has estimated a general lowering of the rate of inflation of 0.7 per cent in the 1990s.

8 This is the line of argumentation in, for example, Krugman (1997).

9 In the case of Krugman, see, for instance, Krugman (1986, 1990).

10 For a discussion of the assumptions underlying the theory of comparative advantages, see e.g. Grimwade (1989).

11 This is, for instance, the understanding of the Commission itself: see European Commission (1996), which is presented as 'an updated and revised Action Plan in order to launch a second phase of the EU information society strategy'.

REFERENCES

Aglietta, Michel (1979) A *Theory of Capitalist Regulation*. London: New Left Books.

Allen, Paul (1995) 'Standardization policies for network technologies', in Richard Hawkins, Robin Mansek and Jim Skea (eds), *Standards, Innovation and Competitiveness*. Cheltenham: Elgar.

Bairoch, Paul (1996) 'Globalization myths and realities', in Robert Boyer and Daniel Drache (eds), *States against Markets*. London: Routledge. pp. 173–92.

Baldwin, Thomas, McVoy, Stevens and Steinfield, Charles (1996) *Convergence: Integrating Media, Information and Communication Systems*. London: Sage.

Beck, Ulrich (2000) *What is Globalization?* Oxford: Blackwell.

Bell, Daniel (1973) *The Coming of Post-industrial Society*. New York: Basic.

Besen, Stanley (1995) 'The standard processes in telecommunication and information technology', in Richard Hawkins et al. (eds), *Standards, Innovation and Competitiveness*. Cheltenham: Elgar.

Bhagwati, J. (2004) *In Defence of Globalization*. Oxford: Oxford University Press.

Boyer, Robert (1990) *The Regulation School: A Critical Introduction*. New York: Columbia University Press.

Boyer, Robert and Drache, Daniel (eds) (1996) *States against Markets*. London: Routledge.

Castells, Manuel (1996) *The Rise of the Network Society*. Oxford: Blackwell.

Castells, Manuel (1997) *The Power of Identity*. Malden, MA; Oxford: Blackwell.

Commission of the European Communities (2002) *eEurope 2005: An Information Society for All*, COM(2002) 263 final. Brussels: CEC.

Dosi, Giovanni (1984) *Technical Change and Industrial Transformation*. London: Macmillan.

Dosi, Giovanni, Pavitt, Keith and Soete, Luc (1990) *The Economics of Technical Change and International Trade*. Brighton: Harvester-Wheatsheaf.

Drucker, Peter (1969/1994) *The Age of Discontinuity*. New Brunswick, NJ: Transaction.

Duff, Alistair (1998) 'Daniel Bell's theory of the information society', *Journal of Information Science*, 24 (6): 373–93.

Duff, Alistair, Craig, David and McNeill, David (1996) 'A note on the origins of the "information society"', *Journal of Information Science*, 22 (2): 117–22.

Eliasson, G. (1998) *The Macroeconomic Effects of the Computer and Communications Technology*. Stockholm: KTH.

European Commission (1994) *Europe's Way to the Information Society: An Action Plan*. COM(94) 347. Brussels: EC.

European Commission (1996) *Europe at the Forefront of the Global Information Society: Rolling Action Plan*. COM(96)607. Brussels: EC.

Freeman, Christopher and Soete, Luc (1982) *The Economics of Industrial Innovation*. London: Pinter.

Garnham, Nicholas (1996) 'Constraints on multimedia convergence', in William Dutton (ed.), *Information and Communication Technologies: Visions and Realities*. Oxford: Oxford University Press. pp. 103–19.

Giddens, Anthony (1999) *How Globalization Is Reshaping Our Lives*. London: Profile Books.

Gramsci, Antonio (1971) 'Americanism and Fordism', in A. Gramsci, *Selections from the Prison Notebooks*. London: Lawrence & Wishart.

Grimwade, Nigel (1989) *International Trade: New Patterns of Trade*. London: Routledge.

Hardt, Michael and Negri, Antonio (2001) *Empire*. Cambridge, MA: Harvard University Press.

Hirst, Paul and Thompson, Grahame (1996) *Globalization in Question*. Cambridge: Polity.

Hirst, Paul and Zeitlin, Jonathan (1992) 'The problem of "globalisation"', *Economy and Society*, 21 (4): 357–96.

HLEG (1997) *Building the European Information Society for Us All*. DG V. Brussels: European Commission.

Klein, Noami (2000) *No Logo: No Space, No Choice, No Jobs*. London: Flamingo.

Kondratieff, N. (1925) 'The long wave in economic life', *Review of Economic Statistics*, 17: 105–15.

Krugman, Paul (ed.) (1986) *Strategic Trade Policy and the New Internnational Economics*. Cambridge, MA: MIT Press.

Krugman, Paul (1990) *Rethinking International Trade*. Cambridge, MA: MIT Press.

Krugman, Paul (1997) *Pop Internationalism*. Cambridge, MA: MIT Press.

Kuhn, Thomas (1962) *The Structure of Scientific Revolutions*. Chicago: Chicago University Press.

Lipietz, Alain (1987) *Mirages and Miracles: The Crisis of Global Fordism*. London: Verso.

Lundvall, Bengt-Åke (1992) *National Systems of Innovation: Towards a Theory of Innovation and Interactive Learning*. London: Pinter.

Machlup, Fritz (1962) *The Production and Distribution of Knowledge in the United States*. Princeton, NJ: Princeton University Press.

Martin, H.-P. and Schumann, H. (1996) *Die Globaliserungsfalle: Der Angriff auf Demokratie und Wohlstand*. Reinbek: Rowohlt.

May, Christopher (2000) *The Information Society: A Sceptical View*. Cambridge: Polity Press.

Melody, William (1997) *Telecom Reform: Principles, Policies and Regulatory Practices*. Lyngby: Technical University of Denmark.

Monbiot, George (2003) *The Age of Consent: A Manifesto for a New World Order*. London: HarperCollins.

Naisbitt, John (1982) *Megatrends: Ten New Directions Transforming Our Lives*. New York: Warner.

Negroponte, Nicholas (1995) *Being Digital*. New York: Knopf.

Nelson, R.R. and Winter, S.G. (1982) *An Evolutionary Theory of Economic Change*. Cambridge, MA: Harvard University Press.

OECD (1999) *The Economic and Social Impact of Electronic Commerce*. Paris: OECD.

OECD (2004) *OECD ICT Key Indicators*. Paris: OECD.

Ohmae, K. (1990) *The Borderless World*. New York: Harper.

Piore, Michael and Sabel, Charles (1984) *The Second Industrial Divide: Possibilities for Prosperity*. New York: Basic.

Porat, Marc Uri (1977) *The Information Economy: Definition and Measurement*. Washington, DC: US Department of Commerce.

Porter, Michael (1990) *Competitive Advantages of Nations*. London: Macmillan.

Ricardo, David (1817/1947) *The Principles of Political Economy and Taxation*. London: Dent.

Rosenberg, Nathan (1982) *Inside the Black Box: Technology and Economy*. Cambridge: Cambridge University Press.

Schumpeter, Joseph (1939) *Business Cycles: A Theoretical, Historical and Statistical Analysis of the Capitalist Process*. New York: McGraw-Hill.

Shapiro, Carl and Varian, Hal (1999) *Information Rules: A Strategic Guide to the Network Economy*. Cambridge, MA: Harvard Business School Press.

Smith, Adam (1776/1947) *The Wealth of Nations*. London: Dent.

Stiglitz, Joseph (2002) *Globalization and Its Discontents*. London: Penguin.

Toffler, Alvin (1980) *The Third Wave*. London: Collins.

UN (1994) *The Tradability of Banking Services*. ST/CTC/168. Geneva: United Nations.

US Department of Commerce (1999) *The Emerging Digital Economy*. Washington, DC: USDC.

Wayo Seini, A., Abdulai, M.-S. and Kwadwo Asenso-Okyere, W. (1998) *Telematics Usage for Ghana's Development*. A report prepared for the Ghana National Committee for Internet Connectivity (GNCIC). Available online: http:// www.bellanet. org/partners/aisi/nici/ghana/ghanaa

Webster, Frank (1995) *Theories of the Information Society*. London: Routledge.

Wolf, M. (2004) *Why Globalization Works*. New Haven: Yale University Press.

20

The Governance of Media Markets

BELLA MODY, HARRY M. TREBING
AND LAURA STEIN

In *Telecommunications Politics* (1995), Mody and collaborators wrote about the forces and factors that influenced the deregulation and privatization of telecommunication in developing countries, home to two-thirds of the world's population. We focused on the role of intergovernmental organizations like the World Bank, foreign capital, the nation-state and domestic capital. We traced the influences of these forces through national case studies. We warned that privatization alone would not achieve competition, and we urged that state–market relations be conceptualized as adaptive rather than opposed. The real question should be the nature of state intervention rather than how much.

Market-opening telecommunication deregulation has been championed on a global and national scale by growth-oriented industry and governments of the US, Japan and the UK since the 1980s. At the beginning of the twenty-first century, after two decades of promoting deregulation for competition, the tendency seems to be towards an industry characterized by tight oligopoly (defined as four leading firms together controlling 60–100 per cent of the market). The US formula for competition for global prosperity included three essential steps: (1) mandatory unbundling of local networks; (2) establishment of prices for network access and interconnection that do not inhibit competition; and

(3) auctioning the frequency spectrum to promote wireless communication that can compete with wireline networks. Although there has been successful action in some of these areas in some nations, highly competitive networks have not emerged across the board, and industry concentration and/or tight oligopoly are becoming more and more evident on a national and global basis. Strictly economy-focused governance of liberalization that ignores social formations and political constituencies is rootless and insensitive to local conditions. We need a new architecture for the governance of new media markets that is based on consensus building, freely chosen international collaborations, and respect for the unique conditions in individual societies. In a world increasingly connected by the media, new and old, we cannot do media analysis that is single disciplinary, sectoral, technological or economic alone.

Five economic factors alone raise serious questions about the type of deregulated market structures that are evolving. First, there are substantial network economics inherent in the provision of telecommunications services. These lead to high concentration, which, in turn, creates a potential for exercising market and political power that can negate the effects of selective entry through open access. This is especially important when coupled with vertical integration into downstream markets and common ownership of wireline and wireless plant.

Second, unbundling network components for new entrants will not overcome the obstacles confronting such entrants when dealing with an incumbent network providing widespread rebundled retail services. If the new entrant cannot match the wide range of offerings by the incumbent, then it will be confined to niche markets. Niche market rivalry is not a surrogate for workable competition, nor is niche market competition a sufficient constraint on the profits or pricing practices of the incumbent. Where the new entrant is large and has substantial market power, as in the case of new entry by the regional Bell holding companies into long-distance telecommunications markets, there will be a strong incentive for the inter-exchange carrier and the entrant to engage in bilateral oligopoly negotiations that will jeopardize neither the profits nor the discretionary behaviour of either player.

Third, the scope and capital intensity of comprehensive networks create a strong pressure to assure a stream of revenues sufficient to support a capital structure that is heavily weighted by debt capital. This financial burden creates incentives for market differentiation, price leadership and interdependent action. This serves as a further inducement for oligopoly behaviour.

Fourth, the prospects for developing generally accepted 'neutral' pricing guidelines for access appear to be remote. Incumbent telephone companies want high access charges covering profits forgone from not serving retail markets, a contribution to overhead costs, and the incremental cost of interconnection. Entrants want low access charges covering little more than bare-bones incremental costs. The outlook for a swift and straightforward reconciliation by national regulators is far from promising.

Fifth, successful rationing of the frequency spectrum to promote competition depends on the market structure in which auctioning takes place. In a tight oligopoly, the firm has an incentive to buy and withhold the spectrum in anticipation of high prices and profits at a later date, especially if this is necessary to secure a

place in a market where future success is dependent on being a major full service provider capable of offering bundled wireline and wireless services. With few restrictions on licensees, oligopolists would be free to exploit such strategies to maximize advantage.

Why worry about oligopoly in telecommunication? Is it not superior to regulated private monopoly or to inefficient public monopolies? The rhetoric promoting market openings did not include the adverse consequences of tight oligopolies that are not amenable to light regulation through price caps, incentive allowances and open access. The first adverse consequence is the strong incentive for oligopolies to engage in an aggressive programme of mergers, acquisitions and various forms of collaborative behaviour such as alliances and joint ventures. Second, prices will no longer track costs. There will be strong incentives to engage in price discrimination and cross-subsidization between markets, to grant price concessions to large buyers, and to resort to patterns of price leadership to stabilize revenues wherever possible. Third, cost savings will not be distributed to final customer classes in a manner that is commensurate with their role in making such savings possible. Fourth, profit levels will be higher over time than those that would be expected to prevail under effective competition. This has been demonstrated in economies like New Zealand where privatization/deregulation programmes have been put in place. Fifth, network technology will be driven by the requirements of the largest users (multinational corporations) at the expense of a universal network designed to serve all classes. Sixth, network denigration and service deterioration are distinct possibilities under tight oligopoly and light regulation. The firm will have a strong incentive to redeploy assets based on profitability expectations. This can result in an incentive to underprovide quality service in many residual markets. Finally, tight oligopoly provides an excellent opportunity to promote new centres of economic and political power. Success in creating a centre of power in telecommunications will depend upon achieving three important goals; (1) the creation of an optimal mix of basic services and new growth-oriented services; (2) the capture of all inherent network economies and technological advances involved in providing these services; and (3) an ability to fully exploit the demand and supply characteristics of differentiated markets in a fashion that will foreclose or circumscribe new entry while maintaining high levels of economic profits. Tight oligopolists will also have the advantage of possessing resources sufficient to shape public policies to achieve these goals.[1]

The rhetoric for competition has not resulted in competitive market structures, and advances in technology have not provided suitable solutions to these problems. Indeed, high levels of market concentration have persisted as the telecommunications industry has evolved from analogue to digital and then to Internet protocol technology. At the same time, regulatory attempts to address these problems through the promotion of competitive access have failed to create market structures that can be described as competitive (5–6 independent firms of equal size with no significant barriers to entry or exit).[2] A reform of the regulatory process is needed to deal with tight oligopoly through a system of monitoring corporate concentration, together with new innovative programmes that negate the adverse consequences of oligopoly in pricing, investment and marketing (Trebing, 2004). We should expect nothing less from regulatory agencies who are supposed to be custodians of the public interest.

Disappointment with the nation-state as the supposedly public interested service provider, and the availability of eager, willing and able foreign firms looking for new markets has led to intergovernmental agreements on equal treatment of all carriers and sources of capital. Service providers are protecting themselves from competition through mergers and alliances, layoffs (Yoo and Mody, 2000), the introduction of new technologies, and diversification into content provision. Firms are seeking to differentiate themselves on the features of their products and services rather than on price.

What is the status of telecommunication policy and regulation around the world? The lack of symmetry in regulation between content provision and carriage is being questioned

as technological development blurs market boundaries. With broadband technology and increased use of data, mobile and leased lines over voice services, pricing regulation and rebalancing local and long-distance rates is now an issue. Some combinations of regulatory assurance of interconnectivity and determination of rates with industry-based access undertakings have emerged in many countries. Some nations have no explicit policies to promote innovation in the information and communication service industries while many others have used government procurement incentives, research and development programmes and taxation incentives. The Internet as innovation came from innovators free from network control; some worry that the AOL–Time-Warner merger will allow cable to control broadband access and compromise the promise of the Internet. National market stimulation policies have been limited to expanding the use of existing technologies through education and public access via telecentres, schools and libraries. Novel applications to meet unmet citizen needs are few and far between, e.g. graphic interfaces for illiterate users interested in information on employment opportunities for unskilled workers. National universal service policies have been premised on social equity more often than on human rights and economic development issues. New policy and regulatory approaches are needed to balance efficiency, distribution and fairness goals. National policy, regulatory measures and their impacts reflect the distinct social and economic conditions in which telecommunication infrastructure is embedded. These range from application of general competition, trade practices law and consumer protection across sectors, to the creation of an industry-specific regulator, to regulation separated from service provision, to maintenance of the traditional organization of service provision and regulation within the same government agency. Competition in the Danish telecommunication market has come further than competition in the EU countries in general partly because of sector-specific regulation. The Finnish conception of economic and electronic equity differs from that of the

US; thus Finland has the world's highest PC
penetration and Internet usage rates. For 80 per
cent of the world's population who live on
20 per cent of the world's income, (about
4.8 million people) arguably, e-equity should
be at least as important as e-commerce.

REGULATION AND REGULABILITY
OF NEW MEDIA

Whether government regulation of new media
is desirable or possible is a point of contention
in both popular and academic discourse.[3]
Many view these media as natural agents of
economic, cultural and political progress. This
viewpoint, described variously as technological determinism, technological utopianism or
technological optimism, holds that new technologies possess inherent characteristics that
naturally tend toward beneficial outcomes.
While some view these characteristics as so
intractable as to override attempts at regulation altogether, others argue simply that new
technologies should be allowed, whenever
possible, to develop free from government or
market regulation.[4] With regards to computer
networks, examples of such thinking can be
found in the works of Cate (1995) and Labunski
(1997), who argue that the openness of
computer networks, the presence of multiple
Internet service providers (ISPs), and the capacity of these networks to carry large amounts
of data, guarantee that individual rights are
well protected in the absence of government
regulation. Similarly, Johnson and Post (1997)
hold that the ability of global communication
systems to traverse national borders undermines the ability of nations to regulate them
and negates the benefits of global commerce
for those countries who attempt to do so.
Others, such as Samorski et al. (1997: 155–6)
and Froomkin (1997), hold that the decentralized nature of the Internet, the volume of data
it carries, and the ability of users to communicate anonymously, render government regulation of the network too costly and inefficient.
These scholars draw a causal connection
between the apparent characteristics of new

technologies and political, economic and
social betterment.

Sceptics of network regulability also point
out that government regulation can be circum-
vented in a number of ways. Users can configure their network connections to appear to
reside somewhere else or make use of remailers
which allow anonymous and untraceable communication (Johnson and Post, 1997: 9). In
1993, Canadian citizens used an anonymous
remailer to establish a Usenet group that carried foreign news coverage of an ongoing high-
profile criminal trial which under Canadian
law could not be covered by the national press
(Froomkin, 1997: 146–7). Government regulation can also be thwarted by the existence of
countries, such as Anguilla, Bermuda and the
aspiring 'Sealand', willing to act as data havens
for the transmission and storage of communication that other countries designate as illegal
(Garfinkel, 2000: 232; Gellman, 1997: 267;
Mayer-Schönberger and Foster, 1997: 241).
Finally, network users in regions that enforce
significant content restrictions, such as China,
the Middle East and North Africa, can access
Internet service providers in foreign countries
(Human Rights Watch, 1999: 27; Taubman,
1998: 266), or use proxy servers which act as
gateways into otherwise censored websites
(Human Rights Watch, 1999: 27).

Others reject the characterization of computer networks as inherently unregulable and
uniformly beneficial. They argue for a more
nuanced view of the relationship between
technology and social outcomes, one which
evaluates technology within the context of
larger political, economic and social forces,
and which acknowledges the malleability of
allegedly innate characteristics. For example,
scholars working in the tradition of critical
political economy, such as Bettig (1997: 138),
McChesney (1996: 99), Mosco (1989: 25) and
Schiller (1999: 37), argue that computer networks are tools for the extension of a global
market system which seeks to commodify and
control information and its uses. From this
perspective, new technologies are more likely
to facilitate repressive political and economic
relations than to transform them. In this view,
the potential for computer networks to further

positive values, like political participation and equality, can only be achieved by protecting public principles and practices that are not served by the marketplace.

In addition, several historians and theorists of technology highlight the socially constructed nature of technology and its uses. These scholars argue that technology is not an independent artifact, with an inherent or instrumental logic, that inevitably will be developed and deployed in socially efficient and rational ways (Fischer, 1992: 12; Slack, 1984: 59). Rather, technology embodies and reflects the complex social systems within which it is produced and developed. Individual technologies may favour certain uses, but the uses to which technologies ultimately are put cannot be surmised solely by examining their characteristics. For example, Sassen (1998) maintains that the relationship between computer networks and global economic and social processes can be best observed by examining the concrete sites in which that relationship materializes. For Sassen, the information infrastructures implemented in global cities, such as New York, London, Tokyo, Paris, Frankfurt, Zurich, Amsterdam, Sydney, Hong Kong, Buenos Aires, Taipei, Bombay and Mexico City, among others, are useful sites for analyses.

Further, the presumption that communication technology alone can bring about political or social change is communicentric and technocentric (Slack, 1984: 144). The development and use of specific technologies are the result not of the artifact itself, but of social struggles and negotiations among numerous parties, including investors, competitors, customers and government agents (Castells, 1996: 5; Fischer, 1992: 18; McOmber, 1999). While it may be somewhat reductive, for the purpose of theoretical differentiation, we will call those who reject the position that technology has an inevitable trajectory apart from larger social forces 'technological constructivists'.

From a technological constructivist perspective, what appear to be the technological *characteristics* of a medium at any given moment are actually a subset of that medium's technological *capabilities*. Thus, within certain parameters, computer networks can be structured

to serve different interests and values, to enable or disrupt various political, economic and cultural practices, and to permit different degrees of regulation. The particular set of capabilities that come to the fore in any given technology is an outcome of a complex interplay between a technology and the political, economic and social context in which its capabilities are embedded. This argument is well developed by Lessig (1999: 89), who points out that all computer code, or the human-made software and hardware that structure the environment of computer networks, necessarily constrains or enables different behaviours. Code formalizes such choices as whether data are collected, whether anonymity is possible, who is granted access, and what speech can be heard (1999: 217). Government intervention can shape code by mandating that certain choices be made in the deployment of computer networks. Code can also be shaped and conditioned by private commercial interests who seek to control and exploit information and communication.

Lessig attributes the current freedom of the Internet to its open and non-proprietary protocols that do not condition access on the personal identification of users. He notes, however, that closed, private networks can be layered on top of this otherwise open architecture. These private networks can control access by demanding that all users be authorized, by conditioning access to data on users' credentials, and by monitoring the nature of the data being transmitted. Numerous tools for verifying the identity of Internet users are already in use, including passwords, cookie files placed on users' hard disks by browsers, and digital signatures or certificates that authenticate information about users or their machines (1999: 34–5). Both government and commerce have strong incentives to design more control into the system, and the malleability of the technology makes it possible for them to do so.[5] Lessig (1999: 57, 2001) further notes that a second-generation Internet, with an architecture even more conducive to regulation, would allow governments and commerce effective control over users, even if some opportunities for regulatory circumvention prevent absolute control.

Technological constructivism suggests that technology and its uses are shaped by human agents. Since technology has no inevitable outcomes, citizens and their governments are not consigned to the role of passive observers of technological development. Moreover, while technological determinism rejects the notion that public policy might help determine the social uses of new technologies, technological constructivism posits an affirmative role for communication policies which are based on empirical investigations into the social contexts surrounding specific technologies (Carey, 1988; Fischer, 1992; Slack, 1984). From this perspective, public policy is a necessary and desirable response to the social choices that inevitably accompany the introduction of new technologies. Once we accept the notion that technology is inscribed with social choices and values, the question of whether technology can or will be regulated is rendered irrelevant. The real questions are, rather, which values and interests will technology be designed to serve, and whether those values will be defined publicly or privately, nationally or globally.

New global media are the impetus for a reconsideration of law and policy across many areas of information and communication practice. Nations around the world must decide how to respond to the social conflicts engendered by these media, whether that response is to let market forces resolve these issues or to reassert the role of government in defining and enforcing public service values. As Castells (1996: 7) points out, governments can either frustrate the development of technologies or accelerate their development and change the pace of national modernization and economic development. We are at a formative moment in the development of new global media. As many scholars note, policy decisions that are taken now can help shape the long-term infrastructures, institutions, goals, values and outcomes of global information and communication technologies (Carey, 1998: 34; Klopfenstein, 1998: 35; McChesney, 1996: 100; Melody, 1990: 31, 33; Neuman et al., 1993: 77–8).

While governments may have an important role to play in the development of national policies that determine the trajectory of the growth and development of ICT, there is considerable disagreement among scholars about what determines the ability of states to effectively formulate national policies. Typically, studies of national policy-making have been conducted at one of three major analytical levels: at the level of the international system, at the level of the state itself and at the level of civil society (Krasner, 1976; Singer, 1961; Waltz, 1979). These levels are differentiated in terms of the assumptions about the influence of factors operating at the domestic and/or international level on state behaviour (Cafruny, 1995).

For 'internationalist' approaches, the state is considered to act more or less independently of domestic social forces. The explanation is sought primarily at the international systemic level and in terms of the imperatives of a given configuration of the international system (Bousquet, 1980; Chase-Dunn, 1998; Frank, 1969; Gilpin, 1987; Krasner, 1991; Wallerstein, 1980). National communication policies are considered outcomes of, at one extreme, the 'globalization' of new media and interactive communication technologies and, on the other, the manifestations of new forms of cultural imperialism and economic domination by a handful of developed economies. For 'civil society' approaches the state is conceptualized as subordinate to the dominant economic forces in societies, and the struggle among competing economic forces and interest groups is the primary causal variable that explains state actions and behaviour (Jessop, 1989; Miliband, 1968; Poulantzas, 1969, 1973, 1976, 1978). Here national communication policies represent the interests of dominant economic formations, typically manifested in the growing concentration of media ownership and content in capitalist economies (Herman and Chomsky, 1988; Schiller, 1985). In contrast to the internationalist and civil society approaches, state-centred theorists argue that the state is a collection of institutions with a unique centrality in both national and international formations (Evans et al., 1985; Mann, 1983; Nordlinger, 1981; Skocpol, 1977). The state is a force in its own right and does not simply reflect the dynamics of either civil society or the international system. National communication policies, from this perspective, are to be considered as exemplars of state action to promote and protect national goals and objectives (Hamelink, 1983; Katz, 1988; Noll, 1986; Petrazzini, 1993; Sinha, 1995; Tehranian et al., 1977).

A number of scholars have offered theoretical and empirical accounts of national policy-making that identify the continuities between social forces and the changing nature of the state and global relations. These scholars reject the assumption of the causal primacy of the international system and the corollary assumption of the analytical separation of state and society (Almond, 1988; Cafruny, 1995; Cox, 1986; Palan, 1992; Schmitter, 1985). From this perspective, national communication policies are the outcome of the complex interplay of forces operating within the international arena, the state and civil society (McAnany and Wilkinson, 1996; McDowell, 1994; Sinclair, 1996; Sinha, 1994, 1998). This type of analytical approach may be the most promising for examining issues relating to national policy-making in new media and interactive communication technologies.

We know a lot about *market* fundamentals. The International Labour Organization advocates also looking at the fundamentals in *people's lives*. Economic and social policies are not dichotomous. Telecommunication policies are made by men and women; they can be changed to go beyond the theoretical fundamentalism of foreign dictates and be integrated with a nation's need to eradicate poverty and social exclusion, and to create jobs. First and foremost, we must establish national and international principles to ensure that information and communication technologies are designed to serve collectively defined political, economic and social goals.

NOTES

1 In both the US and Canada, the large regional Bell holding companies (RBHCs) and the incumbent provincial telecommunications carriers (such as Bell Canada and Telus) not only have established themselves as tight oligopolies, but also appear to be emerging as new centres of power. The RBHCs have diversified into all phases of telecommunications, going beyond the provision of local wireline telephone service to include long-distance, wireless service, broadband service, voice over Internet protocol, high-speed data and video service (Trebing, 2004). They have also significantly constrained public-sector provision of telecommunications services by securing passage of laws in 11 states that specifically forbid municipal utilities from providing telecommunications services. Tight oligopoly also prevails in wireless markets at the national level, where three RBHCs, through their wireless affiliates, now serve almost 70 per cent of all US wireless customers. In Canada, the incumbent provincial carriers dominate the entire wireline market, large business long-distance service, wholesale long-distance data and private line service, and international service. Concurrently, the wireless (mobile) market remains a tight oligopoly, with Bell Canada, Telus and Rogers Wireless holding approximately equal shares of that market. In addition, Bell Canada (BCE Inc.) provides direct broadcast satellite service and commercial television, and has a major investment in the *Globe and Mail* newspaper (CRTC, 2004; Trebing, 2004).

2 The Telecommunications Act of 1996 was designed in part to introduce pervasive competition at the local exchange level in the US. This would be accomplished by compelling local exchange carriers, especially RBHCs, to lease or supply local hoops, switches and transport to competitive entrants to enable them to reach final customers. To accomplish this goal, the FCC introduced unbundled network elements incorporated into platforms designated as UNE-Ps which were to be sold at prices based on total element long run incremental cost. In March 2004, the US Court of appeals of the District of Columbia remanded the FCC's Triennial Review Order dealing with access issues for revision. In December 2004, the FCC drastically reduced its access requirements imposed on the RBHCs and other incumbent local exchange carriers. Switching would no longer be a UNE and access to high capacity fibre would be severely restricted or eliminated. Only local subloop copper would have to be leased but the new entrant would have difficulty getting access to this element. These revisions essentially left matters of access and access pricing to bilateral negotiations between a potential entrant and an incumbent carrier. Given the asymmetric distribution of power favoring the incumbent, the outcome of such a process is clear. Public policy makers would now appear to be placing primary reliance on new technology to constrain market dominance. Undoubtedly, the FCC's permissive merger policy is designed to facilitate new technologies which would presumably sweep away existing market power and promote innovation and change. This argument ignores the ability of centres of power to incorporate new technology within their ambit of control.

Mention should also be made of the efforts of AT&T to bypass the local exchange by employing a different technology. AT&T spent $100 billion to acquire cable properties to reach the final customer. But this effort failed and AT&T had to sell these properties to Comcast at a significant loss. Subsequently, AT&T has suffered 16 quarters of declining revenues and its credit rating was reduced to junk status in 2004.

3 We use the term 'regulation' to refer generally to rules that govern, control or direct behaviour to desired ends. Agents of regulation may include governments, the marketplace, the self and others. The term 'government regulation' refers more specifically to government action designed in theory to control or direct behaviour in order to achieve goals deemed socially desirable (Rogerson and Thomas, 1998: 430). 'Regulability' refers to the capability of certain behaviours or practices to be regulated (Lessig, 1999: 14).

4 For the latter view, see Litan and Niskanen (1998). De Sola Pool (1983: 5) terms those who believe that government and other institutional forces can alter the otherwise benevolent course of technology 'soft technological determinists'.

5 Governments could use identification tools to verify attributes about computer users, such as age or place of residence, and determine whether their laws apply to that user. Different government jurisdictions would have an incentive to cooperate with one another to ensure that their laws are applied to their citizens when they engage in activities outside their jurisdiction (Lessig, 1999: 55–6). Commerce, for its part, favours user identification in order to engage in secure and safe transactions (1999: 39).

REFERENCES

Almond, G. (1988) 'The return to the state', *American Political Science Review*, 82 (3): 853–74.

Bettig, Ronald V. (1997) 'The enclosure of cyberspace', *Critical Studies in Mass Communication*, 14: 138–57.

Bousquet, N. (1980) 'From hegemony to competition: cycles of the core', in Terence Hopkins and Immanuel Wallerstein (eds), *Processes of the World System: Political Economy of the World System Annuals*. Beverly Hills: Sage. pp. 46–83.

Cafruny, A. (1995) 'Class, state, and world systems: the transformation of international maritime relations', *Review of International Political Economy*, 2 (2): 283–314.

Canadian Radio-television and Telecommunications Commission [CRTC] (2004) 'Report to the Governor in Council: status of competition in Canadian telecommunications markets', November.

Carey, James W. (1988) *Communication as Culture: Essays on Media and Society*. Boston: Unwin Hyman.

Carey, James W. (1998) 'The Internet and the end of the national communication system: uncertain predictions of an uncertain future', *Journalism and Mass Communication Quarterly*, 75 (1): 23–34.

Castells, Manuel (1996) *The Rise of the Network Society*. Malden, MA: Blackwell.

Cate, Fred H. (1995) 'The First Amendment and the national information infrastructure', *Wake Forest Law Review*, 30 (1): 1–50.

Chase-Dunn, Christopher (1998) *Global Formation: Structures of the World Economy*. Oxford: Blackwell.

Cox, R.W. (1986) 'Social forces, states and world orders: beyond international relations theory', in Robert Keohane (ed.), *Neorealism and Its Critics*. New York: Columbia University Press. pp. 204–54.

Evans, P., Rueschmayer, D. and Skocpol, T. (eds) (1985) *Bringing the State Back In*. Cambridge: Cambridge University Press.

Fischer, Claude S. (1992) *America Calling: A Social History of the Telephone to 1940*. Berkeley, CA: University of California Press.

Frank, André Gundar (1969) *The Development of Underdevelopment*. New York: Monthly Review Press.

Froomkin, A. Michael (1997) 'The Internet as a source of regulatory arbitrage', in Brian Kahin and Charles Nesson (eds), *Borders in Cyberspace: Information Policy and the Global Information Infrastructure*. Cambridge, MA: MIT Press. pp. 129–63.

Garfinkel, Simson (2000) 'Welcome to Sealand. Now bugger off', 8(7), July: *Wired*, 230–9.

Gellman, Robert (1997) 'Conflict and overlap in privacy regulation: national, international, and private', in Brian Kahin and Charles Nesson (eds), *Borders in Cyberspace: Information Policy and the Global Information Infrastructure*. Cambridge, MA: MIT Press. pp. 255–82.

Gilpin, R. (1987) *The Political Economy of International Relations*. Princeton, NJ: Princeton University Press.

Hamelink, Cees (1983) *Cultural Autonomy in Global Communications: Planning National Information Policy*. New York: Longman.

Herman, Edward S. and Chomsky, Noam (1988) *Manufacturing Consent*. New York: Pantheon.

Human Rights Watch (1999) *The Internet in the Mideast and North Africa: Free Expression and Censorship*. New York: Human Rights Watch.

Jessop, P. (1989) 'Capitalism, nation-states and surveillance', in David Held and John Thompson (eds), *Social Theory of Modern Societies: Anthony Giddens and his Critics*. Cambridge: Cambridge University Press. pp. 103–28.

Johnson, David R. and Post, David G. (1997) 'The rise of law on the global network', in Brian Kahin and Charles Nesson (eds), *Borders in Cyberspace: Information Policy and the Global Information*

Infrastructure. Cambridge, MA: MIT Press. pp. 3–47.

Katz, R. (1988) *The Information Society: An International Perspective.* Cambridge, MA: Harvard University Press.

Klopfenstein, Bruce C. (1998) 'Internet economics: an annotated bibliography', *Journal of Media Economics*, 11 (1): 3–48.

Krasner, S. (1976) 'State power and the structure of international trade', *World Politics*, 28: 317–47.

Krasner, S. (1991) 'Global communications and national power: life on the Pareto frontier', *World Politics*, 47 (3), April: 336–66.

Labunski, Richard (1997) 'The First Amendment at the crossroads: free expression and new media technology', *Communication Law and Policy*, 2 (2): 165–212.

Lessig, Lawrence (1999) *Code and Other Laws of Cyberspace.* New York: Basic.

Lessig, Lawrence (2001) *The Future of Ideas: The Fate of the Commons in a Connected World.* New York: Random House.

Litan, Robert E. and Niskanen, William A. (1998) *Going Digital!* Washington, DC: Brookings Institution Press and Cato Institute.

Mann, M. (1983) 'The autonomous power of the state', *Archives européenes de sociologie*, 25 (2): 185–213.

Mayer-Schönberger, Viktor and Foster, Teree E. (1997) 'A regulatory web: free speech and the global information infrastructure', in Brian Kahin and Charles Nesson (eds), *Borders in Cyberspace: Information Policy and the Global Information Infrastructure.* Cambridge, MA: MIT Press. pp. 235–54.

McAnany, Emile and Wilkinson, Karin (eds) (1996) *Mass Media and Free Trade: NAFTA and the Cultural Industries.* Austin, TX: University of Texas Press.

McChesney, Robert W. (1996) 'The Internet and U.S. communication policy-making in historical and critical perspective', *Journal of Communication*, 46 (1): 98–124.

McDowell, S. (1994) 'India, the LDCs and GATT negotiations on trade and investment services', in R. Stubbs and G. Underhill (eds), *Political Economy and the Changing Global Order.* New York: St Martin's Press. pp. 497–510.

McOmber, James B. (1999) 'Technological autonomy and three definitions of technology', *Journal of Communication*, 49 (3): 137–53.

Melody, William H. (1990) 'Communication policy in the global information economy: whither the public interest?', in Marjorie Ferguson (ed.), *Public Communication: The New Imperatives.* Newbury Park, CA: Sage. pp. 16–39.

Miliband, R. (1968) *The State in Capitalist Society.* London: Weidenfeld & Nicolson.

Mody, Bella, Bauer, Johannes, M. and Straubhaar, Joseph D. (eds) (1995) *Telecommunications Politics: Ownership and Control of the Information Highway in Developing Countries.* Mahwah, NJ: Erlbaum.

Mosco, Vincent (1989) *The Pay-per Society: Computers and Communication in the Information Age.* Norwood, NJ: Ablex.

Neuman, W. Russell, McKnight, Lee and Solomon, Richard Jay (1993) 'The politics of a paradigm shift: telecommunications regulation and the communication revolution', *Political Communication*, 10 (1): 77–94.

Noll, R. (1986) 'The political and institutional context of communications policy', in M. Snow (ed.), *Market-place for Telecommunications.* New York: Longman. pp. 42–65.

Nordlinger, E. (1981) *On the Autonomy of the Democratic State.* New Haven, CT: Yale University Press.

Palan, R. (1992) 'The second structuralist theories of international relations: a research note', *International Studies Notes*, 17 (3): 32–56.

Petrazzini, B. (1993) 'The politics of telecommunications reform in developing countries', *Pacific Telecommunications Review*, March: 4–23.

Pool, Ithiel de Sola (1983) *Technologies of Freedom.* Cambridge, MA: Harvard University Press.

Poulantzas, N. (1969) 'The problem of the capitalist state', *New Left Review*, 58: 67–78.

Poulantzas, N. (1973) *Political Power and Social Classes.* London: New Left Books.

Poulantzas, N. (1976) *Crisis of the Dictatorships.* London: New Left Review.

Poulantzas, N. (1978) *State, Power, Socialism.* London: New Left Books.

Rogerson, Kenneth S. and Thomas, G. Dale (1998) 'Internet regulation process model: the effect of societies, communities, and governments', *Political Communication*, 15 (4): 427–44.

Samorski, Jan H., Huffman, John L. and Trauth, Denise M. (1997) 'The v-chip and cyber cops: technology vs. regulation', *Communication Law and Policy*, 2 (1): 143–64.

Sassen, Saskia (1998) *Globalization and Its Discontents.* New York: New Press.

Schiller, Dan (1999) *Digital Capitalism: Networking the Global Market System.* Cambridge, MA: MIT Press.

Schiller, Herbert, I. (1985) *Information and the Crisis Economy.* Norwood, NJ: Ablex.

Schmitter, P. (1985) 'Neocorporatism and the state', in Wyn Grant (ed.), *The Political Economy of Corporatism*. New York: St Martin's Press. pp. 32–62.

Sinclair, John (1996) 'Culture and trade: some theoretical and practical considerations', in Emile McAnany and Karin Wilkinson (eds), *Mass Media and Free Trade: NAFTA and the Cultural Industries*. Austin, TX: University of Texas Press. pp. 30–60.

Singer, J. (1961) 'The level of analysis problem in international relations', in K. Knorr and S. Verba (eds), *The International System: Theoretical Essays*. Princeton, NJ: Princeton University Press. pp. 77–92.

Sinha, Nikhil (1994) 'Information technology, economic development and technological unemployment in developing countries', *Revue Tiers Monde*, April–June: 411–24.

Sinha, Nikhil (1995) 'Telecommunications regulatory reform in the Third World: an institutional perspective', in Bella Mody, Joseph Straubhaar and Johannes Bauer (eds), *Telecommunications Politics: Ownership and Control of the Information Highway in Developing Countries*. New York: Erlbaum. pp. 297–308.

Sinha, Nikhil (1998) 'Telecommunications reforms and the changing role of the state in India'. Paper presented at the 48th Annual Conference of the International Communication Association, Jerusalem, 20–24 July.

Skocpol, T. (1977) 'Wallerstein's world capitalist system: a theoretical and historical critique', *American Journal of Sociology*, 82: 1075–89.

Slack, Jennifer D. (1984) *Communication Technologies and Society: Conceptions of Causality and the Politics of Technological Intervention*. Norwood, NJ: Ablex.

Taubman, Geoffrey (1998) 'A not-so World Wide Web: the Internet, China, and the challenges to nondemocratic rule', *Political Communication*, 15 (2): 255–72.

Tehranian, Majid, Hakimzadeh, Farhad and Vidale, Marcello (1977) *Communications Policy for National Development: A Comparative Perspective*. London: Routledge & Kegan Paul.

Trebing, Harry M. (2004) 'Assessing deregulation: the clash between promise and reality', *Journal of Economic Issues*, 38 (1), March: 1–27.

Wallerstein, Immanuel (1980) *The Modern World System*. New York: Academic.

Waltz, K. (1979) *Theory of International Politics*. Reading, MA: Addison-Wesley.

Yoo, H. and Mody, B. (2000) 'Predictors of downsizing in the US local telephone industry', *The Information Society*, 16 (1): 23–33.

21

New Global Media and the Role of the State

LAURA STEIN AND NIKHIL SINHA

Global information and communication technologies (ICTs) could precipitate extraordinary political, cultural and economic transformations over the twenty-first century. Carey (1998: 28) predicts that global communication systems such as the Internet will alter physical and symbolic environments worldwide just as the telegraph, telephones and railroads altered national and international landscapes throughout the nineteenth and early twentieth centuries. While most scholars agree that global media can facilitate change on a global scale, they differ sharply over the nature of these changes. Will these new media facilitate freedom of expression and access to knowledge and information, or will they deepen and intensify the control and commodification of information on a national and transnational scale? What values and principles will global communication systems serve and what role can or should national governments play in determining the structure and use of these media?

Indeed, regulation of information and communication systems is critical to nation-states for several reasons. First, communication systems are central to political processes. Democracies and non-democracies alike recognize the role of communication systems in conveying information to their citizens.

Democracies depend on communication systems to generate the social knowledge necessary to collective decision-making processes (Barber, 1984: 197; Dewey, 1954: 155; Entman, 1989; Enzensberger, 1974; Rucinski, 1991) and to ensure citizens' communication rights (Melody, 1990: 19; Zhao, 2000: 43). At the same time, global media and interactions have worldwide effects that are in the interests of all nations to regulate. Yet, the mechanisms for representing, discussing, evaluating and collectively responding to these phenomena among affected populations are insufficient or lacking altogether. In this sense, global ICTs, as well as globalization generally, create a crisis of representation for political institutions and processes worldwide (Carey, 1998: 34). Second, ICTs are enmeshed in the social and cultural fabric of nations. Information and communication are part of the shared national symbolic environment, as well as the environment of other social or communal formations (Babe, 1995: 40). Consequently, many nations are concerned with how ICTs may impact their social and cultural life. For example, many nations fear that the availability of obscene, racist or blasphemous speech on the Internet will have a corrupting influence on their societies. A third and related reason why effective regulation of global media has relevance to nation-states is the ultimate inseparability of real and virtual spaces. Although global ICTs host virtual transborder activities, virtual activities are experienced by real citizens rooted in real places. As such, nation-states have an interest in regulating these activities (Lessig, 1999: 190). Research which insists that virtual activities exist in 'cyberspace', rather than in real space, reifies network activity and prematurely dismisses the power and jurisdiction of nation-states to regulate it.[1]

This chapter addresses some of the challenges faced by nation-states in devising communication policies for the new global ICTs. Since a comprehensive discussion of global ICT policy would be too vast and unwieldy, we focus exclusively on computer networks, a prominent and growing sector of ICTs that have a potentially global reach. Computer networks are sets of computers that are linked at physical and logical levels (Schiller, 1999: xv). Computer networks, including the Internet, constitute new media in that they enable the convergence of formerly separate media forms onto a common delivery platform (Melody, 1990: 16; Schiller, 1999: 74). Drawing on aspects of other media, including print, audio, video and voice-based communications, computer networks allow for the creation of new media forms with new characteristics. These networks, along with the practices and policies that surround them, offer a vantage point from which to view the challenges new media pose to national regulators.

We begin by examining three key areas of legal and policy conflict over computer networks; namely, intellectual property, privacy and freedom of expression. Legal and regulatory trends and developments in these areas reveal how new technologies are destabilizing existing policy regimes and demanding a rethinking of communication policy on the part of national governments. The chapter concludes by examining some policy principles and new models of regulation proposed by scholars to adapt national governance mechanisms for the effective regulation of global media. The discussion recognizes that national policies are the outcome of a complex

interplay of domestic and international forces. The nature and character of the state, the strengths of its institutional framework and its relationship to domestic and international forces will largely determine the form and content of such policies.

THREE AREAS OF POLICY DEVELOPMENT: INTELLECTUAL PROPERTY, PRIVACY AND FREEDOM OF EXPRESSION

Global computer networks raise challenging questions for law and policy on intellectual property, privacy and freedom of expression. A comprehensive analysis of these questions is beyond the scope of this chapter. Nevertheless, a broad sketch of central policy dilemmas in each of these areas, as well as the options open to national regulators, can situate otherwise abstract policy discussions in concrete social conflicts and choices facing many nations. Not only are many social conflicts around computer networks clustered around these key areas of policy development but, perhaps more importantly, law and policy in these areas shape the contours of the public use and exchange of information and communication. Though law and policy in each of these areas is in a state of flux worldwide, it is possible to discern patterns and trends that constitute the roots of policy dilemmas which are likely to play themselves out over the next couple of decades.

As they currently exist, computer networks possess a number of features that represent uncharted territory for governments wishing to implement and enforce policy and regulation. These features include the ability of computer networks to collect, store, process and retrieve vast quantities of information (Branscomb, 1994: 3; *The Economist*, 1999: 21; Johnson, 1994; OECD, 1997: 13; Peterson, 1995: 164); to copy information quickly and easily (Alleyne, 1995: 140; Halbert, 1999: 26); to allow direct and interactive communication between individuals and small groups (Morris and Ogan, 1996: 44); to bypass governmental and non-governmental media gatekeepers (Human

Rights Watch, 1999: 12; Taubman, 1998: 261); to send information along decentralized and unpredictable pathways (Froomkin, 1997: 131; Lessig, 1999: 166); to allow network users to communicate anonymously (Froomkin, 1997: 129; Lessig, 1999: 14); and to permit interactions between persons located in different legal and political jurisdictions (Kahin and Nesson, 1997: x; Lessig, 1999: 192; Reidenberg, 1997: 86; Robinson, 1989: 44). These features have considerable impact on the abilities of governments to regulate and enforce policies applying to computer networks.

Conflicts in the areas of intellectual property and privacy have arisen largely because of the increasing commodification of information. Information has become a valuable asset, and the ability of governments, organizations and individuals to monitor, control and trade information requires laws and policies that clearly delineate the property rights of all actors in the information exchange process. In the absence of comprehensive supranational property rights regimes, the role of defining property rights within networked environments necessarily falls upon national governments. In the case of freedom of expression, tensions have arisen because governments themselves have implemented laws or policies designed to protect national political and normative goals, often to the detriment of the speech rights of their own citizenry or in conflict with the speech rights regimes of other nations. The next three sections examine these conflicts, the ways governments are attempting to address them, and the options available for them to do so.

Intellectual Property

Computer networks intensify the conflict, ever-present in intellectual property law, between expression as a commodity and as a collective good. Intellectual property law grants copyright holders exclusive rights to control copying and other uses of creative works *for a limited period of time*. In this sense, intellectual property is not analogous to material property. Intellectual property law presumes that creativity

is encouraged when copyright holders can benefit financially from their labour, but that the exclusive control of these works eventually becomes a detriment to society (Bettig, 1992: 149; Lessig, 2001). Ultimately, the collective good requires that information, knowledge and creative expression become freely and widely accessible to all. The collective good aspect of intellectual property is also captured in the notion of fair use. Fair use permits non-copyright holders to copy works for the purpose of comment, criticism and other activities which are understood to further the advancement of knowledge. By creating new opportunities both to control information and expression and to evade that control, computer networks invite challenges to both the copyright holder's right to control their work and the public's right to access this work.

Computer network technology can facilitate the extension of copyright controls or the free exchange of information and communication. Scholars are split on whether computer networks will underprotect or overprotect intellectual property. Many scholars note that computer networks enable non-copyright holders to engage in the widespread duplication and dissemination of copyrighted material. The ease with which computer networks permit such activities works to undermine copyright holders' control over intellectual property products (Thurow, 1997: 98–9). This underprotection of property rights results in a loss of domestic and international profits; a decline in the research, development and creation of new products; and a reluctance to engage in global trade among nations that export information-based products and services (Alleyne, 1995: 140; Jussawalla, 1992: 3, 43–4). Those who worry that new technology will underprotect copyrights focus on the need to develop law, policy and new technologies that promote the rights of intellectual property holders on computer networks (Thurow, 1997).

Others argue that computer technology may increase copyright holder control over intellectual property and override collective fair use principles for the sake of private profits (Halbert, 1999; Hunter and Herbeck, 1999; Lessig, 2001). Copyright holders can use software to track and control the uses of a creative work, including how many times a work is viewed and how it can be altered or manipulated. Such software effectively allows copyright holders to disaggregate and charge for every aspect of information use (Halbert, 1999: 128; Lessig, 1999: 136). Copyright holders can also make access to creative works contingent upon private contracts, such as click-wrap or shrink-wrap agreements, which consumers tacitly accept when they view online information or open a software product package. These 'agreements' specify the terms and conditions of access and often demand that consumers relinquish their rights to fair use and collective good protections associated with intellectual property law (Feemster, 2000; Halbert, 1999: 62; Lessig, 1999: 135). In addition, copyright holders can limit the circulation of creative works online to trusted systems that agree to abide by their terms and conditions and that interact exclusively with other systems that agree to do so (Lessig, 1999: 129). Those who believe that computer technology will overprotect copyright argue that new developments in intellectual property law or practice must maintain the public's rights to access ideas.

Global computer networks, and the growing global trade in intellectual property goods, are also sites of tension between developed and developing countries. While there are no 'international copyrights' that enable individuals to protect work throughout the world, most countries are members of the Berne Union for the Protection of Literary and Artistic Property (Berne Convention) and the Universal Copyright Convention, which allow producers of intellectual property to protect their works in countries of which they are not a citizen or national.[2] Fearing information piracy on a global scale, developed nations argue that strong enforcement of intellectual property rights and internationally harmonized legal regimes are necessary to facilitate a global trade in information products (Burk, 1997: 221; Jussawalla, 1992: 4; OECD, 1997: 11–12; White House, 1997: 12). Nations with strong intellectual property regimes have exerted political and economic pressure, often in the form of international treaties and agreements, on countries that fail to enforce copyright (Alleyne, 1995: 34, 133; Bettig, 1997: 150;

Boyle, 1997: 121–3; Burk, 1997: 221; Halbert, 1999: 77). For example, bilateral trade agreements have enabled the US to enact copyright laws in Singapore, Malaysia, Indonesia and South Korea (Jussawalla, 1992: 67). The World Intellectual Property Organization has strengthened the international intellectual property rights regime (May, 1998: 256), and the US succeeded in pushing through strong protections for intellectual property in the Trade Related Intellectual Property (TRIPS) agreement under the auspices of the World Trade Organization (Goldstein, 1994: 195; May, 1998: 256; Sell, 1995). The TRIPS agreement requires member states to comply with certain standards of protection for copyright, trademarks, industrial designs and patents. (Jackson, 1998: 473).

Yet many developing countries are reluctant to uphold intellectual property laws or agreements that make access to information more costly, impede technology transfer and increase the monopoly power of multinational corporations (Alleyne, 1995: 133; Jussawalla, 1992: 39–40, 58). Countries who view intellectual creativity as a collective rather than an individual creation, who themselves hold few copyrights, or who seek to further national and economic development through the cheap and widespread dissemination of intellectual products, see little reason to enforce restrictive copyright laws (Alleyne, 1995: 124; Burk, 1997: 213; Halbert, 1999: 78). However, many developing countries find themselves in a dilemma. While less stringent enforcement of international intellectual property regimes may provide developing countries with greater access to information resources from the more advanced industrial economies, the same rules may allow multinational corporations to extract and exploit economic and commercial information about national industrial and agricultural resources within developing counties. As Thurow (1997: 100, 103) notes, rather than conform to the intellectual property regimes of developed countries, developing countries should ensure that any copyright regime they adopt addresses their particular needs.

As we have earlier stated, computer networks can be used to alter the balance that different countries have achieved between information as a commodity and as a social good. Tensions over intellectual property law both within and between countries revolve largely around where to draw the line between information control and the free flow of information. As trade in online information, products and services grows, copyright holders seek out ways to charge for every use of information, to prevent unauthorized uses, and to assert and extend their ownership over information, ideas and artifacts (Bettig, 1997: 140, 147; Halbert, 1999: 49; Mosco, 1989). Such behaviour is in keeping with the logic of the marketplace and constitutes a modern enclosure movement (similar to that of the enclosure of public lands in England during the first half of the nineteenth century) in which ideas and information are being converted from common goods into private property (Bettig, 1997: 138; Lessig, 2001; Thurow, 1997: 101). The more cultural artifacts and assets are privately controlled and monopolized, the fewer opportunities the public has to participate in the iterative creation and re-creation of social and cultural life (Bettig, 1992: 152; Halbert, 1999: 147). While the commercialization of computer networks and information may be inevitable, as Abrahamson (1998: 14) argues, many fear that unchecked commercialization and commodification will impede information's widespread distribution and the social benefits that come from sharing information (Besser, 1999; Halbert, 1999; Thurow, 1997: 101). From this perspective, too much control over information discourages creativity, commentary and criticism. On an international level, excessive control over intellectual property inhibits the free flow of information between developed and developing countries and leads to a loss in social and economic welfare (Jussawalla, 1992: 86, 110–11). As private parties reach to extend copyright protections locally and globally, societies must ask themselves at what point information control and ownership exceed adequate incentives and rewards for the creation and trade of intellectual artifacts and begin to harm the collective good.

Precisely where to strike this balance is a matter of both law and policy. Governments must decide the extent to which copyright will be protected on computer networks and which rights will be upheld against the technology's ability to negate them. Many nations have been quick to devise laws and legislation that bolster intellectual property protections for copyright holders and strengthen the global trade in information (Bettig, 1997: 150; Halbert, 1999: 37, 43–4). Law and policy will also decide the extent to which the collective good aspects of copyright and the copy duties of copyright holders will be reconfigured by private computer code, business practices and contract law. Governments must also consider whether, and under what conditions, information and knowledge should be publicly available and accessible (Branscomb, 1994: 3; Demac, 1994: 63; Lessig, 1999; Thurow, 1997: 103) and to what extent they will adhere to international agreements, like the TRIPS, in their struggle to access and disseminate global information while protecting potentially valuable local intellectual and information resources. The ability of governments to effectively address these issues varies widely and, as we shall discuss later, is dependent on a variety of international and domestic factors not all of which are subject to governmental control.

Privacy

The ability of computers to collect, search and exchange data feeds a growing market for personal information and harbours the potential to erode personal privacy. Personal information can be collected any time someone writes a cheque, uses a credit or debit card, engages in a financial transaction, views World Wide Web pages, or does anything else that generates a data trail (*The Economist*, 1999; Peterson, 1995: 167), and it includes names, telephone numbers, marital status, education level, job history, credit history, medical records, and any other information that can be linked to specific persons or data subjects (Branscomb, 1994: 4). Often, individuals have little choice but to reveal this information, which is collected without their consent or knowledge, or is a byproduct of a sale or service transaction

(1994: 4; Gandy, 1993: 78, 82; Peterson, 1995: 164). Furthermore, personal information can become the basis for decisions made about an individual by others, such as whether someone is offered a job, targeted for government surveillance or eligible for medical insurance (Branscomb, 1994: 4). As Gandy (1993: 83–4) notes, personal information derives its market value from the signals it gives organizations about the desirability of forming relationships with individuals as consumers, employees or political agents.

The growing trade in personal information has many nations concerned about the privacy rights of their citizens. Though conceptions of privacy vary from country to country, privacy is frequently linked to the rights of individuals to enjoy autonomy, to be left alone, and to determine whether and how information about one's self is revealed to others (Branscomb, 1994: 28; Johnson, 1994: 225; Peterson, 1995: 171; Westin, 1967: 7). A useful definition of privacy is provided by Westin: 'privacy is the claim of individuals, groups and institutions to determine for themselves, when, how and to what extent information about them is communicated to others' (1967: 158). A central privacy concern of many nations, and one which we will focus on here, involves the ability of individuals to access and control how their personal information is used by others (Gellman, 1997: 278; Global Internet Liberty Campaign, 1998: 1; Peterson, 1995: 164). As computer networks provoke more and more privacy conflicts between information subjects and information users, the question of who controls personal information takes on increasing importance. Surveillance of individuals by businesses and governments, the dissemination of personal data across national borders, and the use of information for purposes other than that for which it was originally collected, as well as other uses and abuses of personal information, are prodding many governments to rethink their privacy policies. Governments must determine whether privacy policies are necessary to limit the collection and use of personal information by both governmental and private parties, and, if such policies are necessary, how best to formulate them.

Opponents of government regulation of privacy argue that privacy rights are bad for commerce, technologically unenforceable, and antithetical to free speech. This view, typified by an issue of *The Economist* (1999) focusing on privacy, holds that privacy rights impede the free flow of information by putting constraints on the trafficking of personal information and that the inability to control technology makes the decline of privacy as a value inevitable. The ability of privacy rights to inhibit unfettered trade in personal information is also seen as interfering with free speech, though Peterson (1995: 173) points out that the equation of free trade with free speech comes primarily from businesses who sell personal information and marketing firms who use it to sell products. For many opponents of government privacy regulations, voluntary self-regulation on the part of industries and organizations who control personal information is the best means of addressing privacy concerns. From this perspective, personal information belongs to those who collect it (Branscomb, 1994: 13), and ownership confers the right to determine how it is used. On this view, the only way for governments to balance privacy concerns against free speech and the free flow of information is to allow private companies to self-regulate (Cochran, 1996).

Proponents of stronger privacy regulation argue that privacy is a social value that governments must affirmatively protect. In their view, personal information is a type of asset or property that is rightly controlled by the person who generates it, rather than those who collect it (Branscomb, 1994; Gandy, 1993; Lessig, 1999: 156; Westin, 1967). Indeed, those who collect this information surreptitiously or without fair compensation can be seen as engaging in a type of theft (Gandy, 1993: 82). According to Peterson (1995: 186) and Branscomb (1994: 30), the taking of this asset warrants some form of compensation. However, while Branscomb (1994: 28) believes that responsible companies could offer consumers sufficient incentives to release their personal information, Gandy (1993: 91) maintains that fair or equitable compensation is impossible because individuals have no way of estimating the true value of their information. From this perspective, industry self-regulation is an inadequate means of protecting privacy rights. Self-regulation generates conflicting and complex rules among different industries and sectors that increase the costs of business compliance and that undermine consumer confidence (Green et al., 2000). Public service-oriented government regulation, on the other hand, allows for consistent privacy policies that facilitate the flow of legitimately traded information, bolster electronic commerce and protect human rights (Araki, 1989: 193; Global Internet Liberty Campaign, 1998; Green et al., 2000; OECD, 1997: 15, 18).

The privacy policies of the United States and the European Union (EU) draw on the two approaches to privacy rights outlined above and illustrate two contrasting ways in which governments can respond to privacy concerns. In its 1995 Data Protection Directive, the EU explicitly affirms the right to privacy of EU citizens, and defines a comprehensive set of principles and provisions that adhere to that right. The Directive accords specific rights and responsibilities to data subjects and data processors, protects data subjects' rights to control the collection and use of personal information by both governments and private companies, and harmonizes data protection rules among member countries. Among its many provisions, the Directive requires that companies or agencies wanting to process personal information first gain the unambiguous consent of the data subject.[3] Since data subjects must 'opt into' personal data transactions by granting their free and informed consent, the burden of initiating this process falls on the would-be information processor, and non-consenting data subjects are spared the task of tracking and halting objectionable uses of their information (Peterson, 1995: 180). Another provision, perhaps the most controversial in the Directive, prevents personal data from being exported to countries that do not provide comparable levels of protection. Some view this rule as an impediment to the development of electronic commerce in EU countries and to trade with outside countries, such as the United States, which lack significant

privacy protections (Mitchener, 2000: 32; *The Economist*, 1999: 23). At the very least, the Directive creates pressure on countries who want to trade with European Union members to develop comparable data protection rules (Global Internet Liberty Campaign, 1998).

Unlike the European Union's comprehensive approach to data protection, the United States' approach is characterized by fragmentation. No comprehensive federal privacy policy exists. Instead, the US employs a mixture of narrowly targeted federal legislation, state law and industry self-regulation to address privacy concerns. Federal legislation has focused on specific problems related to particular industries, technologies or types of data. Furthermore, while federal legislation places restraints on how the government can use or process information, these rules do not apply to private organizations who collect information (Branscomb, 1994: 17).[4] Several state constitutions protect information privacy, but these provisions apply only to the public sector (Peterson, 1995: 165). For the most part, the US administration advocates private sector self-regulation and marketplace solutions as the best means to address concerns over personal information (White House, 1997: 19). Among US businesses, the preferred method of privacy protection is to permit consumers to exercise an 'opt-out option', under which personal information may be collected and processed unless consumers request otherwise. Under the US position, the burden of protecting privacy and personal information falls upon the individual, and the corporations and organizations collecting the information have wide latitude in the use and dissemination of information.[5] Tensions between the conflicting privacy approaches of the US and the European Union have resulted in a Safe Harbor agreement, finalized in the spring of 2000, which allows US-based companies to choose between formal oversight by EU regulators or qualifying self-regulatory regimes enforced by the US Federal Trade Commission.[6]

Governments around the world have started to tackle the difficult issue of devising laws and policies to protect the data privacy of their citizens. These positions range from the strong protections offered by the EU to the self-regulation model adopted by the US. However, this remains a constantly shifting legal and policy terrain, and most national positions are still in a state of flux. Instead of describing the state of national policies as they relate to specific countries, we offer a broad schema that allows for the assessment and analysis of national policies and, consequently, the condition of privacy protections offered by national policies. Broadly, governmental attempts to regulate data privacy can be assessed according to the degree of protection offered to citizens in four general categories: consent, disclosure, security and accuracy, and enforcement. *Consent* deals with the right of individuals to decide when, how and what kinds of information others collect about them over a computer network. It also includes the activities for which that information is collected and the clarity with which an individual is made aware that consent is required and being asked for. *Disclosure* deals with the terms, conditions and circumstances under which an agency can collect information and disclose it to others, including the kinds of organizations and activities for which disclosure may be permissible. *Security* and *accuracy* involve the obligation of information-collecting agencies to ensure that the collected information is securely stored and accurately maintained. The obligation to maintain accurate information contains the implicit right of individuals to have access to the information about themselves to ensure its accuracy and demand correction in case of errors. Finally, the effectiveness of privacy and data protection laws depends on their mechanisms for *enforcement*.

Persistent questions about who should control personal information suggest that governments will eventually have to clarify ownership rights and responsibilities. Information has become a major asset and commodity, necessitating the protection and definition of ownership rights (Branscomb, 1994: 1). Law and legislation must ultimately define property rights in information, like property rights in traditional and tangible property (Mensch, 1990: 13, 23; Michelman, 1987: 1319, 1335–6; Streeter, 1996: 207). Streeter (1996: 207) and Boyle (1997: 27) point out that all property rights and entitlements are socially constructed

artifacts of governments who must allocate specific legal powers to some and withhold them from others. In the case of information assets, this allocation of rights is by no means straightforward. As Gandy (1993: 75) argues, personal information is created when someone observes the behaviour of another, and property rights in that information are highly debatable. Whether personal information belongs to those who generate it or those who collect it, and whether anyone has the right to traffic in this information, are political questions that must be determined through the development and application of legislative, policy and regulatory mechanisms.

Freedom of Expression

Freedom of expression is a value that numerous nations endorse as a political or social right. While countries, such as India, the US, Canada and others, protect speech rights in their national constitutions, many others acknowledge this right in international human rights agreements. For instance, both the International Covenant on Civil and Political Rights (1966) and the Universal Declaration of Human Rights (1948) guarantee people 'freedom to seek, receive and impart information and ideas' in all media regardless of geographical frontiers. While it may be true that many nations support freedom of expression in theory rather than practice (Human Rights Watch, 1999: 3), speech rights nevertheless remain an expressed value and goal of many nations.

Computer networks open up new and significant opportunities to engage in expression. Computer networks allow groups within civil society to forge direct connections with one another through electronic mail, web pages, file transfers, real-time messaging, and online newsletters and discussion groups. In this sense, computer networks fill a communicative gap between interpersonal media, like telephones, and mass media, like television (Human Rights Watch, 1999: 14; Kavanaugh, 1998). These networks also enable communication that bypasses media gatekeepers and resists government controls on speech. People around the world can utilize these networks to circulate political and cultural content that is censored or suppressed offline, such as sexually explicit works, politically dissident information and ideologies, hate speech, banned texts, and other materials deemed subversive. Computer networks make it possible, as Taubman (1998: 261) argues, to establish social networks outside official government channels. One reason they can do so is that current computer network technology makes government control of speech in this medium a complex proposition (Froomkin, 1997: 129; Lessig, 1999: 166). The ability to communicate anonymously, to encrypt messages so that only specified senders and receivers can read them, and to distribute data over decentralized routes all make computer network communication difficult to monitor or block. For those with access to them, these networks enable a range of practices conducive to freedom of expression.[7]

The ability to circulate what some governments deem objectionable content has provoked social conflict, and in some cases swift policy responses, in numerous countries. Both the United States and Australia have made bids, successfully in the case of the latter and unsuccessfully in that of the former, to criminalize the distribution of sexually explicit material on the Internet on the grounds that it could be available to children (Murphy, 1999).[8] In China, the government requires Internet service providers (ISPs) to block objectionable pornographic or political sites. Included among these sites are those carrying American news media, news and commentary from Taiwan, appeals to free Tibet, and other content which threatens to disrupt 'public order' (Froomkin, 1997: 145; McCarthy, 2000: 22; Rosenthal, 2000: A1; Smith, 2000: C2; Taubman, 1998: 264–5). In Kuwait, Israel and Saudi Arabia, the Internet has been perceived as a threat to local religious and moral sensibilities (Human Rights Watch, 1999: 21, 24; Wheeler, 1998: 362, 365). Scholars have suggested that government regulation of content may occur for political and ideological reasons or as a response to societal pressures to repress 'immoral' or 'unethical' communication (Rogerson and Thomas, 1998; Taubman, 1998). Although each country has a different definition of what constitutes

objectionable content, these definitions are grounded in the cultural values, political beliefs and historical circumstances of each.

Government attempts to control political and cultural content on computer networks raise questions of how speech rights will be configured in these forums and what content government can legitimately regulate. While some scholars would prefer that computer networks be free from any government regulation that affects content (Cate, 1995: 1; Labunski, 1997: 191–2), others find it unrealistic to expect governments to refrain from content regulation (Mayer-Schönberger and Foster, 1997). For many countries, content regulation is an extension of social and cultural norms and standards. Many countries consider rules that apply offline, such as restricting access to pornography or discouraging speech that insults or degrades racial, ethnic or other social groups, to be equally desirable online. As Wheeler (1998) argues, the cultural values and frameworks of a nation will affect the practices and policies surrounding computer networks.

Scholarship on speech rights and computer networks focuses on three primary concerns that relate to the conditions prohibiting or promoting freedom of expression. First, analysts identify potential methods of government control of information. Although scholars unanimously acknowledge that total control is difficult to achieve, they nevertheless catalogue numerous methods whereby governments can effectively (if not completely) control speech. Second, scholars examine the efforts of authoritarian or non-democratic governments to control political speech. This research scrutinizes the popular assumption that computer networks are inherently democratic and able to deflect government control. Third, scholars examine the jurisdictional questions raised when the social and cultural restrictions on speech in one country clash with those of another. The ability of citizens to access materials that are banned or restricted in their own countries raises the question of whether international cooperation and agreement will be necessary to enforce content regulations or whether such regulations will become increasingly untenable.

The openness of computer network architecture has not prevented governments from pursuing numerous strategies to control or contain access to objectionable content within their borders. As Mayer-Schönberger and Foster (1997: 235) note, national restrictions on freedom of expression are common around the world. In the US, Benkler (2000) found that laws aiming to control information flows were a major category of Internet legislation in the 1990s. Although specific content regulations may change from year to year, most regulations exhibit commonalities that are likely to persist over time. Regulatory restrictions and content containment strategies can be divided into those that attempt to control gateways to content and those that attempt to control the users themselves. Governments have multiple means of controlling or creating content gateways. Many governments require ISPs to filter or block objectionable content on their systems. By limiting the number of ISPs available, licensing them, or managing them outright, governments can keep a close watch on ISP activities. Governments can also establish proxy servers that act as gateways through which users must pass to gain access to global networks. Both ISPs and proxy servers can utilize software that filters content based on criteria such as the e-mail addresses of senders and recipients, Internet protocol addresses which identify message origins or destinations, or characters that appear in the body of a message (Human Rights Watch, 1999: 36; Kavanaugh, 1998: 37). Kuwait, Saudi Arabia, Yemen, the United Arab Emirates, Tunisia, Algeria, the US and China are among the countries who have used these methods to constrain access (Human Rights Watch, 1999: 24; Kavanaugh, 1998: 82, 84; McCarthy, 2000: 21–2; Taubman, 1998: 265; United States v. American Library Association, 2003; Wheeler, 1998: 362–3). In China, Singapore and the United Arab Emirates, governments also mandate the blocking of some of the more well-known anonymous remailer sites which could help citizens circumvent content regulation (Human Rights Watch, 1999: 39). Measures like these counteract the decentralized architecture of computer networks by utilizing or creating centralized access points

that are amenable to control. Governments may also monitor or restrict user access to the network. For example, in Jordan the government restricts user access by keeping the price of Internet service artificially high (Human Rights Watch, 1999), while in Myanmar only those who are close to the ruling party are authorized to use e-mail (Barron, 2000). Other nations, such as Iraq, Libya, Syria and Saudi Arabia, have chosen to deny their citizens access altogether (Human Rights Watch, 1999: 27; Schneider, 2000: A1). Finally, Chinese Internet users and publishers risk criminal penalties if they fail to register with the government (Taubman, 1998: 264).

Several studies, including Human Rights Watch's (1999) study on the Middle East and North Africa, Kavanaugh's (1998) study on North Africa, and Taubman's (1998) study on China, suggest that non-democratic governments can project their political and cultural will onto computer networks. These studies collectively argue that non-democratic governments are able to increase access to the medium while simultaneously militating against the potential unintended effects of exposing citizens to what Taubman (1998: 257–8) terms 'ideational pluralism'. Ideational pluralism, or multiple sources of ideas and information, threatens the ability of non-democratic governments to maintain hegemony over information and ideology within their borders. It also offers politically discontent groups access to viewpoints and perspectives that could help foment opposition movements. Cognizant of the threats to centralized power posed by computer networks, many non-democratic governments attempt to strike a balance between the control of information and the diffusion of technology seen as promoting economic and social advancement. While these strategies help to maintain the primacy of state-controlled information in the short term, whether they will be able to successfully control content in the long run remains to be seen. Nevertheless, all of these studies presume that network technology will be the Trojan horse that foils government control of content. There is already some evidence of the successful use of the Internet to 'subvert' the political control governments have sought to exercise over dissenting movements. During the Tiananmen Square uprising in 1989 and the attempted coup in the Soviet Union in 1990, phone, fax and computer networks provided alternative sources of information to the outside world (Fredrick, 1993, 293; Quarterman, 1990: xxiii–xxiv). In Mexico, a representative for the Zapatista movement, Subcommandante Marcos, was able to use the Internet to communicate with his supporters and the rest of the world (Ford and Gil, 2001). Similarly, during the Kosovo war, the dissident radio station B92 was able to continue broadcasting by using the Internet even after the station was closed down by Serbian police (Hibbert, 1999: 401).

Diverse and contradictory content regulations also raise questions about whether a nation's rules have jurisdiction over content that originates elsewhere. Examples of jurisdictional conflict over content include a 1995 attempt by the German government to force the global access provider CompuServe to block German users' access to 200 sexually explicit computer discussion groups and a subsequent effort on the part of the French government to pressure the search engine Yahoo! into preventing French citizens from viewing Nazi memorabilia on its English-language auction sites (Associated Press, 2000; Delaney, 2000: B10; Rogerson and Thomas, 1998: 247: *Yahoo! Inc. v. Le Ligue Contre le Racisme*, 2001). Both cases raised, but have yet to answer, the question of exactly whose laws should apply to communication that regularly crosses national borders. At present, contradictory national laws govern global computer networks (Mayer-Schönberger and Foster, 1997). Such laws are a concern of companies who worry about their liability for data that regularly travel through multiple countries with diverse policies (White House, 1997). Contradictory laws and unclear jurisdictions are also a concern of countries who seek to protect national norms and values.

Unlike the dilemmas new technologies have precipitated in intellectual property and privacy policies, tensions over political and cultural content are the result not of conflicts over information ownership but over the social, cultural and political environment of different countries. Ultimately, these conflicts beg the question of whether governments can or should regulate content over computer networks in order to protect national values, given the political and cultural diversity both among and within nations. For many countries, the ability of citizens to communicate over computer networks destabilizes existing balances between the free flow of information and information control. While some analysts argue that computer networks are ultimately incompatible with government controls and authoritarian rule (Froomkin, 1997: 141; Wriston, 1994), others are less certain that governments will fail to assert control over these networks (Goldsmith, 1998: 1200; Kavanaugh, 1998: xiii). Research in this area must continue to ask whether and under what conditions regulations affecting freedom of expression are appropriate and sustainable, and whether the current openness of computer networks engenders freedom of expression, or whether social and cultural practices and values will instead reshape the architecture of computer networks.

POLICY PRINCIPLES AND MODELS OF GLOBAL MEDIA REGULATION

Computer networks have already precipitated serious social conflicts in the areas of intellectual property, privacy and speech rights. Although computer technology and services are constantly evolving, many of the conflicts they engender will persist through successive incarnations of the technology. For this reason, governments must define the purposes, principles and values that should animate their communication systems. Making these social choices now will allow these decisions to be incorporated into technology and industry as they develop, rather than forcing costly and inefficient changes later. Thoughtful policy choices should also ensure that valued rights are respected and protected throughout this period of technological innovation and change brought on by global computer networks. This section explores models of regulation and policy principles that can be applied to computer networks. Several policy models exist for managing and resolving conflicts over computer networks, including marketplace and private sector regulation, national public service or interest regulation, and international or multinational regulatory regimes. None of these options are mutually exclusive; they can be used in combination to supplement and counterbalance each other's protections. Moreover, none of these models circumvent the need for government regulation, since even the marketplace requires governments to structure and enforce its terms and conditions, while international regimes require the support of participating nations. Nevertheless, we will discuss these models separately in order to highlight the distinctions between them and to examine their respective advantages and disadvantages. After reviewing these models, we go on to consider the principles and guidelines that might successfully steer future developments in intellectual property, privacy, and speech rights law and policy.

Given that computer networks can and will be regulated, nation-states must determine what methods of regulation to employ, whether these are public service or market-oriented, based on national laws and normative systems, or subject to international agreements and covenants. To be effective, regulations must be enforceable and achieve collectively desired outcomes. Yet, global communication systems challenge the ability of nation-states to regulate effectively and to exercise their sovereignty. Sovereignty refers to a ruling body's power to make and enforce policies that affect people or territories within its jurisdiction. One challenge comes from market participants that increasingly assert their claim to privately regulate transactions over these networks. Another comes from the ability of communication and information to regularly cross national borders, thereby calling the jurisdictional limits of nation-states into question. Furthermore, the increasing ability of individuals and organizations to communicate globally begs the question of whether international instruments would be more effective agents of regulation than nation-states: and, if so, how these

instruments would incorporate participation, attain legitimacy, and provide accountability for those affected by their actions. These factors put pressure on nation-states to redefine their role in formulating and enforcing communication policy.

Whether future communication policies are market or public interest driven, or the product of national or international regulatory regimes, scholarship suggests that these policies require a socially agreed set of principles at their core. Principles are general rules or propositions on which subsequent actions can be based. In addition, they are a jargon-free way of expressing policy goals (Proceedings of the Annenberg Washington Program Panel Two, 1995: 84–5). Defining the core principles of national and international communication policy has several advantages. First, principles can underscore the values that nations wish to privilege with regards to privacy, intellectual property, speech rights and other policy areas. Principles can help nations protect access to communication systems and content, set minimum standards of conduct among data processors and collectors, and delineate spheres of public knowledge and information. Defining principles at the outset of technological development allows governments to shape communication systems before special interests become entrenched and change becomes more difficult (Kirby, 1983: 13). Principles also provide a firm foundation on which to build coordinated and comprehensive legislation. For Branscomb (1994: 84), principles are a superior basis for legislation to their alternative – narrowly conceived laws formulated in response to narrowly framed problems. Principles can also foster the linkages necessary to coordinate between national and international policy, law and technological development. Socially sanctioned principles can facilitate the harmonization of domestic laws among nations (OECD, 1997: 11), treaty negotiations among countries (Kirby, 1983: 14), and the overall development of global communication systems (OECD, 1997: 4). Finally, nations that have an express commitment to communication policy principles possess clearer benchmarks for assessing whether specific regulations achieve their desired goals.[9] Without larger principles or goals in mind, any policy can become an end in itself.

Identifying principles is a critical step towards setting national and international policy goals. Yet, it is only the first step. Once principles are determined, nations must decide how to apply them. Principles must be incorporated into national and international law and legislation if they are to have any force or effect. Meshing international and other guidelines, which do not have the force of law, with legal traditions and practices in individual countries will be challenging (Kirby, 1983: 17–18). Nations will also have to decide the domains in which to apply these principles. For example, while EU privacy principles apply across all information processing, marketplace policies focus on specific industries, technologies and other sectoral divisions. In the area of speech rights, scholars disagree over whether access principles should be applied according to the specific technology involved (Cate, 1995; Labunski, 1997), the functions of the medium (Melody, 1990; Plotkin, 1996: 238), or the classification of an entity as a content provider or transmission facility (OECD, 1997: 4). Despite these difficulties, the process of harmonizing and coordinating national and international policy cannot succeed without attention to the fundamental principles that will guide these policies and shape global communication systems.

Market-based Regulation

Marketplace regulation of computer networks, through code and contracts, limits the sovereign powers of nations by reducing their role to enforcing market structures. The use of competitive markets to allocate communication resources is favoured by many scholars and policy-makers. According to supporters of marketplace regulation, markets are responsive to fluctuating demands for products and services, can measure the value individuals assign to various communication services, and 'depoliticize' decision-making by allowing private actors within the marketplace to determine resource allocation (de Sola Pool, 1983;

Kahn, 1988: Preface). The primary goal of market systems is economic efficiency, and the ability of economic efficiency to maximize the wealth of nations is equated with the overall public interest and beneficial social outcomes (Office of Technology Assessment, 1990: 21–2). From this perspective, marketplace regulation is preferred to socially determined, public interest regulation which is seen as hindering the efficient allocation of resources, as well as improvements in products and services (Hilton, 1972; Kahn, 1988; MacAvoy, 1979).

Market regulation, also referred to as private sector or self-regulation, allows private actors operating within competitive markets to settle social conflicts over communication (Mosco, 1988). Under a market model, businesses can develop their own rules, standards and practices (Glickman and Carney, 2000: 196), and consumers are free to patronize those businesses whose rules and practices they favour. The legitimacy of this model rests on the assumption that consumers can choose at any time to 'exit' a relationship that involves one set of rules in order to form a new relationship under another rule set (Johnson and Post, 1997: 32). In this model, the role of government is limited to establishing a legal framework that facilitates commerce, providing industries with incentives to regulate themselves, and maintaining marketplace competition and consumer choice. Extending the argument to the international arena, market theorists maintain that an international market economy, institutionalized in international economic regimes characterized by self-regulating norms and rules, would constitute a public good for all participating nations because it would ensure the greatest economic benefit for the greatest number (Gilpin, 1987; Kindleberger, 1978; Krasner, 1991; Waltz 1979). This is the preferred model of the US, which would like the private sector to build and control computer networks (Bettig, 1997: 146; White House, 1997: 18–19).

Johnson and Post (1997), Reidenberg (1997: 100) and others argue that computer networks are good candidates for private sector self-regulation. In their view, computer networks constitute distinct spaces, clearly demarcated from the real world, with their own unique problems. They argue that computer network providers and infrastructure organizations can take on their own sovereign powers by creating their own borders and rules of order. Network users and system operators could devise their own rules for controlling behaviour in these spaces, and system operators could ban users who didn't follow their rules. Banned or dis- contented users would be able to establish new relationships with other system operators, pre- sumably under better conditions and terms of service. Johnson and Post suggest that, except- ing cases where network activities affect the vital interests of nation-states, national govern- ments could defer their authority over behav- iour in these spaces to network self-regulation. While Reidenberg (1997: 96) believes that governments must continue to protect the public interest over computer networks, he also suggests that they reallocate some of their authority to the virtual world. On a similar note, Louveaux et al. (1999) suggest that 'cyber-tribunals' or 'virtual magistrates' be set up online to provide non-judicial dispute res- olution for conflicts that occur over computer networks.

Private sector regulations may be imple- mented through voluntary standards and codes, contracts between service or access providers and consumers, and the conscious design of network architecture. While private sector regulations allow businesses to determine the methods and values behind network regula- tion, they risk short-changing the public good aspects of communication law and policy. Voluntary standards and codes allow businesses maximum flexibility in regulating their own behaviour over computer networks. However, voluntary rules can easily result in overlapping and conflicting guidelines, especially since these rules can apply variously to individual companies, industry sectors, particular corpo- rate functions, professional associations or the technology itself (Gellman, 1997: 256, 260). Poorly structured private sector regulations can also leave significant gaps in the areas and prac- tices they cover. Furthermore, since there are no penalties for failing to enforce voluntary rules, incentives to adhere to them are weak.

Regulation of behaviour over computer networks can also be achieved through the use of private contracts. Access or service providers can subject network users to contractual arrangements as part of their terms of service (Bing et al., 1983: 114; Proceedings of the Annenberg Washington Program Panel One, 1995: 26). These contracts effectively establish private law and policy on computer networks. For example, copyright holders increasingly employ contracts to lay out conditions and terms of service. These contracts may specify acceptable uses of their products and require consumers to waive their rights under intellec- tual property law, such as the right of fair use or first sale (Lessig, 1999: 135). Thus, while con- tracts can be used to resolve conflicts sur- rounding information flows over computer networks, they can also be used to displace or circumvent rights established under public law.

Finally, the private sector can use technology to solve problems associated with intellectual property, privacy and freedom of expression. Lessig (1999: 7) argues that, without govern- ment intervention, code, or the software and hardware that make up these systems, will reg- ulate computer networks. There are many examples of regulation through network tech- nology. Technological means, such as filtering or age verification systems, can be used to control access to objectionable expression over com- puter networks (1999: 175–6; White House, 1997: 25). Software programs can be used to protect privacy by determining a user's privacy preferences and alerting the user when com- puter sites don't meet their standards (Global Internet Liberty Campaign, 1998; Green et al., 2000: 94; Lessig, 1999: 160). Technology can also be used to extend the control of copyright holders over intellectual property by tracking and controlling copies of materials or by designing technology in a way that limits its potential uses. For example, digital audiotape (DAT) is designed to degrade in quality with successive copies, even though DAT is techni- cally capable of producing an infinite number of perfect copies (Lessig, 1999: 128). While technology can solve problems brought on by computer networks, it will solve these prob- lems according to who has power in the marketplace and who controls or owns the technology (Lessig, 1999: 7). In some cases, consumers may be able to use technology to protect their rights and preferences, as with privacy software or filtering programs implemented by the end user. Conversely, technology may be used to strip consumers and citizens of rights they hold under public law, as in the case of some intellectual property technologies or content filters imposed by companies, service providers or governments rather than freely chosen by end users. In the case of content filters, end users may be unaware that regulations are being applied and, therefore, be incapable of challenging them. Given the potential of technology to override public values, many analysts believe that governments must have a role in monitoring and penalizing network practices which fail to conform to accepted rights and standards (Global Internet Liberty Campaign, 1998; Green et al., 2000: 94; Lessig, 1999: 160).

Critics of marketplace regulation argue that allowing businesses to determine the social purposes of computer networks results in the erosion of public service values traditionally maintained by governments (Lessig, 1999: 59; Schiller, 1999: 59, 87). By defining economic efficiency as the end goal of communication systems, market regimes reduce information and communication to mere commodities, and fail to recognize the other roles they play in social, cultural and political life (Babe, 1995: 18). Regulating behaviour on computer networks through contract and code takes areas of regulation, including privacy, intellectual property and speech rights, out of the domain of public political processes and into that of private decision-making. Rights that exist in the public realm of government will not necessarily find protection in the private realm of commerce. Governments' role in regulating media is dramatically transformed. Whereas a public service model of government regulation expects governments to ensure access to and availability of services and technology, affordable prices for essential services, and the rights of media owners and users (Office of Technology Assessment, 1990: 23), the market model views governments as enforcers of market rules and

requirements, such as property rights, contracts and information flows. Citizens who are dissatisfied with the terms of service can seek out another service provider, but they do not have the opportunity to change those terms by having a 'voice' in those systems (Hirschman, 1986: 77: Lessig, 1999: 201). Lessig (1999: 199) argues that governments which allow market regulation to control the architecture of the Internet will undoubtedly experience a loss of sovereignty.

Private sector regulation of computer networks is problematic in a number of other regards. As articulated by Johnson and Post (1997), network self-regulation presumes that online behaviour takes place in a unique space that is detached from the real world. This line of reasoning reifies computer networks and the activities that take place over them. In fact, as scholars such as Lessig (1999: 190) and Mayer-Schönberger and Foster (1997: 238) point out, these networks are not extraterritorial. Behaviour that takes place in online space simultaneously occurs in real geographic space. Consequently, both spaces have a degree of control over network actors. The marketplace model also characterizes network actors as consumers who are free to change rule sets whenever they become dissatisfied with conditions under a particular network service or access or content provider. Yet, for many network users, the label of consumer falls short of accurately characterizing their relationship to online spaces. As Lessig (1999: 201–3) points out, people become members of online communities; they spend time there, build relationships and establish social capital. Given these circumstances, moving to another rule set can constitute a significant burden, and human dignity may demand that people have some opportunity to shape these spaces (1999: 217). Finally, private sector regulation has additional disadvantages. Unlike socially determined government regulations that are transparent in the sense that they are publicly discussed and scrutinized, private sector regulations are often non-transparent. Private regulators can be less forthcoming and less accountable than their public counterparts (1999: 178–1). Private sector regulations are also less likely to achieve the kind of coordinated and predictable network environment many business users seek. While these regulations may resolve some conflicts over information and communication, they may also work to achieve private goals, like the extension of control over information, that disregard public values. Even with private sector regulations in play, citizens must call on governments to resolve disputes that arise and to ensure the preservation of public values associated with law on intellectual property, privacy and speech rights, as well as other areas of social life.

National Public Service Regulation

National politically determined, public service regulation of communication policy can be set through national laws, legislation and rule-making bodies. Policy may be written into government constitutions, as is the case with speech rights protections in many countries. Newer constitutions may even include rights associated with data protection, such as the right to access and control personal information found in the constitutions of Hungary and South Africa. National legislation allows countries to systematically consider different policy options and to collectively choose the values animating their communication systems. National judiciaries can adjudicate conflicts that arise according to the legal traditions and customs of a given country.

National public service regulation allows for political choices to be made on a scale commensurate with citizen participation and with government accountability. National governments possess the tools to devise and enact policies that protect public values and interests (Reidenberg, 1997: 96). For example, as research on data protection shows, comprehensive national regulation is key to controlling abuses of information privacy (Lessig, 1999: 163; Peterson, 1995: 164; Reidenberg, 1997: 95). Governments also define the rules that govern communication markets and act as a line of defence against private actors who use contracts, technology or other methods to erode public rights in favour of private interests.

Hence, Lessig (1999: 197–9) argues that governments must ultimately decide the degree of protection to give to values that are called into question by new technologies, as well as the appropriate balance between the rights and responsibilities of network users and network owners.

Notwithstanding the importance of the role governments can and in many cases should play in the governance of new communication technologies, of significant concern is their very ability to devise and enforce effective regulations. The main dilemma being faced by governments is how to respond to the growing technological and economic pressures brought about by global computer networks, while safeguarding important social and political goals and objectives. While there is no correct blueprint for what makes government oversight successful, there are certain themes and characteristics that will determine the effectiveness and credibility of national regulation. First, the development of national policies toward communication technologies is a political process, and the nature of the political system and the dominant political ideology will be key factors in determining the nature and substance of the policy process. Second, the strength of the legal system, including the nature of contractual laws and the property rights regime within a country, will be critical for providing stability and enforceability of national policies. Finally, the nature and effectiveness of safeguarding institutions like the judiciary and the regulatory agencies and instruments developed to oversee computer networks will be crucial to determining the effectiveness of the management of these new technologies. Many countries lack the institutional framework required to effectively develop and implement national policies and regulations.

Another challenge to national sovereignty stems from the ability of computer networks to facilitate interactions between people and organizations residing in different legal jurisdictions. Legal differences between jurisdictions cut across multiple areas of law, including privacy, freedom of expression and intellectual property, and are often related to the different culture, history and attitudes of specific countries

(Kirby, 1983: 11–12). When communication crosses many jurisdictions and has effects in many places, including outside its country of origin, the authority of any one territorial sovereign to apply laws becomes questionable. The ability of computer network communication to regularly cross national borders makes it difficult for governments to determine whether an activity or actor falls within their jurisdiction (Rogerson and Thomas, 1998: 430). In addition, the architecture of global computer networks, with its possibilities of anonymity and decentralized communication, can frustrate governments' attempts to identify and locate people engaged in illegal behaviour (Lessig, 1999: 19). In effect, these features of global communication systems weaken the relationship between sovereignty and geographical territory (Gellman, 1997: 271; Kirby, 1983: 12; Reidenberg, 1977: 85). Sovereign power has traditionally depended on the ability to regulate behaviour within a particular geographic territory and on the implicit or explicit consent of those governed (Johnson and Post, 1997: 5–6; Perritt, 1997). These aspects of sovereignty do not readily translate into a context in which behaviour involves multiple jurisdictions.

Such international interactions and transactions are increasingly being seen as part of the emergence of a global or transnational civil society (Braman and Sreberny-Mohammadi, 1996; Calabrese, 1999; Frederick, 1993; Hamelink, 1991). Defining civil society as that part of collective social life that is free from both the power of the state and the market, these scholars document the impact of computer networks on growing trans-border cooperation between various types of citizens groups especially in the areas of human rights, consumer protection, peace, gender equality, racial justice, environmental activism, consumer protection and workers' rights (Frederick, 1993: 285). These new social movements, non-governmental organizations (NGOs) and citizen advocacy groups have taken advantage of networks such as the Association for Progressive Communications (a network connecting dozens of smaller networks such as Econet, PeaceNet, ConflictNet, and WorkNet) to provide alternative mechanisms for citizens to support and participate in a variety of global activities. A number of scholars have documented the use of communication technologies in general and computer networks in particular to foster transnational progressive, alternative and radical social movements (Bennett, 2003; Calabrese, 1999; Downing, 2001; Ford and Gil, 2001; Waterman, 1998). Though there is no doubt that computer networks have increased the scope for global civic engagement by citizens often in opposition to the positions taken by their own national governments, the long-term impact of both new technologies and new social movements on the overwhelming power of states and markets is as yet undetermined. Although legal and jurisdictional conflicts may weaken the ability of nations to regulate, they do not render national regulation altogether ineffective. Nations can still assert control over network users, operators and infrastructures within their jurisdictions (Reidenberg, 1997: 99). For example, data havens, or countries which apply few or no rules to computer network communication, may not be able to shield computer network communication from the jurisdictional claims of other countries. Other nations may succeed in claiming jurisdiction over the network equipment and facilities which allow data havens to achieve connectivity outside their territory, or over the network users and operators who maintain citizenship outside the data haven (Garfinkel, 2000: 238–9).

While national government regulation is both unavoidable and, in many cases, desirable, it also has significant weak points. If not kept in check by a strong conception of public rights, governments may go beyond maintaining the structures that protect rights and instead become a prime violator of these rights. As we have noted, authoritarian regimes continue to limit the range of information and ideas that they want circulating within their civil societies and view computer networks as real threats to their ability to control the nature and flow of information within their societies. Further, for governments who fail to set national policy in a comprehensive or coordinated way, conflicting rules can hinder electronic commerce and create uncertainty for network users (Gellman, 1997: 256–7). Finally, national regulation alone cannot solve problems that arise when communication crosses numerous jurisdictions with conflicting policies. Such cases call for international and multilateral policy responses. Nevertheless, the authority of nations to regulate across jurisdictions remains precarious, and national rules will be harder to assert over global computer networks absent an amenable network architecture and international cooperation.

International and Multinational Regimes

Effective regulation of global computer networks may require the development or refinement of international instruments and institutions for communication policy-making. Many scholars point out the growing links between national and international policy. Domestic policies in one country can easily have effects on other countries (Michalski, 1989: 15; OECD, 1995: 4). Transnational laws, such as the European Union Privacy Directive, have ramifications for countries both inside and outside their jurisdiction (Kirby, 1983: 52; OECD, 1995: 5). And global transactions raise transnational problems whose solutions require international cooperation and coordination (Kirby, 1989: 167; Lessig, 1999: 205–6; Mayer-Schönberger and Foster, 1997: 243; OECD, 1997: 5). Proponents of the global marketplace argue that international organizations should be used to harmonize conflicting commercial regulations and to set the rules of the global market game (Bitterman, 1989: 308; Cate, 1994; Glickman and Carney, 2000). From this perspective, international ICT policy is necessary to rationalize and refine global competition. From another angle, Lessig (1999: 205) argues that global ICTs open up new communicative spaces in which citizens from around the world can participate. As activity in such spaces increases, more questions are raised about our legal status there (1999: 226). For Lessig, clarification of the rights and responsibilities that adhere to international spaces and international life is essential for the fair and humane treatment of all network users and participants.

Conflicting legal rules have created pressures to harmonize regulation across countries or to find some method of coordinating or cooperating among multiple jurisdictions (Glickman and Carney, 2000: 195; Hudson, 1994: 141; Lessig, 1999: 192). In other words, nations must accept laws that apply across multiple jurisdictions or agree on a way to determine, in case of conflict, whose laws apply. International cooperation could come in many forms. Countries could mandate the regulability of network architecture, and mutually agree to enforce one another's laws by instituting mandatory electronic identification and zoning (Lessig, 1999: 207). Nations could cede some of their sovereign powers to third parties, such as international regulatory agencies, arbitrators or courts (Johnson and Post, 1997) – though, in this case, national legal systems would be necessary to implement, enforce or interpret third-party decisions (Perritt, 1997). Whichever mechanisms or methods are chosen, cooperation and coordination will require the establishment of international policy principles that serve as a common denominator between countries and/or that indicate the circumstances in which sovereignty should be deferred. Establishing these principles requires that nations come to some agreement on the political and economic goals of international society and international life (Alleyne, 1995: 17).

Global information flows, along with the jurisdictional limitations of nation-states, necessitate the development of transnational regimes for communication law and policy. The majority of communication and legal scholars support the idea that the protection of legitimate rights and interests on global communication systems requires international cooperation (Bitterman, 1989: 308; Blumenthal, 1999: 550; Cate, 1994; Glickman and Carney, 2000; Kirby, 1989: 167; Lessig, 1999: 205–6; Mayer-Schönberger and Foster, 1997: 243; OECD, 1997: 14; Thurow, 1997: 100). What these scholars disagree on, as our earlier discussions on speech rights, intellectual property and privacy suggest, are the normative goals of international cooperation and how these goals are best achieved. Since these perspectives have already been covered at length in earlier sections, our purpose here will be to briefly survey the current landscape of transnational treaties, agreements and organizations, along with the promises and pitfalls they hold for global media regulation.

Transnational communication regimes are nearly as old as the earliest global media, the mail and the telegraph. To date, international rule makings and organizations have centred largely on the areas of telecommunications, the mail and intellectual property (Alleyne, 1995: 21). In 1849, multinational agreements were forged to rationalize the transnational use of the telegraph, and in 1865, 20 countries signed a multilateral treaty that created the International Telegraph Union (ITU), an organization designed to set the rules for international telegraphy. Later renamed the International Telecommunication Union and incorporated into the United Nations, the ITU makes binding decisions regarding the technical regulation of telecommunications, including the protocols used for modems. In the case of the mail, the formation of an organization in 1874 that would eventually become the Universal Postal Union (UPU) heralded the beginning of a multinational postal regime. The UPU today encourages worldwide international cooperation and standardization of postal services (Bing et al., 1983: 133). Intellectual property law has been subject to multilateral copyright agreements since 1886 when several countries, including Japan, Germany, France and the United Kingdom, adopted the Berne Convention for the Protection of Literary and Artistic Works. The Berne Convention sought to establish international norms for intellectual property protection by requiring member states to accord the same intellectual property protections to nationals from other member states as exist for their own citizens, a concept known as the national treatment standard (Berne Convention, 1886; Braunstein, 1989; Goldstein, 1994: 183–4).

The preponderance of international intellectual property agreements and organizations is due largely to the desire of copyright-holding countries to protect their intellectual goods against piracy and fraud. International agreements generally aim to establish and harmonize international intellectual property principles and laws (Bing et al., 1983: 134; Jussawalla, 1992: 4). In addition to the Berne Convention, intellectual property protections have been part of numerous bilateral and multilateral agreements, including the Universal Copyright Convention (UCC), the World Trade Organization (WTO), the North American Free Trade Agreement (NAFTA), the US–Canada Free Trade Agreement, and many others. Since 1967, the Berne Convention has been administered by the World Intellectual Property Organization (WIPO).[10] Another prominent international intellectual property agreement, the Universal Copyright Convention (UCC), was created in 1952 to impose minimum intellectual property requirements on the US, Latin America, Europe, Asia and Africa. Administered by the United Nations Educational, Scientific and Cultural Organization (UNESCO), the UCC acts as the smallest common denominator for intellectual property law at the international level (Bing et al., 1983: 79). In 1996, the Berne Convention was updated to include the WIPO Copyright Treaty and the WIPO Performances and Phonograms Treaty. These two treaties sought to strengthen intellectual property rules in relation to digital communication and to encourage online commerce (White House, 1997: 13). Another international intellectual property organization, the Internet Corporation for Assigned Names and Numbers (ICANN), was established in the late 1990s in order to administer Internet domain names and intellectual property addresses. Unlike all of the aforementioned organizations which are publicly funded and maintained, ICANN is a private, non-profit group.

Countries have been slower to forge transnational agreements on privacy issues and speech rights. Two transnational organizations, the Organization for Economic Cooperation and Development (OECD) and the Council of Europe, have devised privacy guidelines for transnational information flows based on fair information practices (Gellman, 1997: 265). OECD and Council of Europe guidelines have become the foundation for numerous countries' privacy policies. In addition, the European Union leads the world in promoting international cooperation and harmonization of privacy policies. The EU Privacy Directive, like other EU Directives, formulates centralized policy objectives and standards at the European level and asks EU member states to implement these in their respective nations. Although Directives do not create transnational rights that citizens can draw on directly, they do allow member countries to implement uniform rules in such areas as data protection and intellectual property (Reidenberg, 1997: 94–5). In the case of the Privacy Directive, the EU has been able to coordinate information policy among its member nations and to pressure many nations outside the EU to conform to higher privacy standards. Finally, several international rights covenants exist which include speech rights clauses, such as the Universal Declaration of Human Rights, the International Covenant on Civil and Political Rights, and the (European) Convention for the Protection of Human Rights (Cate, 1994: 470). These agreements declare the intentions of their signatories to uphold the values of freedom of expression and information.

International and multinational agreements and organizations exist in various states of development in countries across the world, with intellectual property rights regimes tending to be more developed, speech rights less so, and privacy rights somewhere in between. While these efforts represent necessary first steps in ensuring global communication rights regimes that can keep pace with global communication processes, they also highlight several issues that need to be addressed if nations are to pursue more equitable international policies. These issues include how such regimes will affect included and excluded countries, how representative they are of the world's citizens and countries, and how their rules will be coordinated, monitored and enforced. First, multinational regimes are prone to inclusion and exclusion problems. As we saw with the EU data protection rules and some intellectual property rules, excluded countries that did not ascribe to an agreement's norms and standards felt pressured to conform nevertheless. This issue is particularly pronounced for developing countries who are pressured to adhere to restrictive intellectual property rights that do

little to promote the growth of knowledge and information in their home countries. Conversely, countries that are party to these agreements have difficulty protecting their rights in outside territories. Protecting rights globally may require some uniform standards that all countries can agree to, but which leave room for flexibility and experimentation. As Burk (1997: 226, 231) suggests, international agreements should create minimum standards of protection which at the same time permit innovation and variation. One example of such flexibility is the inclusion of a global 'fair use' clause in the Berne Convention and UCC. Supported by African, Asian and Latin American countries, this clause allows for the circulation of copyrighted works for the purposes of teaching, scholarship or research if member countries obtain licences and provide reasonable remuneration (Goldstein, 1994: 187–9).

A second issue, and one to which less attention has been paid, concerns the representative aspects of international regimes. Ideally, international regimes should allow participating countries to coordinate law and policy so as to further the common good for all involved and should be representative of, and accountable to, those who fall under their regulations. In practice, these regimes may be unduly affected by differentials in political and economic power so that the stronger powers dominate the rule-making and policy processes (Alleyne, 1995: 152). Representation may also turn out to be a problematic aspect of private, non-profit regulatory bodies, such as ICANN. ICANN is responsible for assigning name and address spaces on the Internet, essentially delegating property rights to specific individuals. While Glickman and Carney (2000: 196) laud ICANN as a new model of international regulation, Mueller (1999: 517, 519) argues that ICANN's private status allowed it to avoid public input and scrutiny during its formation and ultimately led to public demands for procedural safeguards like those applying to government organizations. For Mueller (1999), the rhetoric of private regulation simply masks a policy process in which valuable rights and assets are allocated without adequate public representation and accountability. Lastly, international regimes may need to be consolidated, clarified or made more effective. At present, there are numerous organizations, treaties and agreements regulating various aspects of intellectual property, privacy and speech rights law. For example, in the area of intellectual property, Kirby (1983: 49) notes that there are a number of pre-existing organizations capable of dealing with intellectual property issues, and Jussawalla (1992: 56) sees a need to specify relations between TRIPS, WIPO and the UCC. In addition, regimes can only be effective to the extent that they monitor and enforce the principles and rules they set forth. Yet, the link between some regimes and mechanisms for monitoring or enforcing policy is weak. For example, while many international rights covenants protect speech rights, none sponsors organizations that monitor speech rights violations or enforce speech rights protections.

International Policy Principles

Arriving at internationally accepted principles will be a formidable task. One method might be for nations to examine the principles contained in existing policy agreements. Yet, while Bing et al. (1983: 81) review contemporary policy instruments for indications of global communications principles, they also suggest that relying on established principles is insufficient. Global communication systems raise new and unanswered questions. In some cases decision-makers may be able to apply old principles in a new context, but in others new principles will have to be developed in accord with social, cultural and political values. In this section, we briefly lay out some suggested policy principles for intellectual property, privacy and speech rights.

In the area of intellectual property, nations must determine what principles will define the public use and availability of information and knowledge. Will fair use and first-sale principles be extended into global communication systems, or will these principles be swept away by technological design, legal means or industry practices? What length of time should

copyright holders enjoy monopoly rights over intellectual goods, and at what point does this monopoly become a detriment to society? Scholars suggest that principles must protect the fundamental philosophical aim of copyright law, the promotion and dissemination of knowledge and creativity throughout society (Halbert, 1999; Lessig, 1999; Thurow, 1997). Halbert (1999: 158) argues that copyright rules should strike a balance between the public good and private gain; copyright holders should be able to profit from their work, but not at the expense of the greater common good. Lessig (1999: 141; 2001) and Thurow (1997: 102) maintain that copyright principles should effectively demarcate public from private knowledge and establish a public domain or intellectual commons in which knowledge and information are broadly accessible. This public domain might include basic scientific knowledge (Thurow, 1997: 102), computer software code that enacts basic functions or processes (Jussawalla, 1992: 112), and cultural symbols that have already duly profited their copyright holders (Halbert, 1999).

Numerous countries have already developed privacy principles, defining the values associated with the collection and use of personal information. Many of these countries have data protection or information privacy laws which are based on guidelines set forth by the OECD and the Council of Europe and on general principles of fair information practices (Council of Europe, 1981; Gandy, 1993: 7; Gellman, 1997: 265; Global Internet Liberty Campaign, 1998; OECD, 1981). These principles generally favour the values of openness and transparency in information collection and processing. Among the principles set forth on privacy are that individuals should have the right to control their own data, to have data about them collected fairly and lawfully, to opt into (rather than out of) data processing and sharing, to access and correct inaccurate data about themselves, and to limit secondary uses of personal data (Branscomb, 1994: 24; Global Internet Liberty Campaign, 1998; Hausman, 1994: 138; Lessig, 1999: 156; Maxeiner, 1995: 99; OECD, 1997: 14; Peterson, 1995: 184). In addition, countries should require data collectors to disclose their information and privacy practices, impose penalties on those who fail to comply with privacy rules, and assign a government agency the task of monitoring and enforcing privacy policy (EU Data Protection Directive, 1995; Green et al., 2000: 84; OECD, 1981).

Speech rights principles cover access to communication systems, resources and content. Some scholars, such as Hudson (1994: 137) and Melody (1990: 30), argue that universal access must be a core principle of communication policy. Melody (1990) favours the application of universal service principles to all communication systems that constitute essential facilities. The concept of universal service mandates non-discriminatory access to, and pricing of, communication systems and services. Others favour this concept as a means of preventing system gatekeepers and owners from charging monopoly prices for their services, giving special treatment to favoured content and service providers, or discriminating among those who wish to interconnect with their systems (Human Rights Watch, 1999: 5, 7). Analysts also suggest that governments should eschew centralized content censorship. For speech rights absolutists, there is no justification for government regulation of speech. For others, such as the OECD (1997: 15), governments must promote the free flow of information in a way that respects both speech and privacy rights. One principle which seeks to contain unwelcome government content censorship, put forth by Samorski et al. (1997: 163) and Human Rights Watch (1999: 4), holds that control over content should, whenever possible, be delegated to end users. Receiver-based software allows individual users to set their own parameters for filtering unwanted content and could reduce pressures on service providers to act as content gatekeepers. Human Rights Watch (1999: 6) further suggests that government surveillance be subject to due process and judicial supervision so that it doesn't unduly infringe on individuals' privacy or civil rights. Additional speech rights principles have been set out in UNESCO's new world information and communication order (NWICO) initiative of the 1970s, which advocates a plurality of information sources,

freedom and responsibility of communication workers, and the rights of all citizens to participate in international information exchanges and communication processes (Alleyne, 1995: 123). More recently, the United Nation's World Summit on the Information Society (WSIS) reaffirmed international principles related to free speech, including media independence, pluralism and diversity; freedom to receive and impart information; media responsibility; diversity of media ownership; and the closing of the gap in communication skills and resources between nations (United Nations, 2003: article 53).

CONCLUSION

New media, and the practices and institutions surrounding them, pose significant challenges to regulatory regimes around the world. National control over communication systems is complicated by technologies whose reach and effects extend beyond the jurisdictional boundaries of nation-states. Many governments fear the loss of political and economic sovereignty, others the loss of cultural identity. New media highlight a gap that now exists between life and governance; people can interact in supranational or global arenas that as of yet have no definitive mode of governance. Global networks offer a vast array of options to people, corporations and organizations for the pursuit of political, economic and cultural activities. Nations who wish to determine the goals and values that animate global media systems must pursue effective legal and legislative frameworks both nationally and internationally. In addition to transgressing jurisdictional boundaries, new media also test the conceptual and definitional boundaries of policy regimes affecting intellectual property, privacy and speech rights. Social conflicts in each of these areas demand policy responses that demarcate public rights, set behavioural standards and curtail abusive practices. New global media raise fundamental questions and concerns about who will control communication systems and the terms and conditions of access to them. These concerns cannot be addressed simply by turning to legal precedent or technological solutions. Rather, nations must declare the principles that will define or redefine the social values and purposes of media systems in today's world.

Communication and legal scholars have been charting and surveying shifts in the regulatory landscape, assessing these shifts in normative terms, and seeking workable models of global media regulation. This scholarship tracks the tremors that occur as technologies, processes of commodification or private sector regulation collide with national norms, values and practices. Communication scholars identify the characteristics and practices accompanying new technologies, examine their social and political effects, and look for indications of whether these technologies will aid or abate social control. Legal scholars observe the conflicts new technologies are already creating in national and international life and explore various tools and mechanisms that might reconcile national policy goals with jurisdictional concerns.

Monitoring and assessing the changing landscape of communication systems is a critical task in this era of rapid technological and industrial change. Only by doing so can we determine how these systems interact with global political economic processes, how human agents are configuring and developing their structures, and how national and international policy-makers can act to protect socially determined goals. Global media systems like the Internet raise a classic problem of political organization. As the effects and consequences of global technology extend beyond the mechanisms for governing them, we must investigate the terms under which national and international governance mechanisms can claim to legitimately represent the world's nations and citizenry. Scholars of political communication and the philosophy of communication should investigate the institutional and communicative resources and requirements necessary for global governance. Scholars must also examine the real practices and effects of existing national and international policy instruments and institutions. Closer study of these areas will fill the gaps that currently exist in our knowledge of how new media are affecting the regulatory landscape and help point the way towards sensible, humane and representative global communications policy.

NOTES

1 An example of such research can be found in Johnson and Post (1997), who argue that global networks constitute their own spaces with their own sovereignty. These authors underplay the fact that those who communicate over ICTs are already subject to real-world sovereigns who have an obligation to protect their citizens.

2 Under these treaties, the following works may be protected: (1) both unpublished and published works of an author who is a national or resident of a country that is a member of these treaties; or (2) published works, with permission, of an author who is not a national or resident of a country that is a member of these treaties.

3 For more details on the Directive, see the Directive on the Protection of Individuals with Regard to the Processing of Personal Data and on the Free Movement of Such Data. For a concise summary of the Directive's provisions, see Rosenoer (1997: 156– 60).

4 For example, the Privacy Act of 1974 (5 U.S.C. § 552a) mandates limited privacy protections for government-maintained databases, including the right of individuals to review and correct personal information stored in government records. The rules do not apply to privately held databases.

5 Although the US continues to advocate self-regulation and narrow sectoral rules, numerous analysts have deemed the US approach a failure (Branscomb, 1994; Gellman, 1997; Global Internet Liberty Campaign, 1998; Green et al., 2000; *The Economist*, 1999). US privacy protections are a patchwork of inconsistent, weak and inadequately enforced rules which leave US citizens with no substantive protections for personal information. No federal agency oversees or enforces data protection in the US, and support for such rules among the business community is weak (Gellman, 1997: 267, 274; Mitchener, 2000).

6 Under the agreement, any organization must offer individuals the opportunity to choose (opt out) whether and how personal information they provide is used or disclosed to third parties. For sensitive information (i.e. personal information about medical or health conditions, racial or ethnic origin, political opinions, religious or philosophical beliefs, trade union membership or information specifying the sex life of the individual) they must be given affirmative or explicit (opt in) choice if the information is to be used for a purpose other than those for which it was originally collected. Organizations are required to take reasonable precautions to protect information from loss, misuse and unauthorized access, disclosure, alteration and destruction and to take reasonable steps to ensure individuals have access to personal information about them and are able to correct, amend or delete that information where it is inaccurate.

7 This section focuses on speech rights restrictions posed by national governments. Freedom of expression and access to communication resources can also be restricted by non-governmental actors, such as system operators or network infrastructure owners (Office of Technology Assessment, 1990: 169). While this type of censorship is rare and ineffective at present owing to the competitive market for network access and services and the current open network architecture, it may figure more prominently in the future (Cooper, 2000; Lessig, 1999: 167). Although not our focus here, we believe that any private sector developments that threaten freedom of expression should be closely examined by policy-makers and corrected when necessary.

8 Although the US rules were struck down in the resulting Supreme Court case of *Reno v. ACLU* (1997), the US Congress has continued to pursue legislation that aims to restrict the availability of pornography on the Internet. Congress has mandated that public schools and libraries who accept designated government technology subsidies use filtering software to censor indecent content when providing Internet access to students and library patrons (*United States v. American Library Association*, 2003).

9 For example, while markets systems have as their primary goal the efficient allocation of resources, efficiency is only one value among many that most countries would apply to communication systems. Markets and other models of regulation must be evaluated against the range of goals which countries aim to achieve, including those related to privacy, access and speech rights.

10 WIPO also helps countries create and reform intellectual property rules, comply with international intellectual property treaties, and encourage more specialists to enter the intellectual property field (Alleyne, 1995: 30). In the 1990s, WIPO took on the additional role of investigating Internet domain name trademark conflicts, making recommendations on how to resolve top-level domain disputes, and otherwise managing the international domain name trademark regime (Mueller, 1999: 505–6).

REFERENCES

Abrahamson, David (1998) 'The visible hand: money, markets, and media evolution', *Journalism and Mass Communication Quarterly*, 75 (1): 14–18.

Alleyne, Mark D. (1995) *International Power and International Communication*. New York: St Martin's Press.

Araki, Toshihiro (1989) 'Information technology and legal issues', in Meheroo Jussawalla, Tadayuki Okuma and Toshihiro Araki (eds), *Information Technology and Global Interdependence*. New York: Greenwood. pp. 193–6.

Associated Press (2000) 'French court says Yahoo! broke racial law', *New York Times*, 23 May (online).

Babe, Robert E. (1995) *Communication and the Transformation of Economics: Essays in Information, Public Policy, and Political Economy*. Boulder, CO: Westview.

Barber, Benjamin R. (1984) *Strong Democracy: Participatory Politics for a New Age*. Berkeley, CA: University of California Press.

Barron, Sandy (2000) 'Myanmar works hard to keep the Internet out', *New York Times*, 14 July (online).

Benkler, Yochai (2000) 'Net regulation: taking stock and looking forward', *University of Colorado Law Review*, 71: 1203–61.

Bennett, W. Lance (2003) 'Communicating global activism: strengths and vulnerabilities of networked politics', *Information, Communication & Society*, 6 (2): 143–68.

Berne Convention (1886) Berne Convention for the Protection of Literary and Artistic Works, 9 September 1886, 828 U.N.T.S. 221 (1972).

Besser, Howard (1999) 'Will copyright protect the public interest?', *Peace Review*, 11 (1): 25–31.

Bettig, Ronald V. (1992) 'Critical perspectives on the history and philosophy of copyright', *Critical Studies in Mass Communication*, 9 (2): 131–55.

Bettig, Ronald V. (1997) 'The enclosure of cyberspace', *Critical Studies in Mass Communication*, 14 (2): 138–57.

Bing, J., Forsberg, P. and Nygaard, E. (1983) 'Legal problems related to transborder data flows', in Organization for Economic Cooperation and Development (ed.), *An Exploration of Legal Issues in Information and Communication Technologies*, 8. Paris: OECD. pp. 59–135.

Bitterman, Mary G.F. (1989) 'Conclusions from TIDE II', in Meheroo Jussawalla, Tadayuki Okuma and Toshihiro Araki (eds), *Information Technology and Global Interdependence*. New York: Greenwood. pp. 307–8.

Blumenthal, Marjory S. (1999) 'The politics and policies of enhancing trustworthiness for information systems', *Communication Law and Policy*, 4 (4): 513–55.

Boyle, James (1997) *Shamans, Software, and Spleens: Law and the Construction of the Information Society*. Cambridge, MA: Harvard University Press.

Braman, Sandra and Sreberny-Mohammadi, Annebelle (1996) *Communication and Transnational Civil Society*. Creskill, NJ: Hampton.

Branscomb, Anne Wells (1994) *Who Owns Information? From Privacy to Public Access*. New York: Basic.

Braunstein, Yale M. (1989) 'Economics on intellectual property rights in the international arena', in Meheroo Jussawalla, Tadayuki Okuma and Toshihiro Araki (eds), *Information Technology and Global Interdependence*. New York: Greenwood. pp. 183–92.

Burk, Dan L. (1997) 'The market for digital piracy', in Brian Kahin and Charles Nesson (eds), *Borders in Cyberspace: Information Policy and the Global Information Infrastructure*. Cambridge, MA: MIT Press. pp. 205–34.

Calabrese, Andrew (1999) 'Communication and the end of sovereignty', *Info*, 1 (4): 313–26.

Carey, James W. (1998) 'The Internet and the end of the national communication system: uncertain predictions of an uncertain future', *Journalism and Mass Communication Quarterly*, 75 (1): 23–34.

Cate, Fred H. (1994) 'Global information policy-making and domestic law', *Indiana Journal of Global Legal Studies*, 1 (2): 467–87.

Cate, Fred H. (1995) 'The First Amendment and the national information infrastructure', *Wake Forest Law Review*, 30 (1): 1–50.

Cochran, Wendell (1996) 'Computers, privacy, and journalists: a suggested code of information practices', *Journal of Mass Media Ethics*, 11 (4): 210–22.

Cooper, Mark (2000) 'Open access to the broadband Internet: technical and economic discrimination in closed proprietary networks', *University of Colorado Law Review*, 71: 1011–69.

Council of Europe (1981) Convention for the Protection of Individuals with Regard to the Automatic Processing of Personal Data, ETS No. 108, Strasburg.

Delaney, Kevin J. (2000) 'Yahoo! returns to French court to address Nazi paraphernalia', *Wall Street Journal*, 11 August: B10.

Demac, Donna A. (1994) 'Multimedia and intellectual property rights', *Media Studies Journal*, 8 (1): 59– 63.

Dewey, John (1954) *The Public and Its Problems* (1927). Athens, OH: Ohio University Press.

Downing, John D.H. (2001) *Radical Media: Rebellious Communication and Social Movements*. Thousand Oaks, CA: Sage.

Entman, Robert (1989) *Democracy without Citizens*. New York: Oxford University Press.

Enzensberger, Hans Magnus (1974) *The Consciousness Industry*. New York: Seabury.

EU Data Protection Directive (1995) Directive 95/46/EC of the European Parliament and of the Council of 24 October 1995 on the Protection of Individuals with Regard to the Processing of Personal Data and the Free Movement of Such Data. Available online: http://www.privacy.org/pi/intl_orgs/ec/final_EU_Data_Protection.html

Feemster, Ron (2000) 'When libraries faced the future', *University Business*, February. Available online: http://www.universitybusiness.com/0002/library.html

Ford, Tamara V. and Gil, Genève (2001) 'Radical Internet use', in John D.H. Downing (ed.), *Radical Media: Rebellious Communication and Social Movements*. Thousand Oaks, CA: Sage. pp. 201–34.

Frederick, Howard (1993) 'Networks and emergence of global civil society', in Linda M. Harasim (ed.), *Global Networks: Computers and International Communication*. Cambridge, MA: MIT Press. pp. 283–95.

Froomkin, A. Michael (1997) 'The Internet as a source of regulatory arbitrage', in Brian Kahin and Charles Nesson (eds), *Borders in Cyberspace: Information Policy and the Global Information Infrastructure*. Cambridge, MA: MIT Press. pp. 129–63.

Gandy, Oscar H. (1993) 'Toward a political economy of personal information', *Critical Studies in Mass Communication*, 10: 70–97.

Garfinkel, Simson (2000) 'Welcome to Sealand. Now bugger off', *Wired*, July: 230–9.

Gellman, Robert (1997) 'Conflict and overlap in privacy regulation: national, international, and private', in Brian Kahin and Charles Nesson (eds), *Borders in Cyberspace: Information Policy and the Global Information Infrastructure*. Cambridge, MA: MIT Press. pp. 255–82.

Gilpin, Robert (1987) *The Political Economy of International Relations*. Princeton, NJ: Princeton University Press.

Glickman, Howard and Carney, Dan (2000) 'Watching over the World Wide Web', *Business Week*, 28 August: 195–6.

Global Internet Liberty Campaign (1998) 'Privacy and Human Rights: An International Survey of Privacy Laws and Practice'. Available online: http://www.gilc.org/privacy/survey/intro.html

Goldsmith, Jack L. (1998) 'Against cyberanarchy', *The University of Chicago Law Review*, 65 (4): 1199–250.

Goldstein, Paul (1994) *Copyright's Highway: The Law and Lore of Copyright from Gutenberg to the Celestial Jukebox*. New York: Hill & Wang.

Green, H., France, M., Stepanek, M. and Borrus, A. (2000) 'Online privacy: it's time for rules in Wonderland', *Business Week*, 20 March: 83–8, 92.

Halbert, Debora J. (1999) *Intellectual Property in the Information Age*. Westport, CT: Quorum.

Hamelink, Cees (1991) *Communication: The Most Violated Human Right*. Stockholm: Inter Press Service Dispatch.

Hausman, Carl (1994) 'Information age ethics: privacy ground rules for navigating in cyberspace', *Journal of Mass Media Ethics*, 9 (3): 135–44.

Hibbert, Bill (1999) 'Regulation of electronic publishing and commerce', *Info*, 1 (5): 393–404.

Hilton, George W. (1972) 'The basic behavior of regulatory commissions', *American Economic Review*, 62 (2): 47–54.

Hirschman, Albert O. (1986) *Rival Views of Market Society and Other Recent Essays*. New York: Viking.

Hudson, Heather (1994) 'Toward universal access to information', *Media Studies Journal*, 8 (1): 137–42.

Human Rights Watch (1999) *The Internet in the Mideast and North Africa: Free Expression and Censorship*. New York: Human Rights Watch.

Hunter, Christopher D. and Herbeck, Dale (1999) 'From LaMacchia to the No Electronic Theft Act: criminal copyright infringement and the freedom of expression'. Paper presented at the Annual Meeting of the International Communication Association, San Francisco, CA.

International Covenant on Civil and Political Rights (1966), G.A. Res. 2200, U.N. GAOR, 21st Sess., Supp. No. 16, at 52, U.N. Doc. A/6316, art. 19.

Jackson, Margaret (1998) 'Keeping secrets: international developments to protect undisclosed business information and trade secrets', *Information, Communication & Society*, 1 (4): 467–87.

Johnson, David R. and Post, David G. (1997) 'The rise of law on the global network', in Brian Kahin and Charles Nesson (eds), *Borders in Cyberspace: Information Policy and the Global Information Infrastructure*. Cambridge, MA: MIT Press. pp. 3–47.

Johnson, J.T. (1994) 'The private I, you, they', *Journal of Mass Media Ethics*, 9 (4): 223–8.

Jussawalla, Meheroo (1992) *The Economics of Intellectual Property in a World without Frontiers*. New York: Greenwood.

Kahin, Brian and Nesson, Charles (1997) 'Preface', in Brian Kahin and Charles Nesson (eds), *Borders in Cyberspace: Information Policy and the Global Information Infrastructure*. Cambridge, MA: MIT Press. pp. vii–xi.

Kahn, Alfred E. (1988) *The Economics of Regulation: Principles and Institutions*. Cambridge, MA: MIT Press.

Kavanaugh, Andrea L. (1998) *The Social Control of Technology in North Africa*. Westport, CT: Praeger.

Kindleberger, Charles P. (1978) *International Economics*, 6th edn (1st edn 1958). Homewood, IL: Irwin.

Kirby, Michael D. (1983) 'Legal aspects of information technology', in Organization for Economic Cooperation and Development (ed.), *An Exploration of Legal Issues in Information and Communication Technologies*, 8. Paris: OECD. pp. 9–57.

Kirby, Michael D. (1989) 'Informatics and democratic society: beyond the Tokyo Summit', in Meheroo Jussawalla, Tadayuki Okuma and Toshihiro Araki (eds), *Information Technology and Global Interdependence*. New York: Greenwood. pp. 157–71.

Krasner, Stephen D. (1991) 'Global communications and national power: life on the Pareto optimal curve', *World Politics*, 43 (3): 336–66.

Labunski, Richard (1997) 'The First Amendment at the crossroads: free expression and new media technology', *Communication Law and Policy*, 2 (2): 165–212.

Lessig, Lawrence (1999) *Code and Other Laws of Cyberspace*. New York: Basic.

Lessig, Lawrence (2001) *The Future of Ideas: The Fate of the Commons in a Connected World*. New York: Random House.

Louveaux, S., Salaün, A. and Poullet, Y. (1999) 'User protection in cyberspace', *Info*, 1 (6): 521–37.

MacAvoy, Paul W. (1979) *The Regulated Industries and the Economy*. New York: Norton.

Maxeiner, James R. (1995) 'Freedom of information and the EU Data Protection Directive', *Federal Communications Law Journal*, 48 (1): 93–104.

May, Christopher (1998) 'Capital, knowledge and ownership', *Information, Communication & Society*, 1 (3): 246–69.

Mayer-Schönberger, Viktor and Foster, Teree E. (1997) 'A regulatory web: free speech and the global information infrastructure', in Brian Kahin and Charles Nesson (eds), *Borders in Cyberspace: Information Policy and the Global Information Infrastructure*. Cambridge, MA: MIT Press. pp. 235–54.

McCarthy, Terry (2000) 'China dot now', *Time*, 28 February: 16–23.

Melody, William H. (1990) 'Communication policy in the global information economy: whither the public interest?', in Marjorie Ferguson (ed.), *Public Communication: The New Imperatives*. Newbury Park, CA: Sage. pp. 16–39.

Mensch, Elizabeth (1990) 'The history of mainstream legal thought', in David Kairys (ed.), *The Politics of Law: A Progressive Critique*. New York: Pantheon. pp. 13–37.

Michalski, Wolfgang (1989) 'Advanced information technologies: challenges and opportunities', in Meheroo Jussawalla, Tadayuki Okuma and Toshihiro Araki (eds), *Information Technology and Global Interdependence.* New York: Greenwood. pp. 9–18.

Michelman, Frank I. (1987) 'Possession vs. distribution in the constitutional idea of property', *Iowa Law Review*, 72: 1319–50.

Mitchener, Brandon (2000) 'EU privacy rules carry a cost', *Wall Street Journal*, 14–15 April: 29, 32.

Morris, Merrill and Ogan, Christine (1996) 'The Internet as mass medium', *Journal of Communication*, 46 (1): 39–50.

Mosco, Vincent (1988) 'Toward a theory of the state and telecommunications policy', *Journal of Communication*, 38: 107–25.

Mosco, Vincent (1989) *The Pay-per Society: Computers and Communication in the Information Age.* Norwood, NJ: Ablex.

Mueller, Milton (1999) 'ICANN and Internet governance: sorting through the debris of "self-regulation"', *Info*, 1 (6): 497–520.

Murphy, Jamie (1999) 'Australia passes law on limiting the Internet', *New York Times*, 1 July (online).

Office of Technology Assessment (1990) *Critical Connections: Communications for the Future.* Washington, DC: US Government Printing Office.

OECD (1981) *Guidelines Governing the Protection of Privacy and Transborder Data Flows of Personal Data.* Paris: OECD.

OECD (1995) *Information Technology Policies: Organizational Structure in Member Countries*, 3 (43). Paris: OECD.

OECD (1997) *Global Information Infrastructure – Global Information Society (GII–GIS): Policy Recommendations for Action*, 81 (5). Paris: OECD.

Perritt, Henry H., Jr (1997) 'Jurisdiction in cyberspace: the role of intermediaries', in Brian Kahin and Charles Nesson (eds), *Borders in Cyberspace: Information Policy and the Global Information Infrastructure.* Cambridge, MA: MIT Press. pp. 164–202.

Peterson, Sandra Byrd (1995) 'Your life as an open book: has technology rendered personal privacy virtually obsolete?', *Federal Communications Law Journal*, 48 (1): 163–86.

Plotkin, Adam S. (1996) 'The First Amendment and democracy: the challenge of new technology', *Journal of Mass Media Ethics*, 11 (4): 236–45.

Pool, Ithiel de Sola (1983) *Technologies of Freedom.* Cambridge, MA: Harvard University Press.

Privacy Act (1974) 5 U.S.C. § 552a.

Proceedings of the Annenberg Washington Program Panel One (1995) 'Information issues: intellectual property, privacy, integrity, interoperability, and the economics of information', *Federal Communications Law Journal*, 48 (1): 5–55.

Proceedings of the Annenberg Washington Program Panel Two (1995) 'Information policy making', *Federal Communications Law Journal*, 48 (1): 57–91.

Quaterman, John S. (1990) *The Matrix: Computer Networks and Conferencing Systems Worldwide.* Bedford, MA: Digital.

Reidenberg, Joel R. (1997) 'Governing networks and rule-making in cyberspace', in Brian Kahin and Charles Nesson (eds), *Borders in Cyberspace: Information Policy and the Global Information Infrastructure.* Cambridge, MA: MIT Press. pp. 84–105.

Reno (1997) *Reno, Attorney General of the United States, et al. v. American Civil Liberties Union et al.*, 521U.S. 844.

Robinson, Peter (1989) 'Information technology and the relationship among OECD countries', in Meheroo Jussawalla, Tadayuki Okuma and Toshihiro Araki (eds), *Information Technology and Global Interdependence.* New York: Greenwood. pp. 40–6.

Rogerson, Kenneth S. and Thomas, G. Dale (1998) 'Internet regulation process model: the effect of societies, communities, and governments', *Political Communication*, 15 (4): 427–44.

Rosenoer, Jonathan (1997) *CyberLaw: The Law of the Internet.* New York: Springer.

Rosenthal, Elizabeth (2000) 'China issues rules to limit e-mail and web content', *New York Times*, 27 January: A1.

Rucinski, Dianne (1991) 'The centrality of reciprocity to communication and democracy', *Critical Studies in Mass Communication*, 9 (2): 184–94.

Samorski, Jan H., Huffman, John L. and Trauth, Denise M. (1997) 'The V-chip and cyber cops: technology vs. regulation', *Communication Law and Policy*, 2 (1): 143–64.

Schiller, Dan (1999) *Digital Capitalism: Networking the Global Market System.* Cambridge, MA: MIT Press.

Schneider, Howard (2000) 'Syria advances cautiously into the online age', *Washington Post*, 27 April: A1.

Sell, Susan K. (1995) 'The origins of a trade-based approach to intellectual protection: the role of industry organizations', *Science Communication*, 17 (2): 163–85.

Smith, Craig (2000) 'Tough new rules don't faze Chinese Internet start-ups', *New York Times*, 4 October: C2.

Streeter, Thomas (1996) *Selling the Air: A Critique of the Policy of Commercial Broadcasting in the United States.* Chicago: University of Chicago Press.

Taubman, Geoffrey (1998) 'A not-so World Wide Web: the Internet, China, and the challenges to nondemocratic rule', *Political Communication*, 15 (2): 255–72.

The Economist (1999) 'The end of privacy', 1 May: 15, 21–3.

Thurow, Lester C. (1997) 'Needed: a new system of intellectual property rights', *Harvard Business Review*, September–October: 95–103.

United Nations (2003) International Telecommunications Union: Declaration of Principles: Building the Information Society: A Global Challenge in the New Millenium. 12 December 2003, 12 January 2005. Available online: http:www.itu.int/wsis/docs/geneva/official/dop.html

United States v. American Library Association (2003) 156 Supreme Court Reports, Lawyers' Edition 2d. 221.

Universal Declaration of Human Rights (1948) G.A. Res. 217 (III), U.N. Doc. A/810, art. 19.

Waltz, K. (1979) *Theory of International Politics*. Reading, MA: Addison-Wesley.

Waterman, Peter (1998) *Globalization, Social Movements and the New Internationalism*. London: Mansell.

Westin, Alan F. (1967) *Privacy and Freedom*. New York: Atheneum.

Wheeler, Deborah L. (1998) 'Global culture or culture clash: new information technologies in the Islamic world – a view from Kuwait', *Communication Research*, 25 (4): 359–76.

White House (1997) 'A framework for global electronic commerce'. 1 July.

Wriston, Walter B. (1994) 'The inevitable global conversation', *Media Studies Journal*, 8 (1): 17–25.

Yahoo! Inc. v. Le Ligue Contre le Racisme (2001) 169 F.Supp. 2d. 1181 (N.D. Cal. 2001).

Zhao, Yuezhi (2000) 'Caught in the web: the public interest and the battle for control of China's information superhighway', *Info*, 2 (1): 41–66.

22

The Information Society Revisited

FRANK WEBSTER

The term 'information society' is widely used both inside academia and in the wider society. One has but to pick up the newspapers or turn on the television to encounter references to a new information age, or to browse the shelves of bookshops to come across titles displaying the words. There are several reasons why this should be so, but most prominent among them is surely the prevalence of information itself in the present era. There is simply a very great deal more information about than hitherto: perhaps most obviously in an explosion of media and media products (from cable TV channels to compact disk records, from mobile telephones to the Internet), but also importantly in the rapid and accelerating permeation of computerized technologies throughout society, in the increased provision and take-up of education in most social systems, and in the growth of occupations that deal, for the most part, with information (clerks, professionals, instructors and so on). Experiencing such developments, it is not surprising that many observers have come to describe our age in terms of one of its most palpable features: hence, logically, the information society.

In 1995 I published the first edition of a book, *Theories of the Information Society*, that brought together a range of social theories which attempted to account for the significance of information over recent decades. The presumption was that in this chapter the book's arguments would be updated to take account of new thinking that has come from debate on and consideration of the development of more recent phenomena such as cyberspace and cyborgs. It is certain that the rapid development of these new technologies as well as of digital television and mobile telecommunications, and the take-up of personal computers, e-mail and e-commerce, have further stimulated talk of an information age having come upon us. Again, the fact that there is now a great deal more information around than even a decade ago, and that this is demonstrable from everyday experiences (from watching television round the clock, through electronic banking services, to a significant increase in the information intensity of a good deal of modern-day work), has encouraged commentators to declare, more confidently than ever, that we inhabit an information society.

It is in this context that this chapter reviews and evaluates conceptions of an information society. At the outset I state plainly my own view on the salience of the term. My conclusion is that most of the conceptions of an 'information society' are of limited use to social scientists, and still less to the wider public's understanding of transformations in the world today. I shall reveal why I have come to this conclusion in the course of this chapter, but, bluntly put, the reasons are as follows. I find most conceptions of information society unsatisfactory because of:

- inconsistencies and lack of clarity as regards criteria used to distinguish an information society;
- imprecise use of the term 'information';
- the unsupportable supposition of information society theorists that quantitative increases in information lead to qualitative social changes.

These objections neither mean that I find the massive spread of information unworthy of study, nor even that I reject all conceptions of the 'information society'. Indeed, it seems to me that, in one particular way (the sixth definition I review later), information has become so important and consequential for how we live that it is valid to conceive of us inhabiting an information society. Nonetheless, most definitions of an 'information society' I do find unconvincing, especially because they presuppose mistakenly that the enormous growth of information and virtuoso ways of handling it leads to a new social order.

DEFINITIONS OF AN INFORMATION SOCIETY

It is possible to identify six ways of distinguishing an information society. Five of these focus on measures of one or other of the following phenomena:

- technological innovation and diffusion;
- occupational change;
- economic value;
- information flows;
- the expansion of symbols and signs.

These are not mutually exclusive, though scholars place different emphases on each dimension (Duff, 2000). All of these conceptions rely on a quantitative assessment of a particular phenomenon to argue that its expansion has brought about a qualitatively different form of social organization. In this way each theorization adopts a form of reasoning which is *ex post*

facto: there is evidence of there being more information in society today, therefore we have an information society. As we shall see, there are serious difficulties with this form of argument (May, 2002). Nonetheless, it is undeniable that it has an immediate, even commonsensical, appeal, and it is a familiar form of reasoning. For example, it is frequently suggested that, just as a decline in the numbers of farm workers and a rise in factory employment signalled the end of agricultural society and the emergence of industrialism, so too are quantitative changes in information indicative of the coming of an information society. I criticize this form of argument later.

The sixth definition of an information society is singular in that it refers, not to the fact of there being more information, but to changes in the ways in which life is now conducted because of information. The argument offered here, that theoretical information/ knowledge is the fulcrum of contemporary life, suggests a distinct conception of the information society. In my view, this is the most persuasive (if the least commonly mooted) argument for the applicability of the concept of information society and it is one that I would commend to scholars and students alike.

I propose now to examine each of the first five definitions in turn. I then consider the questions of quantity and quality, and the nature of information, before examining the sixth definition.

Technology

Technological conceptions centre on an array of innovations that have appeared over the past 20 years or so. New technologies are one of the most visible indicators of new times, and accordingly are frequently taken to signal the coming of an information society. These include cable and satellite television, computer-to-computer communications, PCs, new office technologies – notably online information services and word processors – and CD-ROM facilities. The suggestion is, simply, that such a volume of technological innovations must lead to a reconstitution of the social world because its impact is so profound.

During the late 1970s and early 1980s commentators got excited about the 'mighty micro's' capacity to revolutionize our way of life (Evans, 1979; Martin, 1978; McHale, 1976), and none more so than the world's leading futurist, Alvin Toffler (1980). His suggestion, in a memorable metaphor, is that, over time, the world has been decisively shaped by three waves of technological innovation, each as unstoppable as the mightiest tidal force. The first was the agricultural revolution and the second the industrial revolution. The third is the information revolution that is engulfing us now and which presages a new way of living (which, attests Toffler, will turn out fine if only we ride with the wave).

More recently, futurism's enthusiasms have been boosted by computing's capacity to transform telecommunications, to in effect merge the two technologies (Toffler, 1990). It is this spread of computer communications technologies (e-mail, data and text communications, online information exchange, etc.) that currently inspires most speculation about a new society in the making (Dertouzos, 1997; Gates, 1995; Negroponte, 1995). The rapid growth of the Internet especially, with its capacities for simultaneously promoting economic success, education and the democratic process, has stimulated much commentary. Media regularly feature accounts of the arrival of an information 'superhighway' on which the populace must become adept at driving. Authoritative voices are raised to announce that 'a new order ... is being forced upon an unsuspecting world by advances in telecommunications. The future is being born in the so-called *Information Superhighways* ... [and] anyone bypassed by these highways faces ruin' (Angell, 1995: 10).

More soberly, the spread of national, international and genuinely global information exchanges between and within banks, corporations, governments, universities and voluntary bodies indicates a similar trend towards the establishment of a technological infrastructure that allows instant computer communications at any time of day in any place that is suitably equipped (Connors, 1993).

Most academic analysts, while avoiding the exaggerated language of futurists and politicians, have nonetheless adopted what is at root a similar approach (Feather, 1998). For instance, from Japan there have been attempts to measure the growth of *joho shakai* (information society) since the 1960s (Duff et al., 1996). The Japanese Ministry of Posts and Telecommunications (MPT) commenced a census in 1975 which endeavours to track changes in the volume (e.g. numbers of telephone messages) and vehicles (e.g. penetration of telecommunications equipment) of information using sophisticated techniques (Ito, 1991, 1994). In Britain, a much respected school of thought has devised a neo-Schumpeterian approach to change. Combining Schumpeter's argument that major technological innovations bring about 'creative destruction' with Kondratieff's theme of 'long waves' of economic development, these researchers contend that information and communications technologies represent the establishment of a new epoch (Freeman, 1987) which will be uncomfortable during its earlier phases, but over the longer term will be economically beneficial. This new 'technoeconomic paradigm' constitutes the 'information age' which is set to mature early in this new century (cf. Hall and Preston, 1988).

Occupational Change

This is the approach most favoured by sociologists. It is also one closely associated, with good reason, with the work of Daniel Bell (1973) who is the most important theorist of 'post-industrial society' (a term virtually synonymous with information society, and used as such in much of Bell's own writing). Here the occupational structure is examined over time and patterns of change are observed. The suggestion is that we have achieved an information society when the preponderance of occupations is found in information work. The decline of manufacturing employment and the rise of service sector employment is interpreted as the loss of manual jobs and its replacement with white-collar work. Since the raw material of non-manual labour is information (as opposed to the brawn and dexterity plus machinery characteristic of manual labour), substantial increases in such informational work can be said to announce the arrival of an information society.

There is *prima facie* evidence for this: in Western European and North American nations over 70 per cent of the workforce is now found in the service sector of the economy, and white-collar occupations are now a majority. On these grounds alone it would seem plausible to argue that we inhabit an information society since the 'predominant group (of occupations) consists of information workers' (Bell, 1979: 183).

An emphasis on occupational change as the marker of an information society has displaced once dominant concerns with technology in recent years. It should also be understood that this conception of the 'information society' is quite different from that which suggests it is information and communications *technologies* which distinguish the new age. A focus on occupational change is one which stresses the transformative power of information itself rather than the influence of information technologies, information being what is drawn upon and generated in occupations or embodied in people through education and experiences. Charles Leadbetter (1999) titled a book to highlight the insight that it is information which is foundational in the present epoch. 'Living on thin air' was once a familiar admonition by the worldly-wise to those reluctant to earn a living by the sweat of their brows. But all such advice is now outdated, Leadbetter arguing that this is exactly how to make one's livelihood in the information age. *Living on Thin Air* proclaims that 'thinking smart', being 'inventive', and having the capacity to develop and exploit 'networks' are actually the key to the new 'weightless' economy (Coyne, 1997; Dertouzos, 1997), since wealth production comes, not from physical effort, but from 'ideas, knowledge, skills, talent and creativity' (Leadbetter, 1999: 18). His book highlights examples of such successes: designers, deal-makers, image-creators, musicians, biotechnologists, genetic engineers and niche-finders abound.

Leadbetter puts into popular parlance what many thinkers now argue as a matter of course.

A range of influential writers, from Robert Reich (1992) and Peter Drucker (1993) to Manuel Castells (1996–8), suggest that the economy today is led and energized by people whose major characteristic is the capacity to manipulate information. Preferred terms vary between authors, from 'symbolic analysts' and 'knowledge experts' to 'informational labour', but in all one message is constant: today's movers and shakers are those whose work involves creating and using information. Twenty per cent (and expanding) of the US workforce (Reich, 1992: 179) is constituted by this group which manages, designs, creates and refines information, this being the raw material of our globalized and fast-changing world.

All analysts agree that information operatives vary enormously in what they actually do. For instance, many manage corporate affairs in various capacities, some handle financial networks, others work in a burgeoning media sector, or in the law, or higher education, or accounting, or public relations, or local government, while still others are in design where they are occupied with adding value to mundane materials. Despite such diversity, all share a propensity to reskill themselves as a matter of routine. In this way they are at one with the flexible world economy which demands constant change on all sides. This commitment to what others have called 'lifelong learning' ensures that informational labour keeps ahead of the game, capable of building a portfolio of experience on various projects while ever ready to adapt positively to novel situations.

A corollary of this is that informational labour, whatever particular differences are in evidence, shares talents most commonly nurtured in higher education. Specific skills learned in universities do matter, but they quickly date and the graduate must constantly retrain to keep abreast of things. Much more important then is the 'human capital' nurtured in the experience of higher education, something which expresses itself in a heightened capacity to communicate effectively, to analyse situations dispassionately, to come up with a strategy for advance, to broker deals with other actors, to identify strengths and weaknesses in a given milieu, and so on (Reich, 1992: 178–9).

The inculcation of such qualities places an especial premium on higher education and, in this light, it is scarcely surprising that the calibre and capabilities of a nation's education system have become central to government policy (Brown and Lauder, 1995). The *leitmotiv* of Tony Blair's UK administration from its outset in 1997 has been 'education, education, education', a litany repeated in all advanced nations which intend to see their citizenry capture a high proportion of 'symbolic analysis' jobs in the future (Seltzer and Bentley, 1999). Not surprisingly, then, a system of mass higher education is taken to be an indicator of an information society.

Economy

This approach charts the growth in economic worth of informational activities. If one is able to plot an increase in the proportion of gross national product (GNP) accounted for by the information business then logically there comes a point at which one may declare the achievement of an information economy. Once the greater part of economic activity is taken up by information activity rather than say subsistence agriculture or industrial manufacture, then it follows that we may speak of an information society (Jonscher, 1999).

In principle straightforward, but in practice an extraordinarily complex econometric exercise, much of the pioneering work was done by Fritz Machlup (1902–83) of Princeton University (Machlup, 1962). His identification of information industries such as education, law, publishing, media and computer manufacture, and his attempt to estimate their changing economic worth, have been refined by Marc Porat (1977a, 1977b).

Porat distinguished the primary and secondary information sectors of the economy, the former being susceptible to ready economic valuation since it had an ascribable market price, the latter being harder to price but nonetheless essential to all modern-day organizations, involving informational activities within companies and state institutions (for example, the personnel wings of a company, the research and development sections of a business). In this way Porat is able to distinguish the two informational sectors, then to consolidate them, to separate out the non-informational elements of the economy and, by reaggregrating national economic statistics, to conclude that, with almost half the US's GNP accounted for by these combined informational sectors, 'the United States is now an information-based economy'. As such it is an 'information society [where] the major arenas of economic activity are the information goods and service producers, and the public and private (secondary information sector) bureaucracies' (Porat, 1978: 32).

Space

This conception of the information society, while it does draw on economics and sociology, has at its core the geographer's distinctive stress on space. Here the major emphasis is on information networks which connect locations and in consequence can have profound effects on the organization of time and space. It has become an especially popular index of the information society throughout the 1990s as information networks have become increasingly prominent features of social organization.

It is usual to stress the centrality of information networks that may link together different locations within and between an office, a town, a region, a continent and indeed the entire world. As the electricity grid runs through an entire country to be accessed at will by individuals with the appropriate connections, so too may we imagine now a 'wired society' operating at the national, international and global level to provide an 'information ring main' (Barron and Curnow, 1979) to each home, shop, university and office – and even to the mobile individual who has his laptop and modem in his briefcase.

Increasingly we are all connected to networks of one sort or another – and they themselves are expanding their reach and capabilities in an exponential manner (Urry, 2000). We come across them personally at many levels: in electronic point of sale terminals in shops and restaurants, in accessing data across continents, in e-mailing colleagues, or in exchanging information on the Internet. We may not personally have experienced this realm of 'cyberspace', but the information ring main functions still more frantically at the level of international banks, intergovernmental agencies and corporate relationships.

A popular idea here is that the electronic highways result in a new emphasis on the flow of information (Castells, 1996–8), something which leads to a radical revision of time/space relations. In a 'network society' constraints of the clock and of distance have been radically relieved, the corporations and even the individual being capable of managing their affairs effectively on a global scale. The academic researcher no longer needs to travel from the university to consult the Library of Congress since she can interrogate it on the Internet; the business corporation no longer needs to fly out its managers to find out what is happening in their Far East outlets because computer communications enable routine and systematic surveillance from afar. The suggestion of many is that this heralds a major transformation of our social order (Mulgan, 1991), sufficient to mark even a revolutionary change.

Culture

The final conception of an information society is easily acknowledged. Each of us is aware from our everyday lives that there has been an extraordinary increase in the information in social circulation. For instance, television programming is round-the-clock. There are also several broadcast channels available, and the TV receiver has been enhanced to incorporate video technologies, cable and satellite, and even computerized information services. More recently, an avalanche of computerized games has become attached to PCs and 'virtual reality' products have begun to enter the home. There is very much more radio output available now than even a decade ago, at local, national and international level. And radios are no longer fixed in the front room, but spread through the home, in the car, in the office and, with the

Walkman, everywhere. Movies have long been an important part of people's information environment. Though over the years attendances at cinemas have declined, movies are today very much more prevalent than ever: available still at cinema outlets, broadcast on television, readily borrowed from video rental shops, cheaply purchased from the shelves of chain stores. Walk along any street and it is almost impossible to miss the advertising hoardings, the billboards, the window displays in shops. Visit any railway or bus station and one cannot but be struck by the widespread availability of paperback books and inexpensive magazines. In addition, audiotape, compact disk and radio all offer more, and more readily available, music, poetry, drama, humour and education to the general public. Newspapers are extensively available and a good many new titles fall on our doorsteps as free sheets. Junk mail is delivered daily. And so forth.

The informational features of our world are more thoroughly penetrative than a short list of television, radio and other media systems suggests. This sort of listing implies that new media surround us, presenting us with messages to which we may or may not respond. In truth the informational environment is a great deal more intimate, more constitutive of us, than this suggests. One may consider, for example, the informational dimensions of the clothes we wear, the styling of our hair and faces, the very ways in which nowadays we work at our image (from body shape to speech, people are intensely aware of the messages they may be projecting and how they feel about themselves in certain clothes, with a particular hairstyle, etc.). Reflection on the complexities of fashion, the intricacy of the ways in which we design ourselves for everyday presentation, makes one well aware that social intercourse nowadays involves a greater degree of informational content than previously.

Contemporary culture is manifestly more heavily information laden than any of its predecessors. We exist in a media-saturated environment which means that life is quintessentially about symbolization, about exchanging and receiving – or trying to exchange and resisting reception of – messages about ourselves and others. It is in acknowledgement of this explosion of signification that many writers conceive of our having entered an information society, one where everything that we see and do is simulated (Poster, 1990, 1995).

FROM QUANTITY TO QUALITY?

Critiques of information society scenarios revolve around a discontent with quantitative measures when they are used to designate profound, systemic change. The central criticism is that quantitative indices of the spread of information and information technologies cannot be interpreted as evidence of really deep-seated social change. On the contrary, they can be regarded as the consolidation and extension of established patterns of interest and control (Beniger, 1986; Webster and Robins, 1986).

Definitions of the information society offer a quantitative measure (numbers of white-collar workers, percentage of GNP devoted to information, etc.) and assume that, at some unspecified point, we enter an information society when this begins to predominate. But there are no clear grounds for designating as a new type of society one in which all we witness is greater quantities of information in circulation and storage. If there is just more information then it is hard to understand why anyone should suggest that we have before us something radically new. This is a point made well by Anthony Giddens (1985: 178) when he observes that all societies, as soon as they are formed into nation-states, are information societies in so far as routine gathering, storage and control of information about population and resources are essential to their operation. On this axis all that differentiates the present era from, say, seventeenth-century England, is much greater quantities of information that are amassed, dissembled and processed. If what we are experiencing in the informational realm today is but an extrapolation and intensification of trends established long ago, then it is hard to see on what basis it can be alleged that these developments are bringing about a new sort of society.

Furthermore, it is at least intellectually possible to imagine a radically different sort of society coming into being, one that may even merit the title 'information society', though this transformation may be manifested in only small quantitative increases of information. That is, it may be feasible to describe as a new sort of society one in which it is possible to locate information of a qualitatively different order, though the information changes appear quantitatively minor. This does not require that we discover that a majority of the workforce is engaged in information occupations or that the economy generates a specified sum from informational activity. For example, it is theoretically possible to imagine an information society where only a small minority of information experts holds decisive power. Science fiction writers from H.G. Wells to Kurt Vonnegut have frequently suggested just this. On a quantitative measure, say of occupational patterns, this would not qualify for information society status, but we could feel impelled to so designate it because of the decisive role of information/knowledge in the power structure and direction of social change.

Bluntly, quantitative measures – simply more information – cannot of themselves identify a break with previous systems, while it is at least theoretically possible to regard small but decisive qualitative changes as marking a system break. Further, it is especially odd that so many of those who identify an information society as a new type of society do so by presuming that this qualitative change can be defined simply by calculating how much information is in circulation, how many people work in information jobs and so on. What we have here is the assumption that quantitative increases transform – in unspecified ways – into qualitative changes in the social system. But to argue that a plethora of personal computers or a preponderance of white-collar occupations means we have an information society is tautologous. We have been presented with no argument as to why more information should result in the coming of a new era; we have had only the unfounded assertion that more information defines a new society.

Moreover, quantitative measures tend to homogenize highly disparate activities. For example, in totalling the value of information activities in the economy and arriving at a given sum, information society theorists arguably overlook crucial qualitative differences within information. For instance, sales of a single tabloid newspaper in Britain are vastly greater than those of all the quality broadsheets combined. But who would suggest that these newspapers can be lumped together in the same category? The crucial issue to most observers is the quality of the information, of news, reportage and opinion, that these newspapers contain. Indeed, so crucial is the issue of quality here that it is possible to present a credible argument that contends that a mass circulation tabloid or entertainment-dominated television represents the very antithesis of an information society, with a 'dumbed down' audience being swamped by garbage information (Postman, 1985; Washburn and Thornton, 1996).

This example alerts us to a related matter, the tendency for quantitative measures to overlook strategic issues (Mosco, 2004). For instance, a raw count of information occupations is blind to the differences between groups, equating, say, social workers and stock exchange dealers, schoolteachers and corporate executives, clerks and lawyers. All are, of course, information workers, and hence equal in terms of the statistician's categories, but some of them clearly are very much more equal than others. In a cognate manner, postmodernist Jean Baudrillard's (1983) willingness to announce the 'implosion' of meaning in the realm of the sign in effect puts light entertainment, news and documentary programming on the same plane – all artifacts that can be experienced by audiences in any way they feel disposed.

There are a good many criticisms to be made of the methods used to measure an information society. All return to the issue that, while finished statistics may appear precise and firm, behind them lies a great deal of subjectivity and variable interpretation. For instance, discriminating between informational and non-informational occupations is a difficult task, involving distinctions of degree rather than of kind. Thus a photocopier repair person is deemed to be an information worker

by virtue of working with advanced technologies, while the farmhand is seen as merely manual, though it is likely that a good deal of information will be required in the performance of their duties. The point is, we need to be sceptical of apparently conclusive figures which are the outcomes of researchers' perceptions of where occupations are to be most appropriately categorized.

There are related complaints to be made about technological measures of the information society. At first sight technologies seem to be especially robust measures, but what is to count as a relevant technology? PCs, computer-to-computer facilities, video, telephone exchanges, cable, camcorders, satellites, Gameboy toys, Exocet missiles, CD players – as soon as one begins the list, problems arise. Again, which of the long list of potential technologies might take priority over others? Networked systems over free-standing PCs? Further, how is one to count computers: by processing power, by use (machines in larger offices are likely to be much more exactingly used than those in the home), or by cost? And how can one assess the role of software packages in the expansion of information technology?

Finally, but by no means least, even when one is alert to the difficulties that come with trying to establish what technologies are to be counted and how they are to be weighted against one another, there looms the vexing question: how much technology must there be in place to enable commentators to describe something as an information society? It is not frivolous to ask whether an information society is one in which everyone has a PC in the home, or whether it is more appropriate to designate this as three-quarters of the way towards a mature information society compared with those that have an established information network in place (but then again, when is a network a network?)

A connected and familiar criticism of technological conceptions of an information society is that they are determinist (Dickson, 1974). First, they assume that technology is the major force in social change – hence arguments which refer to the 'world the steam engine made', 'the atomic age', the 'computer society'. A moment's reflection reveals that history is much more complicated. For example, it is clearly the case that climate, mineralogical deposits, economics, education, war and a host of other factors have contributed to social change, some of these being, at the least, powerful forces influencing technological innovation itself (consider, for example, the influence of war and defence pressures on the development of high technology). Second, technological determinists work with a model which holds to a clear separation of technology and society, the former being in some way apart from social influence yet destined to have the most profound social effects. Technology here is at once sealed from the social world yet capable of shattering established social relations. Perhaps for this reason, technological development is frequently presented as an unworldly thing, led by eccentric inventors or possessed boffins, which yet impacts society dramatically when it is launched on the unsuspecting public. Again, however, it is not difficult to appreciate that technology is a part of society, subject to social shaping by factors such as investment priorities from corporate and government bodies, market opportunities and value commitments. Accepting this position casts doubt on those thinkers who would have it that technological innovations are such as to define a new type of information society (MacKenzie, 1996).

WHAT IS INFORMATION?

When one first encounters statistical series which chart increases in information, it might appear that we are using a term that is precise and widely understood. Initially at least it does seem unproblematical to observe that information increase is identifiable in, say, growth in numbers of magazine titles available, in book issues from public libraries, in the volume of telephone traffic, in enrolment on advanced education courses, in television sales, in hits on websites, in the scale of exchange rate flows, in the expansion of online databases, in take-up of PCs and so forth.

However, a difficulty here is the profligate way in which the term 'information' is used. When bundled in this manner, different definitions of the word are collapsed. The closer one looks at what is meant by 'information', the more awkward does it seem to find a precise and unambiguous definition. Commentators write as if the meaning of the term is self-evident, but in this they are mistaken. Indeed, Norman Stevens concludes that 'so diverse are the definitions of information today ... that it is impossible to reconcile them', and, he continues, 'there is little consistency in the way in which the term information is used ... resulting in an assumption, probably incorrect, that there is a broad underlying definition of information that encompasses all uses of the term in all fields that is commonly and directly understood' (1986: 5).

Among the diversity of definitions of information in play, Zhang Yuexiao (1988: 400) reports that there have been identified some 400 conceptions of information presented by researchers in various fields and cultures. Most significant is the divide between those approaches which conceive of information in non-semantic ways and those which insist in its being something that has meaning. The latter is the most widely understood lay definition, information being regarded as data and ideas that are identifiable, organized in some way, often communicated, stored in various forms (books, television, etc.) and used in a meaningful way (Stevens, 1986: 9). However, it is important to appreciate that this is not the engineer's understanding of information, which is a matter of measuring signals (Shannon and Weaver, 1964 [1949]). Thus measures of information increase that focus on the processing power of computers or the acceleration of transmission rates by telecommunications exchanges invoke one definition of the term, that of the technologist which evacuates content. Commentators who define information in semantic terms, and perhaps look to the extension of signs and symbols in advertising and on television, are operationalizing a quite different conception of information. Elsewhere, those who take the growth in economic import of information – say, the expansion of the publishing business or trading in video materials – adopt a conception of the subject that is amenable to assessment by price, but which is a definition that elides questions of semantics. Again, one of the most common ways of identifying an information society is by counting the number of information workers in employment, a definition of information which centres on a process rather than a product, focusing on what people do rather than on what is produced. This may be intrinsically interesting, but it is a quite different notion of information from one which would emphasize its expression in artifacts such as books and computers.

This lack of precision, and the habit of aggregating highly diverse conceptions into the single category, ought to encourage closer scrutiny of a blanket term that has been used rather promiscuously in recent years. That said, Theodore Roszak's (1986: x) observation that it is the 'very emptiness' of the word 'information' which paradoxically has allowed it 'to be filled with mesmerizing glamour' merits serious consideration. Indeed, when one encounters writers who insist that more information makes for an information society, it is as well to query just what it is they are counting as information here. Michel Foucault (1980) urged scholars to scrutinize ways in which things get talked about, arguing that examination of the construction of 'discourses' can be illuminating as well as somewhat subversive. A Foucauldian account of the genealogy of 'information', one which looks attentively at variable ways in which the term is conceived and applied by information theorists, computer scientists, semiologists, librarians, sociologists and economists, would make for an instructive read. Not least, it would lead one to hesitate before making sweeping statements along the lines that 'information' is transforming the very foundations of life as we know it.

THEORETICAL KNOWLEDGE

There is another suggestion, intriguing if somewhat imprecise, which contends that we are on the point of entry into a distinctly novel information society, yet without a need to reflect on the meanings of the information so developed. This proposition has it that we no longer need to seek quantitative measures of information expansion (information employees, tradeable information, etc.), because a decisive qualitative change has taken place as regards the ways in which information is used. This marks such a break with the past that we may legitimately refer to the coming of an information society.

From this point of view an information society is regarded as one in which theoretical knowledge takes on a pre-eminence which it has hitherto lacked. The theme that unites what is in fact rather a disparate range of thinkers is that, in this information society (though frequently 'knowledge society' is preferred, for the obvious reason that it conjures much more than agglomerated bits of information), affairs are organized and arranged in such a way as to prioritize theory.

It is worth noting that Daniel Bell presents this as an 'axial principle' of post-industrial society and that, although the weight of his analysis leans towards quantitative increases in service (i.e. information) occupations as indicators of post-industrialism, he is emphatic that 'what is radically new today is the codification of theoretical knowledge and its centrality for innovation' (1979: 189).

It is easy enough to understand what Bell means by this when we contrast today's post-industrialism with its predecessor industrial society. In the past, it is argued, innovations were made, on the whole, by 'inspired and talented tinkerers who were indifferent to science and the fundamental laws underlying their investigations' (Bell, 1973: 20). In contrast to this decidedly practical and problem-solving orientation, it is suggested by Bell that nowadays innovations start from theoretical premises. That is, now that we have arrived at a situation in which it is possible to codify known scientific principles, our knowledge of these becomes the starting point of action. In this way, what was once dismissed as useless – as just 'theory' – has becomes the axis of practical innovations.

Again, it is not difficult to find illustrations of this 'change in the character of knowledge itself' (1973: 20). For instance, Alan Turing's paper 'On computable numbers', published in 1937, set out mathematical principles which underpin later applications in computer science; the development of integrated circuits that enabled the 'microelectronics revolution' to get under way in the late 1970s was founded on known principles of solid-state physics; and innovations in areas as diverse as compact disk technology, lasers and nuclear energy were reliant on breakthroughs in theoretical physics which were regarded, initially as least, as being without practical consequence. In fact, it is rather difficult to think of technological applications nowadays which do not hinge on theoretical knowledge, whether it is calculating the needs of households for supply of potable water, constructing aircraft, building bridges or generating energy. Not surprisingly, perhaps, we find historian Eric Hobsbawm confirming Bell's perception, concluding that during this century 'the theorists [have been] in the driving seat ... telling the practitioners what they were to look for and should find in the light of their theories' (1994: 534–5).

Bell takes his argument for what he terms the 'primacy of theoretical knowledge' considerably further, to suggest that it is pre-eminent not only in the realm of technological innovation, but even in social and political affairs. For instance, governments today introduce policies based on theoretical models of the economy. These are variable – Keynesian, monetarist, supply side, *laissez-faire*, collectivist – but each underpins the day-to-day decisions that ministers may make in response to practical exigencies. Alternatively, it is salutary to reflect on contemporary policies oriented towards resolving environmental problems. It quickly becomes evident that these are not merely responses to particularly pressing problems (an oil spillage at sea, desertification). They do involve such contingencies, of course, but they are also proposals developed on the basis of theoretical models of the ecosystem's sustainability. Thus, for instance, environmental debates are routinely informed by theoretical projections on matters such as population growth, fish stocks and the condition of the ozone layer. Practical policies are only imaginable on the basis of these sorts of theoretical

model: for example, appropriate reactions to a noticeably dry or warmer summer in the UK are comprehensible only in a context of theoretical models of the long-term likelihood of and consequences of global warming. To be sure, such models are at present inchoate and unrefined, but they and other instances help us to appreciate that, while theoretical knowledge does not have to be 'true' in any absolute sense, it does play a decisive part in our lives.

Theoretical knowledge is undeniably an arresting idea, one which *prima facie* defines a new type of society which hinges on the generation and use of information/knowledge. If theory is at the point of initiation of developments, in contrast to one-time practical demands, then such knowledge could be said to herald a new sort of society. Moreover, we are talking here not merely of more white-collar workers or more bits of information being produced, but of a new foundational principle of social life.

Nonetheless, a major difficulty with this notion is defining with any precision what is meant by theoretical knowledge (Kumar, 1978: 219–30). Theory evokes abstract and generalizable rules, laws and procedures and, with this, there can be agreement that advances, especially in scientific knowledge, have resulted in their codification in texts which are learned by would-be practitioners and which in turn become integrated into their practical work. This principle can reasonably be thought to be at the heart of research and development projects at the forefront of innovations, but it is clearly in evidence too in a large range of professions such as architecture, building, handling of food and even the design of much clothing.

However, there are those who would extend the notion of theoretical knowledge to encompass a much vaster range, all of which could be cited as evidence of a knowledge-based society. Here, for example, one might include the training of many white-collar employees in law, social services, accountancy, etc. as evidence of the primacy of knowledge in the contemporary world. Indeed, one might argue that the whole of higher education, at the least, is concerned with transmitting theoretical knowledge. After all, it is a common refrain, in Britain at least, that the rapid transition to mass higher education (with about 30 per cent of the age group attending universities) has been required by the need to equip appropriately large numbers of people to operate successfully in the 'knowledge society' (Webster, 2000). Such knowledge as is transmitted is undoubtedly codified and generally abstracted from practical applications, and it is even generalizable, though it is surely of a different order of magnitude to the theoretical knowledge expounded in sciences such as chemistry and physics.

Nico Stehr (1994), proposing that we now inhabit a 'knowledge society', does extend the definition of theory in such a way, arguing that nowadays knowledge has come to be constitutive of the way that we live. Recourse to theoretical knowledge is now central to virtually everything that we do, from designing new technologies and producing everyday artifacts to making sense of our own lives when we draw upon large repositories of knowledge to help us better understand our own location.

Here we are extending the idea of theoretical knowledge a very great deal, but it is helpful in so far as Stehr echoes themes in the work of social theorist Anthony Giddens that merit comment. Stehr proposes a threefold typology of the development of knowledge: *meaningful,* that is the Enlightenment ideal of knowledge for better understanding; *productive,* that is knowledge applied to industry; and *action,* where knowledge is intimately connected to production with, for example, the inclusion of intelligent devices, and where it influences the performance of one's everyday activities. This last form of knowledge appears close to Giddens' emphasis on what he refers to as the *intensified reflexivity* of 'late modern' existence. What Giddens highlights here is that, increasingly, modernity has been a story of people's release from the strictures of nature and certain forms of community, where it appeared that one had to do what one did as it was a matter of 'fate', towards individuals and groups making choices about their own and collective destinies in circumstances of 'manufactured uncertainty'. That is, the world increasingly is not bounded by fixed and unchangeable limits,

but is rather recognized as malleable and the outcome of human decisions. A requisite of this is heightened self and collective interrogation, otherwise reflexivity, though this is not to be perceived as some trend towards self-absorption. Quite the contrary, it is premised on openness to ideas, information and theories from very diverse realms, which are examined and incorporated as circumstances and people so decide (Lash, 2002).

A key point here is that a 'post-traditional' (Giddens, 1994) society which is characterized by intensified reflexivity of actors and institutions hinges on information/knowledge. Of course, some of this is local and particular (one's biography reflected upon, a company carefully scrutinizing its sales and stock records), but a great deal is also abstract, emanating especially from electronic media and from other, notably educational, institutions. If one accepts Giddens' argument that we do inhabit a world of 'high modernity' in which reflexivity is much more pronounced than hitherto, then it is feasible to conceive of this as heightening the import of information and knowledge in contemporary life. A world of choices, for both organizations and individuals, is reliant on the availability and generation of detailed and rich information. If one follows Giddens' contention that ours is an era of intensified reflexivity on the basis of which we forge our material as well as social conditions, then it follows that this will sustain and will demand a complex and deep information environment. It is perhaps not quite the same sort of theoretical knowledge as that which Daniel Bell has proposed, but in so far as it is abstract and codified then it could find inclusion in a suitably widened category.

Nevertheless, there are reasons why we should hesitate to depict any novel information society in these terms. Not least is that Anthony Giddens himself is reluctant to do so. While he does emphasize that a 'world of intensified reflexivity is a world of *clever people*' (1994: 7), he appears unwilling to present this as other than an extension of long-term trends. Life today is certainly more information intensive, but this may not be sufficient to justify projections that it represents a new sort of society.

In addition, Giddens has also raised doubts about the novelty of theoretical knowledge. Several years ago he observed that 'there is nothing which is specifically new in the application of "theoretical knowledge" … Indeed … rationality of technique … is the primary factor which from the beginning has distinguished industrialism from all preceding forms of social order' (1981: 262). This being so, we return to the problem of designating as novel today's society in which theoretical knowledge is prevalent.

Giddens' objection also begs the key question: just what do commentators mean by theoretical knowledge? It is clear, from the quotation above, that Giddens feels that the classical sociologist Max Weber's conception of formal rationality which underpins purposive action (most famously manifested in the growth of bureaucratic structures) might apply on one definition. After all, it involves abstract and codifiable principles, rules and regulations (the entire bureaucratic machine), as well as requiring from participants the command of abstract knowledge (how the system works). Theoretical knowledge, in these terms, is not much more than learning the rules and procedures of how bureaucracies function. If so, then one is forced also to ask what is especially new about this.

This leads us to the wider complaint about the imprecision of the term 'theoretical knowledge'. If, for instance, the 'primacy of theoretical knowledge' is taken to refer to known scientific principles (the boiling point of water, the conductivity of elements, etc.) which are codified in texts, then this is one matter. However, if theoretical knowledge is taken to include hypothetical models such as the relation between inflation and unemployment, poverty and life chances, or social class and educational opportunity, then this surely is another matter. It may be that such theoretical knowledge is distinguishable from laws of physics only by degree, but this remains an important difference nonetheless. If theoretical knowledge is perceived as the prominence in modern life of expert systems that operate services such as water and sewerage, air traffic control and the telephone networks, through the systematic monitoring of activities which are (re)organized on the basis of established principles (of toxicity, safety of margins and so forth), then this too is another thing. Alternatively, if theoretical knowledge is to be understood as a trend towards very much more intensified reflexivity amongst individuals as well as institutions, on the basis of which they then shape their future courses of action, then this is another thing again. Finally, if the rise of theoretical knowledge is to be chartered by the spread of educational certification – a common strategy – then this is to introduce still another significantly different definition. Such imprecisions may lead one to be wary of theoretical knowledge as a sound means of distinguishing an information society, albeit that a decisive shift towards the primacy of theory does appear to be a marked feature of recent history. It is, in my view, the most credible conception of an information society available.

CONCLUSION

This chapter has examined six analytically separable conceptions of the information society. It has argued that all are suspect to a greater or lesser degree, so much so that the idea of an information society, on most measures, cannot be sustained. In each case defining criteria are imprecise and vague. Moreover, the claim that the information society marks a profound transformation in our ways of life cannot be supported on the basis of the quantitative indices that are typically advanced. There can be no doubt that, in advanced nations, information and communication technologies are now pervasive and that information has grown in economic significance, as the substance of much work, and in amounts of symbolic output. But the idea that all such might signal the shift towards a new society, an information society, is mistaken. Indeed, what is most striking are the continuities of the present age with previous social and economic arrangements, informational developments being heavily influenced by familiar constraints and priorities (H. Schiller, 1981, 1984, 1996; D. Schiller, 1999). As Krishan Kumar has concluded, the information explosion 'has not produced a radical shift in the way industrial societies are organized, or in the direction in which they have been moving. The imperatives of profit, power and control seem as predominant now as they have ever been in the history of capitalist industrialism. The difference lies in the greater range and intensity of their applications ... not in any change in the principles themselves' (1995[2005]: 154). It is ironic that the most persuasive conception of an information society, that which centres on the role of theoretical knowledge, is the least commonly suggested by information society adherents.

REFERENCES

Angell, Ian (1995) 'Winners and losers in the information age', *LSE Magazine*, 7 (1): 10–12.

Barron, Iann and Curnow, Ray (1979) *The Future with Microelectronics: Forecasting the Effects of Information Technology*. London: Pinter.

Baudrillard, Jean (1983) *In the Shadow of the Silent Majorities*. New York: Semiotext(e).

Bell, Daniel (1973) *The Coming of Post-industrial Society: A Venture in Social Forecasting*. Harmondsworth: Penguin.

Bell, Daniel (1979) 'The social framework of the information society', in Michael L. Dertouzos and Joel Moses (eds), *The Computer Age: A Twenty-year View*. Cambridge, MA: MIT Press. pp. 163–211.

Beniger, James R. (1986) *The Control Revolution: Technological and Economic Origins of the Information Society*. Cambridge, MA: Harvard University Press.

Brown, Phillip and Lauder, Hugh (1995) 'Post-Fordist possibilities: education, training, and national development', in L. Bash and A. Green (eds), *World Yearbook of Education 1995: Youth, Education and Work*, vol. 2. London: Kogan Page. pp. 19–32.

Castells, Manuel (1996–8) *The Information Age*, 3 vols. Vol. 1: *The Rise of the Network Society* (1996). Vol. 2: *The Power of Identity* (1997). Vol. 3: *End of Millennium* (1998). Oxford: Blackwell.

Connors, Michael (1993) *The Race to the Intelligent State*. Oxford: Blackwell.

Coyne, Diane (1997) *The Weightless Economy*. Oxford: Capstone.

Dertouzos, Michael (1997) *What Will Be: How the New World of Information Will Change Our Lives*. London: Piatkus.

Dickson, David (1974) *Alternative Technology and the Politics of Technical Change*. London: Fontana.

Drucker, Peter (1993) *Post-capitalist Society*. New York: HarperCollins.

Duff, Alistair (2000) *Information Society Studies*. London: Routledge.

Duff, Alistair, Craig, D. and McNeill, D.A. (1996) 'A note on the origins of the information society', *Journal of Information Science*, 22 (2): 117–22.

Evans, Christopher (1979) *The Mighty Micro: The Impact of the Micro-chip Revolution*. London: Gollancz.

Feather, John (1998) *The Information Society: A Study of Continuity and Change*, 2nd edn. London: Library Association.

Foucault, Michel (1980) 'Two lectures', in *Power/Knowledge*. Brighton: Harvester.

Freeman, Christopher (1987) *Technology Policy and Economic Performance*. London: Pinter.

Gates, Bill (1995) *The Road Ahead*. Harmondsworth: Penguin.

Giddens, Anthony (1981) *The Class Structure of the Advanced Societies*, 2nd edn. London: Hutchinson.

Giddens, Anthony (1985) *The Nation State and Violence: Volume Two of a Contemporary Critique of Historical Materialism*. Cambridge: Polity.

Giddens, Anthony (1994) *Beyond Left and Right*. Cambridge: Polity.

Hall, Peter and Preston, Paschal (1988) *The Carrier Wave: New Information Technology and the Geography of Innovation, 1846–2003*. London: Unwin Hyman.

Hobsbawm, Eric (1994) *Age of Extremes: The Short Twentieth Century*. London: Joseph.

Ito, Y. (1991) 'Birth of *joho shakia* and *johaka* concepts in Japan and their diffusion outside Japan', *KEIO Communication Review*, 13: 3–12.

Ito, Y. (1994) 'Japan', in Georgette Wang (ed.), *Treading Different Paths: Informatization in Asian Nations*. Norwood, NJ: Ablex. pp. 68–98.

Jonscher, Charles (1999) *Wired Life*. New York: Bantam.

Kumar, Krishan (1978) *Prophecy and Progress: The Sociology of Industrial and Post-industrial Society*. London: Allen Lane.

Kumar, Krishan (1995 [2005]) *From Post-industrial to Postmodern Society*. 2nd edn. Oxford: Blackwell.

Lash, Scott (2002) *Critique of Information*. London: Sage.

Leadbetter, Charles (1999) *Living on Thin Air: The New Economy*. London: Hodder & Stoughton.

Lyon, David (1988) *The Information Society: Issues and Illusions*. Cambridge: Polity.

Machlup, Fritz (1962) *The Production and Distribution of Knowledge in the United States*. Princeton, NJ: Princeton University Press.

MacKenzie, Donald (1996) *Knowing Machines: Essays on Technical Change*. Cambridge, MA: MIT Press.

Martin, James (1978) *The Wired Society*. Englewood Cliffs, NJ: Prentice-Hall.

May, Christopher (2002) *The Information Society: A Sceptical View*. Cambridge: Polity.

McHale, John (1976) *The Changing Information Environment*. London: Elek.

Mosco, Vincent (2004) *The Digital Sublime: Myth, Power, and Cyberspace*. Cambridge, MA: MIT Press.

Mulgan, Geoff J. (1991) *Communication and Control: Networks and the New Economies of Communication*. Cambridge: Polity.

Negroponte, Nicholas (1995) *Being Digital*. London: Hodder & Stoughton.

Porat, Marc Uri (1977a) *The Information Economy: Definition and Measurement* (executive summary and major findings). OT Special Publication 77–12 (1). Washington, DC: US Department of Commerce, Office of Telecommunications.

Porat, Marc Uri (1977b) *The Information Economy: Sources and Methods for Measuring the Primary Information Sector* (detailed industry reports). OT Special Publication 77–12 (2). Washington, DC: US Department of Commerce, Office of Telecommunications.

Porat, Marc Uri (1978) 'Communication policy in an information society', in G.O. Robinson (ed.), *Communications for Tomorrow*. New York: Praeger. pp. 3–60.

Poster, Mark (1990) *The Mode of Information: Poststructuralism and Social Context*. Cambridge: Polity.

Poster, Mark (1995) *The Second Media Age*. Cambridge: Polity.

Postman, Neil (1985) *Amusing Ourselves to Death: Public Discourse in the Age of Show Business*. New York: Penguin.

Reich, R. (1992) *The Work of Nations: Preparing Ourselves for 21st Century Capitalism*. New York: Vintage.

Roszak, Theodore (1986) *The Cult of Information: The Folklore of Computers and the True Art of Thinking*. Cambridge: Lutterworth.

Schiller, Dan (1999) *Digital Capitalism: Networking the Global Market System*. Cambridge, MA: MIT Press.

Schiller, Herbert I. (1981) *Who Knows: Information in the Age of the Fortune 500*. Norwood, NJ: Ablex.

Schiller, Herbert I. (1984) *Information and the Crisis Economy*. Norwood, NJ: Ablex.

Schiller, Herbert I. (1996) *Information Inequality*. New York: Routledge.

Seltzer, Kimberley and Bentley, Tom (1999) *The Creative Age: Knowledge and Skills for the New Economy*. London: Demos.

Shannon, C. and Weaver, W. (1964 [1949]) *The Mathematical Theory of Communication*. Urbana, IL: University of Illinois Press.

Stehr, Nico (1994) *Knowledge Societies*. London: Sage.

Stevens, Norman (1986) 'The history of information', *Advances in Librarianship*, 14: 1–48.

Toffler, Alvin (1980) *The Third Wave*. New York: Morrow.

Toffler, Alvin (1990) *Powershift: Knowledge, Wealth, and Violence at the Edge of the 21st Century*. New York: Bantam.

Urry, John (2000) *Sociology beyond Societies: Mobilities for the 21st Century*. London: Routledge.

Washburn, Katherine and Thornton, John (eds) (1996) *Dumbing Down: Essays on the Strip-mining of American Culture*. New York: Norton.

Webster, Frank (1995 [2002]) *Theories of the Information Society*. 2nd edn. London: Routledge.

Webster, Frank (2000) 'Higher education', in G. Browning, A. Halcli and F. Webster (eds), *Understanding Contemporary Society: Theories of the Present*. London: Sage. pp. 312–27.

Webster, Frank and Robins, Kevin (1986) *Information Technology: A Luddite Analysis*. Norwood, NJ: Ablex.

Zhang, Yuexiao (1988) 'Definitions and sciences of information', *Information Processing and Management*, 24 (4): 479–91.

Index

Abbate, J., 254
Abbott, C., 85
Aboriginal culture, 150
Abrahamson, D., 419
absolute advantages, 397, 398
access, 6, 25
    children's, 77–8, 87, 103–4
    and demand, 314–16
    digital divide, 6, 25, 93–5, 107, 152, 168, 311
    electronic islands, 313
    freedom of expression, 436
    and gender, 78, 79, 82, 93, 94, 240
    importance of, 310
    policies, 316–19, 418, 424
    and socioeconomic status, 77–8, 93–4, 311, 315, 319
    technological trends, 313–14
    to e-mail, 93, 253, 254, 316
    to games, 82
    to infrastructure, 239–41
    to Internet see Internet
    to telephones, 6, 295, 307–8, 311–12, 315, 316–19
    trends, 319
    universal, 6, 307–10, 312–13, 436
accumulation regime, 391
Acland, C., 148
actor-network theory (ANT), 146, 147, 250, 258
actors, 146, 259, 268
actual knowledge networks, 129
adaptive structuration theory (AST), 118, 123–4, 125
adoption threshold, 250
Advanced Communication Technologies and Services
    (ACTS), 388
advertisements, 101, 198, 199
    see also marketing
affect, 155
Africa, 316–17
age, 84–5, 94, 96, 105
agency, 8, 145–7, 154–5, 157
agents, 114, 128–9, 157
Agre, P., 4
Aiken, H., 194
airline computerized reservation systems, 357–9
Al-Jazeera, 293
Alaska, 318–19
aliases, 254
alliances, 375, 380
allocution, 334
Alloway, N., 82
Altman, I., 43
American Airlines, 358

Americans with Disabilities Act (1990), 95
analogue television, 332, 337
Anderson, B., 289
Ang, I., 296
Annenberg School for Communication, 18
anonymity, 38, 41, 43, 76, 84, 121, 126, 200
Antonelli, C., 251
AOL (America Online), 97, 103, 104, 267, 271
APIs (application program interfaces), 235
Appadurai, A., 4, 289
appropriation, 123, 125
Arabic-language broadcasting, 293
archetypes, 233
Argyle, M., 209
ARPANET, 189–90, 253, 254, 260
Arrow, H., 125
Arrow, K., 17, 365–6
artefacts, 2–3, 9, 23
articulation, 142, 146, 147, 148, 149
Asia, 297, 316, 318, 396
Association of Internet Researchers, 59
Association for Progressive Communications, 431
associationism, 279, 284
AST see adaptive structuration theory
asynchronous CMC, 35, 38, 116
AT&T, 22, 189, 307–8
audience
    for children, 86, 87
    concept of, 2–3, 8, 27
    globalization, 296
    interactivity, 211, 214
    studies, 7
    see also users
Austin (Texas), 272
Australia, 329, 423
authoritarian regimes, 380, 424–5, 431
automated industrial production, 187–8

Babbage, C., 191
backwards compatibility, 241
Bairoch, P., 388
Bakos, Y.J., 354
Bales, R.F., 36, 37, 210
Ball-Rokeach, S., 45
Balsamo, A., 155
Bangemann, M., 400
Bangladesh, 316, 318
Bar, F., 195–6
Bargh, J.A., 41, 42, 45
Barker, C., 289

Barlow, D., 65
Barnett, G., 20
Baron, N., 35, 39, 40, 46
Baudelaire, C., 196
Baudrillard, J., 450
Baym, N.K., 41, 43, 63, 68, 102
BBC (British Broadcasting Corporation), 255, 292
Beck, U., 170, 172
Becker, H.S., 233
Bell, D., 17, 390, 445, 452, 453
Beniger, J., 17, 98, 192–3, 212, 214
Benjamin, R., 358
Benkler, Y., 339
Berger, C.R., 209–10
Berkowitz, S.D., 251
Berne Convention, 418, 433
Bettig, R.V., 298
bias, pro-innovation, 252
bias of technology, 150–2, 153, 366–7
Bijker, W.E., 249
Bildschirmtext, 255, 256
binary distinctions, 144
Bing, J., 435
Biocca, F., 217
biotechnological matrix, 146
biotechnology, 154–5
biotechnology firms, 267
BITNET, 253, 254
Blacksburg Electronic Village (BEV), 65, 100
blocking, 338, 344
blogs, 5, 84, 216
Bloor, D., 249
Blumer, H., 210
Boal, I., 150, 155
Bober, M., 77–8
Boddewyn, J.J., 340–1
Boddy, W., 27
body, 154–5
Bordewijk, J.L., 333
boundary objects, 188–9, 249
bounded rationality, 353
Bourdieu, P., 19
Bowker, G.C., 233
Boyd-Barrett, O., 293
Braczyk, H., 269
Brail, S., 280
Brand, S., 241
Branscomb, A. Wells, 420, 426
Brazil, 316
Bretz, R., 215
55 Broad Street (New York), 279–80
broadband, 320, 337
broadcast media
    regulation, 22, 335, 337
    see also radio; television
broadcasting networks, 24
Brook, J., 155
Brousseau, E., 357
Brown, J.S., 98

Browning, G., 175
Brynjolfsson, E., 352
Bucciarelli, L.L., 230, 247
Buchman, D., 81
Buckingham, D., 86
Bull, M., 139
Burgoon, J.K., 127, 207
Burk, D.L., 434
Bush, George W., 292

Cairncross, F., 291
California, 275, 280
Cambridge, 274
Canada, 18, 65–6, 100, 255, 256, 280–1
capacity, 308
capitalism, 171–2
car industry, 357, 359
Cardiff (Wales), 281–3
Carey, J., 61–2, 288–9
carriers, 317–19
Carter, S., 177
case studies, 67–8
Cash, J.I., 359
Cassell, J., 82
Castells, M., 277, 288, 289–90, 339, 355, 390
Cathcart, R., 206, 212
causality, 143, 144–5, 376
CB radio, 214
CCIS (Craigmillar Community Information
    Service), 100–1
CCIT (Consultative Committee on International
    Telegraphy and Telephony), 254
Ceefax, 255, 256
cell phones see mobile phones
cellular technology, 321
centralization bias, 150
Cerulo, K., 99
Chaffee, S.H., 206
chat rooms, 35, 84, 96, 97, 101, 201
Cherny, L., 46, 63–4, 100
Chicago School, 57, 248
childhood, 77
children
    access to new media, 77–8, 87, 103–4
    computer games, 78–84
    education potential of media, 85–7
    and innovation, 199–200
    Internet use, 49, 76–8, 84–5, 101,
        103–4, 343–4
    online culture, 84–5
    policy, 87, 343–4
    relationship with new media,
        75–7, 85–7
    social use of new media, 77–85
Chile, 317
China, 423, 424
choice, 118, 119–21, 259
cinema, 148, 197
    see also film industry

citizen-government communication, 372
citizen's band (CB) radio, 214
citizenship, 299
civic involvement, 95–8, 107
civil society, 410, 431
Clark, A., 145–6
class *see* socioeconomic status
classification, 234
Clemons, E.K., 359
Clerkenwell (London), 279
Clinton, W., 148
clusters, 266, 267, 270, 271–8, 284
    industry trajectory, 278–83
CNN, 291
co-presence, 209
coalitions, 375, 380
coaxial cable, 320
Cobb, J., 106
code, 338–9, 409
codes of conduct, 46, 338, 343
cognitive knowledge networks, 129
Coleman, S., 65
collective good, 417, 419
Collins, F., 191
colonialism, 240
commodification of information, 417, 419, 429
communication
    definition, 8
    direction, 211–12, 216
    see also computer-mediated communication;
        face-to-face communication; group
        interaction; interpersonal interaction;
        telecommunications
communication infrastructures, 231
communication networks, 129
communication research, 17–18, 250, 251
communication technologies *see* ICTs
Communications Act (1934) (USA), 22, 307
communicators, 266
communities
    changing concepts, 59–64
    CMC concept, 45, 46–7
    Internet and involvement, 98–101, 107
    learning communities, 85
    relationship with media, 55–9
    research on new media and, 64–9
community access, 313, 316–17
community information networks, 59
community media, 58, 64–5, 150
community of practice, 64
comparative advantages, 397–8
comparative research, 20
competition, 309, 314, 318–19, 359,
    394–5, 398
    and deregulation, 394–5, 405, 406, 407
complexity theory, 118, 124–6
compressed video, 323
compressed voice, 322
computer conferencing, 114, 121

computer games, 5, 40, 76
    children's use of, 78–84
    and gender, 81–3
    as texts, 83–4
computer games industry, 79, 269
computer networks, 416
    policy, 416–17
    regulation, 408–9
    see also global computer network regulation
computer-based messaging, 17
computer-mediated communication (CMC)
    cues-filtered-out perspective, 36–7
    forms, 35–6
    identity, 41–3, 101, 200
    impact, 163
    information richness, 122
    interaction, 211, 212, 217–20
    language use, 40–1
    media characteristics, 37–9
    personal relationships, 43–5
    popularity, 36
    research, 17, 18
    social groups, 45–7
    vs. face-to-face, 36–7, 39, 43–5, 121,
        122, 126–8
    vs. other media, 39–40
    see also Internet
computer-mediated identities, 41–3
computerized reservation systems
    (CRSs), 357–9
computers
    access, 77–8, 93–5, 239–41, 311
    and children, 76–8
    convergence with television, 332
    e-mail development, 252, 253–5
    educational potential, 85–6
    and information society, 445
    innovation history, 188–9, 190–1, 193–6,
        200–1, 351, 394
    and productivity, 373–4
    as projective devices, 17
    user-to-system interactivity, 217–21
    vs. videotex, 257
consequences *see* effects of technology
consolidation, 309
consultation, 334
Consultative Committee on International Telegraphy
    and Telephony (CCITT), 254
consumer sovereignty, 300
content convergence, 332
content creation, 214–15, 216–17
content creators, 211, 213–14
content regulation, 329–31, 334–9, 423–5
    self-regulation, 339–45
context
    and culture, 142
    interpersonal, 37, 42–3, 49–50
contingency, 142, 148, 247, 258–61
    see also uncertainty

continuous development, 24
Contractor, N.S., 118, 124–5, 128
contracts, 428
control
    and interaction, 212, 213, 215, 216, 218, 219
    see also regulation; surveillance
control revolution, 17, 97, 192–3, 212
control technologies, 156–7
Convention for the Protection of Human
        Rights, 434
convergence
    infrastructure, 350, 351, 376–7
    move toward, 268, 269, 283–4, 308–9
    and regulation, 329, 332, 336, 337
    theories of, 395
conversation, 39, 210, 334
Cooke, P., 281
Cooper, M., 94
coordination, 374, 377
coordination network, 125–6
copyright, 298, 301, 344, 417–19, 428, 433, 434, 435
cordless communication, 321
corporate power, 171
corporations
    clusters, 272–3
    global, 291–2, 293
    new media, 270–1
    telecommunications, 309
    transnational, 297–8
corporeality, 154–5
Council of Europe, 433
Covent Garden (London), 279
Cowan, R.S., 151
Craigmillar Community Information Service
        (CCIS), 100–1
Crawford, C., 218
creative industries strategies, 301–2
critical mass, 250
critical studies, 18–19, 135–6
CSNET, 253
cues, 36–7, 121, 126
cues-filtered-out perspective, 36–7
Culnan, M.J., 36, 116
Cultural Access Group, 100
cultural domination models, 292–3
cultural imperialism, 291–4
cultural studies, 18–19, 141, 157–8
    bias of technology, 150–2
    causality and agency, 144–7
    identity, 149–50, 151–2
    nature of, 142–4
    politics, 150, 151–3
    progress and genealogy, 147–9
    social space and corporeality, 153–7
culture
    children online, 84–5
    debates and concepts, 134–40
    game play, 78–9
    and globalization, 296

culture *cont.*
    and information society, 448–9
    regulation, 423
    and technology, 141, 143
        causality and agency, 144–7
        identity, politics and bias, 149–53
        progress and genealogy, 147–9
        social space and corporeality, 153–7
    see also political culture
Cunningham, S., 296
Curtis, P., 42
cybercafés, 316
CyberPatrol, 344
cyberspace
    and culture, 135–7
    and embodiment, 155
    and political culture *see* political culture
    regulation, 338–9, 416
    see also Internet; virtual communities; World
        Wide Web

Daft, R.L., 119
DAMA (demand assignment multiple access), 322
Danet, B., 40, 41
data havens, 408, 431
data processing, 194
Data Protection Directive (1995) (EU), 421
databases, 236, 237–8
David, P., 189, 233
Day, G.S., 212
Deacon, D., 26
decentralization, 150, 190, 191
decision-making *see* group decision
        support systems
DECT (digital European cordless telephone), 321
Deibert, R.J., 166
delegation, 152
Deleuze, G., 147, 156
demand, 314–16, 371–3, 379
demand assignment multiple access (DAMA), 322
democracy, 150–1, 154, 169, 175, 291, 415
    and regulation, 380, 423, 424–5
depersonalization, 121
deregulation, 341–2, 405–7
    see also liberalization
Dertouzos, M., 173
Dery, M., 155
DeSanctis, G., 123
Descartes, R., 137
Deshpande, S.P., 219
design, 187–92, 217–18, 232–4, 241–2, 247
determination, 247, 258–61
determinism *see* social determinism;
        technological determinism
developing countries, 313, 316–17
    access, 239–40, 311, 314
    demand, 372–3
    globalization, 299, 302, 398–9
    ICT industry in, 396

developing countries, *cont.*
  intellectual property, 418, 434
  NWICO debate, 292–3
development, information in, 310
development communication, 299
diffusion of innovations theory, 18, 246, 247–8,
    250–2, 258, 261
Digital, 276
digital audiotape (DAT), 428
digital community networks, 65–6, 68, 100
digital content regulation, 329–31, 334–9
  self regulation, 339–45
digital divide, 6, 25, 93–5, 107, 152, 168, 311
  see also access
digital European cordless telephone (DECT), 321
digital network technology, in workplace,
    195–6, 350, 353–60
digital services, 313, 322–3
digital subscriber line (DSL), 320
digitalization, 56, 308, 331–2
disability, 95, 234, 241
discourse analysis, 39
discourse communities, 64
disembodiment, 41, 42
disinhibition, 36, 37, 121, 126
disintermediation, 98, 333, 336, 345, 355, 358
distributed knowledge, 129
distributive mechanisms, 259–60
divergence, 269–70
diversity on Internet, 67, 96, 106
documents, 213–17
DOS, 235
Dosi, G., 393
dot.com revolution, 267, 270
Douglas, S., 191–2
Downer, A., 290
Doyle, G., 294
dropouts, 94
Drotner, K., 200
Drucker, P., 390
DSL (digital subscriber line), 320
Dublin Core, 238
Dudley, L., 374
dynamics of information exchange, 371–2
dynamics of innovation, 259

e-commerce, 174, 421
e-lancers, 128
e-mail
  access, 93, 253, 254, 316
  demand, 372
  design and development, 232, 246, 252, 253–5,
    260–1, 313
  interaction, 35, 45, 102, 103, 105, 216, 218
  media richness, 119, 120
  standards, 234
  user perceptions, 40
E-Society Programme, 19–20
Ebo, B., 135
ECHO, 100

economic development, 18, 376–7
economic efficiency, 427
Economic and Social Research Council, 19
economics of information, 17, 364,
    365–6, 378–80
  demand, 371–3, 379
  development, 376–7
  distorted images, 378
  language, 376
  market, 370–1
  organization, 374–6
  policy, 377–8
  productivity, 373–4
  property rights, 369–70
economics of language, 376
economy
  culture of, 135
  diffusion theory, 250–1, 252
  effect of ICTs on, 288
  ICT innovation, 174, 192–3, 257, 258
  information economy, 23, 351–2, 366–8
  and information society, 447
  market system, 364, 370–1
  and political culture, 171–2
  theories of, 401
  see also globalization; new media industry
EDI (electronic data interchange), 356–7
education
  CMC in, 212
  higher, 275, 277, 446–7, 453–4
  and information society, 446–7, 453–4
  learning communities, 85
  potential of media, 75–6, 80, 85–7, 103
educational background, 94, 96, 319
EFF (Electronic Frontier Foundation),
    56, 172
effectiveness, 310
effects of technology, 18, 20, 144, 260, 336
  on children, 76, 80–1
  on groups, 118, 121–2
  see also social consequences of ICTs
efficiency, 310, 427
Egan, E., 269
Eisenstein, E., 153
electric eye door opener, 146
electricity networks, 232–3
electronic brokerage effect, 354–5
electronic community media, 57–8
electronic data interchange (EDI), 356–7
Electronic Frontier Foundation (EFF), 56, 172
electronic hierarchies, 354
electronic integration effect, 354
electronic islands, 313
electronic markets, 354–5
ELIZA program, 217
embodiment, 41, 42, 154–5
emergent perspective, 118
encryption, 344
engineering, 248–9
ensemble, 23

entertainment innovation, 196–9
entertainment potential of new media, 76, 86, 105
entertainment sector, 269, 270, 278, 279, 282–3, 294
environmental policy, 453
equality, 67
equity, 310
Erbring, L., 48, 101
Erikson, E., 137
ethics, 239
ethnicity and race, 78, 93, 96, 100, 152, 168, 240–1
ethnography, 26, 68
ethnoscape, 4
Europe
 ICT innovation in, 193
 ICT policy, 388, 400
 information society policy, 400
 liberalization and rise of ICT in, 394
 privacy policy, 421, 433–4
 regulation in, 330
 research in, 18–19, 20, 388
European Commission, 329, 336, 400
Everard, J., 177
extranets, 117

face-to-face communication
 conversation, 210
 information richness, 122
 Internet as alternative, 105
 personal relationships, 43, 44–5
 social presence, 119
 vs. CMC, 36–7, 39, 43–5, 121, 122, 126–8
fair use, 417–18, 434, 435
faithful appropriation, 123
Fallows, J., 97
Federal Geographic Data Committee (FGDC), 238
feedback, 210–11
feminism, 82, 106, 240
Ferguson, D., 105
Fernback, J., 62
Ferrara, K., 40
fiction, 216
film industry, 269, 278, 279, 282, 294
 see also cinema
filtering, 338, 343–4, 345
financescapes, 4
Finland, 275, 318, 407–8
Fiske, J., 83
flaming, 36, 37, 254
flexibility, 241
flexible accumulation, 167
flexible specialization, 390, 392–3
flow, 219, 220, 293, 333–4
Floyd, K., 43, 44
Fordism, 391
formal properties of innovation, 259
forms of life, 145
Foucault, M., 19, 137, 149, 156, 165, 452

France
 early research, 17
 regulation, 333, 425
 technopoles, 274, 276–7
 videotex, 188, 255, 256, 260
France Télécom, 188
Franzen, A., 105
free trade, 397
freedom, 96
freedom of expression, 22, 96, 338, 417, 420, 422–5, 428, 434, 436
Freeman, C., 252, 393
freenets, 240
Fulk, J., 120, 218
functional proximity, 278
Funk, J., 81

Gailey, C.W., 82
Galegher, J., 39, 46
game studies, 83
games see computer games
Gandy, O.H., 420, 422
Gans, H., 60
Garfinkel, S., 298
Garnham, N., 19
Gates, Bill, 170, 171
Gavin, J., 44
GCSS see group communication support systems
GDSS see group decision support systems
Geertz, C., 366
Gellner, E., 289
Gemeinschaft, 60
gender, 138
 access, 78, 79, 82, 93, 94, 240
 bias of technology, 151–2
 children's computer use, 78, 79
 computer games, 76, 81–3
 Internet use, 93, 94, 96
gender identities, 41, 42, 151–2
genealogy, 148–9
General Agreement on Trade in Services (GATS), 299
genome project, 367
geographical location
 and access, 303, 306, 311, 314, 318–19
 and community, 60, 65, 66, 99
 of ICT sector, 278, 396
 of innovation, 301
 see also clusters; space
geosynchronous earth orbiting (GEO) satellites, 322
Germany, 255, 256, 425
Gertler, M., 280
Gesellschaft, 60
Ghani, J.A., 219
Ghozati, K., 47
Giacquinta, J.B., 86
Gidari, A., 341
Giddens, A., 17, 123, 289, 449, 454–5
Gilbert, P., 82
GILC (Global Internet Liberty Campaign), 172

Gilder, G., 171
Gilder's law, 333
GISS *see* group information support systems
global civil society, 431
global computer network regulation,
        416–17, 425–7
    freedom of expression, 422–5
    intellectual property, 417–19
    international and multinational regimes, 432–5
    international policy principles, 435–6
    market-based regulation, 427–30
    national public service regulation, 430–2
    privacy, 419–22
global information society, 300–1
Global Internet Liberty Campaign (GILC), 172
global media flows, 293
global mobile personal communications systems
        (GMPCS), 322
globalization, 157, 376
    concept of, 287–8, 398
    industry structures and spaces, 272, 294, 375
    media debates, 291–4
    policies, 296–302, 333, 391, 415–16
        see also global computer network regulation
    political economy, 289–91, 292
    role of communications media, 288–9
    role of telecommunications, 294–6, 297
    see also internationalization
Goffman, E., 209
Gordon, D., 290
Gordon, R.J., 373
government
    communication with, 372
    utility ownership, 309
    see also national policy
governmentality, Netizenship, 174–8
GPSS *see* group performance support systems
Graham, M., 188
Graham, S., 156
graphic user worlds, 36
Greenfield, P., 80
Gregory, J., 237
gross national product (GNP), 447
Grossberg, L., 147, 157–8
group communication support systems (GCSS), 116
group decision support systems (GDSS), 117–18, 123,
        124–5, 127–8
group external support systems (GXSS), 117
group information support systems (GISS), 117
group interaction, 210
    role of technology, 115–18
        empirical findings, 126–8
        knowledge networks, 128–30
        theories, 118–26
group performance support systems (GPSS), 117–18
groups, 114–15
    as complex systems, 118, 124–6
    computer-mediated, 45–7
Guattari, F., 147
Gulia, M., 44, 47, 48, 56, 68, 102

Gumpert, G., 206, 212
Gurak, L., 64

Ha, L., 212
Haber, S., 380
hackers, 190–1
Haddon, L., 95
Halbert, D.J., 435
Hall, P., 277
Hall, S., 146, 148, 291
Hamman, R., 102
Hampton, K., 66, 67, 100
Hanssen, L., 212
Haraway, D., 138, 146
Harcourt, W., 106
Harrison, T.M., 154
Harvey, D., 167
Hayles, N.K., 171
health support groups, 102, 106, 236
Healy, J., 86
Heeter, C., 208
Herman, E., 293
Hesse, B.W., 211
Heydebrand, W., 270, 279
hierarchies, 46, 353, 354, 356–7, 358
higher education, 275, 277, 446–7, 453–4
Hill, K.A., 95–6, 97
Hillery, G., 59
Hiltz, S.R., 17, 37, 121, 190
Hirokawa, R.Y., 210
Hirst, P., 290
history, and culture, 136–7
history of ICT innovation, 187–92, 452–3
    private sphere, 196–201
    professional sphere, 192–6
history of infrastructure, 232–4
history of new media research, 16–20
Hitt, L.M., 352
Hobart, M., 136
Hobsbawm, E., 453
Hoffman-Reim, W., 335
Hoffsaes, C., 194
Holeton, R., 240
Hollander, E., 68
Hollingshead, A.B., 116, 121–2
home, ICT innovation in, 196–201
Horn, S., 100
Horton, D., 213–14
hotlines, 344–5
Houlberg, R., 214
household access, 313
Howard, P., 93
Howkins, J., 301
Hughes, G., 281
Hughes, J., 95–6, 97
Hughes, T., 232
Huhtamo, E., 206
human rights, 422, 434, 436
Human Rights Watch, 436
human-computer interaction (HCI), 218–19

humour, 40–1
Hutchinson, T., 199
hybrid fibre/coax (HFC), 320–1
hybridization, 4–5, 23–4
Hyde, M.J., 148
hyperpersonal interaction, 44–5
hypertext, 219
hypertext transfer protocol (HTTP), 254

I-Generation, 166
IBM, 189, 194
ICANN *see* Internet Corporation for Assigned Names
    and Numbers
ICT industry, 393–6
  see also new media industry
ICT skills, 93, 200
ICTs
  access to *see* access
  bias, 150–1, 366–7
  definition, 21
  disengagement from, 94, 98
  and economic development, 376
  engagement with, 7–8, 27, 319–20, 359–60
  and globalization, 288
  and groups *see* group interaction
  innovation *see* history of ICT innovation
  and internationalization, 396
  research and policy, 388
  social consequences of, 6–7, 25, 26–7
  social shaping of, 3–6, 23–5, 26–7
  see also telecommunications
ideational pluralism, 424
identity
  and agency, 147
  children's, 84, 85
  computer-mediated, 41–3, 101, 200
  and culture, 149–50, 151–2
  gender, 41, 42, 151–2
  and political culture, 176–7
  use of term, 137–8
  see also anonymity
ideoscapes, 4
IMAX, 148
impacts *see* effects of technology
imperialism, 291–4
IMS (Information Management System), 194
income, 94, 311, 315
India, 297, 396
individual, use of term, 137–8
Indonesia, 316
industrial change, 364, 370, 390–3
industrial organization, 350–1
  emergence of networks, 351–3
  impact of new media, 353–60
  see also clusters
industrial society, 452
industry *see* economics of information; industrial
    organization; new media industry; trade
    and industry policy
inequality, 77–8, 93–5

informatics, 166
information
  as commodity/collective good, 417, 419, 429
  concept of, 8, 368–9, 451–2
  defining, 8
  economics of *see* economics of information
  importance of access, 310
  measures, 375, 378, 444, 449–51
information brokers, 316
information and communication technologies *see* ICTs
information economy, 23, 351–2, 366–8, 389–90
information flow, 293, 333–4
information gaps, 310–12
information management programs, 117, 194
information networks
  and information society, 447–8
  strategic use of, 350, 359–60
  see also computer networks
information revolution, 367
information richness, 122
information sector, 308–9, 310, 389, 396, 446, 450
information society
  assessment and change, 449–51
  concepts of, 386, 443–9, 452–5
  debate origins, 389–90
  globalization, 300–1
  internationalization, 396–9
  johoka index, 17
  policy plans, 399–400, 401–2
  subjects of debate, 387–9
  theoretical knowledge, 452–5
  trade and industry policy, 400–2
  videotex, 257
Information Society Technologies (IST), 388
information technology (IT) productivity paradox,
    233, 352, 373–4
information utilities, 257
information workers *see* information sector
informational society, 288
infrastructural inversion, 233
infrastructure
  access and usability, 239–41, 312
  concept of, 2–3, 9, 23, 230–1
  design, 241–2
  features, 234–9
  globalization, 295, 297
  information economy, 376–7
  information networks, 350
  sociohistorical analysis, 232–4
  telecommunications, 295
Innis, H., 150, 153
innovation
  diffusion theory, 18, 246, 247–8, 250–2,
    258, 261
  e-mail, 252, 253–5
  and economics of information, 370
  history *see* history of ICT innovation
  and information society, 444–5
  infrastructure, 237
  moments of development, 258–60

innovation *cont.*
  and new media industry, 272–3, 275–6
  policy, 407
  in private sphere, 196–201
  in professional sphere, 192–6
  recombination, 4–5, 23–4
  trends and access, 313–14
  videotex, 252, 255–8
innovation economics, 393
instant messaging, 36
institutional access, 313
instrumentalism, 135, 169
Intel, 189
intellectual property rights
  globalization, 298, 301, 417–19, 433, 434
  information economy, 369–70, 377, 380
  personal information, 422
  regulation, 344, 417–19, 428, 433, 434–5
interactionism, 248
interactive cable systems, 320
interactive fiction, 216
interactive television, 216
interactivity, 7, 25, 205, 207–9, 220–1, 270
  user-to-documents, 213–17, 220–1
  user-to-system, 217–21
  user-to-user, 209–13, 220–1
  see also group interaction; interpersonal interaction
intermediaries, 98, 332–3, 336, 345, 354–5, 358–9
International Covenant on Civil and Political Rights, 422, 434
International Development Research Centre (IRDC), 373
International Monetary Fund, 290
international policy, 410, 426, 432–5
international research, 20
International Telecommunication Union (ITU), 295, 433
International Telegraph Union, 433
internationalization, 387–8, 396–9, 400, 401
  see also globalization
Internet
  access, 92–5, 107, 240–1
    children's, 77–8
    design, 234, 409
    location, 295, 311–12, 313, 319
    origins, 190
    policies, 316, 318–19, 409
    technology, 313–14
    universal, 313
  airline reservations, 358–9
  bias of, 150–2
  children's use of, 49, 76–8, 84–5, 101, 103–4, 343–4
  civic involvement, 95–8, 107, 372
  and community, 56, 59, 66–7, 98–101, 107
  concept of user, 8
  and culture, 84–5, 135–7, 147
  definition, 21–2
  and democracy, 150–1, 154, 175, 380, 424–5
  displacement by, 104–5
  and globalization, 296, 298–9

Internet *cont.*
  governance, 164–5
  and ICT industry, 395
  and identity, 41–3, 84–5, 151–2
  and individual control, 97, 235–6, 334
  and information society, 445
  infrastructure, 235–6
  innovation history, 189–90, 192, 201
  language use, 40–1
  motivations for use, 105
  and political culture *see* political culture
  in private sphere, 200, 201
  regulation
    access, 407, 409
    government policy, 407, 408, 423, 424–5
    privacy, 22, 298–9
    self-regulation, 337–8, 339–45
  social groups, 45–7
  social interaction, 35–6, 38–9, 40–9, 101–8, 216
  standards, 234, 235–6
  studies, 2
  via satellite, 322
  see also computer networks; e-mail; virtual communities; World Wide Web
Internet Architecture Board (IAB), 164, 171
Internet Content Rating for Europe (INCORE), 343
Internet Corporation for Assigned Names and Numbers (ICANN), 164, 341, 343, 433, 434
Internet dropouts, 94
Internet Engineering Task Force (IETF), 164, 171
Internet games industry, 269
Internet Industry Association Australia (IIA), 341
Internet relay chat (IRC), 41, 84
  see also chat rooms
Internet Service Providers' Association (ISPA), 341
internet service providers (ISPs), 340, 341, 424
Internet Society (ISOC), 164, 171, 190
Internet telephony, 322
interpersonal consequences of Internet, 47–9
interpersonal interaction, 209–10, 211, 212, 217–20
  computer-mediated, 35–6, 49–50
    compared with other media, 39–40
    cues-filtered-out perspective, 36–7
    identity, 41–3
    language use, 40–1
    media characteristics, 37–9
    personal relationships, 43–5
    social groups, 45–7
  and group performance, 127
interpretive flexibility, 249, 260
intranets, 117, 129, 195–6
invasiveness of media, 335
invention, 259
  see also innovation
IRDC (International Development Research Centre), 373
ironic appropriation, 123
isolation, 101, 105–6, 200

ISPs *see* Internet service providers
Ito, Y., 17
ITU (International Telecommunication Union),
    295, 433

James, L., 104, 212
James, M., 104
Jameson, F., 138, 167–8
Jankowski, N., 58
Janowitz, M., 57
Japan, 17, 274, 277–8, 329, 445
Jenkins, H., 82–3
Johansen, R., 17
Johnson, D.R., 428, 429
Johnson, S., 100, 101, 106
joho shakai, 445
johoka shakai, 17
Jones, S., 61–2, 93, 105
Jonscher, C., 17
Jorgenson, D.W., 373, 374
journalism, 216
Joyrich, L., 138, 139

Kanfer, A., 102
Katz, J., 42, 76, 94, 102
Kay, A., 217
Kayany, J., 104
Keeble, D., 279
Kestnbaum, M., 48
Kiesler, S., 17, 121, 212
Kinder, M., 79
Klein, A., 271
Klein, M., 83
knowledge, 375, 378, 452–5
knowledge economy, 390
knowledge management, 128
knowledge networks, 128–30
knowledge space, 23
Kolko, B.E., 152
Kollock, P., 47
Komito, L., 47
Kondratieff, N., 393, 445
Konsynski, B.R., 359
Koontz, V., 252
Kraut, R., 35, 43, 48
Kress, G., 26
Krugman, P., 290, 388
Kuhn, T., 329, 393
Kumar, K., 455–6
Kuwait, 423

labour force *see* workforce
labour market mobility, 276–7
Laffitte, P., 276
Lamberton, D., 17
Landow, G.P., 212, 216
language, 39–41, 154, 374, 376
large technical systems (LTS), 249
LaRose, R., 215
Lasswell, H.D., 288

Latour, B., 146, 152–3, 232
Laurel, B., 218–19
Lea, M., 37, 40, 42, 43, 44, 45, 46
Leadbetter, C., 446
learning communities, 85
Lefebvre, H., 155
legal jurisdiction, 425, 430
legislation, 22, 95, 308, 313, 314
Lengel, R.H., 119
Lent, J., 296
Leone, R., 96, 97, 98, 100, 101
Leonhirth, W.J., 206
Lessig, L., 338–9, 380, 409, 428, 432, 435
Levy, M.R., 208, 214
Lévy, P., 23, 106
Lewis, C.A., 198
liberalism, 390, 400–1
liberalization, 294–5, 318, 389, 394–5, 401, 405–7
linguistics, 63–4
literacy, 288
Livingstone, S., 77–8
locality *see* geographical location
Lockard, J., 47
London, 278–9
London Internet Exchange (LINX), 341
Longhi, C., 276, 277
Loomis, D.G., 371
Los Angeles, 280
Louveaux, S., 428
Love, G., 37
low earth orbiting (LEO) satellites, 322
Lumière, L., 197
Lyotard, J.-F., 138, 167, 171, 172, 174

McCarthy, A., 139
McChesney, R., 293
MacDonald, S., 375
McGrath, J.E., 116, 121–2, 125, 212
Machlup, F., 17, 365, 366–7, 377, 378, 389, 447
Macintosh computers, 188–9
McKenna, K.Y.A., 41, 45
McKenney, J.L., 123
MacKenzie, D., 26, 237
McLaughlin, M.L., 46
McLuhan, M., 5, 268
McMillan, J.J., 148
McPherson, T., 152
McQuail, D., 56
Mahler, A., 212
Mahood, C., 208
mailing lists, 35
mainframe computing, 193–5
Malone, T.W., 354
management, 193, 194–5, 374–5
Mann, S., 157
mapping, 142, 148
market-based regulation, 426, 427–30
    see also self-regulation
marketing, 76, 79, 87
    see also advertisements

markets, 353, 354, 357–9, 364, 366–8, 370–1, 405–11
Markus, M.L., 36, 116
Martin, C., 166
Martin-Barbero, J., 294
Marvin, C., 206
Marvin, S., 156
Marx, L., 379
Marxism, 19, 149
mass society theories, 2–3, 5, 20, 27
    decline of, 7, 8, 9, 18
Massey, B.L., 208
Massively Multiplayer Online Games (MMOG), 296
Matei, S., 45
Mattelart, A., 300
Matternes, J.H., 374
media choice, 118, 119–21
media dependency theory, 214
media effects see effects of technology
media globalization, 291–4
media imperialism, 292
media industry
    globalization, 294–9
    see also new media industry
media representations of innovation, 191–2
media richness theory, 36, 119–20, 218
mediascapes, 4, 289
mediated communication, 7–9
    see also computer-mediated communication
Meier, R., 365
Melody, W., 23, 300, 436
Merton, R.K., 57
message boards, 35
messageries roses, 256
meta-tags, 370
metadata, 238
Metcalfe's law, 333
methodology, 25–8, 36–7, 49, 67–8, 80–1, 444, 449–51
Mexico, 317
Meyrowitz, J., 289
Michaels, E., 150
microcomputing, 195
microfiche, 237
Microsoft, 189, 297
Microsoft Outlook, 117
millennium bug, 157
Miller, D., 296
Miller, L., 151
MIME (multipurpose Internet mail extensions protocol), 234
Minc, A., 17
Ministry of Posts and Telecommunications (MPT), 445
minitel, 188, 200, 255, 256
Mitchell, C., 64–5
Mitchell, J.C., 248
mobile phones, 200, 270, 295, 323
mobile technologies, 6–7, 321–2
mode of regulation, 391
modernity, 4, 167

Mody, B., 405
moments of technological development, 258–60
monitoring see surveillance
monopoly, 309, 406
Moore's law, 333, 394
MOOs, 35–6, 43, 44, 46
Morley, D., 200, 291
Morse, M., 135–6
MUDs, 35–6, 41, 42, 43, 46–7, 63–4, 201
Mueller, M., 434
multi-access radio, 321
multimedia, 206, 266–7, 268–9
    see also new media
multinational regulation, 432–5
multiple identities, 41
multitheoretical multilevel (MTML) models, 129
Murdoch, R., 291
Murray, J.H., 206, 207
music, 198, 199–200
Myers, D., 40, 41, 43
mythinformation, 145

N-Gen, 103
Nachum, L., 279
Nass, C., 207, 211, 219
nation
    and globalization, 291, 293
    impact of communications media on, 289
    importance of regulation, 415–16
    and Netizenship, 174–8
national differences in Internet access, 92
national policy, 405–11
    cluster formation, 273–8
    and economics of information, 377–8
    freedom of expression, 22, 422–5
    and globalization, 291, 296–302
    intellectual property, 417–19
    principles and models, 425–32
    privacy, 419–22
    state and self-regulation, 340, 341, 342
    theory underlying, 453
    universal service, 87, 314–19
    see also international policy; trade and industry policy
negative regulation, 331
Negroponte, N., 56, 165, 169–70, 206
Nelson, C., 142
neoliberal theories, 299
netiquette, 255
Netizenship, 169, 174–8
Netville, 65–6, 100
network analysis, 60–1, 248, 251
network externalities, 24–5, 235, 251, 357
network metaphor, 5–6, 24–5
network organizations, 355–6
network society, 166
networking, 190

networks
in clusters, 273, 276, 277
community networks, 59, 65–6, 68
electronic islands, 313
and information society, 447–8
knowledge networks, 128–30
and media choice, 120
and organizations, 350–1
emergence of networks, 351–3
impact of new media, 353–60
and political culture, 169–74
regulation of, 408–9
unbundling, 406
workplace innovation, 195–6
see also global computer network regulation
Neu, C.R., 93
new media
definitions, 2–3, 20–5, 56–7, 206
engagement with, 7–8, 27
evolution, 1–2, 206–7, 266
nature of, 268–71
new media industry
convergence and divergence, 266–7, 268–71, 283–4
globalization, 294–302
see also clusters; ICT industry; industrial organization;
self-regulation; trade and industry policy
new media research methodology, 25–8, 67–8
new media studies, 1–2, 7, 15–20
new mediation ecology, 9
new world information and communication order
(NWICO), 292–3, 299, 436
New York, 270, 279–80
New York Information Technology Center, 279, 280
Newhagen, J.E., 212
News Corporation, 291–2
newsgroups, 35, 41, 114
see also Usenet
newspapers, 57, 58, 104, 196, 211, 450
Nie, N.H., 48, 101
Nielsen, J., 212
Nietzsche, F., 137
Nisbet, R., 59, 147–8
Noble, D., 148, 187–8
Nokia, 275
Nonaka, I., 278
Nora, S., 17
Norlund, J.-E., 214
NSFnet, 253
numerical control machines, 187–8
Nunes, M., 139–40
NWICO (new world information and communication
order), 292–3, 299, 436
Nye, J.S.(Jr.), 294

Oakley, K., 302
O'Brien, J., 41
occupational change, 445–7, 450
Odzer, C., 106
OECD see Organization for Economic Cooperation
and Development

oligopoly, 405, 406–7
Ong, W., 154
online communities see virtual communities
online culture, children's, 84–5
open entry, 309
open innovation, 273
open source movement, 235
opportunism, 353
optical fibre, 314, 320, 321
Oreja, M., 335
organic communities, 62, 63, 98–9
organization
and economics of information, 374–6
see also groups; industrial organization
Organization for Economic Cooperation and
Development (OECD), 329, 398, 433
organizational imperative, 118
organizations
computer innovation, 194
knowledge networks, 128
and media choice, 119
see also corporations
origins of innovation, 258–9
Otaku-Zoku, 76
Otlet, P., 237
OURMedia, 58
overpersonalization, 98
ownership
of telecommunications, 309
see also intellectual property rights

Papacharissi, Z., 105
Papert, S., 76, 79–80, 85
paradigm shifts, 329
in regulation, 330, 334–9
self regulation, 339–45
underpinnings, 331–4
paradigms, technoeconomic, 390, 393, 445
parasocial interaction, 98, 213–14
parental support, 86
Park, R.E., 57
Parker, E., 18
Parks, M.R., 42, 43, 44, 102
participant structure, 38
participation equalization effect, 126–7
participatory design, 65, 241–2
path dependency, 189–90
Pathé, C., 197
patient support groups, 102, 106, 236
Pavlik, J.V., 206, 211
payphones, 316, 321
pedagogy, 85, 86
PENs (public education networks), 59
people, 8
see also audience; users
perceived interactivity, 207–8, 220–1
performance, in CMC tasks, 127–8
performativity, 41, 135, 167
Perse, E., 105
personal information, 419–22, 435–6

personal relationships, 43–5, 78–9
Perterson, S.B., 420
Peru, 318
pervasiveness of media, 335
Pew Internet and American Life Project, 36, 49, 102, 255
Philippines, 317
phonograph, 198, 199
photography, 196–7
piano, 198
PICT (Programme on Information and Communication
    Technologies), 19–20
Piore, M., 392
Platform for Internet Content Selection (PICS), 344
Plato, 144
Poland, 318
policy see international policy; national policy; regulation
policy studies, 18
policy-oriented research, 20
political content regulation, 423, 424–5
political culture, 163–9
    Netizenship, 174–8
    networks, 169–74
political economy, 19, 289–91, 292
political involvement, 95–8, 107
politics of technology, 150, 151–3
Pool, I.de S., 21
Poole, M.S., 123, 124
Porat, M.U., 17, 389–90, 447
Porter, M., 272, 273
Post, D.G., 428, 429
post-Fordism, 391, 392
post-industrial society, 17, 390, 445, 452
postal service, 309, 433
Poster, M., 154
postmodernism, 41, 138–9, 154–5, 167, 172
power, 150, 153, 294
    see also political culture
practices, 2–3, 9, 23
Preece, J., 47
Prehn, O., 58
prescription, 152–3
Prestel, 255
pricing, 359, 406
Prigogine, I., 124
printing press, 268, 288
privacy, 239, 298–9, 417, 419–22, 428,
    433–4, 435–6
private sphere, ICT innovation in, 196–201
private-sector regulation see self-regulation
privatization, 294–5, 309, 405
pro-innovation bias, 252
production, 2–3, 388, 392, 393
productivity, 273, 352
productivity paradox, 233, 352, 373–4
Programme on Information and Communication
    Technologies (PICT), 19–20
progress, 143, 147–8
property see intellectual property rights
protocols, 234–5, 254
    see also standards

Provenzo, E., 81, 84
pseudo-community, 98, 214
PTT (post, telephone and telegraph), 309
public access broadcasting, 58, 150
public discussion, 66–7
public education networks (PENs), 59
public service regulation, 426, 430–2
public sphere, 66, 196–8
    see also workplace
publicness, of media, 336
Putnam, R., 99

qualitative approach, 26, 67, 68
qualitative change, 444, 449–51
quality, in newsgroups, 67
quantitative approach, 67, 444, 449–51
Quéré, M., 276, 277
QWERTY keyboard, 231, 235

race see ethnicity and race
radical contextuality, 142
radio
    community, 55, 64–5
    innovation, 192, 198, 199–200
    interaction, 211, 214, 215
    multi-access, 321
    regulation, 22
Rafaeli, S., 45, 205, 208, 214, 215
Rainie, L., 93
Rash, W., 97, 176
rating, 343–4
Raymond, E., 241
RCA, 188
reach, 310
reciprocity, 67
recombination, 4–5, 23–4
record players, 199–200
Redfield, R., 60
Reeves, B., 211, 219
reflexivity, 454
registration, 334
regulation
    by industry see self-regulation
    by state see international policy; national policy
    and children, 87, 343–4
    paradigm shift, 330, 331–9
    technological means, 338, 343–4, 428–9
    see also surveillance
regulation school, 390–2
Reid, E.M., 41
Reidenberg, J.R., 428
Reinmöller, P., 278
reintermediation, 336, 345
religion, 106
remailers, 408, 424
remediation, 5
representation, 155–6
Research in Advanced Communications in Europe
    (RACE), 388
responsibility, 157

reterritorialization, 296
reverse salients, 232
Rheingold, H., 56, 61, 97, 100, 155, 192
Ricardo, D., 397
Rice, R., 15, 21, 37, 94, 102, 252
Riedel, E., 64
Riphagen, J., 102
Roberts, L.D., 42, 43, 44
Robertson, D., 106
Robins, K., 19, 23, 291
Robinson, J., 48, 104
Rogers, E.M., 18, 212, 252
Rojas, V., 95
Ross, A., 153
Rostow, E., 307–8
Roszak, T., 452
Rubin, A., 105
Rudin, W., 280
Ruggieri, R., 290
Ruhleder, K., 231
rural areas, 311, 313, 314, 316, 318–19
Russ, A., 279

Sabel, C., 392
Saco, D., 175
Safe Harbor agreement, 298, 421
Sakr, N., 293
Samorski, J.H., 436
San Francisco, 280
Sassen, S., 409
satellite technology, 297, 314, 322
Saxenian, A., 269
scaffolding, 145–6
scarcity, 332–3, 336, 345–6
Schaffer, S., 191
Scherer, K., 48, 49, 102
Schiffman, Z., 136
Schiller, H.I., 292
Schlesinger, P., 297
Schmitz, J., 120, 218
Schneider, S., 66, 67
Schramm, W., 21
Schudson, M., 210
Schultz, T., 208
Schumpeter, J., 17, 393, 445
science and technology parks, 275–6
science, technology and society (STS), 144
science and technology studies (STS), 232
Scott, A., 268–9
Screen Wales, 282
Seattle Community Network, 65
Sefton-Green, J., 86
Seibold, D.R., 124–5
self, 135, 137–8, 157–8, 340–1
self-categorization theory, 42
self-concepts, 81
self-organizing systems theory (SOST), 124–5
self-regulation, 331, 337–45, 420–1, 426, 427–30
semiconductors, 275
Senegal, 316

Sennett, R., 196
service sector, 308–9, 310, 389, 396
sexual content, 423
Shapiro, A., 96, 97, 98, 100, 101, 150–1, 334
Short, J., 17, 119, 218
SIDE (social individuation and deindividuation)
    model, 42
Siepmann, C., 199
signification, 136, 155
Silicon Alley, 270, 279
Silicon Valley, 275, 280
Silver, D., 65
Silverstone, R., 9
Simmel, G., 248
Sinclair, J., 293, 294, 296
Skirrow, G., 83
Skocpol, T., 99
Slack, J.D., 139, 146, 155
Slack, R.S., 100
Slater, D., 296
smart cards, 315, 323
Smith, Adam, 397
Smith, Anthony, 291
Smith, M., 59
social arrangements, 2–3, 9, 23
social capital, 64, 106
social change, 444, 449–51
social consequences of ICTs, 6–7, 25, 26–7, 47–9
    see also effects of technology
social construction of technology (SCOT), 248, 249, 409
    see also social shaping of technology
social cues, 36–7, 121, 126
social determinism, 4
    see also social shaping of technology
social economy, 106
social good, 417, 419
social hierarchies, 46
social individuation and deindividuation (SIDE)
    model, 42
social influence model, 120
social informatics, 249
social interaction, 210
    domestic computer use, 86, 103, 200
    games, 78–9
    Internet, 101–8
    virtual communities, 99, 100
    see also group interaction; interpersonal interaction
social movements, 431
social network analysis, 61, 248, 251
social presence theory, 36, 119, 120, 218
social psychology, 17
social shaping of ICTs, 3–6, 23–5, 26–7
social shaping of technology (SST), 21, 246, 247–50,
    258, 261
    see also social construction of technology
social ties, 60–1, 66
socioeconomic status
    and access, 77–8, 93–4, 311, 315, 319
    and identity, 149
    and use, 96

socioemotional communication, 37, 96
sociology, 17, 59–61, 250, 251
sociology of scientific knowledge (SSK), 249
sociotechnical paradigms, 251, 258
Soete, L., 393
soft power, 294
software, 278–9, 338, 343–4, 350, 396, 428
Soho (London), 278–9
Sophia Antipolis, 276–7
SOST (self-organizing systems theory), 124–5
South Africa, 316
sovereignty, 177, 426, 430–1
space, 17, 38, 83, 139–40, 153–7, 447–8
    see also clusters; geographical location
spatiality, 167
Spears, R., 42, 43, 44, 45
speech communities, 64
speech rights see freedom of expression
Spender, D., 151–2
Spigel, L., 199
spillovers, 266, 279, 373
spirituality, 106
Sproull, L., 17
SST see social shaping of technology
stability of technology, 237
Stacey, M., 60
Stafford, L., 45
Stallybrass, J., 83
Stamm, K.R., 57
Standage, T., 215
standards, 234–9, 254, 356–7, 370, 395
Stanford Industrial Park, 275
Star, S.L., 231, 249
state
    culture of, 135
    and self-regulation, 340, 341, 342
    see also government; national policy
status
    in groups, 121, 126
    see also socioeconomic status
Stefik, M., 165, 233
Stehr, N., 454
Stein, L., 65
Stephen, T., 154
Stern, S., 84
Sterne, J., 147, 158
Stevens, N., 451
Stigler, G.J., 365
Stiroh, K.J., 373, 374
Stone, A.R., 62
strategic trade policies, 398
Stratton, J., 151, 157
Straubhaar, J., 215, 296
Straus, S., 102
Streeter, T., 422
strong globalization theories, 290
subject, 137–8
subjectivity, 157–8
subsidies, 308, 315, 317–18
Sudweeks, F., 40, 45

support, 46, 86, 103, 200
surveillance, 156–7, 255, 420
Sutton, J., 370–1
symbolic interaction, 210, 218
symbolization, 448–9
synchronous CMC, 35, 38, 39, 116
synergy, 274–5
system, user-to-system interactivity, 217–20

tacit knowledge, 375
talk shows, 214
Tapscott, D., 76, 101, 103
task performance, 116, 117–18, 122, 127
Tattersall, I., 374
Taubman, G., 424
Taylor, D.A., 43
Taylor, L.D., 43, 371, 372
technoeconomic paradigms, 390, 393, 445
technological constructivism, 410
technological dependence, 143
technological determinism
    concept of, 21, 187, 248
    and cultural studies, 143, 152, 153
    diffusion theory, 252
    impact on children, 77
    information society, 450–1
    Internet, 48
    media effects research, 122
    regulation, 408
    rejection of, 4, 21, 248
technological imperative, 118
technology
    bias, 150–1, 366–7
    causality and agency, 144–7
    identity, 149–50, 151–2
    information economy, 366–8
    information society, 444–5, 450
    politics of, 150
    progress and genealogy, 147–9
    as a project, 246
    regulation using, 338, 343–4, 428–9
    relationship with culture see culture
    role in group interaction see group interaction
    space and corporeality, 139–40, 153–7
    trends, 313–14
    see also ICTs; innovation; social shaping
        of technology
technopoles, 273–8
technoscape, 4
telecentres, 316
telecommunications
    convergence with computing, 351
    demand studies, 371–2
    and economic development, 376
    liberalization and regulation, 394–5, 405–8
    role in globalization, 294–6, 297
    utilization, 319–20
telecommunications access, 307–8, 311–12
    electronic islands and ghettos, 313
    policies to increase, 316–19

women
  role of Internet for, 106
  use of ICTs, 320
women's community radio, 64–5
Woolgar, S., 232
workforce
  in clusters, 280
  ICT skills, 93
  and information society, 445–7, 450
  mobility, 276–7
  work teams, 114, 128
  see also information sector
workplace
  ICT innovation in, 192–6
  see also industrial organization; new media industry
World Brain project, 236–7
World Intellectual Property Organization (WIPO), 418, 433
World Summit on the Information Society (WSIS), 436

World Trade Organization (WTO), 290, 398
World Wide Web (WWW)
  access, 234
  infrastructure, 233
  interaction, 208
  privacy, 419
  see also Internet; virtual communities
writing, 136, 193
Wu, G., 207
Wynn, E., 42

X.25 standard, 254

Yates, J., 193, 234
Yelsma, P., 104

Z39.50 standard, 236
Zack, M.H., 123
Zhang, Y., 451
zoning, 344